ROBERT'S RULES OF ORDER
NEWLY REVISED

10TH EDITION

GENERAL HENRY M. ROBERT
U.S. Army

A New and Enlarged Edition by
SARAH CORBIN ROBERT
HENRY M. ROBERT III
WILLIAM J. EVANS
DANIEL H. HONEMANN
THOMAS J. BALCH

PERSEUS PUBLISHING
Cambridge, Massachusetts

Cataloging-in-Publication Data is available from
the Library of Congress
ISBN 0-7382-0384-X

For questions and answers and further information on parliamentary
procedure visit http://www.robertsrules.com

Perseus Publishing is a member of the Perseus Books Group.

Find us on the World Wide Web at http://www.perseuspublishing.com

Perseus Publishing books are available at special discounts for bulk
purchases in the U.S. by corporations, institutions, and other organizations. For more information, please contact the Special Markets De-
partment at HarperCollins Publishers, 10 East 53rd Street, New York,
NY 10022, or call 1-212-207-7528.

Text design by Rachel Hegarty
Set in 9.5-point Galliard by Perseus Publishing Services

First printing of the 10th edition, October 2000
2 3 4 5 6 7 8 9 10—03 02 01

*Where there is no law, but every man
does what is right in his own eyes,
there is the least of real liberty.*

—HENRY M. ROBERT

*It is difficult to find another branch of
knowledge where a small amount of study
produces such great results in increased
efficiency in a country where the people
rule, as in parliamentary law.*

—HENRY M. ROBERT

THE EDITIONS OF THIS MANUAL

		POCKET MANUAL OF RULES OF ORDER FOR DELIBERATIVE ASSEMBLIES
First Edition	February 1876	
Second Edition	July 1876	
Third Edition	1893	

(Cover short title: ROBERT'S RULES OF ORDER)

Fourth Edition	1915	
(Completely reworked and 75 percent enlarged by original author)		ROBERT'S RULES OF ORDER REVISED
Fifth Edition	1943	
Sixth Edition	1951	
("Seventy-Fifth Anniversary")		

Seventh Edition	1970	
(Enlarged more than twofold and totally recast to be made self-explanatory)		ROBERT'S RULES OF ORDER NEWLY REVISED
Eighth Edition	1981	
Ninth Edition	1990	
TENTH EDITION	2000	
("Millenium." Thoroughly re-edited to refine conceptual clarity and consistency of statement.)		

Inclusive of Robert's Rules of Order and Robert's Rules of Order Revised more than Five Million copies in print

CONTENTS

I

THE DELIBERATIVE ASSEMBLY: ITS TYPES AND THEIR RULES

II

THE CONDUCT OF BUSINESS IN A DELIBERATIVE ASSEMBLY

III

DESCRIPTION OF MOTIONS
IN ALL CLASSIFICATIONS

IV

MEETING AND SESSION

—
V
—

THE MAIN MOTION

—
VI
—

SUBSIDIARY MOTIONS

VII

PRIVILEGED MOTIONS

VIII

INCIDENTAL MOTIONS

IX

―

MOTIONS THAT BRING A QUESTION AGAIN BEFORE THE ASSEMBLY

―

X

―

RENEWAL OF MOTIONS; DILATORY AND IMPROPER MOTIONS

XI

QUORUM; ORDER OF BUSINESS AND RELATED CONCEPTS

XII

ASSIGNMENT OF THE FLOOR; DEBATE

XIII

VOTING

XIV

NOMINATIONS AND ELECTIONS

XV

OFFICERS; MINUTES AND OFFICERS' REPORTS

XVI

BOARDS AND COMMITTEES

XVII

MASS MEETINGS; ORGANIZATION OF A PERMANENT SOCIETY

XVIII

BYLAWS

XIX

CONVENTIONS

XX

DISCIPLINARY PROCEDURES

CHARTS, TABLES AND LISTS

PREFACE

to the Tenth Edition

The issuance of this Millennium Edition of *Robert's Rules of Order Newly Revised* marks a century and a quarter in the life of the series of books, comprising ten editions in all, familiarly known as "Robert's Rules of Order." Its authors are happy to have Perseus Books now become its official publisher after its identification with the name of Scott, Foresman and Company through most of the past century as the mark of current authenticity of each succeeding edition.

A complete list of the editions is shown facing the first page of the Table of Contents, and their history is told in the Introduction. This tenth edition in the entire series is the fourth edition of the second complete reworking of the subject matter first published in 1970. It is the only book in print containing the completely developed body of parliamentary rules understood as "Robert's Rules of Order."

In this edition, a new quotation from the original author, Henry M. Robert, appears on the epigraph page at the beginning of the book, below the now familiar one on "real liberty." It refers to the great value of "a small amount of study" in the field of parliamentary procedure.

A manual suitable for adoption by organizations as a parliamentary authority must necessarily acquire some complexity. Otherwise, in practical cases, questions are sure to arise that it fails to answer. But one of the greatest needs in parliamentary procedure today is for an increased yet relatively small, basic portion of it to become the common property of everyone, much as the rules of baseball.

This core of the subject matter is a little more developed than can be known just by applying ordinary common sense. It does need to be learned, though it is really quite simple. Seeming complexities enter in only when the less usual situations they cover arise.

While this book contains considerable detail, it is written to be as readable as possible, consistent with necessary technical accuracy. It is also designed to lead the reader step-by-step to an understanding of parliamentary procedure. These goals were among the intended hallmarks of the 1970 general revision.

Even the novice has much to gain by reading this book through, particularly the first five chapters, simply skimming over what he or she does not at first understand. What the user needs after doing that is to know *where to find* the answers.

The process of arriving at additional content through the technique of interpretation continues, as situations occurring in assemblies point to a need for more fully developed rules to go by in particular cases. In the preparation of this edition, the entire text of the work has been subjected to a thorough review, seeking to ferret out any remaining inconsistencies or ambiguities in concept or statement.

The coming of the Internet and the widespread use of e-mail and the fax machine have stirred interest in the concept of an "electronic meeting." This edition notes that the opportunity for simultaneous aural communication among all participants is central to the deliberative character of a meeting. It recognizes, therefore, that meetings may be conducted by videoconference or teleconference, when authorized by the bylaws and when regulated by appropriate special rules of order and standing rules specifying such things as how recognition is to be sought and the floor obtained. On the other hand, it warns that although e-mail or faxes may provide a suitable substitute for postal mail in the issuance of calls for meetings or the conduct of mail voting, they are not suited for the conduct of the deliberative process under the precedents and procedures common to parliamentary law.

Some of the other more important points of revision are the following:

- The role of "established custom" in relation to written rules has been clarified.
- An explanation of the so-called "friendly amendment" is presented in a new subsection.
- New provisions relating to the notice and call of meetings have been added, and a precise rule for the counting of days of notice required has been provided.

- A new subsection on the conduct of "public sessions" in appropriate bodies has been added.
- Notice has been taken of the use of such variations as "chair" or "chairperson" in place of "chairman."
- Clarification has been provided concerning the effect of referral of a motion to a committee on the freedom of the committee (and the assembly itself) to deal with amendments to the motion which were acted upon by the assembly prior to referral, including any with respect to which a motion to reconsider was pending at the time of referral.
- A rule prohibiting ballot votes "for" or "against" a candidate, as distinguished from a motion, has been introduced.
- References to federal, state, and local laws are restricted, wherever appropriate, to procedural rules prescribed by such laws, in recognition of the fact that rules of parliamentary procedure are concerned with the process by which a deliberative assembly arrives at a decision, and not with the wisdom, or even legality, of the decision itself. For similar reasons, the rule prohibiting rescission of a motion which is in the nature of a contract has been eliminated.
- The meaning of the term "majority of the entire membership" has been more clearly defined, and greater prominence has been given to the cases in which it may be applied.
- Modified rules for Lay on the Table make it clear that, while this motion may never be used with the purpose of killing the pending motion without debate, it is proper to use it to set aside the pending question in order to bring up another motion which the majority considers more urgently important.
- New treatment of the motion to Fix the Time to Which to Adjourn establishes that the motion may not be used to set an additional meeting before an already-scheduled meeting within the same session.
- Greater specification has been given of the cases in which an action is null and void so that a Point of Order may be raised to invalidate it without regard to the usual timeliness requirement.
- More comprehensive rules have been provided explaining when Suspend the Rules may not be used because doing so would violate a fundamental principle of parliamentary law or a basic right of an individual member.

- Provisions regarding Request to Be Excused from a Duty have been removed from the section on Requests and Inquiries and placed in a new, separate section.
- The rule establishing the time limits for a motion to Reconsider in a session of more than one day has been modified so as more accurately to reflect the purpose of the rule.
- The rules relating to reconsideration of negative votes on the motions to Commit or Refer, Postpone to a Certain Time, Limit or Extend Limits of Debate, for the Previous Question, and to Lay on the Table have been modified to give full effect to the rule that the motion to Reconsider cannot be applied to any motion which can be renewed.

In addition, the Tenth Edition clarifies:

- The definition of a deliberative assembly.
- The vote required to adopt a parliamentary authority in varying circumstances.
- That the chair's wording of a motion when it is put to a vote is the definitive version to be included in the minutes.
- The custom of "standing at ease," which has been distinguished from a recess.
- The difference in effect between recessing and adjourning.
- What may be considered at a special meeting.
- The propriety of motions to refrain from doing something.
- The undesirability of having "co-chairmen."
- The vote required to adjourn earlier than the time scheduled in an adopted agenda.
- When an adjourned meeting may be scheduled in relation to the next regular meeting.
- The circumstances under which a motion that conflicts with something previously adopted without being processed as a motion to Rescind or Amend Something Previously Adopted is, or is not, null and void.
- That Suspend the Rules may not be used with regard to rules that have their application outside a meeting context.
- The rules concerning Division of a Question with respect to which motions can and cannot be divided.

- The procedure to be followed when there is objection to a Request to Modify a Motion.
- Standard Descriptive Characteristic 2 of the motions to Rescind and to Amend Something Previously Adopted in order to reflect the manner in which these motions are most frequently applied.
- The rules respecting amendment of motions for which previous notice has been given.
- That the motion to Discharge a Committee may be used in a committee to discharge a subcommittee.
- That it is possible to move to reconsider a vote taken by secret ballot.
- The proper treatment to be accorded a motion to reconsider a vote on an adhering subsidiary or incidental motion which is made after the main motion to which the subsidiary or incidental motion adheres has been temporarily disposed of.
- Where corrections to the minutes are recorded.
- The vote needed to change an agenda or program previously adopted.
- The rules concerning preference in recognition to take account of the right to give previous notice of a motion.
- That members cannot be compelled to abstain from voting on the grounds of personal interest, even though they should do so.
- The time within which a member may change his or her vote.
- The proper use of "voting cards."
- Voting procedure when electing several members to a single office, such as directors, and in counting ballots with votes for more than one office or question.
- The recording of roll-call votes and the conduct of electronic roll-call votes.
- That a motion to take an informal straw poll is improper.
- That notice is not required before completing an election when a person who has been elected declines.
- The duties of the parliamentarian.
- Possible procedures for audits.
- The procedure for removal or replacement of committee members.
- Rules concerning amendments to the report of the Credentials Committee at a convention.
- The right of a member to appeal the action of the chair in ordering the removal of a nonmember.

The authors wish to acknowledge their indebtedness to Lisa M. Blanch for secretarial work in connection with the manuscript and for the editorial assistance of Marnie Cochran, Marco Pavia, and Norman Ware of the staff of Perseus Books.

Henry M. Robert III
William J. Evans
Daniel H. Honemann
Thomas J. Balch

INTRODUCTION

This book embodies a codification of the present-day general parliamentary law (omitting provisions having no application outside legislative bodies). The book is also designed as a manual to be adopted by organizations or assemblies as their parliamentary authority. When the manual has been thus adopted, the rules within it, together with any special rules of procedure that may also be adopted, are binding upon the body and constitute that body's rules of order.

Parliamentary law originally was the name given to the rules and customs for carrying on business in the English Parliament that were developed through a continuing process of decisions and precedents somewhat like the growth of the common law. These rules and customs, as brought to America with the settling of the New World, became the basic substance from which the practice of legislative bodies in the United States evolved. Out of early American legislative procedure and paralleling it in further development has come the *general parliamentary law*, or *common parliamentary law*, of today, which is adapted to the needs of organizations and assemblies of widely differing purposes and conditions. In legislative bodies, there is often recourse to the general parliamentary law in situations not covered by the rules or precedents of the particular body—although some of the necessary procedure in such a case must be proper to that type of assembly alone.

The kind of gathering in which parliamentary law is applicable is known as a *deliberative assembly*. This expression was used by Edmund Burke to describe the English Parliament, in a speech to the electorate at Bristol in 1774; and it became the basic term for a body of persons meeting (under conditions detailed on pp. 1–2) to discuss and determine upon common action.

Acting under the general parliamentary law, any deliberative assembly can formally adopt written rules of procedure which, as fully explained on pages 15ff., can confirm, add to, or deviate from parliamentary law itself. As indicated above, the term *rules of order*, in its proper sense, refers to any written parliamentary rules so adopted, whether they are contained in a manual or have been specially composed by the adopting body. The term *parliamentary procedure*, although frequently used synonymously with *parliamentary law*, refers in this book to parliamentary law as it is followed in any given assembly or organization, *together with* whatever rules of order the body may have adopted.

Thomas Jefferson speaks of "the Parliamentary branch of the law." From this country's beginning, it has been an underlying assumption of our culture that what has been authoritatively established as parliamentary law is *law*—in the sense of being binding within all assemblies except as they may adopt special rules varying from the general parliamentary law. But since there has not always been complete agreement as to what constitutes parliamentary law, no society or assembly should attempt to transact business without having adopted some standard manual on the subject as its authority in all cases not covered by its own special rules.

Early Origins of the English Parliament

The holding of assemblies of the elders, fighting men, or people of a tribe, community, or city to make decisions or render opinions on important matters is doubtless a custom older than history. According to a widely held view, our own tradition of parliamentary process may be traced to ways of life in Anglo-Saxon tribes before their migration to the island of Britain starting in the fifth century A.D. Among these peoples on the continent of Europe, the tribe was the largest regularly existing political unit. From analogy with the customs of other Germanic tribes, it is supposed that freemen were accustomed to come together in the "Village-moot," to make "bye-laws" for their village and to administer justice. These groups also chose men to represent them at the "Hundred-moot," of the district, which acted as a court of appeal and arbitrated intervillage disputes. Still higher in authority, and similarly constituted, was the "Folk-moot," which was also the citizen army of the tribe.

The same institutions, it is believed, were carried into Anglo-Saxon England, where the Folk-moot became the "Shire-moot." There is little historical knowledge of events in the island of Britain during the two hundred years after the first Anglo-Saxon invasions early in the fifth century. When a picture of Anglo-Saxon England in its formative stages does emerge, the Shire-moot—later called the "Shire Court"—is found to be an instrument of local government subject to crown supervision, under a king advised by a national assembly known as the "witan," or "witenagemot." Originally established in each of the separate early English kingdoms and supposed to include all freemen who held land, the witenagemot in the united and Christianized England normally met at the call of the king and was composed of such major landholders, ealdormen, king's officers, bishops, and abbots as he might wish to summon. Although the witenagemot was not in practice a democratic institution, the king's authority was held to derive from its consent, and it might exert influence in the choice of a new king.

The Norman Conquest in 1066 brought England under tight military control by a French-speaking administration, but the structure of Anglo-Saxon governmental machinery was left largely intact.

The Norman kings assembled councils composed of court officials, barons, and prelates—of whom the number present depended on the importance of the business to be discussed. In its fullest form this assembly was known as the "Great Council," and was looked upon as constitutionally a continuation of the witenagemot. Under the feudal system, it was the duty of each baron to advise the king on any matter on which he might request the baron's opinion. The early Great Councils were feudal assemblies summoned by the king for the purpose of obtaining such advice.

The conversion of the Great Council into what we now know as Parliament came about during the thirteenth and early fourteenth centuries. The word *parliament* was in use slightly earlier to describe any important meeting held for the purpose of discussion. This word was first officially applied to certain Great Councils of a particular character in the time of Henry III (reigned 1216–1272). The distinguishing feature of the early parliaments was the fact that the barons of the Council were invited not only to express their opinions individually on matters laid before them by the king, but to discuss, *with each other*, the overall "state of the realm"—the business "of king and kingdom" rather than only "the king's business." The earliest parliament clearly identifiable as of this character was held in 1258.

A second important change in the English national assembly began soon afterward with the introduction into Parliament of representatives of the shires (knights) and of the towns or boroughs (burgesses)—that is, taken together, representatives of the *communities,* or *Commons.* Although a number of precedents for such a step had been set earlier, the first national parliament in which the Commons were included was that held by Edward I in 1275. Initially, the primary purpose in summoning the Commons was usually to obtain their approval for measures of taxation, and they were included in Parliament only on occasions when such support was desired. After 1311, however, the Commons were in attendance at every parliament. Separation of Parliament into the two branches which later became known as the House of Lords and the House of Commons took place by degrees and was completed shortly after 1340.

Development of Procedure in Parliament

"The proceedings of parliament in ancient times, and for a long while," Thomas Jefferson wrote more than four and a half centuries later (in the preface to his famous *Manual,* discussed below), "were crude, multiform, and embarrassing. They have been however constantly advancing towards uniformity and accuracy. . . ."*

Many of the advances in the parliamentary system alluded to by Jefferson occurred from the latter part of the sixteenth century through the seventeenth century. This was a period of prolonged internal conflict over the prerogatives of Parliament—as opposed to those of the king—which stimulated an increased interest in procedure, especially in the House of Commons. During this same time, the Journal of the House of Commons, which was first undertaken by the clerk of the House on his own initiative in 1547, became established as a source of precedent on matters of procedure. The first recorded instance of such use of this Journal was in 1580 or 1581. The Journal was given official status as a document of the Commons about 1623.

Roughly concurrent with the initiation of the Journal of the House of Commons was the development of a body of writing on its procedure. The earliest formal treatment of the Commons' procedure in

---

*Thomas Jefferson, preface to *A Manual of Parliamentary Practice for the Use of the Senate of the United States* (1801; reprint, Old Saybrook, Ct.: Applewood Books, 1993), p. xv.

English was written between 1562 and 1566 by Sir Thomas Smyth and was published in 1583, six years after the author's death, as part of a larger work, *De Repvblica Anglorvm: The manner of Gouernement or policie of the realme of England*. Activity by other authors in writing treatises on parliamentary precedents and practices followed. In 1689, George Petyt listed as references for his small book, *Lex Parliamentaria* (London), thirty-five earlier parliamentary works or sources. In his book—a pocket manual prepared for the convenience of members of Parliament—Petyt includes entries from the Journal of the House of Commons relating to procedure, of which the following examples illustrate the gradual evolution of parliamentary law and are readily recognized as early wordings of present-day principles and rules:

- *One subject at a time:* 1581. When a Motion has been made that Matter must receive a Determination by the Question, or be laid aside by the general Sense of the House, before another be entertain'd. (p. 158.)
- *Alternation between opposite points of view in assignment of the floor:* 1592. It was made a Rule, That the Chair-man shall ask the Parties that would speak, on which side they would speak . . . and the Party that speaketh against the last Speaker, is to be heard first. (p. 209.)
- *Requirement that the chair always call for the negative vote:* 1604. [I]t is no full Question without the Negative part be put, as well as the Affirmative. (p. 161.)
- *Decorum and avoidance of personalities in debate:* 1604. He that digresseth from the Matter, to fall upon the Person, ought to be suppressed by the Speaker. . . . No reviling or nipping words must be used. (p. 157.)
- *Confinement of debate to the merits of the pending question:* 1610. A Member speaking, and his speech, seeming impertinent, and there being much hissing and spitting, it was conceived for a Rule, that Mr. Speaker may stay impertinent Speeches. (p. 156.)
- *Division of a question:* 1640. If a Question upon a Debate contains more Parts than one, and Members seem to be for one Part, and not for the other; it may be moved, that the same may be divided into two, or more Questions: as Dec. 2, 1640, the Debate about the Election of two Knights was divided into two Questions. (p. 169.)

The Parliamentary Process Brought to America

The same period when the procedure of the House of Commons was undergoing its new development was also the time during which permanent English colonies were established in the Western Hemisphere, beginning with Virginia in 1607. The founding of this colony was soon followed by the institution of the first representative assembly in America, authorized for Virginia by the governor acting for the London Company in 1619. This body consisted of a House of Burgesses as an elected lower chamber and a small Governor's Council as an upper chamber. As additional colonies were founded, similar assemblies were established in them, and succeeding generations of English settlers brought along the parliamentary processes they had known in the old country.

Into each legislature—into county, town, and parish meeting—the colonists transplanted the rules and customs of Parliament, as far as these rules and customs were applicable under the particular company charter, proprietary grant, or similar instrument by which the colony was established. This new type of self-government, through general parliamentary principles operating under specifications contained in a written basic document, represented a phase in the development of parliamentary law that was peculiar to America, since in England the Constitution was unwritten. Thus, each colony acquired the beginning of a body of experience later to go into the framing of individual state constitutions. The manner in which these rules and customs were adapted to meet the situation within each colony may account for the local variance in parliamentary tradition which persisted among people in America long after the founding of the United States, and that would eventually be one of the conditions that led to the writing of *Robert's Rules of Order*.

When policies of the mother country in the 1700s had gradually changed with the growth of the British Empire in such a way as to set the stage for the American Revolution, representatives of the different colonies considered common resistance to the actions of Parliament. In these deliberations, the colonists were able to function effectively by depending on procedures originally developed in Parliament itself!

The First Continental Congress, convening in Philadelphia on September 5, 1774, was made up of delegates largely unacquainted with the representatives of colonies other than their own, and most of the advance planning among the colonies had been by correspondence. Thus, the accomplishments of the first two days of the Congress are worth mentioning as an indication of the grounding and experience of the members in parliamentary methods, and of the thoroughness of their preparation. By September 7 the Continental Congress had: (1) examined the credentials of, and certified as delegates, the accredited representatives; (2) completed its own organization by adopting four "rules of conduct to be observed in debating and determining the questions"; and (3) made progress toward carrying out its purposes to the extent of adopting resolutions for the appointing of committees to study the colonies' rights and to examine statutes affecting their trade and manufactures.

Under existing rules and customs, the Second Continental Congress carried on the war; it also directed the framing of, and adopted, the Declaration of Independence. In assemblies in each state, through similar proceedings somewhat modified by local tradition, colonial charters were amended to conform to an independent status, or new state constitutions were drafted. Many of the provisions thus codified had been gradually arrived at by the separate colonies over periods of more than a hundred years. These state constitutions in turn—stemming from a common experience with English law and adapting that law to the new conditions—provided the material from which the Constitution of the United States was produced at the Constitutional Convention in 1787, in the face of seemingly deep and discouraging disagreements.

By the close of the eighteenth century, the stages through which the parent English parliamentary methods had passed in America may be summarized as follows:

- the use, within each colony, of such parliamentary rules as were applicable under its individual charter or other authorization for the establishment of the colony;
- the application of these same practices in intercolonial gatherings when representatives of the colonies met to act in their common interest; and
- the use of parliamentary procedure as an instrument for implementing the processes of representative government under a written constitution.

Jefferson's *Manual*

Despite this progress, the parliamentary system of the young United States needed further codification. As presiding officer of the Senate while serving as Vice-President of the United States (1797–1801),

Thomas Jefferson saw this need, which he described—with respect to the situation in the Senate—in this way:

> The Constitution of the United States . . . authorizes each branch of [the Congress] "to determine the rules of its own proceedings." The Senate have accordingly formed some rules for their own government; but these going only to few cases, they have referred to the decision of their President, without debate and without appeal, all questions of order arising either under their own rules or where they have provided none. This places under the discretion of the President [of the Senate] a very extensive field of decision . . . which, irregularly exercised, would have a powerful effect on the proceedings and determinations. . . . The President must feel . . . the necessity of recurring . . . to some known system of rules. . . . But to what system . . . is he to recur, as supplementary to [the rules] of the Senate?*

Parliament, Jefferson concluded, provided the most practical model for the Congress. It had "served as a prototype to most of" the existing state legislatures. It was "the model which we have all studied, while we are little acquainted with the modifications of it in our several states. . . . Its rules are probably as wisely constructed for governing the debates of a deliberative body, and obtaining its true sense, as any which can become known to us. . . . (p. xiv.)

"Considering therefore the law of proceedings in the Senate as composed of the precepts of the constitution, the regulations of the Senate, and, where these are silent, of the rules of Parliament,"** Jefferson compiled his *Manual of Parliamentary Practice,* published in 1801. In it, he extensively cited about fifty English works and documents on parliamentary law and related subjects. Among his sources, however, Jefferson in his preface to the *Manual* (p. xv) acknowledges primary indebtedness to *Precedents of Proceedings in the House of Commons* by John Hatsell, who was clerk of the House of Commons from 1768 to 1820. First published in 1781, Hatsell's work is today the best authority on eighteenth-century procedure in the House of Commons.

The position of Jefferson's *Manual* is unchallenged as the first to define and interpret parliamentary principles for our democratic republic

---

*Jefferson, *Manual*, pp. xiii, xiv.
**Ibid., p. xiv.

and to offer a basic pattern of rules and a measure of uniformity for the legislative processes of the United States. The authority of the *Manual* became established through its adoption by state legislatures and by other groups. The House of Representatives also adopted Jefferson's *Manual;* however, differences between the House and the Senate would cause the House to develop and become governed by a separate body of rules and practices largely superseding Jefferson's work.

Cushing's *Manual*

Within a few decades after Jefferson wrote his *Manual,* the formation of societies of various kinds—political, cultural, scientific, charitable, and religious—began to create an increasing need for a body of rules adapted to the requirements of nonlegislative organizations. It seems to have been early recognized that such societies have a deliberative character which calls for the application of essentially the same principles of decision as in a legislative body. Yet certain differences in their conditions—as compared with those of the legislative body—must be taken into account in the formulation of any system of rules suitable for the occasional meeting or the nonlegislative organization. For example:

- Congress and most state legislatures are composed of two Houses, with sessions (p. 80) usually lasting from several months to nearly a year; but sessions of an ordinary local society rarely last longer than one meeting of two or three hours.
- The members of a legislative body are generally paid to attend its daily meetings and can be legally compelled to do so, so that the quorum—in Congress, for example—is a majority of the members; but the quorum in a voluntary society must be much less if the organization is to be able to function.
- The business of a legislative body is vastly greater in volume and more complex than that of the typical ordinary society, so that most of the work in legislative bodies is done in standing committees, whereas in a local society it is handled by the assembly or, if necessary, is assigned to special committees.

The first author who attempted to meet the procedural needs of the country's growing number of voluntary societies was Luther S.

Cushing (1803–1856), Clerk of the Massachusetts House of Representatives and a noted jurist. His small volume, *Manual of Parliamentary Practice: Rules of Proceeding and Debate in Deliberative Assemblies*—which became known as "Cushing's Manual"—was published in 1845, with a section of further notes being added in 1847. This work, the author said, was intended for "assemblies of every description, but more especially for those which are not legislative in their character."* Cushing accordingly omitted from his manual rules applicable only to lawmaking bodies, but he included those that he considered suitable for both legislative and lay assemblies.

Among Cushing's observations and conclusions with respect to nonlegislative assemblies in particular were the following:

1. The general parliamentary rules in Jefferson's *Manual* formed "the basis of the common parliamentary law of this country." (p. 4.)
2. Through modifications by state legislatures, "a system of parliamentary rules [had] been established in each state, different in some particulars from those of every other state." (p. 13.)
3. Some ordinary meetings were conducted "not merely according to the general parliamentary law" but also following the system of the individual state. (p. 14.)
4. For such societies to be considered bound by the parliamentary practice of a particular state legislature in this way, Cushing held, was "erroneous." (p. 14.)
5. The "occasional assembly" or ordinary organization was properly subject only to the common parliamentary law and to such rules as the body would specially adopt for itself. (p. 14.)

In adherence to the last proposition, Cushing confined his book to what he considered "common parliamentary law," and prescribed that on all other necessary matters of procedure, each organization or assembly should adopt rules of its own *(rules of order)*—much as Congress and legislatures do.

Although Cushing's *Manual* was concisely written, was well received, and became a classic accepted as standard, it was to prove in-

---

*Luther Cushing, *Manual of Parliamentary Practice: Rules of Proceeding and Debate in Deliberative Assemblies,* 7th ed. (Boston: Taggard & Thompson, 1847), p. 4.

sufficient to the needs of the assemblies for which it was intended. The devising of an adequate supplementary system of rules of order by each assembly for its own use—as envisioned by Cushing—was to prove a task beyond the capacity of the average organization. In the years following the Civil War, the confusion that still existed in parliamentary practice among the multiplying number of lay associations and meetings became a matter of concern to Henry Martyn Robert.

Genesis of *Robert's Rules of Order*

Henry Martyn Robert (1837–1923) was an engineering officer in the regular army—finally attaining the rank of Brigadier General as chief of his corps—who was active in church organizations and civic and educational work wherever he was stationed, as much as military duties allowed him time. His interest in parliamentary law—as he often related—had been precipitated in 1863 at New Bedford, Massachusetts, where he had been transferred from more strenuous war duty after a recurrence of tropical fever. Without warning, he was asked to preside over a meeting, and did not know how. But he felt that the worst thing he could do would be to decline. "My embarrassment was supreme," he wrote. "I plunged in, trusting to Providence that the assembly would behave itself. But with the plunge went the determination that I would never attend another meeting until I knew something of . . . parliamentary law."*

Afterward, in a small book on another subject he found a few pages of "rules for deliberative assemblies." From these he copied information "showing four or five motions according to rank" (see pp. 59–61), "two or three . . . that could not be debated and some that could not be amended" and carried it on a slip of paper in his wallet for several years afterward. With this, he hoped he would be safe.

In 1867 Robert was promoted to Major and ordered to San Francisco, which was then a turbulent community made up of people recently arrived from every state. As he and his wife worked with persons from different parts of the country in several organizations seeking to

---

*Henry Martyn Robert, notes for a lecture in Cincinnati, c. 1916, in Henry M. Robert Papers, Library of Congress. Further quotations of remarks by General Robert are from the same source, except as noted.

improve social conditions there, they found themselves in the midst of a strange situation. Remarking on it many years later, in a lecture in Cincinnati, he stated that "Friction as to what constituted parliamentary law was indeed no uncommon thing." Each member of these organizations had brought from his home state different and often strong convictions as to what were correct parliamentary rules, and a presiding officer usually followed the customs of the locality from which he came. Under these conditions, confusion and misunderstanding had reached a point where issues of procedure consumed time that should have gone into the real work of the societies.

Robert doubted that these organizations would be able to function efficiently until there could be better agreement as to what constituted parliamentary law. In his words:

> So I inquired at the largest book store for the best books on the subject. *Cushing's Manual* was handed me and also *Wilson's Digest,* a book containing about 2400 decisions made in the English Parliament and our Congress. Then I sent for the *Congressional Manual,* which contained *Jefferson's Manual—*. . .[,] The Rules of the House of Representatives and Barclay's *Digest of Rules and Practice of the House.* . . .
>
> A careful reading of these books showed that it was not an easy matter to decide what was parliamentary law. . . . For instance, both Jefferson and Cushing gave an equal rank to the motions for the Previous Question, and to Postpone Definitely, and Indefinitely, and to Commit; the House of Representatives makes them rank thus: Previous Question, Postpone Definitely, Commit, Amend, and Postpone Indefinitely at the foot of the list; and the Senate does not allow the Previous Question and instead of placing Indefinitely Postpone at the foot, it puts it at the head of the list. Also if a motion to strike out a paragraph is lost, the paragraph can afterwards be amended according to the rules and practice of both Houses of Congress, but it could not be amended according to Jefferson and Cushing and the practice of the English Parliament. In Congress the question would be stated and put on striking out the paragraph whereas according to the other authorities it should be put on whether the paragraph shall stand as a part of the resolution.
>
> Again, as to debate: The U.S. Senate allowed each member to speak twice on the same day to the same question without any

limit as to time; all the other authorities allowed only one speech from each member on any question, and the House of Representatives also limited that speech to one hour. Also in Congress certain motions are undebatable, whereas the other authorities did not allude to such a thing as an undebatable motion, except that Cushing said in a note that legislative bodies usually, to quote, "provide that certain questions, as for example, to Adjourn, to Lay on the Table, for the Previous Question, or as to the Order of Business, shall be decided without debate."

These examples will . . . show the difficulties in the way of [anyone] . . . who was anxious to know enough [parliamentary law] to enable him to cooperate with others in effective work in lines in which he was interested.

Robert decided to prepare a few rules of order—expected to run to about sixteen pages—which he hoped would be suitable for the societies to which he and his wife belonged. If these organizations adopted such rules, "each member could know what motions could be debated and amended, which ones required a two-thirds vote, and what was the order of precedence."* When a few sheets had been printed, he began to try them out. The reception was encouraging, but the pamphlet was never completed. He came to the conclusion that the real problem would not be solved by "a half dozen societies having a system of parliamentary law of their own."

At about this time (1871), Robert was transferred to duty based in Portland, Oregon. Although he was obliged to lay aside parliamentary studies because of heavier responsibilities, such contact with organizations as he had time for strengthened ideas which had begun to crystallize in San Francisco: (1) In the country at large, the average society would find it difficult to have an adequate set of rules of order prepared specially for its own use, as Cushing had apparently expected it to do. Few ordinary organizations had, in fact, done so. (2) Even if a society were in a position to work out a satisfactory set of rules, this would only create further multiplicity. *The need was the reverse—to enable civic-minded people to belong to several organizations or to move to new localities*

---

*That is, which motions can be made when which others are pending (see p. 58).

without constantly encountering different parliamentary rules. (3) Conditions in ordinary societies, different as the purposes of those societies might be, were sufficiently similar from a parliamentary point of view to be guided by practically the same rules of order. (4) As far as any trend could be seen, it appeared that the best presiding officers were following the practice of the U.S. House of Representatives on basic points, such as the order of precedence of motions, which motions could be debated, and so on. The practice of the House was then approaching an established form after marked evolution during the preceding decades—during which it had become considerably different from the "old common parliamentary law" as laid down by Jefferson and Cushing.

Robert thus became convinced of the need for a new kind of parliamentary manual, *"based, in its general principles, upon the rules and practice of Congress, and adapted, in its details, to the use of ordinary societies.* Such a work should give, not only the methods of organizing and conducting the meetings, the duties of the officers and the names of the ordinary motions, but in addition, should state in a systematic manner, in reference to each motion, its object and effect; whether it can be amended or debated; if debatable, the extent to which it opens the main question to debate; the circumstances under which it can be made, and what other motions can be made when it is pending."*

Writing such a manual as Robert envisioned would amount to weaving into a single whole a statement of existing parliamentary law and a set of proposed rules of order. His idea was that the book should be written in a form suitable for adoption by any society, without interfering with the organization's right to adopt any special rules it might require. In the manual, rules taken from the practice of the House should be used except in specific cases where analysis showed that some other rule was better for the conditions in an ordinary organization—which did not, for example, have the enormous volume of business to be handled, the sharp division along party lines, or the extended length of congressional sessions with daily meetings. Sometimes the Senate practice might be preferable, such as allowing each member to speak twice to the same question on the same day.

---

*Henry M. Robert, preface to *Pocket Manual of Rules of Order for Deliberative Assemblies*, 1st ed. (Chicago: S.C. Griggs & Company, 1876), p. 3 (carried with but slight variation in several succeeding editions (emphasis added).

Robert had no time to begin writing until January 1874 in Milwaukee, when a severe winter tied up army engineering services along Lake Michigan for about three months. By October he had a revised manuscript of the rules of order proper, for which he was ready to seek a publisher. This manuscript, which would have made up the complete book as he originally conceived it, became the first part of the work that was finally published. When early efforts to obtain a publisher failed, he decided to have 4,000 copies made by a job printer at his own expense and under his direction. Since Robert's military duties often would not permit him to correct proofs promptly, the printer could only spare enough type to set and print sixteen pages at a time— the type then being distributed and used again for the next sixteen pages.

The printing slowly progressed in this manner through most of the year 1875. Soon after it began, Robert—having concluded, at least partly through his wife's influence, that more information should be added for the benefit of persons with no experience in meetings— wrote and added a second part, to which he gave the title "Organization and Conduct of Business." Because of its purpose and the nature of its contents, Part II was written in a simpler style, and it contained such repetition of material from Part I as the author thought would be useful to the intended reader. By the end of 1875, the printing of the two parts of the *Pocket Manual of Rules of Order for Deliberative Assemblies* (176 pages) was completed.

Even then, with his 4,000 "ready-printed" copies, the author was able to obtain a contract with a publisher only by making unusual concessions. In the face of the latter's skepticism as to the demand for such a work, Robert agreed to pay for binding the 4,000 copies and to bear the expense of giving 1,000 copies of the book to parliamentarians, educators, legislators, and church leaders throughout the country. The first edition of the manual accordingly was published by S. C. Griggs and Company of Chicago on February 19, 1876. The publisher placed on the cover the title *Robert's Rules of Order*. That first edition is now long a rare book.

Robert expected the 3,000 copies available for sale to last two years, during which he planned to prepare a revision on the basis of comments and suggestions from users. But the edition—received with immediate and enthusiastic acclaim—was sold out in four months. Six weeks after the original publication, work was begun on a second edition, with sixteen more pages, which was ready at the end of July 1876.

The following year, the portions of the second 1876 edition comprising the elementary Part II, "Organization and Conduct of Business," and the "Table of Rules Relating to Motions"—which, with continuing development, has been found in all editions but was originally a new and unique feature of the *Pocket Manual*—were also offered separately in paperback under the title *Parliamentary Guide* (price twenty-five cents). The *Guide* did not remain long in print, however, as the demand apparently was for the complete *Robert's Rules of Order* (then priced at seventy-five cents). The latter volume gained another twenty-six pages through changes and additions made by the author in a third edition issued in 1893.

In 1896, when the Griggs firm went out of business, the then recently formed Scott, Foresman and Company purchased the former publisher's list and thus acquired the publishing rights to *Robert's Rules of Order*. The designation "Robert's Rules of Order," the short title printed on the cover of the *Pocket Manual,* properly refers only to the three earliest editions, the last of which was superseded in 1915. At that time, the three editions of the *Pocket Manual* had totaled more than a half million copies.

Subsequent Revisions

Robert's Rules of Order Revised, the first complete revision, was the product of three years of the original author's full-time effort, beginning in 1912, with his second wife, Isabel Hoagland Robert, a former teacher, acting as his secretary and editorial assistant. (His first wife, Helen Thresher Robert, who influenced him to include the elementary portion in the first edition, had died in 1895.) The revision was published on May 5, 1915. Shortly afterward, General Robert wrote that much more work had been put into it than into the three previous editions combined. The 1915 revision, expanded by 75 percent from the 1893 edition, had less than one fourth of its content taken directly from that edition. The reorganization, expansion, and clarification represented by *Robert's Rules of Order Revised* was largely the outgrowth of hundreds of letters received by the author over the years, submitting questions of parliamentary law arising in organizations and not covered in the earlier editions.

Upon General Robert's death in 1923, his only son, Henry M. Robert, Jr.—a professor of mathematics, and later economics, at the United States Naval Academy, who also taught parliamentary law at Columbia University during each summer session—took over the author's office under a trust that his father had established. In that capacity, Henry Jr. continued his father's practice of replying to parliamentary questions from users of the book. It had been the original author's wish that after his death his son should further revise the manual as developments might dictate. Henry Jr. looked forward to doing this following his retirement from the Naval Academy, but he died in 1937 before that time came.

The trusteeship of *Robert's Rules of Order Revised* then passed to Henry Jr.'s widow, Sarah Corbin Robert—like Isabel, a former teacher. At General Robert's request, she had served as a critical reader in the preparation of his last two books, the elementary text, *Parliamentary Practice* (1921), and the work he considered his definitive explanatory effort, *Parliamentary Law* (1923). She had also substituted in teaching her husband's courses at Columbia when Henry Jr. had to give up doing so because of an increased workload at the Naval Academy.

In 1943, changes that General Robert had recorded between 1915 and the time of his death, for inclusion in the next revision of the manual, were incorporated within the 1915 pagination with Isabel and Sarah Robert serving as editors. Under their authorship, additional front and end matter was inserted and further in-page changes were made for the Seventy-fifth Anniversary Edition of 1951. Under the title of *Robert's Rules of Order Revised,* the manual thus remained in basically the 1915 typesetting until 1970, by which time a combined total of 2.65 million copies of all editions issued until then had had been in use.

About 1960, work was begun on a second complete revision of the book under the direction of Sarah Corbin Robert. She was joined in this project by her son, Henry M. Robert III, and by William J. Evans, a Baltimore lawyer, with James W. Cleary later serving as an editorial adviser to the publisher. This undertaking had a twofold goal: (1) a thorough overhauling of the parliamentary content dictated by two generations' use of the then-existing work, and (2) the new development of a reference book that would both be suitable for adoption by organizations as their parliamentary authority, and at the same time be as readable and as near to completely self-explanatory as possible—equally useful to a presiding officer, organization member, parliamentarian, and instructor in parliamentary procedure. Achieving this dual goal to the authors' best ability proved to be a task whose magnitude was only dimly perceived at the outset. The resulting general revision of the book was published as *Robert's Rules of Order Newly Revised* on the ninety-fourth anniversary of the publication of the first edition, February 19, 1970. As the original author stated that more work had been put into the 1915 revision than into the three previous editions combined, so it is believed that more work went into the production of the 1970 edition of *Robert's Rules of Order Newly Revised* than into all six editions brought out previously.

An additional key figure in guiding the authorship affairs of the book since that time, particularly in their commercial aspect, has been John Robert Redgrave, a great-grandson of the original author and the business representative of The Robert's Rules Association, which replaced the first trust after the death of General Robert's last surviving child.

Consistent with the earlier practice of publishing partial revisions containing in-page changes within the same pagination, a 1981 edition prepared by Henry M. Robert III and William J. Evans made a number of clarifications throughout the work. These changes were the result of experience in using the book in the eleven-year period following the 1970 revision. Some of the more important areas of clarification related to the *Previous Question,* the motion to *Lay on the Table,* the nature of a board as a form of assembly, the rule prohibiting interruption of actual voting, and the rules governing amendment at the expiration of the allotted time under different kinds of orders limiting debate or setting a time for voting. The 1981 edition was issued additionally in paperback format by Scott, Foresman and Company in 1984. This was the first time that a current edition of the complete manual had been offered in paperback.

In 1990, the same process was carried further with the issuance of a ninth edition of the work, again authored by Henry M. Robert III and William J. Evans, with Daniel H. Honemann, also a Baltimore attorney, then joining to assist them. Under new technology applied to that edition, however, a complete resetting of the book became for the first time an easy matter. This fact permitted a greater variety of changes and the incorporation of more additional material than would otherwise have been feasible. A listing of some of the more important areas of revision in the 1990 edition appears in its preface. Two of the most significant of these were the reinsertion, in improved form, of a subsection on hints to inexperienced presiding officers found in earlier editions, and a new treatment of some standard principles of interpretation of by-laws and other documents.

This tenth edition is published as the Millennium Edition of the year 2000. It responds anew to the ever continuing need for further refinement of interpretation and for answering newly arising questions. This edition is the work of four coauthors, Henry M. Robert III, William J. Evans, Daniel H. Honemann, and now Thomas J. Balch, a member of the Illinois bar residing in Virginia.

All editions of the work issued after the death of the original author have thus been prepared by persons who either knew and worked with him or are connected to such persons in a direct continuity of professional association.

An accompanying development since the appearance of the 1990 edition relates to the publisher. For most of the century now drawn to a close—for all but the first twenty years of the work's long life—the name of Robert's Rules of Order has been synonymous with that of Scott, Foresman and Company, much as the names of Merriam and Webster. As changes in the economics of publishing have dictated the sale and division of companies since 1990, however, the publishing rights in the book have successively passed to HarperCollins and then to Addison, Wesley, Longman. And now, for this Millennium Edition, The Robert's Rules Association is happy to welcome Perseus Books as the new official publisher of this standard manual.

Influence of Robert

The crux of *Robert's Rules of Order*'s initial contribution was in making it possible for assemblies and societies to free themselves from confusion and dispute over rules governing the use of the different motions of parliamentary law. In this respect the book filled the need that the author accurately stated in the quotation from his preface found on page xxxviii of this introduction.

In basing his rules on the practice of the U.S. House of Representatives in the manner already described, Robert stated that this practice—except where obviously unsuited to ordinary societies—had come to determine the actual common parliamentary law of the country, just as the practice of the House of Commons had done in England. Within any assembly or organization, however, it was his idea that the authority of his rules should rest on formal adoption of his manual by the particular body. But the book was soon cited increasingly as an authority apart from individual adoption—in such a manner as to constitute acknowledgment of its rules as parliamentary law itself. Thus Robert—by offering a codification of the rules and practices of the House of Representatives adapted to ordinary societies—gave formal direction to a movement toward establishing a more complete common parliamentary law, built upon congressional practice. In this way, Robert had a central role in bringing the parliamentary law of the United States to a stability and a stage of development that led former House parliamentarian Clarence Cannon to describe it as a "system of procedure adapted to the wants of deliberative assemblies generally and which, though variously interpreted in minor details by different writers, is now in the main standardized and authoritatively established."*

In an often quoted statement, the original author said: "The great lesson for democracies to learn is for the majority to give to the minority a full, free opportunity to present their side of the case, and then for the minority, having failed to win a majority to their views, gracefully to submit and to recognize the action as that of the entire organization, and cheerfully to assist in carrying it out, until they can secure its repeal."** But this same man, as he headed many engineering boards in the later phases of his professional career, became known for guiding them to produce reports that were unanimously concurred in by the board members. His record as a leader in civic, social-service, and church activities was similar. He was loath to settle for less.

This was not the contradiction that it may at first seem. Robert was surely aware of the early evolutionary development of parliamentary procedure in the English House of Lords resulting in a movement from "consensus," in its original sense of unanimous agreement, toward a decision by majority vote as we know it today. This evolution came about from a recognition that a requirement of unanimity or near unanimity can become a form of tyranny in itself. In an assembly that tries to make

---

* *Encyclopaedia Britannica*, 1958 ed., s.v. "Rules of Order."
**Henry M. Robert, *Parliamentary Law* (1923; reprint, New York: Irvington Publications, 1975), p. 4.

such a requirement the norm, a variety of misguided feelings—reluctance to be seen as opposing the leadership, a notion that causing controversy will be frowned upon, fear of seeming an obstacle to unity—can easily lead to decisions being taken with a pseudoconsensus which in reality implies elements of default, which satisfies no one, and for which no one really assumes responsibility. Robert saw, on the other hand, that the evolution of majority vote in tandem with lucid and clarifying debate—resulting in a decision representing the view of the deliberate majority—far more clearly ferrets out and demonstrates the will of an assembly. It is through the application of genuine persuasion and parliamentary technique that General Robert was able to achieve decisions in meetings he led which were so free of divisiveness within the group.

PRINCIPLES UNDERLYING PARLIAMENTARY LAW

The rules of parliamentary law found in this book will, on analysis, be seen to be constructed upon a careful balance of the rights of persons or subgroups within an organization's or an sssembly's total membership. That is, these rules are based on a regard for the rights:

- of the majority,
- of the minority, especially a strong minority—greater than one third,
- of individual members,
- of absentees, and
- of all these together.

The means of protecting all of these rights in appropriate measure forms much of the substance of parliamentary law, and the need for this protection dictates the degree of development that the subject has undergone.

Parliamentary procedure enables the overall membership of an organization—expressing its general will through the assembly of its members—both to establish and empower an effective leadership as it wishes, and at the same time to retain exactly the degree of direct control over its affairs that it chooses to reserve to itself.

Ultimately, it is the majority taking part in the assembly who decide the general will, but only following upon the opportunity for a deliberative process of full and free discussion. Only two thirds or more of those present and voting may deny a minority or any member the right of such discussion.

In this connection, there is an underlying assumption of a *right* that *exists* even though it may not always be prudent or helpful for it to be exercised. Each individual or subgroup has the right to make the maximum effort to have his, her, or its position declared the will of the assembly to the extent that can be tolerated in the interests of the entire body.

Another important principle is that, as a protection against instability—arising, for example, from such factors as slight variations in attendance—the requirements for changing a previous action are greater than those for taking the action in the first place.

Fundamentally, under the rules of parliamentary law, a deliberative body is a free agent—free to do what it wants to do with the greatest measure of protection to itself and of consideration for the rights of its members.

The application of parliamentary law is the best method yet devised to enable assemblies of any size, with due regard for every member's opinion, to arrive at the general will on the maximum number of questions of varying complexity in a minimum amount of time and under all kinds of internal climate ranging from total harmony to hardened or impassioned division of opinion.

THE DELIBERATIVE ASSEMBLY: ITS TYPES AND THEIR RULES

§1. THE DELIBERATIVE ASSEMBLY

1

Nature of the Deliberative Assembly

A *deliberative assembly*—the kind of gathering to which parliamentary law is generally understood to apply—has the *5* following distinguishing characteristics:

- It is a group of people, having or assuming freedom to act in concert, meeting to determine, in full and free discussion, courses of action to be taken in the name of *10* the entire group.
- The group meets in a single room or area or under equivalent conditions of opportunity for simultaneous aural communication among all participants.
- The group is of such size—usually any number of per- *15* sons more than about a dozen—that a degree of formality is necessary in its proceedings.

- Persons having the right to participate—that is, the members—are ordinarily free to act within the assembly according to their own judgment.
- In any decision made, the opinion of each member present has equal weight as expressed by vote—through which the voting member joins in assuming direct personal responsibility for the decision, should his or her vote be on the prevailing side.
- Failure to concur in a decision of the body does not constitute withdrawal from the body.
- If there are absentee members—as there usually are in any formally organized assembly such as a legislative body or the assembly of an ordinary society—the members present at a regular or properly called meeting act for the entire membership, subject only to such limitations as may be established by the body's governing rules (see "quorum of members," however, pp. 20–21; also **40**).

The rules in this book are principally applicable to meeting bodies possessing all of the foregoing characteristics. Certain of these parliamentary rules or customs may sometimes also find application in other gatherings which, although resembling the deliberative assembly in varying degrees, do not have all of its attributes as listed above.*

The distinction should be noted between the *assembly* (that is, the *body of people* who assemble) and the *meeting* (which is the *event* of their being assembled to transact business). The relation between these terms, however, is

---

*Efforts to conduct the deliberative process by postal or electronic mail or facsimile (fax) transmission–which are not recommended–must be expressly authorized by the bylaws and should be supported by special rules of order and standing rules as appropriate, since so many situations unprecedented in parliamentary law may arise and since many procedures common to parliamentary law are not applicable (see pp. 482–83).

such that their application may coincide; a "mass meeting," for example, is described below as one type of assembly. The term *meeting* is also distinguished from *session*, according to definitions stated in **8.** A session may be loosely described as a single complete course of an assembly's engagement in the conduct of business, and may consist of one or more meetings.

A *member* of an assembly, in the parliamentary sense, as mentioned above, is a person having the right to full participation in its proceedings—that is, as explained in **3** and **4,** the right to *make motions,* to speak in *debate* on them, and to *vote.* Some organized societies define different classes of "membership," not all of which may include this status. Whenever the term *member* is used in this book, it refers to full participating membership in the assembly unless otherwise specified. Such members are also described as "voting members" when it is necessary to make a distinction.

A deliberative assembly that has not adopted any rules is commonly understood to hold itself bound by the rules and customs of the *general parliamentary law*—or *common parliamentary law* (as discussed in the Introduction)—to the extent that there is agreement in the meeting body as to what these rules and practices are. Most assemblies operate subject to one or more classes of written rules, however, that the particular body—or, sometimes, a higher authority under which it is constituted—has formally adopted. Taken as a whole, such rules may relate to the establishment of the organization or society of which the assembly is the meeting body, they may interpret or supplement the general parliamentary law, or they may involve provisions not directly related to the transaction of business. The classes of rules that an assembly or an organization may adopt and the position that the rules in this book assume within such a body's overall system of rules are initially explained in **2.** Aside from rules of parliamentary procedure and the par-

1 ticular rules of an assembly, the actions of any deliberative
body are also subject to applicable procedural rules prescribed by local, state, or national law and would be null
and void if in violation of such law.*

5   The basic principle of decision in a deliberative assembly is that, to become the act or choice of the body, a
proposition must be adopted by a *majority vote;* that is, direct approval—implying assumption of responsibility for
the act—must be registered by more than half of the mem-
10 bers present and voting on the particular matter, in a regular or properly called meeting at which the necessary
minimum number of members, known as a quorum (pp.
20–21), is present (see also p. 387). Modifications of the
foregoing principle that impose a requirement of more than
15 a majority vote arise: (a) where required by law; (b) where
provided by special rule of a particular organization or assembly as dictated by its own conditions; or (c) where required under the general parliamentary law in the case of
certain steps or procedures that impinge on the normal
20 rights of the minority, of absentees, or of some other group
within the assembly's membership.

When a decision is to be based on more than a majority, the requirement most commonly specified is a *two-
thirds vote*—that is, the expressed approval of at least two
25 thirds of those present and voting. Under certain circumstances, whatever the vote required, there may be an additional requirement of *previous notice,* which means that
notice of the proposal to be brought up—at least briefly describing its substance–must be announced at the preceding
30 meeting or must be included in the "call" of the meeting at

---

*If the assembly is itself a lawmaking body, its actions are subject to ap-
plicable law of a higher authority—as, for example, the acts of a state legislature in the United States, which must not be in conflict with the constitution
of that state, with national law, or with the national constitution.

which it is to be considered (see also pp. 116–18). The call *1* of a meeting is a written notice of the time and place, which is mailed or distributed to all members of the organization a reasonable time in advance. Other bases for decision which find use in certain cases are defined in **44,** such as a *5* *majority of the entire membership*—that is, more than half of all the members.

Types of Deliberative Assembly

10

The deliberative assembly may exist in many forms. Among the principal types that it is convenient to distinguish for the purposes of parliamentary law are: (1) the *mass meeting;* (2) the *assembly of an organized society,* particularly when meeting at the local or lowest subdivisional *15* level; (3) the *convention;* (4) the *legislative body;* and (5) the *board.* A brief introductory explanation of the five principal types of deliberative assembly is given below.

THE MASS MEETING.   The mass meeting is the *20* simplest form of assembly in principle, although not the one most frequently encountered. A mass meeting is a meeting of an unorganized group that is announced as open to everyone (or everyone within a specified sector of the population) interested in a particular problem or pur- *25* pose defined by the meeting's sponsors, and that is called with a view to appropriate action to be decided on and taken by the meeting body. A series of connected meetings making up a session may be held on such a basis. The class of persons invited might be, for example, supporters of a *30* given political party, homeowners residing within a certain city, persons opposed to a tax increase, or any similar group. Admittance may be limited to the invited category if desired. Everyone who attends a mass meeting has the right to participate in the proceedings as a member of the assem- *35* bly, upon the understanding that he is in general sympathy with the announced object of the meeting.

It should be noted that a large attendance is not an essential feature of the mass meeting, although it may usually be desired. A series of meetings held for the purpose of organizing a society are in the nature of mass meetings until the society has been formed.

Mass meetings are particularly treated in **53.**

THE LOCAL ASSEMBLY OF AN ORGANIZED SOCIETY.   The assembly at the meetings of an organized permanent society existing as a local club or local branch is the type of assembly with which the average person is most likely to have direct experience. As the highest authority within such a society or branch (subject only to the provisions of the *bylaws* or other basic document establishing the organization), this body acts for the total membership in the transaction of its business. Such an assembly's membership is limited to persons who are recorded on the rolls of the society as voting members in good standing. The bylaws of an organized local society (see pp. 12–14) usually provide that it shall hold regular meetings at stated intervals—such as weekly, monthly, quarterly, or sometimes even annually—and also that it shall establish a procedure for calling special meetings as needed (see pp. 89–90). Each of these meetings in such an organization normally is a separate session (**8**).

THE CONVENTION.   A convention is an assembly of *delegates* (other than a permanently established public lawmaking body) chosen, normally for one session only, as representatives of constituent units or subdivisions of a much larger body of people in whose name the convention sits and acts.

The most common type of convention is that of an organized state or national society—held, for example, annually or biennially—in which the delegates are selected by, and from among the members of, each local branch. A convention is sometimes also called for the purpose of forming an association or federation; or, like a mass meeting, it may be convened to draw interested parties or representatives of interested organizations together in acting upon a common problem. The ordinary convention seldom lasts longer than a week. In principle, however, there is no limit on the length of the convention session. A constitutional convention, for example—convoked to draft a proposed new state constitution—may continue for weeks or months.

The voting membership of a convention consists of persons who hold proper credentials as delegates or as persons in some other way entitled to such membership, which must be certified and reported to the convention by its Credentials Committee. Whenever the term "majority of the entire membership" is used in this book, it means, in the case of a convention of delegates, a majority of the total number of convention members entitled to vote, as set forth in the official roll of voting members of the convention (pp. 390–91, 598–99).

The conclusion of the convention session normally dissolves the assembly. In the case of a state or national society, when another convention convenes a year or two later, it is a new assembly.

Conventions are particularly treated in **58, 59,** and **60**.

THE LEGISLATIVE BODY. The term *legislative body* refers to a constitutionally established public lawmaking body of representatives chosen by the electorate for a fixed term of office—such as Congress or a state legislature. Such a body typically (though not always) consists of two assemblies, or "houses." Its sessions may last for months, during which it meets daily and its members are paid to devote their full time to its work and can be legally compelled to attend its meetings.

Each state or national legislative assembly generally has its own well-developed body of rules, interpretations, and precedents, so that the exact procedure for a particular legislative house can be found only in its own manual.

In this connection, however, it should be noted that certain smaller public bodies may serve a lawmaking function yet not assume the character of a full-scale legislative assembly, and instead may somewhat resemble a board or the assembly of a society. An example of such a body might be a city council that meets weekly or monthly and whose members continue their own full-time occupations during their term of service.

THE BOARD. A board, in the general sense of the term, is an administrative, managerial, or quasi-judicial body of elected or appointed persons that has the character of a deliberative assembly (as described on pp. 1–2) with the following variations:

a) boards have no minimum size and are frequently smaller than most other assemblies; and
b) while a board may or may not function autonomously, its operation is determined by responsibilities and powers delegated to it or conferred on it by authority outside itself.

A board may be assigned a particular function on behalf of a national, state, or local government, as a village board that operates like a small city council, a board of education, or a board of examiners. In a nonstock corporation that has no assembly or body of persons constituting a general voting membership, as a university or foundation, the board of directors, managers, trustees, or governors is the supreme governing body of the institution. Similarly, in a stock corporation, although the board of directors is elected by stockholders who hold an annual meeting, it constitutes the highest authority in the management of the corporation. A board within an organized society is an instrumentality of the society's full assembly, to which it is subordinate. Boards are discussed in greater detail in **49.**

Applicability of Modified Parliamentary Rules in Small Boards and Committees

The distinction between a *board* and a *committee* must be briefly noted here for an understanding of what follows. A board of any size is a form of assembly as just explained. Committees, on the other hand, are bodies that are often, but not necessarily, very small, and that are subordinate instruments of an assembly or are accountable to a higher authority in some way not characteristic of an assembly. A large board, and a large committee, generally follow parliamentary procedure the same as any assembly. In small boards and committees, most parliamentary rules apply, but certain modifications permitting greater flexibility and informality are commonly allowed. Whenever it is stated in this book that a particular rule applies to "small boards and committees," the size implied will depend somewhat on conditions, but such a group is usually to be understood as consisting of not more than about a dozen persons. The distinguishing characteristics of boards and committees are discussed in **49** and **50.**

§2. RULES OF AN ASSEMBLY OR ORGANIZATION

An organized society requires certain rules to establish its basic structure and manner of operation. In addition, a need

1 for formally adopted rules of procedure arises in any assembly, principally because there may be disagreement or a lack
of understanding as to what is parliamentary law regarding
points that can affect the outcome of substantive issues.

5   Experience has shown that some of the rules of a society
should be made more difficult to change, or to suspend—
that is, to set aside for a specific purpose—than others. Upon
this principle, the rules which an established organization
may have are commonly divided into classes—some of which
10 are needed by every society, while others may be required
only as conditions warrant. Within this framework under the
general parliamentary law, an assembly or society is free to
adopt any rules it may wish (even rules deviating from parliamentary law) provided that, in the procedure of adopting
15 them, it conforms to parliamentary law or its own existing
rules. The only limitations upon the rules that such a body
can thus adopt might arise from the rules of a parent body (as
those of a national society restricting its state or local
branches), or from national, state, or local law affecting the
20 particular type of organization.

        The various kinds of rules which a society may for-
mally adopt include the following: Corporate Charter,
Constitution and/or Bylaws, Rules of Order (which include a standard work on parliamentary law adopted as
25 the society's Parliamentary Authority, and any Special
Rules of Order), and Standing Rules. Each of these types
of rules is discussed below. (For a more complete treatment of constitution and/or bylaws, see **56** and **57.**)

30   **Corporate Charter**

        The Corporate Charter (in different states variously
called the *Certificate of Incorporation, Articles of Incorporation, Articles of Association,* etc.) is a legal instrument that sets
forth the name and object of the society and whatever other

information is needed for incorporating the society under the *1*
laws of the particular state—or under federal law in the case
of a few special types of organizations. Incorporation is sometimes necessary or may be advisable, depending upon the differing laws of each state, if the organization is to hold *5*
property, inherit a legacy, make legally binding contracts, hire
employees, be in a position to sue or be sued as a society, protect its officers and members from personal liability, or the
like. Apart from this consideration, in general, a society need
not be incorporated unless incorporation is dictated by a law *10*
relating to the society's contemplated activities.

A corporate charter should be drafted by an attorney
and must then be processed in accordance with the legal
procedure for incorporation in the state (or under federal
law if applicable). Any later amendments (that is, changes in *15*
the charter) are subject to the requirements of law and any
limitations placed in the charter itself.

In an incorporated organization, the corporate charter
supersedes all its other rules, none of which can legally
contain anything in conflict with the charter. Nothing in *20*
the charter can be suspended by the organization itself
unless the charter so provides. For these reasons, a corporate charter generally should contain only what is necessary to obtain it, and to establish the desired status of the
organization under law—leaving as much as possible to *25*
the bylaws or to lower-ranking rules if appropriate in accordance with the principles explained below and in **56.***

---

*The word *charter* may also refer to a certificate issued by a national
or state organization, granting the right to form a particular local or subordinate unit. While such a charter is not an instrument of incorporation
and is usually quite general in its terms, it supersedes any rules the subordinate body may adopt, because it carries with it the requirement that the
subordinate unit adopt no rules that conflict with those of the grantor.

Constitution; Bylaws

In general, the constitution or the bylaws—or both—of a society are the documents that contain its own basic rules relating principally to itself as an organization, rather than to the parliamentary procedure that it follows. In the ordinary case, it is now the recommended practice that all of a society's rules of this kind be combined into a single instrument, usually called the "bylaws," although in some societies called the "constitution"—or the "constitution and bylaws," even when it is only one document. The term *bylaws,* as used in this book, refers to this single, combination-type instrument—by whatever name the particular organization may describe it—which:

1) should have essentially the same form and content whether or not the society is incorporated (except for the omission or inclusion of articles on the name and object as noted below);

2) defines the primary characteristics of the organization—in such a way that the bylaws serve as the fundamental instrument establishing an unincorporated society, or conform to the corporate charter if there is one;

3) prescribes how the society functions; and

4) includes all rules that the society considers so important that they (a) cannot be changed without previous notice to the members and the vote of a specified large majority (such as a two-thirds vote), and (b) cannot be suspended (with the exception of clauses that provide for their own suspension under specified conditions, or clauses in the nature of rules of order as described on p. 17, l. 22–24; see also pp. 254–55, 562–64).

While the number of articles in the bylaws will be determined by the size and activities of the organization, the general nature of the subjects covered will be indicated by the following list of articles, typical of those found in the bylaws of the average unincorporated society: (1) Name of the organization; (2) its Object; (3) Members; (4) Officers; (5) Meetings; (6) Executive Board (if needed); (7) Committees; (8) Parliamentary Authority (that is, the name of the manual of parliamentary procedure that the organization is to follow; see below); and (9) Amendment (prescribing the procedure for making changes in the bylaws). If the society is incorporated, its name and its object are usually set forth in the corporate charter, in which case the first two articles listed above should be omitted from the bylaws. The appropriate content of bylaws is discussed in detail in **56.**

It formerly was common practice to divide the basic rules of an organization into two documents, in order that one of them—the *constitution*—might be made more difficult to amend than the other, to which the name *bylaws* was applied. In such a case, the constitution would generally contain the most essential provisions relating to the first five items listed in the preceding paragraph (leaving additional details to the bylaws), and would prescribe the procedure for amending the constitution. Such an arrangement may still be found in cases where a national, state, or local law applying to the particular type of organization requires a constitution separate from the bylaws, or in older organizations that have had little occasion to change their existing rules. Unless the constitution is made more difficult to amend than the bylaws, however, no purpose is served by separating these two sets of rules. In an incorporated society there gener-

1 ally should not be a constitution separate from the bylaws, since in such a case the constitution would duplicate
much of the corporate charter. Although it is not improper, in an unincorporated society, to have both a con-
5 stitution and bylaws as separate documents (provided
that the constitution is made more difficult to amend),
there are decided advantages in keeping all of the provisions relating to each subject under one heading within a
single instrument—which results in fewer problems of
10 duplication or inconsistency, and gives a more under-
standable and workable body of rules.

Except for the corporate charter in an incorporated society, the bylaws (as the single, combination-type instrument is called in this book) comprise the highest body of
15 rules in societies as normally established today. Such an instrument supersedes all other rules of the society, except the
corporate charter, if there is one. In organizations that have
both a constitution and bylaws as separate documents,
however, the constitution is the higher of the two bodies of
20 rules and supersedes the bylaws.

The bylaws, by their nature, necessarily contain whatever limitations are placed on the powers of the assembly of
a society (that is, the members attending a particular one of
its meetings) with respect to the society as a whole. Simi-
25 larly, the provisions of the bylaws have direct bearing on the
rights of members within the organization—whether present or absent from the assembly. It is a good policy for
every member on joining the society to be given a copy of
the bylaws, printed together with the corporate charter, if
30 there is one, and any special rules of order or standing rules
that the society may have adopted as explained below. A
member should become familiar with the contents of these
rules if he looks toward full participation in the society's
affairs.

Rules of Order

The term *rules of order* refers to written rules of parliamentary procedure formally adopted by an assembly or an organization. Such rules relate to the orderly transaction of business in meetings and to the duties of officers in that connection. The object of rules of order is to facilitate the smooth functioning of the assembly and to provide a firm basis for resolving questions of procedure that may arise.

In contrast to bylaws, rules of order derive their proper substance largely from the general nature of the parliamentary process rather than from the circumstances of a particular assembly. Consequently, although the tone of application of rules of order may vary, there is little reason why most of these rules themselves should not be the same in all ordinary societies and should not closely correspond to the common parliamentary law. The usual method by which an ordinary society now provides itself with suitable rules of order is therefore to include in its bylaws a provision prescribing that the current edition of a specified and generally accepted manual of parliamentary law shall be the organization's *parliamentary authority,* and then to adopt only such *special rules of order* as it finds needed to supplement or modify rules contained in that manual. If a society has already adopted bylaws that do not designate a parliamentary authority, one may be adopted by the same vote as a special rule of order. In a mass meeting or a meeting of a body not yet organized, adoption of a parliamentary authority (or individual rules of order) may take place at the beginning of the meeting by majority vote. Special rules of order supersede any rules in the parliamentary authority with which they may conflict. The average society that has adopted a suitable parliamentary authority seldom needs special rules of order,

1 however, with the exception—in certain cases—of a rule establishing the society's own order of business (see p. 24), and a rule relating to the length or number of speeches permitted each member in debate. These rules
5 are usually adopted in the form of *resolutions* (pp. 32, 100–105), but when they are printed, the enacting words ("*Resolved,* That") are dropped.

When a society or an assembly has adopted a particular parliamentary manual—such as this book—as its au-
10 thority, the rules contained in that manual are binding upon it in all cases where they are not inconsistent with the bylaws (or constitution) or any special rules of order of the body, or any provisions of local, state, or national law applying to the particular type of organization. What
15 another manual may have to say in conflict with the adopted parliamentary authority then has no bearing on the case. In matters on which an organization's adopted parliamentary authority is silent, provisions found in other works on parliamentary law may be *persuasive*—that is,
20 they may carry weight in the absence of overriding reasons for following a different course—but they are not binding on the body.

Although it is unwise for an assembly or a society to attempt to function without formally adopted rules of order,
25 a recognized parliamentary manual may be cited under such conditions as persuasive. Or, by being followed through long-established custom in an organization, a particular manual may acquire a status within the body similar to that of an adopted parliamentary authority.

30 Any special rules of order should be adopted separately from the bylaws and should be printed in the same booklet with, but under a heading separate from, the bylaws. Although rules in the nature of special rules of order are sometimes placed within the bylaws—as occurs most fre-
35 quently when a society prescribes its own order of busi-

ness—such an arrangement is less desirable, since it may   *1*
lead to cases of uncertainty as to whether a particular rule
can be suspended.

In some organizations a particular practice may sometimes come to be followed as a matter of established custom   *5*
so that it is treated practically as if it were prescribed by a
rule of order. However, if such a practice is or becomes in
conflict with the parliamentary authority or any written
rule of the organization, and a *Point of Order* (**23**) citing
the conflict is raised at any time, the custom falls to the   *10*
ground, and the conflicting provision in the parliamentary
authority or written rule must thereafter be complied with,
unless a special rule of order (or, in appropriate circumstances, a standing rule) is added or amended to incorpo-
rate the custom. If there is no contrary provision in the   *15*
parliamentary authority or written rules, the established
custom should be adhered to unless the assembly, by a majority vote, agrees to do otherwise.

Rules of order—whether contained in the parliamentary authority or adopted as special rules of order—can be   *20*
suspended by a two-thirds vote as explained in **25** (with
the exceptions there specified). Rules clearly identifiable
as in the nature of rules of order that are placed within the
bylaws can also be suspended by a two-thirds vote; but,
except for such rules and for clauses that provide for their   *25*
own suspension, as stated above, bylaws cannot be suspended.

Adoption or amendment of special rules of order that
are separate from the bylaws requires either (a) previous notice (pp. 116–18) and a two-thirds vote or (b) a vote of a   *30*
majority of the entire membership. After the bylaws of a society have been initially adopted when the organization is
formed, the adoption or amendment of special rules of
order placed within the bylaws is subject to the procedure
for amending the bylaws (see **57**).   *35*

1   **Standing Rules**

Standing rules, as understood in this book except in the
case of conventions, are rules (1) which are related to the
5   details of the administration of a society rather than to parliamentary procedure, and (2) which can be adopted or
changed upon the same conditions as any ordinary act of
the society. An example of such a rule might be one setting
the hour at which meetings are to begin, or one relating to
10 the maintenance of a guest register. Standing rules generally
are not adopted at the time a society is organized, but individually if and when the need arises. Like special rules of
order, standing rules may be printed under a separate heading in the booklet containing the bylaws, and in such a case,
15 any enacting words such as "*Resolved,* That" should be
dropped. A standing rule can be adopted by a majority vote
at any business meeting without previous notice. Although
such a rule remains in effect until rescinded or amended, it
does not bind future sessions if a majority desires to sus-
20 pend it temporarily for the duration of a particular session.
(For the requirements for rescinding or amending such a
rule, see p. 295, l. 24–31.)

Standing rules in conventions differ from ordinary
standing rules in some respects, as explained on pages
25 599–601. Some assemblies, particularly legislative bodies,
also apply the name *standing rules* to their rules of order.
Whatever names an assembly may apply to its various rules,
the vote required to adopt, amend, or suspend a particular
rule is determined by the nature of its content according to
30 the definitions given above.

THE CONDUCT OF BUSINESS IN A DELIBERATIVE ASSEMBLY

§3. BASIC PROVISIONS AND PROCEDURES

The basic parliamentary concepts and practices are interconnected in such a way that a complete statement of the rules that relate to any one of them frequently involves reference to several other concepts. This section contains an initial explanation of a number of these topics, which are given a more detailed treatment later in this book.

In reading all that follows throughout this manual, it should be borne in mind that—as in any treatment of any subject—a statement of a rule generally cannot include all possible exceptions to the rule. Whenever a particular statement appears to conflict with a more general statement elsewhere in the book, therefore, the particular statement-

1 governs in the matter to which it states that it applies (see
also p. 571).

Minimum Composition of a Deliberative Assembly

5   QUORUM OF MEMBERS.   The minimum number
of members who must be present at the meetings of a deliberative assembly for business to be legally transacted is the
quorum of the assembly. The requirement of a quorum is a
10 protection against totally unrepresentative action in the
name of the body by an unduly small number of persons. In
both houses of Congress, the quorum is a majority of the
members, by the United States Constitution. Such a quorum is appropriate in legislative bodies but too large in most
15 voluntary societies. In an ordinary society, therefore, a provision of the bylaws should specify the number of members
that shall constitute a quorum, which should approximate
the largest number that can be depended on to attend any
meeting except in very bad weather or other extremely un-
20 favorable conditions. In the absence of such a provision in a
society or assembly whose real membership can be accurately determined at any time—that is, in a body having an
enrolled membership composed only of persons who maintain their status as members in a prescribed manner—the
25 quorum is a majority of the entire membership, by the
common parliamentary law. In the meetings of a convention, unless the bylaws of the organization provide otherwise, the quorum is a majority of the delegates who have
been registered at the convention as in attendance, irrespec-
30 tive of whether some may have departed. In a mass meeting,
or in a regular or properly called meeting of an organization
whose bylaws do not prescribe a quorum and whose membership is loosely determined (as, for example, in many
church congregations or alumni associations), there is no
35 minimum number of members who must be present for the

valid transaction of business, or—as it is usually expressed—   1
the quorum consists of those who attend the meeting. (The
rules relating to the quorum are more fully stated in **40.**)

MINIMUM OFFICERS.   The minimum essential of-   5
ficers for the conduct of business in a deliberative assembly
are a *presiding officer,* who conducts the meeting and sees
that the rules are observed, and a *secretary,* or *clerk,* who
makes a written record of what is done—usually called "the
minutes." If the officers are members of the assembly—as   10
they usually are in ordinary societies—they are counted in
determining whether a quorum is present.

The presiding officer should be placed so that, even when
he is seated—on a high stool if necessary when behind a
lectern—he can see the entire hall and all present can see him   15
(see also p. 433). The presiding officer's official place or station (usually in the center of the platform or stage, if there is
one) is called "the chair." During meetings, whoever is presiding is said to be "in the chair" (whether standing or seated
at the time), and he is also referred to as "the chair." The   20
phrase "the chair" thus applies both to the person presiding
and to his station in the hall from which he presides. The secretary's desk should be placed so that papers can easily be
passed to him from the chair during the meeting.

The duties of the presiding officer, the secretary, and   25
other officers that an assembly or society may have are described in **47.**

Pattern of Formality
30
Customs of formality that are followed by the presiding
officer and members under parliamentary procedure serve
to maintain the chair's necessary position of impartiality
and help to preserve an objective and impersonal approach,
especially when serious divisions of opinion arise.   35

1   CUSTOMS OBSERVED BY MEMBERS. The president or chief officer of an organized society, who normally presides at its meetings, is then addressed as "Mr. President" or "Madam President" (whether a married or un-
5 married woman), "Mr. [or Madam] Moderator," or by whatever may be his or her official title. In the lower house of a legislative body, this officer is most commonly "Mr. [or Madam] Speaker." A vice-president is addressed as "Mr. President" or "Madam President" while actually presiding.
10 (A possible exception may arise where the usual form would make the meaning unclear—for example, when the vice-president is in the chair while the president is also on the platform. In such an instance, the vice-president should be addressed as "Mr. [or Madam] Vice-President.") A person
15 presiding at a meeting who has no regular title or whose position is only temporary is addressed as "Mr. [or Madam] Chairman" by long-established usage. Several variations of this form—such as "chairperson" or "chair"—are now frequently encountered, however, and may be in use as the
20 general practice in particular assemblies. Even in a small meeting, the presiding officer of an assembly should not be addressed or referred to by name. (The only exceptions that might arise in an *assembly** would be in cases of a testimonial nature, such as in the presentation of a gift to a presi-
25 dent who is about to go out of office.) With nearly the same strictness of observance, he should not be addressed by the personal pronoun "you"—although occasional exceptions may occur in ordinary societies if brief administrative consultation takes place during a meeting. As a general rule,
30 when additional reference to the presiding officer is necessary in connection with addressing him by his official title,

---

*As distinguished from a small committee, where some relaxation of this rule may be appropriate, depending on the conditions.

members speak of him as "the chair"—as in, "Mr. President, do I understand the chair to state . . . ?"

Members address only the chair, or address each other through the chair. In the parliamentary transaction of business—within a latitude appropriate to the conditions of the particular body—members generally should try to avoid mentioning another member's name whenever the person involved can be described in some other way, as in, "Mr. President, may I ask the member to explain . . . ," or, "Mr. Chairman, I hope that the gentleman who last spoke will think of the probable consequences . . ." With a very limited number of particular exceptions, and except in small boards and committees, a member never speaks while seated; and with a slightly larger number of exceptions, a member does not speak (unless in a small board or a committee) without first having risen, addressed the chair, and *obtained the floor* as described on pages 28–30.

CUSTOMS OBSERVED BY THE PRESIDING OFFICER. The presiding officer speaks of himself only in the third person—that is, he never uses the personal pronoun "I." In actual parliamentary proceedings he always refers to himself as "the chair"—as in, "The chair rules that . . ." At other times during meetings—such as when he makes a report to the members in the capacity of an administrative officer of the organization rather than as presiding officer of the assembly—he may, if he wishes, describe himself by his official title, as in, "Your President is pleased to report . . ." Strictly speaking, the chair does not mention a member's name and does not address an individual member as "you," except in connection with certain disciplinary procedures (see p. 627). Instead he may say, for example, "The chair must ask the member to confine his remarks to the merits of the pending question." In practice in an ordinary lay assembly, however, there are a number of

1   occasions where the chair often refers to members by name,
     such as when assigning the *floor* (that is, the exclusive right
     to be heard at that time, as explained on pp. 28–30), or
     when announcing the members of a committee.

5   (For more complete explanations of the general forms
     observed by the presiding officer and members in an as-
     sembly, see **42** and **43**.)

10   **Call to Order; Order of Business**

         When the time of a meeting has arrived, the presiding
     officer opens it, after he has determined that a quorum is
     present, by *calling the meeting to order*. He takes the chair
15   (that is, occupies the presiding officer's station in the hall),
     waits or signals for quiet, and, while standing, announces in
     a clear voice, "The meeting will come to order," or, "The
     meeting will be in order." (For the procedure to be fol-
     lowed when a quorum of members do not appear, see pp.
20   336–37.) The call to order may be immediately followed by
     religious or patriotic exercises or other opening ceremonies.
         The initial procedures in a mass meeting or in one called
     to form a society are described in **53** and **54**. Sessions (**8**) of
     permanently organized bodies usually follow an established
25   *order of business* that specifies the sequence in which certain
     general types or classes of business are to be brought up or
     permitted to be introduced. If the assembly has no binding
     order of business, any member who obtains the floor (see pp.
     28–30) can introduce any legitimate matter he desires
30   (within the objects of the organization as defined in its by-
     laws) at any time when no business is before the assembly for
     consideration. A society may follow the order of business
     given in the manual that the bylaws of the organization des-
     ignate as its parliamentary authority, or it may have adopted
35   its own particular order of business. Although an organiza-
     tion has no binding order of business until it has either

adopted its own or has adopted a parliamentary authority that specifies one, the following order of business (which is fully explained in **41**) has come to be regarded as usual or standard for one-meeting sessions of ordinary societies:

1) Reading and Approval of Minutes*
2) Reports of Officers, Boards, and Standing (that is, permanently established) Committees
3) Reports of Special (Select or Ad Hoc) Committees (that is, committees appointed to exist only until they have completed a specified task)
4) Special Orders (that is, matters which have previously been assigned a type of special priority, as explained in **14** and **41**)
5) Unfinished Business and General Orders (that is, matters previously introduced which have come over from the preceding meeting)
6) New Business (that is, matters initiated in the present meeting)

In a meeting where an established order of business is being followed, the chair calls for the different classes of business in the prescribed order.

A mass meeting usually requires no order of business, since, referring to the headings listed above, there is nothing but new business to be brought up (unless the meeting is one within a series).

---

*The order of business is separate and distinct from the procedure of calling a meeting to order, which is not a part of the order of business. A meeting opens by being called to order even when it has no established order of business. Additional "calls to order" may occur during the order of business at various times not specified in advance, if the assembly takes a recess (**8**, **20**) or adjourns to a future time (**8**, **22**) before the order of business is completed. For these reasons, it is not proper to list a "call to order" as the first item in an order of business or agenda, as is often incorrectly done.

1   A convention commonly adopts its own order of business—which often specifies the exact hours at which certain
important questions are to be taken up. The order of business of a convention is known as the *program,* or the
5   *agenda,* depending on whether it is interwoven with, or
separate from, the overall schedule of convention meetings,
events, etc. (see **41, 59**).

A legislative body usually has a more elaborate order of
business suited to its own needs.

10

Means by Which Business Is Brought Before the Assembly

MOTIONS.   Business is brought before an assembly
15   by the *motion* of a member. A motion may itself bring its
subject to the assembly's attention, or the motion may follow upon the presentation of a report or other communication.

A motion is a formal proposal by a member, in a meet-
20   ing, that the assembly take certain action. The proposed action may be of a substantive nature, or it may express a
certain view or direct that a particular investigation be conducted and the findings be reported to the assembly for
possible further action, or the like.

25   The basic form of motion—the only one whose introduction brings business before the assembly—is a *main motion.* There are also many other separate parliamentary
motions that have evolved for specific purposes. While all of
these motions propose some form of action and while all of
30   them are said to be brought "before the assembly" when
they are placed under consideration, most of them do not
bring business before it in the sense described above—as a
main motion does. Many of these motions involve procedural steps relating to a main motion already being consid-
35   ered.

The main motion sets a pattern from which all other *1*
motions are derived. In the remainder of this chapter, rules
and explanations relating to "motions" have the main motion as their frame of reference. The manner in which a
main motion is brought before the assembly is explained on *5*
pages 31ff.

MOTIONS GROWING OUT OF REPORTS OR
COMMUNICATIONS. After the presentation of the report of an officer, a board, or a committee, one or more *10*
motions to carry out recommendations contained in the report may be introduced. (For the procedures in such cases,
see **41** and **51**.)

A motion may also grow out of the presentation of a
written communication to the assembly. This may be in the *15*
form of a letter or memorandum from a member who is not
present, from a superior body (such as a state or national
executive board to a local chapter), or from an outside
source. A communication normally is addressed to the president or secretary and is read aloud by the secretary—unless *20*
the presiding officer properly should read it because of special importance of the content or source.

It is not customary to make a motion to *receive* a communication or a committee report, which means only to
permit or cause such a paper to be read. This is an example *25*
of a case in the ordinary routine of business where the formality of a motion is dispensed with. It should be noted
that a motion "to receive" a communication after it has
been read is meaningless and should therefore be avoided.

The reading of a communication does not in itself for- *30*
mally bring a question before the assembly. After the reading, or at the time provided by the order of business, a
motion can be offered proposing appropriate action. If no
member feels that anything needs to be done, the matter is
dropped without a motion. *35*

1   BUSINESS THAT COMES UP WITHOUT A MO-
TION, BECAUSE OF PREVIOUS ACTION. Business
may come up automatically at a certain time, without a motion *at that time,* if the motion by which it was introduced
5 has previously been postponed (**14**) or made a special order
(**41**). In such cases, the business is announced at the proper
time by the chair.

Obtaining and Assigning the Floor
10

    Before a member in an assembly can make a motion or
speak in *debate*—the parliamentary name given to any
form of discussion of the merits of a motion—he must *obtain the floor;* that is, he must be *recognized* by the chair as
15 having the exclusive right to be heard at that time.* (For
the parliamentary motions that can be made without obtaining the floor, see tinted pp. 42–43.) The chair must
recognize any member who seeks the floor while entitled
to it.
20   To claim the floor, a member rises at his place when no
one else has the floor (or goes to a microphone in a large
hall), faces the chair, and says, "Mr. President," or "Mr.
Chairman," or "Madam Chairman," or whatever is the
chair's proper title. If the member is entitled to the floor at
25 the time, the chair recognizes him—normally by announcing, as applicable, the person's name or title, or the place or
unit that he represents. This member then has the floor**

---

    *This rule generally need not be adhered to in a small board or a com-
mittee.

    **The expression "privileges of the floor," sometimes used in legisla-
tive bodies or conventions, has nothing to do with *having the floor,* but
means merely that a person is permitted to enter the hall. It carries no right
to speak or any other right of membership, except as may be determined by
rules or action of the body.

and can remain standing and speak in debate or make a
motion as permitted under the rules in this book depending on the parliamentary situation at the time. If only one
person is seeking the floor in a small meeting where all
present know and can clearly see one another, the chair
can recognize the member merely by nodding to him. On
the other hand, if a speech is prearranged, or if several
members are attempting to claim the floor at once in a
large meeting, presiding officers often use the formal
wording, "The chair recognizes Mr. Smith." When the
names of the members are not generally known, a person
addressing the chair to claim the floor should state his
name and any necessary identification as soon as the presiding officer turns toward him, as "Edward Wells, Delegate, Crescent County." The chair then assigns the floor
by repeating the member's name or identification. When
the member finishes speaking, he *yields* the floor by resuming his seat.

If two or more rise at about the same time, the general
rule is that, all other things being equal, the member who
rose and addressed the chair first *after the floor was yielded* is
entitled to be recognized. A member cannot establish "prior
claim" to the floor by rising before it has been yielded. In
principle, it is out of order to rise or be standing while another person has the floor—except for the purpose of making
one of the motions or taking one of the parliamentary steps
that can legitimately interrupt at such a time (tinted pp.
42–43). In a very large assembly, if members must walk some
distance to microphones, it may be necessary to vary from
the preceding rule as dictated by conditions in the particular
hall. Some arrangements used in large assemblies are outlined
on page 371.

While a motion is open to debate, there are three important cases where the floor should be assigned to a person who may not have been the first to rise and address the

chair (but who did so before anyone had actually been recognized). These cases are as follows:

1) If the member who made the motion claims the floor and has not already spoken on the question, he is entitled to be recognized in preference to other members.
2) No one is entitled to the floor a second time in debate on the same motion on the same day as long as any other member who has not spoken on this motion desires the floor.
3) In cases where the chair knows that persons seeking the floor have opposite opinions on the question (and the member to be recognized is not determined by [1] or [2] above), the chair should let the floor alternate, as far as possible, between those favoring and those opposing the measure.

A member cannot rise for the purpose of claiming *preference in being recognized* (as this right is called in all of the above cases) after the chair has recognized another member. If at any time the chair makes a mistake, however, and assigns the floor to the wrong person—when preference in recognition was timely claimed or in any other case—his attention can be called to it by raising a *Point of Order* (**23**), and he should immediately correct the error.

The preceding rules usually are adequate for assigning the floor in most business meetings. In great assemblies or conventions, or in bodies that must handle a heavy agenda (**41**) or complex issues, additional situations often occur where the best interests of the assembly require the floor to be assigned to a claimant who was not the first to rise and address the chair. (For the rules governing these cases, see **42**.)

§4. THE HANDLING OF A MOTION

The handling of a motion varies in certain details according to conditions. In the ordinary case, especially under new business, there are six essential steps—three by which the motion is *brought before the assembly,* and three in the *consideration* of the motion.

How a Motion Is Brought Before the Assembly

The three steps by which a motion is normally brought before the assembly are as follows:

1) A member *makes* the motion. (The words *move* and *offer* also refer to this step. A person is said to "make a motion," but he uses the word "move" when he does so. He is also said "to move" a particular proposal, as in "to move a postponement.")
2) Another member *seconds* the motion.
3) The chair *states the question on the motion.* (The step of stating the question on the motion should not be confused with *putting the question,* which takes place later and means putting the motion to a vote.)

Neither the making nor the seconding of a motion places it before the assembly; only the chair can do that, by the third step (stating the question). When the chair has stated the question, the motion is *pending,* that is, "on the floor." It is then open to debate (if it is a main motion or one of several other *debatable* parliamentary motions, which are described in later chapters). If the assembly decides to do what a motion proposes, it *adopts* the motion, or the motion is *carried;* if the assembly expressly decides against doing what the motion proposes, the motion is *lost,* or *rejected.*

1   MAKING A MOTION.   To make a main motion, a member must obtain the floor, as explained above, when no other question is pending and when business of the kind represented by the motion is in order. The member then makes

5   his motion, in simple cases by saying, "I move that . . . [announcing what he proposes in a wording intended to become the assembly's official statement of the action taken]." For more important or complex questions, or when greater formality is desired, he presents the motion in the form of a *res-*

10 *olution.* The usual wording then is, "I move the adoption of the following resolution: '*Resolved,* That . . . '"; or, "I offer the following resolution: '*Resolved,* That . . . '" A resolution or a long or complicated motion should be prepared in advance of the meeting, if possible, and should be put into writ-

15 ing before it is offered. The mover then passes it to the chair as soon as he has offered it. If conditions make it impractical for a member offering a written resolution to read it himself, he should sign it and pass or send it to the chair ahead of time (in a large meeting, often by page or messenger), or he can

20 deliver it to the secretary before the meeting. In such a case the member offers his resolution by saying, "I move the adoption of the resolution relating to . . . which I have sent to the chair [or "have delivered to the Secretary"]." The chair then says, "The resolution offered by Mrs. A is as fol-

25 lows: . . . [or, "The Secretary will read the resolution offered by Mrs. A"]." (For additional information on the proper form for main motions and resolutions, see **10.**)

        As soon as a member has made a motion, he resumes his seat. He will have the right to speak first in debate, if he

30 wishes, after the chair has stated the question. If the motion has not been heard or is not clear, another member can ask that it be repeated, which the chair can request the maker or the secretary to do, or can do himself.

        Under parliamentary procedure, strictly speaking, discus-

35 sion of any subject is permitted only with reference to a pending motion. When necessary, a motion can be prefaced by a

few words of explanation, which must not become a speech; 1
or a member can first request information, or he can indicate
briefly what he wishes to propose and can ask the chair to assist him in wording an appropriate motion. In general, however, when a member has obtained the floor while no motion 5
is pending—unless it is for a special purpose, such as to ask a
question—he makes a motion immediately. Any desired im-
provements upon the member's proposal can be accomplished by several methods after the motion has been made
(for a summary, see pp. 108–11). For a member to begin to 10
discuss a matter while no question is pending, without
promptly leading to a motion, implies an unusual circumstance and requires permission of the assembly (see pp. 287–
88) in addition to obtaining the floor. In larger assemblies, this
rule requires firm enforcement. In smaller meetings, it may 15
sometimes be relaxed with constructive effect if the members
are not accustomed to working under the standard rule. Unless the assembly has specifically authorized that a particular
subject be discussed while no motion is pending, however,
such a discussion can be entered into only at the sufferance of 20
the chair or until a point of order is made; and in the latter
case, the chair must immediately require that a motion be offered or the discussion cease. The general rule against discussion without a motion is one of parliamentary procedure's
powerful tools for keeping business "on track," and an obser- 25
vance of its spirit can be an important factor in making even a
very small meeting rapidly moving and interesting.*

---

*In the very early development of parliamentary procedure, a presiding
officer was expected to distill from the debate the essence of a motion and, in
conclusion, take a vote on that motion. It was found in the House of Lords
in England that, when there was no definite motion pending, it was not possible to tell whether debate was germane, and the debate itself often became
discursive and lengthy. In addition, the presiding officer might not digest the
debate into a motion in a way satisfactory to most of the members. In such a
case, there was little opportunity to put the motion in proper form before voting, since the chair's formulation of it occurred at the conclusion.

SECONDING A MOTION. After a motion has been made, another member who wishes it to be considered says, "I second the motion," or, "I second it," or even, "Second!"—without obtaining the floor, and in small assemblies without rising.* In large assemblies, and especially in those where nonmembers may be seated in the hall, the seconder should stand, and without waiting to be recognized should state his name (with other identification, if appropriate) and say, "Mr. President [or "Mr. Chairman"], I second the motion." In some organizations, especially labor unions, the word "support" is used in place of "second."

If no member seconds the motion, the chair must be sure that all have heard it before proceeding to other business. In such a case the chair normally asks, "Is there a second to the motion?" In a large hall he may repeat the motion before doing so. Or, if a resolution was submitted in writing and read by the chair or the secretary rather than by the mover (as described on p. 32), the chair may say, "Miss A has moved the adoption of the resolution just read. Is there a second to the resolution?" If there still is no second, the chair says, "The motion [or "resolution"] is not seconded"; or, "Since there is no second, the motion is not before this meeting." Then he immediately says, "The next item of business is . . . "; or, if appropriate, "Is there any further business?"

A second merely implies that the seconder agrees that the motion should *come before the meeting* and not that he necessarily favors the motion. A member may second a motion (even if using the word "support" as indicated above) because he would like to see the assembly go on record as *rejecting* the proposal, if he believes a vote on

---

*Motions need not be seconded in a small board or a committee.

the motion would have such a result. A motion made by   *1*
direction of a board or duly appointed committee of the
assembly requires no second from the floor (provided the
subordinate group is composed of more than one person),
since the motion's introduction has been directed by a   *5*
majority vote within the board or committee and is therefore desired by at least two assembly members or elected
or appointed persons to whose opinion the assembly is
presumed to give weight regarding the board's or committee's concerns. (For rules governing the appointment   *10*
of non–assembly members to committees, see pp. 167,
475, 478–79.)

The requirement of a second is for the chair's guidance as
to whether he should state the question on the motion, thus
placing it before the assembly. Its purpose is to prevent time   *15*
from being consumed by the assembly's having to dispose of
a motion that only one person wants to see introduced.

In handling routine motions, less attention is paid to
the requirement of a second. If the chair is certain that a
motion meets with wide approval but members are slow in   *20*
seconding it, he can state the question without waiting for
a second. However, until debate has begun in such a case—
or, if there is no debate, until the chair begins to take the
vote and any member has voted—a point of order (see **23**)
can be raised that the motion has not been seconded; and   *25*
then the chair must proceed formally and ask if there is a
second. Such a point of order should not be made only for
the sake of form, if it is clear that more than one member
wishes to take up the motion. After debate has begun or, if
there is no debate, after any member has voted, the lack of   *30*
a second has become immaterial and it is too late to make a
point of order that the motion has not been seconded. If a
motion is considered and adopted without having been seconded—even in a case where there was no reason for the

1 chair to overlook this requirement—the absence of a second does not affect the validity of the motion's adoption.

(For lists of certain parliamentary motions that do not
require a second, see tinted pp. 42–43.)

5

THE STATING OF THE QUESTION BY THE
CHAIR.   When a motion that is in order has been made
and seconded, the chair formally places it before the assembly by *stating the question;* that is, he states the exact mo-
10 tion and indicates that it is open to debate (and certain
other parliamentary processes to be explained in **5** and **6**)
in the manner indicated below as appropriate to the case:

- The basic form used by the chair in stating the question
15   on an ordinary motion is, "It is moved and seconded that
[or "to"] . . . [repeating the motion]." The chair then
normally turns toward the maker of the motion to see if
he wishes to be assigned the floor. If the maker does not
claim the floor and, after a pause, no one else does, the
20   chair may ask, "Are you ready for the question?"* For example, "It is moved and seconded that the Society allocate fifty dollars for . . . "; or, ". . . that fifty dollars be
allocated . . . "; or, "It is moved and seconded to allocate
fifty dollars for . . . The chair recognizes Mr. A."
25 - In the case of a resolution, the chair may state the question by saying, "It is moved and seconded to adopt the
following resolution [or, ". . . that the following resolution be adopted"]; '*Resolved,* That . . . [reading the res-
olution].'"
30 - If the chair, in stating the question on a written resolution or motion, wishes the secretary to read it, he may

---

*In stating the question on one of the parliamentary motions that can
be neither debated nor amended (see **6**), the chair never includes the words
"Are you ready for the question?" but *puts the question* (that is, puts it to a
vote) immediately after stating it.

state the question as follows: "It is moved and seconded *1*
to adopt the resolution which the Secretary will now
read." Secretary reads resolution, after which chair continues: "The question is on the adoption of the resolution just read." *5*

- If a written resolution was not read by the mover but
was read by the chair or the secretary before being seconded, the chair may state the question thus: "It is
moved and seconded to adopt the resolution just read."

- The chair at his discretion may also use the form given *10*
immediately above in cases where the member offering
a resolution has read it clearly and the chair is confident
that all members have understood it. In such a case,
however, any member has the right to have the motion
or resolution read again when the question is stated. *15*

In principle, the chair must state the question on a motion immediately after it has been made and seconded, unless he is obliged to rule that the motion is out of order or
unless, in his opinion, the wording is not clear. *20*

Rules and explanations relating to the conditions under
which various motions are out of order will be found particularly in **5, 6,** and **7;** in **10** (pp. 106–108); and in the first
three of the "Standard Descriptive Characteristics" given in
the sections on each of the parliamentary motions (**11–37**). *25*
When a member who has legitimately obtained the floor offers a motion which is not in order, the chair may be able, in
certain instances, to suggest an alternative motion which
would be in order and would carry out the desired intent to
the satisfaction of the maker. If the chair is obliged to rule that *30*
the motion is out of order, he should say, "The chair rules
that the motion is out of order [or "not in order"] because
. . . [briefly stating the reason]." (He should not say, "You
are out of order," nor, "Your motion is out of order." To state
that a *member* is out of order implies that the member is *35*

1   guilty of a breach of decorum or other misconduct in a meeting; and even in such a case, the chair does not normally address the member in the second person. See pp. 23–24; also **61**.) If the chair rules that a motion is out of order, his deci-
5   sion is subject to an appeal to the judgment of the assembly. (For procedure regarding *Appeal,* see **24**.)

    If a motion is offered in a wording that is not clear or that requires smoothing before it can be recorded in the minutes, it is the duty of the chair to see that the motion is
10   put into suitable form—preserving the content to the satisfaction of the mover—*before* the question is stated. The chair should not admit a motion that the secretary would have to paraphrase for the record. The chair—either on his own initiative or at the secretary's request—can require any
15   main motion, amendment (**10, 12**), or instructions to a committee to be in writing before he states the question.

    Until the chair states the question, the maker has the right to modify his motion as he pleases or to withdraw it entirely. After the question has been stated by the chair, the
20   motion becomes the property of the assembly, and then its maker can do neither of these things without the assembly's consent (see pp. 283–86); but while the motion is pending the assembly can change the wording of the motion by the process of *amendment* (**12**) before acting upon it.

25   After a motion has been made but before the chair states it or rules that it is out of order, no debate is in order. At such a time, however, any member can quickly rise and, without waiting to be recognized, can say, "Mr. President, I would like to ask the maker of the motion if he will accept
30   the following modification: . . . [or, ". . . if he would be willing to change the words . . . to . . . "]." The maker then answers, "Mr. President, I accept [or "do not accept," or "cannot accept"] the modification"; or, he can respond by making a different modification: "Mr. President, I will
35   modify the motion as follows: . . . "

If the maker of a motion modifies it before the question is stated, a person who has seconded it has the right to withdraw his second; but if a modification is accepted *as suggested by another member*—either before or after the motion has been seconded—the suggester has in effect seconded the modified motion, so that no other second is necessary. Under any circumstances where a second is withdrawn but it is clear that another member favors consideration of the motion in its modified form, the chair treats the motion as seconded. If the maker makes any change in his motion and it remains, in effect, seconded, or (if necessary) is then seconded, the chair says, "It is moved and seconded . . . ," stating the question on the modified motion just as if it had been so moved originally. If a modification is suggested and the maker declines to make any change, the chair says, "The modification is not accepted," and (provided that the motion has been seconded) he states the question on it as it was moved by the maker.

Modifications of a motion that are suggested before the question is stated should usually be limited to changes that are likely to be generally acceptable to the members present—or, in other words, changes that probably would not occasion debate if proposed as amendments while the motion was pending.

In a similar manner, before the question on a motion has been stated, any member who believes that the maker will immediately withdraw the motion if a certain fact is pointed out to him can quickly rise and say (without waiting for recognition), "Mr. Chairman, I would like to ask if the member would be willing to withdraw his motion in view of . . . [stating the reasons for the suggested withdrawal]." The maker responds, "I withdraw [or "decline to withdraw"] the motion." If the maker withdraws his motion, the chair says, "The motion is withdrawn," and proceeds to the next business. If the purpose of the withdrawal

1 was to deal with a more urgent matter first, the chair immediately recognizes the appropriate member to bring it
up. If the maker is unwilling to withdraw his motion, the
chair says, "The member declines to withdraw the motion,"
5 and (if the motion has been seconded) he then states the
question.

Strictly speaking, before the question is stated no comment should accompany suggestions that a motion be modified or withdrawn. In ordinary meetings, however, time
10 can often be saved by brief informal consultation—which
the chair can permit at his discretion, provided that he is
careful to see that this privilege is not abused or allowed to
run into debate. The chair can frequently maintain the necessary control over such informal consultation by standing
15 while it takes place (in contrast to the rule that he should
normally be seated during debate unless it would obstruct
his view of the members; see pp. 435–36).

20 **The Consideration of a Main Motion: Basic Steps**

Once a main motion has been brought before the assembly through the three steps described above, there are
three further basic steps by which the motion is considered
in the ordinary and simplest case (unless it is adopted by
25 *unanimous consent,* as explained on pp. 51–53). These normal steps are as follows:

1) Members *debate* the motion (unless no member claims
   the floor for that purpose).
30 2) The chair *puts the question* (that is, puts it to a vote).
3) The chair *announces the result* of the vote.

In addition, while the motion is open to debate, the assembly may wish to take a number of actions as a part of the
35 motion's consideration—which can themselves be the sub-

ject of certain parliamentary motions, as explained in **5** and   1
6. In the following description of the three principal steps
in the consideration of a main motion, it is assumed that
none of these other motions are introduced.

                                                                        5

DEBATE ON THE QUESTION.   Immediately after
stating the question, the chair should turn toward the
maker of the motion to see if he wishes to be assigned the
floor first in debate—to which the maker has the right if he
claims it before anyone else has been recognized, even   10
though others may have risen and addressed the chair first.

Except in a small board or a committee, a member who
desires to speak in debate must obtain the floor as described
on pages 28–30. The chair in assigning the floor should be
guided by the principles explained in the same pages, and in   15
42. In the debate, each member has the right to speak twice
on the same question on the same day,* but cannot make a
second speech on the same question so long as any member
who has not spoken on that question desires the floor. A
member who has spoken twice on a particular question on   20
the same day has *exhausted his right to debate* that question
for that day.

Without the permission of the assembly, no one can
speak longer than permitted by the rules of the body—or,
in a nonlegislative assembly that has no rule of its own re-   25
lating to the length of speeches, longer than ten minutes.

Debate must be confined to the merits of the pending
question. Speakers must address their remarks to the chair,
maintain a courteous tone, and—especially in reference to
any divergence of opinion—should avoid injecting a per-   30
sonal note into debate. To this end, they must never attack
or make any allusion to the motives of members. As already

---

*For procedures where greater freedom of debate is desired, see **15**
and **52.**

noted, speakers should refer to officers only by title and should avoid the mention of other members' names as much as possible.

Except in small boards and committees, the presiding officer should not enter into discussion of the merits of pending questions (unless, in rare instances, he leaves the chair until the pending business has been disposed of, as described on pp. 382–83). While members are speaking in debate, the presiding officer should remain seated unless the view between him and the members would be obstructed. In the latter case, he should step back slightly while a member is speaking. Although the presiding officer should give close attention to each speaker's remarks during debate, he cannot interrupt the person who has the floor so long as that person does not violate any of the assembly's rules and no disorder arises. The presiding officer must never interrupt a speaker simply because he knows more about the matter than the speaker does.

The presiding officer cannot close debate so long as any member who has not exhausted his right to debate desires the floor, except by order of the assembly, which requires a two-thirds vote (**15, 16, 43**).

(For additional rules and information related to debate, see **43.**)

PUTTING THE QUESTION.   When the debate appears to have closed, the chair may ask, "Are you ready for the question?" If no one then rises to claim the floor, the chair proceeds to put the question—that is, he puts it to a vote after once more making clear the exact question the assembly is called upon to decide. If the chair's wording of the question is erroneous, a point of order may be made until any member has actually voted. Except as it may be corrected in response to such a point of order, the exact wording the chair uses in putting the question is definitive, and the wording in the minutes should be the same. Where there is any possibility of confusion, the chair, before calling for the vote, should make sure that the members understand the effect of an "aye" vote and of a "no" vote. In putting the question, the chair should stand (except in a small board or a committee) and should especially project his voice to be sure that all are aware that the vote is being taken. The vote on a motion is normally taken by *voice* (or *viva voce*),* unless, under certain conditions, it is taken by *rising* or—sometimes in committees, or in small boards, or other very small assemblies—by a *show of hands*. In putting the question by any of these methods, the chair calls first for the affirmative vote, and all who wish to vote in favor of the motion so indicate in the manner specified; then he calls for the negative vote. The chair must always call for the negative vote, no matter how nearly unanimous the affirmative vote may appear, except that this rule is commonly relaxed in the case of noncontroversial motions of a complimentary or courtesy nature; but even in such a case, if any member objects, the chair must call for the negative vote. A further exception arises when the negative vote is intrinsically irrelevant, as, for example, when "a vote of one fifth of the members present" is required, and the number who have voted in the affirmative is clearly greater than one fifth of those present (see p. 390). The chair should not call for abstentions in taking a vote, since the number of members who respond to such a call is meaningless. To "abstain" means not to vote at all, and a member who makes no response if "abstentions" are called for abstains just as much as one who responds to that effect (see also p. 394).

The three methods of putting the question stated in the preceding paragraph are described below. Other methods of taking a formal vote (as distinguished from adopting a

*Pronounced VIE-vuh VOE-see.

1   motion by unanimous consent, pp. 51–53) are used only
when expressly ordered by the assembly or prescribed by its
rules; they are described in **45.**

    Form for Taking a Voice Vote.   A vote by voice is the
5   regular method of voting on any motion that does not require more than a majority vote for its adoption (see p. 4;
44). In taking a voice vote, the chair puts the question by
saying, "The question is on the adoption of the motion to
[or "that"] . . . [repeating or clearly identifying the mo-
10   tion]. Those in favor of the motion, say *aye.** [Pausing for
response,] . . . Those opposed, say *no.*" (Alternative forms
are: "All those in favor . . . "; "All in favor . . . "; or the
wording formerly prescribed in Congress, "As many as are
in favor . . .") In the case of a resolution, the question may
15   be put as follows: "The question is on the adoption of the
following resolution: [reading it]. Those in favor of adopting the resolution that was just read, say *aye.* . . . Those opposed, say *no.*" If the resolution has been read very recently
and there appears to be no desire to have it read again, the
20   chair may use this form: "The question is on the adoption
of the resolution last read. Those in favor of adopting the
resolution, say *aye.* . . . Those opposed, say *no.*"

    Form for Taking a Rising (Division) Vote.   The simple
rising vote (in which the number of members voting on each
25   side is not counted) is used principally in cases where a voice
vote has been taken with an inconclusive result, and as the
normal method of voting on motions requiring a two-thirds
vote for adoption (see *Chair's Announcement of the Voting
Result,* etc., below). When only a majority is required, how-
30   ever, time may sometimes be saved by taking a rising vote initially, if the chair believes in advance that a voice vote *will be*
inconclusive. In all such cases the vote can be taken in a form
like this: "Those in favor of the motion to invite Mr. Jones to

---

*United States House of Representatives Rule I **§6.** Revision of 106th
Congress, 1999.

be guest speaker at our next meeting will rise. [Or, "stand."] *1*
... Be seated. ... Those opposed will rise. ... Be seated."

If a rising vote remains inconclusive, the chair or the assembly can order the vote to be counted (see p. 50; **30;** pp. 396–97). The form then used is, for example: "The question is on the motion to limit all speeches at this meeting to two minutes. Those in favor of the motion will rise and remain standing until counted. ... Be seated. Those opposed will rise and remain standing until counted. ... Be seated." *10*

Form for Taking a Vote by Show of Hands. As an alternative to voting by voice, a vote by show of hands can be used as the basic voting method in small boards or committees, and it is so used in some assemblies. An inconclusive voice vote is also sometimes verified by this method. *15* For either of these purposes, the use of voting by show of hands in *assemblies* should be limited to very small meetings where every member can clearly see every other member present. In voting by this method, the question can be put, for example, as follows: "The question is on the motion *20* that the bill for building repairs be paid as rendered. All those in favor of the motion will raise the right hand. ... Lower hands. [Or, nodding, "Thank you."] Those opposed will raise the right hand. ... Lower hands."

25

CHAIR'S ANNOUNCEMENT OF THE VOTING RESULT; VERIFICATION PROCEDURES AND CASES WHERE THE CHAIR VOTES. The chair, remaining standing, announces the result of the vote immediately after putting the question—that is, as soon as he has paused to *30* permit response to his call for the negative vote. A majority vote in the affirmative adopts any motion unless it is one of the particular motions that require a larger vote under parliamentary law or the rules of the organization. (For the parliamentary motions that require a two-thirds vote, see tinted *35*

p. 46). Under all of the voting methods described above except a counted rising vote (or a counted show of hands), the result is determined by the chair's judgment as to the more numerous side—which it is his duty, in doubtful cases, to verify beyond reasonable doubt, and to the satisfaction of the members, by the procedures described below.

In voting by any of these methods (including a counted rising vote), a member has the right to change his vote up to the time the result is finally announced. After that, he can make the change only by unanimous permission of the assembly. (See p. 395, and see pp. 51–53 regarding the granting of such permission by unanimous consent.)

Content of Complete Announcement.   In general (that is, as applying to main motions and other types of motions explained in later chapters), the chair's announcement of the result of the vote should include the following:

1) Report of the voting itself, stating which side "has it"—that is, which side is more numerous—or, in the case of a motion requiring a two-thirds vote for adoption, whether there are two thirds in the affirmative. If the vote has been counted, the chair should first give the count before announcing the prevailing side.

2) Declaration that the motion is adopted or lost.

3) Statement indicating the effect of the vote, or ordering its execution, if needed or appropriate (see p. 115 for an example).

4) Where applicable, announcement of the next item of business, or (in the case of "secondary" motions, which are described in the next chapter) stating of the question on the next motion that consequently comes up for a vote.

Form of Announcement.   The four points generally covered by the chair's announcement of the voting result as listed above are normally spoken without separation into distinct elements. Standard forms can be given only for the part of the announcement covered by the first two points as shown below. The form of the latter portion is determined by the particular motion and the circumstances under which it was moved. (For illustrations of the complete announcement as applicable to the different motions, see p. 115 and also *Form and Example* in **11–37**.) Depending on the voting method and the vote required for adoption of the motion, the chair makes the standard portion of the announcement as follows:

- *For a voice vote:* ". . . The ayes have it and the motion is adopted [or "agreed to" or "carried"]. . . ."* Or, ". . . The noes have it and the motion is lost. . . . "
- *For a rising vote (uncounted) or a vote by show of hands:* ". . . The affirmative has it and the motion is adopted. . . . " Or, ". . . The negative has it and the motion is lost. . . . "
- *For a rising vote or a show of hands on which a count has been ordered:* ". . . There are 32 in the affirmative and 30 in the negative. The affirmative has it and the motion is adopted. . . . " Or, ". . . There are 29 in the affirmative and 33 in the negative. The negative has it and the motion is lost. . . . "
- *For a motion requiring a two-thirds vote for adoption (where an uncounted rising vote is conclusive):* ". . . There are two thirds in the affirmative and the motion is adopted. . . . " Or, ". . . There are less than two thirds in the affirmative and the motion is lost. . . . "

---

*The ellipsis points (dots) before and after each form indicate that it follows immediately after the putting of the question, and is immediately followed by the remainder of the announcement of the result, as described above.

1   • *For a motion requiring a two-thirds vote for adoption
       (where a count of the vote is taken):* ". . . There are 51 in
       the affirmative and 23 in the negative. There are two
       thirds in the affirmative and the motion is adopted.
5   . . . " Or, ". . . There are 48 in the affirmative and 26 in
       the negative. There are less than two thirds in the affir-
       mative and the motion is lost. . . . "

    • *When the chair votes where his vote will affect the result*
       (see below): ". . . There are 35 in the affirmative and 35
10   in the negative. The chair votes in the affirmative, mak-
       ing 36 in the affirmative and 35 in the negative, so that
       the affirmative has it and the motion is adopted. . . . "
       Or, ". . . There are 39 in the affirmative and 38 in the
       negative. The chair votes in the negative, making 39 in
15   the affirmative and 39 in the negative, so that there is
       less than a majority in the affirmative and the motion is
       lost. . . . "

    • *When the chair votes where his vote will affect the result on
       a motion requiring a two-thirds vote for adoption:*
20   ". . . There are 59 in the affirmative and 30 in the neg-
       ative. The chair votes in the affirmative, making 60 in
       the affirmative and 30 in the negative, so that there are
       two thirds in the affirmative and the motion is adopted.
       . . . " Or, ". . . There are 60 in the affirmative and 30 in
25   the negative. The chair votes in the negative, making 60
       in the affirmative and 31 in the negative, so that there
       are less than two thirds in the affirmative and the mo-
       tion is lost. . . . "

30   *Verifying an Inconclusive Vote.*   A voice vote—or, in
     larger meetings, even a vote by show of hands—may some-
     times be inconclusive, either because the voting is close or
     because a significant number of members have failed to
     vote. If the chair feels that members may question a some-
35   what close result of which he is reasonably convinced, he

can first say, "The ayes [or "the noes"] *seem* to have it." The
chair then pauses, and any member who doubts the result
is thus invited to demand verification of the vote by a *division,* as explained below. If no member makes such a demand or states that he doubts the result, the chair
continues, "The ayes have it . . . ," as shown above. If the
chair is in actual doubt in the case of such a vote, however,
he should not announce a result, but should immediately
retake the vote—strictly speaking, always as a rising vote.
(Regarding use of a show of hands as a method of verifying
an inconclusive voice vote, however, see below.) If it appears when those in the affirmative rise that the vote will be
close enough to require a count, the chair should count the
vote, or direct the secretary to do so, or (in a large assembly) appoint a convenient number of tellers—preferably an
even number equally divided between members known to
be in favor of the motion and those opposed to it. If, after
a vote has been retaken as an uncounted rising vote, the
chair finds himself still unable to determine the result, he
should take the vote a third time as a *counted* rising vote.

Division of the Assembly. Whether or not the chair
pauses to say, "The ayes seem to have it . . . ," any member
(without a second) has the right to require that a voice vote
(or even a vote by show of hands) be retaken as a rising vote,
so long as he does not use the procedure as a dilatory tactic
when there clearly has been a full vote and there can be no
reasonable doubt of the result. A vote retaken by rising at the
demand of a member is called a *Division of the Assembly,* or
simply "a division." A member can demand a division from
the moment the negative votes have been cast until the announcement of the result is complete and (if such a point is
reached promptly) until the question is stated on another
motion. To do so, the member, without obtaining the floor,
calls out the single word "Division!" or "I call for [or "demand"] a division," or "I doubt the result of the vote." The

1 chair must then immediately take the rising vote. Either the
chair on his own initiative or the assembly by a majority vote
can order such a vote to be counted. If a division appears
doubtfully close and the chair does not order a count, a
5 member, as soon as the chair has declared the result, can rise
and address the chair, and is entitled to preference in recognition for the purpose of moving that the vote be counted. If
such a motion is made and is seconded, the chair puts the
question (by a voice vote) on whether a count shall be or-
10 dered. If a count is ordered, the chair takes the doubtfully
close division again by a counted rising vote. (For additional
information regarding *Division of the Assembly* and motions
relating to voting, see **29** and **30**.)

  Verification by Show of Hands.   In very small assem-
15 blies where everyone present can clearly see everyone else,
an inconclusive voice vote may sometimes be verified satisfactorily by a show of hands if no member objects. A show
of hands is not a division, however, and it is not always as
effective in causing a maximum number of members to vote
20 when some have not done so. In small meetings, a voice
vote can be retaken by a show of hands at the initiative of
the chair; or, during the same time that it is in order to demand a division, any member can call out, "Mr. President,
may we have a show of hands?" In either case, any other
25 member still has the right to demand a division, which requires the chair to take a rising vote. The chair can also immediately take a rising vote in response to a request for a
show of hands.

  Chair's Vote As Part of the Announcement, Where It Af-
30 *fects the Result.*   If the presiding officer is a member of the
assembly or voting body, he has the same voting *right* as any
other member. Except in a small board or committee, however—unless the vote is secret (that is, unless it is by ballot;
45)—the chair protects his impartial position by exercising
35 his voting right only when his vote would affect the out-

come, in which case he can either vote and thereby change *1*
the result, or he can abstain. If he abstains, he simply announces the result with no mention of his own vote. In a
counted rising vote (or a count of hands) on a motion requiring a majority vote for adoption, the outcome will be *5*
determined by the chair's action in cases where, without his
vote, there is (a) a tie, or (b) one more in the affirmative
than in the negative.* Since a majority in the affirmative is
necessary to adopt the motion in the case mentioned, a final
result in the form of a tie rejects it. When there is a tie with- *10*
out the chair's vote, the chair can vote in the affirmative, and
such a vote adopts the motion; but if the chair abstains from
voting, the motion is lost. When there is one more in the affirmative than in the negative without the chair's vote, the
motion is adopted if the chair abstains; but if he votes in the *15*
negative, the result is thereby tied and the motion is lost.

(For additional information regarding the procedures
used in voting, see **44** and **45**.)

Adoption of a Motion or Action Without a *20*
Motion, by Unanimous (or General) Consent

In cases where there seems to be no opposition in routine business or on questions of little importance, time can
often be saved by the procedure of *unanimous consent,* or as *25*
it is also called, *general consent.* Action in this manner is in
accord with the principle that rules are designed for the
protection of the minority and generally need not be strictly
enforced when there is no minority to protect. Under these
conditions, the method of unanimous consent can be used *30*
either to adopt a motion without the steps of stating the

---

*For a discussion of the conditions under which the chair's vote affects
the result in the case of motions requiring a two-thirds vote for adoption,
see page 393.

1 question and putting the motion to a formal vote, or it can
   be used to take action without even the formality of a motion. To obtain unanimous consent in either case, the chair
   states that "If there is no objection . . . [or, "Without ob-
5 jection . . . "],," the action that he mentions will be taken;
   or he may ask, "Is there any objection to . . . ?" He then
   pauses, and if no member calls out, "I object," the chair announces that, "Since there is no objection . . . ," the action
   is decided upon. If any member objects, the chair must
10 state the question on the motion, allow any desired debate
   (unless it is an "undebatable" parliamentary motion—see **6**
   and tinted pp. 44–45), and put the question in the regular
   manner. Or—if no motion has been made—the chair must
   first ask, "Is there a motion to . . . [stating the proposed
15 action]"; or he must at least put the question, assuming
   such a motion. If an objection is made with reasonable
   promptness, even though the chair may have already announced the result as one of "no objection," he should disregard such an announcement and proceed to state the
20 question in the usual manner.

   "Unanimous consent" does not necessarily imply that
   every member is in favor of the proposed action; it may only
   mean that the opposition, feeling that it is useless to oppose
   or discuss the matter, simply acquiesces. Similarly, when a
25 member responds to the chair's inquiry, "Is there any objection . . . ?" with "I object," he may not necessarily oppose the motion itself, but may believe that it is wise to take
   a formal vote under the circumstances. In other words, the
   objection is raised, not to the proposed action, but to the
30 action's being taken without a formal vote. No member
   should hesitate to object if he feels it is desirable to do so,
   but he should not object merely for dilatory purposes. If a
   member is uncertain of the effect of an action proposed for
   unanimous consent, he can call out, "I reserve the right to
35 object," or, "Reserving the right to object, . . . " After brief

consultation he can then object or withdraw his reservation.   *1*

The correction and approval of minutes (p. 343) is an example of business that is normally handled by unanimous consent. As a second example, assume that a speaker whose time has expired in debate on a motion asks for two additional minutes. If the chair thinks that all members will approve, he may handle the matter as follows: *5*

CHAIR: If there is no objection, the member's time will be extended two minutes ... [pause]. Since there is no objection, the member's time is extended two minutes.   *10*

Or:

CHAIR: Is there any objection to the member's time being extended two minutes? ... [pause]. The chair hears no objection, and it is so ordered.   *15*

Or, particularly if no objection is anticipated:

    20

CHAIR: Without objection, the member's time is extended two minutes.

In cases where unanimous consent is already apparent, the chair may sometimes assume it. For example, if everyone is obviously absorbed in listening to a speaker who seems near the end of his remarks, the chair may allow him to conclude without interruption, although his time has expired.   *25*

Whenever it is stated in this book that a certain action or the adoption of a certain motion "requires a two-thirds vote," the same action can, in principle, also be taken by unanimous consent. If much hinges on the outcome, however, it is usually better to take a formal vote. Action by unanimous consent requires the presence of a quorum, just as for the transaction of business by any other method.   *30*

    35

Relation of Other Motions to the Main Motion

As already noted, the foregoing initial description of the handling of motions refers principally to the *main motion*—the basic form of motion by which business is brought up and by which the assembly takes substantive action. As also stated above, the consideration of a main motion can involve a number of other procedures not yet described—which are nevertheless in the nature of action by the assembly and are themselves properly the subject of motions. In the same way there are a number of "privileged" motions, which are not associated with the main question but can nevertheless be introduced while it is pending because they relate to certain urgent matters that may arise and warrant immediate determination at such a time. Except for interrupting consideration of the main motion, motions of this type have no direct effect on its disposition. Finally, there are motions by which business can be brought before the assembly under a number of special circumstances involving an earlier question. For each of the permissible processes in all of these categories, there has evolved a particular motion with its own name and rules governing its use—resembling or differing from the main motion in varying degrees. All such derived forms of motions, proposing procedural steps specifically defined under parliamentary law, are loosely referred to for descriptive purposes in this book as "parliamentary" motions.

The next chapter contains a brief statement of the purpose of each of the parliamentary motions, together with an explanation of the classes into which all motions are divided. The main motion is more fully treated in **10,** as are each of the other motions in **11–37.**

DESCRIPTION OF MOTIONS
IN ALL CLASSIFICATIONS

§5. BASIC CLASSIFICATIONS; ORDER
OF PRECEDENCE OF MOTIONS

Classes of Motions

As noted in Chapter II, the word *motion* refers to a formal proposal by a member, in a meeting, that the assembly take certain action. Before a subject can be considered, it must be placed before the assembly in the form of a motion. From the basic type of motion known as the main motion, as also noted in the preceding chapter, many other specific motions have been derived and have become defined under parliamentary law.

For convenience in description, motions may be classified as shown at the top of the next page. (As indicated to the right of the list, the motions in the second, third, and fourth classes—subsidiary, privileged, and incidental motions taken together—are also called "secondary motions.")*

---

*Secondary motions must not be confused with secondary *amendments,* a much more specialized concept explained on pp. 126–28.

1. Main motions
    a. Original main motions
    b. Incidental main motions
2. Subsidiary motions ⎫
3. Privileged motions ⎬ Secondary
4. Incidental motions ⎭ motions
5. Motions that bring a question again before the assembly

Secondary Motions as an Underlying Concept

NATURE OF SECONDARY MOTIONS.   The concept of *secondary motions* serves as a starting point for the division of motions into the classes shown. It also throws light on the *order of precedence of motions,* which, as explained below, is a basic element of the rules under which these motions are used in the transaction of business.

Secondary motions may be seen as related to the following fundamental principle of parliamentary law: *Only one question can be considered at a time; once a motion is before the assembly, it must be adopted or rejected by a vote, or the assembly must take action disposing of the question in some other way, before any other business (except certain matters called "privileged questions") can be brought up.* By this principle, a main motion can be made only when no other motion is pending. Thus, however, the need for a number of particular *secondary* motions arises.

A secondary motion is one whose relationship to the main question, or whose procedural or emergency character, is such that:

1) it can be made and considered while a main motion is pending (or, occasionally, it is applicable just before or after a related main question is pending)—without vio-

lating the principle of taking up only one question at a
time; and

2) when the secondary motion has been made and has
been admitted by the chair as *in order* (that is, as being
legitimately able to come before the assembly at the
time according to the rules affecting its use), it must be
acted upon or disposed of before direct consideration of
the main question can be continued.

Secondary motions generally are made and seconded
and are stated by the chair, as a main motion would be—except that certain of them are in order while another member has the floor, and most of the motions in this latter
group do not require a second (see tinted pp. 42–43).

When a secondary motion is placed before the assembly, it becomes the *immediately pending question;* the main
motion remains pending while the secondary motion is
also pending. A main motion is the immediately pending
question whenever it is pending with no secondary motion. Whenever the chair has occasion to inform the assembly as to what is the immediately pending question,
however, he does not use this phrase, but employs the parliamentary form, "The question is on the motion to . . ."
The latter form is used even when more than one motion
is pending.

TAKING OF PRECEDENCE BY ONE MOTION
OVER ANOTHER. If two motions "A" and "B" are related under rules of parliamentary procedure in such a way
that motion "B" can be made while motion "A" is pending
and, when stated by the chair, can thus temporarily replace
"A" as the immediately pending question, motion "B" *takes
precedence** over (or *takes precedence of*) motion "A," and mo-

---

*Pronounced pree-SEED-n's.

1 tion "A" *yields to** motion "B." A secondary motion thus takes precedence over the main motion; and a main motion takes precedence over nothing and yields to all applicable secondary motions.

5   Certain secondary motions also take precedence over others, so that it is possible for more than one secondary motion to be pending at a time (together with the main motion). In such a case, the motion most recently stated by the chair (among those that have not been voted on) is the
10 immediately pending question.

ORDER OF PRECEDENCE OF MOTIONS; RANK. The rules under which secondary motions take precedence over one another have been gradually evolved through ex-
15 perience. While these rules are proper to each of the specific motions, they follow patterns that are related to the division of secondary motions into the classes of *subsidiary, privileged,* and *incidental* motions.

    Viewed apart from incidental motions and with modifi-
20 cations under particular conditions explained on pages 62–63, the main motion, the seven subsidiary motions, and the five privileged motions fall into a definite *order of precedence,* which gives a particular *rank* to each of these thirteen motions. The main motion—which does not take
25 precedence over anything—ranks lowest. Each of the other twelve motions has its proper position in the order, taking precedence over the motions that rank below it and yielding to those that rank above it. The privileged motions rank above all other motions. The manner in which the order of
30 precedence of motions operates is illustrated in the summaries of subsidiary and privileged motions given in the next section (see also the chart on tinted pp. 3–5).

---

*The word *yield* as used in this sense has no connection with *yielding the floor* as explained on page 29.

The incidental motions each have a certain relationship to the order of precedence of motions; but this relationship can be fully discussed only in terms of the rules governing the individual motions. Other factors also affect the conditions under which these motions are in order, as described on pages 66–71. When a particular incidental motion is in order, it takes precedence over the main motion and any other motions that may be pending. Incidental motions have no rank among themselves, and none of them can be assigned a *position* in the order of precedence of motions.

The rank of the motions in the fifth classification as listed at the beginning of this chapter—that is, the *motions that bring a question again before the assembly*—is discussed in the description of these motions beginning on page 72.

§6. DESCRIPTION OF CLASSES AND INDIVIDUAL MOTIONS

Main Motions

A *main motion* is a motion whose introduction brings business before the assembly. As already noted, a main motion can be made only when no other motion is pending, and it ranks lowest in the order of precedence of motions.

It is usual to distinguish between *original main motions* and *incidental main motions*—which differ principally in the nature of their subject matter. The difference in the rules governing the use of main motions in these two subclasses is only slight. It should be noted that incidental main motions form a category completely separate from *incidental motions*—the fourth general class of motions. (The distinction between original main motions and incidental main motions is fully discussed on pages 95–97.)

Subsidiary Motions

Subsidiary motions assist the assembly in treating or disposing of a main motion (and sometimes other motions).

MANNER OF LISTING THE MOTIONS. Each of the subsidiary motions is briefly described below in terms of the type of situation where it is of use, in a manner that may convey a suggestion of how the order of precedence of motions was arrived at. In the case of the subsidiary motions only, their distinguishing characteristics as a class are explained *after* this description of the individual motions, since these characteristics will be more easily understood if the material is read in that order. The subsidiary motions are listed below in reverse order of rank—which is the chronological order in which they would be moved if all of them became pending at one time. Each of the motions listed takes precedence over—that is, ranks above—the main motion, and also any or all of the motions listed before it.

LISTING OF INDIVIDUAL SUBSIDIARY MOTIONS. The subsidiary motions, briefly described by function, are as follows:

1) If an embarrassing main motion has been brought before the assembly, a member can propose to dispose of this question without bringing it to a direct vote, by moving to *Postpone Indefinitely* (**11**).

2) If a main motion might be more suitable or acceptable in an altered form, a proposal to change its wording (either to clarify or, within limits, to modify the meaning) before the main motion is voted on can be introduced by moving to *Amend* (**12**).

3) But it may be that much time would be required to amend the main motion properly, or that additional in-

formation is needed, so that it would be better to turn the motion or resolution over to a committee for study or redrafting before the assembly considers it further. Such action can be proposed by moving to *Commit* the main question—or *Refer* it to a committee (**13**).

4) If the assembly might prefer to consider the main motion later in the same meeting or at another meeting, this can be proposed by moving to *Postpone to a Certain Time*—also called the motion to *Postpone Definitely,* or simply to *Postpone* (**14**).

5) If it is desired to continue consideration of a motion but debate is consuming too much time, a member can move to place a limit on the debate; on the other hand, if special circumstances make it advisable to permit more or longer speeches than under the usual rules, a motion to do so can be made; or, it may sometimes be desirable to combine the elements of limitation and extension, as in limiting the length of speeches but allowing more speeches per member. All such modifications of the normal limits of debate on a pending motion are proposed by means of the motion to *Limit or Extend Limits of Debate* (**15**).

6) If it is desired to close debate and amendment of a pending motion so that it will come to an immediate vote, this can be proposed by moving the *Previous Question* (**16**).

7) If there is reason for the assembly to lay the main motion aside temporarily without setting a time for resuming its consideration, but with the provision that it can be taken up again whenever a majority so decides, this can be proposed by the motion to *Lay on the Table* (**17**).

CHARACTERISTICS OF SUBSIDIARY MOTIONS AS A CLASS. Subsidiary motions as a class are distinguished by having *all four* of the following characteristics:

1   (1) They are always *applied* to another motion while it is
pending, to aid in treating or disposing of it; the adoption of
one of them always *does something to* this other motion—that
is, changes its status in some way—without adopting or ex-
5   pressly rejecting it. (2) They can be applied to *any* main motion. (Regarding other applications, see below.) (3) They fit
into an order of precedence, as already explained. (4) The
time when they are in order extends from the moment the
question on a motion to which they can be applied is stated
10 by the chair, until he begins to take the vote on that motion,
the only limitations within this period being as follows:

a) the subsidiary motion must be admissible at the time,
according to the order of precedence of motions;
15 b) the question presented by the subsidiary motion must
not be absurd or substantially the same as one already
decided (**38, 39**); and
c) after a vote has been ordered by the adoption of a motion for the *Previous Question* and before this vote has
20   been taken, no subsidiary motion can be made—except
Lay on the Table (which is of higher rank than the *Previous Question*).

CASES WHERE ONE SUBSIDIARY MOTION CAN
25 BE APPLIED TO ANOTHER.   The subsidiary motion
to *Amend* is applicable to many other motions in addition
to the main motion. All of the subsidiary motions can be
amended except *Postpone Indefinitely,* the *Previous Question,* and *Lay on the Table* (which, by the nature of what
30 they propose, do not lend themselves to amendment).
When the motion to *Amend* is applied to another subsidiary motion, its rank is modified so that it takes precedence over the motion to which it is applied, even if that
motion ranks higher than *Amend* in the regular order of
35 precedence of motions. For example, suppose that a motion

to *Postpone* the main question to a certain time is immedi- 1
ately pending. In such a case, motions to *Limit or Extend
Limits of Debate*, for the *Previous Question*, and to *Lay on
the Table* are in order; motions to *Postpone Indefinitely*, to
Amend, and to *Commit*, on the other hand, may have be- 5
come pending before the motion to *Postpone Definitely* was
moved, but none of these three motions can now be
made—*except* that it is in order to move to amend the motion to *Postpone*, while it is immediately pending.

Debate can also be limited or extended on any debatable 10
motion* that is immediately pending (or on a specified series
of pending motions including the immediately pending question, **15**); and, similarly, debate and amendment can be
closed on a motion or series of motions that are debatable
and amendable, or amendment can be closed on motions 15
that can be amended but not debated (**16**). The four lowest-
ranking subsidiary motions can be debated (except that
Amend is undebatable when it is applied to an undebatable
motion). Debate of the three highest-ranking subsidiary motions is not permitted, since that would defeat their purpose. 20
From these rules, it follows that the motion to *Limit or Extend Limits of Debate* can be applied to any of the four subsidiary motions of lower rank (but not to the two that rank
above it), while the *Previous Question* can be applied to any
of the five subsidiary motions that rank below it (but not to 25
the one subsidiary motion that ranks above it).

INCIDENTAL MAIN MOTIONS CORRESPOND-
ING TO SUBSIDIARY MOTIONS.   For each of the first
five subsidiary motions (that is, for all except the *Previous* 30
Question and *Lay on the Table*), there is a corresponding in-

---

*See explanation in **7**; rules governing the individual motions, **11–37**;
Table of Rules Relating to Motions, tinted pages **6–29**; and lists, tinted
pages **44–45**.

cidental main motion (p. 96) of the same name that can be made when no other motion is pending.

(Each of the subsidiary motions is fully discussed in **11–17.**)

Privileged Motions

CHARACTERISTICS OF PRIVILEGED MOTIONS AS A CLASS. Unlike subsidiary or incidental motions, *privileged motions* do not relate to the pending business, but have to do with special matters of immediate and overriding importance which, without debate, should be allowed to interrupt the consideration of anything else. Like subsidiary motions, however, the five privileged motions fit into an order of precedence. All of them take precedence over motions of any other class (except in certain instances where the immediately pending question may be a motion to *Amend,* a motion for the *Previous Question,* or an incidental motion that was moved while a still higher-ranking privileged motion was immediately pending). The privileged motions as a class are also known as "privileged questions," which should not be confused with "questions of privilege," as described in connection with the second motion listed below.

LISTING OF INDIVIDUAL PRIVILEGED MOTIONS. The privileged motions are listed below in ascending order of rank. Each of the succeeding motions takes precedence over any or all of the motions listed before it.

1) If the adopted program or order of business is not being followed, or if consideration of a question has been set for the present time and is now in order but the matter is not being taken up, a single member, by making a *Call for the*

Orders of the Day (**18**), can require such a schedule to be enforced—unless the assembly decides by a two-thirds vote (**25**) to set the orders of the day aside.

2) If a pressing situation is affecting a right or privilege of the assembly or of an individual member (for example, noise, inadequate ventilation, introduction of a confidential subject in the presence of guests, etc.), a member can *Raise a Question of Privilege* (**19**), which permits him to interrupt pending business to state an urgent request or motion. If the matter is not simple enough to be taken care of informally, the chair then makes a ruling as to whether it is admitted as a question of privilege and whether it requires consideration before the pending business is resumed.

3) A short intermission in a meeting, even while business is pending, can be proposed by moving to *Recess* (**20**) for a specified length of time.

4) A member can propose to close the meeting entirely by moving to *Adjourn* (**21**). This motion can be made and the assembly can adjourn even while business is pending, provided that the time for the next meeting is established by a rule of the society or has been set by the assembly. (In such a case, unfinished business [p. 346] is carried over to the next meeting.)

5) Under certain conditions while business is pending, the assembly—before adjourning or postponing the pending business—may wish to fix a date and hour, and sometimes the place, for another meeting, or (in an established society) for another meeting before the next regular meeting. In cases of this kind, the motion to *Fix the Time to Which to Adjourn* (**22**) can be made—even while a matter is pending—unless another meeting is already scheduled for the same or the next day. This is the highest ranking of all motions.

INCIDENTAL MAIN MOTIONS CORRESPONDING TO PRIVILEGED MOTIONS.   For the motions to *Recess,* to *Adjourn,** and to *Fix the Time to Which to Adjourn,* there are corresponding incidental main motions of the same names (p. 96). Questions of privilege can also be brought up while no motion is pending, and at such times they are moved just as any main motion.

(Each of the privileged motions is fully discussed in **18–22.**)

Incidental Motions

CHARACTERISTICS OF INCIDENTAL MOTIONS AS A CLASS.   *Incidental motions* relate, in different ways, to the pending business or to business otherwise at hand—some of them with varying degrees of resemblance to subsidiary motions, but none of them possessing all four of the characteristics listed on pages 61–62. As a class, incidental motions deal with questions of procedure *arising out of:* (1) commonly, another pending motion; but also (2) sometimes, another motion or item of business

a) that it is desired to introduce,
b) that has been made but has not yet been stated by the chair, or
c) that has just been pending.

An incidental motion is said to be *incidental to* the other motion or matter out of which it arises. With but few

---

*The distinction between the main and the privileged motions to adjourn is different from any other case where an incidental main motion corresponds to a secondary motion of the same name, since a motion "to adjourn" can retain "privileged" characteristics even when no question is pending (see **21**).

exceptions, incidental motions are related to the main ques-   *1*
tion in such a way that they must be decided immediately,
before business can proceed. Most incidental motions are
undebatable.

Each of the incidental motions is applicable only in its   *5*
own type of special circumstance—which may be a particular characteristic present in the motion to which it is incidental, or a particular point in time or possible occurrence
during the assembly's involvement with the other motion
or matter. This is an important respect in which incidental   *10*
motions differ from subsidiary motions, since subsidiary
motions—in principle and with certain qualifications already noted (p. 62, l. 13–22)—are applicable to any main
motion over the entire time that it is pending.

15

LISTING OF INDIVIDUAL INCIDENTAL MO-
TIONS.   The order in which the incidental motions are
listed below, unlike that in which the subsidiary and privileged motions are presented above, has no relation to what
other motions they may take precedence over or yield to   *20*
(see discussion beginning on p. 70). The incidental motions
arise as follows:

1) Although the presiding officer has the responsibility of
    enforcing the rules, any member who believes he has   *25*
    noticed a case where the chair is failing to do so can, at
    the time the breach occurs, call attention to it by mak-
    ing a *Point of Order* (**23**); the effect is to require the
    chair to make a ruling on the question involved.
2) Although the duty of ruling on all questions of parlia-   *30*
    mentary procedure affecting the assembly's proceedings
    rests with the chair, any two members, by moving and
    seconding an *Appeal* (**24**) immediately after the chair
    has made such a ruling, can require him to submit the
    matter to a vote of the assembly.   *35*

1   3) When it is desired that the assembly take up a question or do something that would be in violation of a rule that applies, it can be proposed in some cases to *Suspend the Rules* (**25**) to permit accomplishment of the desired
5   purpose.

  4) If an original main motion has been made and a member believes that it would do harm for the motion even to be discussed in the meeting, he can raise an *Objection to the Consideration of the Question* (**26**), provided he does so
10   before debate has begun or any subsidiary motion has been stated; the assembly then votes on whether the main motion shall be considered (and if there is a two-thirds vote against consideration, the motion is dropped).

  5) If a pending main motion (or an amendment to it) con-
15   tains two or more parts capable of standing as separate questions, the assembly can vote to treat each part accordingly in succession; such a course is proposed by the motion for *Division of a Question* (**27**).

  6) If the main motion is in the form of a resolution or doc-
20   ument containing several paragraphs or sections which (although not separate questions) could be most efficiently handled by opening each paragraph or section to amendment one at a time (before the whole is finally voted on), such a procedure can be proposed by the mo-
25   tion for *Consideration by Paragraph or Seriatim* (**28**).

  7) If a member doubts the accuracy of the chair's announcement of the result of a voice vote (or even a vote by show of hands)—or doubts that a representative number of persons voted—he can demand a *Division of the*
30   *Assembly* (**29**); a single member thus has the power to require a standing vote, but not to order a count, which only the chair or the assembly can do (see next item).

  8) A member can move that a vote be taken (a) by ballot, (b) by roll call, or (c) by a counted standing vote, espe-
35   cially if a division of the assembly has appeared incon-

clusive and the chair neglects to order a count. This
grouping also includes a motion (d) that the polls be
closed or reopened in a ballot vote or an election. All
these motions are grouped under the heading of *Motions Relating to Methods of Voting and the Polls* (**30**).

9) If the bylaws or rules of the organization do not prescribe how nominations are to be made, and if the assembly has taken no action to do so prior to an election, any member can move while the election is pending (a) to specify one of various methods by which the candidates shall be nominated; or, if the need arises, (b) to close nominations, or (c) to reopen them; these are the *Motions Relating to Nominations* (**31**).

10) A member may *Request to Be Excused from a Duty* (**32**) if he wishes to be relieved from an obligation imposed upon him by the bylaws or by virtue of some position or office he holds.

11) There are several other types of *Requests and Inquiries* (**33**) which a member can make in connection with business that someone desires to introduce, or which is pending or has just been pending. These include:

   a) *Parliamentary Inquiry* (a request for the chair's opinion on a matter of parliamentary procedure as it relates to the business at hand—not involving a ruling).

   b) *Point of Information* (an inquiry as to facts affecting the business at hand—directed to the chair or, through the chair, to a member).

   c) *Request for Permission (or Leave) to Withdraw or Modify a Motion* (after it has been stated by the chair).

   d) *Request to Read Papers.*

   e) *Request for Any Other Privilege.*

The first two types of inquiry are responded to by the chair, or by a member at the direction of the chair; the other requests can be granted only by the assembly.

1 CONDITIONS UNDER WHICH INCIDENTAL
MOTIONS TAKE PRECEDENCE OVER, OR YIELD
TO, OTHER MOTIONS.   Incidental motions take precedence over other motions according to the following princi-
5 ple: *An incidental motion is in order only when it is
legitimately incidental to another pending motion, or when it
is legitimately incidental in some other way to business at hand*
(see pp. 66–67); *it then takes precedence over any other motions
that are pending.* Each incidental motion has its own rules
10 that determine the conditions under which it is incidental—
that is, the motions or situations to which it can be applied,
and the circumstances or stage of consideration at which this
can be done. Usually, but not always, an incidental motion is
legitimately incidental to another *pending* motion only while
15 the other motion is immediately pending.

As stated above, incidental motions have no rank
among themselves and cannot be assigned positions within
the order of precedence of motions, although they have individual relationships to that order which are described in
20 the sections dealing with these motions (**23–33**). With the
exception of a *Division of the Assembly,* incidental motions
yield to the privileged motions and generally yield to the
motion to *Lay on the Table,* unless the incidental motion
arose out of a motion of higher rank than the one to which
25 it would otherwise yield (see also second paragraph below).
By the principle stated in the preceding paragraph, an incidental motion yields to any motion legitimately incidental
to itself—as all motions do. For example, a motion for a *Division of a Question,* or one to *Suspend the Rules,* would
30 yield to a *Point of Order* arising in connection with itself.

Whenever it is stated in this book that "incidental motions" or "all incidental motions" take precedence over a
certain motion, or that a certain motion yields to "all applicable incidental motions," it must be understood that the
35 incidental motions referred to are only those that are legit-

imately incidental at the time they are made. For example,   *1*
"Incidental motions always take precedence over the main
motion"; but an *Objection to the Consideration of a Question*
is legitimate only against an *original* main motion, and the
objection is no longer in order after debate has begun or a   *5*
subsidiary motion has been stated by the chair—even
though an original main motion is immediately pending
(**26**). Similarly, "A *Point of Order* takes precedence over any
pending question (of no matter how high a rank) out of
which it arises"—but it does so only at the time the breach   *10*
of order occurs.

In connection with motions that can be incidental to
motions of any rank (such as *Point of Order, Appeal, Suspend the Rules, Motions Relating to Voting,* and certain types
of *Requests and Inquiries*), whenever it is stated that one of   *15*
these motions yields to "all motions" above a certain rank,
the incidental motion nevertheless does not yield to any
motion ranking below the one out of which it arises. For
example, "A *Point of Order* yields to the motion to *Lay on
the Table,* and to all privileged motions." This statement is   *20*
true without qualification if the point of order is in connection with a motion ranking lower than *Lay on the Table*
(that is, a main motion or any other subsidiary motion); but
a point of order arising from a motion to *Recess* would yield
only to the two higher-ranking privileged motions—to *Ad-*   *25*
journ and to *Fix the Time to Which to Adjourn.*

While a series consisting of a main motion and a number of subsidiary or privileged motions is being considered,
it is possible for some of the incidental motions—such as a
Point of Order, an *Appeal,* or a *Division of the Assembly*—to   *30*
arise more than once, in connection with different motions
in the series.

INCIDENTAL MAIN MOTIONS CORRESPOND-
ING TO INCIDENTAL MOTIONS.   Counterparts of   *35*

1 some of the incidental motions may occur as incidental
   main motions. For example, a *standing rule* (**2**) can be suspended for the duration of a session (**8**); and a motion for
   such a suspension, made when no business is pending, is an
5 incidental main motion. Similarly, a motion prescribing
   how nominations shall be made is an incidental main motion if it is moved while no election is pending.

   (Each of the incidental motions is fully discussed in
   23–33.)
10

Motions That Bring a Question
Again Before the Assembly

   BASIS OF THIS CLASSIFICATION.   Four motions
15 are grouped in this book as *motions that bring a question
   again before the assembly* since, either by their adoption or by
   their introduction, they serve the function described by the
   name of the class. Two of these motions—and a third in certain applications—cannot be satisfactorily placed in any other
20 classification. The remaining motion in the group and, in its
   other applications, the third just mentioned are incidental
   main motions having special characteristics. Like main motions, all of the motions that bring a question again before
   the assembly are usually made (and three of them can only be
25 made) while no business is pending. The existence of these
   motions as a separate category may be seen as related to the
   following principles of parliamentary law:

   a) *During the meeting or series of connected meetings (called*
30   *a "session," 8) in which the assembly has decided a ques-*
       tion, the same or substantially the same question cannot be
       brought up again, except through special procedures that
       imply an unusual circumstance.
   b) *While a question is temporarily disposed of (by any of sev-*
35   *eral methods described in this and later chapters) but is*

not finally settled, no similar or conflicting motion whose   1
adoption would restrict the assembly in acting on the first
question can be introduced.

c) *To change what the assembly has adopted requires some-*
thing more (in the way of a vote or previous notice to the   5
members) than was necessary to adopt it in the first
place.

No motion violating principles (a), (b), or (c) is in order.
But the motions that bring a question again before the as-   10
sembly enable the assembly for good reason to reopen a
completed question during the same session, or to take up
one that has been temporarily disposed of, or to change
something previously adopted and still in force.

   15

LISTING OF INDIVIDUAL MOTIONS IN THIS
CLASS. The order in which these motions are listed
below has no relation to the order of precedence of motions. The first three of these motions are either main motions or have the same low rank as main motions, and the   20
fourth has special characteristics relating to rank (see pp.
76, 306–307). The motions that bring a question again before the assembly, briefly described by function, are as follows:

   25

1) If it is desired to resume consideration of a main motion
(with or without a series of *adhering* motions—see pp.
112–13) which lies on the table, it can be proposed by
means of the motion to *Take from the Table* (**34**) that
the motion or series become pending again. (A main   30
motion is said to lie on the table if it was laid on the
table earlier in the present session, or in the last previous session with no more than a quarterly time interval
having intervened [see p. 88], and it has not yet been finally disposed of.)   35

2) If it is desired to strike out an entire main motion, resolution, rule, bylaw, section, or paragraph that has been adopted, such action can be proposed by means of the motion to *Rescind* (or *Repeal*, or *Annul*, **35**); and by another form of the same parliamentary motion—that is, the motion to *Amend Something Previously Adopted* (**35**)—it can be proposed to modify only a part of the wording or text previously adopted, or to substitute a different version.

3) If a question has been referred, or a task has been assigned, to a committee that has not yet made its final report, and it is desired to take the matter out of the committee's hands, either so that the assembly itself can consider or act upon it or so that it can be dropped, such action can be proposed by means of the motion to *Discharge a Committee* (**36**).

4) If, in the same session that a motion has been voted on but no later than the same day or the next day on which a business meeting is held, new information or a changed situation makes it appear that a different result might reflect the true will of the assembly, a member who voted with the prevailing side can propose to *Reconsider* (**37**) the vote; that is, he can move that the question shall come before the assembly again as if it had not previously been considered.

RELATIONSHIPS AMONG MOTIONS IN THIS CLASS.   The motions that bring a question again before the assembly have a number of differences among themselves, and they may be variously subgrouped depending on the point of view, as follows:

- The motion that takes the form either to *Rescind* or to *Amend Something Previously Adopted* is an incidental main motion because (a) it brings *business* before the as-

sembly by its *introduction* and (b) when it is voted on, 1
business thereby ceases to be pending. By contrast, two
other motions in this class, *Reconsider* (as applied to a
main motion) and *Take from the Table,* do not bring a
question again before the assembly by their introduc- 5
tion, but by their *adoption,* which automatically causes
a main question to *become* pending. The remaining motion, *Discharge a Committee,* either shares this same
characteristic with the motions to *Take from the Table*
and to *Reconsider,* or else it is in effect a particular case 10
of the incidental main motion to *Rescind* or to *Amend
Something Previously Adopted*—depending on whether
the matter to be taken out of the committee's hands
was in the form of a pending motion referred by means
of the subsidiary motion to *Commit,* or was a task as- 15
signed to the committee by means of a main motion
(see pp. 160–61).

• From another point of view, the motion to *Discharge a
Committee*—even when applied to cause a previously referred motion to become pending again—is similar to 20
the motion to *Rescind* or to *Amend Something Previously Adopted* in regard to the rules governing its use.
Both of these motions have special requirements for
their adoption—that is, both require either notice or
more than a majority vote (see pp. 295–96, 301). 25

• Again, the motion to *Discharge a Committee* (as applied
to a *motion* that was referred) and the motion to *Take
from the Table* have the common feature of proposing
that the assembly take up a matter still "within its control" (see pp. 88, 329–30) that was *temporarily* 30
disposed of. On the other hand, the motion to *Rescind*
or to *Amend Something Previously Adopted* and the
motion to *Reconsider* are both applied to a motion that
has been finally voted on. However, the motion to
Rescind or to *Amend Something Previously Adopted* can 35

be applied only to a motion on which the vote was affirmative, and it proposes a specified change in a decision that may have been made at any time previously. By contrast, the motion to *Reconsider* can, with certain exceptions, be applied to a vote that was either affirmative or negative, within a limited time after that vote, and it proposes no specific change in a decision but simply proposes that the original question be reopened.

- The motion to *Reconsider* can be applied to several of the subsidiary, privileged, or incidental motions; and in certain cases when so applied, it assumes the character of a secondary motion—that is, a motion that can be made and considered while other motions are pending. It is the only one of the four motions in this class that can be applied to anything except a main question. Because of the time limit on making the motion to *Reconsider,* the *making* of this motion takes precedence over all others (even the highest-ranking motion in the regular order of precedence of motions, *Fix the Time to Which to Adjourn*); but its consideration has only the rank of the motion proposed to be reconsidered. The motion to *Reconsider* thus cannot always be taken up at the time it is made. This feature of the motion is one of its unique characteristics.

(Each of the motions that bring a question again before the assembly is fully discussed in **34–37.**)

§7. STANDARD DESCRIPTIVE CHARACTERISTICS OF MOTIONS

Many of the most important rules governing the use of the individual motions described in this chapter reduce to eight *standard descriptive characteristics*. In addition to

containing basic rules of procedure for each motion, these
characteristics serve as points of comparison showing how
the motion resembles or differs from a main motion.

The standard descriptive characteristics of a motion are
the following:

1. Over what motions, if any, it takes precedence (that is,
   what motions can be pending without causing this motion to be out of order); also, to what motions it yields
   (that is, what motions can be made and considered
   while this motion is pending). (The main motion, ranking lowest, takes precedence over no other motion and
   yields to all subsidiary motions, all privileged motions,
   and all applicable incidental motions.)
2. To what motions or to what type of situation it is applicable; also, what motions, particularly subsidiary motions, are applicable to it, if any. (The main motion is
   applicable to no other motion; and all subsidiary motions, and certain incidental motions under various conditions, are applicable to it.)
3. Whether it is in order when another has the floor. (A
   main motion is not.)
4. Whether it requires a second. (A main motion does.
   Whenever it is stated in this book that a certain motion
   "must" be seconded, or "requires" a second, the precise
   meaning is as explained on pp. 34–36, and the requirement does not apply when the motion is made by direction of a board or committee.)
5. Whether it is debatable—that is, whether debate on its
   merits is permitted while it is immediately pending. (A
   main motion is.)
6. Whether it is amendable. (A main motion is.)
7. What vote is required for its adoption. (A main motion
   requires a majority vote, except as noted on pp. 98–
   99.)

8. Whether it can be reconsidered. (A main motion can.)

The standard descriptive characteristics of the main motion are more fully stated in **10**, and those of the other parliamentary motions are given in **11–37**. In addition, key facts with regard to Standard Descriptive Characteristics 1 and 2 are shown in Chart I, tinted pages 3–5, and with regard to Standard Descriptive Characteristics 3 through 8 are shown in Chart II, tinted pages 6–29.

Additional background for the detailed treatment of the motions in **10–37** is provided by the discussion of the topics "meeting" and "session" in **8** and **9**.

MEETING AND SESSION

§8. MEETING, SESSION, RECESS, ADJOURNMENT

Explanation of Terms

In an assembly, as alluded to above on pages 2–3 and 24, each event of the members' being assembled to transact business constitutes a separate *meeting;* but the complete unit of engagement in proceedings by the assembly is a *session,* which (in the general case covering all types of assemblies) consists of one or more connected meetings. The term *session* is a fundamental concept entering into many important parliamentary rules.

In parliamentary law and as understood in this book, the terms defined below have distinct meanings:

- A *meeting* of an assembly is a single official gathering of its members in one room or area to transact business for a length of time during which there is no cessation of proceedings and the members do not separate, unless for a short *recess,* as defined below. (For modification of the "one-room-or-area" requirement when the bylaws authorize meeting by videoconference or teleconference, see pages 482–83.) Depending on the business to be transacted, a meeting may last from a few minutes to several hours. (See footnote, p. 2, with respect to the impracticality of attempting to conduct business by written communication.)

• A *session* of an assembly, unless otherwise defined by the bylaws or governing rules of the particular organization or body, is a meeting or series of connected meetings devoted to a single order of business, program, agenda, or announced purpose, in which—when there is more than one meeting—each succeeding meeting is scheduled with a view to continuing business at the point where it was left off at the previous meeting (see also discussion of distinction between recess and adjournment, p. 83).

• A *recess,* strictly speaking, is a short intermission or break within a meeting that does not end the meeting or destroy its continuity as a single gathering, and after which proceedings are immediately resumed at the point where they were interrupted. During the recess, members may leave the hall or room in which the meeting is being held, but they are expected to remain nearby. A recess frequently has a purpose connected with the business of the meeting itself—such as to count ballots, to permit consultation among members, or the like. (For the motion to *Recess,* see **20.**)

• A meeting is said to *stand at ease* if the chair, without objection, simply permits a brief pause, without a declaration of recess. In such a case there is technically no interruption of the meeting, and members remain in their places. Quiet conversation among neighboring members may take place, but it must cease immediately when the chair declares the meeting again in

order or any member objects to continuing to stand at   *1*
ease.

- An *adjournment* (that is, the act of the assembly's adjourning) terminates a meeting; it may also end the session. If another meeting to continue the same business   *5*
or order of business has been set for a definite time (or
to be "at the call of the chair"), the adjournment does
not end the session. (See also pp. 90–91 for the use of
the word *adjournment* as applied to an *adjourned meeting;* for the motion to *Adjourn* see **21.**)   *10*

- The term *adjournment sine die** (or *adjournment without day*) usually refers to the close of a session of several
meetings: (a) where the adjournment dissolves the assembly—as in a series of mass meetings or in an annual
or biennial convention for which the delegates are sep-   *15*
arately chosen for each convention; or (b) where, unless
called into special session, the body will not be convened again until a time prescribed by the bylaws or
constitution—as in the case of a session of a legislature.
In cases where the words *sine die* are applicable, they   *20*
may be, but are not always, mentioned in the motion to
adjourn or the chair's declaration of the adjournment.

Interrelation of the Concepts
    25

NUMBER OF MEETINGS IN A SESSION.   The
length of a session or the number of meetings included
within it varies depending on the type of assembly.

In a permanent society whose bylaws provide for regular weekly, monthly, or quarterly meetings that go through   *30*
an established order of business in a single afternoon or
evening, each "meeting" of this kind normally completes a
separate session—unless the assembly at such a meeting

---

*Pronounced SIGN-ee- DYE-ee.

1　schedules an *adjourned meeting* as explained on pages
90–91. This rule is the common parliamentary law and
holds except where a special rule in the bylaws provides
otherwise. Although any society has the right to define, in
5　its bylaws, what shall constitute a session of the organization, it is usually unwise in ordinary societies to adopt a rule
making regular sessions last over a long period of time.
Such a rule would make it possible for the hands of the organization to be tied during that time, since the same ques-
10　tion cannot be brought up again during the same session
after it is too late to reconsider (**37**) a vote that has finally
disposed of a motion without adopting it (that is, a vote
that has rejected or indefinitely postponed it or has sustained an objection to its consideration; see **11, 26**).

15　　In the case of a state or national organization that holds
annual or biennial conventions, each convention constitutes
a session of the organization—having one agenda or program—which may be broken up into separate meetings in
the morning, afternoon, and evening, or into many meet-
20　ings held over several days. In Congress a session may comprise hundreds of almost daily meetings, sometimes
continuing for nearly a year.

DEPARTURE FROM PARLIAMENTARY MEAN-
25　INGS IN ORDINARY SPEECH.　Because of the fact
that a meeting and a session usually coincide in ordinary
local societies or branches, these two terms often tend to
become confused or used interchangeably in everyday
speech. Whenever either word is used, the context should
30　be noted in the light of the explanations in this section. A
similar situation exists regarding the terms *recess, adjournment,* and *adjournment sine die.* It is common, especially in
conventions, to hear the word *recess* also applied to a longer
break that *does* terminate a meeting and that consequently
35　should be understood as an adjournment, as in "to recess

until tomorrow." On the other hand, assemblies sometimes
"adjourn" or provide in the program or agenda for an "adjournment" when only a short recess is intended. The use
of the word *recess* to describe the interval between regular
sessions of an organization or assembly, as in "the summer
recess of Congress," is a colloquialism that has no relationship to the parliamentary meaning of the term.

COMPARATIVE EFFECTS OF RECESS AND AD-
JOURNMENT WITHIN A SESSION.   The distinction
between *recess* and *adjournment* may in some cases become
thin so that it must be judged in the individual context. For
example, according to the definitions given above, a break in
the proceedings of a convention for lunch may be more in
the nature of a recess, or of an adjournment, depending on
the time and the extent of dispersion of the members that is
required for them to be served. From the viewpoint of the effect of a recess or an adjournment on the procedure the next
time the assembly is called to order, the difference is that at
the conclusion of a recess there never are any "opening" proceedings, but business is always immediately resumed where
it was left off, just as if there had been no recess. At the beginning of any meeting (after the first meeting in a session),
on the other hand, the resumption of business at the point
where it was left off may be, but is not necessarily, preceded
by brief opening ceremonies and the reading of minutes.
Normally in a session lasting several days, the minutes are
read at the beginning of the first meeting each day; and the
beginning of a later meeting the same day may be virtually in-
distinguishable from the conclusion of a recess.*

---

*If the assembly recesses rather than adjourns, that may preclude cer-
tain motions to *Suspend the Rules*, (see "Renewal of the Motion" p. 254)
and to *Reconsider and Enter on the Minutes* (see p. 323, l. 17–22).

1   HOW MEETINGS TO CONTINUE A SESSION ARE
SCHEDULED.   When a meeting adjourns without ending
the session, this necessarily means that the time for another
meeting to continue the same business or order of business
5 has already been set (or that provision has been made for
such a meeting to be held "at the call of the chair"). The time
or provision for this next meeting of the session may have
been established by one of the following methods (which are
listed in order of frequency of occurrence): (a) through a
10 program adopted at the beginning of a convention; (b) by
the adoption in the present meeting of a motion (main or
privileged, depending on when it is moved) to fix the time to
which to adjourn; or (c) by a specification in the motion to
adjourn, *if* that motion was made as a main motion while no
15 other question was pending.

ORDINARY PRACTICE IN ADJOURNING.   In
ordinary practice a meeting is closed by adopting a motion
simply "to adjourn"; or under certain conditions the chair
20 can declare the adjournment without a motion, as explained on pages 232-33. The society meets again at the
time provided in its bylaws or other rules, or as already established by the adoption of an earlier motion. If it does not
expect to convene until the next "regular meeting" pre-
25 scribed by rule or bylaw, the chair declares that the meeting
"is adjourned," and such an adjournment closes the session.
On the other hand, if another meeting in the same session
has been scheduled by any of the methods listed in the preceding paragraph, the chair announces the time as he de-
30 clares the adjournment, saying, for example, that the
"meeting is adjourned until 4 P.M. tomorrow."
In the event of fire, riot, or other extreme emergency, if
the chair believes taking time for a vote on adjourning
would be dangerous to those present, he should declare the
35 meeting adjourned—to a suitable time and place for an ad-

journed meeting (if he is able), or to meet at the call of the chair.

Significance of Session

The principle significance of the session as a complete unit of an assembly's engagement in proceedings lies in the freedom of each new session, as contrasted with the limitations placed upon a session in progress by decisions it has made. Some of the consequences of this characteristic of the session are described in the following paragraphs.

FREEDOM OF EACH NEW SESSION. As a general principle, one session cannot tie the hands of the majority at any later session, or place a question beyond the reach of such a majority, except through the process of adopting a special rule of order or an amendment to the bylaws (either of which requires more than a majority vote; see immediately below). It is improper, for example, to postpone anything beyond the next session—which would be an attempt to prevent the next session from considering the question. The principle stated applies in qualified form to cases in which a majority rescinds or amends something adopted at an earlier session, or discharges a committee from further consideration of a question referred to it at an earlier session—which a majority can do provided that previous notice was given. (See p. 295, l. 24 to p. 295, l. 10 and p. 301, l. 3–15 for the vote required for these actions without previous notice.)

RELATION OF A SESSION'S FREEDOM TO THE RULES OF AN ORGANIZATION. The application of the same principle to the case of *standing rules* (which, as the term is understood in this book, should not deal with parliamentary procedure; see **2**) is as follows: Although a

1   standing rule can be adopted by a majority vote at any session and continues in force until it is rescinded or amended, such a rule does not interfere materially with the freedom of a later session, since it can be suspended for the 5   duration of any session (but not for longer) by a majority vote.

     Bylaws, on the other hand—and *special rules of order,* which *do* deal with parliamentary procedure—contain the provisions that are expected to have stability from session 10 to session, and to represent the judgment of the whole society as distinguished from the members voting at any particular session. These rules therefore require both previous notice and a two-thirds vote for amendment (with a vote of a majority of the entire membership as an 15 allowable alternative); and rules of order require a two-thirds vote for suspension, while bylaws cannot be suspended.

     RELATION OF A SESSION'S FREEDOM TO THE 20 RENEWABILITY OF MOTIONS. The conditions under which a motion can be *renewed*—that is, can be introduced as if new after having previously been made and disposed of without adoption—are closely related to the freedom of each new session, and to the distinction be- 25 tween a meeting and a session. As stated in **38** and on page 82, the same or substantially the same question cannot be brought up a second time during the same session except by means of the parliamentary motions that bring a question again before the assembly. At any later session, on the 30 other hand, any motion that is still applicable can normally be renewed unless it has *come over from the previous session* (by one of the four procedures mentioned on page 88 under *Regular Meeting,* below) as *not finally disposed of* (see also **38,** where the renewal of motions is fully dis- 35 cussed).

RELATION OF A SESSION'S FREEDOM TO LIM-
ITATION ON APPOINTMENT AS CHAIRMAN PRO
TEM.   If the assembly is to elect a chairman pro tem to
hold office beyond the current session (in the event of ill-
ness or disability of both the regular presiding officer and
his alternate), notice must be given at the preceding meeting or in the call of the meeting that elects him. One session cannot interfere with the freedom of each new session
to choose its own chairman pro tem except by an election
held with previous notice (pp. 116–18).

§9. PARTICULAR TYPES OF BUSINESS MEET-
INGS

Regular Meeting

The term *regular meeting* (or *stated meeting*) refers to the
periodic business meeting of a permanent society, local
branch, or board, held at weekly, monthly, quarterly, or similar intervals, for which the day (as, "the first Tuesday of each
month") should be prescribed by the bylaws and the hour
should be fixed by a standing rule of the society. If, instead, an
organization follows the practice of scheduling the dates of its
regular meetings by resolution, notice must be sent to all
members in advance of each regular meeting, and the number
of days' notice required should be prescribed by the bylaws (p.
558). Each regular meeting normally completes a separate session, as explained on pages 81–82 (see *Adjourned Meeting,*
pp. 90–91 below, however). Some societies have frequent
meetings for social or cultural purposes at which business may
be transacted, and also hold a session every month or quarter
especially for business. In such societies, the term *regular
meeting* applies particularly to the regular business session.

Important rules relating to the continuance of a question from one session to the next depend on whether *no*

1   *more than a quarterly time interval* intervenes between the
    two sessions. In this book, two consecutive sessions are un-
    derstood to be separated by no more than a quarterly time
    interval if the second session occurs at any time during the
5   calendar month three months later than the calendar month
    in which the first session was held. For example, with refer-
    ence to a session held at any time during the month of Jan-
    uary, no more than a quarterly time interval has intervened
    since the most recent previous session if that session was
10 held on or after October 1st of the preceding calendar year;
    and no more than a quarterly time interval will intervene
    until the next session if that session will be held on or be-
    fore April 30th of the current year.

    When two consecutive business sessions of an organiza-
15 tion are not separated by more than a quarterly time inter-
    val, there are four processes by which a main question can
    go over from the earlier session to the next one, as a mo-
    tion *temporarily but not finally disposed of* that is thus said
    to remain *within the control of the assembly:* (1) by being
20 postponed or made a special order (**14, 41**); (2) by lying on
    the table (**17**); (3) by being the subject of a motion to *Re-
    consider* that has been made and seconded at a time when it
    could not be considered, and that has not been *called up*
    (**37**); and (4) by being referred to a committee with in-
25 structions to report at a later session (**13**). In cases where
    the next session will not be held until after more than a
    quarterly time interval has elapsed, the only means by
    which a motion can go over to another session is by refer-
    ral to a committee* (see also pp. 329–30).

---

*It should be noted that if some, but not all, of an organization's
regular business sessions are separated by no more than quarterly time
intervals, it is only between meetings which are that close together that a
question can go over from one session to the next by any means other
than referral to a committee. If a society holds regular monthly business

Any business that falls within the objects of the society *1* as defined in its bylaws (or, in the case of a board, any business within the authority of the board) can be transacted at any regular meeting (provided that the parliamentary rules relating to action already taken, or to matters not finally disposed of and remaining within the control of the assembly, *5* are complied with in cases where they apply; compare pp. 106–108; see also **35** and **38**).

Special Meeting

A *special meeting* (or *called meeting*) is a separate session of a society held at a time different from that of any regular meeting, and convened only to consider one or more items of business specified in the call of the meeting. Notice of the *15* time, place, and exact purpose of the meeting must be mailed to all members a reasonable number of days in advance. The reason for special meetings is to deal with important matters that may arise between regular meetings and that urgently require action by the society before the next regular meeting. *20* As in the case of a regular meeting, the session of a special meeting in an ordinary society is normally concluded in a single meeting, unless the assembly at the special meeting schedules an adjourned meeting (see below).

The section of the bylaws that authorizes the calling of *25* special meetings (without which special meetings cannot properly be called; see p. 558) should prescribe:

1) by whom such a meeting is to be called—which provision is usually in the form of a statement that the presi- *30*

---

meetings from September through May, for example, but does not meet during the summer, a question can be postponed until the next meeting at any of the meetings from September through April, but such a question cannot be postponed at the May meeting until the September meeting.

1   dent (or, in large organizations, the president with the approval of the board) can call a special meeting, and that he shall call a special meeting at the written request of a specific number of members; and

5   2) the number of days' notice required. Unless otherwise provided in the bylaws, the number of days is computed by counting all calendar days (including holidays and weekends), excluding the day of the meeting but including the day of the mailing.

10

The presiding officer directs the secretary to mail the notice of the special meeting to all members at the society's expense in compliance with the bylaws no later than the required number of days in advance, making sure that it con-

15 tains all the necessary information.

With the exception of motions that relate to procedure without direct reference to a particular substantive item of business,* only business mentioned in the call of a special meeting can be transacted at such a meeting. If, at a special

20 meeting, it becomes urgent in an emergency to take action for which no notice was given, that action, to become legal, must be ratified (see pp. 118–20) by the organization at a regular meeting (or, if ratification also cannot wait, at another special meeting properly called for that purpose).

25

Adjourned Meeting

An *adjourned meeting* is a meeting in continuation of the session of the immediately preceding regular or special

30 meeting. The name *adjourned meeting* means that the meeting is scheduled for a particular time (and place, if it is not otherwise established) by the assembly's "adjourning to" or "adjourning until" that time and place. If a reg-

---

*Motions covering such cases are *incidental main motions* relating to procedure. See p. 96, l. 27–28.

ular meeting or a special meeting is unable to complete its
work, an adjourned meeting can be scheduled for later the
same day or some other convenient time before the next
regular meeting, by the adoption (as applicable) of a main
or a privileged motion to fix the time to which to adjourn,
or a main motion to adjourn until the specified time (see
21, 22). In such a case, the adjourned meeting is sometimes spoken of as "an adjournment of" the regular or
special meeting. This usage should not be confused with
the act of adjourning.

When common expressions such as "regular [or
"stated"] meeting," "special [or "called"] meeting," and
"annual meeting" (see below) are used in the bylaws, rules,
or resolutions adopted by an organization, the word *meeting* is understood to mean *session* in the parliamentary
sense, and therefore covers all adjourned meetings.

An adjourned meeting takes up its work at the point
where it was interrupted in the order of business or in the
consideration of the question that was postponed to the adjourned meeting, except that the minutes of the preceding
meeting are first read.

Annual Meeting

The term *annual meeting* is used in two senses.

Certain types of societies may hold only one business
meeting of the general membership each year, perhaps leaving the management of the organization's affairs in the
meantime to a board. Such a meeting is then the annual
meeting of the society.

In local organizations that hold regular business meetings throughout the year, however, the bylaws may provide
that one of these regular meetings held at a specified time
each year shall be known as the annual meeting. The only
difference between this kind of annual meeting and the other
regular meetings is that the annual reports of officers and

standing committees, the election of officers, and any other items of business that the bylaws may prescribe for the annual meeting are in order, besides the ordinary business that may come up. The minutes of the previous regular meeting are read and approved as usual at the annual meeting, and the minutes of the annual meeting are read and approved at the next regular meeting. Minutes of one annual meeting should not be held for action until the next one a year later.

Business that is legally required to be done "at the annual meeting" can be done at any time (when it is in order) during the session of the annual meeting, or, in other words, either at that meeting as originally convened or at any adjournment of it. If such an item of business has actually been taken up as required and proves impossible or impractical to complete during the session of the annual meeting in a case where no more than a quarterly time interval (see p. 88) will elapse until the next regular business session, the matter can also be postponed to the next regular session for completion.

Executive Session

An *executive session* in general parliamentary usage has come to mean any meeting of a deliberative assembly, or a portion of a meeting, at which the proceedings are secret. This term originally referred to the consideration of executive business—that is, presidential nominations to appointive offices, and treaties—behind closed doors in the United States Senate. The practice of organizations operating under the lodge system is equivalent to holding all regular meetings in executive session. In any society, matters relating to discipline—particularly trials—properly should be handled only in executive session. In most organizations, except those operating under the lodge system, by practice

or sometimes by rule, membership meetings are open to
the public, but board or committee meetings are customarily held in executive session. In the latter case, members of
the organization who are not members of the board or
committee, and sometimes nonmembers, may be invited to
attend, perhaps to give a report, but they are not *entitled* to
attend.

A motion to go into executive session is a question of
privilege (**19**), and therefore is adopted by a majority vote.
Only members, special invitees, and such employees or staff
members as the assembly or its rules may determine to be
necessary are allowed to remain in the hall.

A member can be punished under disciplinary procedure (**61**) if he violates the secrecy of an executive session.
Anyone else permitted to be present is honor-bound not to
divulge anything that occurred. The minutes, or record of
proceedings, of an executive session must be read and acted
upon only in executive session, unless that which would be
reported in the minutes—that is, the action taken, as distinct from that which was said in debate—was not secret, or
secrecy has been lifted by the assembly. When the minutes
of an executive session must be considered for approval at
an executive session held solely for that purpose, the brief
minutes of the latter meeting are, or are assumed to be, approved by that meeting.

Public Session

This type of meeting is the opposite of an executive session. Many public and semipublic bodies are governed by
sunshine laws—that is, they must be open to the public.
Normally, such laws have no application to private, non-
governmental bodies.

In meetings of many public bodies, such as school
boards, the public may attend. Similarly, in some private or-

1 ganizations such as church councils, parishioners may be permitted to attend. These attendees are not members of the meeting body and ordinarily have no right to partici-pate. Some bodies, especially public ones, may invite non-

5 members to express their views, but this is done under the control of the presiding officer subject to any relevant rules adopted by the body and subject to appeal by a member. Often, by rule or practice, time limits are placed on speak-ers and relevance is closely monitored.

THE MAIN MOTION

§10. THE MAIN MOTION

As explained in **3–6,** a *main motion* is a motion whose introduction brings business before the assembly; such a motion can be made only while no other motion is pending.

Distinction Between Original Main and Incidental Main Motions

The division of main motions into *original* and *incidental* main motions was mentioned in **6** and is discussed below.

An *original main motion* is a main motion that introduces a substantive question as a new subject. This is the motion most often used, and is the basic device by which a matter is presented to the assembly for possible action, as ". . . that the Club contribute $50 to the centennial celebration"; or ". . . that the Society go on record as favoring the Popular Run route for the proposed new beltway"; or ". . . to adopt the following resolution: '*Resolved,* That the Northridge Improvement Association

1

5

10

15

20

oppose a municipal tax increase at this time.'" It may be more suitable for an original main motion to be made orally, or to be submitted in writing, depending on its length, complexity, or importance. (See *Making a Motion,* p. 32, where many of the statements apply especially to original main motions.)

An *incidental main motion* is a main motion that is incidental to or relates to the business of the assembly, or its past or future action. Such a motion is distinguished by the following characteristics:

1) It proposes an action specifically defined under parliamentary law and described by a particular parliamentary term. There are thus a definite number of incidental main motions somewhat as in the case of the secondary motions (subsidiary, privileged, and incidental) and the motions that bring a question again before the assembly.

2) It does *not* mark the beginning of a particular involvement of the assembly in a substantive matter, as an original main motion does. (Like all main motions, however, it can be made only when nothing is pending, and it brings business before the assembly.) Action that can be proposed by the incidental main motions may relate: (a) to further steps in dealing with a substantive matter in which the assembly's involvement has begun earlier; or (b) to procedure, without direct reference to a particular substantive item of business.

An incidental main motion involving a subject already entered into might be a motion to *adopt* recommendations which a committee has prepared upon instructions (not relating to a referred *motion*), or a motion to *ratify* emergency action taken at a meeting when no quorum was present. An example of an incidental main motion relating to procedure without reference to an item of business would be a motion to take a *recess*, made when no business is pending, or a motion to place a special *limit* on the length of speeches throughout a meeting. In each of the examples just mentioned, the italicized word—*adopt, ratify, limit, recess*—is the parliamentary term that describes the motion.

An incidental main motion is usually made orally. The chief difference in the rules governing original and incidental main motions is that an *Objection to the Consideration of a Question* (**26**) can be applied only to original main and not to incidental main motions. The reason is that, in the case of an incidental main motion dealing with a subject previously entered into, the involvement has already begun and it is too late to object; and in the case of an incidental main motion involving only procedure, an objection to its consideration has no legitimate purpose. In conventions, incidental main motions are not referred to a resolutions committee. The form in which an original main motion is written does not determine in any way what must be referred to a "resolutions committee," nor does it affect the form of the motions reported by such a committee (see, for example, "platform," pp. 617–18).

Most of the incidental main motions closely correspond to secondary (subsidiary, privileged, or incidental) motions described by the same or similar names—as in the last two of the four examples above. (Compare the subsidiary motion to *Limit or Extend Limits of Debate*, **15,** and the privileged motion to *Recess*, **20**.) Referring to the Table of Rules Relating to Motions on tinted pages 6–29, most of the motions listed as "main"—with the exception of No. 1 (original main motion)—are incidental main motions in their usual application. The motions to *adopt* and to *ratify* are briefly discussed at the end of this chapter.

Standard Descriptive Characteristics

A main motion:

1. Takes precedence of nothing—that is, it cannot be moved when any other question is pending. It yields to all subsidiary, all privileged, and all applicable incidental motions; that is, any subsidiary or privileged motion, and any incidental motion that is applicable in the particular case at the particular time, can be moved while a main motion is pending.

2. Can be applied to no other motion. All subsidiary motions can be applied to it. If it is postponed to a certain time or laid on the table, it carries with it any subsidiary motions that may also be pending. If it is referred to a committee, the only subsidiary motions that it carries with it to the committee are pending amendments (so that a motion to *Postpone Indefinitely,* if pending, is dropped). An *Objection to the Consideration of a Question* can be applied only to an original main motion, not to an incidental main motion.

3. Is out of order when another has the floor.

4. Must be seconded.

5. Is debatable.

6. Is amendable.

7. Requires a majority vote, except:

   a) when the motion proposes an action for which the bylaws prescribe a requirement of more than a majority vote (such as a two-thirds vote, or previous notice [pp. 116–18], or both)—as may be the case, for example, for motions proposing admission to membership, the purchase or sale of real estate, etc.;

   b) when adoption of the motion would have the effect of suspending a rule of order or a parliamentary right of members, in which case it requires a two-

thirds vote—as, for example, a motion to place a
special limit on the length or number of speeches
per member during a meeting or a session; or

c) when adoption of the motion would have the effect
of changing something already adopted, as in a motion to postpone an event previously scheduled by
vote of the assembly, or to discharge a committee
(from an uncompleted task previously assigned to it
by means of a main motion, before the committee
is ready to report)—in which case the vote required
is as stated on pages 295–96 under Standard
Characteristic 7 of the motion that takes the form
either to *Rescind* or to *Amend Something Previously
Adopted.*

8. Can be reconsidered. (See, however, Standard Characteristic 8 of the motion that takes the form either to *Rescind* or to *Amend Something Previously Adopted,* p.
296; with reference to the adoption of bylaws, see p.
542, l. 28–29, and p. 574, l. 5–6.)

The Framing of Main Motions

WORDING OF A MAIN MOTION.   If a main mo-
tion is adopted, it becomes the officially recorded statement
of an action taken by the assembly. A motion should therefore be worded in a concise, unambiguous, and complete
form appropriate to such a purpose. It cannot employ language that is not allowed in debate (**43**). A member making
a motion embodying something that has just been said by the
chair or another member in informal consultation during a
meeting should avoid statements such as "I so move," and
should himself recite the complete motion that he offers.

A motion whose only effect is to propose that the assembly *refrain* from doing something should not be offered if the same result can be accomplished by adopting no

1   motion at all. It is incorrect, for example, to move "that no
response be made" to a request for a contribution to a fund,
or "that our delegates be given no instructions," unless
some purpose would be served by adoption of such a mo-
5   tion. This could be the case, for example, if the membership
of an organization wishes to make certain that a subordinate body, such as its executive board, will not take such action at a later date, or if the motion expresses an opinion or
reason as to why no action should be taken.

10   Motions to "reaffirm" a position previously taken by
adopting a motion or resolution are not in order. Such a
motion serves no useful purpose because the original motion is still in effect; also, possible attempts to amend a motion to reaffirm would come into conflict with the rules for
15   the motion to *Amend Something Previously Adopted* (**35**);
and if such a motion to reaffirm failed, it would create an
ambiguous situation.

It is preferable to avoid a motion containing a negative
statement even in cases where it would have a meaning, since
20   members may become confused as to the effect of voting for
or against such a motion. Rather than moving, for example,
that the association go on record as "not in favor of the proposed public bond issue," it should be moved that the association "oppose" or "declare its opposition to" the bond
25   issue. In this connection, it should be noted that voting
down a motion or resolution that would express a particular
opinion is not the same as adopting a motion expressing the
opposite opinion, since—if the motion is voted down—no
opinion has been expressed. A member may be in complete
30   agreement with the views contained in a resolution yet feel
that his organization should remain silent on the matter, and
he may vote against the resolution for such a reason.

MOTIONS SUBMITTED IN WRITING: RESOLU-
35   TIONS.   As previously stated, a main motion—particu-

larly an original main motion—is frequently offered as a *res-*   *1*
olution, either because of its importance or because of its
length or complexity. Any resolution—and any long or
complicated motion, whether cast as a resolution or not—
should always be submitted in writing as described on   *5*
page 32. In preparing an important written motion or resolution (which should be done in advance of the meeting if
possible), it is often advisable to consult with members who
can be of assistance in perfecting it, and also with those
whose support is likely to be necessary for its adoption. If   *10*
such a motion is not offered as a resolution, it can simply be
written out in the form in which it would be moved orally
(beginning with the word "That"); for example, "That the
Merchants' Association sponsor an essay contest open to
high school students of the city, to be conducted according   *15*
to the following specifications: . . . ." If put in the form of
a resolution, the preceding example would be written, "*Re-*
solved, That the Merchants' Association sponsor an essay
contest . . . ." In a resolution, the name of the adopting organization can also be made a part of the enacting words,   *20*
as in "*Resolved by the International Benevolent Association*
in convention assembled, That . . . ."

An example of a simple resolution expressing an opinion or position of an organized society is given on page
95, l. 20, to page 96, l. 1. If the resolution is offered in   *25*
a mass meeting (or in any meeting where there is no established organization whose act the adopted resolution
would become), it may begin, "*Resolved,* That it is the
sense of this meeting that . . ." A resolution can consist
of more than one resolving clause, as in the following ex-   *30*
ample:

> *Resolved,* That it is the sense of this meeting that the
> existing zoning ordinance should undergo a general
> revision; and   *35*

Resolved, That the Secretary be requested to send a copy of this resolution, and of the report already presented at this meeting, to the Mayor and to each member of the City Council.

USE OF A PREAMBLE.   It is usually inadvisable to attempt to include reasons for a motion's adoption within the motion itself. To do so may encumber the motion and may weigh against its adoption—since some members who approve of the action it proposes may dislike voting for it if it states reasons with which they disagree. When special circumstances make it desirable to include a brief statement of background, the motion should be cast in the form of a resolution, with the background or reasons incorporated in a *preamble* that is placed before the resolving clauses. A preamble consists of one or more clauses beginning "Whereas, ..." *It should be emphasized that neither rule nor custom requires a resolution to have a preamble, and one should not be used merely for the sake of form.* In general, the use of a preamble should be limited to cases where it provides little-known information without which the point or the merits of a resolution are likely to be poorly understood, where unusual importance is attached to making certain reasons for an action a matter of record, or the like.

An example of a resolution with an appropriate preamble might be the following:

Whereas, A privately conducted survey by experts engaged by the Association reveals conditions constituting a serious fire hazard throughout the lower office-building area bordering the waterfront;

    Resolved, That a committee of seven consisting of [names of four], and three others to be named by the chair, be appointed to draw up recommendations

whereby the Association may bring to bear all possible *1*
influence to secure proper enforcement of city fire regulations and any revision of them that may be found
to be appropriate.

5

To avoid detracting from the force of the resolution itself, a preamble generally should contain no more clauses
than are strictly necessary. In cases where an elaborate resolution (consisting of several preamble clauses and several
resolving clauses) cannot be avoided, however, the follow- *10*
ing skeleton example will serve as a guide:

Whereas, The . . . [text of the first preamble
clause];
. . . . *15*
Whereas, . . . [text of the next to the last preamble
clause]; and
Whereas, . . . [text of the last preamble clause];
Resolved, That . . . [stating action to be taken];
Resolved, That . . . [stating further action to be
taken]; and *20*
Resolved, That . . . [stating still further action to
be taken].

In the consideration of a resolution having a preamble, *25*
the preamble is always amended last, since changes in the
resolving clauses may require changes in the preamble. In
moving the adoption of a resolution, the preamble is not
usually mentioned, since it is included in the resolution.
When the *Previous Question* (**16**) is ordered on the resolu- *30*
tion before the preamble has been considered for amendment, however, the *Previous Question* does not apply to the
preamble, which becomes open to debate and amendment
unless the *Previous Question* is then separately ordered on
it also. *35*

DETAILS OF FORM AND VARIATIONS IN RESOLUTIONS. The following details regarding the usual form for writing resolutions, and the variations that are used, should be noted:

If there is a preamble, each clause, written as a separate paragraph, begins with the word "Whereas" followed by a comma, and the next word should begin with a capital letter. The preamble, regardless of how many paragraphs it has, should never contain a period. Each of its paragraphs should close with a semicolon, followed, in the case of the next to the last paragraph, by the word "and" (which is optional for the preceding paragraphs also). The last paragraph of the preamble should close with a semicolon, after which a connecting expression such as "therefore" or "therefore, be it" or "now, therefore, be it" is sometimes added. When one of these phrases is included, no punctuation should follow it, and it should always be placed at the end of the preamble paragraph, never at the beginning of the resolving paragraph, thus:

> Whereas, The . . . [text of the preamble]; now, therefore, be it
> *Resolved*, That . . . [stating action to be taken].

A resolution is often more forceful with a minimum of connecting words, however, as in the earlier examples above.

The word *"Resolved"* is underlined or printed in italics, and is followed by a comma and the word "That"—which begins with a capital "T." If there is more than one resolving clause, each of them should be a separate paragraph. Unless the paragraphs are numbered as in the alternative form described below, each paragraph begins with the words *"Resolved*, That," just as the first resolving clause. Each resolving paragraph may close with a semicolon (followed by the word "and" at least in the case of the next to the last, as in the example already shown); or each resolving paragraph may end with a period. A resolving paragraph should not contain a period within its structure, though observance of this rule is becoming less strict. As an alternative form, separate paragraphs, except the first, may be numbered and begin with the word "That"—as follows:

> *Resolved,* That . . .
> 2. That . . .
> 3. That . . .

(For the format used in a *platform,* see pp. 617–18.)

ORDERS (INSTRUCTIONS TO EMPLOYEES). In organizations with employees, the assembly or the board can give instructions to an employee in the form of an *order,* which is written just as a resolution except that the word *"Ordered"* is used in place of the word *"Resolved."* An example would be: "*Ordered,* That the steward obtain impoundment of all unauthorized vehicles found parked on the club premises."

SERIES OF RESOLUTIONS OFFERED BY A SINGLE MAIN MOTION. If a single composite proposal for taking a number of actions in reference to a particular subject has too many elements to be conveniently written into one resolution (even of several clauses), it can be set forth in a series of separate resolutions that can be numbered and offered by means of a single main motion, thus: "Mr. President, I move the adoption of [or "I offer"] the following resolutions: . . . " Such a series of resolutions can include orders as described above. In the case of a series of resolutions relating to a single subject, if members desire one or more of the resolutions to be considered separately, the motion for *Division of a Question* (**27**) must be made

1 and adopted by a majority vote. Sometimes a series of independent resolutions relating to completely different subjects is offered by a single main motion in the same way. In
the latter case—where the subjects are independent—any
5 resolution in the series must be taken up and voted on separately at the demand of a single member. Such a demand
can be made even when another has the floor, at any time
until the vote has been taken on adopting the series. A
member wishing to make this demand rises and says, for ex-
10 ample, "Mr. President, I call for a separate vote on Resolution No. 2."

Main Motions That Are Not in Order

15   Below are stated a number of characteristics or conditions that cause a particular main motion to be out of order,
and—where applicable—the alternative courses that are
open for accomplishing the desired result:

20 1) No main motion is in order that conflicts with the bylaws (or constitution) or rules of the organization or assembly, and to the extent that procedural rules
applicable to the organization or assembly are prescribed by federal, state, or local law, no main motion is
25   in order that conflicts with such rules.
2) No main motion is in order that presents substantially
the same question as a motion previously rejected during the same session; and, apart from a motion to *Rescind* or to *Amend Something Previously Adopted* (**35**),
30   no main motion is in order that conflicts with a motion
previously adopted at any time and still in force.* If a
main motion that interferes with a desired action has

---

*Unless an adopted main motion specifies a time for the termination
of its effect, it continues in force until it is rescinded.

been adopted, a motion to reconsider (**37**) the vote on
it can be made for a limited time during the same session; and if it is reconsidered, it can be voted down or
amended as desired, in the reconsideration. Although
reconsideration is the preferable procedure in such a
case when possible, an adopted main motion, at any
time before or after it is too late to reconsider it, can be
changed by means of the motion to *Amend Something
Previously Adopted*, or it can be rescinded and the desired new motion can then be introduced. If a main motion to take a desired action has already been rejected
during the current session, it can be renewed (**38**)—
that is, the same question can be introduced again as if
new—at any later session.

3) No main motion is in order that would conflict with or
that presents substantially the same question as one
which has been *temporarily but not finally disposed of*—
whether in the same or the preceding session (see pp. 88,
329–30)—and which remains *within the control of the assembly*. Referring to the four possible processes by which
a main motion may have been placed in such status, if it
interferes with the introduction of another main motion,
it can be brought before the assembly again and can be
amended to encompass the idea of the desired new motion, as follows:

a) if it has been postponed to (or made a special order
for) a later time (**14, 41**), the rules can be suspended
(**25**) and it can be taken up;

b) if it has been laid on the table (**17**), it can be taken
from the table (**34**);

c) if a reconsideration of it has been moved but has not
been taken up, the motion to *Reconsider* can be
called up (**37**), which causes the first motion either
to be reconsidered or to become finally disposed of
without a reconsideration; or

d) if the first motion was referred to a committee that has not finally reported (**13**), the committee can be discharged from further consideration of the question (**36**).

4) A main motion that proposes action outside the scope of the organization's object as defined in the bylaws or corporate charter is out of order unless the assembly by a two-thirds vote authorizes its introduction.

Many of the alternative courses for obtaining a result that cannot be directly reached through a main motion, as described in items (2) and (3) above, involve parliamentary motions having special requirements (such as a two-thirds vote or previous notice, pp. 116–18) for their adoption. The rules relating to the motions to *Suspend the Rules* (**25**), *Take from the Table* (**34**), *Rescind or Amend Something Previously Adopted* (**35**), *Discharge a Committee* (**36**), and *Reconsider* (**37**), and the rules relating to the renewal of motions (**38**), should be read in connection with the application of these methods.

Treatment of Main Motions

The basic procedure by which main motions are introduced and considered is described in detail in **4**. Additional points to be noted in connection with the handling of main motions are as follows:

PROCEDURES BY WHICH THE PROPOSAL CONTAINED IN A MAIN MOTION CAN BE IMPROVED UPON BEFORE ACTION IS TAKEN. As previously noted (pp. 32–33), it is a general parliamentary rule that a subject must be brought up in the form of a motion (embodying a specific proposal) before it can be discussed in a meeting of an assembly. A motion should be as well thought out as possible before it is introduced. At the same time, it will frequently happen that the assembly—al-

though desiring to take some kind of action on the subject *1*
that a main motion has brought to its attention—wishes to
make greater or less change in the proposal before voting
on its adoption. There are several means by which such a result can be accomplished, depending on the conditions and *5*
the degree or scope of the changes desired. The courses
that are open in such cases are summarized below:

1) After a main motion has been made and before the
   question has been stated by the chair, any member can *10*
   quickly rise and, with little or no explanatory comment,
   informally suggest one or more modifications in the
   motion, which at this point the maker can accept or reject as he wishes (see pp. 38–39). Application of this
   method should generally be limited to minor changes *15*
   about which there is unlikely to be a difference of opinion.
2) After the question has been stated by the chair—although the assembly, and not the maker of the motion,
   then has control over its wording—the maker can re- *20*
   quest unanimous consent to modify the motion (see
   pp. 283–86). If any member then objects, however, the
   desired modification must be introduced in the form of
   a motion to *Amend,* as noted below.
3) By means of the subsidiary motion to *Amend* (**12**), mem- *25*
   bers can propose changes to be made in the wording and,
   within limits, the meaning of a pending main motion before it is voted on. These amendments must be seconded,
   are debatable, and are adopted by a majority vote. Such
   proposed amendments can take the form of either: *30*
   a) word-by-word or phrase-by-phrase changes in the
      main motion—of which several specific types are per-
      mitted under the rules for the motion to *Amend;* or
   b) a motion to *substitute* an entire new text of the main
      motion in place of the pending version (see pp. *35*
      146–54).

1   Whatever amendments are adopted, the main motion is
then voted on in its amended form.

4) If proper recasting of a main motion will require time or
5   study, the subsidiary motion to *Commit* (**13**), which is
adopted by a majority vote, can be used to refer the main
motion to a committee. When this committee reports, it
normally recommends appropriate amendments for the
assembly's consideration. Such a committee can be a spe-
10   cial committee, appointed only for the particular case, or
it can be one of a number of standing committees that
may be permanently established within the organization
(see **50**). Some assemblies provide in their rules for the
automatic referral of all main motions dealing with cer-
15   tain classes of subjects to specified standing committees as
soon as they are introduced. Bills are handled in this
manner in most legislative bodies. In conventions, the
rules of the organization often require that all resolutions
not reviewed by some other committee be submitted to
20   a Resolutions Committee before coming before the general voting body (see pp. 614–15). Where an assembly is
large and has a volume of business, it is usually desirable
to have every main question go to a committee before
final action is taken.

25 5) If the general problem posed by a main motion might be
better dealt with by an alternative measure that cannot
conveniently be proposed as an amendment in the form of
a substitute (see above), a member speaking in debate can
urge rejection of the pending main motion, saying that if
30   it is voted down he will offer a different main motion
which he can describe briefly and which deals with the
general problem in a substantially different way (see, however, p. 106, l. 26 to p. 107, l. 14). Or, with the same explanation, he may move to postpone the main motion
35   indefinitely (**11**). If the pending motion is thereafter

voted down, or indefinitely postponed, the chair immedi- 1
ately recognizes this member again for the purpose of
making his alternative motion, even if another member
rises to claim the floor first and addresses the chair.

5

INTRODUCTION OF SUBSIDIARY OR INCIDEN-
TAL MOTIONS AS A PART OF—OR PRIVILEGED
MOTIONS AS AN INTERRUPTION OF—THE CON-
SIDERATION OF A MAIN MOTION. While a main
motion is pending, as described in **5** and **6,** one or more 10
subsidiary motions or incidental motions can be introduced
and disposed of an as integral part of the main motion's
consideration, or the introduction of one or more privileged motions can interrupt its consideration. A member
may speak in debate on the main motion and conclude by 15
offering a secondary motion.

Such motions are usually made during the period while
the main motion is open to debate, although certain incidental motions can also arise before or after this stage in its
handling. The precise times and circumstances when each of 20
these motions is in order are determined by the first three of
the motion's standard descriptive characteristics. If the assembly's treatment of a particular main motion involves a
number of these other motions, they may occur in such a way
that each one of them is disposed of before the next is intro- 25
duced, or—depending on the circumstances—several of
them may become pending at one time by operation of the
order of precedence of motions (see pp. 56–59).

In the latter case, when a motion that takes precedence over all pending questions is made, that motion is 30
disposed of first, and then "the question recurs" on the
next-most-recently-moved motion; that is (as far as applicable in the existing parliamentary situation), its consideration is resumed at the point where the higher-ranking
motion interrupted it. This motion is again open to de- 35

bate and amendment if it is a debatable and amendable motion. In this manner, the motions in the series of pending questions are voted on in the reverse of the order in which they were made—with the main motion being voted on last—unless the result of the vote on one of the other motions causes consideration of the remainder of the series to be halted.

This principle may be illustrated by a somewhat more complicated example than may ordinarily occur in practice. Referring to the explanation of subsidiary, privileged, and incidental motions in **6**, assume that the following series of motions is pending and that the motions have been moved in the order shown:

1) a main motion;
2) a motion to postpone the main question indefinitely;
3) an amendment to the main motion;
4) a motion to refer the main question (with the pending amendment) to a committee;
5) a motion to postpone the pending questions to a certain time;
6) a motion to vote on the postponement by ballot;
7) a motion to lay the pending questions on the table; and
8) a motion to take a recess.

In such a case, the motion to *Recess* is voted on first, then the motion to *Lay on the Table*, and so on, proceeding upward through the list above. If any one of the motions (8), (7), (5), (4), or (2) is adopted, however, consideration of the remaining motions stops. These processes, and others that may be employed in or interrupt a main motion's consideration, are explained initially in **6** and are further illustrated in the examples in **11–33**.

A subsidiary or incidental motion *adheres* to a main question if it is related to the main question in such a way

that—once introduced—it must be decided before the
main question can be decided. Adhering motions thus remain connected with the main question if that question is
interrupted or temporarily disposed of, and remain to be
decided first if and when the main question is taken up
again. In the example in the preceding paragraph, motions
(2) through (7) adhere to the main motion—except that
motion (2), to *Postpone Indefinitely,* would cease to adhere
to it if motion (4), to *Commit,* were adopted (see Standard
Descriptive Characteristic 2, p. 98). Motion (8) in the example does not adhere to the main question.

MAIN MOTIONS BROUGHT UP BY MEANS OF A
CALL FOR THE ORDERS OF THE DAY OR BY RAIS-
ING A QUESTION OF PRIVILEGE. Under the
process by which a main motion is normally introduced, as
already explained, it can be moved only while no motion is
pending. Certain questions may come before the assembly
with the status of main motions after having interrupted
other business, however, if they are brought up by means of
either of the two lowest-ranking *privileged* motions. To
Call for the Orders of the Day (**18**) and to *Raise a Question
of Privilege* (**19**) each have privileged rank and can therefore
interrupt pending business. As a result of the application of
one of these devices to interrupt a pending question, an
order of the day (that is, another question previously set as
due to come up automatically at the time) may be taken up,
or an urgent motion relating to the privileges of the assembly or of a member may be admitted as a *question of privilege* to be entertained immediately. But when such an order
of the day or question of privilege has thus become pending, it is treated exactly as any other main motion. (The description of the first two privileged motions on p. 64–65
and the sections on them referred to above should be read
in connection with this paragraph.)

1   NOTES ON EXAMPLE FORMAT THROUGHOUT
THE BOOK.   In the examples for the handling of motions below and throughout this book, methods of notation
used are as follows:

5

• The examples generally show the presiding officer addressed as "Mr. President" or "Madam President."
   While this form corresponds to the chair's designation
   in most organized societies, the presiding officer should
10   be addressed by whatever is his or her official title in the
   particular organization or assembly. Where he or she has
   no special title, or in a meeting of an unorganized body
   such as a mass meeting, the form "Mr. Chairman" or
   "Madam Chairman" should be used (see also pp.
15   22–23).
• The phrase "obtaining the floor" in parentheses before
   words spoken by a member indicates that this member
   must first obtain the floor in the manner explained on
   pages 28–30.
20 • The word "Second" in parentheses after words spoken in
   making a motion indicates that, except in cases where it
   is proposed on behalf of a board or a committee, another
   member must second the motion as described on pages
   34–36, and that it is assumed that this is done.

25

EXAMPLE.   The example below illustrates the handling of a main motion in a case that involves only the basic
forms of the six principal steps—three in bringing the motion before the assembly (p. 31) and three in its considera-
30 tion (p. 40).
Assume that the chair has just asked if there is any new
business (see p. 349).

MEMBER A (obtaining the floor): I move that the Society con-
35 tribute $100 to the Centennial Celebration. (Second.)

CHAIR: It is moved and seconded that the Society contribute $100 to the Centennial Celebration. [Proceeding as shown on pp. 36–37.]   *1*

The chair immediately turns toward Member A (who re-   *5* sumed his seat after making his motion) to see if he wishes the floor first in debate (see p. 30, l. 4–6). Member A is already rising to claim the floor. The chair recognizes him:

CHAIR: Mr. A.   *10*

Member A explains the reasons why the contribution should be made, followed by others who also speak in debate after having obtained the floor. When debate appears to have ended, the chair makes sure that no one else wishes to speak   *15* as by asking, "Are you ready for the question?" and then puts the question—that is, puts the motion to a vote—as follows:

CHAIR: The question is on the motion that the Society contribute $100 to the Centennial Celebration. As many as are in favor of the mo-   *20* tion, say *aye.* [Pausing for response.] . . . Those opposed, say *no.* . . . The ayes have it and the motion is agreed to. The Treasurer will issue the appropriate check and the Secretary will prepare a covering letter forwarding the contribution to the Chairman of the Centennial Commission. Is there further new business?   *25*

If the assembly is taking up business under the heading of Special Orders in the order of business, or that of Unfinished Business and General Orders (rather than New Business as in the above example), the chair, instead of say-   *30* ing, "Is there further new business," announces, "The next item of business is . . . [immediately proceeding to state the question]" (see 346–48).

(See **4** for variations in the steps illustrated above. For examples of the use of subsidiary and incidental motions in the   *35*

1   handling of main motions and the application of privileged motions while a main motion is pending, see **11–33**.)

5   **Previous Notice of Motions**

The term *previous notice* (or *notice*), as applied to necessary conditions for the adoption of certain motions, has a particular meaning in parliamentary law. A requirement of previous notice means that announcement that the motion 10 will be introduced—indicating its exact content as described below—must be included in the call of the meeting (p. 5) at which the motion will be brought up, or, as a permissible alternative, if no more than a quarterly time interval (see p. 88) will have elapsed since the preceding meeting, the announce- 15 ment must be made at the preceding meeting. The call of a meeting is generally mailed to all members a reasonable time in advance, which may be prescribed in the bylaws. In organizations that meet less often than at quarterly time intervals (see p. 88), or that meet as a convention of delegates, the 20 bylaws should require the secretary to issue a call.

Motions that have the effect of changing or nullifying previous action of the assembly—such as the motion to *Rescind* or to *Amend Something Previously Adopted* (**35**), the motion to *Discharge a Committee* (**36**), or a motion to 25 postpone an event already scheduled—require previous notice if they are to be adopted by only a majority vote. The adoption or amendment of special rules of order requires either (a) previous notice *and* a two-thirds vote or (b) a vote of a majority of the entire membership—as does the 30 amendment of bylaws if they do not prescribe the procedure for their amendment, which they should do (see also Table of Rules Relating to Motions, tinted pp. 6–29). Bylaws sometimes also provide a requirement of notice for original main motions dealing with certain subjects (com- 35 pare Standard Characteristic 7[a], p. 98).

Subject to any rules of the organization that provide *1*
how notice shall be given, it can be given as follows:

If previous notice is given *at a meeting,* it can be given
orally unless the rules of the organization require it to be in
writing—which is often the case with notice of amendments *5*
to bylaws. Unless the rules require the full text of the motion,
resolution, or bylaw amendment to be submitted in the notice, only the purport need be indicated; but such a statement
of purport must be accurate and complete—as in "to raise
the annual dues to $20"—since it will determine what *10*
amendments are in order when the motion is considered.
The notice becomes invalid if the motion is amended beyond
the scope of the notice (see also **35, 57**).

When no question is pending, a member desiring to
give a notice is entitled to preference in recognition (but see *15*
pp. 366–70 for circumstances in which others may have a
higher priority for such preference). But if the member
wishing to give the notice is unable to obtain the floor
while no business is pending (as may sometimes happen, for
example, in a convention that is following an adopted *20*
agenda or program, **41,** or in cases where a meeting of an
ordinary society adjourns before completing its regular
order of business), the notice, if necessary, can interrupt
pending business or any other pending motion; the notice
is also in order when another person has been assigned the *25*
floor but has not yet begun to speak, and is in order even
after it has been voted to adjourn, provided that the chair
has not yet declared the meeting adjourned (see also pp.
230–32).

A notice can be given and taken note of in a meeting as *30*
follows:

MEMBER A (obtaining the floor): I give notice that at the next
meeting I will move to rescind the resolution adopted April 17, 20__,
relating to . . . *35*

1   CHAIR: Notice has been given that at the next meeting . . . [repeating the substance of the notice].

5   The secretary then records the notice in the minutes. If the member desiring to give the notice is unable to obtain the floor, the following variations in form can be used as appropriate to the case:

10   MEMBER A (rising and addressing the chair immediately after the chair has recognized another member, Mr. Y, and before the latter has begun to speak—or remaining standing if he has just sought the floor unsuccessfully): Mr. President!

15   CHAIR: For what purpose does the member rise [or, if Member A has remained standing after seeking the floor, "For what purpose does the member address the chair"]?

MEMBER A: I wish to give notice of the following amendment to the bylaws: "To amend Article II, Section 3, by . . . "

CHAIR: Notice has been given of the following amendment to the bylaws: . . . Mr. Y has the floor.

20   Instead of being given at a meeting, a notice can also be sent by mail to every member with the call of the meeting at which the matter is to come up for action, except where the rules of the organization provide otherwise. In such a

25   case, the member desiring to give the notice writes a letter to the secretary alone, requesting that the notice be sent with the call of the next meeting; and the secretary should then do this at the expense of the organization.

30   **Motion to Adopt and Motion to Ratify**

A motion to *adopt* (or *accept* or *agree to*) an officer's or a committee's report or recommendations which the assembly (by means of a main motion) directed the officer or commit-

35   tee to prepare is an incidental main motion. A motion to

adopt or accept a report or the recommendations of a standing committee prepared on the committee's own initiative and dealing with a subject that was not expressly referred to the committee, however, is an original main motion.

A motion to adopt a resolution, bylaws, or any other document can be amended by adding, "and that it be printed and that members be furnished with copies," or, "that it [or "they"] go into effect at the close of this annual meeting," or anything of a similar nature (see also **51**; for the adoption of bylaws, see **56** and p. 553, l. 1–3).

The motion to *ratify* (also called *approve* or *confirm*) is an incidental main motion that is used to confirm or make valid an action already taken that cannot become legally valid until approved by the assembly. Cases where the procedure of ratification is applicable include:

- emergency action taken at a regular or properly called meeting at which no quorum was present;
- emergency action taken by officers, committees, or delegates in excess of their instructions;
- action taken by a local unit that requires approval of the state or national organization; or
- action taken by a state or national society subject to approval by its constituent units.

An assembly can ratify only such actions of its officers, committees, delegates, or subordinate bodies as it would have had the right to authorize in advance. It cannot make valid a voice-vote election when the bylaws require elections to be by ballot; nor can it ratify anything done in violation of procedural rules prescribed by national, state, or local law, or in violation of its own bylaws, except that provision for a quorum in the bylaws does not prevent it from ratifying emergency action taken at a meeting when no quorum was present.

1   A motion to ratify can be amended by substituting a motion of censure, and vice versa, when the action involved has been taken by an officer or other representative of the assembly.

5   Since the motion to ratify (or to censure) is a main motion, it is debatable and opens the entire question to debate.

SUBSIDIARY MOTIONS

*See 6, pages 60ff., for a list of these motions
and a description of their characteristics as a class.*

§11. POSTPONE INDEFINITELY
(To drop the main motion without a direct vote on it)

Postpone Indefinitely is a motion that the assembly decline
to take a position on the main question. Its adoption kills the
main motion (for the duration of the session) and avoids a direct vote on the question. It is useful in disposing of a badly
chosen main motion that cannot be either adopted or expressly rejected without possibly undesirable consequences.

Standard Descriptive Characteristics

The subsidiary motion to *Postpone Indefinitely:*

1. Takes precedence over nothing except the main question to which it is applied. It is the lowest-ranking subsidiary motion and yields to all other subsidiary
   motions, to all privileged motions, and to all applicable
   incidental motions.
2. Can be applied only to the main question and can therefore be made only while a main question is immediately

1   pending. Motions to *Limit or Extend Limits of Debate*
    and for the *Previous Question* can be applied to it with-
    out affecting the main question. It cannot be commit-
    ted (although the motion to *Commit* can be made while
5   it is pending; see below). It cannot be definitely post-
    poned or laid on the table alone, but when it is pend-
    ing, the main question can be definitely postponed or
    laid on the table, and in such a case, the motion to *Post-
    pone Indefinitely* is also postponed to the specified time
10 or carried to the table.

   3. Is out of order when another has the floor.

   4. Must be seconded.

   5. Is debatable; and, unlike the case of any other subsidiary
    motion, debate on the motion to *Postpone Indefinitely*
15 can go fully into the merits of the main question.

   6. Is not amendable.

   7. Requires a majority vote.

   8. An affirmative vote on the motion to *Postpone Indefi-
    nitely* can be reconsidered. A negative vote on it cannot
20 be reconsidered, and after such a vote this motion can-
    not be renewed as to the same main motion, for two
    reasons: (a) by the negative vote on *Postpone Indefi-
    nitely,* the effort to prevent the issue raised by the main
    motion from coming to a head is already lost; and (b)
25 the opponents of the main motion will be given another
    chance to kill it by direct rejection when the vote on
    the main motion is taken.

Further Rules and Explanation

30   EFFECT ON THE PENDING MOTION.   The ef-
    fect of postponing a question indefinitely is to suppress it
    throughout the current session. In a convention or confer-
    ence consisting of several meetings, the suppression contin-
35 ues throughout the entire series of meetings, and in

ordinary societies, throughout the weekly, monthly, or other meeting, as the case may be. Consequently, the adoption of the motion to *Postpone Indefinitely* is in effect an indirect rejection of the main motion.

EFFECT OF REFERRAL (OF THE MAIN MOTION) ON A PENDING MOTION TO POSTPONE INDEFINITELY.   If a main motion is referred to a committee while *Postpone Indefinitely* is pending, the latter motion is ignored and does not go to the committee, since the adoption of the motion to *Commit* indicates that the assembly is not in favor of postponing indefinitely.

OCCASIONAL SPECIAL USE.   The motion to *Postpone Indefinitely* is sometimes employed by strategists to test their strength on a motion they oppose. Making this motion enables members who have exhausted their right of debate on the main question to speak further because, as explained under Standard Characteristic 5, the motion to *Postpone Indefinitely,* though technically a new question, necessarily involves debate of the main question. Its effect, therefore, is to give the opponents of the pending measure a chance to kill it without risking its adoption, as they would be doing if the vote were taken on the main motion itself. If opponents of the main question carry the indefinite postponement, the main question is suppressed for the session; if they fail, they still have a vote on the main question and, having learned their strength by the vote on the indefinite postponement, can form an opinion as to the advisability of continuing their effort.

Form and Example

Assume that the following resolution is pending in a meeting of a local unit of a state professional society:

1   "*Resolved,* That the Ferndale Unit endorse the State President of the Society, James Thornton, for the office of United
States Senator." Debate creates a delicate situation. Members
are loyal to their state president, but in questions of public of-
5   fice they wish to support the nominee of their choice. Yet, for
them to vote *no* on the endorsement might appear to be a re-
pudiation of their state president. Furthermore, a vote on this
question either in the affirmative or in the negative might
tend to create an unfortunate division within the local unit.

10

MEMBER A (obtaining the floor): I move that the resolution be
postponed indefinitely. (Second.)
CHAIR: It is moved and seconded that the resolution pertaining to
the endorsement of James Thornton for United States Senator be
15 postponed indefinitely. The chair recognizes Mr. A.

Debate on the subsidiary motion to *Postpone Indefinitely* will likely involve also the advisability of the resolution itself. When debate ceases, however, the subsidiary
20 motion is voted on first.

CHAIR: The question is on the motion to postpone indefinitely the
resolution, "*Resolved,* That the Ferndale Unit endorse the State President of the Society, James Thornton, for the office of United States
25 Senator." As many as are in favor of postponing the resolution indefinitely, say *aye.* . . . Those opposed, say *no.* . . . The ayes have it and the
resolution is postponed indefinitely.

If the motion to *Postpone Indefinitely* is lost, the chair
30 announces the result and immediately states the question
on the main motion. The wording in this case is:

CHAIR: The noes have it. The motion to postpone indefinitely is
lost. The question is on the resolution, "*Resolved,* That . . . " [Contin-
35 ues as for any main motion.]

§12. AMEND

1

The subsidiary motion to *Amend* is a motion to modify the wording—and within certain limits the meaning—of a pending motion before the pending motion itself is acted upon.

5

Less frequently, it may become desirable to apply a similar process to something already adopted—as bylaws, a program, or a resolution. It should be noted that the motion then used is not the subsidiary motion to *Amend,* but a main motion having particular characteristics. This section deals only with *Amend* as a subsidiary motion. (For the motion to *Amend Something Previously Adopted,* see **35**).

10

Amend is probably the most widely used of the subsidiary motions. Its adoption does *not* adopt the motion thereby amended; that motion remains pending in its modified form. Rejection of a motion to *Amend* leaves the pending motion worded as it was before the amendment was offered.

15

Neither the member who offers an amendment nor the maker of the main motion *amends* or "makes an amendment"; only the assembly can do that. A member's vote on an amendment does not obligate him to vote in a particular way on the motion to which the amendment applies; he is free to vote as he pleases on the main motion, whether it is amended or not.

20

25

An amendment must always be *germane*—that is, closely related to or having bearing on the subject of the motion to be amended. This means that no new subject can be introduced under pretext of being an amendment (see pp. 129–31).

30

Standard Descriptive Characteristics

The subsidiary motion to *Amend:*

35

1. a) *When applied to a main motion:* takes precedence over the main motion and over the subsidiary motion to *Postpone Indefinitely;* yields to all other subsidiary motions except *Postpone Indefinitely,* to all privileged motions, and to all incidental motions except a motion to divide the main question and a motion to consider the main question by paragraph or seriatim.

    b) *When applied to other than main motions:* takes precedence over the motion that it proposes to amend; yields to any other motion that would take precedence over the motion to be amended (except that, if applied to an amendment, it would not yield to a motion to divide that amendment or a motion to consider the amendment by paragraph or seriatim); yields to motions to *Limit or Extend Limits of Debate* or for the *Previous Question* when they are applied to it; and yields to motions incidental to itself.

2. Can be applied to any main motion (but in the case of some incidental main motions only in a limited manner); also can be applied, in different limited ways, to any other motion that legitimately contains a variable factor; for example, can be applied to change the duration of a proposed recess or the hour to which a pending question is to be postponed. (For lists of motions that cannot be amended, see tinted pp. 44–45.)

    Amend can be applied to itself (that is, to a pending *primary* amendment), so that a *secondary amendment** (or "amendment to an amendment") will result, but it cannot be applied to a secondary amendment (see Standard Characteristic 6, below).

    The sections in this book dealing with each individual motion contain under Standard Characteristic 6 a

---

*Secondary amendments must not be confused with secondary *motions,* a much more general concept explained on pages 56ff.

statement of whether *Amend* is applicable to that par-   *1*
ticular motion, and if applicability is limited, in what
manner.

    Motions to *Limit or Extend Limits of Debate* and for
the *Previous Question* can be applied to a pending pri-   *5*
mary amendment or secondary amendment; and these
motions affect only the immediately pending amendment unless otherwise specified (see Standard Characteristic 6, below). A *Division of the Question* can be
applied to the motion to *Amend,* although it is seldom   *10*
useful to do so; the motion for *Consideration by Paragraph or Seriatim* can also be applied to it. The motion
to *Amend* cannot have motions to *Commit, Postpone
Definitely,* or *Lay on the Table* applied to it alone, but
when a primary amendment or a primary and a second-   *15*
ary amendment are pending, the main question can be
committed, postponed, or laid on the table, and the
amendments then undergo the same process with the
main question. The motion to *Amend* cannot be postponed indefinitely.   *20*
3. Is out of order when another has the floor.
4. Must be seconded.
5. Is debatable whenever the motion to which it is applied
   is debatable. Such debate must be confined to the desirability of the amendment, however, and must not ex-   *25*
   tend to the merits of the motion to be amended, except
   as may be necessary to determine whether the amendment is advisable. *Amend* is undebatable whenever the
   motion to be amended is undebatable.
6. Is generally amendable. This characteristic, however, as   *30*
   noted in Standard Characteristic 2 above, creates two
   degrees of amendment—primary and secondary—and a
   secondary amendment cannot be amended. A primary
   amendment applies directly to the main question. A secondary amendment is a change in a pending primary   *35*

1   amendment, to which it must be germane (pp. 129–
     31); the secondary amendment does not apply directly
     to the main question. The terms *amendment of the first
     degree* and *amendment of the second degree,* or *amend-*
5   *ment to the main question* and *amendment to the amend-*
     ment, are correct expressions, but the terms *primary*
     and *secondary* are preferred. An amendment of the third
     degree is not permitted, since it would make the parlia-
     mentary situation too complicated. To accomplish the
10   same purpose, a member can say, while a secondary
     amendment is pending, that if it is voted down, he will
     offer another secondary amendment—which he can
     then indicate briefly—in its place. Only one primary
     amendment and one secondary amendment are permit-
15   ted at a time, but any number of each can be offered in
     succession—so long as they do not again raise questions
     already decided. (See *Filling Blanks,* pp. 155–60, how-
     ever, for a special method of amending highly variable
     factors, such as times, amounts, names, or numbers, by
20   which several alternative proposals can be pending at
     the same time.)

     7. Requires only a majority vote, even in cases where the
        question to be amended takes a two-thirds vote for
        adoption.

25   8. Can be reconsidered.

Further Rules and Explanation (with Forms)

     CLASSIFICATION AS TO FORM.   There are three
30   basic processes of amendment, the third of which is an in-
     divisible combination of the first two. For each of these
     processes, some of the rules are different depending on
     whether it is applied with reference to a few words or to a
     whole paragraph or section; so that each process has two
35   forms, as follows:

1. First process: to *insert,* or to *add.*
   a. To *insert words,* or, if they are placed at the end of the sentence or passage being amended, to *add words.*
   b. To *insert a paragraph,* or, if it is placed at the end, to *add a paragraph.*
2. Second process: to *strike out.**
   a. To *strike out words.*
   b. To *strike out a paragraph.*
3. Third process: an indivisible combination of processes (1) and (2) having the following forms:
   a. To *strike out and insert* (which applies to words).
   b. To *substitute;* that is, in effect, to strike out a paragraph, or the entire text of a resolution or main motion, and insert another. (Note that *substitute* is a technical parliamentary term that is not applied to anything less than a complete paragraph of one or more sentences, so that this term is not applicable to Form 3[a].)

Forms 1(a), 2(a), and 3(a), relating to *words,* can be applied to change the wording within a single sentence, or occasionally within two or more consecutive sentences that make up a *part* of a single paragraph. Forms 1(b), 2(b), and 3(b), relating to a *paragraph,* can also be applied to a section, article, or larger unit.

The rules for each of the different forms of amendment are given in separate subsections beginning on page 133.

DETERMINING THE GERMANENESS OF AN AMENDMENT.   As already stated, an amendment must

---

*It should be noted that the application of the word "delete" to any form of amendment is not a preferred parliamentary usage, but the shortened expression "to strike" is acceptable.

1 be *germane* to be in order. To be *germane,* an amendment
   must *in some way involve* the same question that is raised by
   the motion to which it is applied. A secondary amendment
   must relate to the primary amendment in the same way. An
5 amendment cannot introduce an independent question;
   but an amendment can be hostile to, or even defeat, the
   spirit of the original motion and still be germane.

   Aside from these principles, there is no single, all-
   inclusive test for determining when a proposed amendment
10 is germane and when it is not. A method by which the germaneness of an amendment can often be verified, however,
   grows out of the following general rules of parliamentary
   law:

15 1) During the session in which the assembly has decided a
      question, another main motion raising the same or sub-
      stantially the same question cannot be introduced.
   2) While a motion has been temporarily disposed of (by
      being referred to a committee, postponed, or laid on
20   the table, or by being the subject of a motion to *Recon-*
      sider that has not been called up, **37,** no other motion
      can be admitted that might conflict with one of the pos-
      sible final decisions on the first motion.

25   By these rules, if a proposed amendment is related to
   the main motion in such a way that, after the adoption, rejection, or temporary disposal of the present main motion,
   the essential idea of the amendment could not be introduced as an independent resolution at least during the same
30 session, the amendment is germane and should be admitted, since there will not, or may not, be any opportunity to
   present it later. This test cannot be reliably used to determine that an amendment is *out of* order, since it is sometimes possible for an amendment to be germane even if,
35 regardless of action on the present main motion, the idea

embodied in the amendment could be introduced independently later in the same session.

As an example of a germane amendment, assume that a motion is pending "that the Society authorize the purchase of a new desk for the Secretary." It would be germane and in order to amend by inserting after "desk" the words "and matching chair," since both relate to providing the secretary with the necessary furniture. On the other hand, an amendment to add to the motion the words "and the payment of the President's expenses to the State Convention" is not germane.

Or assume that the following is the pending motion: "that the City Council commend Officer George for his action in . . ." An amendment to strike out "commend" and insert "censure," although antagonistic to the original intent, is germane and *in order* because both ideas deal with the council's opinion of the officer's action. Also, since a motion to censure the officer for the same act could not be introduced independently in the same session after the adoption of a motion to commend him, the amendment to change *commend* to *censure* is germane under the rule given above. It should be noted that *censure* is different from *not commend* (see *Improper Amendments,* below).

There are borderline cases where a presiding officer will find it difficult to judge the germaneness of an amendment. Whenever in doubt, he should admit the amendment or, in important cases, refer the decision to the assembly: "The chair is in doubt and will ask the assembly to decide whether the amendment is germane. [Debate, if any, provided that debate is in order.] The question is on whether the amendment is germane to the resolution [or "to the primary amendment"]. As many as are of the opinion that the amendment *is* germane, say *aye.* . . . Those of the opinion that it is *not* germane, say no . . . , etc." (See also example under *Point of Order,* pp. 246–47.)

IMPROPER AMENDMENTS.   The following types of amendment are out of order:

1) One that is not germane to the question to be amended.
2) One that merely makes the adoption of the amended question equivalent to a rejection of the original motion. Thus, in the motion that "our delegates be instructed to vote in favor of the increase in Federation dues," an amendment to insert "not" before "be" is out of order because an affirmative vote on not giving a certain instruction is identical with a negative vote on giving the same instruction. But it *would* be in order to move to insert "not" before "to" ("instructed not to vote in favor"), since this would change the main motion into one to give different instructions (see, however, p. 99, l. 33 to p. 100, l. 9).
3) One that would make the question as amended identical with, or contrary to, one previously decided by the assembly during the same session, or previously considered and still *"not finally disposed of"* or *"within the control of the assembly"* (see pp. 88, 329–30).
4) One that proposes to change one of the forms of amendment listed on page 129 into another form. A pending primary amendment to "strike out 'oak' before 'furniture,'" for example, cannot be converted into the form *strike out and insert* by moving to add "and insert 'maple.'"
5) One that would have the effect of converting one parliamentary motion into another. For example, a motion to "postpone the question until 2 P.M." cannot be amended by "striking out 'until 2 P.M.' and inserting 'indefinitely,'" since this would convert it into a different kind of motion.
6) One that strikes out the word *"Resolved"* or other enacting words.

7) One that is frivolous or absurd.

8) One that would leave an incoherent wording or a wording containing no rational proposition.

9) One that would convert a primary amendment into an improper form under any of the rules for the different forms of amendment as given below.

NOTE ON AMENDMENT OF PREAMBLE.   When a resolution has a preamble (one or more clauses beginning "Whereas"), the preamble is not opened to amendment until after amendment of the resolving clauses has been completed. After any amendment of the preamble, a single vote is taken on the question of adopting the entire resolution or paper (see also p. 269).

RULES FOR THE DIFFERENT FORMS OF AMENDMENT.   Because *Amend* can be moved in different forms, rules pertaining to each form of the motion are given separately below, with examples. It should first be noted, however, that many of the rules governing the different forms of amendment are particular applications of the following principle: After the assembly has voted that certain words (or a certain paragraph) shall, or shall not, form part of a pending resolution, it is not in order to make another motion to *Amend* that raises the same question of content and effect. Common sense should guide the presiding officer in interpreting the rules, both to give freedom for improvement of the main motion finally to be voted on, and at the same time to protect the assembly from motions for amendment that present questions it has already decided.

1(a). To Insert, or to Add, Words.   A motion to insert words must specify the exact place of insertion by naming the word before or after which, or the words between which, the insertion is to be made—whichever will better

1 locate and point out the effect of the change. For long or
   printed copies, the line number and paragraph number
   should be designated.

       In the consideration of a motion to *insert* certain words,
5 or (if they are to be placed at the end of the passage being
   amended) to *add* certain words, any necessary perfecting of
   the new words should be done by secondary amendment
   before the vote is taken on inserting or adding as proposed
   by the primary amendment. Otherwise there may be no op-
10 portunity to perfect the inserted or added words, for reasons explained in the next paragraph.

       After words have been inserted or added, they cannot
   be changed or struck out, except through a reconsideration
   of the vote (see **37**), or through an amendment presenting
15 a new question in the form of a motion:

   1) To strike out the entire paragraph into which the words
      were inserted.
   2) To strike out a portion of the paragraph, including all or
20   part of the words inserted and enough other words to
      make a different question from the one decided by the
      insertion.
   3) To substitute an entire paragraph for the one into which
      the words were inserted.
25 4) To strike out a portion of the paragraph (including all
      or a part of the words inserted) and insert other words,
      in a way that presents a new question.

       If a motion to insert certain words in a particular place
30 is voted down, it is still in order—provided that it will present an essentially new question—to make a motion:

   1) To insert only a part of the same words.
   2) To insert all or a part of the same words together with
35   some others.

3) To insert the same words *in place of* others (motion to *strike out and insert*).

4) To insert the same words in another place where the effect will be different.

A motion to insert, or to add, words can have applied to it secondary amendments in any of the three forms relating to words—inserting or adding; striking out; or striking out and inserting.

1(b). To Insert or to Add, a Paragraph. The rules for the insertion or addition of a paragraph are essentially the same as those given above, except that after a paragraph has been inserted, words can still be *added* to it (that is, placed at the end of the paragraph only) provided that they do not conflict with or modify anything in the paragraph as already inserted. When a paragraph is to be inserted or added, any necessary perfecting should first be done by secondary amendments. After its insertion or addition, the paragraph cannot be struck out except in connection with other paragraphs that make the question materially different. If a motion to insert or add a paragraph is voted down, its rejection does not preclude any other motion except one that presents essentially the same question. If a rejected paragraph is rewritten or shortened in such a way that its effect is changed, it becomes a different paragraph under the rules for amendment.

Form and Example: 1(a), 1(b). To Insert, or to Add (Words or a Paragraph). Typical forms in which a motion to insert, or to add, may be made are: "I move to amend the resolution by inserting the word 'waterfront' before the word 'property'"; "I move to insert 'plus expenses' after '$100'"; "I move to insert 'permanent' between 'all' and 'employees'"; "I move to insert in Line 5 of the second paragraph, the word 'preferred' before 'stocks'"; "I move to insert after Paragraph 3 the following paragraph: . . . "; "I

1   move to amend by adding the words, 'at a cost not to exceed
    $2,000'"; "I move to add the following paragraph: . . . "

    In stating the question on each motion in any series in-
    volving amendments, and again when putting a motion to
5   vote, the chair should take care that the members understand
    which step is under immediate consideration, as well as the
    effect of each proposed step—in respect to both an affirma-
    tive and a negative result. When putting an amendment to
    vote, the chair may find it advisable to reread the entire mo-
10 tion or resolution (or the paragraph or portion that the
    amendment would affect), the proposed amendment, and
    the motion, resolution, or affected portion as it will stand if
    the amendment is adopted; he should then make it clear once
    more that it is the *amendment* that is to be voted on. In other
15 cases—depending on the length of the resolution and the
    amendment, the nature of the subject matter, the conditions
    of the assembly, etc.—the question may sometimes be clearer
    to the members if the chair restates only the amendment. In
    announcing the result of the vote on an amendment, regard-
20 less of whether it is adopted or rejected, the chair should fully
    state the question that consequently becomes immediately
    pending.

    Assume that the following resolution is pending: "*Re-
    solved,* That in accordance with the recommendations of the
25 Properties Committee, the Association purchase the tract of
    land bordering the thirty-two-hundred block of Westfield
    Boulevard."

    MEMBER A (OBTAINING THE FLOOR): I move to amend by inserting
30 the words "and grade" after "purchase." (Second.)
    CHAIR: It is moved and seconded to insert the words "and grade"
    after "purchase." If the amendment is adopted, the resolution will
    read: "*Resolved,* That in accordance . . . the Association purchase *and
    grade* the tract of land . . . Westfield Boulevard." The question is on
35 inserting the words "and grade."

After debate on the amendment, the chair puts it to vote: *1*

CHAIR: The question is on amending the resolution for the purchase of the Westfield Boulevard property, by inserting the words "and
grade" after "purchase," so that, if the amendment is adopted, the res- *5*
olution will read: [reading it again]. The effect of adopting the amendment will be to include the proposed grading of the property in the
expenditure that the resolution would direct at this time. As many as
are in favor of inserting the words "and grade" in the resolution, say
aye. . . . Those opposed, say *no*. . . . The ayes have it and the amend- *10*
ment is adopted. The question is now on the resolution as amended,
which is "*Resolved,* . . . purchase and grade the tract of land . . . Westfield Boulevard."

Should the amendment fail, the chair's announcement *15*
of the result would be as follows:

CHAIR: The noes have it and the amendment is lost. The question
is now on the resolution: "*Resolved,* That in accordance . . . the Association purchase the tract of land . . . Westfield Boulevard." *20*

At this point, regardless of whether the amendment is
adopted or rejected, the resolution is again open to debate,
and it is in order to offer a different amendment.

Amendments are sometimes so simple or acceptable *25*
that they may be adopted by *unanimous consent* (see pp.
51–53). For example, assume that while a main motion is
pending, "That the Properties Committee be directed to
secure estimates for the necessary building repairs," a member moves "to amend by inserting the words 'at least three' *30*
before 'estimates.'" If the chair senses that there is general
approval, he may say, "If there is no objection, the words
'at least three' will be inserted. The wording would then be
'to secure at least three estimates.' [Pause.] There is no objection; the words are inserted." *35*

1   As an example of *secondary amendment by inserting,* assume that there are pending: (1) a resolution, "*Resolved,*
That the Society purchase the property adjoining the present Headquarters"; and (2) (immediately pending) a pri-
5 mary amendment, "to add the words, 'and convert it into
a parking lot.'" (Details as to probable costs of proposed
phases of the project are assumed to be known.)

MEMBER X (obtaining the floor): I move to insert in the pending
10 amendment the word "landscaped" before "parking lot." (Second.)
CHAIR: It is moved and seconded to amend by inserting in the primary amendment the word "landscaped" before "parking lot." If the
word is inserted, the primary amendment will be, "to add to the resolution for the purchase of the property, the words 'and convert it into
15 a *landscaped* parking lot.'" The question is on inserting the word
"landscaped."

Debate, if any, must be confined to the issue: *If* the conversion to a parking lot is to be included in the project at
20 this time, should the lot be landscaped? When this debate
has ended, the chair puts the secondary amendment to a
vote, announces the result, and states the question before
the assembly, as follows:

25   CHAIR: The question is on inserting in the primary amendment the
word "landscaped" before "parking lot." If the word is inserted, the
primary amendment will be, "To add to the resolution for the purchase
of the adjoining property, the words, 'and convert it into a *landscaped*
parking lot.'" It should be noted that this vote will not decide whether
30 a parking lot is to be part of the project. This vote will determine only
whether the parking lot will be landscaped *if* it is constructed. A vote
of *aye* is *for* landscaping. A vote of *no* is *against* landscaping. As many
as are in favor of inserting the word "landscaped" in the amendment,
say *aye.* . . . Those opposed, say *no.* . . . The ayes have it and the word
35 is inserted. The question is now on the primary amendment as

amended, which is, "to add to the resolution the words, 'and convert it into a landscaped parking lot.'" If the amendment is adopted, the resolution will read, "*Resolved,* That the Society purchase the property adjoining the present Headquarters, *and convert it into a landscaped parking lot.*" Adoption of this amendment will mean that if the property is purchased by the Society, there will be a parking lot—which will be landscaped. The question is on the amendment.

Debate and voting on the question proceed as described above.

2(a). To Strike Out Words. A motion to strike out words must specify their location when it is not otherwise clear.

When a motion to strike out certain words is made, it can be applied only to consecutive words; but the words to be struck out may become separated as a result of secondary amendments, in which case the primary amendment is voted on in a form in which it could not have been moved directly. To strike out separated words, the best method is to make a motion to strike out the entire clause or sentence containing the separated words and insert a new clause or sentence as desired. Separated words can also be struck out by separate motions.

If a motion to strike out certain words is adopted, the same words cannot be inserted again unless the place or the wording is so changed as to make a new proposition. If a motion to strike out certain words fails, it is still in order—subject to the requirement that the words involved must be consecutive—to move:

1) To strike out only a part of the same words.
2) To strike out all or a part of the same words together with some others.
3) To strike out all or a part of the same words and insert different ones.

4) To strike out all or a part of the same words together with some others and insert different words.

It is important to note that: *The motion to amend by striking out certain words can be amended only by striking out words from the primary amendment.* The effect of such a secondary amendment is that words struck out of the primary amendment will remain in the main motion regardless of whether the primary amendment is adopted or rejected. For example, assume that the following are pending: (1) a main motion directing the secretary to write to Congressmen Altman, Brock, Crowley, Davidson, and Edwards; (2) a primary amendment to strike out "Brock, Crowley, Davidson"; and (3) a secondary amendment to strike out "Crowley" from the primary amendment. If the secondary amendment is adopted, the primary amendment then becomes "to strike out 'Brock' and 'Davidson'" from the main motion—so that Crowley's name will remain in the main motion regardless of the outcome of the vote on the primary amendment, which no longer affects him. As a consequence of the rule stated at the beginning of this paragraph, a primary amendment to strike out a single word cannot be amended.

When a motion is made to strike out a sentence that might desirably be retained with some changes, the form of secondary amendment allowed for motions to strike out certain words may not be readily applicable. In such a case, a member can say in debate on the primary amendment that he believes the sentence should be reworded in a way which he can then state, and that if the motion to strike out the present sentence is adopted he will move to insert his new version. If the motion to strike out is lost, he can also move to strike out the present sentence and insert his new version.

2(b). To Strike Out a Paragraph.   There is an essential difference between the motion to strike out a paragraph and the motion to strike out certain words, which lies in the rules and effect of secondary amendment. When it is moved to *strike out an entire paragraph,* the paragraph that would be struck out is opened to improvement by *secondary amendment in any of the three forms relating to words* (inserting or adding; striking out; or striking out and inserting) before the vote is taken on the primary amendment. If the primary amendment to strike out is voted down, the paragraph then remains in the resolution *with any changes that were made by secondary amendment.* The following differences in the effect of a *secondary amendment to strike out*—dependent on whether the primary amendment to strike out involves only certain words or a paragraph—should be particularly noted:

- If the primary amendment is to strike out certain *words,* then words struck out of the primary amendment will remain *in* the resolution regardless of the final vote on the primary amendment (as explained under *Strike Out Words,* above).
- But if the primary amendment is to strike out a *paragraph,* then words struck out of that paragraph in the process of secondary amendment are *out of* the resolution regardless of the final vote on the primary amendment.

After a paragraph has been struck out, it cannot be inserted again unless the wording (or, possibly, the place) is changed in a way that presents an essentially new question. After a motion to strike out a particular paragraph has been voted down, any amendment presenting a materially new question involving the same paragraph, or any part of it, is still in order.

Form and Example: 2(a), 2(b). To Strike Out (Words or a Paragraph). The motion to strike out may be made in such forms as "I move to strike out the word 'concrete' before 'pavement' in Line 5"; or "I move to strike out the third paragraph of the platform statement." Variations similar to those given for inserting or adding (pp. 135–36) are applicable.

1   Assume that the following main motion is pending:
"That the Bowling League establish a division open to the
juniors and seniors of Southwood High School."

5   MEMBER A (obtaining the floor): I move to amend by striking out
the words "juniors and." (Second.)
         CHAIR: It is moved and seconded to amend by striking out the
words "juniors and." If the amendment is adopted, the main motion
will be "to establish a division open to the seniors of Southwood High
10   School." The question is on striking out the words "juniors and."

         From this point, the procedure is similar to that already
illustrated for inserting or adding.
         3(a). To Strike Out and Insert (applying to words).   The
15   motion to strike out and insert is especially applicable in situations where it may be impossible to secure the desired result without making the act of "striking out" inseparable
from that of "inserting"—as may happen if some members
are unwilling to vote for the one unless assured of the other.
20   The two parts of this motion cannot be separated, either by
secondary amendment or by a *Division of the Question.*
         To avoid confusion with the form of amendment
known as *Substitute* (p. 146, #3[b]), which applies to paragraphs or longer elements, the word *substitute* should not
25   be used in connection with the motion to *strike out and insert,* which applies to words.
         Motions to strike out and insert fall into two types:

   • those by which a different wording is inserted in the
30   same place; and
   • those by which the same wording struck out of one
      place is inserted in a different place.

         It is not in order to move to strike out something from
35   one place and insert something materially different in another place by a single action, unless the mover receives

unanimous consent to make these two separate motions at the same time.

The first type of the motion to strike out and insert—the kind that proposes to insert a different wording in the same place—is perhaps more common.

When such a primary amendment is offered, the chair states the question on it and lets debate of its merits begin in the usual way. For purposes of secondary amendment, however, this type of motion is treated as if resolved into its two elements, with secondary amendment of each element following the rules that would apply to two separate motions for primary amendment—one to strike out (amendable only by striking out) and another to insert (amendable in any of three forms relating to words). A single secondary amendment involving both elements of a primary amendment to strike out and insert is not in order. If a motion to strike out and insert involves enough words that several secondary amendments—particularly to the words to be struck out—might be possible, it is often best to take any amendments to the words to be struck out first, because members who wish to perfect the words to be inserted by secondary amendment may need to know exactly what language those words will replace, to be able to perfect them effectively. Amendments to the words to be inserted are then taken up after amendments to the words to be struck out have been disposed of. But the chair should make a judgment depending on the conditions as to whether the assembly wishes to follow this procedure or will find it helpful. In any event, the primary amendment remains open to debate at all times while it is pending with no secondary amendment pending, and this debate goes into the merits of both parts of the motion viewed as a single whole.

While a primary amendment to strike out and insert certain words is pending, if an admissible secondary amendment to the words to be struck out is introduced and no amend-

1 ments to the words to be inserted have been proposed, the chair simply proceeds to entertain the secondary amendment, letting debate on the primary amendment resume after the secondary amendment has been dealt with. But the first
5 time that a secondary amendment to the words to be inserted is offered—assuming a number of amendments to the words to be struck out might be possible—the chair has the option, as described in the preceding paragraph, of saying: "The chair believes it would be better to follow the proce-
10 dure of taking any amendments to the words to be struck out first, as permitted under the rules." Accordingly, before entertaining the amendment just offered, the chair will ask, "Are there any amendments [or "any further amendments"] to the words to be struck out?" When it appears that no one
15 else wishes to propose an amendment to the words to be struck out, the chair then says: "The primary amendment as amended is open to debate, and secondary amendments to the words to be inserted are now in order." After reasonable opportunity to offer any amendments of the latter type has
20 been given, secondary amendments to either element are in order. When these and any further debate have concluded, the vote is taken on the motion to strike out and insert as it stands after secondary amendment.

After a motion to strike out and insert has been adopted,
25 what has been struck out and what has been inserted are subject to the same rules regarding further amendment, as if the striking out and the inserting had been done by separate motions: The inserted matter cannot be struck out, and the matter that has been struck out cannot be inserted again, except
30 through a reconsideration of the vote on the amendment, or through changes in the wording or the place in a way that presents a new question (under the rules already given for *Insert, or Add,* and for *Strike Out*).

If a motion to strike out and insert is voted down, it is
35 still in order:

- to make either of the separate motions to *strike out,* or to *insert,* the same words that would have been struck out or inserted by the combined motion that was lost; or
- to make another motion to *strike out and insert*—provided that the change in either the wording to be struck out or the wording to be inserted presents a question materially different from the one that was voted down.

When a primary amendment to strike out a passage of any length or complexity and insert a new version is pending and some members would prefer to insert something different or keep something closer to the original, it may be difficult or impossible to reach the desired end by secondary amendment. Situations of this kind can occur especially when the amendment relates to one or more complete sentences that do not constitute an entire paragraph. In such a case, a member should speak against the pending primary amendment and say that if it is rejected he will offer a new motion to strike out the same passage and insert the version he desires—which he should then state. He should present his case as strongly as possible, because if the first proposed version is inserted, it cannot be changed afterward except in connection with a different question.

As already explained in connection with the rules for the motion to *strike out,* the motion to *strike out and insert* can be used to obtain the effect of striking out or modifying separated words. To do this, a member can move to strike out of the resolution a passage long enough to include all of the words to be removed or changed, and insert the revised passage. If several changes in a paragraph are desired, it is usually better to rewrite the paragraph and offer the new version as a *substitute,* as explained below.

Form and Example: 3(a). To Strike Out and Insert (applying to words). As an example of a motion to strike out and insert, assume that the following resolution is pending:

1   "*Resolved,* That the Citizens' Association endorse the
Rockville site for the new Community College."

MEMBER A (obtaining the floor): I move to amend by striking out
5   "Rockville" and inserting "Chatham." (Second.)
CHAIR: It is moved and seconded to strike out "Rockville" and insert "Chatham." If the amendment is adopted, the resolution will be
to "endorse the Chatham site for the new Community College."

10   Debate on the amendment is limited to the relative advantages of the two sites. After the amendment is debated, the
chair puts it to vote, as in the case already illustrated for *Insert
or Add.* Debate on the resolution can go into the question of
whether the association should express approval of any site.
15   *3(b). To Substitute.*   A motion to *Amend* by striking out
an entire paragraph, section, or article—or a complete main
motion or resolution—and inserting a different paragraph or
other unit in its place is called a motion to *substitute,* and the
paragraph or resolution to be inserted is said to be offered (or
20   proposed) as "a substitute." A substitute can be offered for a
paragraph or a main motion of only one sentence, and in
such a case the paragraph proposed as a substitute can contain several sentences. (For the replacement of sentences
within a paragraph, see below.) A substitute offered for a
25   main motion or resolution, or for a paragraph within a resolution, is a primary amendment and can therefore be moved
only when no other amendment is pending. If a motion proposes to replace one or more paragraphs that are involved in
a pending primary amendment, it is a secondary amendment
30   to which the term *substitute* is also applicable.*
A primary amendment to *substitute* is treated similarly
to a motion to *strike out and insert* as described on pages

---

*It is thus possible to introduce a proposed "substitute for a substi-
tute," which cannot be amended, since it is a secondary amendment.

142–45. It is open to debate at all times while it is pending with no secondary amendment pending; and such debate may go fully into the merits of both the original text and the substitute, since this is necessary to determine the desirability of the primary amendment. But for purposes of secondary amendment, the motion to substitute is looked upon as resolved into its two elements, the paragraph to be struck out and the paragraph to be inserted. In contrast to the rules for striking out and inserting *words,* however, when a motion to *substitute* is under consideration the paragraph to be struck out as well as the paragraph to be inserted can be perfected by secondary amendment in any of the three basic forms (inserting or adding; striking out; or striking out and inserting), since this is the procedure when either of the separate motions to *insert* or to *strike out* is applied to the paragraph. For this reason, the paragraph to be struck out will practically always be susceptible to secondary amendment. As in the case of a motion to strike out and insert words, the chair has the option of accepting only amendments to the paragraph to be struck out first, and then only amendments to the proposed substitute, thereafter accepting either type of secondary amendment. Following this procedure is likely to be more often indicated in the case of a motion to substitute, particularly if a substantive issue hangs on such a motion, as in the example given below. After all secondary amendments have been disposed of and after any further debate on the motion to substitute, the vote is taken on whether to make this substitution.

For replacing an unbroken *part* of a paragraph when the part to be replaced consists of (or contains) one or more complete sentences, there is an option between offering the amendment as a motion to strike out the part and insert the new matter (that is, as a motion to *strike out and insert*), or moving it in the form of a substitute for the entire paragraph with only the desired part changed. Either of these

1 motions, as applied to the same case, will present substantially the same question when it is made, but the effect of each of them is different as to permissible secondary amendment. If much of the paragraph is involved in such a
5 case, it is generally better to offer the desired amendment in the form of a substitute. If this method is used, however, secondary amendment can also involve the portion of the paragraph in which no change was proposed initially.

In taking the vote on whether to make the substitution,
10 the chair should first read both the paragraph of the original text and the proposed substitute—*as they stand at the time* as amended. Even if the entire resolution or main motion is replaced, adopting the motion to *substitute* only *amends* the resolution, which remains pending as amended.
15 After a paragraph, section, or version of a resolution has been substituted for another, the substituted paragraph or resolution cannot be amended except by *adding* something that does not modify the paragraph's existing content—as is true of any paragraph that has been inserted. The para-
20 graph that has been replaced cannot be inserted again unless a material change in the wording (or possibly, the place) makes a new question—as is true of any paragraph that has been struck out.

If a motion to substitute is lost, the assembly has de-
25 cided only that the paragraph proposed as a substitute shall not replace the one specified. The same proposed new paragraph can still replace a different one, or can simply be inserted. On the other hand, the paragraph that was retained in the resolution can be further amended, or struck
30 out (if it is not the entire resolution); or it still can be replaced by a different substitute.

When a question is being considered *by paragraph or seriatim* (**28**), it is in order to move a substitute for any paragraph or section at the time that the paragraph or section is
35 opened to amendment. But it is not in order to move a sub-

stitute for the entire document until all of the paragraphs or
sections have been individually considered and the point is
reached when the chair announces that the entire paper is
open to amendment.

If a resolution is referred to a committee while a primary
amendment—or a primary and a secondary amendment—are
pending, the committee can report by recommending a substitute for the resolution, even though the substitute cannot
become pending until the other amendments have been
voted on in their normal order. Thus, when a committee has
so reported, the chair first states the question on the secondary amendment that was pending when the resolution was
committed, puts the secondary amendment to vote, and then
continues with the primary amendment to which it applied.
As soon as this primary amendment is disposed of, the chair
states the question on the substitute recommended by the
committee, and proceeds as he would with any other motion
to substitute.

In a similar way, if a resolution is referred to a committee while a substitute and a secondary amendment (either
to the original or to the substitute) are pending, the committee can report in favor of either version, with any desired
recommendation as to secondary amendment; or the committee can recommend rejection of the pending substitute
and propose a new substitute in its place. In all such cases,
the chair starts with the parliamentary situation as it was
when the resolution was committed; he then proceeds as
with any motion to substitute, and states the question on
any new amendment (recommended by the committee) as
soon as it is in order for that amendment to be pending
under the usual rules.

The motion to *substitute* often provides a convenient and
timesaving method for handling a poorly framed resolution,
or for introducing a different and better approach to the real
question raised by a main motion. While changes by separate

1 amendments are in progress, a member who feels that he has
a better solution by substitution can indicate its features
briefly and announce his intention of offering the substitute
as soon as no other amendment is pending. If the member
5 wishing to propose the substitute thinks it appropriate, he
can try to bring the pending amendments to an immediate
vote by moving the *Previous Question* (**16**) on them.

An amendment in the form of a substitute can also be
used to defeat or work against the purpose of the measure
10 originally introduced. Such a stratagem can be utilized with
a view either to converting the measure into a weakened
form before its final adoption, or to substituting a version
that is likely to be rejected in the final vote. It should be
noted that a vote in favor of substituting an entire resolution
15 or main motion is ordinarily a vote to kill any provisions of
the original version that are not included in the substitute.

Properly applied, the rules for the treatment of motions
to *substitute* automatically operate in fairness to both sides
when there is disagreement as to the preferability of the
20 original or the substitute. Under the procedure of initially
accepting amendments to each element of the primary
amendment exclusively—which is generally indicated
whenever such disagreement exists—the proponents of the
original version are first given the opportunity to amend
25 their proposition into a more acceptable form in the light of
conditions revealed by the introduction of the substitute.
When this process is correctly handled as described on
pages 143–44 and 146–47, it tends to ensure that the provisions of the version first offered receive appropriate con-
30 sideration, without impeding free debate of the proposal to
substitute. By the requirement that internal amendment of
the substitute be done before the vote on the motion to
make the substitution, the members are protected from
having to decide whether to reject the original version with-
35 out knowing what may finally replace it.

Form and Example: 3(b). To Substitute. As an example of a motion to substitute, assume that the following resolution is pending: "*Resolved,* That the Parish Federation undertake the construction and equipping of a new service wing for the Parish House, to be financed as far as possible by a mortgage on the present building."

Debate points strongly to a need for further investigation, but many members are determined to secure immediate authorization. The meeting seems evenly divided, and the outcome is unpredictable.

MEMBER A (obtaining the floor): I move to substitute for the pending resolution the following: "*Resolved,* That the Parish Board be directed to engage appropriate professional consultants to make a survey of, and prepare a complete report on, the need, probable cost, feasible methods of financing, and maintenance of a new service wing for the Parish House." (Second.)

CHAIR: It is moved and seconded to amend by substituting for the pending resolution the following: [reading the substitute submitted by Member A]. The motion to substitute proposes that the resolution just read shall come before the assembly in place of the pending resolution. [Debate.]

MEMBER L (who favors the *pending* resolution and is, therefore, opposed to the motion to substitute—obtaining the floor): I move to amend the proposed substitute by adding the words "within twenty days." (Second.)

CHAIR: The chair believes it will be preferable to take any amendments to the pending resolution first, as permitted under the rules. Such amendments, if adopted, will affect the wording in which the pending resolution will come to a final vote if the motion to substitute fails.* Accordingly, before entertaining the amendment just offered, the chair will call for any amendments to the pending resolution, which

---

*If the members are familiar with the procedure for handling motions to substitute, the chair may omit the sentence preceding the asterisk.

he will first reread. The pending resolution is as follows: "*Resolved,* That the Parish Federation undertake the construction and equipping of a new service wing for the Parish House, to be financed as far as possible by a mortgage on the present building." Are there any amendments to the pending resolution?

MEMBER X (obtaining the floor): I move to amend the pending resolution by striking out everything after the word "undertake" and inserting the words "a campaign to raise funds for the construction and equipping of a new service wing for the Parish House." (Second.)

The chair states the question on this amendment, making its effect clear, and, after debate, puts it to vote. For purposes of the example, assume that the proponents of the original resolution differ on the amendment, some voting for it, others opposing it. Also, since the adoption of this amendment presumably would make the pending resolution *less* objectionable to those who feel that the proposed project is presently ill advised and who therefore hope that the substitution will be made, most of those members probably vote for the amendment. Assume that it is adopted. The chair announces the result as follows:

CHAIR: The ayes have it and the amendment is adopted. The pending resolution now reads, "*Resolved,* That the Parish Federation undertake a campaign to raise funds for the construction and equipping of a new service wing for the Parish House." The question is on the motion to substitute. (Further debate on the relative merits of the pending resolution and the proposed substitute.)

MEMBER L (who favors the *pending* resolution—obtaining the floor): I move to amend the substitute by adding "within twenty days." (Second.)

CHAIR: Before entertaining the amendment just offered, the chair will again ask: Are there any further amendments to the pending resolution? [Pause.] There being none, it is moved and seconded to amend the proposed substitute by adding the words "within twenty days."

Brief debate shows that the proposed survey could not *1*
be properly carried out in twenty days. Assume that this
amendment is voted down.

MEMBER B (who is in favor of the motion to substitute, but fears it *5*
will fail unless some time limit is specified—obtaining the floor): I
move to amend the substitute by adding "within sixty days." (Second.)

The chair states the question on this amendment and (after
brief debate) puts it to vote. Assume that the amendment is *10*
adopted. In announcing the result, the chair continues:

CHAIR: The ayes have it and the amendment is adopted. The proposed substitute now reads, "*Resolved,* . . . " Are you ready for the
question on the motion to substitute? *15*

After any debate (during which the substitute may be further amended), the chair puts to vote the motion to substitute.
Both resolutions are read, usually by the chair—the pending
resolution first, then the resolution proposed as a substitute. *20*

CHAIR: The question is on the motion to substitute. The chair will
read the pending resolution first, then the resolution proposed as a
substitute. The pending resolution is: "*Resolved,* That the Parish Federation undertake a campaign to raise funds for the construction and *25*
equipping of a new service wing for the Parish House." The resolution
proposed as a substitute is: "*Resolved,* That the Parish Board be directed to engage appropriate professional consultants to make a survey
of, and prepare a complete report on, the need, probable cost, . . .
within sixty days." The question is: Shall the resolution last read be *30*
substituted for the pending resolution? As many as are in favor of the
motion to substitute, say *aye.* . . . Those opposed, say *no.* . . .

The chair announces the result of the vote and states the
question on whichever resolution is left pending, as follows: *35*

1   CHAIR: The ayes have it and the motion to substitute is adopted. The question is now on the resolution: [reading the resolution directing the employment of professional consultants].

5   Or:

     CHAIR: The noes have it and the motion to substitute is lost. The question is now on the resolution: [reading the resolution for a fundraising campaign].

10

Regardless of which resolution is now pending, there may be further debate. If the motion to substitute has been adopted, the resolution now pending is in the position of a paragraph that has been inserted, and it can no longer be 15 amended except by *adding* nonmodifying matter. On the other hand, if the motion to substitute has been lost, the resolution for the fund drive can be further amended; but in determining whether an amendment now offered presents a new question and can therefore be admitted, ac- 20 count must be taken of any motions to amend that were voted on before the motion to substitute was introduced, or while it was pending.

FRIENDLY AMENDMENTS. The term "friendly 25 amendment" is often used to describe an amendment offered by someone who is in sympathy with the purposes of the main motion, in the belief that the amendment will either improve the statement or effect of the main motion, presumably to the satisfaction of its maker, or will increase 30 the chances of the main motion's adoption. Regardless of whether or not the maker of the main motion "accepts" the amendment, it must be opened to debate and voted on formally (unless adopted by unanimous consent) and is handled under the same rules as amendments generally (see 35 also pp. 283–86).

Filling Blanks

1

Filling blanks, although not a form of amendment in itself, is a closely related device by which an unlimited number of alternative choices for a particular specification in a main motion or primary amendment can be pending at the same time. In effect, it permits an exception to the rule (in Standard Characteristic 6) that only one primary and one secondary amendment can be pending at a time, and in certain cases it has distinct advantages.

5

10

In amending by the ordinary method, a maximum of three alternatives can be pending at once, and the last one moved must be voted on first. In filling blanks, the number of alternatives is not limited; members have an opportunity to weigh all choices before voting and to vote on them in a fair and logical order. Among cases adapted to such treatment are main motions or primary amendments containing names of persons or places, dates, numbers, or amounts.

15

CREATING A BLANK.   A blank to be filled can be created in one of three ways:

20

a) A member can offer a motion or an amendment containing a blank: for example, "*Resolved,* That Lodge No. 432 build a new headquarters at a cost not to exceed $_____"; or an amendment to a main motion can propose "to add 'provided that estimates be received on or before _____.'"

25

b) A member can move that a blank be created. For example, assume that the pending resolution is: "*Resolved,* That Lodge No. 432 build a new headquarters at a cost not to exceed $300,000." Any member can move "to create a blank by striking out of the pending resolution the sum '$300,000.'" If such a motion is adopted, the specification struck out to create the blank automati-

30

35

cally becomes one of the proposals for filling it—as "$300,000" in the example. Although the motion to create a blank may appear to resemble a motion to amend by striking out and inserting, it is in fact an incidental motion (see pp. 66–67). The motion to create a blank requires a second, but it is neither debatable nor amendable; it can also be made and voted on while a primary or a secondary amendment relating to the subject specification is pending. For example, assuming the same pending resolution as above, the identical motion to create a blank by striking out "$300,000" can be made while a primary amendment "to strike out '$300,000' and insert '$350,000'" is also pending. Adoption of the motion to create a blank in such a case (before the amendment is voted on) causes both specifications—the one in the pending resolution and the corresponding one in the amendment—to become proposals for filling the blank; as "$300,000" and "$350,000" in the example.

c) The chair can suggest the creation of a blank, as follows: "The chair suggests creating a blank by striking out '$300,000.' If there is no objection, a blank will be created. [Pause.] There is no objection; the blank is created." If a member objects, the chair puts the question to a vote, treating the question just as he would treat a motion to create a blank made as described above.

When a blank exists or has been created, any number of members can suggest, without a second, a different name, place, number, date, or amount for filling it. No member can suggest more than one proposal for filling the blank unless he receives unanimous consent to do so. Each proposal is debatable and is treated as an independent original to be voted on separately until one is approved by a majority.

FILLING A BLANK WITH NAMES. The following *1*
principles apply to the process of filling a blank with one or
more names:

a) The procedure for filling a blank with one name is prac- *5*
   tically the same as for making nominations. The chair repeats each name as it is proposed, and finally takes a vote
   on each in that same order, until one receives a majority.
b) If the blank is to be filled with more than one name and
   no more are suggested than are required, the names can *10*
   be inserted by unanimous consent.
c) If more names are suggested than are required, the
   chair takes a vote on each in the order of its proposal
   until enough to fill the blank have received a majority
   vote. The names remaining in the list as proposed are *15*
   ignored, since the assembly has decided which names
   shall fill the blank.
d) If the number of names is not specified, the chair takes
   a vote on each name suggested; and all names approved
   by a majority vote are inserted. *20*

FILLING A BLANK WITH AMOUNTS OF
MONEY. Sometimes the particular nature of the blank
determines the order in which proposals for filling it should *25*
be put to vote. Typical instances of this kind are blanks to
be filled with amounts of money. In such cases it is advisable, whenever a logical order is apparent, to arrange the
proposed entries so that *the one least likely to be acceptable
will be voted on first,* and so on. New supporters may then *30*
be gained with each succeeding vote until a majority in
favor of one entry is reached.
   As an example of the procedure for filling a blank with
an amount of money, assume that a resolution to build a
new headquarters "at a cost not to exceed $_____" is *35*

1 pending, and that it is proposed to fill the blank with the
following amounts: $350,000, $250,000, $400,000, and
$300,000. The character of this measure—to *spend*
money—indicates that the amounts should be arranged and
5 voted on in order from the highest to lowest. If $400,000
is rejected, the vote is taken next on $350,000; and if that
is not adopted, the chair puts the question on $300,000. If
that amount is adopted, no vote is taken on $250,000, and
the chair immediately says, "The amount of $300,000 fills
10 the blank. The question is now on the resolution: '*Resolved,*
That . . . at a cost not to exceed $300,000.'" Note that if
the smallest sum had been voted on first, it might have been
adopted, with the result that those who preferred the added
advantages possible through a larger expenditure would
15 have been cut off from considering larger sums.

On the other hand, suppose that the motion or resolution is "to sell the headquarters for an amount not less than
$_____." In the case of such a motion—to *accept* a sum of
money in *settlement*—the amounts being considered should
20 be arranged and voted on in order from the smallest to the
largest. Thus, those who are willing to sell for the smallest
amount, and some additional members, will be willing to
sell for the next larger sum, and so on, until the smallest
sum for which the majority is willing to sell is reached.
25

FILLING A BLANK WITH PLACES, DATES, OR
NUMBERS.   When a blank is to be filled with a place,
date, or number, a choice of methods for arranging and
voting on the proposals can be made as follows:
30

a) Voting on the suggestions in the order in which they are
offered, as when filling a blank with names.
b) Voting on the proposals in the order of their probable
acceptability, beginning with the least popular choice, as
35 when filling a blank with an amount.

c) (If there is no clear-cut reason why either increasing or decreasing order would be preferable), voting first on the largest number, longest time, or most distant date, and so on.

The particular circumstances must determine the order to be used.

If an amount has been struck out in order to create a blank, that amount is voted on in its proper place in the logical sequence among the other amounts. If a name has been struck out to create a blank, however, it comes first in the order of names to be voted on.

The suggestions for filling a blank can be voted on by any of the regular methods (pp. 42ff., 395ff.) Voting by ballot or roll call is seldom used except in the case of names, however, unless there is keen competition—for example, among several cities seeking a convention. When names are being voted on, the ballot has an advantage in more truly revealing the will of the voting body; frequently when the vote is by voice, members vote for those nominated first.

It should be noted that the vote that fills a blank does not decide the main question. When the blank is filled, the chair must immediately state the question on the adoption of the completed motion.

The *Previous Question* cannot be ordered on a motion to create a blank or to stop the debate on suggestions for filling the blank. The same result may be accomplished, however, by a motion to *Close Suggestions* which is identical to a motion to Close *Nominations* (**31**). It may be adopted by a two-thirds vote and is in order if an excessive number of suggestions are being submitted.

Normally, blanks should be filled before voting on the motion itself; but if a large majority is confident that the measure will be rejected in any case, time may be saved by

1 ordering the *Previous Question* on *all* applicable pending
questions before the blank is filled. This brings the assembly to an immediate vote on suggestions already made to fill
the blank, if any, and on the main motion or on the
5 amendment containing the blank. If by chance the motion
is nevertheless adopted, the blank should be filled and the
motion completed before any other business is taken up.

(For further examples of both creating and filling a blank,
see pp. 163, l. 13–15, p. 164, l. 30–32, p. 166, l. 6–19, p.
10 171, p. 263, l. 4–8, p. 276, l. 25–32.)

§13. COMMIT OR REFER

The subsidiary motion to *Commit* or *Refer* is generally
15 used to send a pending question to a relatively small group
of selected persons—a committee—so that the question
may be carefully investigated and put into better condition
for the assembly to consider.

The motion to *Commit* also has three *variations* whose
20 object is not to turn the main question over to a smaller
group, but to permit the assembly's full meeting body to
consider it with the greater freedom of debate that is allowed
in committees—that is, with no limit on the number of times
a member can speak. These forms of the motion are:

25

a) to "go into a committee of the whole";
b) to "go into quasi committee of the whole" (or, to "consider as if in committee of the whole"); and
c) to "consider informally."

30

"Informal consideration" is the simplest of the three
methods and is usually the best in ordinary societies whose
meetings are not large (see pp. 523-24).

The term *recommit* is applied to a motion that proposes
35 to refer a question a second time, either to the same committee that previously considered it or to a different one.

All of the rules in this section, except when stated to the contrary, apply equally to variations (a), (b), and (c) above, and to a motion to recommit.

When a motion proposes to assign a task or refer a matter to a committee when no question is pending, such a motion is not the subsidiary motion to *Commit*, but is a main motion. It is an incidental main motion if the assignment or referral is pursuant to a subject on which the assembly has already taken some action; but it is an original main motion if the matter to be assigned or referred relates to a new subject.

Standard Descriptive Characteristics

The subsidiary motion to *Commit* or *Refer:*

1. Takes precedence over the main motion, over the subsidiary motions to *Postpone Indefinitely* and to *Amend,* and over the incidental motions for *Division of a Question* and for *Consideration by Paragraph or Seriatim*. It also takes precedence over a debatable appeal (or a point of order which has been referred by the chair to the judgment of the assembly and that is debatable when so referred, p. 242, l. 7–13) under either of the following conditions: (a) if the appeal or question of order does not adhere to the main question; or (b) if no other motions except those named in the preceding sentence are pending or involved in the appeal or question of order. It yields to the subsidiary motions to *Postpone Definitely,* to *Limit or Extend Limits of Debate,* for the *Previous Question,* and to *Lay on the Table;* to all privileged motions; and to all applicable incidental motions.

2. Can be applied to main motions, with any amendments that may be pending; can be thus applied to *orders of the day* (**18, 41**) or *questions of privilege* (**19**) while they are actually pending as main motions, and such an applica-

1   tion is independent of, and does not affect, any other
    matter that they may have interrupted; can be applied
    to debatable appeals (or points of order referred by the
    chair to the judgment of the assembly that are debatable
5   when so referred, p. 242, l. 7–13), but if such an appeal
    adheres (pp. 112–13) to the main question (that is, if
    the appeal must be decided before the main question is
    decided), the motion to *Commit* can be applied to the
    appeal only in connection with the main question,
10 which also goes to the committee (see also p. 169); and
    can be applied to nonadhering debatable appeals sepa-
    rately, without affecting the status of any other ques-
    tions that may be pending. It cannot be applied to an
    undebatable appeal. It cannot be applied to the motion
15 to *Reconsider* alone—that is, it cannot be applied to a
    motion to reconsider a main question; and if a main
    question is committed while a motion to reconsider an
    amendment is pending, such a motion to *Reconsider* is
    thereafter ignored. It cannot be applied to any sub-
20 sidiary motion, except that its application to a main
    question also affects any motions to *Amend* that may be
    pending, as noted above. It cannot be moved after the
    adoption of a motion to close debate on the main ques-
    tion at a definite hour or to limit the total time allowed
25 for debate; but it remains in order if only a limitation on
    the length of speeches is in force (see **15**). Motions to
    Amend, to *Limit or Extend Limits of Debate,* and for the
    Previous Question can be applied to it without affecting
    the main question. The motion to *Commit* cannot be
30 definitely postponed or laid on the table alone, but
    when it is pending the main question can be definitely
    postponed or laid on the table, and in such a case, the
    motion to *Commit* is also postponed or carried to the
    table. It cannot be postponed indefinitely.
35 3. Is out of order when another has the floor.

4. Must be seconded.

5. Is debatable. The debate can extend only to the desirability of committing the main question and to the appropriate details of the motion to *Commit,* as explained below, however, and not to the merits of the main question.

6. Is amendable as follows: in the case of a standing committee, as to the committee to which the main question is to be referred; in the case of a special committee, as to the committee's composition and manner of selection; and in the case of any form of committee, as to any instructions the committee is to follow. It can be amended so as to change from any one of the five forms of the motion (listed on p. 166, l. 10–15) to another, or a blank can be created (pp. 155–60) and the suggested forms voted on in the order given on page 166. A motion to consider informally is not amendable.

7. Requires a majority vote.

8. An affirmative vote on the motion to *Commit* can be reconsidered if the committee has not begun consideration of the question. Thereafter, if the assembly wishes to take the question out of the hands of the committee, the motion to *Discharge a Committee* (**36**) must be used. A negative vote on the motion to *Commit* can be reconsidered only until such time as progress in business or debate has been sufficient to make it essentially a new question. Thereafter, the motion can be renewed (see pp. 328–29).

Further Rules and Explanation

NECESSARY DETAILS OF THE MOTION.   The motion to *Commit* usually should include all necessary details:

- If the main question is to be considered in a committee of the whole, or in quasi committee of the whole ("as if in committee of the whole"), or if it is to be considered informally, the motion should specify which of these methods is to be used.

- If the main question is to be sent to a standing committee (see **50**), the motion should specify the name of the committee.

- If the main question is to go to a special (select, or ad hoc) committee (see **50**), the motion should specify the number of committee members, and the method of their selection unless the method is prescribed by the bylaws; or, if preferred, the motion can name the members of the special committee. (The word *special*, or *select*, or *ad hoc*, is not generally used in a motion to refer to a special committee; the motion is worded, for example, "to refer the question to a committee of five to be appointed by . . ." See also forms of the motion on pp. 170–71.)

- Instructions to the committee can also be included in the motion to *Commit*, whether the committee is to be a standing or a special one, or a committee of the whole. These instructions, which are binding on the committee, may involve such matters as when the committee should meet, how it should consider the question, whether it should employ an expert consultant, and when it should report. The committee can be given "full power" to act for the society in a specific case and can be authorized to spend money or even to add to its own membership.

Although these details can be changed by ordinary amendments, they can often be handled more efficiently by treating them as in filling blanks (pp. 155–60, 171).

DILATORY MOTION TO COMMIT. The chair should rule out of order, as dilatory, any motion to *Commit* that is obviously absurd or unreasonable—such as one that *1* (because of the time involved or any other reason) would have the effect of defeating the purpose of the main question.

ALTERNATIVE PROCEDURES WHEN THE *5* MOTION IS INCOMPLETE.   When a motion to *Commit* merely lacks essential details—for example, when the motion is made simply "to refer the main question to a committee"—the chair should not rule it out of order. Instead, these two courses are open: *10*

a) Members can offer suggestions or formal amendments to complete the required details, or the chair can call for them.
b) The chair can put the motion to *Commit* to vote at once *15* in its simple form.

The second alternative is appropriate if no one is seeking recognition and the chair believes that the motion to *Commit* is not likely to be adopted, in which case time spent in *20* completing the details would be wasted. Opponents of the motion to *Commit* may try to bring about the same result (that is, obtaining an immediate vote on the referral) by moving the *Previous Question* on it (see **16**). If the necessary two thirds (of those voting) vote to order the *Previous Question* *25* on an incomplete motion to *Commit,* the motion is almost certain to be rejected, whatever details might be added.

In the event that any of the above procedures results in the adoption of an incomplete motion "to refer the question to a committee," the details must be completed as de- *30* scribed in the following paragraphs, before any other business is taken up.

COMPLETING AN INCOMPLETE MOTION TO COMMIT.   In completing a motion that simply refers *35*

1 "the main question to a committee"—either while the motion to *Commit* is pending or after it is adopted—the chair first asks, "To what committee shall the question be referred?" If only one suggestion is made, he assumes that
5 this is the will of the assembly, and he states that it is inserted into the motion to *Commit*. But if different proposals are made, either in the form of primary and secondary amendments or simply as suggestions, the chair treats them as proposals to fill a blank (pp. 155–60) and puts them to
10 vote in the following order until one receives a majority: (1) committee of the whole; (2) quasi committee of the whole (or "as if in committee of the whole"); (3) consider informally; (4) standing committees, in the order in which they are proposed; and (5) special (select, or ad hoc) commit-
15 tees, the one containing the largest number of members being voted on first. A proposal to recommit to the same standing or special committee that previously considered the question should be voted on before other proposals for standing or special committees are voted on.
20 If it is decided that the committee is to be a special one, the chair then asks—unless the rules provide the method— "How shall the committee be appointed?" Again, if only one suggestion is made, it is inserted by unanimous consent, but if different methods are suggested or moved, they
25 are voted on in the following order: (1) election by ballot; (2) nominations from the floor ("open nominations") with viva-voce election; (3) nominations by the chair; and (4) appointment by the chair (see also pp. 474ff.). The first of these methods of selection that receives a majority vote is
30 then inserted into the motion to *Commit* and the remainder are ignored.

If the motion to *Commit* lacks any other detail, the chair proceeds in a similar fashion to obtain completion of the motion. As soon as it is completed, if it is a *pending* mo-
35 tion to *Commit,* the chair states the question on it, thus

opening it to additional debate during which any member
can move—or the chair himself can suggest—that it be
amended by adding instructions. By a majority vote, instructions can also be added to a motion to *Commit* that is
being completed after its adoption.

NAMING MEMBERS TO A SPECIAL COMMIT-
TEE.   A standing or special committee may include, or
even have as its chairman, one or more persons who are not
members of the assembly or the society; but if the chair appoints the committee, the names of all such nonmembers
being appointed must be submitted to the assembly for approval, unless the bylaws or the motion to appoint the committee specifically authorizes the presiding officer to
appoint nonmembers (see also pp. 475, 478–79). When a
motion to refer to a special committee has been adopted,
no business except privileged matters can intervene until selection of the committee members is completed—except
that if the chair is to appoint the committee, he can, if he
wishes and time permits, state that he will announce the
names of its members later. In such a case, however, the
committee must be left with reasonable time to accomplish
its purpose after the names of its members have been announced for the record and any non–society members have
been approved as necessary under the rule stated at the beginning of this paragraph in a meeting of the assembly. The
committee cannot act before such an announcement of its
membership is made, unless otherwise authorized by vote
of the assembly.

Although it is not necessary to place on a special committee the member who made the motion to *Commit*, it is
usual to do so when such a person is interested and qualified. For a discussion of the appropriate size and personnel
of committees under various circumstances, see pages
480–81.

DESIGNATING THE COMMITTEE CHAIRMAN. If the chair appoints or nominates the committee, he has the duty to select its chairman—which he does by naming that person to the committee first—and the committee cannot elect another. The chair should not state the name of any committee member until he has decided his preference for chairman. The chair should specifically mention as chairman the first committee member he names, but if he neglects to state this fact, the designation nevertheless is automatic unless the first-named member immediately declines the chairmanship (which the member can do, and remain on the committee). If the first-named member declines to serve as chairman, the chair then names his next choice for this position. If the committee's task is heavy and will require some time to complete, it often is advisable to appoint a vice-chairman. The anomalous title "co-chairman" should be avoided, as it causes impossible dilemmas in attempts to share the functions of a single position.

If the committee is named by a power other than the chair (such as the assembly or the executive board), the body that elects the committee members has the power, at the time the appointments are made, to designate any one of them as chairman. If a chairman is not designated when the committee is appointed, the committee has the right to elect its own chairman. In the latter case, the first-named member has the duty of calling the committee together and of acting as temporary chairman until the committee elects a chairman. Since such a committee may confirm its first-named member in the chairmanship, it is important that this person be qualified and dependable.

FREEDOM OF ACTION AFTER REFERRAL. Once a committee to which a resolution or other main motion has been referred commences its deliberations, the committee is free to consider, and recommend for adoption, any amendment to the resolution or motion so referred, without regard to whether or not the assembly, prior to the referral, considered the same or a similar amendment and either adopted or rejected it. When the committee reports, even if to the same meeting that made the referral, the matter stands before the assembly as if introduced for the first time, and the assembly itself, therefore, is also free to consider any such amendment, whether considered by the committee or not.*

EFFECT ON MOTIONS ADHERING TO THE REFERRED QUESTION.   If the motion to *Postpone Indefinitely* is pending when a main motion is referred to a committee, the motion for indefinite postponement is dropped from further consideration. Pending amendments and any adhering debatable appeals (**24**), on the other hand, go to the committee with the main motion, and are reported with it.

SUBSEQUENT INSTRUCTIONS.   After a question has been referred to a committee and at any time before the committee submits its report, even at another session, the assembly by a majority vote can give the committee additional instructions in reference to the referred question.

VACANCIES IN A COMMITTEE.   The power to appoint a committee includes the power to fill any vacancy that may arise in it. Unless the bylaws provide otherwise (see pp. 479–80, 642), the appointing authority has the power to remove or replace members of the committee: If a single per-

---

*The provisions of this paragraph do not apply, however, with respect to informal consideration (pp. 160, 523–24).

1   son, such as the president, has the power of appointment, he
    has the power to remove or replace a member so appointed;
    but if the assembly has the power of selection, removal or re-
    placement can take place only under rules applicable to the
5   motions to *Rescind* or *Amend Something Previously Adopted*
    (see p. 480). Committee members are presumed to serve
    until their successors are appointed.

PROCEDURE WHEN A COMMITTEE REPORTS.

10 For the procedure when a committee submits its report
    on a referred question, see **51**; see also page 149.

Form and Example

15   The motion to *Commit* or *Refer* may be made in
    many forms. The following are typical: "I move to refer
    the motion to a committee"; "I move to recommit the
    resolution"; "I move that the motion be referred to the
    Social Committee"; "I move that the resolution be re-
20 ferred to a committee of three to be appointed by the
    chair" [or "nominated by the chair," or "elected from
    open nominations"]; "I move that the question be re-
    ferred to the Executive Board with full power"; "I move
    to refer the resolution to a committee of seven, the chair-
25 man to be Mr. Brownley, six members to be elected by
    ballot from open nominations, and the committee to be
    instructed to report at the April meeting"; "I move that
    the Club now resolve itself into [or "go into"] a com-
    mittee of the whole to consider the resolution"; "I move
30 that the resolution be considered in quasi committee of
    the whole" [or "considered as if in committee of the
    whole"]; and "I move that the motion be considered in-
    formally."
        Assume that a resolution is pending which, after debate,
35 apparently requires careful amendment before the assembly

will be willing to act on it. However, the assembly is pressed for time. *1*

MEMBER A (obtaining the floor): I move that the resolution be referred to a committee to be appointed by the chair. (Second.) *5*

CHAIR: It is moved and seconded that the resolution be referred to a committee to be appointed by the chair. [Pause.] Are you ready for the question? [No response.] Of how many members shall the committee consist?

MEMBER B (obtaining the floor): I move to amend the motion to *10* commit by inserting after the word "committee" the words "of three." (Second.)

CHAIR: It is moved and seconded to amend the motion by inserting after the word "committee" the words "of three."

MEMBER C (obtaining the floor): I move to amend the amendment *15* by striking out "three" and inserting "seven." (Second.)

CHAIR: If there is no objection, the chair suggests that the number of committee members be decided upon by the method of filling blanks. [Pause.] There is no objection and it is so ordered. It has been suggested that the committee be composed of seven and also three *20* members. Are there additional suggestions?

MEMBER D (calling from his seat): I suggest five.

CHAIR: Five is also suggested. Are there other suggestions? [No response.] If not, the different numbers of members suggested for the proposed committee are seven, five, and three. These will be voted on in *25* descending order. As many as are in favor of seven members, say *aye.* . . . Those opposed, say *no.* . . . The noes have it and the number seven is not adopted. As many as are in favor of five members, say *aye.* . . . Those opposed, say *no.* . . . The ayes have it and the number five is chosen for the committee membership. The question is now on the motion "to refer *30* the resolution to a committee of five to be appointed by the chair." [Pause. No response.] As many as are in favor of referring the resolution to such a committee, say *aye.* . . . Those opposed, say *no.* . . . The ayes have it and the motion is adopted. The chair appoints Mr. Johnson as chairman, Dr. Donaldson, Mrs. Applegarth, Mr. Frank, Miss Dillon. *35*

§14. POSTPONE TO A CERTAIN TIME (OR DEFINITELY)

The subsidiary motion to *Postpone to a Certain Time* (or *Postpone Definitely,* or *Postpone*) is the motion by which action on a pending question can be put off, within limits, to a definite day, meeting, or hour, or until after a certain event. (The expression "to defer" should be avoided, since it is often subject to vague usage.) This motion can be moved regardless of how much debate there has been on the motion it proposes to postpone. A question may be postponed either so that it may be considered at a more convenient time, or because debate has shown reasons for holding off a decision until later. This motion should not be confused with *Postpone Indefinitely,* which, as explained earlier (**11**), does not actually postpone the pending question, but kills it.

When a motion proposes to postpone a matter that is not pending—for example, the hearing of a committee's report—such a motion is not the subsidiary motion to *Postpone,* but is an incidental main motion (**10**). If the effect would be to change action already taken by the assembly, as, for example, "to postpone for three weeks the dinner scheduled for October 15," such a motion is a particular case of the motion to *Amend Something Previously Adopted* (**35**).

Standard Descriptive Characteristics

The subsidiary motion to *Postpone to a Certain Time:*

1. Takes precedence over the main motion; over the subsidiary motions to *Postpone Indefinitely,* to *Amend,* and to *Commit;* and over the incidental motions for *Division of the Question* and for *Consideration by Paragraph or Seriatim.* It also takes precedence over a debatable appeal (or a point of order which has been referred by the chair

to the judgment of the assembly and which is debatable   *1*
when so referred, p. 242, l. 22–24) under either of the following conditions: (a) if the appeal does not adhere to the
main question; or (b) if no other motions except those
named in the preceding sentence are pending or involved   *5*
in the appeal or question of order. It takes precedence
over a debatable motion to *Reconsider* when it is in order
to apply it to that motion under the conditions stated in
Standard Characteristic 2 below. It yields to the subsidiary
motions to *Limit or Extend Limits of Debate,* for the *Pre-*   *10*
vious Question, or to *Lay on the Table;* to all privileged motions; and to all applicable incidental motions.

2. Can be applied to main motions, with any motions to
   Postpone Indefinitely, Amend, or *Commit* that may be
   pending; can be thus applied to *orders of the day* (pp.   *15*
   177–80; **41**) or *questions of privilege* (**19**) while they are
   actually pending as main motions, and such an application
   is independent of, and does not affect, any other matter
   that they may have interrupted; can be applied to debatable appeals (or points of order referred by the chair to   *20*
   the judgment of the assembly that are debatable when so
   referred, p. 242, l. 22–24), but if such an appeal adheres
   (pp. 112–13) to the main question (that is, if the appeal
   must be decided before the main question is decided), the
   motion to *Postpone* can be applied to the appeal only in   *25*
   connection with the main question, which is thus also
   postponed (see also pp. 180–81); can be applied to nonadhering debatable appeals separately, without affecting
   the status of any other questions that may be pending;
   and can be applied to an immediately pending, debatable   *30*
   motion to *Reconsider* (**37**) when it is in order to postpone
   the question or series of adhering questions containing
   the motion(s) to be reconsidered, in which case all such
   questions and adhering motions are postponed with the
   motion to *Reconsider.* It cannot be applied to an unde-   *35*

1   batable appeal or to an undebatable motion to *Recon-
    sider;* and it cannot be applied to any subsidiary motion,
    except that its application to a main question also affects
    any motions to *Postpone Indefinitely, Amend,* or *Commit*
5   that may be pending, as noted above. It cannot be moved
    after the adoption of a motion to close debate on the
    main question at a definite hour or of a motion to limit
    the total time allowed for debate; but it remains in order
    if only a limitation on the length of speeches is in force
10 (see **15**). Motions to *Amend,* to *Limit or Extend Limits
    of Debate,* and for the *Previous Question* can be applied to
    it without affecting the main question. The motion to
    Postpone cannot be laid on the table alone, but when it is
    pending the main question can be laid on the table, car-
15 rying to the table also the motion to *Postpone.* It cannot
    be postponed indefinitely or committed.

3. Is out of order when another has the floor.

4. Must be seconded.

5. Is debatable; but debate is limited in that is must not
20 go into the merits of the main question any more than
    is necessary to enable the assembly to decide whether
    the main question should be postponed and to what
    time.

6. Is amendable as to the time to which the main question
25 is to be postponed, and as to making the postponed
    question a *special order* (see pp. 177–180; **41**).

7. Requires a majority vote in its simple and usual form. If
    (as originally moved or as a result of amendment) it
    makes a question a *special order,* however, the motion to
30 *Postpone* then requires a two-thirds vote, because it sus-
    pends any rules that will interfere with the question's
    consideration at the time specified. An amendment to the
    motion to *Postpone* requires only a majority vote, even if
    it would add a provision to make the postponed question
35 a special order and would consequently change to two

thirds the vote necessary for adoption of the motion to *Postpone*.

8. An affirmative vote on the motion to *Postpone* can be reconsidered. A negative vote on this motion can be reconsidered only until such time as progress in business or debate has been sufficient to make it essentially a new question. Thereafter, the motion can be renewed (see p. 329, l. 1–8).

Further Rules and Explanation

LIMITS ON POSTPONEMENT AND THEIR RELATION TO MEETING AND SESSION.   Rules limiting the time to which a question can be postponed are related to the terms *meeting* and *session* (**8**), as follows:

In a case where more than a quarterly time interval (see p. 88) will elapse between meetings (for example, in an annual convention of delegates or in a local society that holds only an annual meeting), a question cannot be postponed beyond the end of the present session. In cases where no more than a quarterly time interval (see p. 88) will elapse between sessions, a question can be postponed until, but not beyond, the next regular business session. For example, in a society that holds regular business meetings on the same day of each week, a question cannot, at one meeting, be postponed for longer than a week.

If it is desired to postpone a question to a time between regular meetings, it is necessary first to provide for an *adjourned meeting,* which is a continuation of the session scheduling it; then the question can be postponed to that meeting. If a motion to postpone a question to a regular meeting is already pending, the privileged motion to *Fix the Time to Which to Adjourn* (**22**) can be used to set an adjourned meeting, and the motion to *Postpone* can then be amended so that the proposed postponement will be to the

1 adjourned meeting. Some societies have frequent sessions for social or cultural purposes at which business may be transacted, and also hold a session every month or quarter especially for business. In such societies these rules apply
5 particularly to the regular business sessions, to which questions can be postponed from the previous regular business session or from any intervening meeting.

When the time to which a question has been postponed arrives and the question is taken up, it can be postponed
10 again if the additional delay will not interfere with the proper handling of the postponed motion.

Neither the motion to *Postpone to a Certain Time* nor any amendment to it is in order if the effect would be the same as that of the motion to *Postpone Indefinitely*—that is, if it
15 would kill the measure. For example, a motion to postpone until tomorrow a pending question of accepting an invitation to a banquet tonight cannot be recognized as a motion to *Postpone to a Certain Time*. The chair must either rule this motion out of order or, if the motion to *Postpone Indefinitely*
20 is in order at the time, he can state the motion as such at his discretion. The same would apply to a motion to postpone a question from one regular business session to the next in cases where the next business session will not be held within a quarterly time interval (see p. 88).
25

RULE AGAINST POSTPONEMENT OF A CLASS OF SUBJECTS.   As already noted, the subsidiary motion to *Postpone* can be applied only to a question that is actually pending; but an individual item of business that is not
30 pending can, when appropriate, be postponed by means of a main motion.

It is not in order, either through a subsidiary motion or a main motion, to postpone a class of business composed of several items or subjects, such as reports of offi-
35 cers or reports of committees (see *Order of Business,* **41**);

but each report can be postponed separately as it is an-   1
nounced or called for.* If it is desired to reach an item immediately but it falls at a later point in the regular order
of business, the assembly, by a two-thirds vote or by unanimous consent (pp. 51–53), can adopt either a motion to   5
"suspend the rules and take up" the desired question, or
a motion "to pass" one or more items or classes of subjects in the order of business. After a question taken up
out of its proper order by either of these methods has
been disposed of, the regular order of business is resumed   10
at the point where it was left off (see motion to *Suspend
the Rules,* **25**).

POSTPONEMENT OF A SUBJECT THAT THE BY-
LAWS SET FOR A PARTICULAR SESSION.   A matter   15
that the bylaws require to be attended to at a specified session, such as the election of officers, cannot, in advance and
through a main motion, be postponed to another session;
but when the election or other matter is actually pending, it
can be postponed to an adjourned meeting in the manner ex-   20
plained above, after first adopting a motion to *Fix the Time to
Which to Adjourn.* The adjourned meeting, as already stated,
is a continuation of the same session. This procedure is sometimes advisable, as in an annual meeting for the election of officers on a stormy night when the attendance is abnormally   25
small, even though a quorum is present.

PRIORITY OF POSTPONED ITEMS AND ITS RE-
LATION TO ORDER OF BUSINESS AND ORDERS
OF THE DAY.   When a question is due to come up after   30
postponement, it may be subject to a priority that depends
on the form in which the motion to *Postpone* was adopted.

---

*It should be noted that a similar rule applies to the subsidiary motion
to *Lay on the Table* (see pp. 203, 207–8, 351–52).

1   Rules affecting the postponement of more than one item of
business to the same or conflicting times are closely related
to *order of business* and *orders of the day* (**41**), according to
principles that may be summarized as follows:

5   A postponed question becomes an *order of the day* for
the time to which it is postponed. An order of the day cannot be taken up before the time for which it is set, except
by reconsidering (**37**) the vote that established the order, or
by suspending the rules by a two-thirds vote. Orders of the
10 day consist of *general orders* and *special orders.* Special orders have precedence over general orders. If a question is
postponed without making it a special order, it is a general
order for the time to which it is postponed.

        An order of the day can be made for a definite session,
15 day, or meeting, or for a particular hour. When set for *a session, day, or meeting,* special orders and general orders usually have their established places in the order of business.
Special orders that are not set for a particular hour normally
are taken up after reports of special committees are heard.
20 General orders are taken up after unfinished business is disposed of but are grouped with it under the heading, "Unfinished Business and General Orders." The effect of setting
an order of the day for a particular *hour* depends on
whether it is a general order or a special order.

25   The effect of postponing a question to a specified hour or
until after a particular event in a meeting (making it a *general
order for that hour*) is: (1) to ensure that the question cannot
come up before the predetermined time except by a two-
thirds vote or through a reconsideration of the postpone-
30 ment; and (2) to provide that it will come up at the time
named, or later, depending on certain circumstances. Such an
order of the day cannot interrupt pending questions, and
(except by a two-thirds vote) it cannot come up before general orders have been reached in the order of business, even
35 if the time named has arrived or passed; but it is automatically

taken up at the time named or as soon thereafter as general
orders have been reached and any of the following matters,
all of which have precedence over it, have been disposed of:
(1) a question pending at the time named; (2) a special order
for a particular hour that comes into conflict; (3) a motion to
Reconsider that is called up (**37**); or (4) any other orders of
the day for the same time, or coming into conflict, that *were
made before this general order was made.*

Any number of questions can be postponed to the same
time (provided that they are not made special orders for the
same or obviously conflicting hours). Such questions, or
other postponed questions that come into conflict, are taken
up in the order in which they were postponed. If a matter
that has been postponed to a meeting, or to an hour during
a meeting, is not disposed of before adjournment, it becomes
a part of unfinished business, unless it was a special order (in
which case it becomes an unfinished special order).

Making a question a special order for a certain time
(which can be done only by a two-thirds vote unless in connection with the adoption of an agenda or program, **41,
59**) suspends any rules that may interfere with consideration of the question at the time specified—except those relating: (a) to adjournment or recess; (b) to questions of
privilege; (c) to special orders made before this special order
was made; or (d) to *the* special order for a meeting, as explained below. As previously stated, if a matter is made *a*
special order for a definite day or meeting without naming
an hour, it is taken up, along with any unfinished special orders, under that heading in the order of business; and it
thus has precedence over unfinished business and general
orders. But if a matter is made a special order for a particular *hour,* it will interrupt or have precedence over any other
business then pending or set for the same time, except: (1)
another special order made before it was; or (2) *the* special
order for a meeting.

1   A matter can be made *the* special order for a meeting if it is desired to reserve an entire meeting, or as much of it as necessary, for the consideration of a single subject. At the appointed meeting, the chair announces the special order as 5 the pending business immediately after the minutes have been disposed of. At the time that a matter is made *the* special order for a meeting, any other special orders that were made earlier and are likely to come into conflict with *the* special order should be adjusted to different times. If this 10 has been neglected, however, *the* special order for a meeting has precedence over any other form of special order.

EFFECT ON MOTIONS ADHERING TO A POST-PONED QUESTION.   When a main motion is post-15 poned, motions to *Postpone Indefinitely, Amend,* and *Commit* may be pending, and debate may have been limited or closed. All such adhering or attached motions are postponed with the main question, and when consideration of that question is resumed at the specified time, the business 20 is in the same condition as it was immediately before the postponement, with the following exception: If the consideration is not resumed until the next session, any limitation on or curtailment of debate is exhausted and therefore ignored. Similarly, when a main motion is postponed, it also 25 carries with it any adhering debatable appeals (**24**)—that is, debatable appeals that are related to the main question in such a way that they must be decided before the main question is acted upon. The main question cannot be postponed while an undebatable appeal is pending.

30   Except for the effect of an unexhausted order limiting or closing debate, as explained in the preceding paragraph, when a question is taken up *on a different day* from the one on which it was postponed, the right of members to debate it begins over again, as if the question had not previously 35 been debated; that is, each person can again speak twice to

each debatable question, regardless of whether he may have *1*
already done so before the postponement (see **43**).

Form and Example
5

The form used in making this motion depends on the
desired object:

a) Simply to postpone the question to the next meeting,
   when it will have precedence over new business: "I *10*
   move to postpone the motion [or "that the question be
   postponed"] to the next meeting."
b) To specify an hour before which the question will not
   be taken up (unless by a two-thirds vote or through reconsideration), and when it will come up automatically *15*
   as soon as no business is pending and any remaining
   matters that have precedence over it have been disposed
   of: "I move that the resolution be postponed until 3
   P.M." [or ". . . until 9 P.M. at the meeting scheduled for
   February 15"]. *20*
c) To postpone consideration of a motion until after a certain event in a meeting, when it will immediately be
   taken up (unless a special order intervenes): "I move to
   postpone the question until after the address by our
   guest speaker." *25*
d) To ensure that the question will come up at the next
   meeting and will not be crowded out by other matters:
   "I move that the question be postponed to the next
   meeting and be made a special order." (Two-thirds vote
   required for adoption.) *30*
e) To ensure that the matter will come up at precisely a
   certain hour, even if it interrupts pending business: "I
   move that the resolution be postponed and be made a
   special order for 3 P.M. tomorrow." (Two-thirds vote required for adoption.) *35*

1   f) To postpone a subject—such as a revision of the bylaws—to an adjourned meeting at which the entire time
can be devoted to it if necessary, a motion to *Fix the
Time to Which to Adjourn* should first be made and
5   adopted, and then the motion to *Postpone* should be
made in this form: "I move that the question be postponed and made *the* special order for the adjourned
meeting set for next Tuesday evening." (Two-thirds
vote required for adoption.)

10

Assume that a controversial resolution is pending at a
convention and that many of the delegates who are most interested and best informed on the subject will not be able
to be present until tomorrow.

15

    MEMBER A (obtaining the floor): I move to postpone the resolu-
tion until eleven o'clock tomorrow morning. (Second.)
    CHAIR: It is moved and seconded that the resolution be postponed
until eleven o'clock tomorrow morning. [Pause.]
20   MEMBER B (after obtaining the floor and stating that in his opinion
further consideration of the resolution should under no circumstances
be delayed *beyond* 11 A.M. the next day): I move to amend the motion
to postpone, by adding "and make it a special order." (Second.)
    CHAIR: It is moved and seconded to amend the motion to post-
25 pone the resolution until eleven o'clock tomorrow morning by adding
"and make it a special order." [Debate, if any.] The question is on
amending the motion to postpone by adding "and make it a special
order." As many as are in favor of the amendment, say *aye*. . . . Those
opposed, say *no*. . . . The ayes have it and the amendment is adopted.
30 The question now is on the motion, as amended, to postpone the resolution until eleven o'clock tomorrow morning and make it a special
order. This motion now requires a two-thirds vote. [Pause.] Are you
ready for the question? [Pause. No further debate.] As many as are in
favor of the motion to postpone the resolution until eleven o'clock to-
35 morrow morning and make it a special order, will rise. . . . Be seated.

Those opposed, rise. . . . Be seated. There are two thirds in the affirmative and the motion is adopted. The resolution is a special order for 11 A.M. tomorrow. The next item of business is . . .

If the amendment to make a special order is rejected, the chair proceeds in the usual manner to take a voice vote on the *unamended* motion to postpone. If the motion to postpone is not adopted, he again states the question on the resolution. But if the resolution *has* been made a special order for the following day at 11 A.M., as in the above example, then at the appointed time the chair says:

CHAIR: It is now eleven o'clock. The following resolution was made a special order for this time. "*Resolved,* That . . ." The question is on the adoption of the resolution. . . .

§15. LIMIT OR EXTEND LIMITS OF DEBATE

The subsidiary motion to *Limit or Extend Limits of Debate* is one of the two motions by means of which an assembly can exercise special control over debate on a pending question or on a series of pending questions. (The other motion serving such a purpose is the *Previous Question,* **16.** Neither of these motions is allowed in committees; see **50.**)

The motion to *Limit or Extend Limits of Debate* can *limit* debate by: (1) reducing the number or length of speeches permitted, but without including specific provision for closing debate; or (2) requiring that, at a certain later hour or after debate for a specified length of time, debate shall be closed and the question shall be put to vote. It can *extend the limits* of debate by allowing more and longer speeches than under the regular rules (see pp. 375–77). It cannot impose an immediate closing of debate, which requires a different motion—the *Previous Question.*

When an assembly adopts a motion to *Limit or Extend Limits of Debate,* it is said to adopt an "order" taking such action. (The word *order* as applied in this sense should not be confused with the technical terms *order of the day, general order,* and *special order* as used in **3, 14,** and **41.**) When an order limiting or extending the limits of debate finally ceases to be in force as relates to all the motions it affected, the order is said to be "exhausted" (see pp. 187–88).

If a motion proposing to change the regular limits of debate (for any length of time or during the consideration of one or more particular subjects) is made while no question is pending, such a motion is not the subsidiary motion to *Limit or Extend Limits of Debate,* but is an incidental main motion (although it requires a two-thirds vote for its adoption, just as the subsidiary motion does).

Standard Descriptive Characteristics

The subsidiary motion to *Limit or Extend Limits of Debate:*

1. Takes precedence over all debatable motions. It yields to the subsidiary motions for the *Previous Question* and to *Lay on the Table;* to all privileged motions; and to all applicable incidental motions.
2. Can be applied to any immediately pending debatable motion, to an entire series of pending debatable motions, or to any consecutive part of such a series beginning with the immediately pending question. (It therefore can be made only while a debatable motion is immediately pending. If a series of debatable questions is pending and an undebatable incidental motion is immediately pending, the latter must be disposed of before any motion to *Limit or Extend Limits of Debate* can be made.) Motions to *Amend* and (for the purpose of

stopping amendment) the motion for the *Previous Question* can be applied to it without affecting the main question. The motion to *Limit or Extend Limits of Debate* cannot be laid on the table alone, but when it is pending the main question can be laid on the table, carrying to the table also the motion to *Limit or Extend Limits of Debate.*

3. Is out of order when another has the floor.
4. Must be seconded.
5. Is not debatable.
6. Is amendable, but any amendment, like the motion itself, is undebatable.
7. Requires a two-thirds vote—because it suspends the rules, and because limiting debate takes away the basic rights of all members to full discussion and may restrict a minority's right to present its case.
8. Can be reconsidered, without debate, at any time before the order limiting or extending limits of debate is exhausted (see pp. 187–88). If the order has been partially carried out, only the unexecuted part can be subject to reconsideration. A negative vote on the motion to *Limit or Extend Limits of Debate* can be reconsidered only until such time as progress in debate has been sufficient to make it essentially a new question, after which it can simply be renewed (see p. 329, l. 1–8).

Further Rules and Explanation

EFFECT ON PENDING AND SUBSEQUENT MOTIONS. This motion's effect upon other pending and subsequent motions depends on the nature of its specific provisions, and is closely related to its position in the order of precedence of motions (**5**), as follows:

If a series of debatable questions is pending and a motion to *Limit or Extend Limits of Debate* does not specify

1   the motions to which it is to apply, then only the immediately pending question is affected. An order *limiting* debate
applies not only to the motion(s) on which the limitation is
ordered, but also to any debatable subsidiary motions, mo-
5   tions to *Reconsider,* or debatable appeals that may be made
subsequently while the order is in force. An order *extending
limits* of debate, on the other hand, does not affect any motion that was not pending when the order was adopted.

While a motion to *Limit or Extend Limits of Debate* is
10   *pending,* its precedence prevents the making of subsidiary
motions of lower rank (*Postpone Indefinitely, Amend, Commit, Postpone to a Certain Time*). This situation should not
be confused with the situation after the motion's *adoption.*
If the limitation or extension that has been ordered does
15   not provide for *closing* debate, it has no effect on what subsidiary motions can be made. On the other hand, after the
adoption of an order providing a time for the close of debate—by specifying either the hour at which the vote shall
be taken or the total amount of time allowed for debate—
20   motions to *Commit* or to *Postpone to a Certain Time* cannot be made unless the vote establishing the order is
reconsidered and reversed, since these motions would be in
conflict with the purpose of that order. The main question
and any adhering motions can be laid on the table, how-
25   ever, even while the order setting a time for the close of debate is in effect. If motions to *Commit* or to *Postpone* were
already part of a series that was pending when an order
scheduling the close of debate was adopted, the remaining
questions may be postponed or committed at the time the
30   motions for such action come to a vote.

Unlike the case of main motions and lower-ranking subsidiary motions (*Postpone Indefinitely, Amend, Commit,
Postpone*), the adoption of one motion limiting or extending debate in a certain way does not cause another such
35   conflicting motion to be out of order. A motion to set dif-

ferent limitation(s) or extension(s), or to change from one   1
to the other, or to order the *Previous Question* (**16**), can be
made at any time that it is in order under the order of
precedence of motions, until the pending questions affected have been finally disposed of. The reason is that the   5
two-thirds vote necessary for the adoption of any motion to
modify the limits of debate also fulfills the requirement for
changing something previously adopted (see **35**).

CONDITIONS FOR EXHAUSTION OF ITS EF-   10
FECT.   An order limiting or extending limits of debate is
exhausted: (1) when all of the questions on which it was imposed have been voted on; (2) when those questions affected
by the order and not yet voted on have been either referred
to a committee or postponed indefinitely; or (3) at the con-   15
clusion of the session in which the order has been adopted—
whichever occurs first. If any of the questions to which the
order applies are postponed definitely or laid on the table,
and are taken up again later during the same session, the unexecuted part of the order remains in effect. If it was ordered   20
that debate on a main motion be closed *and the vote be taken*
at a certain hour—as in (a) under Form and Example
below—and that hour has passed, no further debate on any
pending question is allowed, no further amendments can be
offered, and all pending questions must be voted on imme-   25
diately unless the vote that limited debate is reconsidered and
reversed or the time is set forward. On the other hand, after
the expiration of the allotted time under any order limiting
debate *without specifying when the vote shall be taken,* amendments and motions to dispose of the main motion are in   30
order, but they are then undebatable unless the limitation of
debate is changed as just indicated. Any questions affected by
an order modifying limits of debate that in any way go over
to the next session—or that are referred to a committee and
reported back, even in the same session in which commit-   35

1 ted—become open to debate under the regular rules. An order limiting or extending limits of debate applies to reconsiderations of the affected questions before, but not after, exhaustion of the order.

5

Form and Example

The forms in which this motion may be made depend on the desired object, as follows:

10

a) To fix the hour for closing debate and putting the question: "I move that at 9 P.M. debate be closed and the question on the resolution be put."

b) To limit time spent in debate: ". . . that debate on the *15*   pending amendment be limited to twenty minutes."

c) To reduce or increase the number or length of speeches: ". . . that debate be limited to one speech of five minutes for each member"; or ". . . that Mr. Lee's time be extended three minutes"; or "I ask unanimous consent *20*   that Mr. Lee's time . . . " (see pp. 51–53).

d) To combine several of the above objects: "I move that _____ and _____ [the leaders on the two sides] each be allowed twenty minutes, which may be divided between two speeches, and that other members be lim-*25*   ited to one speech of two minutes each, provided that all pending questions shall be put at 4 P.M." (see also example on p. 620).

The form of *stating* the question on this amendable but *30* undebatable motion is:

CHAIR: It is moved and seconded that no later than 9 P.M. debate be closed and the question on the resolution be put. The motion to limit or extend limits of debate is not debatable, but it can be amended. [Pause; or, "Are you ready for the question on . . . "; or, "Are there any amendments to . . . "] the motion to limit debate?

The words at the end of the last sentence, ". . . the motion to . . . ," can be varied depending on the particular form in which the motion was made.

Unless the motion to *Limit or Extend Limits of Debate* is adopted by unanimous consent (pp. 51–53), the chair puts it to a vote taken by rising, as in the example shown for a motion to postpone a question and make it a special order, on pages 182–83. In announcing the result, the chair states the parliamentary situation as it then exists:

CHAIR (after taking a rising vote): There are two thirds in the affirmative and the motion is adopted. The resolution will therefore be put to a vote no later than 9 P.M. and debate cannot continue beyond that hour. The question is on [stating the immediately pending question].

§16. PREVIOUS QUESTION
(Immediately to close debate and the making of subsidiary motions except the motion to Lay on the Table)

The *Previous Question* is the motion used to bring the assembly to an immediate vote on one or more pending questions; its adoption does this with certain exceptions.

Adopting or "ordering" the *Previous Question:*

1) immediately closes debate on, and stops amendment of, the immediately pending question and such other pending questions as the motion may specify (in consecutive series; see Standard Characteristic 2); and

2) prevents the making of any other subsidiary motions except the higher-ranking (**5**) *Lay on the Table.**

The adoption of an order for the *Previous Question* does not prevent the making of privileged or incidental motions (**6**) as applicable, and, strictly speaking, it does not prevent a special order set for a particular hour (**14, 41**) from interrupting the pending business (see also pp. 194–96).

The motion for the *Previous Question* has nothing to do with the last question previously considered by the assembly and has a long history of gradually changing purpose.

The *Previous Question* is not allowed in committees (**50**).

Standard Descriptive Characteristics

The subsidiary motion for the *Previous Question:*

1. Takes precedence over all debatable or amendable motions to which it is applied, and over the subsidiary motion to *Limit or Extend Limits of Debate;* and, if adopted, it supersedes the effect of an unexhausted order limiting or extending debate, with respect to the motions to which it is applied. It yields to the subsidiary motion to *Lay on the Table,* to all privileged motions, and to all applicable incidental motions.
2. Can be applied to any immediately pending debatable or amendable motion; to an entire series of pending debatable or amendable motions; and to any consecutive

---

*In practice it is seldom appropriate to move to lay a pending question or series of questions on the table after the *Previous Question* has been ordered on them; but a legitimate need to do so may sometimes arise, particularly in a large assembly if the vote(s) are to be taken by a method such as by ballot, standing for a count, or roll call (see also **45,** and *Misuses of the Motion to Lay on the Table,* pp. 207–8).

part of such a series, beginning with the immediately pending question. (Under this rule it can be applied to motions that are amendable but not debatable,* for the purpose of stopping amendment; see tinted p. 45.) It supersedes any earlier order for the closing of debate at a future time and can be applied while such an order is in effect. In practice, this motion usually is made in an unqualified form, such as "I move the previous question," and then it applies only to the immediately pending question. In its qualified form, however, it can be applied to include consecutively any series beginning with the immediately pending question. For example, the following motions might be pending: (a) a resolution; (b) an amendment to the resolution; (c) a motion to refer the resolution and its pending amendment to a committee; and (d) an immediately pending motion to postpone all of these questions to a definite time. In this case, an unqualified motion for the *Previous Question* will apply only to (d). Such a motion can be qualified to apply to (d) and (c); to (d), (c), and (b); or to (d), (c), (b), and (a). It cannot include only (d) and (b); only (d), (b), and (a); only (d), (c), and (a); or only (d) and (a); and no motion for the *Previous Question* excluding the immediately pending question (d) can be made until (d) has been voted on. No subsidiary motion can be applied to the *Previous Question,* except that when it is pending the main question can be laid on the table, carrying to the table also all adhering motions, including the motion for the *Previous Question.*

3. Is out of order when another has the floor.
4. Must be seconded.
5. Is not debatable.

---

*An example of such a motion is the motion to *Limit or Extend Limits of Debate* (**15**).

6. Is not amendable. However, it has a special characteristic that permits an effect similar to amendment when
the motion is applied while a series of questions is
pending. When a motion for the *Previous Question* is
immediately pending in such a case, it can be made
again with more or fewer pending questions included
(subject to the restrictions shown in Standard Characteristic 2, above), *before* the first motion for the *Previous Question* is voted on. The procedure resembles
filling blanks (see pp. 155–60) except that each of the
motions must be made by a member who has obtained
the floor, and each must be seconded.* For example,
if one member has made this motion in the unqualified form when a series of questions is pending (so that
it would apply only to the question immediately pending at that time), another member can move it on part
of the series and still another can move it on *all* pending questions. The vote is taken first on the motion
that would order the *Previous Question* on the largest
number of motions; if this fails, then on the next
smaller number, and so on, until one is adopted (by a
two-thirds vote), or until all of the motions for the
Previous Question are rejected.

7. Requires a two-thirds vote. (If a motion for the *Previous Question* fails to gain the necessary two-thirds vote,
debate continues as if this motion had not been
made.) In ordinary bodies, the requirement of a two-
thirds vote for ordering the *Previous Question* is important in protecting the democratic process. If this
rule were not observed, a temporary majority of only
one vote could deny the remaining members all op-

---

*For the form to be followed by the chair in granting limited recogni-
tion to a member who seeks the floor at such a time, see pages
200–201.

portunity to discuss any measure that such a majority wished to adopt or kill.*

8. Can be reconsidered before any vote has been taken under the order of the *Previous Question,* but (in contrast to the motion to *Limit or Extend Limits of Debate*) it cannot be reconsidered after the order has been partly executed;** see also pages 197–98. A negative vote on the motion for the *Previous Question* can be reconsidered only until such time as it has become essentially a new question—that is, if it is reasonable to assume that debate or action on any of the motions involved may have made more members desire to vote immediately on some or all of the questions still pending. Thereafter, it can be renewed (see p. 329, l. 1–6).

Further Rules and Explanation

EQUAL APPLICATION OF RULES TO COLLO-QUIAL FORMS SUCH AS "CALL FOR THE QUES-TION." A motion such as "I call for [or "call"] the

---

*Although the rules of the United States House of Representatives permit the *Previous Question* to be ordered by a majority vote, there are differences between the conditions in that body and in the ordinary organization that should be understood. Because of another House rule, an order for the *Previous Question* does not actually bring a measure to an immediate vote in Congress unless it has already been debated. If no discussion of the measure has taken place on the floor of the House, forty minutes' debate is allowed after adoption of the *Previous Question*—twenty minutes for each of the opposing sides. These rules derive from the great volume of business and the fact that under the two-party system of government by elected representatives, opposing sides often become nearly equal. At the same time, this system creates special conditions that make it unlikely that there will be unfair use of the power to curtail debate. The United States Senate does not admit the *Previous Question*, although it permits debate to be limited by means of a motion for cloture.

**When the *Previous Question* has been ordered on a number of motions, the order is said to be partly executed (or partly carried out) if one or more, but not all, of these motions have been voted on. When all of the motions specified in the order have been voted on, it is fully executed.

1 question" or "I move we vote now" is simply a motion for
   the *Previous Question* made in nonstandard form, and it is
   subject to all of the rules in this section. Care should be
   taken that failure to understand this fact does not lead to vi-
5 olation of members' rights of debate.

   Sometimes the mere making of a motion for the *Previous Question* or "call for the question" may motivate unanimous consent to ending debate. Before or after such a motion has been seconded, the chair may ask if there is any
10 objection to closing debate. If member(s) object or try to get the floor, he should ask if there is a second to the motion or call; or, if it has already been seconded, he must immediately take a vote on *whether to order* the *Previous Question*. But *regardless of the wording of a motion or "call"*
15 *seeking to close debate, it always requires a second and a two-thirds vote, taken separately from and before the vote(s) on the motion(s) to which it is applied, to shut off debate against the will of even one member who wishes to speak and has not exhausted his right to debate* (see pp. 42, 375–77).

20

EXEMPTION OF UNDEBATED PREAMBLE FROM THE PREVIOUS QUESTION UNLESS SEPARATELY ORDERED.   When a resolution having a preamble (one or more explanatory clauses beginning
25 "Whereas, . . . ") is pending, if the *Previous Question* is ordered on the resolution before consideration of the preamble has been reached (pp. 102ff., 133, 269), the order does not apply to debate and amendment of the preamble, to which the assembly proceeds immediately. After the chair
30 has declared the preamble open to debate and amendment in such a case, the entire resolution can be brought to an immediate vote, if desired, by then ordering the *Previous Question* on the preamble.

35 VOTING ON A SERIES OF MOTIONS UNDER THE PREVIOUS QUESTION; INTERRUPTION OF

EXECUTION. When the *Previous Question* is ordered on a series of pending motions as explained above under Standard Characteristic 2, they are voted on in order of rank beginning with the immediately pending question—that is, in reverse of the order in which they were made. If the series includes motions to *Postpone Definitely,* to *Commit,* or to *Postpone Indefinitely* and one of these motions is adopted, further voting stops—regardless of how many of the remaining questions were, or were not, included under the order for the *Previous Question.* But if voting is not stopped in such a manner, then, when all of the motions on which the *Previous Question* was ordered have been voted on, consideration of any questions still pending resumes under the regular rules.

If a question or series of questions (including motions on which the *Previous Question* has been ordered) *ceases to be the pending business* before all of the motions affected by the order have been voted on, *execution* of the order is said to be *interrupted.* Interruption of the execution of an order for the *Previous Question* may occur as follows:

- If a motion to *Postpone,* to *Commit,* or to *Postpone Indefinitely* on which the *Previous Question* has been ordered is adopted (as in the preceding paragraph) in a case where one or more of the remaining questions *were also included* under the order, execution of the order is thus *interrupted after it has been partly carried out.*

- *Before or after* an order for the *Previous Question* has been *partly carried out,* as already noted, it is also possible for its execution to be interrupted as a result of the question(s)'s being laid on the table, or by the intervention of a special order set for a particular hour (**14, 41**), a question of privilege (**19**), a recess (**8, 20**), or an adjournment (**8, 21**). (If the hour set for a special order, a recess, or an adjournment has arrived and the *Previous Question* has been ordered on one or more pending motions, however,

1   there usually will be no objection to the chair's putting
them all to a vote in succession before he announces the
matter that intervenes, unless the votes are to be taken by
a method requiring time.)

5

EXHAUSTION OF THE PREVIOUS QUESTION.
The *Previous Question* is said to be *exhausted* (in reference
to a particular order for it) when all of the motions on
which it was ordered have been finally disposed of, or when
10   any motions not yet finally disposed of are no longer affected by the order. The conditions for exhaustion of the
Previous Question are the same as for an order limiting or
extending limits of debate—that is: (1) when all motions on
which the *Previous Question* was ordered have been voted
15   on; (2) when those not yet voted on have either been committed or postponed indefinitely; or (3) at the end of the
session in which the *Previous Question* was ordered—
whichever occurs first. After the *Previous Question* is exhausted, any remaining questions that come up again are
20   open to debate and amendment just as if there had been no
order for the *Previous Question*.
If the execution of an order for the *Previous Question* is
interrupted and if the motion or motions that were pending come up again later, the rules in the foregoing para-
25   graph apply as follows:

• If the questions were *referred to a committee* and are
later reported, the *Previous Question* is *exhausted* and
the motions are open to debate and amendment, even
30   if it is during the same session.
• But if the interruption of execution occurred by any *other
means than referral* and the questions come up again
during the *same session,* the order *remains in effect;* all
motions on which the *Previous Question* was ordered
35   must be voted on immediately (unless a reconsideration

of the order is possible and a motion to reconsider it has been made, or is then made; see below).

- If the questions do not come up again until a *later session*, the *Previous Question* is *always exhausted*, regardless of how the interruption of execution occurred.

RECONSIDERATION OF A VOTE THAT HAS ORDERED THE PREVIOUS QUESTION.   As noted in Standard Characteristic 8, a vote that has ordered the *Previous Question* can be reconsidered before, but not after, any of the motions affected by the order have been voted on. Consequently, it will frequently happen that a motion to reconsider an affirmative vote on the *Previous Question* itself can be made only in the brief moment after the vote ordering the *Previous Question* is completed and before the first vote is taken under the order (see also p. 201).

If the execution of an order for the *Previous Question* was interrupted before any vote was taken under the order, and if the questions come up again during the same session, a motion to reconsider the order (if not made earlier) can be made only in the moment after the chair has announced these questions as the pending business and before any of them are voted on. In addition, the regular time limits for making a motion to *Reconsider* apply (see **37**).

It should be noted that if a motion or series of motions that is under an order for the *Previous Question* comes up after having been *postponed*, there can never be a reconsideration of the order. The reason is that the motion to *Postpone* can only have been made before the *Previous Question* was ordered, so that the order for the *Previous Question* will always have been partly executed by the vote that caused the postponement.

In practice, if a motion to reconsider an affirmative vote on the *Previous Question* prevails, the subsequent procedure is abbreviated as follows: The vote that adopted the motion to *Reconsider* is also presumed to have carried out the reconsideration and to have reversed the vote that is reconsidered; that is, the *Previous Question* is not presumed to be rejected and is not voted on again, for this reason: In such a case, only members opposed to the *Previous Question* would vote to reconsider it after it had been adopted; consequently, if a majority have voted for reconsideration, it will be impossible to obtain a two-thirds vote in favor of the *Previous Question*.

RECONSIDERATION OF A VOTE TAKEN UNDER THE PREVIOUS QUESTION. If a vote *ordered by* adopting a motion for the *Previous Question* is reconsidered before the *Previous Question* is exhausted, the motion to *Reconsider* is undebatable and the motion reconsidered cannot be debated or amended. But if the reconsideration occurs after the *Previous Question* is exhausted, the motion to *Reconsider* and the question to be reconsidered are no longer affected by the *Previous Question*.

EFFECT ON APPEALS. An appeal is undebatable if it is made after the *Previous Question* has been moved or ordered and before the order is exhausted.

EFFECT ON SUBSEQUENT MOTIONS GENERALLY. The general rules as to the effect of an unexhausted order for the *Previous Question* on subsequent motions that would normally be debatable or amendable are as follows:

- While one or more *motions on which the Previous Question has been ordered remain pending*, the order also applies to any other motions that may take precedence over these pending questions. (The rules stated in the two preceding paragraphs—for motions to reconsider a vote taken under the *Previous Question* and for appeals—are applications of this principle.)

- But if a *question of privilege* is raised and is admitted for immediate consideration (see **19**), or if a special order set for a particular hour intervenes, these questions are independent of an unexhausted order for the *Previous Question* applying to business that they interrupt.

Form and Example

The forms used in making this motion include: "I move the previous question" (to apply only to the immediately pending question); "I move [or "demand," or "call for"] the previous question on the motion to commit and its amendment"; "I demand the previous question on all pending questions"; and so on. Calls of "Question!" by members from their seats are not motions for the *Previous Question* and are disorderly if another member is speaking or seeking recognition.

In stating the question on this undebatable, nonamendable motion, the chair does not pause or ask, "Are you ready for the question?" but *puts* the question for a rising vote on the motion for the *Previous Question* immediately as shown below. Similarly, in announcing an affirmative result, he at once states the question on the motion that is then immediately pending.

Assume that a series of several debatable and amendable motions is pending.

MEMBER A (obtaining the floor): I move the previous question on [specifying the motions, unless he desires that only the immediately pending question be affected]. (Second.)

CHAIR: The previous question is moved on [naming the motions, unless none was specified]. As many as are in favor of ordering the

1 previous question on [repeating the motions], rise. . . . Be seated.
Those opposed, rise. . . . Be seated. There are two thirds in the affirmative and the previous question is ordered on [naming again the
motions to which the order applies]. The question is now on the
5 adoption of the motion to . . . [stating in full the immediately pending question]. As many as are in favor [and so on, putting to vote in
proper sequence all motions on which the *Previous Question* has been
ordered].

10   If there are less than two thirds in the affirmative, the
chair announces the result of the vote on the motion for the
Previous Question as follows:

  CHAIR: There are less than two thirds in the affirmative and the
15 motion for the previous question is lost. The question is now on . . .
[stating the question on the immediately pending motion. Debate may
now resume. The chair does not say, "Are you ready for the question?"
here, since the assembly has just shown that it is not ready.]

20   The following example shows the forms used in handling alternative motions for the *Previous Question* that
specify different numbers of pending questions in a series,
as described under Standard Characteristic 6.
    Assume that a resolution, an amendment to the resolu-
25 tion, and a motion to *Commit* are pending (in which case the
motion to *Commit* is the immediately pending question).

  MEMBER X (obtaining the floor): I move the previous question.
(Second. In this case only the motion to *Commit* is affected.)
30 CHAIR: The previous question is demanded. As many as are in
favor of ordering . . .
  MEMBER Y (quickly rising and interrupting the chair): Mr. President.
  CHAIR: For what purpose does the member rise?
  MEMBER Y: I move the previous question on all pending questions.
35 (Second.)

CHAIR: The previous question is also moved on all pending ques-   *1*
tions. The question is now on the demand for the previous question
on all pending questions. As many . . .

MEMBER Z (quickly rising): Mr. President.

CHAIR: For what purpose does the member rise?   *5*

MEMBER Z: I move the previous question on the motion to commit and on the amendment to the resolution. (Second.)

CHAIR: The previous question is also demanded on the motion to
commit and on the amendment to the resolution. The question is first,
however, on the motion to order the previous question on all pending   *10*
questions. As many as are in favor of ordering . . . [and so on. Alternative motions for the *Previous Question* are voted on in order beginning with the one that would apply to the largest number of pending
questions. Therefore, after admitting Member Y's motion, the chair
starts to put the question on it first; but after admitting Member Z's,   *15*
he returns to taking a vote on Member Y's. If one of these motions for
the *Previous Question* is adopted, any remaining ones are ignored.]

If a member wishes to make a higher-ranking motion or
to move a reconsideration while a motion for the *Previous*   *20*
Question is pending or after the *Previous Question* has been
ordered, he seeks limited recognition by rising and interrupting the chair just as in the example above.

§17. LAY ON THE TABLE   *25*
(To interrupt the pending business so as to permit
doing something else immediately)

The motion to *Lay on the Table* enables the assembly to
lay the pending question aside temporarily *when something*   *30*
else of immediate urgency has arisen, in such a way that:

- there is *no set time* for taking the matter up again;
- but (until the expiration of time limits explained on p.
  206) its consideration *can be resumed at the will of a*   *35*

majority and in preference to any new questions that
may then be competing with it for consideration.

This motion is commonly misused in ordinary assem-
blies—in place of the motion to *Postpone Indefinitely* (**11**), to
Postpone to a Certain Time (**14**), or other motions. Particularly in such misuses, it also is known as a motion "to table."
By adopting the motion to *Lay on the Table,* a majority has
the power to halt consideration of a question immediately
without debate. Such action violates the rights of the minority and individual members if it is for any other purpose than
the one stated in the first sentence of this section. In ordinary
assemblies, the motion to *Lay on the Table* is out of order if the
evident intent is to kill or avoid dealing with a measure. If a
time for resuming consideration is specified in making the
motion, it can be admitted only as a motion to *Postpone* (**14**),
in which case it is debatable (see also pp. 207–209).

Standard Descriptive Characteristics

The subsidiary motion to *Lay on the Table:*

1. Takes precedence over all subsidiary motions, and over
   any incidental motions that are pending when it is
   made. It yields to all privileged motions, and to motions
   that are incidental to itself.
2. Can be applied to main motions, with any other subsidiary motions that may be pending; can be thus applied to *orders of the day* (**14, 41**) or *questions of
   privilege* (**19**) while they are actually pending as main
   motions, and such an application is independent of, and
   does not carry to the table, any other matter that they
   may have interrupted; can be separately applied to debatable appeals that do not adhere (pp. 112–13) to the
   main question (or to nonadhering points of order re-

ferred by the chair to the judgment of the assembly that
are debatable when so referred), and this application has
no effect on the status of any other questions that may
be pending; can be applied to adhering appeals—
whether debatable or undebatable—only by laying the
main question on the table, in which case the appeal
and all other adhering motions go to the table also; and
can be applied to an immediately pending motion to
Reconsider (**37**), whenever *Lay on the Table* would be
applicable if the motion to be reconsidered were immediately pending, and in such a case, it carries to the table
also the motion to be reconsidered, or the series of
questions adhering to the latter motion. It cannot be
applied to an undebatable appeal that does not adhere
to the main question; and it cannot be applied to any
subsidiary motion except in connection with application
to the main question. No motion or motions can be laid
on the table apart from motions which adhere to them,
or to which they adhere; and if any one of them is laid
on the table, all such motions go to the table together.
The motion to *Lay on the Table* can be made while an
order limiting debate or an order for the *Previous Ques-*
tion is in force (see also below). No subsidiary motion
can be applied to the motion to *Lay on the Table*.

    Since the motion to *Lay on the Table* can be applied
only to a question that is actually *pending,* a class or
group of main questions such as orders of the day, unfinished business, or committee reports *cannot be laid*
on the table as a unit. (An item of business can be
reached in such a case, however, by methods that are explained on pp. 207–8, 351–52.)

3. Is out of order when another has the floor.
4. Must be seconded.
5. Is not debatable. It is proper for, and the chair can ask, the
maker of this motion to state his reason first, however, as:

1

"Our speaker must catch an early flight," or "Laying this
question aside temporarily will ensure adequate time to
consider the next item of business, which must be decided
5   at this meeting." (The urgency and the legitimate intent
of the motion can thus be established; but mentioning its
purpose imposes no requirement as to when or whether
the assembly will take the question from the table. An essential feature of this motion is that it cannot be qualified
10   in any way and that, so long as the question remains on
the table, the decision as to when—or if—it will be taken
up is left open. For the limitations on the length of time
that a question can lie on the table, see p. 206.)

6. Is not amendable.
15   7. Requires a majority vote.
8. A vote adopting the motion to *Lay on the Table* cannot be
reconsidered because it is easier and more direct to move
to take the question from the table (see below). A negative vote on this motion can be reconsidered only until
20   such time as it can be renewed (as explained on pp.
205–206) because either (a) progress in business or debate has been sufficient to make it essentially a new question, or (b) something urgent has arisen that was not
known when the assembly rejected this motion.

25

Further Rules and Explanation

LAYING THE PENDING QUESTIONS ON THE
TABLE AFTER DEBATE HAS BEEN CLOSED.   If de-
30   bate has been closed by ordering the *Previous Question* or
by the expiration of the time to which debate was limited,
then up until the moment of taking the last vote under the
order, the questions still before the assembly can be laid on
the table. Thus, while a resolution and an amendment are
35   pending, if the *Previous Question* is ordered on both mo-

tions, it is in order to lay the resolution on the table, carry- *1*
ing with it the adhering amendment. If the amendment had
already been voted on, it would likewise have been in order
to lay the resolution on the table.

5

TAKING A QUESTION FROM THE TABLE.   Rules
affecting the motion to *Lay on the Table* are closely related to
the motion to *Take from the Table* (**34**). After a question has
been laid on the table, it can be taken from the table by a majority vote as soon as the interrupting business is disposed of   *10*
and whenever no question is pending, provided that business
of the same class as the question on the table, unfinished
business, general orders, or new business is in order.

Any member can move to take a question from the table
in a *regular* meeting or in a meeting that is an adjournment   *15*
(**9**) of a regular meeting. A question can be taken from the
table at a *special* meeting only if it has been laid on the table
at that meeting or if previous notice of such intention has
been stated in the call of the meeting. When a question is
taken from the table, everything is in the same condition,   *20*
so far as possible, as it was when laid on the table, except
that if the motion is not taken up until the next session, the
effect of an order limiting or extending the limits of debate
or the *Previous Question* is exhausted (pp. 187–88,
196–97).   *25*

RENEWAL OF THE MOTION TO LAY ON THE
TABLE; LAYING A QUESTION ON THE TABLE
AGAIN.   A motion to *Lay on the Table* that has been
voted down can be renewed, or a question that has been   *30*
taken from the table can be laid on the table again, subject
to the following condition in either case: Another motion
made the same day to lay the same question on the table is
in order only after material progress in business or debate
has been made, or when an unforeseen urgent matter re-   *35*
quires immediate attention. (This rule is a consequence of

1 the fact that the rejection of a motion to *Lay on the Table* or
the taking of a question from the table means that the assembly wishes to consider the matter at that time.) Motions
to *Recess* (**20**) or to *Adjourn* (**21**) that have been made and
5 lost do not justify a new motion to lay the same question on
the table, but the renewal might be justified after a vote on
an important amendment or on a motion to *Commit*.

PARTICULAR EFFECTS OF THE MOTION.   The
10 effects of the adoption of a motion to *Lay on the Table* are
as follows:

It places on the table—that is, in the care of the secretary—the pending question and everything adhering to it.
Thus, if a resolution with a proposed amendment and a mo-
15 tion to *Commit* are pending and the resolution is laid on the
table, all of these questions go to the table at the same time
and, if taken from the table, all will return together. But a
proposed amendment to anything previously adopted—existing bylaws, for example—is a main motion and when laid
20 on the table does not carry with it what it proposes to amend.

In cases in which the next regular business session will
be held before a quarterly time interval has elapsed (see p.
88), a question laid on the table remains there until taken
from the table or until the close of the next regular session;
25 if not taken up by that time, the question dies. In cases in
which the lapse of time between regular business sessions is
greater than a quarterly time interval (see p. 88), a question
laid on the table can remain there only until the end of the
current session; and unless taken from the table earlier, the
30 matter dies with the close of that session.

Since a motion that has been laid on the table is still
within the control of the assembly (pp. 329–30), no other motion on the same subject is in order that would either conflict
with, or present substantially the same question as, the mo-
35 tion that is lying on the table. To consider another motion on

the same subject, it is necessary first to take the question from
the table and then to move the new proposal as a substitute,
or to make whatever other motion is appropriate to the case.

Laying a question on the table with the idea of attending to something else does not suspend any rules or set
aside an order of business that may interfere with doing the
thing desired at the time. Taking up the desired business
may require an additional motion after the question has
been laid on the table (see *Suspend the Rules,* **25**).

MISUSES OF THE MOTION.   As stated at the beginning of this section, the motion to *Lay on the Table* is
subject to a number of incorrect uses that should be
avoided.*

It is out of order to move to lay a pending question on
the table if there is evidently no other matter urgently requiring immediate attention. However, if members who
command a majority wish to bring up a measure out of its
order but lack the two thirds required to suspend the rules
to do so, they may lay each intervening matter on the table
in succession, until the desired matter is reached. This is
proper because their evident object is not to suppress without debate the items laid on the table, but instead to advance consideration of something they consider more

---

*Some misuses of the motion to *Lay on the Table* probably arise from
a misunderstanding of the practice of the United States House of Representatives, where this motion has gradually become converted to a special
purpose that is not applicable in ordinary assemblies. The press of legisla-
tion in the House is so great that only a fraction of the bills introduced each
year can be considered. With this volume of work under the two-party system in such a large body, the majority must be given power to suppress a
measure without debate, and the agenda must be tightly regulated. The
House rules therefore do not allow a question to be taken from the table
without first suspending the rules by a two-thirds vote. Consequently, when
a matter is laid on the table in the House it is virtually killed.

urgent (see pp. 351–52). At a special meeting, it is dilatory (**39**) and out of order to move to lay on the table the matter for which the meeting has been called.

The motion to *Lay on the Table* is often incorrectly used and wrongly admitted as in order with the intention of either killing an embarrassing question without a direct vote, or of suppressing a question without debate. The first of these two uses is unsafe if there is any contest on the issue; the second is in violation of a basic principle of general parliamentary law that only a two-thirds vote can rightfully suppress a main question without allowing free debate.

If the majority were to lay a question on the table, erroneously supposing that it thereby becomes dead, some of those who voted with the majority might leave before the time of final adjournment and the minority might all stay. The real minority might thus become a temporary majority, take the question from the table, and act upon it in the absence of many interested parties. They also might take the question from the table at the next session in cases where that session is held at least within the next quarterly time interval (see p. 88).

CORRECT PROCEDURES IN LIEU OF MISUSES.

In the situations that give rise to improper use of the motion to *Lay on the Table,* the correct procedures are as follows:

If it is desired to dispose of a question without a direct vote, the suitable method is to use the motion to *Postpone Indefinitely.* If it is desired to do this without further debate, the motion to *Postpone Indefinitely* can be followed immediately by a motion for the *Previous Question.* A motion that has been indefinitely postponed is killed for the remainder of the session, but is no more difficult to renew at a later session than any other motion that is subject to such renewal (p. 326).

If it is believed that any discussion of a particular orig- *1*
inal main motion might do harm, the proper course is to
raise *Objection to the Consideration of the Question* (**26**)
before its consideration has begun. For cases where *Post-*
pone (**14**) is the proper motion in lieu of an incorrectly *5*
used motion to *Lay on the Table,* see "Form and Example," below.

Form and Example

10

Forms used in making this motion are: "I move to lay
the question on the table"; or "I move that the resolution
be laid on the table." (It is preferable to avoid moving "to
table" a motion, or "that the motion be tabled.")*

This motion, as explained earlier, is undebatable and *15*
cannot be qualified in any way. In moving it, a member can
mention its intended purpose or name a time at which he
plans to move that the question be taken from the table,
but he cannot move to lay a question "on the table until
after the completion of . . . ," or, "on the table until 2 *20*
P.M." Rather than always ruling such a motion out of order,
however, the chair should properly treat it as a motion "to
postpone the question until . . . "; that is, he should state
the motion as admitted in that form unless the motion to
Postpone is out of order at the time. *25*

Since the motion to *Lay on the Table* can be neither debated nor amended, the chair puts it to a vote immediately
after stating the question on it, as follows:

---

*In the United States, the word *table* used as a verb often suggests the
improper application of the motion to *Lay on the Table,* as explained on
207–08. In British usage, on the other hand, the same expression has an entirely different meaning and refers not to a subsidiary motion but to the introduction of a proposed resolution or document to be placed among items
of business waiting to be considered.

CHAIR: It is moved and seconded to lay the pending question(s) on the table. As many as are in favor of laying the pending question(s) on the table, say *aye.* . . . Those opposed, say *no.* . . . [and so on, as in the examples already given for motions requiring a majority vote for adoption].

For certain limited purposes not involving debate or amendment—such as to make a privileged motion or a motion to *Reconsider* (**37**)—a member can claim the floor while the motion to *Lay on the Table* is pending. To do so, the member rises and interrupts the chair by calling out "Mr. President!"—immediately *after* the chair has said, "It is moved and seconded to lay the pending question(s) on the table," and *before* the vote is taken. The chair grants the member limited recognition by answering, "For what purpose does the member rise?"

After a question has been laid on the table, if further action by the assembly is needed to reach the desired business, the chair immediately says, for example, "Is there a motion to suspend the rules that interfere with hearing the speaker at this time?" (Or, "The chair will entertain a motion to . . . ")

PRIVILEGED MOTIONS

*See 6, pages 64ff., for a list of these motions
and a description of their characteristics as a class.*

§18. CALL FOR THE ORDERS OF THE DAY
(To demand to take up the proper business in order)

A *Call for the Orders of the Day* is a privileged motion by which a member can require the assembly to conform to its agenda, program, or order of business, or to take up a general or special order that is due to come up at the time (**14, 41**), unless two thirds of those voting wish to do otherwise.

Taking up business in the prescribed order is of substantial importance, especially in conventions—which must follow a closely regulated schedule with much of the underlying work taking place off the convention floor in conferences and committees. For business to receive proper consideration, officers, committee members, and the delegates who are principally involved in major questions must be able to know the approximate times at which subjects will come up.

If the presiding officer consistently performs his duty of announcing the business to come before the assembly in its

1 proper order, there will be no occasion for calling for the orders of the day. But the chair may fail to notice that the time assigned for a general or special order has arrived, or he may skip an item in the order of business by mistake, or
5 delay announcing a special order set for that time because he thinks the assembly is so interested in the pending question that it does not yet wish to take up the special order. In these cases, any member has the right to call for the orders of the day. The call must be simply "for the orders of
10 the day" and not for a specified one, as this motion is only a demand that the proper schedule of business—whatever it is—be followed. In other words, while the member may remind the chair of what is scheduled, he cannot by this call obtain consideration of an order of the day that does not
15 have first priority for consideration at that time.

Standard Descriptive Characteristics

The privileged *Call for the Orders of the Day:*

20
1. Takes precedence over all motions except (a) other privileged motions and (b) a motion to *Suspend the Rules* (**25**) that relates to the priority of business—although it can interrupt a *pending* question only if the neglect of a
25 special order is involved (see below). It yields to all other privileged motions, and to any applicable incidental motions that may arise and that must be disposed of before it is disposed of. Except when a special order must be taken up, this call also yields to a motion to *Re-*
30 *consider* or to the calling up (**37**) of a motion to *Reconsider* that has been made previously.
2. Is not applied *to* any motion, but is applicable as follows: (a) when the agenda, program, or order of business is being varied from; (b) when a general order that
35 is in order at the time is not being taken up; or (c) when

the time for considering a special order has arrived or *1*
passed and it is not being taken up. (For a statement of
the precise times at which a *Call for the Orders of the
Day* is in order, see below.) No subsidiary motion can
be applied to this call. *5*

3. If in order at the time, is in order when another has the
floor, even if it interrupts a person speaking.

4. Does not require a second.

5. Is not debatable.

6. Is not amendable. *10*

7. Upon a call by a single member the orders of the day
must be enforced, except that a two-thirds vote can set
them aside. (That is, the orders of the day can be set
aside: either by a vote of two thirds in the negative on a
question put by the chair as to the assembly's desire to *15*
proceed to the orders of the day; or by a vote of two
thirds in the affirmative on a motion by a member to extend the time for considering the pending question, or
to suspend the rules and take up the desired question;
see below.) *20*

8. Cannot be reconsidered.

Further Rules and Explanation

TIMES WHEN A CALL FOR THE ORDERS OF THE *25*
DAY IS IN ORDER. The particular conditions under
which a *Call for the Orders of the Day* is in order are as
follows:

- Referring to cases (a) and (b) under Standard Charac- *30*
teristic 2, which do not involve the neglect of a special
order: As soon as it is evident that the agenda, program,
or order of business is being varied from, or that the
time for the consideration of a postponed motion has
arrived or passed, a *Call for the Orders of the Day* is in *35*

1   order whenever no question is pending. In such a case
where no special order is involved, if a member starts to
make a motion departing from the correct order of
business, or if the chair announces a wrong item, the
5   call must be made before any motion is stated by the
chair; otherwise, it cannot be made until after the motion has been disposed of.

- Referring, on the other hand, to case (c) under Standard Characteristic 2: If the chair does not immediately
10   announce a special order when the time set for its consideration has arrived, a *Call for the Orders of the Day*
can be made at once—even while another question is
pending, unless the pending question is itself a special
order that was made before the one set for the present
15   time was made (see **14, 41**). From the time when a particular special order becomes the proper order of business and until it is announced, a *Call for the Orders of
the Day* is in order.

20   A *Call for the Orders of the Day* cannot be made in a
committee of the whole (see **52**).

STATUS OF AN ORDER OF THE DAY AS A MAIN
MOTION.   In contrast to the privileged *Call for the Or-*
25   *ders of the Day,* an order of the day which such a call may
bring before the assembly is itself invariably a main motion,
and when it is announced and pending, it is debatable and
amendable, and all of the other rules governing main motions apply to it. The orders of the day as a whole cannot be
30   laid on the table or postponed, but an individual order of
the day when actually pending can be so disposed of. As
soon as the orders of the day that have interrupted business
that was pending are completed, the interrupted business is
taken up again at the point at which it was discontinued.

SETTING ASIDE THE ORDERS OF THE DAY.
When the orders of the day are called for, the chair can, and
ordinarily should, immediately announce as the newly
pending business the subject that is then in order. But
sometimes the chair or a member may sense that the assembly would prefer to continue consideration of the
presently pending question or take up another matter first.
In such cases, the assembly by a two-thirds vote can set
aside the orders of the day, as follows:

a) *At the initiative of the chair:* Instead of announcing the
orders of the day when they are called for, the chair can
put the question on proceeding to them: "The orders of
the day are called for. The orders of the day are [identi-
fying the business that is in order]. The question is: Will
the assembly proceed to the orders of the day? As many
as are in favor of proceeding to the orders of the day
. . . [and so on, taking a rising vote]." Since to refuse
to proceed to the orders of the day is an interference
with the order of business similar to suspending the
rules, two thirds in the *negative* are required to vote
down this question and refuse to take up the orders of
the day. Once the assembly has refused to proceed to
the orders of the day, they cannot be called for again
until the pending business is disposed of.

b) *At the initiative of a member:* When the orders of the
day are called for or announced, a member can move
(depending on the case) "that the time for considering
the pending question be extended" a certain number of
minutes, or "that the rules be suspended and" the desired question be taken up (see **25**). These motions require a two-thirds vote in the *affirmative* for their
adoption, since they change the order of business,
agenda, or program.

1   **Form and Example**

The form of the motion is as follows: To call for the orders of the day, a member rises and, addressing the chair
5   without waiting for recognition, says, "Mr. President, I call
for the orders of the day," or "Madam President, I demand
the regular order." The member can, if necessary, remind
the chair of the matter set for that time.

Assume that at yesterday's meeting of a convention, a
10 resolution was postponed and made a special order for
11:30 A.M. today. That time has now arrived, but a member
is speaking on a pending question.

MEMBER A (rising and addressing the chair): Madam President, I
15 call for the orders of the day.

CHAIR: The orders of the day are called for. Yesterday the convention postponed the resolution relating to tax reform to 11:30 A.M.
today, and made it a special order. It is now 11:30. The question is on
the resolution, "*Resolved,* That . . . "
20

After consideration of the resolution is completed, the
former business is resumed where it was left off:

CHAIR: When the orders of the day were called for, the convention
25 was considering the resolution "*Resolved,* That . . ." Mr. Henley had
the floor at that time. The chair recognizes Mr. Henley.

§19. RAISE A QUESTION OF PRIVILEGE

30   To *Raise a Question of Privilege* is a device that permits
a *request or main motion relating to the rights and privileges
of the assembly or any of its members* to be brought up for
possible immediate consideration because of its urgency,
while business is pending and the request or motion would

otherwise be out of order. (For types and examples of ques-   *1*
tions of privilege,* see pp. 219–222.)

This device operates as follows: A member rises and addresses the chair saying that he "rises to a question of privilege . . . " (as explained on p. 220), and the chair   *5*
immediately directs the member to state his question of privilege; the chair must then rule (subject to appeal, **24**)
whether the request or motion is in fact a question of privilege and, if so, whether it is urgent enough to interrupt the
pending business.   *10*

It is important to understand the distinction between the
device *Raise a Question of Privilege* and the question of privilege itself. The point to be decided in connection with the
former is whether a certain question shall be admitted for
consideration with the status and priority of the latter. The   *15*
"raising" of a question of privilege is governed by rules appropriate to the device's high rank in the order of precedence
of motions. When a question of privilege is taken up after it
has been raised and has been admitted by the chair, however,
depending on the form in which it was introduced, it is han-   *20*
dled as a *request* (**33**), or it is treated as a main motion and is
debatable and amendable and can have any subsidiary motion applied to it—regardless of whether it interrupted, or
awaited the disposal of, the pending business. Questions of
privilege can also be introduced while no motion is pending,   *25*
either as requests or by being moved and seconded just as any
other main motion; in that case, the device of "raising" a
question of privilege does not enter in.

Questions of privilege or motions growing out of them
should not be confused with "privileged motions" (or   *30*

---

*The term *question of privilege* is applied to any request or motion relating to the rights and privileges of the assembly or its members, whether
or not it is introduced by means of the device *Raise a Question of Privilege*.

"privileged questions"). The latter comprise the five high-est-ranking motions in the order of precedence, among which *Raise a Question of Privilege* is assigned a position.

The eight characteristics below apply only to the device of *raising* a question of privilege; that is, to a member's obtaining recognition to state his urgent motion or request while business is pending, and to the chair's ruling on the question's admissibility as noted above (and described on p. 220).

Standard Descriptive Characteristics

The privileged device *Raise a Question of Privilege:*

1. Takes precedence over all other motions except the three higher-ranking privileged motions to *Recess,* to *Adjourn,* and to *Fix the Time to Which to Adjourn.* It yields to these three privileged motions, and to any applicable incidental motions that may arise and that *must* be disposed of before it is disposed of.

2. Cannot be applied to any other motion, and no subsidiary motion can be applied to it.

3. Is in order when another has the floor if warranted by the urgency of the situation. (In such cases, the raising of a question of privilege is in order after another has been assigned the floor and before he has begun to speak; it should not interrupt a member who is actually speaking unless the object of the question of privilege would otherwise be defeated—as it would be, however, in each of the two examples at the end of this section, pages 221–22. The raising of a question of privilege cannot interrupt voting or verifying a vote.)

4. Does not require a second, as relates to *raising* the question of privilege; that is, no second is required at any step in the process unless (after the chair has directed the member to state his question of privilege) the

member states it in the form of a motion; such a motion *1*
must be seconded.

5. Is not debatable; that is, there can be no debate as to
   admitting the request or motion that has been raised as
   a question of privilege. (But a motion that is pending *5*
   after having been admitted as a question of privilege is
   debatable.)

6. Is not amendable; that is, the motion to *Amend* is not
   applicable to the process of raising a question of privilege. (But a motion that is pending after having been *10*
   admitted as a question of privilege can be amended.)

7. Is ruled upon by the chair. No vote on the question's
   admissibility is taken unless the chair's ruling is appealed
   (**24**).

8. The chair's ruling on whether to admit the request or *15*
   motion that has been raised as a question of privilege
   cannot be reconsidered.

Further Rules and Explanation

20

TYPES OF QUESTIONS OF PRIVILEGE.
Questions of privilege are of two types: (1) those relating
to the privileges of the assembly as a whole; and (2) questions of personal privilege. If the two come into competition, the former take precedence over the latter. *25*
Questions of the privileges of the assembly may relate to
its organization or existence; to the comfort of its members with respect to heating, ventilation, lighting, and
noise or other disturbance; to the conduct of its officers
and employees, or of visitors; to the punishment of its *30*
members; or to the accuracy of published reports of its
proceedings; etc. A motion to go into executive session
(**9**) is a question of the privileges of the assembly. Questions of personal privilege—which seldom arise in ordinary societies and even more rarely justify interruption of *35*

1 pending business—may relate, for example, to an incorrect record of a member's participation in a meeting contained in minutes approved in his absence, or to charges circulated against a member's character.

5   STEPS IN RAISING AND DISPOSING OF A QUESTION OF PRIVILEGE.   In raising a question of privilege, a member rises, addresses the chair without waiting for recognition, and says, "I rise to a question of privilege
10 affecting the assembly," or ". . . to a question of personal privilege."

   The chair, even if he has assigned the floor to another person, directs the member to state his question of privilege. Depending on the case, the member then either (a)
15 describes the situation briefly and asks that it be remedied, or (b) if he believes that the matter will require formal action by the assembly, makes a motion covering his question of privilege, and another member seconds it. The chair at his discretion can ask a member to put into the
20 form of a motion a question of privilege that the member has stated as a request. Unless the point is simple enough to be promptly adjusted (as in the first example, below) or unless it is in the form of a motion and is not seconded, the chair rules whether the question is a question of priv-
25 ilege, and, if so, whether it is of sufficient urgency to warrant interruption of the existing parliamentary situation. From this ruling an undebatable appeal can be taken.

   If the motion made as a question of privilege is seconded, and if the chair admits it as such and decides that it
30 should be entertained immediately, he states the question on it and proceeds as with any other main motion. When the question of privilege has been disposed of, business is resumed at exactly the point at which it was interrupted. If a member had the floor when the question of privilege was
35 raised, the chair assigns him the floor again.

Form and Example

1

The forms used in raising a question of privilege include: "I rise to a question of privilege affecting [or "relating to"] the assembly" (or "to a question of the privileges *5* of the assembly"), and "I rise to a question of personal privilege." The preceding forms should always be adhered to in cases where it is necessary to interrupt a person speaking. When a question of the privileges of the assembly is raised in a small meeting without interrupting a speaker, a varia- *10* tion such as "A question of privilege, Mr. President!" is permissible.

The following is an example of a question relating to the privileges of the assembly that can be stated as an informal request and that can be routinely adjusted by the chair: *15*

Assume that, while an important speech is in progress at a meeting in a large hall with upper windows, workmen begin to operate jackhammers in an alley beside the building. Member A rises and interrupts, addressing the chair:

20

MEMBER A: Mr. President, I rise to a question of privilege affecting the assembly.

CHAIR: The gentleman will state his question.

MEMBER A: Mr. President, I don't think we're going to be able to hear unless some of the windows are closed. *25*

CHAIR: Will one of the ushers ask the building engineer to have the windows closed on the left side. May we have the sound turned up a little until the windows are closed.

The next example illustrates a question of the privileges *30* of the assembly requiring a formal motion which interrupts pending business. In an ordinary society these occasions are rare, but in a convention or large assembly a situation of unforeseen complications may cause such a motion to become appropriate. *35*

1   Assume that, to hear a prominent speaker, an association has opened one of its meetings to the public. Because
of the speaker's commitments at a later hour, his address
was given first, preceding the business meeting—which was
5 expected to be brief and routine. But Member X has sur-
prised this meeting by introducing a resolution dealing with
a delicate matter of obvious importance that may call for
prompt action by the association.

    Member Y, sensing that consideration of this question
10 should be kept within the organization, interrupts Member
X's speech on the pending resolution by rising "to a question of privilege relating to the assembly." As directed by
the president, he states the question of privilege:

15   MEMBER Y: Mr. President, I believe this is a question we should
consider in a closed meeting. With apologies to our guests, I move that
the open portion of this meeting be declared ended and that our guests
be excused. (Second.)

    CHAIR: The chair rules that the question is one of privilege to be
20 entertained immediately. It is moved and seconded that [stating the
question on the motion to go into executive session].

    Debate or amendment follows, if needed; then the ques-
tion is put to a vote. After announcing the result, the president
25 expresses appreciation to guests. As soon as they have left, he
states the resolution that was interrupted by the question of
privilege, and recognizes Member X, who had the floor.

§20. RECESS

30   A *recess* is a short intermission in the assembly's proceedings, commonly of only a few minutes, which does not
close the meeting and after which business will immediately
be resumed at exactly the point where it was interrupted.*

---

*For an explanation of the distinction between *recess* and *adjournment*,
see **8**, esp. p. 83.

A recess may be taken, for example, to count ballots, to   *1*
secure information, or to allow for informal consultation.

The *privileged* motion to *Recess* (or to *Take a Recess*) is
a motion that a recess begin *immediately,* made *while another question is pending.*   *5*

A motion to recess that is made *when no question is
pending* (whether the recess is to begin immediately or at a
future time) is a *main motion,* and the eight characteristics
given below do not apply to it. Consequently, a motion to
recess is privileged only when another question is pending;   *10*
and a motion to take a recess at a future time is in order
only when no question is pending.

The eight characteristics below apply only to the *privileged* motion to *Recess.*

15

Standard Descriptive Characteristics

The privileged motion to *Recess:*

20

1. Takes precedence over all subsidiary and incidental motions, and over all privileged motions except those to
   Adjourn and to *Fix the Time to Which to Adjourn.* It
   yields to the *privileged* motions to *Adjourn* and to *Fix
   the Time to Which to Adjourn* (but in the cases where   *25*
   motions to adjourn or to set a time for meeting again
   are "not privileged"—that is, are main motions—it
   takes precedence over these motions; see **21** and **22**). It
   also yields to any applicable incidental motions that may
   arise and that *must* be disposed of before the motion to   *30*
   Recess is voted on.
2. Is not applied *to* any motion. Motions to *Amend* can be
   applied to it. The *Previous Question* can also be applied
   to it to prevent amendments being moved, although
   this situation rarely arises in ordinary societies. No other   *35*
   subsidiary motion can be applied to it.

3. Is out of order when another has the floor.
4. Must be seconded.
5. Is not debatable.
6. Is amendable as to the length of the recess; any such amendment is undebatable.
7. Requires a majority vote.
8. Cannot be reconsidered.

Further Rules and Explanation

DECLARING A RECESS WHEN IT HAS BEEN PROVIDED FOR IN THE AGENDA OR PROGRAM. If a recess is provided for in the adopted agenda or program of a convention or other meeting, the chair, without further action by the assembly, announces the fact and simply declares the assembly in recess when the specified time arrives. If the chair does not announce the recess at the scheduled time, a member can call for the orders of the day (**18**), thereby demanding that the recess be declared.

POSTPONING THE TIME FOR TAKING A PRESCHEDULED RECESS. The time for taking a prescheduled recess can be postponed by a two-thirds vote if, when that time arrives, the assembly does not wish to recess. In the latter event, the taking of the recess is treated just as any other order of the day that is due to be taken up, and it can be set aside by any of the procedures described on page 215.

Form and Example

Forms in which this motion may be made are: "I move that the meeting recess [or "take a recess"] until 2 P.M."; "I move to recess for ten minutes"; or "I move to recess until called to order by the chair."

If such a motion is adopted, the chair announces the result as follows:

CHAIR: The ayes have it and the meeting stands recessed [or, "in recess"] for fifteen minutes [rapping once with the gavel, if desired].

At the end of the specified time, the chair gains the attention of the assembly and begins:

CHAIR: The convention [or "meeting"] will come to order. The time of recess has expired. The question is on the resolution . . . [Or, if the recess was taken following the vote on a question or an election but before the result had been announced, the first business would be the announcement of the vote.]

§21. ADJOURN

To *adjourn* means to close the meeting (8). A motion to adjourn may be a privileged or a main motion depending on a number of conditions. The motion to adjourn that commonly occurs in meetings of ordinary societies is the privileged motion. The adoption of any motion to adjourn closes the meeting immediately unless the motion specifies a later time for adjourning (but if it does specify such a time it is not a privileged motion).

The *privileged* motion to *Adjourn* (which is always moved in an unqualified form with no mention of a time either for adjourning or for meeting again) is a motion to close the meeting immediately, made under conditions where some other provision for another meeting exists (so that the adjournment will not have the effect of dissolving the assembly), and where no time for adjourning the present meeting has already been set. In such a case, regardless of whether business is pending, a majority should not be forced to continue in session substantially longer than it de-

1 sires, and even if no business is pending, a decision as to
whether to close the meeting should not be allowed to consume time. For this reason, when there is provision for another meeting and no time for adjourning is already set, an
5 unqualified motion "to adjourn" is afforded sufficiently
high privilege to interrupt the pending question and, on
adoption, to close the meeting before the pending business
is disposed of. And for the same reason, such a motion has
the unique characteristic that, *even if it is made while no*
10 *question is pending,* it is not debatable or amendable and it
remains subject to all of the rules governing the privileged
motion to *Adjourn* (except those that relate to making the
motion while business is pending; see *Standard Descriptive
Characteristics*). Under the conditions just described, a mo-
15 tion to *Adjourn* is therefore said to be "privileged" or to be
"a privileged motion" even when no question is pending.

A motion to adjourn is always a privileged motion *except* in the following cases:

20 1) When the motion is qualified in any way, as in the case
of a motion to adjourn at, or to, a future time.
2) When a time for adjourning is already established, either
because the assembly has adopted a motion or a program setting such a time, or because the order of busi-
25 ness, the bylaws, or other governing rules prescribe it.
3) When the effect of the motion to adjourn, if adopted,
would be to dissolve the assembly with no provision for
another meeting, as is usually the case in a mass meeting or the last meeting of a convention.*
30

Under any of conditions (1) through (3) above, a motion to adjourn is not privileged and is treated just as any

---

*In state or national organizations where subordinate units choose del-
egates each time an annual or biennial convention is held, each convention
is a separate assembly, since it is made up of a different body of delegates.

other main motion. Consequently, a motion to adjourn at *1*
or to a future time is always out of order while business is
pending in any assembly; and any motion to adjourn at all
is out of order while business is pending under either of
conditions (2) or (3)—which, however, do not commonly *5*
apply to meetings of ordinary societies.

In ordinary societies having bylaws that provide for several regular meetings during the year and having no fixed
hour for adjournment, a motion "to adjourn," when unqualified, is always a privileged motion. In meetings of *10*
these organizations, such a motion to *Adjourn* is in order
regardless of whether business is pending; and even when
business is not pending, this motion is undebatable and is
subject to the rules given below.

The following eight characteristics apply only to the *15*
privileged motion to *Adjourn*.

Standard Descriptive Characteristics

The privileged motion to *Adjourn*: *20*

1. Takes precedence over all motions except the *privileged*
   motion to *Fix the Time to Which to Adjourn;* but it is not
   in order while the assembly is engaged in voting or verifying a vote, or before the result of a vote has been announced by the chair, except that, in the case of a vote *25*
   taken by ballot, a motion to *Adjourn* is in order after the
   ballots have been collected by the tellers and before the
   result has been announced.* It yields to the *privileged*
   motion to *Fix the Time to Which to Adjourn* (but it takes *30*
   precedence over a motion to set a time for meeting again

---

*When much time may be consumed in counting ballots, it is generally better to take a recess, but the assembly can adjourn if it has previously
appointed a time for the next meeting. In any case, the result of the ballot
vote should be announced as soon as business is resumed.

in the cases where such a motion is "not privileged"—
that is, is a main motion; see **22**). It also yields to any applicable incidental motions that may arise and that *must*
be disposed of before the motion to *Adjourn* is voted on;
but an incidental motion that can wait should not be entertained after a motion to *Adjourn* has been made.

2. Is not applied *to* any motion, and no motion can be applied to it.

3. Is out of order when another has the floor.

4. Must be seconded.

5. Is not debatable (see pp. 230–32, however).

6. Is not amendable.

7. Requires a majority vote.

8. Cannot be reconsidered (but see p. 232 regarding its
renewal).

Further Rules and Explanation

EFFECT OF ADJOURNMENT ON PENDING
BUSINESS OR ON AN UNCOMPLETED ORDER OF
BUSINESS.   Except as the assembly may have adopted
rules providing otherwise, the effect of an adjournment on a
pending motion or an uncompleted order of business is as
follows:

a) *When the adjournment does not close the session* (as when
an adjourned meeting [**9**] has been set, or in any meeting of a convention except the last one): Business is immediately resumed at the next meeting at the point
where it left off, except that there may first be brief
opening ceremonies or reading of the minutes (see **41**).

b) *When the adjournment closes the session in an assembly
having its next regular business session within a quarterly
time interval* (see p. 88), *and having no members
whose terms of membership expire before the next regular*

session (for example, in ordinary clubs and societies that hold frequent "regular meetings"): The complete order of business is followed at the next regular session. If a question was pending at the time of adjournment, it is taken up as the first item under unfinished business (or under special orders, if it was a special order)—resuming the question at exactly where it was previously interrupted. Any general or special order that was not reached is also taken up under unfinished business or under special orders, respectively (see **41**).

c) *When the adjournment closes a session in a body that will not have another regular session within a quarterly time interval* (see p. 88), *or closes a session that ends the term of all or some of the members* (as may happen in an elected legislative assembly or in a board): The business that is unfinished at the time of adjournment falls to the ground. It can be introduced at the next session, however, the same as if it had never before been brought up.

ADJOURNMENT OF BODIES WITHOUT REGU- LARLY SCHEDULED MEETINGS.   The adjournment of a mass meeting or the last meeting of a convention dissolves the assembly unless provision has been made whereby it will, or may, be later reconvened. When adjournment would dissolve an assembly, the motion to adjourn is a main motion. A motion to close the session in an assembly that will thereby be dissolved, or will not meet again for a long time unless called into authorized special session under the bylaws or other governing rule, is often referred to as a motion to "adjourn sine die," which means to "adjourn without day" (see also p. 81). If the bylaws of an organization provide for the calling of a special convention after the regular convention session has been held, this assembly should meet as a distinct session with a body of delegates and alternates that must be chosen anew under

1 provisions established in the bylaws. However, program items normally associated with conventions of the organization need not be provided for.

In boards or committees where no provision has been 5 made for future meetings, an adjournment, unless otherwise specified in the motion, is always "to meet at the call of the chair." Consequently, since there usually is no fixed hour for adjournment, the motion to adjourn is nearly always privileged in boards or committees. When a special 10 committee or a committee of the whole has completed the business referred to it, however, it "rises" and reports, which is equivalent to the main motion to adjourn.

PARLIAMENTARY STEPS THAT ARE IN ORDER 15 WHILE THE PRIVILEGED MOTION TO ADJOURN IS PENDING, OR AFTER THE ASSEMBLY HAS VOTED TO ADJOURN.   Although the privileged motion to *Adjourn* is undebatable, the following parliamentary steps are in order while it is pending:

20
  • to inform the assembly of business requiring attention before adjournment;
  • to make important announcements;
  • to *make* (but not to take up*) a motion to reconsider a
25   previous vote;

---

*Because of time limits on moving a reconsideration, a motion to *Reconsider* is allowed to be *made* and recorded (but *not* to be *considered*) while a motion to *Adjourn* is pending, or even after it has been voted to adjourn and before the chair has declared the assembly adjourned. A motion to *Reconsider* that is made at such a time normally must wait to be *called up* at a later meeting, unless it is made before the motion to *Adjourn* to voted on and that motion is withdrawn or voted down. If the reconsideration is moved after it has been voted to adjourn and it appears to require immediate attention, however, the chair should retake the vote on the motion to *Adjourn* (see *unique characteristics* of the motion to *Reconsider,* pp. 304–306).

- to make a motion to *Reconsider and Enter on the Minutes* (pp. 321–24);
- to give notice of a motion to be made at the next meeting (or on the next day, in a session consisting of daily meetings) where the motion requires *previous notice* (see pp. 116–18); and
- to move to set a time for an adjourned meeting (**9, 22**) if there is no meeting scheduled for later within the same session.

Any of the above steps that are desired should be taken care of earlier, if possible; but there may sometimes be no such opportunity, particularly in a convention or a session of several meetings that is following an adopted agenda or program (**41**), or in cases where a meeting of an ordinary society adjourns before completing its regular order of business. If any matters of the types listed above arise after it has been moved to adjourn, the chair should state the facts briefly, or a member who rises and addresses the chair for the purpose should be allowed to do so—or to make the necessary motion or give the desired notice—before the vote is taken on the motion to *Adjourn*. If something requires action before adjournment, the member who moved to adjourn can be requested to withdraw his motion.

Regardless of the type of motion by which it is voted to adjourn, the meeting is not closed until the chair has declared that the meeting "is adjourned" (or "stands adjourned"), and members should not leave their seats until this declaration has been made. After it has been voted to adjourn but before the chair has declared the meeting adjourned, it is still in order to take any of the steps listed in the preceding paragraph, if necessary. In announcing an affirmative vote on a motion to adjourn, the chair should usually pause before declaring the meeting adjourned, saying: "The ayes seem to have it. [Pausing and resuming slowly:]

1 The ayes have it, and the meeting is adjourned." The pause
affords time for members to demand a division (**29**) on the
vote to adjourn, or to take any of the other steps just described. If the chair learns, immediately after declaring the
5 assembly adjourned, that a member seeking the floor for
one of these purposes had risen and addressed the chair before the adjournment was declared, it is his duty to call the
meeting back to order, disregarding his declaration of adjournment—but only long enough for the purpose for
10 which the member legitimately sought the floor at such a
time.

LEGITIMATE RENEWAL OF THE PRIVILEGED
MOTION AND ITS ABUSES.   Since a motion to *Ad-*
15 *journ* may be voted down because a majority wish to hear
one speech or take one vote, this motion must be renewable
as soon as there has been any progress in business or even
material progress in debate. But this privilege of renewal
and the high rank of the motion are sometimes abused to
20 the annoyance of the assembly. The chair should therefore
refuse to entertain a motion to *Adjourn* that is obviously
made for obstructive purposes—for example, when a motion to *Adjourn* has just been voted down and nothing has
taken place since to indicate that the assembly may now
25 wish to close the meeting. If a member who has not properly obtained the floor calls out, "I move to adjourn," such
a call cannot be entertained as a motion except by unanimous consent (see *Dilatory Motions,* **39**).

30   CASES WHERE THE ASSEMBLY CAN ADJOURN
WITHOUT A MOTION.   If an hour for adjourning a
meeting within a convention or other session of more than
one meeting has been prescheduled—either in an agenda or
program or by the adoption of a motion setting a time—no
35 motion to adjourn is necessary when that hour arrives. The

chair simply announces the fact and declares the meeting
adjourned, as described for a recess on page 224. If the assembly does not then wish to adjourn, the matter is handled
as a case of setting aside the orders of the day, as explained
on page 215 (see also p. 359). If such a meeting wishes to
adjourn earlier, it is done by a main motion, which, however, can be adopted by a majority vote (see pp. 226–27).
The rules stated above regarding parliamentary steps that
are in order after it has been voted to adjourn are applicable in this case also.

When it appears that there is no further business in a
meeting of an ordinary local society that normally goes
through a complete order of business (**41**) at each regular
meeting (**9**), the chair, instead of waiting or calling for a
motion to adjourn, can ask, "Is there any further business?" If there is no response, the chair can then say,
"Since there is no further business, the meeting is adjourned."

Form and Example

The following forms may be used for either a privileged
or a main motion: "I move to adjourn," or "I move that the
meeting ["now"] adjourn." Additional forms in order as a
main motion are: "I move that the club now adjourn to
meet at 8 P.M. on April 10," or "I move that the convention
adjourn *sine die* [or "adjourn without day"]."

Assume that while a resolution is pending in a regular
monthly meeting of a local society, a member obtains the
floor and moves to adjourn, and the motion is seconded.
Since this motion is privileged and therefore undebatable,
the chair immediately puts the question.

CHAIR: It is moved and seconded to adjourn. As many as are in
favor, say *aye* [continuing to take the vote as described on p. 44].

1   If the motion is adopted, the chair announces the result and declares the meeting adjourned (first making sure that no member is seeking the floor, as described on pp. 231–32). If the motion is lost, the chair, after announcing
5 the result, immediately restates the resolution that was pending when the motion to *Adjourn* was made.

    After the pending resolution has been disposed of, or if there has been sufficient debate to show that the assembly now wishes to adjourn, a new motion to adjourn is in order.
10 If such a motion is made and seconded and there is no other business, the chair, if he senses a general desire to adjourn, can suggest unanimous consent (pp. 51–53), as follows:

    CHAIR: If there is no objection, the meeting will now adjourn.
15 [Pause.] Since there is no objection, the meeting is adjourned.

    The adjournment may be signaled by a single rap of the gavel, if desired.

20 ## §22. FIX THE TIME TO WHICH TO ADJOURN

    The object of the motion to *Fix the Time to Which to Adjourn* (also referred to as the motion to "fix the time for an adjourned meeting") is to set the time, and sometimes
25 the place, for another meeting to continue business of the session, with no effect on when the present meeting will adjourn.

    A motion to *Fix the Time to Which to Adjourn* is in order only if at the time it is offered there is no meeting
30 scheduled for later within the same session. If there is such a meeting, additional meetings within the same session may be set by a motion either to *Suspend the Rules* (**25**) or to *Amend Something Previously Adopted* (**35**), namely, the previously adopted agenda or program for the session.
35   A motion to fix the time to which to adjourn is privileged only when it is made while a question is pending.

If a motion to fix the time to which to adjourn is made in any assembly when no question is pending, it is in order and is debatable and subject to all of the other rules applicable to main motions. If feasible, any desired motion to fix the time to which to adjourn should be made while no other question is pending. But situations may arise in which immediate establishment of the time for an adjourned meeting is important, yet there is no opportunity to make a main motion. The privileged motion to *Fix the Time to Which to Adjourn* can then be used.

The following eight characteristics apply only to the *privileged* motion to *Fix the Time to Which to Adjourn.*

Standard Descriptive Characteristics

The privileged motion to *Fix the Time to Which to Adjourn:*

1. Takes precedence over all other motions and yields to nothing, except that, while it is pending: (a) certain incidental motions, such as a *Point of Order,* may arise and can be disposed of; and (b) the motion to *Reconsider* can be made, but not considered (see **37**). The privileged motion to *Fix the Time to Which to Adjourn* can be moved even after the assembly has voted to adjourn, provided that the chair has not yet declared the assembly adjourned.
2. Is not applied *to* any motion. Motions to *Amend* can be applied to it. The *Previous Question* can also be moved on it to prevent amendments, although this seldom serves a useful purpose.
3. Is out of order when another has the floor.
4. Must be seconded.
5. Is not debatable.
6. Is amendable as to the date, hour, or place; such amendments are undebatable.

7. Requires a majority vote.

8. Can be reconsidered.

Further Rules and Explanation

PROVISIONS AS TO TIME AND PLACE.   In an organized society, the adjourned meeting scheduled by adoption of this motion (privileged or main) must be set for a time before that of the next regular meeting. When the assembly has no fixed place for its meetings, the motion should include the place as well as the time of the adjourned meeting.

If an assembly holding regularly scheduled business meetings adjourns to meet "at the call of the chair," an adjourned meeting called accordingly is a continuation of the same session; but, if no such meeting is held before the next regular session, the adjournment of the previous session becomes final retrospectively as of the date the last meeting adjourned, and the chair's authority to call an adjourned meeting expires.

EFFECT OF THE MOTION.   Whether introduced as a privileged or a main motion, the effect of this motion is to establish an *adjourned meeting*—that is, another meeting that will be legally a continuation of the meeting at which the motion is adopted and, together with that meeting, will make up one session. Unlike a special meeting, an adjourned meeting does not require notice, although it is desirable to give such notice if feasible. An adjourned meeting should not be confused with a *special meeting,* which is a separate session called, in ordinary societies, as prescribed by the bylaws.

Because of the nature of the situations that give rise to use of the privileged motion to *Fix the Time to Which to Adjourn,* adoption of this motion is often followed by immediate introduction of a motion to *Postpone,* or of the privileged motion to *Adjourn,* depending on the purpose, as shown in the examples below. At the adjourned meeting, except for the reading of the minutes, business will be taken up from the point at which the previous meeting adjourned or at which questions were postponed.

It should be noted that the adoption of this motion does not adjourn the present meeting or set a time for its adjournment; thus, it has no direct effect on when the present meeting shall adjourn, and is very different from a motion to fix the time *at* which to adjourn (which is always a main motion).

Form and Example

Forms in which this motion may be made are: "I move that when this meeting adjourns, it adjourn to meet at 2:00 P.M. tomorrow"; "I move that when this meeting adjourns, it stand adjourned to meet at 8:00 P.M. on Wednesday, April 2, at the Riggs Hotel"; or "I move that on adjournment, the meeting adjourn to meet at the call of the chair."

In announcing an affirmative result, the chair says, for instance, "The ayes have it. When the meeting adjourns this evening, it will adjourn to meet at 2 P.M. tomorrow."

As a first example, assume that a number of members wish to set up an adjourned meeting to deal with an involved pending question, so that the remaining order of business can be completed now.

MEMBER A (obtaining the floor): Madam President, I believe the pending resolution will require longer discussion than we have time for this evening. I move that when the meeting adjourns, it adjourn to meet here next Tuesday at 8:15 P.M. (Second.)

The chair states the question on this motion. Amendment as to time and place is possible, but no debate is in order. The chair then puts to vote the motion to *Fix the Time to Which to Adjourn*. After announcing the result—

1 whether adoption or rejection—she says that the question
is on the resolution, which she rereads or indicates by descriptive title. If the motion to *Fix the Time to Which to Adjourn* has been adopted, Member A rises once more.

5

MEMBER A (obtaining the floor): I move to postpone the pending resolution to the adjourned meeting set for next Tuesday evening. (Second.)

The motion to postpone is considered in the usual man-
10 ner. If it is adopted, the chair continues:

CHAIR: The ayes have it and the resolution is postponed to the adjourned meeting. The next item of business is . . .

15 As a second example, assume that the motion to *Fix the
Time to Which to Adjourn* is to be made with a view to immediate adjournment to a specified time, when this purpose
cannot be reached by a main motion:
At the annual meeting of a society, the hour is growing
20 late. A controversial bylaw amendment is pending, on
which a strong minority is determined to continue debate.

MEMBER X (obtaining the floor): I move that when this meeting adjourns, it adjourn to meet at the same time tomorrow evening. (Second.)
25

The motion is treated as in the first example. If it is
adopted, Member X, after the question has been restated
on the pending bylaw amendment, again rises and addresses
the chair.
30

MEMBER X (obtaining the floor): I move that the club now adjourn. (Second.)

The chair states the question on the motion to *Adjourn*   1
and immediately puts it to vote. If it is adopted, the chair
announces the result, as follows:

CHAIR: The ayes have it and the club stands adjourned until eight   5
o'clock tomorrow evening.

INCIDENTAL MOTIONS

*See 6, pages 66ff., for a list of these motions and
a description of their characteristics as a class.*

§23. POINT OF ORDER

When a member thinks that the rules of the assembly
are being violated, he can make a *Point of Order* (or "raise
a question of order," as it is sometimes expressed), thereby
calling upon the chair for a ruling and an enforcement of
the regular rules.

Standard Descriptive Characteristics

A *Point of Order:*

1. Takes precedence over any pending question out of which
it may arise. It yields to all privileged motions and (if it adheres to pending question[s], pp. 112–13) it yields to a
motion to lay the main question on the table, in cases
where these motions are in order at the time according to
the order of precedence of motions. Except for yielding
to the motion to *Lay on the Table* when it adheres to
pending question(s) as just stated, it does not yield to any

subsidiary motion so long as it is handled in the normal manner—that is, by being ruled upon by the chair without debate. Consequently, under this normal procedure:

- If a point of order which adheres to pending question(s) is raised while any one of the six lower-ranking subsidiary motions is immediate pending, no other subsidiary motion except *Lay on the Table* can be made until the point of order is disposed of; but in such a case, *Lay on the Table* or any privileged motion can be moved and must be considered before the point of order is ruled upon.

- If a point of order which does not adhere to pending question(s) is raised while *any* subsidiary motion is immediately pending, *no* subsidiary motion can be made until the point of order is disposed of, but any privileged motion can be moved and must be considered first.

- With reference to either of the above cases, on the other hand, if a motion to *Lay on the Table* or a privileged motion is *pending* and a point of order arises out of the parliamentary situation existing then, the point of order is disposed of first, although it can be interrupted by a still higher-ranking privileged motion.

In cases where the chair, being in doubt, refers the point of order to the judgment of the assembly and where the point thereby becomes debatable (see Standard Characteristic 5, below), it—like a debatable appeal (**24**)—also: yields to the subsidiary motions to *Limit or Extend Limits of Debate* and for the *Previous Question;* yields to the motions to *Commit* and to *Postpone Definitely* provided that they are in order at the time according to the order of precedence of motions; and yields to incidental motions arising out of itself.

2. Can be applied to any breach of the assembly's rules. So long as it is handled in the normal manner by being

1   ruled upon by the chair, no subsidiary motion can be
     applied to it—except that, if it adheres to pending ques-
     tion(s), then (unless the motion to *Lay on the Table* was
     already pending when the point of order arose) the
5   main question can be laid on the table while the point
     of order is pending, and the point of order also goes to
     the table with all adhering motions. If the chair, being
     in doubt, refers the point of order to the judgment of
     the assembly and it thereby becomes debatable (see
10   Standard Characteristic 5, below), the application of
     subsidiary motions to it is governed by the same rules as
     stated for debatable appeals under Standard Character-
     istic 2, pages 248–49.
     3. Is in order when another has the floor, even interrupt-
15   ing a person speaking or reading a report if the point
         genuinely requires attention at such a time (see *Timeli-
         ness Requirement for a Point of Order,* below).
     4. Does not require a second.
     5. Is not debatable—but, with the chair's consent, a mem-
20   ber may be permitted to explain his point and knowl-
         edgeable or interested members can be heard by way of
         explanation. If the chair submits the point to a vote of
         the assembly, the rules governing its debatability are the
         same as for an *Appeal* (see p. 246; see also Standard
25   Characteristic 5, pp. 249–50).
     6. Is not amendable.
     7. Is normally ruled upon by the chair. No vote is taken
         unless the chair is in doubt or his ruling is appealed.
     8. Cannot be reconsidered.
30

Further Rules and Explanation

     GROUNDS FOR A POINT OF ORDER.   It is the
     right of every member who notices a breach of the rules to
35   insist on their enforcement. If the chair notices a breach, he

corrects the matter immediately; but if he fails to do so—through oversight or otherwise—any member can make the appropriate *Point of Order*. The presiding officer may wish to consult the parliamentary authority or the parliamentarian before ruling, and may allow the assembly to stand at ease (see pp. 80–81) while he does so. In any event, when the presiding officer has made a ruling, any two members can appeal (one making the appeal and the other seconding it), as described in **24**.*

If a member is uncertain as to whether there is a breach on which a point of order can be made, he can make a parliamentary inquiry of the chair (see pp. 281–82). In ordinary meetings it is undesirable to raise points of order on minor irregularities of a purely technical character, if it is clear that no one's rights are being infringed upon and no real harm is being done to the proper transaction of business.

TIMELINESS REQUIREMENT FOR A POINT OF ORDER.   If a question of order is to be raised, it must be raised promptly at the time the breach occurs. For example, if the chair is stating the question on a motion that has not been seconded, or on a motion that is out of order in the existing parliamentary situation, the time to raise these points of order is when the chair states the motion. After debate on such a motion has begun—no matter how clearly out of order the motion may be—a point of order is too late. If a member is unsure of his point or wishes to hear what the maker has to say on behalf of the motion before pressing a point of order, he may, with the chair's sufferance, "reserve a point of order" against the motion; but after the maker has spoken, he must insist upon his point of order or withdraw it. Points of order regarding the conduct

---

*There can be no appeal from a ruling on a point of order that is raised while an appeal is pending.

of a vote may be raised immediately following the announcement of the voting result—up until another member has been recognized and has introduced another matter.

The only exceptions to the rule that a point of order must be made at the time of the breach arise in connection with breaches that are of a continuing nature, in which case a point of order can be made at any time during the continuance of the breach. Instances of this kind occur when:

(a) a main motion has been adopted that conflicts with the bylaws (or constitution) of the organization or assembly,*

(b) a main motion has been adopted that conflicts with a main motion previously adopted and still in force, unless the subsequently adopted motion was adopted by the vote required to rescind or amend the previously adopted motion,

(c) any action has been taken in violation of applicable procedural rules prescribed by federal, state, or local law,

(d) any action has been taken in violation of a fundamental principle of parliamentary law (p. 255), or

(e) any action has been taken in violation of either a rule protecting absentees or a rule protecting a basic right of an individual member (p. 255).

In all such cases, it is never too late to raise a point of order since any action so taken is null and void.

Form and Example

When a member notices a breach of order that may do harm if allowed to pass, he rises and, without waiting for recognition, immediately addresses the chair as follows:

---

*Unless the conflict is with a rule in the nature of a rule of order as described on page 17, lines 22–24, in which case a point of order must be timely.

MEMBER A: I rise to a point of order. [Or, "Point of order!"]   *1*

Anyone who is speaking takes his seat. If the point relates to a transgression of the rules of debate, the form used may be: *5*

MEMBER A: Mr. President, I call the gentleman to order.

The chair then asks the member to state his point of order, or what words in the debate he objects to.   *10*

MEMBER A: I make the point of order that . . .

On completing his statement, the member resumes his seat. The chair then rules whether "the point of order is   *15* well taken" or "is not well taken," stating briefly his reasons, which should be recorded in the minutes. If the chair desires, he can review the parliamentary situation without leaving the chair, but standing, before giving his ruling.

If the chair's decision requires any action and no appeal is   *20* made, he sees that the necessary action is taken before proceeding with the pending business. Thus, if the point of order relates to a breach of decorum in debate that is not serious, the chair can allow the member to continue his speech. But if the member's remarks are decided to be improper and anyone   *25* objects, the member cannot continue speaking without a vote of the assembly to that effect (see pp. 626–27).

Before rendering his decision, the chair can consult the parliamentarian, if there is one. The chair can also request the advice of experienced members, but no one has the   *30* right to express such opinions in the meeting unless requested to do so by the chair.

When the chair is in doubt as to how to rule on an important point, he can submit it to the assembly for decision in some such manner as: *35*

1   CHAIR: Mr. Downey raises a point of order that the amendment is
not germane to the resolution. The chair is in doubt and submits the
question to the assembly. The resolution is [reading it]. The proposed
amendment is [reading it]. The question is, "Is the amendment ger-
5 mane to the resolution?"

Since no appeal can be made from a decision of the assembly itself, this question is open to debate whenever an
appeal would be—that is, the question submitted by the
10 chair to the assembly for decision is debatable except
when it relates to indecorum or transgression of the rules
of speaking, or to the priority of business, or when it is
made while an undebatable question is pending. As in the
case of debate on an appeal (**24**), when a point of order
15 that is submitted to a vote is debatable, no member can
speak more than once in the debate except the chair, who
can speak in preference to other members the first time,
and who is also entitled to speak a second time at the close
of debate.

20   In the example given above, the question may be put as
follows:

CHAIR: As many as are of the opinion that the amendment is germane, say *aye*. . . . Those of the opinion that it is not germane, say *no*.
25 . . . The ayes have it and the amendment is in order. The question is
on the adoption of the amendment.

Or:

30   CHAIR: . . . The noes have it and the amendment is out of order.
The question is on the adoption of the resolution.

When a point of order is submitted to a vote of the assembly and the point relates to stopping something from
35 being done, it is usually best to put the question so that an

affirmative vote will be in favor of allowing the proceedings
to continue as if the point had not been raised. Thus, if a
point is made that the chair is admitting a motion which is
out of order, the question should be put so that an affirmative result of the vote will mean that the motion is in
order—as in the example above, or as follows: ". . . As
many as are of the opinion that the motion is in order, say
aye. . . ; etc." When a member has been called to order because of indecorum in debate, the corresponding form is:
". . . As many as are of the opinion that the member should
be allowed to resume speaking, say *aye*. . . . " If the foregoing principle has no clear application to the case, the question can be put so that an affirmative result will uphold the
point of order: ". . . As many as are of the opinion that the
point is well taken, say *aye*. . . . "*

§24. APPEAL

By electing a presiding officer, the assembly delegates to
him the authority and duty to make necessary rulings on
questions of parliamentary law. But any two members have
the right to *Appeal* from his decision on such a question. By
one member making (or "taking") the appeal and another
seconding it, the question is taken from the chair and vested
in the assembly for final decision.

Members have no right to criticize a ruling of the chair
unless they appeal from his decision.

---

*It should be noted that the latter method of putting the question may
often be the opposite of the first method in cases where the first method is
applicable. Thus, in the example of a point of order that an amendment is
not germane, as shown above, the question is put so that a vote of *aye* is a
vote that the amendment *is* germane; but in that case, a vote of *aye* is a vote
that the point is *not* well taken.

1 **Standard Descriptive Characteristics**

An *Appeal*:

5 1. Takes precedence over any question pending at the time
the chair makes a ruling from which the appeal is made.
It yields to all privileged motions (provided that they
are in order at the time according to the order of precedence of motions), and it yields to incidental motions
10 arising out of itself. If it is debatable (see Standard
Characteristic 5, below), it also yields to the subsidiary
motions to *Limit or Extend Limits of Debate* and for the
Previous Question, and yields to the motions to *Commit,*
to *Postpone Definitely,* and to *Lay on the Table,* provided
15 that they are in order at the time according to the order
of precedence of motions. If it is undebatable and adheres to pending question(s), it does not yield to any
subsidiary motion except to *Lay on the Table;* and if it is
undebatable and does *not* adhere to pending ques-
20 tion(s), it yields to no subsidiary motion.

2. Can be applied to any ruling by the presiding officer except that:

a) if a point of order is raised while an appeal is pending, there is no appeal from the chair's decision on
25 this point of order, although the correctness of the
ruling can be brought up later by a motion covering
the case; and

b) when the chair rules on a question about which
there cannot possibly be two reasonable opinions,
30 an appeal would be dilatory and is not allowed.

Rules governing the applicability of subsidiary motions
to *debatable appeals* are as follows: A motion limiting or
extending debate or a motion for the *Previous Question*
can be applied to a debatable appeal without affecting
35 any other pending question. Also:

- When a *debatable* appeal *does not adhere* to pending question(s)—that is, when the decision on it would in no way affect pending question(s)—such a debatable appeal can have any of the subsidiary motions applied to it except *Postpone Indefinitely* and *Amend*.
- But when a *debatable* appeal *adheres* to pending question(s)—as in the case of an appeal from a ruling that an amendment is not germane—the subsidiary motions, except the motions affecting debate, cannot be applied to the appeal alone. However, they can be applied to the main question, and if the latter is committed, postponed, or laid on the table, the appeal goes with this main question.

In the case of *undebatable* appeals:

- When an *undebatable* appeal *does not adhere* to pending question(s), no subsidiary motion can be applied to it; however,
- When an *undebatable* appeal *adheres* to pending question(s), no subsidiary motion can be applied to it alone; but the main question can be laid on the table, and the appeal then goes to the table with the main question and all adhering motions.

3. Is in order when another has the floor, but the appeal must be made at the time of the ruling. If any debate or business has intervened, it is too late to appeal.

4. Must be seconded.

5. Is debatable, unless it (a) relates to indecorum or a transgression of the rules of speaking; (b) relates to the priority of business; or (c) is made while the immediately pending question is undebatable. When an appeal is debatable, no member is allowed to speak more than once except the presiding officer—who need not leave the chair while **so** speaking, but should stand. The first time the chair speaks in debate on the appeal, he is entitled to preference over other members seeking recog-

1 nition. He can answer arguments against the decision or give additional reasons by speaking a second time at the close of the debate. He may announce his intention to speak in rebuttal and ask if there are others who wish to

5 speak first. Even when the appeal is not debatable, the chair can, when stating the question on it, give the reasons for his decision without leaving the chair.

6. Is not amendable.

7. A majority or a tie vote sustains the decision of the chair

10 on the principle that the chair's decision stands until reversed by a majority. If the presiding officer is a member of the assembly, he can vote to create a tie and thus sustain his decision.

8. Can be reconsidered.

15

Further Rules and Explanation

APPROPRIATENESS OF APPEAL.   If a member disagrees with a ruling of the chair affecting any substantial

20 question, he should not hesitate to appeal. The situation is no more delicate than disagreeing with another member in debate. In the case of serious questions when proponents and opponents appear nearly equal, a presiding officer may welcome an appeal from his decision. By relieving the chair of re-

25 sponsibility in a strongly contested situation and placing it on the assembly itself, better relationships are often preserved.

APPLICABILITY LIMITED TO RULINGS.   As explained in Standard Characteristic 2, an appeal is applicable

30 only to a *ruling* by the chair.

No appeal can be made from the chair's response to a parliamentary inquiry or other query, since such a reply is an *opinion* rendered by the chair, not a ruling on a question that has actually arisen. For example, if, in answer to a par-

35 liamentary inquiry, the chair states that a certain motion

would be out of order at the time, this reply is not subject
to appeal. But the point can be put at issue before the assembly by making the motion despite the chair's opinion
and, when he *rules* the motion out of order, appealing from
the chair's decision.

The chair's announcement of the result of a vote also is
not a ruling and is not subject to appeal. If a member
doubts the correctness of such an announced result, however, he should call for a *Division* (see **29**).

Form and Example

A member desiring to appeal rises and, without waiting
to be recognized, addresses the chair as follows:

MEMBER A: I appeal from the decision of the chair. (Second.)

The chair, after stating clearly the exact question at issue,
and the reasons for his decision if he thinks an explanation
necessary, states the question on the appeal as follows:

CHAIR: The question is: "Shall the decision of the chair stand as the
judgment of the assembly [or "club," "society," "board," etc.]?"

Or:

CHAIR: The question is, "Shall the decision of the chair be sustained?"

The question should not be on "sustaining the chair," because the *decision,* not the presiding officer, is in question.

The vote is taken so that the affirmative will be in favor
of sustaining the chair's decision, as follows:

CHAIR: As many as are in favor of sustaining the chair's decision,
say *aye.* . . . Those opposed to sustaining this decision, say *no.* . . .

After the result of the vote is announced, business is resumed in accordance with the situation existing after the action on the appeal.

§25. SUSPEND THE RULES

When an assembly wishes to do something during a meeting that it cannot do without violating one or more of its regular rules, it can adopt a motion to *Suspend the Rules* interfering with the proposed action—provided that the proposal is not in conflict with the organization's bylaws (or constitution), with local, state, or national law prescribing procedural rules applicable to the organization or assembly, or with a fundamental principle of parliamentary law.

Standard Descriptive Characteristics

The incidental motion to *Suspend the Rules:*

1. Can be made at any time that no question is pending. When business is pending, *Suspend the Rules* takes precedence over any motion if it is for a purpose connected with that motion. It yields to the motion to *Lay on the Table* and to all privileged motions when these motions are in order at the time according to the order of precedence of motions—except that if it relates to the priority of business it does not yield to a *Call for the Orders of the Day.* It also yields to incidental motions arising out of itself.

2. Can be applied to any rule of the assembly except bylaws* (or rules contained in a constitution or corporate

---

*Regarding the suspendibility of rules in the nature of rules of order when placed within the bylaws, see page 17, lines 22–24.

charter). No subsidiary motion can be applied to *Suspend the Rules.*

3. Is out of order when another has the floor.
4. Must be seconded.
5. Is not debatable.
6. Is not amendable.
7. Usually requires a two-thirds vote (see below, however). In any case, no rule protecting a minority of a particular size can be suspended in the face of a negative vote as large as the minority protected by the rule.
8. Cannot be reconsidered (see below regarding its renewal).

Further Rules and Explanation

OBJECT AND EFFECT OF THE MOTION. The object of this motion must usually be to suspend one or more rules contained in the parliamentary authority (rules of order), the special rules of order, or the standing rules of the assembly.* A motion to "take up a question out of its proper order," or to consider one before a time to which it has been postponed, is an application of the motion to *Suspend the Rules* (see **14, 41**).

In making the incidental motion to *Suspend the Rules,* the particular rule or rules to be suspended are not mentioned; but the motion must state its specific purpose, and its adoption permits nothing else to be done under the suspension. Such a motion, for instance, may be "to suspend the rules and take up the report of the Building Committee," or "to suspend the rules and agree to [that is, to adopt without debate or amendment] the resolution . . ." When the purpose of a motion to *Suspend the Rules* is to permit the making of another motion, and the adoption of the first

---

*For the classes of rules that an organization or an assembly may adopt, see **2**.

1 motion would obviously be followed by adoption of the
second, the two motions can be combined, as in "to suspend the rules and take from the table (**34**) the question relating to . . ." The foregoing is an exception to the general
5 rule that no member can make two motions at the same
time except with the consent of the assembly—unanimous
consent being required if the two motions are unrelated
(see also pp. 105–106, 265).

If a motion to *Suspend the Rules* is adopted and its object
10 is to allow consideration of business that could not otherwise
have been considered at the time, the chair should immediately recognize the member who moved the suspension of
the rules, to make the appropriate motion that will bring up
the desired business. Or, if no further motion is necessary
15 (for example, if the two motions were combined as indicated
above, or if the question is one that was postponed), the chair
should announce the business as pending.

RENEWAL OF THE MOTION.   If a motion to sus-
20 pend the rules is voted down, it cannot be renewed by moving to suspend the rules for the same purpose at the same
meeting, unless unanimous consent is given. It can, however, be renewed for the same purpose after an adjournment, even if the next meeting is held the same day. Any
25 number of motions to suspend the rules for different purposes can be entertained at the same meeting.

RULES THAT CANNOT BE SUSPENDED.   Rules
contained in the *bylaws* (or constitution) cannot be sus-
30 pended—no matter how large the vote in favor of doing so
or how inconvenient the rule in question may be—unless the
particular rule specifically provides for its own suspension, or
unless the rule properly is in the nature of a rule of order as
described on page 17, lines 22–24. Similarly, no applicable
35 procedural rule prescribed by federal, state, or local law can

be suspended unless the rule specifically provides for its own suspension.

Rules which embody *fundamental principles of parliamentary law,* such as the rule that allows only one question to be considered at a time (p. 56), cannot be suspended. As a further example, since it is a fundamental principle of parliamentary law that the right to vote is limited to the members of an organization who are actually present at the time the vote is taken in a legal meeting (p. 408), the rules cannot be suspended so as to give the right to vote to a nonmember,* or to authorize absentee (pp. 408–409) or cumulative (p. 429) voting, even by a unanimous vote.

Rules *protecting absentees or a basic right of the individual member* cannot be suspended, even by unanimous consent or an actual unanimous vote. For example, the rules requiring the presence of a quorum and previous notice of a proposed amendment to the bylaws protect absentees, and suspension of these rules would violate their rights. Further, the rule requiring officers to be elected by (secret) ballot protects a minority of one from exposing his vote, which he may do if he votes against, or objects to, suspending such a rule (see *Voting by Ballot,* pp. 398–99). Similarly, while generally applicable limits on debate and the making of motions may be imposed by motions such as the *Previous Question,* the rules may not be suspended so as to deny any particular member the right to attend meetings, make motions, speak in debate, and vote, which are basic rights that may be curtailed only through disciplinary proceedings.

At a regular meeting of an organization that has an established order of business, the assembly cannot, even unanimously, vote to *dispense with* that order of business (in the sense of voting, in advance of the time when it adjourns,

---

*In contrast, the rules may be suspended to allow a nonmember to speak in debate.

that the order of business shall not be gone through at all at that meeting). If the assembly, by a two-thirds vote, adopts a motion "to dispense with the regular order of business and proceed to" * a certain subject, it has in effect voted to *pass* all classes in the order of business which normally would precede that subject (see pp. 351–53). In such a case, when the matter taken up out of its proper order has been disposed of, even if it has consumed as much time as the usual meeting, the chair must return to the regular order of business and call for the items in sequence, unless the assembly then votes to adjourn (see **21**).

RULES WHOSE SUSPENSION REQUIRES A TWO-THIRDS VOTE.   The *rules of order* of a society, as contained in the manual established by the bylaws as the parliamentary authority, or as included in any special rules of order adopted by the organization (see **2**), are rules of parliamentary procedure, the suspension of which requires a two-thirds vote. Some societies call all their rules "standing rules." But by whatever name a rule is called, if it relates to parliamentary procedure, it requires either (a) previous notice and a two-thirds vote or (b) a vote of a majority of the entire membership for its amendment; hence, it requires a two-thirds vote for its suspension.

RULES THAT CAN BE SUSPENDED BY A MAJORITY VOTE.   An ordinary** *standing rule,* as the term is used in this book, is a rule that does not relate to parliamentary procedure as such and refers, for example, to such matters as the hour for beginning meetings (in cases where the dates of regular meetings are established by the bylaws).

---

*This usage should be avoided.

**In conventions, the term *standing rule* is used in a special sense that may include parliamentary rules adopted by the convention (see pp. 599ff.).

Standing rules are adopted, as any ordinary motion, by a majority vote, and are amended by a two-thirds vote without previous notice or by a majority vote with such notice; they therefore can be suspended by a majority vote as they do not involve the protection of a minority of a particular size. Through an incidental main motion adopted by a majority vote, a standing rule can be suspended for the duration of the current session. Sometimes standing rules are called "policies," but whatever term is used, if such a rule has its application outside of a meeting context, it cannot be suspended. It can, however, be amended (**35**).

SUSPENSION OF RULES BY UNANIMOUS CONSENT.   Frequently, when the matter is clearly not controversial, time may be saved by asking unanimous consent rather than by making a formal motion to suspend the rules. A member who has obtained the floor can say, for example, "Madam President, I ask unanimous consent to offer the courtesy resolutions before we receive the report of the special committee." The chair then asks if anyone objects and, if so, proceeds to take a vote on suspending the rules, just as if a formal motion had been made.

Form and Example

The usual form of this motion is:

MEMBER A (obtaining the floor): I move that the rules be suspended [or "to suspend the rules"] which interfere with . . . [stating the object of the suspension]. (Second.)

Or:

MEMBER A (obtaining the floor): I move to suspend the rules and take up . . . (Second.)

When the object is to adopt a motion without debate or amendment, the form is:

MEMBER A (obtaining the floor): I move to suspend the rules and adopt [or "agree to"] the following resolution: "*Resolved,* That . . . " (Second.)

If such a motion does not receive the required two-thirds vote, the main motion can be taken up only in the normal way. A member moving to suspend the rules can briefly give sufficient information to enable the members to vote intelligently on his undebatable motion. (For the manner of taking a two-thirds vote, see pp. 44–45, 47–48.) In announcing an affirmative result, the chair says, for example,

CHAIR: There are two thirds in the affirmative and the rules are suspended for the purpose of . . . The chair recognizes Mrs. Watkins.

§26. OBJECTION TO THE CONSIDERATION OF A QUESTION

The purpose of an *Objection to the Consideration of a Question* is to enable the assembly to avoid a particular original main motion altogether when it believes it would be strongly undesirable for the motion even to come before the assembly.

Standard Descriptive Characteristics

An *Objection to the Consideration of a Question:*

1. Takes precedence over original main motions (and over an *unstated* subsidiary motion, except *Lay on the Table*), but the objection can be raised only before there has

been any debate or any subsidiary motion has been
stated by the chair; thereafter, consideration of the main
question has begun and it is too late to object. It yields
to the motion to *Lay on the Table*, to all privileged motions, and to incidental motions arising out of itself.

2. Can be applied to original main motions (p. 95) and to
petitions and communications that are not from a superior body. It cannot be applied to incidental main motions. No subsidiary motion can be applied to it alone,
but while it is pending the main question can be laid on
the table, and the objection then goes to the table with
the main question.

3. Is in order when another has the floor, until consideration of the question has begun, as indicated in Standard
Characteristic 1, above.

4. Does not require a second.

5. Is not debatable.

6. Is not amendable.

7. A two-thirds vote *against consideration* is required to
sustain the objection.

8. A negative vote—that is, a vote sustaining the objection—
can be reconsidered, but not an affirmative vote.

Further Rules and Explanation

RESEMBLANCE TO POINT OF ORDER.   An *Ob-
jection to the Consideration of a Question* is similar in some
ways to a *Point of Order*. The presiding officer, on his own
initiative, can submit his objection of this kind to a vote,
just as he can raise a question of order on his own accord.
An *Objection to the Consideration of a Question* is not used
if a main motion is outside the society's objects as defined
in the bylaws or constitution, or outside the announced
purpose for which a mass meeting has been called; such a
motion should be ruled out of order (p. 108, l. 5–8).

DIFFERENCE FROM OBJECTION IN OTHER CONTEXT. *Objection to the Consideration of a Question* should not be confused with an objection to a request for unanimous consent (see pp. 51–53).

EFFECT OF THE OBJECTION.   If an objection to consideration is sustained, the main motion is dismissed for that session and cannot be renewed during the same session except by unanimous consent or by reconsideration of the vote on the objection. If the objection is not sustained, consideration of the main motion proceeds as if no objection had been made. Even if the objection is sustained, the same main motion can be introduced at any succeeding session.

MANNER OF PUTTING THE QUESTION.   When the objection is put to a vote in its correct form (see *Form and Example,* below), members are asked to vote for or against *consideration* of the question objected to (not for or against sustaining the objection). Therefore, those who wish to *prevent consideration* of the question *vote in the negative.* The objection is sustained if there are at least twice as many negative as affirmative votes.

Form and Example

A member rises, even if another has been assigned the floor, and without waiting to be recognized, addresses the chair as follows:

MEMBER A: Mr. President, I object to the consideration of the question [or "resolution," "motion," etc.].

The chair responds:

CHAIR: The consideration of the question is objected to. Shall the   *1*
question be considered? Those in favor of considering it, rise. . . . Be
seated. Those opposed to considering the question, rise. . . . Be
seated. There are two thirds opposed and the question will not be
considered.   *5*

Or, if the objection is not sustained, the announcement
of the vote may be worded as follows:

CHAIR: There are less than two thirds opposed and the objection is   *10*
not sustained. The question is on the resolution, "*Resolved,* That . . . "

In putting the objection to vote, the chair must be careful *not* to say, "Shall the objection be sustained?" This
would reverse the effect of affirmative and negative votes   *15*
and might cause confusion.

§27. DIVISION OF A QUESTION

When a motion relating to a single subject contains sev-   *20*
eral parts, each of which is capable of standing as a complete
proposition if the others are removed, the parts can be separated to be considered and voted on as if they were distinct
questions—by adoption of the motion for *Division of a
Question* (or "to divide the question").   *25*
There are also certain motions which must be divided
on the demand of a single member, in which case a formal
motion to divide is not used (see p. 265). The eight characteristics below apply only to the incidental *motion* for *Division of a Question.*   *30*

Standard Descriptive Characteristics

The incidental motion for *Division of a Question:*

1. Takes precedence over the main motion and over the subsidiary motion to *Postpone Indefinitely*. If applied to an amendment, it also takes precedence over that amendment; but a motion to divide the main question cannot be made while an amendment to the main question is pending. It yields to all subsidiary motions except *Postpone Indefinitely, Amend,* and *Limit or Extend Limits of Debate;* to all privileged motions; and to all applicable incidental motions. Although it is preferable to divide a question when it is first introduced, a motion to divide can be made at any time that the main motion, an amendment which it is proposed to divide, or the motion to *Postpone Indefinitely* is immediately pending—even after the *Previous Question* has been ordered.

2. Can be applied to main motions and their amendments,* if they are susceptible to division (see below). No subsidiary motion can be applied to it alone except *Amend* and (for the purpose of stopping its amendment) the *Previous Question;* but while it is pending the main question can be committed, postponed, or laid on the table, and it then undergoes the same process with the main question.

3. Is out of order when another has the floor.

4. Must be seconded.

5. Is not debatable.

6. Is amendable.

7. Requires a majority vote.

8. Cannot be reconsidered.

Further Rules and Explanation

SPECIFICATION OF THE MANNER IN WHICH THE QUESTION IS TO BE DIVIDED.   The motion to

---

*Motions to divide amendments, although permissible, are seldom useful.

divide must clearly state the manner in which the question is to be divided. While the motion to divide is pending, another member can propose a different division by moving an amendment. If several different proposals are made, they should be treated as filling blanks; that is, they should be voted on in the order in which they were proposed unless they suggest different numbers of questions, in which case the largest number is voted on first (pp. 155–60). Usually, however, little formality is involved in dividing a question, and it is arranged by unanimous consent.

MOTIONS THAT CANNOT BE DIVIDED. A motion cannot be divided unless each part presents a proper question for the assembly to act upon if none of the other parts is adopted, and unless the effect of adopting all of the parts will be exactly the same—no more, no less—as adoption of the compound main question. Thus, if it is moved to establish a committee and give it instructions, this motion is indivisible because, should the part establishing the committee fail, the part giving the committee instructions would be absurd.

Another type of motion that cannot be divided is one whose parts are not easily separated. The division cannot require a rewriting of the resolution beyond an essentially mechanical separation of it into the required parts. If possible, the division should be carried out by no more than a renumbering of phrases or clauses, prefacing each part with the formal word(s), "That," "*Resolved,* That," or "*Ordered,* That," dropping conjunctions where necessary, or replacing pronouns with the nouns for which they stand, with or without the definite article "the," as required. Depending on how the compound main motion or resolution is worded, however, it may sometimes be necessary to repeat words in more than one part which, in the main motion, appear only once and apply to more than one element of

1 the proposed division. Also needed in this connection may
be slight corrections in syntax or phrase structure in order
to render each part as a complete grammatical sentence free
of awkward wording. These adjustments are permissible
5 provided care is taken to preserve exact logical equivalence
of statement and no new language is introduced.

For example, suppose that the following resolution is
pending: "*Resolved,* That the Society congratulate its member Ernest Dunn on his novel *Crestwood,* and that three
10 copies be purchased for the Society's library." Suppose also
that a member wishes to divide the question so as to consider the purchase of the books separately. The first divided
part obviously would be, "*Resolved,* That the Society congratulate its member Ernest Dunn on his novel *Crestwood.*"
15 The second part, with the wording adjusted no more than
necessary to avoid awkwardness, would have to read, "*Resolved,* That three copies of the novel *Crestwood* by the Society's member Ernest Dunn be purchased for the Society's
library." The phrasing of the second part involves both
20 types of modification described in the last three sentences
of the preceding paragraph.

As indicated in this subsection, if separating the elements of action in a proposed resolution would require recasting the parts more than described above, the resolution
25 cannot be divided.

STRIKING OUT PART OF AN INDIVISIBLE MO-
TION OR SERIES OF MOTIONS.   When a question is
indivisible and a member is opposed to a portion of it, he
30 can seek the desired result by moving to *strike out* (**12**) the
part to which he is opposed. In like manner, when a series
of resolutions is proposed as a substitute for another series,
the substitute series is indivisible if the several resolutions
are not completely parallel, but a motion can be made to
35 strike out of the series any of the component resolutions before the vote is taken on whether to make the substitution.

MOTIONS THAT MUST BE DIVIDED ON DE-
MAND.   Sometimes a series of independent resolutions or
main motions dealing with different subjects is offered in one
motion. In such a case, one or more of the several resolutions
must receive separate consideration and vote at the request of
a single member, and the motion for *Division of a Question* is
not used. Such a demand (which should not be confused
with a demand for a division of the assembly—that is, for a
rising vote) can be made even when another has the floor, as
in, "Mr. President, I call for a separate vote on Resolution
No. 3." This demand must be asserted before the question
on adopting the series has actually been put to vote.

Similarly, when a committee reports a number of
amendments to a resolution referred to it, all the amendments can be adopted by a single vote, except that if any
member demands a separate vote on one or more of them,
those amendments must be considered separately. After the
others have been voted on together, the amendment(s) on
which separate votes were requested are disposed of.

Form and Example

Referring to the example relating to Ernest Dunn's
novel *Crestwood* on page 264, a motion to divide the question may be made either by stating the proposed parts in
their entirety or by using a shorter description of how the
division is to be made, if it is perfectly clear.

In the first instance, the motion would be made thus:

MEMBER A (obtaining the floor): Madam President, I move to divide the resolution into two parts as follows: [repeating them as shown
in the example on p. 264]. (Second.)

The question as to whether to divide the resolution is
voted on first. In this case, the chair would doubtless use
unanimous consent.

1   Under the shorter form of the motion, it may be made instead as follows:

MEMBER A (obtaining the floor): Madam President, I move to di-
5 vide the resolution so as to consider separately the question of purchasing the books. [Or, ". . . so that the question of purchasing the
books be considered separately."] (Second.)

The procedure is then the same as in the first case. If the
10 motion for the division prevails, the chair should state each
of the separated resolutions in full as it is considered.

§28. CONSIDERATION BY PARAGRAPH
15 OR SERIATIM

A report or long motion consisting of a series of resolutions, paragraphs, articles, or sections that are not totally
separate questions can be considered by opening the differ-
20 ent parts to debate and amendment separately, without a division of the question. If the chair does not follow such a
course of his own accord and the assembly wishes to do so,
the procedure can be ordered by adopting a motion to
Consider by Paragraph (or to *Consider Seriatim*). Several
25 distinct main motions *on different subjects* cannot be considered seriatim if a single member objects (see Standard
Characteristic 8, below).

Standard Descriptive Characteristics
30

The incidental motion for *Consideration by Paragraph
or Seriatim:*

1. Takes precedence over the main motion and over the
35   subsidiary motion to *Postpone Indefinitely.* If applied to

an amendment, it also takes precedence over that amendment; but it cannot be applied to the main question while an amendment to the main question is pending. It yields to all subsidiary motions except *Postpone Indefinitely, Amend,* and *Limit or Extend Limits of Debate;* to all privileged motions; and to all applicable incidental motions.

2. Can be applied to main motions and amendments of such length and structure that the method is appropriate. No subsidiary motion can be applied to it alone except *Amend* and (for the purpose of stopping its amendment) the *Previous Question;* but while it is pending the main question can be committed, postponed, or laid on the table, and it then undergoes the same process with the main question.

3. Is out of order when another has the floor.

4. Must be seconded.

5. Is not debatable.

6. Is amendable.

7. Requires a majority vote.

8. Cannot be reconsidered. If it has been decided to consider divisible material seriatim, even if the material was divisible on the demand of a single member, it is too late to move or demand a division of the question.

Further Rules and Explanation

EFFECT OF CONSIDERATION BY PARAGRAPH. The effect of considering a document by paragraph or seriatim is as follows: If a member exhausts his right to debate under the usual rules on one part, his right to debate begins over again as each succeeding part is opened to debate and amendment; yet no vote on adoption is taken until there has been opportunity to perfect all the parts by amend-

1 ment. Keeping all subdivisions of the series open until one final vote avoids the possibility of complications which would result—especially in the case of bylaws—if amendments to later paragraphs necessitated changes in others *5* that had already been adopted.

CASES IN WHICH THE CHAIR NORMALLY APPLIES THE METHOD.   In adopting a set of bylaws or the articles of a platform, consideration by paragraph is the *10* normal and advisable procedure, followed as a matter of course unless the assembly votes to do otherwise. The chair, on his own initiative, can apply this method to any elaborate proposition susceptible to such treatment, unless he thinks the assembly wishes to act on the question as a *15* whole; or the manner of consideration can be settled by unanimous consent. Should the chair neglect this, a member can move "that the resolution be considered by paragraph" (or "seriatim").

20 MOTION TO CONSIDER AS A WHOLE.   If the chair suggests consideration by paragraph and a member feels that time could be saved by acting on it as a whole, the member can move "that it be considered as a whole." This motion is governed by rules identical to those for *Consider-* *25* *ation by Paragraph or Seriatim.*

PROCEDURE FOR CONSIDERATION BY PARAGRAPH.   The procedure in considering by paragraph or seriatim is as follows: The member who moved the adoption of *30* the document, the secretary, or the presiding officer (as the chair may decide) reads the first subdivision, and it is explained by its proponent. The chair then asks, "Is there any debate or amendment to this paragraph [or "section," etc.]?" When there is no further debate or amendment to the first *35* paragraph, each succeeding one is taken up. Amendments are voted on as they arise, but no paragraph as amended is acted upon (as to final adoption or rejection) at that time. After all parts have been considered, the chair opens the entire document to amendment. At this time additional parts can be inserted, or parts can be struck out, or any one of them can be further amended. It is not necessary to amend the numbers of articles, sections, or other subdivisions. It is the duty of the secretary to make all such corrections where they become necessary (see pp. 579–80).

If there is a preamble, it is treated in the same way before the final vote. Then the entire document is acted upon in a single vote. If the *Previous Question* is ordered before the preamble has been considered, it does not apply to the preamble unless expressly so stated.

APPLICATION OF SUBSIDIARY MOTIONS TO THE ENTIRE PROPOSITION DURING CONSIDERATION BY PARAGRAPH.   During the consideration of the separate paragraphs, any motion to *Postpone Indefinitely, Commit, Postpone,* or *Lay on the Table* can apply only to the entire series or proposition. If a motion to *Postpone Indefinitely* is made under these circumstances, it is stated by the chair, but is not debated or voted on until the paragraph-by-paragraph phase of consideration is completed and the entire document has been declared open to amendment. This rule is a consequence of two characteristics of the motion to *Postpone Indefinitely*—that amendments take precedence over it, and that while it is pending the entire main question is open to debate. Motions to *Commit, Postpone* (definitely), or *Lay on the Table,* on the other hand, are taken up as they arise; and, if adopted, they affect the entire main question immediately. If or when the main question comes before the assembly again later, the consideration by paragraph or seriatim is resumed at the point where it was interrupted. The *Previous Question* and

1 *Limit or Extend Limits of Debate* can be applied to amendments or to the entire document but not to the individual paragraphs.

Form and Example

5 When the chair does not initiate seriatim consideration, this form can be used:

10 MEMBER A (obtaining the floor): Mr. President, I move that the resolution [or "the platform," etc.] be considered by paragraph [or "seriatim"]. (Second.)

If the chair suggests consideration by paragraph and a member feels that the proposition could be acted upon as a whole, this form may be used:

MEMBER X (obtaining the floor): Madam President, I move that . . . be considered as a whole. (Second.)

20

§29. DIVISION OF THE ASSEMBLY

Whenever a member doubts the result of a voice (viva-voce) vote or a vote by show of hands—either because the result appears close or because he doubts that a representative number of the members present have voted—he can call for a *Division of the Assembly,* thereby requiring the vote to be taken again by rising.

A voice vote retaken by a show of hands is not a *Division of the Assembly,* since in large assemblies it may be less accurate than a rising vote, and since—even in a small meeting—the rising vote may be more effective in causing a maximum number of members to vote.

On an inconclusive voice vote in a very small meeting where all present can clearly see one another, if, instead of calling for a *Division*, a member asks for a show of hands, this is in the nature of a request, and the chair can retake the vote by this method unless a call for a *Division* is also made. Before or after the vote is thus retaken, however, any member still has the right to demand a *Division* if he believes it will obtain a more conclusive result.

Standard Descriptive Characteristics

A *Division of the Assembly:*

1. Takes precedence over any motion on which a vote is being taken or has just been taken; within the interval immediately following such a vote, it can be called for until, but not after, the *chair has stated the question* on another motion. It does not yield to any motion.
2. Can be applied to any motion on which the assembly is called upon to vote by voice or by a show of hands. No subsidiary motion can be applied to it.
3. Is in order without obtaining the floor, when another has the floor and at any time after the question has been put, even after the vote has been announced.
4. Does not require a second.
5. Is not debatable.
6. Is not amendable.
7. Does not require a vote, since a single member can demand a division.
8. Cannot be reconsidered.

Further Rules and Explanation

PROCEDURE FOR RETAKING A VOTE.   When a *Division* is demanded, the chair immediately takes the vote again, first by having the affirmative rise, then by having the negative rise. If it appears to the chair, when those in the af-

1 firmative rise, that the vote will be close, he can count the
vote or order it to be counted. If a member desires the vote
on the division to be counted, he must make a motion to
that effect, which requires a majority vote (see pp. **49–50,**
5 **396–97; 30**).

VOTE RETAKEN AT CHAIR'S INITIATIVE.   The
chair has the responsibility of obtaining a correct expression
of the will of the assembly. If he is uncertain of the result of
10 a vote or if he feels that the vote is unrepresentative, the chair
can of his own accord take the vote again by a rising vote.

DILATORY USE.   When it is clear that there has
been a full vote and there can be no reasonable doubt as to
15 which side is in the majority, a call for a *Division* is dilatory,
and the chair should not allow the individual member's
right of demanding a *Division* to be abused to the annoyance of the assembly.

20 **Form and Example**

While, or immediately after, the chair announces the result of a vote, "The ayes [or "noes"] have it and . . . ," a
member can call for a division from his seat, without ob-
25 taining the floor:

MEMBER: Division!

Or:

30

MEMBER: I call for [or "demand"] a division.

Or:

35   MEMBER: I doubt the result of the vote.

To such a call in any of these forms, the chair responds:

CHAIR: A division is called for [or "demanded"].

The chair then proceeds to take the rising vote.

§30. MOTIONS RELATING TO METHODS OF VOTING AND THE POLLS

The object of these motions is to obtain a vote on a question in some form other than by voice or *Division* (rising), or to close or reopen the polls. These motions include those that the vote be taken by ballot, that it be taken by roll call (the yeas and nays), and that a standing vote be counted (tellers). Similarly, unusual voting methods are included, such as the use of black and white balls or a signed ballot (see pp. 405–406).

Standard Descriptive Characteristics

Incidental motions relating to methods of voting and the polls:

1. Take precedence over the motion being voted on or to be voted on. When applied to a vote which has just been taken, they can be moved until, but not after, the question on another motion has been *stated*. They can be moved while an order for the *Previous Question* is in effect on the votes to which they apply. They yield to the privileged motions, and to a motion to *Lay on the Table* moved while the question to which they are applied is pending. It is not in order to move that the same question be voted on again under one of the other forms.

2. Can be applied to any motion on which the assembly is called upon to vote. No subsidiary motion can be applied to them except *Amend*.*

3. Are out of order when another has the floor.

4. Must be seconded.

5. Are not debatable.

6. Are amendable.

7. Require a majority vote, except a motion to close the polls, which requires a two-thirds vote.

8. Can be reconsidered, except a motion to close the polls, or an affirmative vote on a motion to reopen the polls. (In the latter cases, the same effect can be obtained by renewal or by the opposite motion.)

Further Rules and Explanation

METHODS OF VOTING.   In practice, the method of taking a vote usually can be agreed upon informally. But when different methods are suggested, they are usually treated not as amendments but as filling blanks, the vote normally being taken first on the one taking the most time. (For ways of voting, see pp. 42–51; **45.**)

A member who believes that a secret vote will give a truer expression of the assembly's will on a pending motion can move that the vote on the motion be taken by ballot. (In regard to ordering a vote to be counted, see p. 50, p. 68, l. 33 to p. 69, l. 5, p. 396; see also *Roll Call Vote*, pp. 405ff.)

CLOSING OR REOPENING THE POLLS.   It is usually better to leave it to the chair to close the polls. When the vote is taken by ballot, as soon as the chair thinks that all have voted who wish to, he inquires if all have

---

*In principle, the *Previous Question* can also be applied to them to stop their amendment, though such a case will rarely arise in practice.

voted. If there is no response, he declares the polls closed, *1*
and the tellers proceed to count the vote.

If a motion is made to close the polls when the voting
has closed naturally, the chair can treat the motion as a
unanimous-consent request and declare the polls closed. In *5*
any case, a formal motion to close the polls should not be
recognized until all have presumably voted. Like motions
relating to the close of debate or nominations, the motion
to close the polls requires a two-thirds vote.

If members enter afterward and it is desired to reopen *10*
the polls, this can be done by a majority vote.

The time at which the polls shall be closed or reopened
can be specified in the motion, or added by amendment.

§31. MOTIONS RELATING TO NOMINATIONS *15*

While an election is pending, a member may wish to
offer a motion to determine the method of making nominations* (when it is not prescribed in the bylaws or rules of
order). Members also may wish to offer motions to close or *20*
reopen nominations.

Standard Descriptive Characteristics

Incidental motions relating to nominations: *25*

1. Take precedence over the pending election for which
   nominations are to be made. (If a member is seeking the
   floor to make a nomination, however, the motion to
   close nominations is out of order.) They yield to the priv- *30*
   ileged motions, and to the motion to *Lay on the Table.*

---

*A motion prescribing the method of nominating is an incidental mo-
tion—and subject to the rules given here—only when the election is pending; otherwise, it is an incidental main motion (see **10**).

2. Apply to any pending election. No subsidiary motion except *Amend** can be applied to them.
3. Are out of order when another has the floor.
4. Must be seconded.
5. Are not debatable.
6. Are amendable.
7. Require a majority vote, except a motion to close nominations, which requires a two-thirds vote because (a) its adoption deprives members of a basic right—to nominate; and (b) the assembly must be protected against attempted abuse of the power to close nominations by a temporary majority.
8. Can be reconsidered, except the motion to close nominations, or an affirmative vote on a motion to reopen nominations. (In the latter cases, the same effect can be obtained by renewal or by the opposite motion.)

Further Rules and Explanation

MOTIONS TO PRESCRIBE METHODS OF NOMINATING.   If no method of making nominations is designated by the bylaws or rules and the assembly has adopted no order on the subject, anyone can make a motion prescribing the method of nomination for an office to be filled. When different methods are proposed, they can be moved as amendments, but are frequently treated as filling blanks (pp. 155–60). In that event, the vote is taken on the various suggested methods of nominating, in this order: (a) by the chair; (b) from the floor (sometimes called "open nominations"); (c) by a committee; (d) by ballot; and (e) by mail (see **46**). It should be noted that not all of these methods are appropriate or desirable in average societies.

---

*See footnote on page 274, which also applies to these motions.

MOTIONS TO CLOSE OR REOPEN NOMINA-
TIONS.   In the average society, a motion to close nominations is not a necessary part of the election procedure and it
should not generally be moved. When nominations have been
made by a committee or from the floor, the chair should in-
quire whether there are any further nominations; and when
there is no response, he declares that nominations are closed.
In very large bodies, the formality of a motion to close nominations is sometimes allowed, but this motion is not in order
until a reasonable opportunity to make nominations has been
given; as noted above, it is out of order if a member is seeking
the floor to make a further nomination, and it always requires
a two-thirds vote. When no one wishes to make a further
nomination, the motion serves no useful purpose.

A legitimate use of the motion to close nominations
would be, for example, to end delay of an election by numbers of nominations obviously intended only to honor persons who have no chance of being elected.

When for any reason it is desired to reopen nominations, this can be done by a majority vote.

The time at which nominations shall be closed or reopened can be specified in the motion, or added by amendment.

§32. REQUEST TO BE EXCUSED FROM A DUTY

Occasionally the bylaws of a society may impose specific
duties on members beyond the mere payment of dues. Members may be obligated to attend a certain number of meetings, to prepare talks or papers, to serve on committees, or
even to accept office if elected. In these cases, a member cannot, as a matter of right, decline such a duty or demand that
he or she be relieved from it, but can request this of the assembly. Except as the bylaws may otherwise provide, the re-

quest can be granted by unanimous consent, or a motion to that effect, which is debatable and amendable, can be offered.

Standard Descriptive Characteristics

A *Request to Be Excused from a Duty:*

1. Takes precedence over any motion with whose purpose it is connected and can also be made at any time when no question is pending. A motion on a request that is pending yields to all subsidiary motions except *Postpone Indefinitely,* to all privileged motions, and to other incidental motions.
2. Can be applied in reference to any motion or parliamentary situation out of which it arises. All subsidiary motions except *Postpone Indefinitely* can be applied to it.
3. Is in order when another has the floor if it requires immediate attention.
4. Does not require a second except when moved formally *by the maker of the request.* A motion to *grant* the request of another member does not require a second since the maker of the request and the maker of the motion—two members—wish the question to be considered.
5. Is debatable.
6. Is amendable.
7. Requires a majority vote, but is frequently settled by unanimous consent.
8. Where the member requesting to be excused from a duty has learned of the action taken on his or her request, only a negative vote can be reconsidered.

Further Rules and Explanation

If a duty is not compulsory, a member can decline when he is first named to it or, if absent at that time, when he first

learns of his election or appointment. At times other than
during a meeting, such a notice of declination can be addressed to the secretary or to the appointing power. Since
in these cases the duty is not compulsory, no motion to ex-
cuse the member is necessary.

A member who remains silent when presumably aware
that he has been named to a duty is regarded as accepting,
and he thereby places himself under the same obligations as
if he had expressly accepted.

If a member who has accepted an office, committee assignment, or other duty finds that he is unable to perform
it, he should submit his resignation—normally in writing—
to the secretary or appointing power. By doing so, he is, in
effect, requesting to be excused from a duty. The chair, on
reading or announcing the resignation, can assume a motion "that the resignation be accepted."

The duties of a position must not be abandoned until a
resignation has been accepted and becomes effective, or at
least until there has been a reasonable opportunity for it to
be accepted.

A request to be excused from a duty *essential to the functioning of a society or assembly* is a question of privilege affecting the organization of the assembly; and so also is the filling
of a vacancy created by the acceptance of a resignation. In
such cases, the assembly can proceed immediately to fill the
vacancy, unless notice is required or other provision for filling
vacancies is made in the bylaws. In the case of a resignation
from office, unless the bylaws provide otherwise, the assembly
cannot proceed to fill the vacancy immediately since notice is
a requirement. But if a member is elected and declines, no
notice is required to complete the election immediately or at
the next meeting (see p. 430).

RESIGNATION FROM MEMBERSHIP.   A mem-
ber in good standing with his dues paid cannot be com-

pelled to continue his membership so that additional obligations are incurred. His resignation should be accepted immediately, and if it is not, he incurs no obligation after his resignation has been sent in, provided he does not avail himself of the privileges of membership. It is different with members who have not paid their dues up to the date of sending in their resignations. Until they have settled their dues, the society is under no obligation to accept their resignations, and thus additional amounts may become due. If their dues are not paid within a reasonable time, instead of accepting their resignations, the society may expel them. A resignation sent in to escape charges need not be accepted. The charges may be preferred, and the trial should proceed the same as if the resignation had not been sent in.

§33. REQUESTS AND INQUIRIES

In connection with business in a meeting, members may wish to obtain information or to do or have something done that requires permission of the assembly. Any member can make the following types of inquiry or request: (a) *Parliamentary Inquiry;* (b) *Point of Information;* (c) *For Permission (or Leave) to Withdraw or Modify a Motion;* (d) *To Read Papers;* and (e) *For Any Other Privilege.*

Standard Descriptive Characteristics

With respect to the requests and inquiries growing out of the business of the assembly that are listed above, the following rules apply:

1. All take precedence over any motion with whose purpose they are connected, and can also be made at any time when no question is pending. A motion on a re-

quest that is pending yields to all privileged motions and to other incidental motions.

2. All can be applied in reference to any motion or parliamentary situation out of which they arise. No subsidiary motion can be applied to any of them.

3. All are in order when another has the floor if they require immediate attention.

4. A *Parliamentary Inquiry* and a *Point of Information* do not require a second. The other requests do not require a second, except when moved formally *by the maker of the request.* A motion to *grant* the request of another member does not require a second, since two members already wish the question to come up—the maker of the request and the maker of the motion.

5. All are not debatable.

6. All are not amendable.

7. No vote is taken on a *Parliamentary Inquiry* and a *Point of Information.* The other requests require a majority vote in order to be granted, and are frequently settled by unanimous consent. When it is too late for renewal, unanimous consent is *required* to grant permission to withdraw a motion to *Reconsider* (p. 306, l. 16–20), or to withdraw previous notice of a proposed motion requiring such notice (pp. 116–18).

8. A *Parliamentary Inquiry* and a *Point of Information* are not subject to reconsideration. The vote on a request *For Permission to Modify a Motion, To Read Papers,* and *For Any Other Privilege* can be reconsidered. On a request *For Permission to Withdraw a Motion,* only a negative vote can be reconsidered.

Further Rules and Explanation (with Forms)

a. PARLIAMENTARY INQUIRY. A *Parliamentary Inquiry* is a question directed to the presiding officer to obtain information on a matter of parliamentary law or the rules of the organization bearing on the business at hand. It is the chair's duty to answer such questions when it may assist a member to make an appropriate motion, raise a proper point of order, or understand the parliamentary situation or the effect of a motion. The chair is not obliged to answer hypothetical questions.

In making an inquiry, the inquirer arises, and without obtaining the floor, addresses the chair as follows:

MEMBER A: Madam President, I rise to a parliamentary inquiry. [Or, "A parliamentary inquiry, please."]

CHAIR: The member will state the inquiry.

MEMBER A: Is it in order at this time to move the previous question?

The chair's reply to a parliamentary inquiry is not subject to an appeal, since it is an opinion, not a ruling. A member has the right to act contrary to this opinion, however, and if ruled out of order, to appeal such a ruling. If an inquiry is made when another member has the floor and an immediate answer is not necessary, the chair can defer a reply until the floor has been yielded.

b. POINT OF INFORMATION. A *Point of Information* is a request directed to the chair, or through the chair to another officer or member, for information relevant to the business at hand but not related to parliamentary procedure. When addressed to the chair, it is treated like a parliamentary inquiry, as follows:

MEMBER A: Mr. President, I rise to a point of information. [Or, "A point of information, please."]

CHAIR: The member will state the point.

MEMBER A: Will the convention delegates report at this meeting?

Or:

MEMBER A: This motion calls for a large expenditure. Will the treasurer state the present balance?

If information is desired of a member who is speaking, the inquirer may use the following form:

MEMBER A: Madam President, will the member yield for a question?

Or:

MEMBER A: Mr. President, I would like to ask the gentleman [or "the member"] a question.

If the speaker consents to the interruption, the time consumed will be taken out of his allowed time. The chair therefore asks if the speaker is willing to be interrupted, and if he consents, directs the inquirer to proceed. Although the presiding officer generally remains silent during the ensuing exchange, the inquiry, the reply, and any resulting colloquy are made in the third person through the chair. To protect decorum, members are not allowed to carry on discussion directly with one another.

An inquiry of this kind may also be for the purpose of reminding a speaker of a point to be made in argument, or it may be intended to rebut his position; but it must always be put in the form of a question.

c. REQUEST FOR PERMISSION (OR LEAVE) TO WITHDRAW OR MODIFY A MOTION. Conditions for withdrawing or modifying a motion depend upon how soon the mover states his wish to withdraw or modify it. *Permission* for him to do so is required only after the motion to which it pertains has been stated by the chair as pending.

Before a motion has been stated by the chair, it is the property of its mover, who can withdraw it or modify it without asking the consent of anyone. Thus, *in the brief interval between the making of a motion and the time when the chair places it before the assembly by stating it,* the maker can withdraw it as follows:

MEMBER A (who made the motion): Madam President, I withdraw the motion.

Or:

MEMBER A (who made the motion): Mr. President, I wish to modify the motion by striking out "demand" and inserting "urge."

In the same interval also, another member can ask if the maker of the motion is willing to withdraw it or accept a change in it, which suggestion the maker can either accept or reject. In such a case the chair either announces, "The motion has been withdrawn," or states the question on the modified motion. If a motion is modified, the seconder can withdraw his second. When the seconder withdraws his second to the modified motion, the member who suggested the modification has, in effect, supplied a second.

After a motion has been stated by the chair, it belongs to the meeting as a whole, and the maker must request the assembly's permission to withdraw or modify his own motion, according to the rules stated in Standard Characteristics 1–8, above. In such cases the procedure is as follows.

To *withdraw* a motion that is before the assembly, the member who made it may use this form:

MEMBER A (who made the motion): Madam President, I ask permission [or "leave"] to withdraw the motion.

The chair treats this first as a unanimous-consent request. That is, if no one objects, the announcement is:

CHAIR: Unless there is objection [pause] the motion is withdrawn.

If there is an objection, the chair of his own accord can put the question on granting the request, or any member other than the one making the request can move "that permission to withdraw the motion be granted." If a member other than the one making the request made the motion, it does not require a second, since the maker of the motion to grant permission and the maker of the request surely both favor it.

A request for permission to withdraw a motion, or a motion to grant such permission, can be made at any time before voting on the question has begun, even though the motion has been amended, and even though subsidiary or incidental motions may be pending. Any such motions that adhere to the main motion cease to be before the assembly and require no further disposition if the main motion is withdrawn. Any member can suggest that the maker of a motion ask permission to withdraw it, which the maker can do or decline to do, as he chooses.

After a question has been divided, one or more of the parts can be withdrawn without affecting the other parts. A motion to *Reconsider* (**37**), or a previous notice of a proposed motion requiring such notice (pp. 116–18), cannot be withdrawn after it is too late for renewal, unless unanimous consent is given.

After a motion has been withdrawn, the situation is as though it had never been made; therefore, the same motion can be made again at the same meeting.

To *modify* a motion after it has been stated by the chair, the maker asks permission to do so, as in the case of withdrawal of a motion. If there is no objection, the chair states

1 the question on the modified motion. If anyone objects, the
chair must then determine whether an amendment equivalent to the requested modification would be in order. If not,
the modification may not be made unless a motion to sus-
5 pend the rules is made and adopted. If a motion for such an
amendment is in order, the chair can assume it or any member can move it formally. The amendment requires a second
if moved by the member who originally made the request.
The rules governing consideration of amendments are fol-
10 lowed (see **12**). A pending motion can be amended only by
vote or unanimous consent of the assembly, even if the maker
of the motion states that he "accepts" the amendment. (See
also treatment of "Friendly Amendments," p. 154.)

15   d. REQUEST TO READ PAPERS.   If any member
objects, a member has no right to read from—or to have
the secretary read from—any paper or book as a part of his
speech without permission of the assembly. This rule is a
protection against the use of reading as a means of pro-
20 longing debate and delaying business. It is customary, however, to permit members to read short, pertinent, printed
extracts in debate so long as they do not abuse the privilege.
If a member wishes to do so, he can, while speaking in debate, say, "If there is no objection, I would like to read . . .
25 [indicating the nature and length of the paper]." The member can then begin to read unless another member objects.*
In such a case, at any time until the speaker has finished
reading, another member can interrupt him by an objection, which must be addressed to the chair. Or, if the
30 speaker desiring to read prefers, he can formally request
permission: "Mr. President, I ask permission to read a statement . . . [briefly describing it, as above]"; and the chair

---

*The procedure of presuming permission to read until objection is
raised is applicable *only in debate on a pending question.*

then asks if there is objection. In either case, if there is an
objection, the chair can, of his own accord, put the question on granting permission, or any member can move
"that permission to read a paper in debate be granted."
This motion requires no second unless moved by the member who made the request. Action of the assembly granting
a request to read a paper can be reconsidered at any time
until the reading has been concluded.

The foregoing paragraph applies only to papers or documents that are not before the assembly for action. When any
paper is laid before the assembly for action, it is a right of
every member that it be read once; and, if there is any debate
or amendment, that it be read again before members are
asked to vote on it. Except as just stated, no member has the
right to have anything read without permission of the assembly. But whenever any member requests that a document that
is before the assembly be read—obviously for information
and not for delay—and no one objects, the chair normally
should direct that it be read. If there is an objection, a majority vote is required to order that it be read. If a member
was absent from the hall when the paper under consideration
was read—even though absent on duty—he cannot insist on
its being read again; in this case, the convenience of the assembly is more important than that of a single member.

e. REQUEST FOR ANY OTHER PRIVILEGE.
When a member desires to make a request not covered by
one of the four types explained above—as, for example, a request to address remarks or make a presentation while no
motion is pending—he rises, addresses the chair, and, as soon
as he catches the presiding officer's attention, states his request. Although he does not have to wait for recognition and
can make his request even though another member has been
assigned the floor, he should never interrupt a member
speaking unless sure that urgency justifies it. Generally, such

1   matters are settled by unanimous consent or informally, but
     if there is an objection, a motion can be made to grant the
     request. If explanation is required, it can be requested or
     given, but this must not extend into debate. These requests
5   should be treated so as to interrupt the proceedings as little
     as is consistent with the demands of justice.

MOTIONS THAT BRING A QUESTION AGAIN BEFORE THE ASSEMBLY

See 6, pages 72ff., for a list of these motions and a description of their characteristics as a group.

§34. TAKE FROM THE TABLE

The object of the motion to *Take from the Table* is to make pending again before the assembly a motion or a series of adhering motions that previously has been laid on the table (see **17**).

Standard Descriptive Characteristics

The motion to *Take from the Table:*

1. Takes precedence over no pending motion, and therefore cannot be moved while any other question is pending; but, subject to the conditions indicated in the next sentence, it takes precedence over a main motion that has been made but has not yet been stated by the chair. Unless it is moved under a suspension of the rules (**25**) it must be moved at a time when no program or rule interferes, and while business of the class to which the

1   subject question belongs, unfinished business, general
     orders, or new business is in order; and it cannot inter-
     rupt a series of motions connected with taking up a sin-
     gle item of business (see below). It yields to privileged
5   and incidental motions but not to subsidiary ones.

2. Can be applied to any question or series of *adhering*
   motions that lies on the table as explained in the first
   paragraph under *Further Rules and Explanations,*
   below. This motion is not in order, however, until some
10   business or interrupting matter has been transacted or
   dealt with since the question was laid on the table; and
   if it is moved and voted down, the motion to *Take from
   the Table* cannot be renewed until some further business
   has been transacted. No subsidiary motion can be ap-
15   plied to the motion to *Take from the Table.*

3. Is out of order when another has the floor; but a member can claim preference in being recognized for the
   purpose of making this motion ahead of a new main
   motion, or he can claim the floor for such a purpose
20   after a new main motion has been made but before the
   new motion has been stated by the chair (see below).

4. Must be seconded.

5. Is not debatable.

6. Is not amenable.

25 7. Requires a majority vote.

8. Cannot be reconsidered—since, if it is adopted, the
   question can be laid on the table again should any legitimate need arise to do so, and since, if it is voted
   down, it can be renewed each time that any business has
30   been transacted.

Further Rules and Explanation

TIME LIMITS ON TAKING A QUESTION FROM
35 THE TABLE.   A question that has been laid on the table

remains there and can be taken from the table during the
same session (**8**), or, if the next regular business session will
be held before a quarterly time interval has elapsed (see p.
88), also at the next session after it was laid on the table. If
not taken from the table within these time limits, the question dies, although it can be reintroduced later as a new
question.

RIGHT OF WAY IN PREFERENCE TO A NEW
MAIN MOTION.   In ordinary assemblies a question is
supposed to be laid on the table only temporarily, with the
expectation that its consideration will be resumed after disposal of the interrupting matter or at a more convenient
time. Consequently, as soon as the business or interrupting
matter has been disposed of, any member can seek recognition for the purpose of moving to take the question from
the table; or, so long as it remains on the table, he can do
so at any time under the classes of business listed in Standard Characteristic 1 above—except while another motion
is pending or while a series of motions connected with one
question is being introduced, as explained in the next paragraph. If the chair recognizes someone else as having risen
and addressed the chair first, a member who rose at about
the same time to move to take the question from the table
should remain standing and say that he rises for this purpose, and the chair should then assign him the floor. Or,
even after a new motion has been made but before it has
been stated by the chair, a member who quickly rises and
says that he does so to move to take the question from the
table should be assigned the floor. The principle is that, if
the assembly so desires, a motion already within its control
by being only temporarily disposed of (pp. 88, 329–30) has
the right of way over a new main motion.

Even if no question is pending, a motion to *Take from
the Table* cannot interrupt a series of motions connected

with bringing up a single item of business, but must wait until the complete series is disposed of. For example, such a series of motions is in process of being dealt with:

- when the assembly has just voted to suspend the rules and permit a certain main motion to be introduced;
- when a question has just been laid on the table for the announced purpose of admitting another motion;
- when a previous action has just been rescinded (**35**) to enable a conflicting main motion to be made; or
- when a main motion has just been voted down after a member stated in debate that in that event he would offer a different motion covering the case.

In each of the above instances, until the main motion that was specified has been made and disposed of, it is not in order to move to take still another question from the table.

STATUS OF A QUESTION TAKEN FROM THE TABLE.   When a question is taken from the table, it is before the assembly, with everything adhering to it, exactly as it was when laid on the table. If amendments and a motion to *Commit* were pending when a resolution was laid on the table, then when it is taken from the table the question is first on the motion to *Commit*. The same would be true if a motion to *Postpone to a Certain Time* were adhering to a resolution, except that if the resolution is not taken from the table until after the time of proposed postponement, the motion to postpone is ignored. If the question is taken up on the same day that it was laid on the table, members who had exhausted their right of debate cannot speak on the question again; but if on another day, no notice is taken of speeches previously made. The *Previous Question* or a limitation or extension of debate is not exhausted, however, if the question to which such an order was applied is taken

from the table at the same session, even on another day—
as in a convention. At the next session any such order is exhausted and the regular rules of debate prevail.

Form and Example

The form used in making this motion is, for example, "I
move to take from the table the resolution relating to . . .
and its amendment."

If Member A, who has risen to seek the floor for the
purpose of making this motion, observes that the chair has
recognized another member who rose at about the same
time and who apparently intends to make a new main motion, the procedure would be as follows:

MEMBER A (remaining standing and interrupting): Mr. President, I
rise for the purpose of moving to take a question from the table.

Upon recognition, Member A then would move
". . . to take from the table the motion relating to . . . "

If Member A did not rise to claim the floor before the
chair recognized another member who already has made a
new motion, then before this question has been stated by the
chair, Member A can quickly rise and address the chair, thus:

MEMBER A: Madam President.

CHAIR: For what purpose does the member rise?

MEMBER A: I rise for the purpose of moving . . . [and so on, as in
the case above].

§35. RESCIND; AMEND SOMETHING PREVIOUSLY ADOPTED

By means of the motions to *Rescind* and to *Amend
Something Previously Adopted*—which are two forms of one

incidental main motion governed by identical rules—the assembly can change an action previously taken or ordered. *Rescind*—also known as *Repeal* or *Annul*—is the motion by which a previous action or order can be canceled or countermanded. The effect of *Rescind* is to strike out an entire main motion, resolution, rule, bylaw, section, or paragraph that has been adopted at some previous time. *Amend Something Previously Adopted* is the motion that can be used if it is desired to change only a part of the text, or to substitute a different version.

Standard Descriptive Characteristics

The motions to *Rescind* and to *Amend Something Previously Adopted*:

1. Take precedence over nothing, and can therefore be moved only when no other motion is pending. *Previous notice* (pp. 116–18) of intent to offer one of these motions at the next meeting can be given while another question is pending, however—provided that it does not interrupt a speaker (see Standard Characteristic 7). These motions yield to subsidiary, privileged, and incidental motions.

2. Can be applied to anything (e.g., bylaw, rule, policy, decision, or choice) which has continuing force and effect and which was made or created at any time or times as the result of the *adoption* of one or more main motions. Can also be applied to any precedent created as a result of a ruling of the chair or an appeal that has been taken from a ruling of the chair. (However, see below for actions that cannot be rescinded or amended.) All of the subsidiary motions can be applied to the motions to *Rescind* and to *Amend Something Previously Adopted*.

3. Are out of order when another has the floor; but previous notice of intent to offer one of these motions at the

next meeting can be given after another member has *1* been assigned the floor, provided that he has not begun to speak.

4. Must be seconded.

5. Are debatable; debate can go into the merits of the *5* question which it is proposed to rescind or amend.

6. Are amendable, by the processes of primary and secondary amendment in any of the forms discussed in **12,** as applicable to the particular case. Thus, a motion to *Rescind* can be amended, for example, to become a mo- *10* tion to strike out only a part of what it was proposed to rescind. But if a motion to *Rescind* or to *Amend Something Previously Adopted* is amended so that the change proposed by the amended motion then exceeds the scope of a previous notice that was given, the effect of *15* the previous notice is destroyed and the motion can no longer be adopted by a majority vote (see Standard Characteristic 7). When these motions *require* previous notice (as may be the case with respect to a motion to rescind or amend a provision of the bylaws or a special *20* rule of order), such a motion cannot be amended so as to make the proposed change greater than that for which notice has been given.

7. In an assembly, except when applied to a constitution, bylaws, or special rules of order, require (a) a two-thirds *25* vote, (b) a majority vote when notice of intent to make the motion, stating the complete substance of the proposed change, has been given at the previous meeting or in the call of the present meeting, or (c) a vote of a majority of the entire membership—whichever is most *30* practical to obtain. In a committee, these motions require a two-thirds vote unless all committee members who voted for the motion to be rescinded or amended are present or have received ample notice, in which case they require a majority vote. A motion to rescind or *35*

1 amend provisions of a constitution or bylaws is subject
to the requirements for amendment as contained in the
constitution or bylaws (see **56, 57**). If the bylaws or
governing instrument contains no provision relating to
5 amendment, a motion to rescind or amend applied to a
constitution or to bylaws is subject to the same voting
requirement as to rescind or amend special rules of
order—that is, it requires (a) previous notice as described above *and* a two-thirds vote or (b) a vote of a
10 majority of the entire membership.
  8. A negative vote on these motions can be reconsidered,
  but not an affirmative vote.

Further Rules and Explanation
15

RIGHT OF ANY MEMBER TO MAKE THE MO-
TIONS, WITHOUT TIME LIMIT.   In contrast to the
case of the motion to *Reconsider,* there is no time limit on
making these motions after the adoption of the measure to
20 which they are applied, and they can be moved by any
member, regardless of how he voted on the original question. When previous notice has been given, it is usual to
wait for the member who gave notice of these motions to
move them; but if he does not, any member can do so.
25

CONDITIONS DETERMINING TYPE OF VOTE
TO BE SOUGHT.   The type of vote (two thirds, a majority when previous notice has been given, or a majority of
the entire membership) to be sought for adopting one of
30 these motions will depend on conditions. Ordinarily it is
desirable to give previous notice if there is a possibility of
serious disagreement. The two-thirds vote without previous
notice may be used for matters requiring emergency action.
In many organizations, a majority of the entire membership
35 may never be obtainable at a meeting; but this may become

the best method in a convention of delegates, or in a small board.

PROPOSED AMENDMENTS BEYOND THE SCOPE OF THE NOTICE.   As noted in Standard Descriptive Characteristic 6 above, when previous notice is a *requirement* for the adoption of a motion to rescind or amend something previously adopted, no subsidiary motion to amend is in order that proposes a change greater than that for which notice was given. This is always the case, for example, when the bylaws of an organization require previous notice for their amendment, which they should do (pp. 562–63). It will also be the case, as a practical matter, whenever a majority of the entire membership is not in attendance at the time the vote is taken on a motion to rescind or amend a provision of the constitution or bylaws, or a special rule of order. In either of the situations described above, no subsidiary motion to amend is in order that proposes a change going beyond the scope of the notice which was given, for the reason that adoption of such a motion will destroy the effect of the notice, and the motion is thus tantamount to a motion to *Postpone Indefinitely.*

ACTIONS THAT CANNOT BE RESCINDED OR AMENDED.   The motions to *Rescind* and to *Amend Something Previously Adopted* are not in order under the following circumstances:

a) When it has previously been moved to reconsider the vote on the main motion, and the question can be reached by calling up the motion to *Reconsider* (**37**).
b) When something has been done, as a result of the vote on the main motion, that is impossible to undo. (The unexecuted part of an order, however, can be rescinded or amended.)

c) When a resignation has been acted upon, or a person has been elected to or expelled from membership or office, and the person was present or has been officially notified of the action. (The only way to reverse an expulsion is to follow whatever procedure is prescribed by the bylaws for admission or reinstatement. For the case of an election, see pp. 642–43 regarding removal of a person from office.)

Form and Example

When previous notice has been given, the motions to *Rescind* or to *Amend Something Previously Adopted* may be made as follows:

MEMBER A (obtaining the floor): In accordance with notice given at the last meeting, I move to rescind the resolution that authorized additional landscaping of the grounds. [Or ". . . to amend the resolution . . . by adding . . . "] (Second.)

In such a case, a majority vote is sufficient.

When no notice of the motion to *Rescind* or to *Amend* has been given, the motions may be made as follows:

MEMBER A (obtaining the floor): I move to rescind the motion relating to . . . adopted at the May meeting. [Or ". . . to amend the motion . . . by inserting . . . "] (Second.)

Without previous notice, the motion requires a two-thirds vote or a majority of the entire membership for its adoption.

In a great many instances, the motion or resolution originally adopted is not referred to, and only the bylaw, rule, or policy to be rescinded or amended is mentioned. For example:

MEMBER A (obtaining the floor): In accordance with the notice given in the call of this meeting, I move to amend Article V, Section 3 of the bylaws by striking out subparagraph (c) thereof. (Second.)

Rescind and Expunge from the Minutes

On extremely rare occasions when it is desired not only to rescind action but also to express the strongest disapproval, a member may move to *Rescind and Expunge from the Minutes* (or *the Record*). Adoption of this motion requires an affirmative vote of a majority of the entire membership, and may be inadvisable unless the support is even greater. Even a unanimous vote at a meeting is insufficient if that vote is not a majority of the entire membership. If such a motion is adopted, the secretary, in the presence of the assembly, draws a single line through or around the offending words in the minutes, and writes across them the words, "Rescinded and Ordered Expunged," with the date and his signature. In the recorded minutes the words that are expunged must not be blotted or cut out so that they cannot be read, since this would make it impossible to verify whether more was expunged than ordered. If the minutes are published, the expunged material is omitted. Rather than expunging, it is usually better to rescind the previous action and then, if advisable, to adopt a resolution condemning the action which has been rescinded.

§36. DISCHARGE A COMMITTEE

By means of the motion to *Discharge a Committee* from further consideration of a question or subject, the assembly can take the matter out of a committee's hands* after referring it to the committee and before the committee has

---

*Or a committee can take it out of a subcommittee's hands.

1 made a final report on it, and the assembly itself can consider it.

So long as a question is in the hands of a committee, the
assembly cannot consider another motion involving practi-
5 cally the same question.

The rules governing this motion are similar to those applying to the motion to *Rescind* or to *Amend Something
Previously Adopted*—of which it is a particular case in certain
applications, as explained on pages 302–303.

10

Standard Descriptive Characteristics

The motion to *Discharge a Committee:*

15 1. Takes precedence over nothing, and therefore can be
moved only when no other question is pending. *Previous notice* of intent to offer the motion at the next meeting can be given while another question is pending,
however—provided that it does not interrupt a speaker.
20 This motion yields to all subsidiary, privileged, and incidental motions.

2. Can be applied to any main motion, or any other matter, that has been referred to a committee and that the
committee has not yet finally reported to the assembly.
25 All of the subsidiary motions can be applied to it.

3. Is out of order when another has the floor; but previous
notice of intent to offer this motion at the next meeting
can be given after another member has been assigned
the floor, provided that he has not begun to speak.

30 4. Must be seconded.

5. Is debatable; debate can go into the merits of the question in the hands of the committee.

6. Is amendable. For example, the motion can be amended
as to the time at which the assembly is to consider the
35 question; or an amendment to the effect that the com-

mittee be instructed to report instead of being discharged can be moved as a substitute.

7. Since the motion would change action already taken by the assembly, requires (a) a two-thirds vote, (b) a majority vote when notice of intent to make the motion has been given at the previous meeting within a quarterly time interval or in the call of the present meeting, or (c) a vote of a majority of the entire membership—whichever is most practical to obtain. To prevent business from being delayed by a committee, however, there are two special circumstances under which the motion requires only a majority vote (even without notice): (a) if the committee fails to report within a prescribed time as instructed, and (b) while the assembly is considering any partial report of the committee.

8. A negative vote can be reconsidered, but not an affirmative vote.

Further Rules and Explanation

CIRCUMSTANCES JUSTIFYING THE MOTION; ALTERNATIVE PROCEDURES.   Action to discharge a committee from further consideration of a question or subject is generally advisable only when the committee has failed to report with appropriate promptness or when, for some urgent reason, the assembly desires to proceed on the matter without further aid from the committee, or wishes to drop the matter.

If the committee to which the matter was referred has not yet taken it up and if it is not too late to move to *Reconsider* (the day of its committal or the next business-meeting day), the appropriate motion is to reconsider the vote on the motion of referral, which requires only a majority vote. The motion of referral may have been a subsidiary motion to *Commit* (**13**) or a main motion, depending on the case, as explained below.

Instead of discharging the committee, the assembly can instruct it to report at a reasonable specified time. A motion to do this is an incidental main motion (unless it is moved as a substitute for a motion to discharge the committee, in which case it is a subsidiary motion; see **12**). If no instruction as to time of reporting has been given previously, this motion requires only a majority vote for adoption. If it changes a previously specified reporting time before that time has arrived, however, the vote required is the same as for the motion to *Discharge a Committee*.

No motion to *Discharge a Committee* is needed when a committee's final report on a referred question or subject has been received by the assembly, since the committee is then automatically discharged from further consideration of the matter.

EFFECT OF DISCHARGING A COMMITTEE. When a committee is discharged from considering a matter, either by the adoption of a motion to discharge it or by the submission of its final report, the committee continues in existence if it is a standing committee, but ceases to exist if it is a special committee that was appointed to take up the matter. In any case, when a committee is thus discharged, its chairman returns to the secretary of the society all papers relating to the referred matter that were previously entrusted to him.

When a committee is discharged from further consideration of a question which was pending at the time of its referral and which was referred by means of the subsidiary motion to *Commit*, the question comes before the assembly automatically at that time (unless the committee is discharged by means of a motion that includes the specification of a later time for considering it). If no later time was specified in the motion, the question can then be postponed, if desired; or if the assembly wishes to drop the matter, the question can be postponed indefinitely. If a motion to *Discharge a Committee* specifies a later time for considering the question and does not make it a special order, the question comes up under the same conditions as if postponed to that time without making it a special order—that is, it is a general order for the time named. If the motion to *Discharge a Committee* includes a provision making the question a special order, it requires a two-thirds vote, just as any other motion to make a special order. (See pp. 177–80 regarding the priority to which a question is subject when it is due to come up after postponement.)

On the other hand, a motion to discharge a committee from further consideration of a subject that was referred to the committee by means of a *main* motion is a particular case of the motion to *Rescind* or to *Amend Something Previously Adopted* (**35**). When such a motion to *Discharge a Committee* has been adopted, another main motion is needed to bring before the assembly the matter that was referred; otherwise it dies.

Form and Example

The form used in making this motion, as applied to a question being considered by a *standing committee,* may be:

MEMBER A (obtaining the floor): I move that the Finance Committee be discharged from further consideration of the resolution relating to . . . (Second.)

In the case of a *special committee,* the following form may be used:

MEMBER A (obtaining the floor): I move that the committee to which was referred the resolution relating to . . . be discharged. (Second.)

If it is desired to take up the question at a later time, there may be added to either of the above forms, for example, the words, "and that the resolution be considered at 4 P.M." (in which case it is a general order for that time), or, "and that it be made a special order for . . . "

If the motion to discharge the committee is adopted and includes no provision for consideration at a later time, and if the question was referred while pending (by means of the subsidiary motion to *Commit*), the chair announces the result and immediately states the question brought out of committee. For example:

CHAIR: There are two thirds in the affirmative and the committee is discharged. The question is now on the resolution, "*Resolved,* . . . "

§37. RECONSIDER

Reconsider—a motion of American origin—enables a majority in an assembly, within a limited time and without notice, to bring back for further consideration a motion which has already been voted on. The purpose of reconsidering a vote is to permit correction of hasty, ill-advised, or erroneous action, or to take into account added information or a changed situation that has developed since the taking of the vote.

To provide both usefulness and protection against abuse, the motion to *Reconsider* has the following *unique characteristics:*

a) It can be made only by a member who voted with the prevailing side. In other words, a reconsideration can be moved only by one who voted *aye* if the motion involved was adopted, or *no* if the motion was lost. (In standing and special committees, the motion to *Reconsider* can be made by any member who did not vote on the losing side—including one who did not vote at all.) It should be noted that it is possible for a minority to be the prevailing side if a motion requiring a two-thirds vote for adoption is lost. A member who voted by ballot may make the motion if he is willing to waive the secrecy of his ballot. Also, if the motion to be reconsidered was adopted by unanimous consent, all the members present at the time of the adoption are in the same position as if they had voted on the prevailing side and qualify to move to reconsider. This requirement for making the motion to *Reconsider* is a protection against its dilatory use by a defeated minority—especially when the motion is debatable (see Standard Characteristic 5, below) and the minority is large enough to prevent adoption of the *Previous Question* (**16**). When a member who cannot move a reconsideration believes there are valid reasons for one, he should try, if there is time or opportunity, to persuade someone who voted with the prevailing side to make such a motion. Otherwise, he can obtain the floor while no business is pending and briefly state his reasons for hoping that a reconsideration will be moved, provided that this does not run into debate; or, if necessary while business is pending, he can request permission to state such reasons (see, *Request for Any Other Privilege,* pp. 287–88).

b) The making of this motion is subject to time limits, as follows: In a session of one day—such as an ordinary meeting of a club or a one-day convention—the motion to *Reconsider* can be made only on the same day the vote to be reconsidered was taken. In a convention or session of more than one day, a reconsideration can be moved only on the same day the original vote was taken or on the next succeeding day within the session on which a business meeting is held. These time limitations do not apply to standing or special committees (see pp. 318–19).

1   c) The *making* of this motion has a higher rank than its
     consideration; that is, the motion can be made and sec-
     onded at times when it is not in order for it to come be-
     fore the assembly for debate or vote. In such a case it
5   can be taken up later, even after it would be too late to
     move it in the first place. If the motion to *Reconsider* is
     introduced at a time when it cannot be taken up, the
     chair does not state the question on it as pending, but
     asks the secretary to record the motion as made and sec-
10   onded. This temporarily suspends any action growing
     out of the vote it is proposed to reconsider. While a mo-
     tion to reconsider the vote on a main motion has this
     status, a member can bring the motion before the as-
     sembly at any time when its consideration is in order.
15   When he does this, he is said to *call up* the motion to
     Reconsider. Except by unanimous consent, a motion to
     Reconsider that has not been finally disposed of cannot
     be withdrawn after it is too late to renew it; that is, it
     can be withdrawn only within the same time limits as for
20   making the motion in the first place.

Standard Descriptive Characteristics

The motion to *Reconsider:*

25

1.   a) With respect to *making* the motion, takes prece-
     dence over any other motion whatever and yields to
     nothing.* The making of this motion is in order
     when any other question is pending, and also after
30   the assembly has voted to adjourn, if the member
     rose and addressed the chair before the chair de-

---

*The motion to *Reconsider* has a special form known as *Reconsider and
Enter on the Minutes,* however, which outranks the regular form of the motion (see pp. 321–24).

clared the meeting adjourned. If a reconsideration
appears to require immediate action in the latter
case, the vote on adjourning should be retaken.
Even while an order for the *Previous Question* is in
effect on a motion which is immediately pending,
until the chair actually begins to take the vote, the
making of a motion to *Reconsider* an earlier vote on
another question is in order.*

b) With respect to its *consideration,* has only the same
rank as that of the motion to be reconsidered, although it has the right of way in preference to any
new motion of equal rank until such a motion has
been stated by the chair as pending. (The procedure
for calling up a motion to *Reconsider* in preference to
a main motion just made by someone else, and relating to another matter, is similar to that described for
moving to *Take from the Table;* see **34**). Provided that
no question is pending, the reconsideration of a vote
disposing of a main motion, either temporarily or
permanently, can be taken up even while the assembly is in the midst of taking up the general orders.

2. Can be applied to the vote on any motion except: (a) a
motion which can be renewed (see pp. 328–29); (b) an
affirmative vote whose provisions have been partly carried out;** (c) an affirmative vote in the nature of a
contract when the party to the contract has been notified of the outcome; (d) any vote which has caused
something to be done that it is impossible to undo; (e)
a vote on a motion to *Reconsider;* or (f) when practically

---

*The *Previous Question* itself can be reconsidered only before any vote
has been taken under it.

**Exception (b) does not apply to a motion to *Limit or Extend Limits
of Debate,* on which the vote can be reconsidered even if such an order has
been partly carried out.

the same result as desired can be obtained by some other parliamentary motion. In the case of subsidiary or incidental motions that adhered to a main motion, however, *Reconsider* can be applied only in such a way that the reconsideration takes place while the main motion to which they adhered is pending—either before the main motion is voted on or when it is being reconsidered at the same time. The same is true where one subsidiary or incidental motion adheres to another; for example, *Reconsider* can be applied to the vote on a secondary amendment only in such a way that the reconsideration takes place before the primary amendment involved is voted on or while the primary amendment is being reconsidered.

By application of these principles, it follows that certain motions cannot be reconsidered, while in the case of others only the vote on an affirmative result can be reconsidered, and with still others, only the vote on a negative result. (See tinted pp. 47–48 for a list of the motions in each of these categories; see also Standard Characteristic 8 in the sections on each individual motion.)

The motion to *Lay on the Table* can be applied to the motion to *Reconsider*. Motions to *Postpone to a Certain Time,* to *Limit or Extend Limits of Debate,* and for the *Previous Question* can also be applied to it when it is debatable (see Standard Characteristic 5). When a motion to *Reconsider* is postponed or laid on the table, all adhering questions are also postponed or go to the table. Motions to *Postpone Indefinitely, Amend,* or *Commit* cannot be applied to a motion to *Reconsider*.

3. Is in order (with respect to *making* the motion) even after another person has been assigned the floor, so long as he has not actually begun to speak. The *calling up* of a motion to *Reconsider* is out of order when another has the floor.

4. Must be seconded at the time it is made. Unlike the making of the motion, which must be done by a person who voted with the prevailing side, the seconding can be done by any member regardless of how he voted on the motion to be reconsidered. The *calling up* of the motion to *Reconsider* does not require a second.

5. Is debatable in all cases in which the motion proposed to be reconsidered is debatable, and when debatable, opens to debate the merits of the question whose reconsideration is proposed. (See pp. 317–18, however, regarding a series of motions proposed to be reconsidered, and the question that is opened to debate in such a case.) When the motion proposed to be reconsidered is not debatable—either because of its nature or because it is subject to an unexhausted order for the *Previous Question* (**16**)—the motion to *Reconsider* is undebatable. Similarly, if the *Previous Question* is in effect on a pending question or series of questions, and if a motion which is proposed to be reconsidered adheres to these pending question(s) in such a way that the reconsideration must be taken up before the *Previous Question* is exhausted, both the motion to *Reconsider* and the motion to be reconsidered are undebatable—even if the latter motion was open to debate as its earlier consideration and the *Previous Question* was ordered later.

6. Is not amendable.

7. Requires only a majority vote, *regardless of the vote necessary to adopt the motion to be reconsidered.* (But see pp. 318–19 for a different rule in the case of standing and special committees.)

8. Cannot be reconsidered. If it is voted on and lost, the motion to *Reconsider* cannot be renewed except by unanimous consent. By the same principle, no question can be reconsidered twice unless it was materially amended during its first reconsideration.

Further Rules and Explanation

EFFECT OF MAKING A MOTION TO RECONSIDER. The effect of *making* a motion to *Reconsider* is the suspension of all action that depends on the result of the vote proposed to be reconsidered, either until the assembly takes up the motion to *Reconsider* or until its effect terminates, as explained below.

Actions That Are Suspended. Cases where the making of a motion to *Reconsider* suspends action are not necessarily limited to the proposed reconsideration of a vote that was affirmative and that authorized or ordered the action that is suspended. A motion to *Reconsider* a negative vote may also cause suspension of some other action that was approved after the motion to be reconsidered was lost, if the adoption of the motion to be reconsidered would make the other action impossible. For example, assume that: (a) A motion to spend all of an available sum of money for library books is voted down. (b) A motion to spend the same money for athletic equipment is then made and adopted. (c) Before this equipment is purchased, it is moved to reconsider the vote on the motion to spend the money for books. If the motion to use the money for books is reconsidered and adopted, it will be impossible to buy athletic equipment. Therefore, the purchase of the athletic equipment must be held up until the reconsideration of the purchase of library books is completed or disposed of.

Termination of the Suspension. When a motion to *Reconsider* is made, any resulting suspension of action remains in effect either (a) until the motion to *Reconsider* has been voted on and, if the motion is adopted, until the reconsideration is completed; or (b) if the motion to *Reconsider* is not taken up, until the suspension terminates as follows: if no more than a quarterly time interval (p. 88) will elapse until the next regular session, the suspension terminates with

the adjournment of the next regular session; but if more than
a quarterly time interval will intervene before the next regular session, the suspension terminates with the end of the
same session in which the motion is made. If the motion to
Reconsider is not called up within these limits of time, the situation becomes the same as if there had been no such motion, and the vote which it was proposed to reconsider—and
any other action held up because of the proposed reconsideration—comes into full force, as if in effect, so far as applicable, from the time the vote was originally taken.

TAKING UP THE MOTION TO RECONSIDER AT
THE TIME IT IS MADE.   If a motion to *Reconsider* is
made at a time when it can be taken up—that is, when the
motion proposed to be reconsidered would be in order initially—the chair immediately states the question on the motion to *Reconsider* as pending before the assembly. In
proposing a reconsideration of the vote on a main motion,
it is usually better to make the motion to *Reconsider* when
no other business is pending and the motion can be taken
up immediately—unless it appears that there may be no
such opportunity or there is an important reason for doing
otherwise.

Whenever the motion to *Reconsider* is taken up, as
noted in Standard Characteristic 5, it is debatable if the motion proposed to be reconsidered is debatable, and debate
can go into the merits of the question proposed to be reconsidered. The right of each member to debate the motion to *Reconsider* is separate from the original
consideration of the motion proposed to be reconsidered.
Therefore, even if a member exhausted his right to debate
in the original consideration and the motion to *Reconsider*
is taken up on the same day, he still has the right to speak
the regular number of times (twice unless the assembly has
a special rule providing otherwise) in debate on the motion

to *Reconsider*. (For rules affecting a member's right to debate in the reconsideration if the motion to *Reconsider* is adopted, see pp. 313–14.)

If a motion to *Reconsider* is voted on and lost, the vote which it proposed to reconsider, and any action held up because of the proposed reconsideration, comes into full force, effective from the time the first vote was taken.

CALLING UP THE MOTION TO RECONSIDER.

If a motion to *Reconsider* that involves a main motion cannot be taken up when it is made, then as long as its suspending effect lasts it can be called up and acted upon, when no question is pending, at any regular or adjourned meeting, or at any special meeting if announced in the call of that meeting. To call it up, a member obtains the floor and says, "Mr. President, I call up the motion to reconsider the vote on the motion . . . [identifying it]." No second is necessary, since the motion to *Reconsider* was seconded at the time it was made. When this motion is called up, the chair immediately states the question on it as pending (see *Form and Example*).

Privilege Accorded the Mover in Regard to the Time at Which Reconsideration Takes Place.   Although any member can call up the motion to *Reconsider* as just described, usually no one but the mover of the reconsideration calls it up on the day the motion is made—at least in cases where the session is to last beyond that day and there is no need for immediate action. The reason is that the mover may wish time to assemble new information, or—if the reconsideration is moved on the same day the original vote was taken—he may want the unrestricted debate that will be allowable if the motion is taken up on another day (see below). So long as business is not unreasonably delayed and the mover of the reconsideration acts in good faith, he is entitled to have it take place at a time he feels will make for the fullest and fairest reexamination of the question. 1

Duty of the Chair When Failure to Call Up the Motion May Do Harm. In cases where a failure to call up a motion to *Reconsider* may do harm, the chair has the duty to 5 point out the situation to the assembly. Suppose, for example, that in a meeting of an ordinary society that will meet within a quarterly time interval (p. 88), there has been a motion to *Reconsider* a vote to do something that can only be done before the next meeting. Should the present meet- 10 ing adjourn without taking up the motion to *Reconsider,* the measure proposed to be reconsidered would be killed unless an adjourned meeting or special meeting were held to consider it. Therefore, if this meeting seems on the point of adjourning before the motion to *Reconsider* has been 15 taken up, the chair should explain the facts and suggest that someone call up the motion. If it has been moved to adjourn under these circumstances, the motion to *Adjourn* can be withdrawn or voted down—or the time can be fixed for an adjourned meeting, which can be done either before 20 or after the vote on adjournment has been taken (see *Fix the Time to Which to Adjourn,* **22**).

EFFECT OF ADOPTION OF THE MOTION TO RECONSIDER; RULES GOVERNING DEBATE ON 25 THE RECONSIDERATION. The effect of the adoption of the motion to *Reconsider* is immediately to place before the assembly again the question on which the vote is to be reconsidered—in the exact position it occupied the moment before it was voted on originally. 30

Rules governing debate on the reconsideration of the vote are as follows:

Reconsideration of a Vote on the Same Day. A member's right to debate the reconsideration of a vote is independent of the extent to which he took part in debate on 35 the motion to *Reconsider*. If the reconsideration takes place on the same day as the first consideration, however, anyone who exhausted his right to debate in the first consideration will not be able to speak on it again during the reconsideration, without permission of the assembly. (But such a member can pursue an equivalent purpose while the motion to *Reconsider* is pending, since the motion proposed to be reconsidered is also open to discussion in debate on the motion to *Reconsider*.)

Reconsideration of a Vote on a Later Day.   Every member's right to debate in the reconsideration of a question begins over again, regardless of speeches made previously, if reconsideration takes place on a day other than that on which the vote to be reconsidered was taken.

Reconsideration Under an Order Limiting or Extending Limits of Debate.   If a vote on one of a series of motions is taken under an order *limiting* debate or for the *Previous Question*, and then is reconsidered before such an order is exhausted (as explained in the sections on those motions, **15** and **16**), the same restrictions continue to apply to debate both on the motion to *Reconsider* and on the reconsideration. In the case of reconsidering a motion similarly covered by an unexhausted order *extending* limits of debate, the extension applies only to the reconsideration itself, not to debate on the motion to *Reconsider*. When reconsideration takes place after exhaustion of the *Previous Question* or a limitation or extension of debate, these orders do not come back into force, and debate or amendment is subject to the ordinary rules.

RECONSIDERATION OF SUBSIDIARY, PRIVILEGED, AND INCIDENTAL MOTIONS.   Conditions under which subsidiary, privileged, or incidental motions can be reconsidered depend on what other motions are pending at the time the reconsideration is moved, as follows:

To Reconsider a Subsidiary, Privileged, or Incidental Mo- 1
tion: Reconsideration Moved While the Main Question Is Pend-
ing.   When a main motion is pending (with or without a
series of adhering motions) and it is moved to reconsider the
vote on a related subsidiary, privileged, or incidental motion, 5
the motion to *Reconsider* becomes (a) immediately pending
or (b) pending at a lower position in the series, depending on
whether the motion proposed to be reconsidered would then
be in order if moved for the first time.

Referring to case (a) above, the motion to *Reconsider* 10
becomes the immediately pending question at once *if no*
other motions that would take precedence over the motion pro-
posed to be reconsidered are also pending (see **5** and **6;** see
also the chart on tinted pp. 3–5). For example, assume that
it is moved and seconded to reconsider a negative vote on 15
a motion to refer the pending main question to a committee. If the main question is now pending alone, or if no
other questions are pending except motions to *Postpone In-*
definitely or to *Amend* (which rank below the motion to
Commit), the chair at once states the question on the mo- 20
tion to *Reconsider* as immediately pending.

On the other hand, referring to case (b) above, if a series of motions is pending with the main question and *one*
or more of them would take precedence over the related motion
whose reconsideration is proposed, the motion to *Reconsider* 25
does not become the immediately pending question when
it is moved, but it becomes pending as one of the series, at
a position corresponding to the rank of the motion proposed to be reconsidered. In such a case, the motion to *Re-*
consider is taken up immediately after voting has been 30
completed on all motions that would take precedence over
the motion to be reconsidered if that were pending. For example, suppose that while a main motion, an amendment,
and a motion to lay the pending questions on the table are
pending, it is moved to reconsider a previous negative vote 35
on referring the same main question and amendment to a

1 committee. The order of rank, from highest to lowest, of
the four motions is: (1) *Lay on the Table,* (2) *Commit,* (3)
Amend, and (4) the main motion. This is the order in
which these motions would be voted on, and the reverse of
5 the order in which they would be made. The procedure in
this instance is as follows: The chair takes note of the fact
that the motion to *Reconsider* has been made and seconded,
instructing the secretary to record it. He then proceeds to
take the vote on the motion to *Lay on the Table.* If that mo-
10 tion is lost, he automatically states the question on the motion to reconsider the vote on the referral to the committee,
since the motion to *Commit* is next lower in rank. If the
motion to *Reconsider* is adopted, the motion to *Commit* is
then reconsidered and voted on again; and if this is lost, the
15 question is then stated on the amendment. (If the motion
to *Lay on the Table* is adopted, then whenever the questions
are taken from the table, the immediately pending question
is the motion to *Reconsider,* and from this point the procedure is the same as above.)
20   If the reconsideration of a primary amendment is
moved while another amendment of the same degree is
pending, the pending amendment is disposed of first. Then
the chair states the question on the motion to reconsider
the amendment previously acted upon.
25   When it is moved to reconsider a debatable subsidiary
or incidental motion which relates to a pending main question or a series of pending questions (in which case the motion to *Reconsider* is debatable, as noted in Standard
Characteristic 5), debate on the motion to *Reconsider* can
30 go into the merits of the motion *proposed to be reconsidered,*
but not into the merits of any other pending question. For
example, in the debate on a motion to reconsider an
amendment to the pending main question, the merits of the
amendment are open to discussion, but not those of the
35 main question apart from the amendment.

To Reconsider an Adhering Subsidiary or Incidental Motion: Reconsideration Moved After the Main Question Has Been Acted Upon. If it is desired to reconsider the vote on a subsidiary or incidental motion (an amendment, for example) after the main question to which it adhered has been finally disposed of (by adoption, rejection, or indefinite postponement), the vote on the main question, or on its indefinite postponement, must also be reconsidered (see also Standard Characteristic 2). In such a case, one motion to *Reconsider* should be made to cover both the vote on the subsidiary or incidental motion whose reconsideration is desired, and the vote on the main question (or its indefinite postponement). The member who makes this motion to *Reconsider* must have voted with the prevailing side in the original vote on the subsidiary or incidental motion—that is, on the motion which will be reconsidered first if the reconsideration takes place.

The same principle applies to the reconsideration of a secondary amendment after the related primary amendment has been voted on. If such a reconsideration is desired while the main question is still pending, the primary amendment must also be reconsidered. If it is desired to reconsider the secondary amendment after the main question has been finally disposed of, the secondary amendment, the primary amendment, and the main question must all be reconsidered, and one motion to *Reconsider* should be made covering the votes of these three motions.

When a motion to *Reconsider* covers the votes on two or more connected motions, not all of these questions can be discussed in debate on the motion to *Reconsider,* but only the one that will be voted on first if the motion to *Reconsider* is adopted. Thus, if the motion is to reconsider the votes on a resolution, a primary amendment, and a secondary amendment, only the secondary amendment is open to debate in connection with debate on the motion to *Reconsider.* If this

1   motion to *Reconsider* is adopted, the chair states the ques-
    tion on the secondary amendment and recognizes the
    mover of the reconsideration as entitled to the floor. The
    question is now in exactly the same condition as it was just
5   before the original vote was taken on the secondary amend-
    ment.

    If a main motion is included in a series covered by a sin-
    gle motion to *Reconsider,* as just described, the reconsider-
    ation is in order at the same times as if it had been moved
10 to reconsider the main motion alone. If the motion to *Re-
    consider* is made at a time when it cannot be taken up, it sus-
    pends action in the way described on pages 310–311 and
    stands until called up, subject to the same conditions as if it
    applied only to the main motion.

15   If a motion to reconsider the vote on an adhering sub-
    sidiary or incidental motion (an amendment, for example)
    is made after the main question to which it adheres has
    been either postponed to a certain time or laid on the table,
    the motion to reconsider is properly noted and is taken up
20 in due course (pp. 320–21) if and when the main motion is
    again brought before the assembly. The same is true if the
    motion to reconsider the adhering subsidiary or incidental
    motion was made before, but was not called up before, the
    main question was postponed or laid on the table. On the
25 other hand, if a main question is referred to a committee,
    no motion to reconsider the vote on an adhering subsidiary
    or incidental motion is in order while the question is in the
    hands of the committee, and any such motion to reconsider
    that was made but not taken up prior to referral is thereafter
30 ignored.

    RECONSIDERATION IN STANDING AND SPE-
    CIAL COMMITTEES.   Reconsideration in a standing or
    a special committee (**50**) differs from reconsideration in a
35 meeting of the assembly in the following respects:

1) A motion to reconsider a vote in the committee can be made and taken up *regardless of the time that has elapsed* since the vote was taken, and there is no limit to the number of times a question can be reconsidered.

2) The motion can be made by any member of the committee who *did not vote with the losing side;* or, in other words, the maker of the motion to *Reconsider* can be one who voted with the prevailing side, or one who did not vote at all, or even was absent.

3) Unless all the members of the committee who voted with the prevailing side are present or have been notified that the reconsideration will be moved, it requires a *two-thirds vote* to adopt the motion to *Reconsider.*

In other respects, reconsideration in a committee is the same as in a meeting of the society or its board. A vote cannot be reconsidered in a committee of the whole.

Form and Example

This motion may be made in forms such as the following:

a) For the reconsideration of a main question: "I move to reconsider the vote on the resolution relating to the annual banquet. I voted for [or "against"] the resolution."

b) To move the reconsideration of a subsidiary, privileged, or incidental motion related to the main question, while the main question is pending: "I move to reconsider the vote on the amendment to strike out 'Friday' and insert 'Saturday.' I voted for [or "against"] the amendment."

c) When the reconsideration of a subsidiary or incidental motion is desired after the main question to which it adhered has been acted upon: "I move to reconsider the votes on the resolution relating to the annual banquet and on the amendment to strike out 'Friday' and

1   insert 'Saturday.' I voted for [or "against"] the
     amendment."

     If the maker of the motion to *Reconsider* fails to state
5   which side he voted on, the chair, before making any other
     response, directs the member to do so:

     CHAIR: The member moving the reconsideration must state how
     he voted on the resolution ["motion," "amendment," etc.].
10

     If the resolution was adopted by unanimous consent,
     the chair should ask whether the member was present at the
     time. If the member did not vote with the prevailing side,
     another member who did so can make the motion to *Re-*
15   *consider,* if he desires. The motion must be seconded.
     If it is in order to take up the motion to *Reconsider* when
     it is made, the chair immediately states the question as follows:

     CHAIR: It is moved and seconded to reconsider the vote on the fol-
20   lowing resolution [reading it].

     If it is not in order to take up the motion to *Reconsider*
     when it is moved, the chair says instead:

25   CHAIR: It is moved and seconded to reconsider the vote on the res-
     olution relating to . . . The secretary will make a note of it.

     He then continues with the pending business.
     When it is in order to call up the motion to *Reconsider*
30   and a member wishes to do so, the member rises and ad-
     dresses the chair:

     MEMBER A (obtaining the floor): I call up the motion to reconsider
     the vote [or "votes"] on . . .
35

     The chair proceeds:

CHAIR: The motion to reconsider the vote [or "votes"] on . . . is *1* called up. The question is on the motion to reconsider . . . [etc.].

If a reconsideration that could not be taken up when it was moved is one that later comes before the assembly au- *5* tomatically, then when that point is reached, the chair says, for example:

CHAIR: The question is now on the motion to reconsider the vote on the amendment to . . . *10*

After debate on a motion to *Reconsider,* assuming that this motion is adopted, the chair puts the question and states the result as follows:

15

CHAIR: As many as are in favor of reconsidering the vote on the resolution relating to the annual banquet, say *aye.* . . . Those opposed, say *no.* . . . The ayes have it and the vote on the resolution is reconsidered. The question is now on the resolution, which is . . . [etc.].

20

Or:

CHAIR: The ayes have it and the votes on the resolution and the amendment are reconsidered. The question is now on the amendment, which is . . . [etc.]. *25*

Note that if the result of the vote on the motion to *Reconsider* is negative, it is the only vote taken. But if the motion to *Reconsider* is adopted, this is followed—after any debate—by the taking of the vote or votes that are conse- *30* quently reconsidered.

Reconsider and Enter on the Minutes

Reconsider and Enter on the Minutes is a special form of *35* the motion to *Reconsider* that has a different object from the regular motion. Its purpose is to prevent a temporary majority from taking advantage of an unrepresentative attendance at a meeting to vote an action that is opposed by a majority of a society's or a convention's membership. The effect of this form of the motion arises from the fact that when it is moved—on the same day that the vote to be reconsidered was taken—it cannot be called up until another day, even if another meeting is held on the same day.* Thus, with a view to obtaining a more representative attendance, it ensures reconsideration of a question on a different day from the one on which the question was put to vote.

DIFFERENCES FROM THE REGULAR FORM OF THE MOTION.   *Reconsider and Enter on the Minutes* differs from the regular form of *Reconsider* in the following respects:

1) It can be moved only on the same day that the vote proposed to be reconsidered was taken. The regular form of the motion to *Reconsider* can be used on the next succeeding day within the session on which a business meeting is held.

2) It takes precedence over the regular motion to *Reconsider*. Also, this motion can be made even after the vote has been taken on the motion to *Reconsider,* provided that the chair has not announced the result of the vote. In this case the regular motion to *Reconsider* is then ignored. If it were not for the rule that the motion to *Reconsider and Enter on the Minutes* takes precedence over the regular motion to *Reconsider,* the motion to *Reconsider and Enter on the Minutes* would generally be forestalled by the regular motion, which would be voted

---

*For an exception, see item (6) below.

down, and then *Reconsider and Enter on the Minutes*   1
could not be moved.

3) It can be applied only to votes that finally dispose of
   main motions; that is, to: (a) an affirmative or negative
   vote on a main motion; (b) an affirmative vote on post-   5
   poning indefinitely; or (c) a negative vote on an objection to the consideration of a question, if the session
   extends beyond that day.

4) It cannot be applied to votes on motions whose object
   would be defeated by a delay of one day. For example,   10
   a motion asking a visitor to address a convention the
   following day cannot have this motion applied to it.

5) If more than a quarterly time interval (p. 88) will intervene before the next regular business session, it cannot
   be moved at the last business meeting of the current   15
   session.

6) It cannot be called up on the day it is made, except that
   when it is moved on the last day—but not the last meeting—of a session of an organization that is not scheduled to meet again within a quarterly time interval (p.   20
   88), it can be called up at the last business meeting of
   the session.

After a motion to *Reconsider and Enter on the Minutes*
has been called up, its treatment is the same as that of the   25
regular motion to *Reconsider*. The name of this form does
not imply that the regular motion to *Reconsider* is not also
recorded in the minutes.

PROCEDURE FOR USE OF THE MOTION.   To   30
illustrate the use of this form of the motion, suppose that at
a long meeting of a county historical society, many members have left, unknowingly leaving a quorum composed
mainly of a small group determined to commit the society
to certain action that a few of those present believe would   35
be opposed by most of the membership. A member in op-

1 position can prevent the vote on such action from becoming final by moving "to reconsider and enter on the minutes the vote on . . ." To be in a position to do this, such a
member—detecting the hopelessness of preventing an affir-
5 mative result on the vote—should vote in the affirmative
himself. If the motion to *Reconsider and Enter on the Minutes* is seconded, all action required by the vote proposed to
be reconsidered is suspended, and there is time to notify absent members of the proposed action.

10   If no member of the temporary minority voted on the
prevailing side and it is too late for anyone to change his
vote (see p. 395), notice can be given that a motion to rescind the vote will be made at the next meeting. At this next
meeting, provided that such notice has been given, the mo-
15 tion to *Rescind* can then be adopted by a majority vote.

PROTECTING AGAINST ABUSES OF THE MO-
TION.   The motion to *Reconsider and Enter on the Minutes* may occasionally be subject to attempted abuse,
20 particularly in ordinary societies with single-meeting sessions, since it gives any two members power to hold up action taken by a meeting. In the average organization this
motion should generally be reserved for extreme cases, and
should be regarded as in order only when final decision on
25 the question could, if necessary, wait until the next regular
meeting, or when an adjourned or special meeting to take
it up is a practical possibility.
        If an actual minority in a representative meeting makes
improper use of this motion by moving to reconsider and
30 enter on the minutes a vote which requires action before the
next regular meeting, the remedy is to fix the time for an adjourned meeting (**9, 22**) on another suitable day when the reconsideration can be called up and disposed of. In such a case,
the mere making of a motion to set an adjourned meeting
35 would likely cause withdrawal of the motion to *Reconsider
and Enter on the Minutes,* since its object would be defeated.

RENEWAL OF MOTIONS; DILATORY AND IMPROPER MOTIONS

§38. RENEWAL OF MOTIONS

If a motion is made and disposed of without being adopted, and is later allowed to come before the assembly after being made again by any member in essentially the *5* same connection, the motion is said to be *renewed*. Renewal of motions is limited by the basic principle that an assembly cannot be asked to decide the same, or substantially the same, question twice during one session—except through a motion to reconsider a vote (**37**) or a motion to rescind an *10* action (**35**), or in connection with amending something already adopted (see also pp. 72–73). A previously considered motion may become a substantially different question through a significant change in the wording or because of a *15* difference in the time or circumstances in which it is proposed, and such a motion may thus be in order when it could not otherwise be renewed.

The rules restricting renewal of motions do not apply to *20* any motion that was last disposed of by being withdrawn. A motion that is withdrawn becomes as if it had never been made and can be renewed whenever it would be originally in order, since the assembly was never asked to decide it.

1   Two general principles govern the renewal of motions:

1) *No motion can be renewed during the same session in*
   which it has already been before the assembly, except where
5   *its renewal is permitted by a specific rule; and such a rule*
   always implies circumstances under which the motion has
   in some respect become a different question. (For a discussion of the rules growing out of this principle, see *Non-*
   renewability During the Same Session, and Exceptions,
10   below.) Whenever it is stated without qualification that
   a particular parliamentary motion "cannot be renewed," such a statement means that the motion cannot be renewed during the same session, or, in the case
   of a subsidiary or incidental motion, not during that
15   session in connection with the same motion to which it
   directly adhered.
2) *Any motion that is still applicable can be renewed at any*
   later session, except where a specific rule prevents its re-
   newal; and such an impediment to renewal at a later ses-
20   *sion normally can exist only when the first motion goes*
   over to that session as not finally disposed of, in which case
   the question can then be reached through the first motion
   (see pp. 88, 329–30).

25
Nonrenewability During the Same Session, and Exceptions

   The following rules are derived from the first principle
   stated above, by which a motion is not renewable at the
30   same session unless the question has become somehow
   different.

   PARTICULAR CASES OF THE GENERAL RULE
   AGAINST RENEWAL.   Applications of the general rule
35   against renewal during the same session include the following:

- A main motion, or a motion for the same amendment to a given motion, cannot be renewed at the same session unless there is a change in wording or circumstances sufficient to present substantially a new question, in which case this becomes technically a different motion. If a series of resolutions voted on together is lost, however, one or more of them can be offered again at the same session, but enough resolutions must be left out to present a genuinely different question from the viewpoint of probable voting result; otherwise this procedure becomes dilatory.

- A motion to *Postpone Indefinitely* cannot be renewed in connection with the same main question during the same session, even if the main motion has been materially amended since the previous vote against indefinite postponement. There will be another opportunity to accomplish the same object—that is, to defeat the main motion—when it comes up for a final vote.

- No motion can be renewed so long as the vote on it can be reconsidered.

- A motion to *Reconsider* that has been rejected cannot be renewed in connection with the same vote. To be able to be reconsidered a second time, the original question must have been materially amended during the first reconsideration—in which case the proposal to reconsider a second time is a new question.

- A motion to *Rescind* that has been voted down cannot be renewed at the same session unless the motion proposed to be rescinded has meanwhile been amended sufficiently to present a new question.

- A motion to divide the same question in substantially the same way cannot be renewed at the same session.

- When a *Question of Privilege* or a *Point of Order* has been ruled on adversely by the chair, it cannot be raised again at the same session unless an appeal is made and the chair's decision is reversed. After a decision of the chair has been sustained on an appeal, no point of order or appeal involving the same principle can be made during that session.

MOTIONS THAT CAN BE RENEWED AT A LATER MEETING OF THE SAME SESSION.

Following are two cases of motions which cannot be renewed at the same *meeting,* but which may have become different questions—and consequently are renewable—at another meeting of the same session (see **8**):

- Although the motion to *Suspend the Rules* for the same purpose cannot be renewed at the same meeting, such a motion can be renewed at the next meeting or any later meeting, even if the next meeting is held on the same day or is part of the same session. This renewal is allowable because by the time of the next meeting the attendance or situation may already have changed sufficiently to justify the renewal. The mere passage of time may make it a new question.
- The same motion to *Fix the Time to Which to Adjourn*—that is, a motion to set the same date, hour, and place for an adjourned meeting—cannot be renewed at the same meeting at which it is voted down; but if, after the first motion is rejected, the assembly decides to set an adjourned meeting for an earlier time than proposed in the first motion, then at that adjourned meeting it is in order to move to set a second adjourned meeting for the same time as originally considered for the first.

MOTIONS THAT CAN BE RENEWED AFTER MATERIAL PROGRESS IN BUSINESS OR DEBATE.

The following motions are renewable if they become new questions as described, even within the same meeting:

- The subsidiary motions to *Commit,* to *Postpone to a Certain Time,* to *Limit or Extend Limits of Debate,* for the *Previous Question,* and to *Lay on the Table* can be renewed whenever progress in business or debate has been such that they are no longer practically the same questions. In addition, a motion to *Lay on the Table* can be renewed if something urgent has arisen that was not known when the assembly rejected this motion.

- A motion to *Take from the Table* that has failed can be renewed after disposal of the business that was taken up following rejection of the motion.

- A *Call for the Orders of the Day* can be renewed after disposal of the business that was taken up when the assembly refused to proceed to the orders of the day.

- A motion to *Adjourn* or to *Recess* can be renewed after material progress in business or in debate—such as an important decision or speech. A vote on a motion to *Recess* or to *Lay on the Table* is not business of a character to justify renewal of a motion to *Adjourn;* and a vote on any of these three motions is not sufficient business to allow renewal of either of the others.

- Motions to close nominations or the polls can be renewed after progress in nominations or voting has been such as to make them essentially new questions.

Conditions That May Impede
Renewal at a Later Session

MAIN MOTIONS THAT GO OVER TO ANOTHER SESSION; MOTIONS WITHIN THE CONTROL OF THE ASSEMBLY, BECAUSE NOT FINALLY DISPOSED OF.   Referring to the second general principle stated on page 326, a main motion that was introduced but not adopted during one session can, except as noted in this paragraph, be renewed at any later session unless it has

1   become absurd. Such exceptions occur only through one of
    the four processes by which, from one session to another, a
    main motion can remain *within the control of the assembly*
    (that is, *temporarily, but not finally, disposed of*), so that *the*
5   *same* motion can be considered at the later session. The first
    three of these procedures, noted below, can arise only in
    cases of organizations where no more than a quarterly time
    interval (see p. 88) will elapse until the next regular session.
    In such societies, a main motion cannot be renewed during
10 the next session after a session at which it was:

1) postponed to the next session (**14**), since the first motion will then come up;
2) laid on the table and not taken from the table (**17, 34**),
15   since the question can still be reached by taking the first
   motion from the table; or
3) voted on and a motion to reconsider the vote was introduced but not called up (**37**), since at the next session the question can still be reached by calling up the
20   motion to *Reconsider*.

Also, in any assembly:

4) a main motion that has been referred to a committee to
25   be reported at a later session cannot be renewed until
   after the session at which the committee reports or is discharged from its consideration (**36**), since the question
   will come up or can be reached by one of these two
   methods.
30

NONRENEWABILITY OF UNSUSTAINED OBJEC-
TION TO THE CONSIDERATION OF A QUESTION.
An unsustained *Objection to the Consideration of a Question*
cannot be renewed in connection with the same main mo-
35 tion—even at a later session if the main motion goes over

to that session through one of the four procedures stated   *1*
immediately above. This rule is simply a consequence of the
fact that an *Objection to the Consideration of a Question* can
be raised only when the main question is first introduced,
and before any consideration of it has begun (see **26**). But   *5*
if an original main motion fails at one session—that is, is
voted down or postponed indefinitely—and is renewed at
the next session, it is then a new motion and its consideration can be objected to, subject to the usual rules.

10

§39. DILATORY AND IMPROPER MOTIONS

Dilatory Motions

A motion is *dilatory* if it seeks to obstruct or thwart the   *15*
will of the assembly as clearly indicated by the existing parliamentary situation.

Parliamentary forms are designed to assist in the transaction of business. Even without adopting a rule on the
subject, every deliberative assembly has the right to protect   *20*
itself from the use of these forms for the opposite purpose.

It is the duty of the presiding officer to prevent members from misusing the legitimate forms of motions, or
abusing the privilege of renewing certain motions, merely
to obstruct business.   *25*

Any main or other motion that is absurd in substance is
dilatory and cannot be introduced. It would also be ridicu-
lous if a minority of two or three members could constantly
raise points of order and appeal from the chair's decisions
on them, or repeatedly move to lay motions on the table,   *30*
or offer frivolous amendments. If a member could demand
a division (**29**) on every vote even when the result was clear,
or move to adjourn again and again when nothing had hap-
pened to justify renewal of such a motion, business could be
brought to a standstill.   *35*

1   Whenever the chair becomes convinced that one or more members are using parliamentary forms for obstructive purposes, he should either not recognize these members or he should rule that such motions are out of order—but he
5 should never adopt such a course merely to *speed up* business, and he should never permit his personal feelings to affect his judgment in such cases. If the chair only *suspects* that a motion is not made in good faith, he should give the maker of the motion the benefit of the doubt. The chair should always
10 be courteous and fair, but at the same time he should be firm in protecting the assembly from imposition.

Improper Motions

15   Motions that conflict with the corporate charter, constitution or bylaws of a society, or with procedural rules prescribed by national, state, or local laws, are out of order, and if any motion of this kind is adopted, it is null and void. Likewise, motions are out of order if they conflict with a
20 motion that has been adopted by the society and has been neither rescinded, nor reconsidered and rejected after adoption. Such conflicting motions, if adopted, are null and void unless adopted by the vote required to rescind or amend the motion previously adopted.

25   Motions are also improper when they present practically the same question as a motion previously decided at the same session. In addition, motions are improper that conflict with, or present practically the same question as, one still within the control of the society because not finally disposed of; that
30 is, one that has been referred to a committee or postponed to a certain time or laid on the table, or one that is subject to a motion to *Reconsider* that can still be called up. If a conflicting motion were allowed in such cases, it would interfere with the freedom of the assembly in acting on the earlier mo-
35 tion when its consideration is resumed.

No motion can be introduced that is outside the object   *1*
of the society or assembly as defined in the bylaws (see p.
554), unless by a two-thirds vote the body agrees to its consideration. Except as may be necessary in the case of a motion of censure or a motion related to disciplinary   *5*
procedures, a motion must not use language that reflects on
a member's conduct or character, or is discourteous, un-
necessarily harsh, or not allowed in debate (see **43, 61**).

CHAPTER
XI

QUORUM; ORDER OF BUSINESS AND RELATED CONCEPTS

§40. QUORUM

As indicated on pages 20–21, a quorum in an assembly is the number of voting members (see definition, p. 3) who must be present in order that business can be legally transacted. The quorum refers to the number of such members *present,* not to the number actually voting on a particular question.

Rules Pertaining to the Quorum

NUMBER OF MEMBERS CONSTITUTING A QUORUM.   Depending on the organization and the provision it adopts in this regard, the number of members constituting a quorum may vary. As discussed below, most voluntary societies should provide for a quorum in their bylaws, but where there is no such provision, the quorum, in accordance with the common parliamentary law, is as follows:

1) In a mass meeting, the quorum is simply the number of persons present at the time, since they constitute the entire membership at that time.

2) In organizations such as many churches or some societies in which there are no required or effective annual dues and the register of members is not generally reliable as a list of the bona-fide members, the quorum at any regular or properly called meeting consists of those who attend.

3) In a body of delegates, such as a convention, the quorum is a majority of the number who have been registered as attending, irrespective of whether some may have departed. This may differ greatly from the number elected or appointed.

4) In any other deliberative assembly with enrolled membership whose bylaws do not specify a quorum, the quorum is a majority of all the members.

To accomplish their work, voluntary societies that have an enrolled membership generally need a provision in their bylaws establishing a relatively small quorum—considerably less than a majority of all the members. In most such organizations, it is rarely possible to obtain the attendance of a majority of the membership at a meeting. Sometimes the specification of a quorum is based on a percentage of the membership; but such a method has the disadvantage of requiring recomputation and may lead to confusion—for example, when the secretary, or other officer who is in a position to certify as to the current number of members for purposes of the percentage calculation, is absent. There is no single number or percentage of members that will be equally suitable as a quorum in all societies. The quorum should be as large a number of members as can reasonably be depended on to be present at any meeting, except in very bad weather or other exceptionally unfavorable conditions.

NOTE ON PROCEDURE IN CHANGING THE QUORUM PROVISION IN BYLAWS. If it becomes

1   necessary to change the quorum provision in a society's bylaws, care should be taken, because if the rule is struck out
first, the quorum will instantly become a majority of the
membership, so that in many cases a quorum could not be
5   obtained to adopt a new rule. The proper procedure is to
strike out the old provision and insert the new provision,
which is moved and voted on as one question.

QUORUM IN BOARDS AND COMMITTEES.   In
10   a committee of the whole or its variations (**52**), the quorum
is the same as in the assembly unless the rules of the assembly or the organization (that is, either its bylaws or its rules
of order) specify otherwise. In all other committees and in
boards, the quorum is a majority of the members of the
15   board or committee unless a different quorum is fixed: (a)
by the bylaws, in the case of a board or standing committee
that the bylaws specifically establish; or (b) by a rule of the
parent body or organization or by the motion establishing
the particular committee, in the case of a committee that is
20   not expressly established by the bylaws. A board or committee does not have the power to determine its quorum
unless the bylaws so provide.

PROCEEDINGS IN THE ABSENCE OF A QUO-
25   RUM.   In the absence of a quorum, any business transacted (except for the procedural actions noted in the next
paragraph) is null and void. But if a quorum fails to appear
at a regular or properly called meeting, the inability to
transact business does not detract from the fact that the so-
30   ciety's rules requiring the meeting to be held were complied with and the meeting was convened—even though it
had to adjourn immediately.
The only action that can legally be taken in the absence
of a quorum is to fix the time to which to adjourn (**22**), ad-
35   journ (**21**), recess (**20**), or take measures to obtain a quo-

rum. The first three of these motions are governed by the Standard Descriptive Characteristics given for them in the numbered sections indicated. A motion that absent members be contacted during a recess would represent a measure in the last category. Motions to obtain a quorum are treated as privileged motions that take precedence over a motion to *Recess* (**20**). Such motions are out of order when another has the floor; must be seconded; are not debatable; are amendable (any amendment being undebatable in accordance with the general rule); require a majority vote; and can be reconsidered. Motions to obtain a quorum are similar to a *Call of the House,* which can be ordered in assemblies having the power to compel attendance (see below).

The prohibition against transacting business in the absence of a quorum cannot be waived even by unanimous consent, and a notice (pp. 116–18) cannot be validly given. If there is important business that should not be delayed, the meeting should fix the time for an adjourned meeting and then adjourn. Where an important opportunity would be lost unless acted upon immediately, the members present can, at their own risk, act in the emergency with the hope that their action will be ratified by a later meeting at which a quorum is present. If a committee of the whole finds itself without a quorum, it can do nothing but rise and report to the assembly, which can then proceed as already described in this paragraph. A quasi committee of the whole or a meeting in informal consideration of a question can itself take any of the four actions permitted an assembly in the absence of a quorum, but a quasi committee of the whole is thereby ended (see **52**).

Manner of Enforcing the Quorum Requirement

Before the presiding officer calls a meeting to order, it is his duty to determine, although he need not announce,

1   that a quorum is present. If a quorum is not present, the
    chair waits until there is one, or until, after a reasonable
    time, there appears to be no prospect that a quorum will as-
    semble. If a quorum cannot be obtained, the chair calls the
5   meeting to order, announces the absence of a quorum, and
    entertains a motion to adjourn or one of the other motions
    allowed, as described above.

       When the chair has called a meeting to order after find-
    ing that a quorum is present, the continued presence of a
10 quorum is presumed unless the chair or a member notices
    that a quorum is no longer present. If the chair notices the
    absence of a quorum, it is his duty to declare the fact, at
    least before taking any vote or stating the question on any
    new motion—which he can no longer do except in connec-
15 tion with the permissible proceedings related to the absence
    of a quorum, as explained above. Any member noticing the
    apparent absence of a quorum can make a point of order to
    that effect at any time so long as he does not interrupt a
    person who is speaking. *Debate* on a question already pend-
20 ing can be allowed to continue at length after a quorum is
    no longer present, however, until a member raises the
    point. Because of the difficulty likely to be encountered in
    determining exactly how long the meeting has been with-
    out a quorum in such cases, a point of order relating to the
25 absence of a quorum is generally not permitted to affect
    prior action; but upon clear and convincing proof, such a
    point of order can be given effect retrospectively by a rul-
    ing of the presiding officer, subject to appeal (**24**).*

---

*What happens to a question that is pending when a meeting adjourns
(because of the loss of a quorum or for any other reason) is determined by
the rules given on pages 228–29. If such a question, however, was introduced as new business and it is proven that there was already no quorum
when it was introduced, its introduction was invalid and, to be considered
at a later meeting, it must again be brought up as new business.

Call of the House

In legislative bodies or other assemblies that have legal power to compel the attendance of their members, a procedure that can be used to obtain a quorum, if necessary, is the motion for a *Call of the House*. This is a motion that unexcused absent members be brought to the meeting under arrest. A *Call of the House* is not applicable in voluntary societies.

Assemblies in which there may be occasion to order a *Call of the House* should adopt a rule governing this motion and providing that if one third, one fifth, or some other number less than a majority of the members or members-elect are present, they can order a *Call of the House* by a majority vote. When a quorum is not present, this motion should take precedence over everything except a motion to *Adjourn* (**21**). If the rule allows the call to be moved while a quorum is actually present (for the purpose of obtaining a *greater* attendance), the motion at such times should rank only with questions of privilege, should require a majority vote for adoption, and, if rejected, should not be allowed to be renewed while a quorum is present.

When a *Call of the House* is ordered, the clerk calls the roll of the members, then calls again the names of the absentees—in whose behalf explanations of absence can be made and excuses can be requested. After this, no member is permitted to leave, the doors are locked, and the sergeant-at-arms, chief of police, or other arresting officer is ordered to take into custody absentees who have not been excused from attendance and bring them before the house. He does this on a warrant signed by the presiding officer and attested by the clerk. When arrested members are brought in, they are arraigned separately, their explanations are heard, and, on motion, they can be excused with or

1 without penalty in the form of payment of a fee. Until a
member has paid such a fee assessed against him, he cannot
vote or be recognized by the chair for any purpose.

    After a *Call of the House* has been ordered, no motion is
5 in order, even by unanimous consent, except motions relating to the call. Motions to adjourn or dispense with further
proceedings under the call, however, can be entertained
after a quorum is present, or after the arresting officer reports that in his opinion a quorum cannot be obtained. An
10 adjournment terminates all proceedings under the *Call of
the House*.

§41. ORDER OF BUSINESS; ORDERS
OF THE DAY; AGENDA OR PROGRAM
15

    The terms *order of business, orders of the day, agenda,*
and *program* refer to closely related concepts having to do
with the order in which business is taken up in a session (**8**)
and the prescheduling of particular business. The meaning
20 of these terms often coincides, although each has its own
applications in common usage.

    An *order of business* is any established sequence in which
it may be prescribed that business shall be taken up at a session of a given assembly. In the case of ordinary societies in
25 which no more than a quarterly time interval (see p. 88)
will elapse between regular meetings, an order of business
that specifies such a sequence only in terms of certain general types or classes of business and gives only the *order* in
which they are to be taken up is normally prescribed for all
30 regular meetings by the rules of the organization. The typical order of business of this kind is described on pages
342–49. In other cases, such as in a convention, an order of
business expressly adopted for a particular session frequently
assigns positions, and even times, to specific subjects or
35 items of business; and to this type of order of business the

terms *agenda* and *program** are applicable, as explained on
pages 360–63. Although the terms *order of business, agenda,*
and *program* relate primarily to the business of an entire session, the same terms are also applied to a part of the whole,
in speaking of "the order of business," "the agenda," or "the
program" of a meeting within a session.

An *order of the day* is an item of business that is prescheduled to be taken up during a given session, day, or meeting,
or at a given hour (unless there is business having precedence
over it that interferes). The methods by which orders of the
day can be made, their division into the classes of *general orders* and *special orders,* and their treatment in cases where they
come into conflict are explained on pages 353ff. General
orders and special orders are also discussed with particular
reference to making them by means of the motion to *Postpone* on pages 177–80 (see also *Call for the Orders of the Day,*
18). Unless designated for particular hours or assigned positions item by item in an agenda or program formally adopted
for a given session, general orders and special orders are taken
up under assigned headings or in customary positions allotted to each of these categories in the order of business. (Note
such headings in the "standard" order of business described
below.)

Within a meeting in which the only items of business
that are in order have been specified and set in sequence in
advance—as might occur, for example, in a particular meeting of a convention—the orders of the day are identical

---

*The term *program* has two senses in parliamentary usage. In the first
sense, as used here, it refers to a type of order of business that may be identical with an agenda, or (in a convention) may include an agenda together
with the times for events outside of the business meetings (see also **59**). In
the second sense, as used on page 351, the term refers to a heading, often
included *within* the order of business for meetings of ordinary societies,
that covers talks, lectures, films, or other features of informational or entertainment value.

1   with the order of business (which, in such a case, is in the
form of an agenda or program).

Usual Order of Business in Ordinary Societies

5

BASIC HEADINGS COVERING BUSINESS
PROPER.   The customary or "standard" order of business for ordinary societies that hold regular business sessions (lasting only a few hours) within at least quarterly
10 time intervals (see p. 88), and that do not have special requirements, comprises the following subdivisions:

1) Reading and Approval of Minutes
2) Reports of Officers, Boards, and Standing Committees
15 3) Reports of Special (Select or Ad Hoc) Committees
4) Special Orders
5) Unfinished Business and General Orders
6) New Business

20   This series of headings is the prescribed order of business for regular meetings of organizations whose bylaws
specify this book as parliamentary authority and which have
not adopted a special order of business. It prescribes only
the sequence of the headings, not the time to be allotted to
25 each—which may vary with every meeting. Certain optional headings are also described following the detailed
discussion of the regular headings below.
      The presiding officer may find it helpful to have at hand
a memorandum of the complete order of business, listing,
30 under headings (2) and (3) as explained below, all known reports which are expected to be presented, and under headings (4) and (5), all matters which the minutes show are due
to come up, arranged in proper sequence or, where applicable, listed with the times for which they have been set. The
35 secretary can prepare, or assist the presiding officer to pre-

pare, such a memorandum. In this connection, regarding the practice in some societies or assemblies of providing each member with a copy of the expected agenda in advance of a meeting, see page 363 at the end of this chapter.

After the presiding officer has called the meeting to order as described on page 24, and after any customary opening ceremonies (see optional headings, p. 349), the meeting proceeds through the different headings in the order of business:

1. *Reading and Approval of Minutes.* The chair says, "The Secretary will read the minutes." In all but the smallest meetings, the minutes are read by the secretary standing. In organizations where copies of the minutes of each previous meeting as prepared by the secretary are sent to all members in advance, the actual reading of them aloud may be waived if no member objects. In either case, the chair then asks, "Are there any corrections to the minutes?" and pauses. Corrections, when proposed, are usually handled by unanimous consent (pp. 51–53). It is generally smoother to do the approval of minutes also by unanimous consent, although a formal motion to approve them is not out of order. Such a motion is normally unnecessary unless, for example, there has been a dispute over the accuracy or propriety of something in the minutes. Whether or not a motion for approval has been offered, the chair may simply say, "If there are no corrections [or "no further corrections"], the minutes stand [or "are"] approved [or "approved as read," or "approved as corrected"]." The actual correction is made in the text of the minutes being approved, and the minutes of the meeting making the correction merely state that a correction was made to the minutes of the prior meeting, without specifying what the correction was. If for any reason there are minutes of other meetings in addition to the last meeting that have not been read previously, they are taken in the order of date.

1   The practice of sending to all members advance copies of the minutes as drafted by the secretary has both advantages and disadvantages. It is natural for the members to prefer to study the minutes beforehand to be better pre-

5 pared to offer corrections; and this procedure generally saves time when the minutes come up for approval. On the other hand, the minutes do not become *the* minutes and assume their essential status as the official record of the proceedings of the society until they have been approved; and

10 before this happens, the secretary's draft may be materially modified in the correction process. Members may miss some of the corrections or neglect to mark them on their copies—or may not get them right unless the chair repeats them very carefully—with the result that many inaccurate

15 copies of the true minutes as finally approved are likely to remain in existence. Only the secretary's corrected copy or a retyping of it is official in such a case. (For "dispensing" with the reading of the minutes, see pp. 456–57.)

   2. Reports of Officers, Boards, and Standing Committees.

20 In most societies it is customary to hear reports from all officers (**47, 48**), boards (**49**), and standing committees (**50**) only at annual meetings. At other meetings the chair calls only on those who have reports to make, as by saying (in calling upon the secretary), "Is there any correspondence?"

25 Or, "May we have the Treasurer's report." Or, "The chair recognizes Mr. Downey, Chairman of the Membership Committee, for a report." If the chair is uncertain, he may ask, for example, "Does the Program Committee have a report?" *Standing committees* listed in the bylaws are called

30 upon in the order in which they are listed.

   If an officer, in reporting, makes a recommendation, he should not himself move its implementation, but such a motion can be made by another member as soon as the officer has concluded his report. In the case of a committee

35 report, on the other hand, the chairman or other reporting member should make any motion(s) necessary to bring the

committee's recommendations before the assembly for consideration. A motion arising out of an officer's, a board's, or a committee's report is taken up immediately, since the object of the order of business is to give priority to the classes of business in the order listed.

If an item of business in this class is on the table (that is, if it was laid on the table at the present session, or at the preceding session if no more than a quarterly time interval has intervened [see p. 88], and if the item has not been taken from the table), it is in order to move to take such business from the table under this heading (see **17, 34**).

(For procedures to be followed in making reports and in handling recommendations arising from reports, see **51**.)

3. Reports of Special Committees. The special committees (**50**) that are to report are called on in the order in which they were appointed. Only those special committees that are prepared, or were instructed, to report on matters referred to them should be called on. Business incident to reports of special committees that is on the table can be taken from the table under this heading (**17, 34**).

4. Special Orders. Under this heading (referring to the explanation of *Orders of the Day* beginning on p. 353) are taken up the following in the order listed:

a) Any unfinished special orders (that is, special orders that were not disposed of at the preceding meeting)—taken in sequence beginning with the special order that was pending when that meeting adjourned if it adjourned while one was pending, and continuing with the remaining unfinished special orders in the order in which they were made (that is, were set by action of the assembly).

b) Items of business that have been made special orders for the present meeting* without being set for specific hours—taken in the order in which they were made.

---

*But not *the* special order (see pp. 359–60).

1 Regarding the interruption of business under this heading
by special orders that have been set for particular hours, see
pages 358ff.

Normally—unless an order of the day was made as a part
5 of an agenda for a session—no motion is necessary at the
time the order comes up, since the introduction of the question has been accomplished previously, as will be seen from
the description of the methods by which orders of the day are
made, on page 354. When a special order that was so intro-
10 duced comes up, the chair announces it as pending, thus: "At
the last meeting, the resolution relating to funds for a new
playground was made a special order for this meeting [or, if
the special order was made by postponement, ". . . was postponed to this meeting and made a special order."]. The res-
15 olution is as follows: '*Resolved*, That . . . [reading it].' The
question is on the adoption of the resolution."

Matters that the bylaws require to be considered at a
particular meeting, such as the nomination and election of
officers, may be regarded as special orders for the meeting
20 and be considered under the heading of *Special Orders* in
the order of business. If a special order is on the table, it is
in order to move to take it from the table under this heading when no question is pending (**17, 34**).

5. *Unfinished Business and General Orders.*   The term
25 *unfinished business,** in cases where the regular business meetings of an organization are not separated by more than a quarterly time interval (p. 88), refers to questions that have come
over from the previous meeting (other than special orders) as
a result of that meeting's having adjourned without complet-
30 ing its order of business (pp. 228–29) and without scheduling
an adjourned meeting (**9, 22**) to complete it.

---

*The expression "old business" should be avoided, since it may incor-
rectly suggest the further consideration of matters that have been finally disposed of.

A *general order* (as explained under *Orders of the Day,* below) is any question which, usually by postponement, has been made an order of the day without being made a special order.

The heading of *Unfinished Business and General Orders* includes items of business in the four categories that are listed below in the order in which they are taken up. Of these, the first three constitute "Unfinished Business," while the fourth consists of "General Orders":

a) The question that was pending when the previous meeting adjourned, if that meeting adjourned while a question other than a special order was pending.

b) Any questions that were unfinished business at the previous meeting but were not reached before it adjourned—taken in the order in which they were due to come up at that meeting as indicated under (a) and (c).

c) Any questions which, by postponement or otherwise, were set as general orders for the previous meeting, or for a particular hour during that meeting, but were not reached before it adjourned—taken in the order in which the general orders were made.

d) Matters that were postponed to, or otherwise made general orders for, the present meeting—taken in the order in which they were made.

Regarding the relationship between this heading in the order of business and general orders for particular hours, see pages 355–57.

The chair should not announce the heading of *Unfinished Business and General Orders* unless the minutes show that there is some business to come up under it. In the latter case, he should have all such subjects listed in correct sequence in a memorandum prepared in advance of the meeting. He should *not* ask, "Is there any unfinished busi-

1 ness?" but should state the question on the first item of
business that is due to come up under this heading; and
when it has been disposed of, he should proceed through
the remaining subjects in their proper order. If a question
5 was pending when the previous meeting adjourned, for example, the chair might begin this heading by saying,
"Under Unfinished Business and General Orders, the first
item of business is the motion relating to use of the parking
facilities, which was pending when the last meeting ad-
10 journed. The question is on the adoption of the motion
'That . . . [stating the motion].'" Later under the same
heading, in announcing a general order that was made by
postponing a question, the chair might say, "The next item
of business is the resolution relating to proposed improve-
15 ment of our newly purchased picnic grounds, which was
postponed to this meeting. The resolution is as follows:
'*Resolved*, That . . . [reading the resolution].' The question
is on the adoption of the resolution."

Any item of business (in whatever class) that is on the
20 table can be taken from the table under this heading at any
time when no question is pending (**17, 34**). To obtain the
floor for the purpose of moving to take a question from the
table at such a time, a member can rise and address the
chair, interrupting him as he starts to announce the next
25 item of business after the previous one is disposed of.

It should be noted that, with the exception indicated in
the preceding paragraph, a subject should not be taken up
under Unfinished Business and General Orders unless it has
acquired such status by one of the formal processes (a), (c),
30 or (d) listed on the preceding page. If brief consultation
during a meeting leads to an informal understanding that a
certain subject should be "brought up at the next meeting," that does not make it unfinished business. Instead, the
matter should be introduced at the next meeting as new
35 business, as explained below.

6. *New Business.* After unfinished business and general orders have been disposed of, the chair asks, "Is there any new business?" Members can then introduce new items of business, or can move to take from the table any matter that is on the table (**17, 34**), in the order in which they are able to obtain the floor when no question is pending, as explained in **3** and **4.** So long as members are reasonably prompt in claiming the floor, the chair cannot prevent the making of legitimate motions or deprive members of the right to introduce legitimate business, by hurrying through the proceedings.

OPTIONAL HEADINGS. In addition to the standard order of business as just described, regular meetings of organizations sometimes include proceedings of the type listed below, which may be regarded as optional in the order of business prescribed by this book.

After the call to order and *before the reading of the minutes,* the next two headings may be included:

Opening Ceremonies or Exercises. Opening ceremonies immediately after the meeting is called to order may include the Invocation (which, if offered, should always be placed first), the singing of the National Anthem, the reciting of the Pledge of Allegiance to the flag, a ritual briefly recalling the objects or ideals of the organization, or the like.

Roll Call. In some organizations it is customary at meetings to call the roll of officers in order to verify their attendance—or, sometimes in very small societies, even to call the roll of members. If there is a roll call of this nature, it should take place at the end of the opening ceremonies unless a special rule of the organization assigns it a different position in the order of business. The chair announces it by saying, "The Secretary will call the roll of officers [or "will call the roll"]."

Consent Calendar. Legislatures, city, town, or county councils, or other assemblies which have a heavy work load

1   including a large number of routine or noncontroversial
matters may find a *consent calendar* a useful tool for disposing of such items of business. Commonly, when such a matter has been introduced or reported by a committee for
5   consideration in the assembly, its sponsor, or, sometimes, an
administrator, may seek to have it placed on the consent
calendar. This calendar is called over periodically *at a point
established in the agenda by special rule of order, at least preceding standing committee reports.* The matters listed on it
10 are taken up in order, unless objected to, in which case they
are restored to the ordinary process by which they are
placed in line for consideration on the regular agenda. The
special rule of order establishing a consent calendar may
provide that, when the matters on the calendar are called
15 up, they may be considered in gross or without debate or
amendment. Otherwise, they are considered under the
rules just as any other business, in which case the "consent"
relates only to permitting the matter to be on the calendar
for consideration without conforming to the usual, more
20 onerous, rules for reaching measures in the body.

    After the completion of new business—that is, when no
one claims the floor to make a motion in response to the
chair's query, "Is there any further new business?"—the
chair may proceed to one or more of the following head-
25 ings, in an order that may be subject to variation determined by the practice of the organization.

    *Good of the Order, General Good and Welfare, or Open
Forum.*   This heading, included by some types of societies
in their order of business, refers to the general welfare of
30 the organization, and may vary in character. Under this
heading (in contrast to the general parliamentary rule that
allows discussion only with reference to a pending motion),
members who obtain the floor commonly are permitted to
offer informal observations regarding the work of the or-
35 ganization, the public reputation of the society or its mem-

bership, or the like. Certain types of announcements may
tend to fall here. Although the Good of the Order often involves no business or motions, the practice of some organizations would place motions or resolutions relating to
formal disciplinary procedures for offenses outside a meeting (**61**) at this point. In some organizations, the program
(see below) is looked upon as a part of the Good of the
Order.

Announcements.   The chair may make, or call upon
other officers or members to make, any necessary announcements; or, if the practice of the organization permits
it, members can briefly obtain the floor for such a purpose.
The placing of general announcements at this point in the
order of business does not prevent the chair from making
an urgent announcement at any time.

Program.   If there is to be a talk, film, or other program of a cultural, educational, or civic nature, it is usually
presented before the meeting is adjourned, since it may
prompt a desire on the part of the assembly to take action.
Although the program is commonly placed at the end of
the order of business in such cases, it can, by special rule or
practice, be received before the minutes are read; or, by suspending the rules (**25**), it can be proceeded to at any time
during the meeting. If, in courtesy to a guest speaker who
is present, the chair wishes the talk to be located at an un-
scheduled point within the business portion of the meeting,
he can usually obtain unanimous consent for a suspension
of the rules by simply announcing, "If there is no objection,
we will hear our speaker's address at this time."

Taking Up Business Out of Its Proper Order

Any particular item of business can be taken up out of
its proper order by adopting a motion to suspend the rules
(**25**) by a two-thirds vote, although this is usually arranged

by unanimous consent (pp. 51–53). Hence, an important committee report or an urgent item of new business can be advanced in order to assure its full and unhurried consideration. If desired, before the completion of the advanced question the regular order of business can be returned to by a majority vote—by adopting a motion to lay the pending question on the table (**17**).

To take up a motion out of its proper order—for example, to introduce an item of new business before that heading is reached—a member who has obtained the floor can say, "I ask unanimous consent to introduce at this time a resolution on financing better schools." If there is any objection, or the member anticipates that there may be, he can say, "I move to suspend the rules that interfere with the introduction at this time of . . ." If unanimous consent is given or if this motion is adopted by a two-thirds vote, the member is immediately recognized to introduce the resolution. If only one or two items stand ahead of the item it is desired to reach, it may be just as simple to lay the intervening items on the table individually (**17**), or to postpone them as they arise (**14**). It is not in order to lay on the table or postpone a *class* of questions, like committee reports, or anything but the question that is actually before the assembly (see pp. 176–77, 203, 207–208, 351–52).

The chair himself cannot depart from the prescribed order of business, which only the assembly can do by at least a two-thirds vote. This is an important protection in cases where some of the members principally involved in a particular question may be unable to be present through an entire meeting. When such a departure from the order of business is justified, however, it is usually easy for the chair to obtain the necessary authorization from the assembly. He can say, for example, "The chair will entertain a motion to suspend the rules, and take up . . . "; or (for obtaining unanimous consent), "If there is no objection, the chair proposes at this time to proceed to take up . . . " (see also illustration under the heading *Program* above).

Orders of the Day

An *order of the day,* as stated above, is a particular subject, question, or item of business that is set in advance to be taken up during a given session, day, or meeting, or at a given hour, provided that no business having precedence over it interferes. In cases where more than a quarterly time interval (p. 88) will elapse before the next regular business session of the organization, an order of the day cannot be made for a time beyond the end of the present session. If the next regular business session will be held within a quarterly time interval, an order of the day cannot be made beyond the end of that next session. An order of the day cannot be taken up before the time for which it is set, except by reconsidering (**37**) the vote that established the order (so long as a reconsideration is possible), or by suspending the rules (**25**) by a two-thirds vote.

Orders of the day are divided into the classes of *general orders* and *special orders*. A special order is an order of the day that is made with the stipulation that any rules interfering with its consideration at the specified time shall be suspended except those relating: (a) to adjournment or recess (**8, 20, 21**); (b) to questions of privilege (**19**); (c) to special orders that were made before this special order was made; or (d) to a question that has been assigned priority over all other business at a meeting by being made *the* special order for the meeting as described on pages 359–60. An important consequence of this suspending effect is that, with the four exceptions just mentioned, a special order for a particular hour interrupts any business that is pending when that hour arrives. Since the making of a special order has the effect of suspending any interfering rules, it requires a two-thirds vote (except where such action is included in the adoption of an agenda or program for a session). Any matter that is made an order of the day without being made a special order is a general order for the time named.

An item of business can be made an order of the day in the following ways:

1) While the question is pending, it can be postponed (**14**) to the specified time by a majority vote (in which case it is a general order); or, by a two-thirds vote, it can be postponed to that time and made a special order.
2) A question that has not yet been brought before the assembly can be made a special order for a future time by means of a main motion adopted by a two-thirds vote. Similarly, it is possible, although less common, to make a question that is not pending a general order for a future time by a majority vote.
3) An agenda or program adopted by a majority vote at the beginning of a session can assign a specific position to the item of business; the subject is then a general order unless it is scheduled (in the agenda or program) for a particular hour, in which case it is a special order for that hour.

FORMS FOR MOTIONS TO MAKE GENERAL OR SPECIAL ORDERS.   The forms in proposing to make a *pending* question an order of the day for a future time by means of the motion to *Postpone* are given on pages 181–82.

When a question that is *not pending* is made an order of the day, it is usually made a special order. A main motion to make a particular subject a special order can be introduced whenever business of its class or new business is in order and nothing is pending. It can be offered in this form: "I move that the following resolution be made a special order

for the next meeting: '*Resolved,* That . . . '"; or, "I offer the
following resolution and move that it be made a special
order for 3 P.M.: '. . .'" In the case of a committee report,
a resolution such as this may be adopted: "*Resolved,* That
the report of the committee on the revision of the bylaws
be made the special order for Wednesday morning and
thereafter until it has been disposed of."

Motions in similar forms can also be used to make a
question that is not pending a general order. In this connection, however, it should be noted that a majority can
thus prevent a matter from coming before the assembly
until a future time, but after a majority has taken such action, nothing less than a two-thirds vote can change it unless it is reconsidered (**37**). If a main motion to make a
question that is not pending an order of the day for a future
time is introduced, any member who would prefer to consider the matter immediately should speak in debate against
the motion that would make it an order of the day. If that
motion is voted down, he can then introduce the subject of
the proposed order as a main question.

RELATION OF ORDERS OF THE DAY TO THE
ESTABLISHED ORDER OF BUSINESS.   In assemblies
that hold regular business sessions within quarterly time intervals (p. 88) and that follow the "standard" order of business explained above, orders of the day for a given session,
day, or meeting that are not set for particular hours are
taken up under the headings of *Special Orders* and *Unfinished Business and General Orders* (see pp. 345–48). In cases
where an ordinary society has adopted its own order of
business for regular meetings, it usually includes similar
headings covering such orders of the day. Where an organization's order of business does not provide such headings,
special orders not set for particular hours are taken up before unfinished business and general orders, or (if there are

1   neither of these), at all events before new business. Under
the same conditions, general orders are taken up after any
unfinished business (that is, business pending at the adjournment of the previous meeting, if any, and orders of the
5   day not disposed of at the time of its adjournment), and before new business unless a later hour is specified (see
below).

    The most common instances of orders of the day set for
particular hours occur in conventions.

10   In any type of assembly, in cases where orders of the day
have been set for particular hours, their consideration at the
proper time may cause interruption or modification of the
order of business as it exists apart from these orders of the
day; and different orders of the day may come into conflict.

15   Rules governing such cases are as follows:

    *Rules of Precedence Affecting General Orders for Partic-
ular Hours.*   As stated above, a general order that has been
set for a particular hour cannot be considered before that
hour unless the rules are suspended by a two-thirds vote, or

20   unless the vote that made the general order can still be reconsidered. This is the principle effect of making a subject
a general order for a particular hour. Since the making of a
general order does not suspend any rules, even if it is designated for a particular hour, delay in its consideration

25   when that hour arrives may arise from a number of causes.
Even though the hour fixed for a general order has arrived,
the order can be taken up only when all of the following
conditions are fulfilled:

30   a) no other business is pending;
    b) general orders not set for particular hours have been
        reached or passed in the order of business;
    c) no special order interferes;
    d) no reconsideration (**37**) that may then be moved or
35   called up interferes; and

e) no general order made before this one, for a particular hour that has arrived or passed, remains undisposed of.

As soon after the designated hour as conditions (a), (b), (c), and (e) are met, the chair should announce the general order as the pending business; but as he starts to do so, any member can rise and address the chair for the purpose of moving or calling up a reconsideration.

The rule that a general order for a particular hour does not interrupt a pending question when that hour arrives holds even when the pending question is a general order that was made later.* But if a general order for an earlier time is not reached by the time set for another general order that was made before it was, the general order that was made first is taken up in preference to the one for the earlier time.

Example. A motion is postponed to 4:30 P.M. Later, another motion is postponed to 4:15 P.M. If the 4:15 motion is taken up at that time (or at least before 4:30) and is not disposed of by 4:30, it continues under consideration and is not interrupted. But if the 4:15 motion is not reached by 4:30, the 4:30 motion, having been postponed first, has preference and will be taken up first. Unless something else affects the situation, the 4:15 motion in such a case will be considered after the disposal of the 4:30 motion.

If several general orders were made for the same time, they are taken up in the order in which they were made. If several general orders were made for the same time in the same motion, they are taken up in the order in which they are listed in the motion. If all of this business is not disposed of before adjournment, it is treated as described on pages 228–29 and 347–48.

---

*If it is desired to take up a general order at its specified hour and a pending question interferes, that pending question can, however, be laid on the table (**17**) or postponed (**14**).

1   *Rules of Precedence Affecting Special Orders for Particular Hours.*   A special order for a particular hour cannot be
considered before that hour except by a two-thirds vote.
But when the designated hour arrives, the special order au-
5 tomatically interrupts any business that may be pending except: (a) a motion relating to adjournment or recess; (b) a
question of privilege; (c) a special order that was made before the special order set for the present hour was made; or
(d) *the* special order for a meeting, as described below. The
10 chair simply announces the special order at the proper time,
as shown on page 183.

With the exception of *the* special order for a meeting,
when special orders that have been made at different times
come into conflict, the one that was made first takes prece-
15 dence over all special orders made afterward, which rank in
the order in which they were made. This rule holds even
when special orders made later have been set for consideration at earlier hours. No special order can interfere with one
that was made earlier than itself. If several special orders
20 have been made at the same time for the same hour, they
rank in the order in which they are listed in the motion by
which they were made. If they were made at the same time
for different hours, each has preference at the hour set for
its consideration and interrupts the pending question, even
25 if that pending question is a special order.

Example.   Assume that a special order has been made
for 3 P.M. Thereafter, one is made for 2 P.M. Still later, one
is made for 4 P.M. At two o'clock, the special order for that
time is taken up, even if it interrupts a general order that is
30 pending. However, if the 2 P.M. special order is still pending at 3 P.M., the 3 P.M. special order is immediately taken
up—interrupting the one that is pending—because it was
made first. Also, because the 3 P.M. order was made first, if
it is still under consideration at four o'clock, it continues re-
35 gardless of the order for that time. Even after the 3 P.M.

order is disposed of, the 4 P.M. order must await completion
of the prior-made 2 P.M. order, which is resumed first. Not
until all of these special orders are disposed of, together
with any others whose times are reached in the meantime,
can the assembly return to its regular order of business, first
resuming consideration of any subject that may have been
interrupted at 2 P.M. It is possible, of course, to rearrange
these special orders by reconsidering the votes that made
them, or, if reconsideration is no longer possible (**37**), by
suspending the rules and taking up each one of them in succession, only to postpone it and make it a special order for
the desired new time. When a series of special orders has
been made at the same time in one motion, it is implied
that the vote on each one will be taken when the hour for
the next special order arrives, but if this is not done the
pending special order is interrupted by its successor.

It should be noted that a special order does not interfere with a recess or adjournment that is prescheduled for a
particular hour. When such an hour arrives, the chair announces it and declares the assembly in recess or adjourned,
even if a special order is pending that was made before the
hour of recess or adjournment was fixed. When the chair
announces the hour, anyone can move to postpone the time
for adjournment, or to extend the time of considering the
pending question for a specified period. These motions are
undebatable and require a two-thirds vote (see also pp.
224, 233).

The Special Order for a Meeting.   When it is desired
to devote an entire meeting to a subject, or as much of the
meeting as may be necessary, the matter can be made *the*
special order for the meeting (as distinguished from *a* special order for the meeting; see pp. 345–46). *The* special
order for the meeting will then be taken up as soon as the
minutes have been approved, and the remainder of the
order of business will not be taken up until this special

1 order has been disposed of. Although *the* special order for
a meeting takes precedence over all other forms of special
orders, even if they were made before it was, the times of
any such orders for particular hours that may come into
5 conflict should be adjusted, as indicated on page 359,
lines 7–12.

Agenda or Program

10   By a single vote, a series of special orders or general
orders—or a mixture of both—can be made; such a series
is called an *agenda*. When an hour is assigned to a particular subject in an agenda, that subject is thereby made a
special order unless, by footnote or other means, it is
15 stated that the time is intended merely for guidance, in
which case the subject is only a general order. Subjects for
which no hour is specified in an agenda are general orders.
Usually an agenda covers an entire session, in which case
it is the order of business for that session and is adopted
20 by a majority vote, even if it contains special orders. If a
series of orders of the day that contains one or more special orders is made by a single vote during the course of a
session that already has an order of business, however, a
two-thirds vote is required. After an agenda or program
25 has been adopted by the assembly, no change can be made
in it except by a two-thirds vote, a vote of a majority of
the entire membership, or unanimous consent. (See *Suspend the Rules* (**25**); *Rescind; Amend Something Previously
Adopted* (**35**).) An affirmative vote to adopt an agenda or
30 program may not be reconsidered. In reference to an
order of business specially adopted for a given session, the
term *program* is often used instead of *agenda;* but while
the latter technically includes only items of business, the
former may include also the times for speakers, meals, and
35 other nonbusiness matters.

ORGANIZATIONS AND MEETINGS IN WHICH ADOPTION OF AN AGENDA IS CUSTOMARY.   It is customary to adopt an agenda or program for each session in organizations whose business sessions are separated by more than a quarterly time interval (see p. 88), and at conventions and other sessions that may last for several days (see **59**). This is also frequently done where, for any reason, neither the standard order of business nor a special order of business established by rule of the organization is practical or applicable. The proposed agenda is followed as a guide by the chair pending its formal adoption. Often an hour is assigned only to such subjects as the calls to order, recesses, adjournments, and particularly important items of business where it is desired to give the members greater assurance that the matter will not be considered before that time. These, then, are special orders for the time stated, and a strict adherence to these times provides a protection to the members and invited speakers, who often come from great distances. Occasionally a time is assigned for every item on the agenda. While this practice may be necessary in some cases, the resulting loss of flexibility often outweighs any benefits that may be gained.

ADVISABILITY OF PROVIDING FOR UNFINISHED BUSINESS.   At intervals or near the end of the session, an agenda should include provision for unfinished business. In agendas in which most or all of the items are special orders for particular times, it may be necessary to provide for unfinished business near the end of each day's sitting. Such provisions give the assembly a recourse whenever it needs a little more time before voting on a question. It can postpone a question to a time provided for unfinished business or, at all events, can conclude consideration of a question during such a period. Otherwise, a pending question that is merely postponed until the disposal of the

1   next item—since it becomes only a general order—may be
severely buffeted by the remaining special orders. Its further consideration would depend upon the next or some
successive items taking less time than allotted, and it might
5   soon be interrupted again by the next subject for which a
time was assigned.

TAKING UP TOPICS IN AN AGENDA.   When the
assigned time for taking up a topic in an agenda arrives, the
10   chair announces that fact. Then he puts to a vote any pending questions without allowing further debate, unless
someone immediately moves to lay the question on the
table, postpone it, or refer it to a committee. If any of these
subsidiary motions are moved, they are likewise put to a
15   vote, together with any amendment to them, without debate. Besides recognizing these subsidiary motions, the
chair also should recognize a motion to extend the time for
considering the pending question, if such a motion is made.
While an extension under these conditions is seldom desir-
20   able and is often unfair to the next topic, it is sometimes
necessary, and a motion for the extension can be adopted
without debate by a two-thirds vote (see also **18**). As soon
as the business that was pending has been disposed of as described, the chair recognizes the member who is to offer the
25   motion or resolution embodying the scheduled topic (unless the question has previously been introduced and has
come over from an earlier time, in which case the chair announces it as the pending business).

30   CARRYING OVER UNFINISHED BUSINESS.   In
agendas for sessions consisting of several meetings, when
most items are general orders, and the time set for adjournment of a meeting arrives before all of the matters
scheduled for that meeting have been considered, the re-
35   maining items of business are carried over to the next meet-

ing. They are taken first in their order before the matters *1*
scheduled for that meeting, provided that no conflict arises
with a special order. Therefore, it is wise to schedule the
more important items of business at a reasonably early
meeting of a convention and not save them for the last *5*
minutes.

AGENDA PROVIDED IN ADVANCE FOR INFOR-
MATION.   In some organizations, it is customary to send
each member, in advance of a meeting, an order of business *10*
or agenda, with some indication of the matters to be considered under each heading. Such an agenda is often provided for information only, with no intention or practice of
submitting it for adoption. Unless a precirculated agenda is
formally adopted at the session to which it applies, it is not *15*
binding as to detail or order of consideration, other than as
it lists preexisting orders of the day (pp. 353ff.) or conforms
to the standard order of business (pp. 24–25, 342ff.) or an
order of business prescribed by the rules of the organization
(pp. 15–17, 24). *20*

ASSIGNMENT OF THE
FLOOR; DEBATE

§42. RULES GOVERNING ASSIGNMENT OF THE FLOOR

The manner in which a member obtains the floor is described on pages 28–30, with an initial treatment of the principal rules governing the assignment of the floor under ordinary conditions in most business meetings. More complete rules affecting the assignment of the floor are contained in this section.

Recognition of a Member

Before a member in an assembly can make a motion or speak in debate, he must claim the floor by rising and addressing the chair as described on page 28, and must be recognized by the chair. The chair must recognize any member who seeks the floor while entitled to it. The chair normally recognizes a member (thereby assigning the floor to him) by announcing, as applicable, the members' name or title, or the place or unit that he represents. If necessary,

the member—either on his own initiative or at the request
of the chair—should state his name, with any appropriate
additional identification, as soon as the presiding officer
turns toward him after he has risen and addressed the chair.
Variations in the granting of recognition are as follows:

- If only one person is seeking the floor in a small meeting where all present can clearly see one another, the
  chair may recognize the member by merely nodding to
  him.
- If a speech is prearranged, or if several members are attempting to claim the floor at once in a large meeting,
  a wording frequently used by the chair in granting
  recognition is, "The chair recognizes Mr. Smith."

Whenever a member rises and addresses the chair at a
time when the floor can be granted only for limited purposes and the chair is not certain that the member under-
stands this fact—for example, when an undebatable
question is immediately pending as explained on page
368—the chair, before recognizing the member, should
ask, "For what purpose does the member [or "the gentleman," or "the lady," or, as in Congress, "the gentle-
woman"] rise?" If members remain seated around a
conference table and do not rise, the chair may ask, "For
what purpose does the member address the chair?"

Except by unanimous consent (pp. 51–53), a motion
can be made only by one who has been recognized by the
chair as having the floor. If a motion is called out by anyone who has not obtained the floor, the chair should ignore
it if another member, by rising promptly and claiming the
floor, shows that unanimous consent has not been given.

When assigned the floor, a member may use it for any
proper purpose, or a combination of purposes; for example,
although a member may have begun by debating a pending

1 motion, he may conclude by moving any secondary motion, including the *Previous Question* (**16**), that is in order at the time.

5 ### Assignment of the Floor When More Than One Person Claims It

If two or more rise at about the same time to claim the floor, the general rule is that, all other things being equal, 10 the member who rose and addressed the chair first *after the floor was yielded* is entitled to be recognized. A member who rises before the floor has been yielded is not entitled to the floor if any other member rises afterward and addresses the chair.*

15 Under a variety of particular conditions, however, when more than one member claims the floor at about the same time, the best interests of the assembly require the floor to be assigned to a claimant who was not the first to rise and address the chair. Such a claimant to the floor in these cases is said to 20 be entitled to "preference in being recognized" or "preference in recognition." A member cannot rise to claim preference in recognition after the chair has actually recognized another member. So long as the person assigned the floor has not actually begun to speak, however, another member may 25 interrupt to give previous notice (p. 117).

The rules governing preference in recognition may be grouped as relating to cases when a debatable question is immediately pending, when an undebatable question is immediately pending, and when no question is pending.

---

*The rules just given in the text represent the basic parliamentary practice. In a large hall where microphones are in use and members must walk some distance to reach one, certain modifications of these rules may be necessary. The basic rules can be followed in cases where ushers are equipped with hand microphones and a microphone is carried to each member who is recognized (see also p. 371).

PREFERENCE IN RECOGNITION WHEN A DE-
BATABLE QUESTION IS IMMEDIATELY PENDING.
While a motion is open to debate:

1) A member may rise to give previous notice of another
   motion (pp. 117–18).
2) If the member who made the motion that is immediately pending claims the floor and has not already spoken on the question, he is entitled to be recognized in
   preference to other members. Under some particular
   cases or variations of this rule, the members entitled to
   preference in recognition are:
   a) in the case of a motion to implement a recommen-
      dation in a committee's report, the reporting mem-
      ber (who presented the committee's report to the
      assembly);
   b) in the case of a question that has been taken from
      the table (**34**), the member who moved to take it
      from the table; and
   c) in the case of a motion to *Reconsider* (**37**), the
      member who *made* the motion to *Reconsider*, not
      necessarily the one who may have called it up (see
      pp. 306, 312–13).
3) No member who has already had the floor in debate on
   the immediately pending question is entitled to it again
   on the same day for debate on the same question so
   long as any member who has not spoken on that question claims the floor.
4) In cases where the chair knows that persons seeking the
   floor have opposite opinions on the question—and the
   member to be recognized is not determined by (1)
   through (3) above—the chair should let the floor alternate, as far as possible, between those favoring and those
   opposing the measure. In large assemblies, various devices are sometimes used to assist the chair in following

this rule, such as having members seeking recognition hold up cards of different colors, go to different microphones "for" and "against," or the like.

When a member has moved to reconsider the vote on a motion for the announced purpose of amending the motion, if the vote is reconsidered he must be recognized in preference to others in order to move his amendment. This rule also applies to reconsiderations of amendable motions that are not debatable (see list on tinted p. 45), as noted below.

PREFERENCE IN RECOGNITION WHEN AN UNDEBATABLE QUESTION IS IMMEDIATELY PENDING.   When the immediately pending question is undebatable (tinted pp. 44–45), the floor can be assigned only to a member who wishes to give previous notice of a motion (pp. 116–18) or make a motion or raise a question that would take precedence over the immediately pending question. In such a case, the mover of the immediately pending question has no preference to the floor. When an undebatable motion that can be amended is reconsidered for that announced purpose, however, the maker of the motion to *Reconsider* (**37**) is entitled to preference in recognition, as explained in the preceding paragraph.

PREFERENCE IN RECOGNITION WHEN NO QUESTION IS PENDING.   Cases where a member is entitled to preference in recognition when no question is pending occur as follows:

1) When a member has been assigned to offer a motion which a special meeting was called to consider, or an important prearranged main motion at any meeting, that member is entitled to prior recognition and no other members should be permitted to intervene in an effort to offer another motion in competition.

2) When a desired object requires a series of motions, each
of which is moved while no question is pending, and
when the assembly has disposed of one motion in such
a series, the next motion in the series has the right of
way; and, for the purpose of making that motion, the
chair should recognize the member who is presenting
the series, even if another member has risen and addressed the chair first. For example:

   a) When a question has been laid on the table (**17**) for
   a legitimate purpose—to enable the assembly to
   take up a more urgent matter—the member who
   moved to lay on the table is entitled to preference
   in recognition to introduce the urgent business.

   b) When the rules have been suspended (**25**) to enable
   a certain motion to be made, the member who
   moved to suspend the rules is entitled to the floor
   to make the motion involved.

3) Similarly, when a motion has been voted down at the
urging of a member who stated in debate that in such
event he would offer a different motion on the same
subject (see pp. 110–11), that member is entitled to
preference in recognition so that he may introduce his
alternative motion.

4) When no question is pending and no series of motions
has been started, and a member has risen seeking the
floor to make a main motion, another member is entitled
to preference in recognition if he addresses the chair and
states that he rises for one of the following purposes:

   a) to make a motion to *Reconsider and Enter on the
   Minutes* (pp. 321–24);

   b) to move to reconsider a vote (**37**);

   c) to call up a motion to *Reconsider* (in its regular or
   special form, [**37**]) that has been made earlier;

   d) to give previous notice (pp. 116–18); or

   e) to move to take a question from the table (**34**)
   when it is in order to do so.

If members come into competition in rising for these purposes, they have preference in the order in which the four actions are listed above. Time limits on making the motion to *Reconsider*—and shorter limits on its special form, to *Reconsider and Enter on the Minutes*—account for first preference of these two motions in such cases.

5) When a motion to appoint a committee for a certain purpose, or to refer a subject to a committee, has been adopted with the omission of necessary details—such as the number of members of the committee, how it shall be appointed, or any instructions to be given it—the member who made this motion has no preference in recognition, since he could have included any desired specifications in his motion. In such a case, however, no new subject (except a privileged one) can be introduced until the assembly has decided all of these related questions.

ASSIGNMENT OF THE FLOOR BY VOTE; APPEALS.   If the chair is in doubt as to who is entitled to the floor, he can allow the assembly to decide the question by a vote, in which case the member receiving the largest vote is entitled to the floor.

If at any time the chair makes a mistake and assigns the floor to the wrong person when more than one member rose and addressed the chair promptly, a *Point of Order* can be raised. Except in a mass meeting, the decision of the chair in assigning the floor can be appealed from by any two members—one making the appeal and the other seconding it (**24**).*

---

*In a mass meeting, the chair's decision in assigning the floor is not subject to appeal. In a very large body other than a mass meeting, if the best interests of the assembly require that the chair be given greater power in assigning the floor, a special rule that there shall be no appeal from his decision in granting recognition can be adopted (see *Rules of Order,* pp. 15–16; see also, in regard to standing rules in a convention, pp. 599ff.).

VARIATIONS IN LARGE CONVENTIONS. In *1* large conventions or similar bodies, some of the rules applicable to the assignment of the floor may require adaptation. For example, members may be asked to line up at numbered microphones. They may be recognized in numerical *5* order, or someone may list them for the chair in the order in which assistant sergeants-at-arms turned on lights affixed to the microphones. A rule may provide that a member who has a priority matter, such as a point of order, may ask the assistant at the microphone to flash the light to so indi- *10* cate. Should a member, called in whatever order is established, move an amendment or other debatable motion, others awaiting a turn should stand aside unless their debate is germane to the new motion. If the Previous Question or a motion to limit debate is moved, members who have been *15* waiting in line cannot validly protest; as in all other cases, the chair cannot choose the occasions when such motions will be in order. He may advise the assembly that, if it wishes to continue debate and hear from those waiting in line, a minority greater than one third has this within its *20* power (see footnote, p. 366).

Interruption of a Member Assigned the Floor

When a member has been assigned the floor and has *25* begun to speak—unless he begins to discuss a subject when no motion is pending or speaks longer in debate than the rules of the assembly allow—he cannot be interrupted by another member or by the chair except for one of the following purposes, and then only when the urgency of the sit- *30* uation justifies it:

a) a *Call for the Orders of the Day* (**18**) when they are not being conformed to,
b) the raising of a question of privilege (**19**), *35*

c) a *Point of Order* or the calling of the member who has the floor to order (**23, 61**)—or the chair's calling this member's attention to the fact that he is failing to observe the rules of speaking (pp. 626–27),

d) a call for a separate vote on one or more of a set of independent resolutions on different subjects that have been offered by a single motion (pp. 106, 265),

e) a request or inquiry (**32, 33**) that requires an immediate response;

or, in certain special circumstances, these additional purposes:

f) an *Appeal* (**24**),

g) an *Objection to the Consideration of a Question* (**26**), or

h) a *Division of the Assembly* (**29**).

After a member has been assigned the floor but before he has begun to speak, it is in order to take any of the steps listed above, and also, if there may be no other opportunity, to rise for the purpose of:

a) giving notice of intent to introduce a motion requiring such notice (pp. 116–18); or

b) making a motion to *Reconsider* (**37**) or to *Reconsider and Enter on the Minutes* (pp. 321–24).

If an interruption occurs for any of the reasons listed above, the member who had the floor does not lose it, although he takes his seat while the interrupting matter is being attended to. As soon as the interruption has been disposed of, the chair directs him to rise and proceed by saying, for example, "Mr. Lewis has the floor."

If a member presenting a committee report or other document to the assembly hands it to the secretary or a reading clerk to be read, the member does not thereby yield the floor, but has it again when the reading is finished.

When a member has risen to claim the floor or has been *1* assigned the floor, it is out of order for another to call out a motion to adjourn, or a motion to lay the pending question on the table. If someone does so, or if calls of "Question!" are made, it is the duty of the chair to obtain order and pro- *5* tect the rights of the member who is entitled to the floor.

§43. RULES GOVERNING DEBATE

Debate, rightly understood, is an essential element in *10* the making of rational decisions of consequence by intelli- gent people. In a deliberative assembly, this term applies to discussion on the merits of a pending question—that is, whether the proposal under consideration should, or should not, be agreed to. That the right of debate is inher- *15* ent in such an assembly is implied by the word *deliberative.*

Debatability is a characteristic of all main motions and of certain other motions, depending on the parliamentary func- tion they serve, according to principles summarized at the end of this section; and from such principles are derived the spe- *20* cific rules stated under Standard Characteristic 5 in **11–37**.

While the amount of debate on a motion in actual prac- tice will depend on such factors as its importance, how strongly it is contested, etc., every member of the assembly has the right to speak to every debatable motion before it is *25* finally acted upon; and subject only to general limitations on debate established by parliamentary law or the rules of the body as explained below, this right cannot be interfered with except by a two-thirds vote.

30

Summary of Procedures Incident to Debate

Until a matter has been brought before the assembly in the form of a motion proposing a specific action, it cannot be debated. As explained in **3** and **4,** the motion must be *35*

1 made by a member who has obtained the floor while no
question is pending (or while the motion is in order, if it is
not a main motion), after which it must be seconded by another member (unless it is made by direction of a board or
5 committee), and must be stated by the chair. The chair may
conclude his statement of the question on the debatable
motion by asking, "Are you ready for the question?" or he
may simply pause and turn toward the maker of the motion
to see if he desires the floor first in debate. After the maker
10 of the motion has had the opportunity to speak first if he
wishes, other members can rise and address the chair to
claim the floor for the purpose of debate, as explained on
pages 28ff. and in **42**.

While debate is in progress, amendments or other sec-
15 ondary (subsidiary, privileged, or incidental) motions can
be introduced and disposed of—and can be debated in the
process, if they are debatable—as explained on pages
111–13. A member may both speak in debate and conclude
by offering a secondary motion, which is a particular appli-
20 cation of the principle that a member having been recognized for *any* legitimate purpose has the floor for *all*
legitimate purposes.

When debate appears to have concluded, the chair may
again ask, "Are you ready for the question?" or if, after a
25 reasonable pause, no one rises to claim the floor, the chair
may assume that no member wishes to speak and, standing,
may proceed to put the question.

It should be noted that, under legitimate parliamentary
procedure, there is no such thing as "gaveling through" a
30 measure. The right of members to debate or introduce secondary motions cannot be cut off by the chair's attempting
to put a question to vote so quickly that no member can get
the floor—either when the chair first states the question or
when he believes debate is ended. Debate is not closed by
35 the presiding officer's rising to put the question. If a vote

has been taken or begun quickly and it is found that a member rose and addressed the chair with reasonable promptness after the chair asked, "Are you ready for the question?" or, by a pause or otherwise, indicated that the floor was open to assignment, then—even if the chair has announced the result of such a vote—the vote must be disregarded, the member is entitled to the floor, and debate begins or resumes. But if the chair gives ample opportunity for members to claim the floor before he puts the question, and no one rises, the right to debate cannot be claimed after the voting has commenced. If, because a member sought the floor in timely fashion, debate is resumed after voting has begun, the question must be put fully again—that is, both the affirmative and the negative votes must called for—regardless of how far the earlier vote had proceeded. When a vote is taken a second time for purposes of verification—as when a *Division* (**29**) is demanded—debate cannot be resumed except by unanimous consent (pp. 51–53).

Length and Number of Speeches

MAXIMUM TIME FOR EACH SPEECH.   In a nonlegislative body or organization that has no special rule relating to the length of speeches (**2**), a member, having obtained the floor while a debatable motion is immediately pending, can speak no longer than ten minutes unless he obtains the consent of the assembly. Such permission can be given by unanimous consent (pp. 51–53), or by means of a motion to *Extend the Limits of Debate* (**15**), which requires a two-thirds vote without debate.

When a member's time is exhausted, the chair rises and—if the member does not immediately conclude his remarks—calls his attention to the fact by an appropriate signal, or by interrupting him if necessary. If it appears that a minute more will afford sufficient time for the member to

1   conclude more gracefully, the chair can ask unanimous con-
     sent to extend the member's time for a short period, or any
     member can do so.

           Rights in regard to debate are not transferable. Unless
5   the organization has a special rule on the subject, a mem-
     ber cannot yield any unexpired portion of his time to an-
     other member, or reserve any portion of his time for a later
     time—that is, if a member yields the floor before speaking
     his full ten minutes, he is presumed to have waived his
10   right to the remaining time.* If a speaker yields to another
     member for a question (*Point of Information*, pp. 282–83),
     the time consumed by the question is charged to the
     speaker.

           A committee chairman or reporting member is not con-
15   sidered to be debating when presenting or reading the
     committee's report, but he is bound to obey the assembly's
     rules relating to debate in any speech made by him in sup-
     port of the motion offered on behalf of the committee.

20   NUMBER OF SPEECHES ON THE SAME QUES-
     TION PER MEMBER PER DAY.   Unless the assembly
     has a special rule providing otherwise, no member can
     speak more than twice to the same question on the same
     day—except that in the case of an *Appeal* (**24**), only the
25   presiding officer can speak twice (the second time at the
     close of the debate), all other members being limited to one
     speech. Merely asking a question or making a brief sugges-
     tion is not counted as speaking in debate; nor is the making

---

*This rule reflects the traditional parliamentary principles. The House
of Representatives has a different rule which permits control of all time by
a single member or the leaders of the opposing sides of the question. The
House rule also prevents members to whom time has been yielded for debate from making motions. See form (d) on page 188 and, especially, the
form on pages 620–21.

of a secondary motion counted as speaking in debate,* so
long as in making the motion the member makes no comment on the then-pending question. It will be seen from
this rule that if debate on a pending motion is continued at
the next meeting, and if that meeting is held on the same
day, members who have already made two speeches on a
question are not allowed to speak on it again without the
assembly's permission. But if the next meeting is held on
another day, all members have their right to debate entirely
renewed with reference to that question. Under this rule,
each debatable motion is a separate question with respect to
members' rights to debate it. Thus, if a series of debatable
questions is pending and a member has, for example, spoken twice that day while the main motion is immediately
pending, he has exhausted his right to debate the main motion; but, even on the same day, he can still speak twice on
a motion to postpone the main question indefinitely, and
twice on each amendment that may be moved, and so on.
As noted under the rules for assigning the floor (**42**), however, a member cannot make a second speech on the same
question the same day until every member who desires to
speak on it has had an opportunity to do so once. If debate
is closed before the member has an opportunity to make a
second speech, none may be made.

Modification of General Limits of Debate

The general rules limiting the length and number of
speeches in debate that are stated above can be modified to
serve the assembly's needs as follows:

---

*Thus a member who has exhausted the number of speeches permit-
ted him on a main motion may still seek recognition to move its referral or
amendment, for example. In such a case the chair should grant limited
recognition by saying, "The member has exhausted his right to debate. For
what purpose does he rise?"

1   ADOPTING A SPECIAL RULE.   The rule allowing each member two speeches of ten minutes' length per day on each debatable question can be made either more restrictive or more liberal for all meetings of a society by *5* adopting a special rule of order by a two-thirds vote after notice, or by a vote of a majority of the entire membership (**2**; see also pp. 116–18). An example of a more restrictive rule might be one setting a limit of not more than one speech of five minutes' length on the same question on the *10* same day for each member.

CHANGING THE LIMITS FOR A SESSION.   An assembly at any session can change the limits of debate, for that session only, by means of a main motion adopted by a *15* two-thirds vote without notice. In a convention—where the limits of debate generally need to be stricter than in a local society—such a modification is usually adopted in the form of a *standing rule of the convention* (**59**), requiring a two-thirds vote in such a case.
20

CHANGING THE LIMITS FOR THE PENDING QUESTIONS(S) ONLY.   While a debatable question is immediately pending, the allowed length or number of speeches can be reduced or increased, for that question only, *25* by means of the subsidiary motion to *Limit or Extend Limits of Debate* (**15**), adopted by a two-thirds vote. This motion can also be used to close debate at a specified future time. If two thirds of those voting wish to close debate immediately, they can do so by adopting the motion for the *Previous Ques-* *30* *tion* (**16**). If a series of adhering debatable questions (pp. 112–13) is pending, either of these motions can also be applied to the entire series or any consecutive part of the series beginning with the immediately pending question. (For forms, see pp. 188–89, 199–201, 620–21.) If it is desired to *35* prevent any discussion of a subject—even by the introducer of the motion, who has the right to the floor first—the only way this can be done is to raise an *Objection to the Consideration of the Question* (**26**) before debate begins or any subsidiary motion is stated. If the objection is sustained by a two-thirds vote, the question cannot be considered in any way at that time or during that session.

On the other hand, if, in considering a particular question, it is desired to retain the usual limit on the length of speeches but remove restrictions on the total number of times members can speak, the assembly by a majority vote can resolve itself into a committee of the whole or into quasi committee of the whole, or it can consider the question informally (see pp. 523–24). Speeches made under these procedures do not count against a member's right to debate the same question if it is further considered by the assembly on the same day under the regular rules. If the question under consideration is composed of a number of sections or paragraphs—as in the case of bylaws, for example—the total number of speeches allowed each member can be greatly increased, but not made unlimited, by considering the document seriatim (**28**), in which case each member can speak twice on each paragraph, section, or unit that is taken up as a separate part.

Decorum in Debate

The following practices and customs observed by speakers and other members in an assembly assist the carrying on of debate in a smooth and orderly manner. The paragraphs under the head *Pattern of Formality* on pages 21–24 should be read in connection with this subject.

CONFINING REMARKS TO THE MERITS OF THE PENDING QUESTION. In debate a member's remarks must be germane to the question before the assembly—that is, his statements must have bearing on whether the pending motion should be adopted (see also *Principles Governing the Debatability of Motions*, pp. 384–86).

1   REFRAINING FROM ATTACKING A MEMBER'S MOTIVES. When a question is pending, a member can condemn the nature or likely consequences of the proposed measure in strong terms, but he must avoid personalities, 5 and under no circumstances can he attack or question the motives of another member. The measure, not the member, is the subject of debate. If a member disagrees with a statement by another in regard to an event that both witnessed, he cannot state in debate that the other's statement "is 10 false." But he might say, "I believe there is strong evidence that the member is mistaken." The moment the chair hears such words as "fraud," "liar," or "lie" used about a member in debate, he must act immediately and decisively to correct the matter and prevent its repetition (see **61**).

15

    ADDRESSING ALL REMARKS THROUGH THE CHAIR. Members of an assembly cannot address one another directly, but must address all remarks through the chair. If, while a member is speaking in debate, another 20 member wishes to address a question to him—which the person speaking can permit or not as he chooses, but which is taken out of his time if he does—the member desiring to ask the question should rise and address the chair, proceeding as explained under *Point of Information* (pp. 282–83).

25

    AVOIDING THE USE OF MEMBERS' NAMES. As much as possible, the use of names of members should be avoided in debate. It is better to describe a member in some other way, as by saying, "the member who spoke 30 last," or, "the delegate from Mason County." The officers of the society should always be referred to by their official titles. There is no need, however, to refer to oneself in debate in the third person as by the use of such expressions as "this member." A member's debate is expected and in- 35 tended to be partial, and the first person is quite acceptable.

REFRAINING FROM SPEAKING ADVERSELY ON A PRIOR ACTION NOT PENDING.   In debate, a member cannot reflect adversely on any prior act of the society that is not then pending, unless a motion to reconsider, rescind, or amend it is pending, or unless he intends to conclude his remarks by making or giving notice of one of these motions.

REFRAINING FROM SPEAKING AGAINST ONE'S OWN MOTION.   In debate, the maker of a motion, while he can vote against it, is not allowed to speak against his own motion. He need not speak at all, but if he does he is obliged to take a favorable position. If he changes his mind while the motion he made is pending, he can, in effect, advise the assembly of this by asking permission to withdraw the motion (pp. 283–86).

READING FROM REPORTS, QUOTATIONS, ETC., ONLY WITHOUT OBJECTION OR WITH PERMISSION.   If any member objects, a member has no right to read from—or to have the secretary read from—any paper or book as part of his speech, without permission of the assembly. Members are usually permitted to read short, pertinent, printed extracts in debate, however, so long as they do not abuse the privilege (see also pp. 286–87).

BEING SEATED DURING AN INTERRUPTION BY THE CHAIR.   If at any time the presiding officer rises to make a ruling, give information, or otherwise speak within his privilege, any member who is speaking should be seated (or should step back slightly if he is standing at a microphone some distance from a seat) until the presiding officer has finished. At that time the member can resume his speech, unless he is denied the right as a disciplinary measure. (Questions of discipline arising from disorderly debate by members are treated in **61**).

1   REFRAINING FROM DISTURBING THE ASSEM-
BLY.   During debate, during remarks by the presiding officer to the assembly, and during voting, no member should
be permitted to disturb the assembly by whispering, walk-
5 ing across the floor, or in any other way. The key words
here are *disturb the assembly*. This rule does not mean,
therefore, that members can never whisper, or walk from
one place to another in the hall during the deliberations of
the assembly. At large meetings it would be impossible to
10 enforce such a rule. However, the presiding officer should
watch that such activity does not disturb the meeting or
hamper the transaction of business.

Rule Against the Chair's Participation in Debate
15

If the presiding officer is a member of the society, he
has—as an individual the same *rights* in debate as any
other member; but the impartiality required of the chair in
an assembly precludes his exercising these rights while he is
20 presiding. Normally, especially in a large body, he should
have nothing to say on the merits of pending questions. On
certain occasions—which should be extremely rare—the
presiding officer may believe that a crucial factor relating to
such a question has been overlooked and that his obligation
25 as a member to call attention to the point outweighs his
duty to preside at that time. To participate in debate, he
must relinquish the chair; and in such a case he should turn
the chair over:

30 (a) to the vice-president;
      (b) to the ranking vice-president present who has not spo-
          ken on the question and does not decline on the
          grounds of wishing to speak on it; or
      (c) if no such vice-president is in the room, to some other
35   member qualified as in (b), whom the chair designates
          (and who is assumed to receive the assembly's approval

by unanimous consent unless member(s) then nominate   1
other person(s), in which case the presiding officer's
choice is also treated as a nominee and the matter is decided by vote).

The presiding officer who relinquished the chair then should   5
not return to it until the pending main question has been disposed of, since he has shown himself to be a partisan as far as
that particular matter is concerned. Indeed, unless a presiding officer is extremely sparing in leaving the chair to take   10
part in debate, he may destroy members' confidence in the
impartiality of his approach to the task of presiding.

In debate on an appeal (**24**) or a point of order (**23**)
that the chair has submitted to the judgment of the assembly (pp. 245–47), the foregoing rule does not apply, and   15
the presiding officer does not leave the chair, since his participation in the debate relates to the function of presiding.

Occasions Justifying Brief Discussion
Outside Debate   20

INFORMAL CONSULTATION TO ASSIST THE
FRAMING OF A MOTION.   As already stated, debate is
permitted only while a debatable question is immediately
pending. Occasionally, however—in small assemblies when   25
a subject is not strongly contested—brief informal consultation or discussion of a subject may assist a member in
framing a proper motion. If the chair permits such discussion, he generally should not allow it to continue more than
a few moments or longer than is reasonably necessary to ar-   30
rive at a motion embodying the member's ideas.

In general, for a member to speak when no question is
pending, without promptly leading to a motion, implies an
unusual circumstance and requires permission *of the assembly*.
But occasionally, in very small bodies, a member who has ob-   35
tained the floor at such a time may state that, if there is no

objection, he would like to give some explanations dealing with a specified subject and to conclude by offering a motion on that subject. If no one objects, the member can then proceed; and the chair, knowing the subject, can hold him to it as he would in debate on a motion (see also p. 33).

ALLOWABLE EXPLANATION OF A PENDING UNDEBATABLE MOTION. Sometimes business may be expedited by allowing a few words of factual explanation while an undebatable motion is pending. The distinction between debate and asking questions or making brief suggestions should be kept in mind in this connection. The chair should be careful not to allow this type of consultation to develop into an extended colloquy between members or to take on the semblance of debate; and he should generally remain standing while the consultation takes place, to show that the floor has not been assigned.

Principles Governing the Debatability of Motions

Rules as to each motion's debatability or undebatability are given under Standard Characteristic 5 in **10–37** and in the Tables of Rules Relating to Motions on tinted pages 6–29. The following is a brief summary of these rules in relation to the principles on which they are based.

Every main motion is debatable, from the nature of the deliberative assembly itself.

With the exception of the two subsidiary motions that have to do with debate, the degree to which each of the subsidiary motions can be debated depends on the extent to which its adoption would restrict the assembly in dealing with the main question.

- Since the motion to *Postpone Indefinitely* (**11**) will kill the main motion if it is adopted, it is fully debatable and leaves the main question open to debate.

- A motion to *Amend* (**12**) is debatable when it is applied   1
  to the main question or to any other debatable motion,
  since it would alter the question it proposes to amend;
  but the debate is limited to the merits of the amendment, and other pending questions can be brought into   5
  the discussion only as necessary in this connection. A
  motion to amend an undebatable motion is undebatable, because to allow debate on it would be contrary to
  the purposes of the other motion's undebatability.
- In the case of the motions to *Commit* (**13**) and to *Post-*   10
  pone to a Certain Time (**14**), debate is quite limited, because the main question will be open to further debate
  when the committee reports or when the time arrives to
  which the question was postponed. Hence, debate is
  confined in the first instance to the wisdom of referring   15
  or to the choice of personnel of the committee and to
  the nature of its instructions, and in the latter instance
  to the wisdom of postponement and the choice of a
  time to which the question will be postponed.
- Motions to *Limit or Extend Limits of Debate* (**15**) and for   20
  the *Previous Question* (**16**) are undebatable inasmuch as
  their very object is to alter the debatability of pending
  question(s), and their purpose would be defeated if they
  were debatable; they arc also in the nature of specialized
  motions to suspend the rules, and any such motion made   25
  while business is pending is undebatable.
- The motion to *Lay on the Table* (**17**) is undebatable because its legitimate purpose would be defeated if it were
  debatable, and because its adoption in no way interferes
  with the right of the majority to take the question from   30
  the table (**34**) and resume debate.

The privileged motions are all undebatable because, if
they were debatable, their high privilege would allow them to
interfere with business. The right of debate is thus incom-   35
patible with high privilege. With reference to the two lowest-

1 ranking privileged motions, it is, of course, the "calling" for
the orders of the day (**18**) or the "raising" of a question of
privilege (**19**) that is undebatable. When the order of the day
or the question of privilege involved in such a case becomes
5 pending, it is a main motion and is therefore debatable.

With the exception of an *Appeal* (**24**), sometimes, and
a *Request to Be Excused from a Duty* (**32**), the incidental
motions are undebatable, because they have high privilege
to interrupt any motions or situations to which they are in-
10 cidental. In the case of an *Appeal* that relates to indecorum,
the rules of debate, or the priority of business, it is assumed
that debate would be a hindrance to business, as it would
be if the appeal were made while the immediately pending
question was undebatable. At all other times an appeal is
15 fully debatable so long as the debate is germane to the subject matter of the appeal. A *Request to Be Excused from a
Duty,* such as a resignation, may require some discussion for
its proper decision, and for this reason it is debatable.

Rules as to the debatability of motions that bring a
20 question again before the assembly may be summarized as
follows:

- The motion to *Take from the Table* (**34**) is undebatable
  because debate would serve no useful purpose and would
25 delay business, and because, if it is voted down, it can be
  renewed each time any business has been transacted.
- The motion to *Rescind* or to *Amend Something Previously Adopted* (**35**) is fully debatable, and it opens to debate the entire motion that it proposes to rescind or to
30 amend. The same is true of the motion to *Discharge a
  Committee* (**36**).
- The motion to *Reconsider* (**37**) is debatable only to the
  extent that the motion proposed to be reconsidered is
  debatable, and it opens the merits of that question to
35 debate. A motion to reconsider an undebatable motion
  is thus undebatable.

VOTING

1

§44. BASES FOR DETERMINING A VOTING RESULT

Majority Vote—the Basic Requirement

As stated on page 4, the basic requirement for approval *5* of an action or choice by a deliberative assembly, except where a rule provides otherwise, is a *majority vote*. The word *majority* means "more than half"; and when the term *majority vote* is used without qualification—as in the case of the basic requirement—it means more than half of the votes *10* cast by persons legally entitled to vote, excluding blanks or abstentions, at a regular or properly called meeting at which a quorum (**40**) is present. For example, at such a meeting (assuming that there are no voters having fractions of a vote, as may occur in some conventions): *15*

- If 19 votes are cast, a majority (more than 9½) is 10.
- If 20 votes are cast, a majority (more than 10) is 11.
- If 21 votes are cast, a majority (more than 10½) is 11.

20

Other bases for determining a voting result, as described below, are required under parliamentary law for certain procedures, or may be prescribed by the rules of the particular body—for decisions in general or for questions of a specified nature (see also Standard Characteristic 7, pp. 98–99). *25*

Two-Thirds Vote

A *two-thirds vote*—when the term is unqualified—means at least two thirds of the votes cast by persons legally entitled to vote, excluding blanks or abstentions, at a regular or properly called meeting at which a quorum is present. For example, at such a meeting (assuming that there are no fractions of votes):

- If 30 votes are cast, a two-thirds vote is 20.
- If 31 votes are cast, a two-thirds vote is 21.
- If 32 votes are cast, a two-thirds vote is 22.
- If 33 votes are cast, a two-thirds vote is 22.

As a compromise between the rights of the individual and the rights of the assembly, the principle has been established that a two-thirds vote is required to adopt any motion that: (a) suspends or modifies a rule of order previously adopted; (b) prevents the introduction of a question for consideration; (c) closes, limits, or extends the limits of debate; (d) closes nominations or the polls, or otherwise limits the freedom of nominating or voting; or (e) takes away membership or office. (For a list of motions that require a two-thirds vote, see tinted p. 46.)

In determining whether a question has obtained two thirds of the votes cast, the chair should take a rising vote (or, in a very small assembly, if he prefers and no one objects, a vote by show of hands), and he should obtain a count of the vote whenever he is in doubt concerning the result.

The chair can obtain a count of the vote initially if it appears—when those in the affirmative rise—that the result will be close; or he can retake it as a counted rising vote if he is afterward in doubt. In an assembly that has no special rule permitting a small fraction (that is, a specified

fraction somewhat less than one third) of the voters to re-   *1*
quire a two-thirds vote to be counted, the chair, in judging whether to obtain a count of the vote at his own
instance, must be particularly careful to leave no room for
anyone to doubt the result in cases where he finds that   *5*
there *are* two thirds on the side that thereby prevails.
Without a count at the chair's instance under these conditions, if he announces that a two-thirds vote has been obtained and those on the losing side doubt the result, they
are powerless to have it verified should those declared the   *10*
winners choose to prevent a count. The reason is that—
whatever may be the true result in view of the closeness of
the vote in such a case—those declared the losers are no
more than approximately one third of those voting, and
therefore cannot command the majority necessary to order   *15*
the vote counted.

Modifications of Usual Bases for Decision

By modifying the concepts of a majority vote and a two-   *20*
thirds vote, other bases for determining a voting result can
be defined and are sometimes prescribed by rule. Two elements enter into the definition of such bases for decision:
(1) the proportion that must concur—as a majority, two
thirds, three fourths, etc.; and (2) the set of members to   *25*
which the proportion applies—which (a) when not stated,
is always the number of members *present and voting* (assuming there are no illegal voters), but (b) can be specified
by rule as the number of members present, the total membership, or some other grouping.   *30*

Assume, for example, that at a meeting of a society with
a total membership of 150 and a quorum of 10, there are
30 members present, of whom 25 participate in a given
counted vote (taken by rising, by show of hands, by roll
call, or by ballot). Then, with respect to that vote: *35*

1	A majority is	13
	A majority of the members present is	16
	A majority of the entire membership is	76
	A two-thirds vote is	17
5	A vote of two thirds of the members present is	20
	A vote of two thirds of the entire membership is	100

10   Regarding these bases for determining a voting result, the following points should be noted:

- Voting requirements based on the number of members present—a majority of those present, two thirds of those

15   present, etc.—while possible, are generally undesirable. Since an abstention in such cases has the same effect as a negative vote, these bases deny members the right to maintain a neutral position by abstaining. For the same reason, members present who fail to vote through indif-

20   ference rather than through deliberate neutrality may affect the result negatively. When such a vote is required, however, the chair must count those present immediately after the affirmative vote is taken, before any change can take place in attendance (see p. 43, l. 25–30).

25   • A *majority of the entire membership** is a majority of the total number of those who are members of the voting body at the time of the vote. (Thus, in a society that has

---

*In the case of a body having a legally fixed membership—for example, a permanent board—it is also possible to define a voting requirement as a majority of the fixed membership, which is greater than a majority of the entire membership if there are vacancies on the board. Thus, in a board whose membership is legally fixed at 12, if 2 members have died and their successors have not been named, a majority of the entire membership is 6, and a majority of the fixed membership is 7. Where a majority of the fixed membership is required for a decision, the body cannot act if half or more of the membership positions are vacant.

both a general membership and an executive board, a *1*
"majority of the entire membership" at a board meeting
refers to a majority of the membership of the board, not
of the society.) In a convention of delegates a majority of
the entire membership means a majority of the total *5*
number of convention members entitled to vote as set
forth in the official roll of voting members of the convention (pp. 7, 598–99). The vote of a majority of the
entire membership is frequently an alternative to a requirement of previous notice, and is required in order to *10*
rescind and expunge from the minutes (see p. 299).
Otherwise, prescribing such a requirement is generally
unsatisfactory in an assembly of an ordinary society, since
it is likely to be impossible to get a majority of the entire
membership even to attend a given meeting, although in *15*
certain instances it may be appropriate in conventions or
in permanent boards where the members are obligated to
attend the meetings.

Whenever it is desired that the basis for decision be *20*
other than a majority vote or (where the normal rules of
parliamentary law require it) a two-thirds vote or a vote of
a majority of the entire membership, the desired basis
should be precisely defined in the bylaws or in a special rule
of order. Whatever voting basis is used, it is also possible to *25*
include a requirement of *previous notice* for specified types
of action. Previous notice means that notice of intent to introduce the proposal must be given at the preceding meeting (in which case the notice can be oral), or in the call of
the meeting at which it is brought up (for a discussion of *30*
previous notice, see pp. 116–18).

Plurality Vote

A *plurality vote* is the largest number of votes to be given *35*
any candidate or proposition when three or more choices are

1 possible; the candidate or proposition receiving the largest
number of votes has a plurality. A plurality that is not a majority never chooses a proposition or elects anyone to office
except by virtue of a special rule previously adopted. If such
5 a rule is to apply to the election of officers, it must be prescribed in the bylaws. A rule that a plurality shall elect is unlikely to be in the best interests of the average organization.
In an international or national society where the election is
conducted by mail ballot, a plurality is sometimes allowed to
10 elect officers, with a view to avoiding the delay and extra expense that would result from additional balloting under these
conditions. A better method in such cases is for the bylaws to
prescribe some form of preferential voting (see pp. 411–14).

15 ### Tie Votes and Cases in Which the Chair's Vote Affects the Result

If the presiding officer is a member of the assembly, he
can vote as any other member when the vote is by ballot (see
20 also p. 400). In all other cases the presiding officer, if a member of the assembly, can (but is not obliged to) vote whenever his vote will affect the result—that is, he can vote either
to break or to cause a tie; or, in a case where a two-thirds vote
is required, he can vote either to cause or to block the at-
25 tainment of the necessary two thirds. In particular:

• On a tie vote, a motion requiring a majority vote for
adoption is lost, since a tie is not a majority. Thus, if
there is a tie without the chair's vote, the presiding of-
30 ficer can, if he is a member, vote in the affirmative,
thereby causing the motion to be adopted; or, if there
is one more in the affirmative than in the negative without the chair's vote (for example, if there are 72 votes
in favor and 71 opposed), he can vote in the negative to
35 create a tie, thus causing the motion to be rejected.

- Similarly, in the case of a motion requiring a two-thirds vote, if, without the chair's vote, the number in the affirmative is one less than twice the number in the negative (for example, if there are 59 in the affirmative and 30 in the negative), the chair, if a member, can vote in the affirmative and thus cause the motion to be adopted; or, if there are exactly two thirds in the affirmative without his vote (for example, if there are 60 in the affirmative and 30 in the negative), the chair can vote in the negative, with the result that the motion is rejected.* Similarly, the chair's vote might affect the result in cases where a *majority of the members* can decide a question.

The chair cannot vote twice, once as a member, then again in his capacity as presiding officer.

In an appeal from the decision of the chair, a tie vote sustains the chair's decision, even though his vote created the tie, on the principle that the decision of the chair can be reversed only by a majority.

§45. VOTING PROCEDURE

Rights and Obligations in Voting

VOTING RIGHTS OF A MEMBER IN ARREARS. A member of a society who is in arrears in payment of his dues, but who has not been formally dropped from the

---

*It should be noted that if, without the chair's vote, the number of negative votes is one more than half the number of affirmative votes, the chair's vote cannot affect the result. Thus, if there are 60 in the affirmative and 31 in the negative without the chair's vote, and he were to vote in the affirmative, the resulting 61 in the affirmative would still fall short of two thirds of the total vote of 92.

membership rolls and is not under a disciplinary suspension, retains the full rights of a voting member and is legally entitled to vote except as the bylaws may otherwise provide.

RIGHT OF ABSTENTION. Although it is the duty of every member who has an opinion on a question to express it by his vote, he can abstain, since he cannot be compelled to vote. By the same token, when an office or position is to be filled by a number of members, as in the case of a committee, or positions on a board, a member may partially abstain by voting for less than all of those for whom he is entitled to vote.

ABSTAINING FROM VOTING ON A QUESTION OF DIRECT PERSONAL INTEREST. No member should vote on a question in which he has a direct personal or pecuniary interest not common to other members of the organization. For example, if a motion proposes that the organization enter into a contract with a commercial firm of which a member of the organization is an officer and from which contract he would derive personal pecuniary profit, the member should abstain from voting on the motion. However, no member can be compelled to refrain from voting in such circumstances.

VOTING ON QUESTIONS AFFECTING ONE-SELF. The rule on abstaining from voting on a question of direct personal interest does not mean that a member should not vote for himself for an office or other position to which members generally are eligible, or should not vote when other members are included with him in a motion. If a member never voted on a question affecting himself, it would be impossible for a society to vote to hold a banquet, or for the majority to prevent a small minority from preferring charges against them and suspending or expelling them (**61**).

RULE AGAINST EXPLANATION BY MEMBERS DURING VOTING.   A member has no right to "explain his vote" during voting, which would be the same as debate at such a time.

CHANGING ONE'S VOTE.   A member has a right to change his vote up to the time the result is announced; after that, he can make the change only by the unanimous consent of the assembly granted without debate (see p. 46).

ASSEMBLY'S PREROGATIVE IN JUDGING VOTING PROCEDURES.   Unless the bylaws provide otherwise, the assembly itself is the judge of all questions arising that are incidental to the voting or the counting of the votes. In an election by ballot, for example, the tellers (p. 402, l. 16–21) should refer to the assembly for decision all questions on which there is any uncertainty.

Regular Methods of Voting on Motions

In Chapter II are described the following methods of voting:

1) by *voice (viva voce)*—the normal method of voting on a motion;
2) by *rising*—used in verifying an inconclusive voice vote, and in voting on motions requiring a two-thirds vote for adoption; and
3) by *show of hands*—an alternative method that can be used in place of a rising vote in very small assemblies if no member objects. In some small groups, a vote by show of hands is also used in place of a voice vote as a

1   normal method of voting. Pages 42–51 should be read
     in connection with these three methods of voting.

     Also described in Chapter II is the procedure of action
5   by *unanimous consent* (or *general consent*). Pages 51–53
     should be read in reference to this method of transacting
     business.
     A characteristic that the three methods of voting listed
     above have in common is that in each case the chair calls
10   first for those voting in the affirmative to indicate the fact
     in a specified manner ("say *aye*," "rise," or "raise the right
     hand"), after which he calls for the negative vote, then
     judges and declares which side prevails.

15   VERIFYING A VOTE.   In connection with the meth-
     ods of voting by voice, by rising, or by show of hands, as
     explained in Chapter II, if the chair is in doubt on a voice
     vote or a vote by show of hands, he should retake it as a ris-
     ing vote and, if necessary to satisfy himself of the result, he
20   should obtain a count of it. Any member, by demanding a
     Division (**29**), can require a voice vote or a vote by show of
     hands to be retaken as a rising vote—but no individual
     member can compel it to be counted. If the chair does not
     obtain a count at his own instance and a member thinks one
25   is desirable, he should move that the vote be counted; and
     if this motion is seconded, the chair must put the question
     on ordering the count. Where no special rule has been
     adopted, a majority vote is required to order a count. In or-
     ganizations where it is desired to allow less than a majority
30   to order a count, a special rule of order establishing the re-
     quired vote should be adopted. Such a rule is particularly
     desirable with reference to motions that require a two-
     thirds vote for adoption (see also pp. 388–89). It should
     be noted that a vote is never retaken by the same form
35   of voting, although, in a counted rising vote, a ballot, or

a roll call, a recapitulation of the tellers' tabulations can be ordered to ensure that the count is precisely correct as reported.

METHOD OF COUNTING A RISING VOTE. In small meetings, the chair can take such a count himself—with or without directing the secretary to make an independent count for verification. In a large assembly, the chair should appoint tellers to take the count. The count is taken by having those in the affirmative rise and stand until counted, then having those in the negative rise and stand until counted. The votes can also be counted by having the members pass between tellers, or having them count off by rows and be seated one at a time, although the latter process is particularly subject to confusion if great care is not exercised by the tellers. Those in the affirmative are always counted first. In all but small assemblies, the doors should be closed and no one should be allowed to enter or leave the hall while a count is being taken. The form used in taking a count is as shown on page 45. In a meeting small enough that each member present can make his own verification of a count on a show of hands, the chair can take the count by this method, if he prefers and no one objects.

VOTING CARDS. Some organizations like to use a brightly colored cardboard card, approximately three inches wide and a foot long, in voting on most or all occasions by raising it when asked to do so by the chair. The authorization of the use of these devices in voting, however, depends on expected conditions in the meeting. If the "voters' cards" have been distributed to the voters in advance, and the chair or a member thinks a simple division vote (as described on page 44, line 24 to page 45, line 2) is called for, the chair may say: "As many as are in favor of the motion, raise your voters' cards. . . . Down. Those opposed, raise your

1 voters' cards. Down. . . . " If a count is desired, however, the chair or the assembly must authorize the count as in the case of a counted division (as described on p. 45, l. 3–10; see also **30**, *Motions Relating to Methods of Voting and the*

5 *Polls*). If this method of voting is to be used, it must be authorized by a special rule of order or, in a convention, by a convention standing rule.

Other Methods of Voting

10   In contrast to the methods of voting mentioned in the preceding subsection, the voting methods described below are, like a count of a rising vote, used only when expressly ordered by the assembly or prescribed by its rules.

15

VOTING BY BALLOT.   Voting by *ballot* (slips of paper on which the voter marks his vote) is used when secrecy of the members' votes is desired. The bylaws of the organization may prescribe that the vote be by ballot in cer-

20 tain cases, as in the election of officers and in admission to membership.* Any vote related to charges or proposed charges before or after a trial of a member or any officer (**61**) should always be by ballot. Except as may be otherwise provided by the bylaws, a vote by ballot can be ordered

25 by a majority vote—which may be desirable in any case where it is believed that members may thereby be more likely to vote their true sentiments.

When the bylaws require a vote to be taken by ballot, this requirement cannot be suspended, even by a unani-

---

*In some organizations—particularly secret societies—black and white balls, deposited in a box out of sight of all but the voter, are used in voting on the admission of candidates to membership—a white ball signifying a *yes* vote and a black one a *no* vote. This method is used principally where one or very few negative votes are to be sufficient to cause a candidate's rejection. This custom, however, is apparently declining.

mous vote. Thus, it is out of order in such a case to move
that one person—the secretary, for example—cast the ballot of the assembly. When a vote is to be taken, or has been
taken, by ballot, whether or not the bylaws require that
form of voting, no motion is in order that would force the
disclosure of a member's vote or views on the matter. A
motion to make unanimous a ballot vote that was not unanimous is out of order, unless that motion is also voted on by
ballot—since any member who openly votes against declaring the first vote unanimous will thereby reveal that he did
not vote for the prevailing choice.

Form of the Ballot.   A ballot can consist of simply a small
slip of paper on which the voter writes his choice in a manner directed by the chair; but if it is known ahead of time that
a vote is to be by ballot and what the exact questions are, the
ballots should be prepared in advance for distribution at the
proper time. In such a case, each question to be voted on appears on the ballot with a list of the possible answers beside
blank spaces or boxes, so that the voter can check the answer
he desires. Two or more questions can be listed on the same
sheet, provided that each is marked in such a way that there
can be no confusion, as illustrated below.

Indicate vote with X.
1. Shall the National Headquarters be moved to
    Thresher City?
                Yes_____
                No_____
2. Meeting place of next convention:
                Seattle_____
                New Orleans_____
                Other_____
                    (Fill in name)

In elections, "for" and "against" spaces or boxes should
not be used. They are applicable only with respect to votes

1 on motions. An election, in effect, is a vote on filling a
blank, and a voter can vote against one candidate only by
voting for another who has been nominated or by writing
in the name of another candidate.

5   *Balloting Procedure.*   In balloting in a meeting where
the voting is in the same room as the meeting, the chair appoints tellers to distribute, collect, and count the ballots,
and to report the vote. The number of tellers is dependent
on the number of voters, and the number of offices to be
10 filled or questions to be answered, or the number of candidates. For a small group, two or three tellers are usually sufficient. The tellers should be chosen for accuracy and
dependability, should have the confidence of the membership, and should not have a direct personal involvement in
15 the question or in the result of the vote to an extent that
they should refrain from voting under the principle stated
on page 394. Often their position with regard to the issue
involved is well known, however, and they are frequently
chosen to protect the interests of each opposing side. They
20 normally vote themselves.

      To ensure accuracy and to enable the tellers when un-
folding the ballots to detect any error, each ballot should be
folded in a manner announced in advance or stated on the
ballot itself.

25   The presiding officer, if a member of the assembly, can always vote in the case of a ballot at the time other members
do. Should he fail to vote before the polls are closed, he cannot then do so without the permission of the assembly.

      When the balloting is completed, the chair directs the
30 tellers to collect the ballots. In collecting the ballots, it is
the tellers' responsibility to see that no member votes more
than once—for the assurance of which the assembly should
adopt some reasonable and orderly method. For example:
(a) In meetings where only voters are present, members can
35 remain in their seats and drop their ballots into a receptacle

passed by a teller, accompanied by another teller as watcher
and checker; (b) they can go to a central ballot box monitored by at least two tellers and deposit their ballots; or (c)
they can hand their ballots to a teller—who judges by the
thickness and feel of the paper that only one ballot is being
cast, and who deposits them in a central ballot box. Whatever method of collecting the ballots is followed, it—like
other details relating to voting—should be fixed by rule or
custom in the organization and should not be subject to
haphazard variation from occasion to occasion.

After all have voted who wish to, the polls can be closed
on the motion of a member by a two-thirds vote (**30**); but it
is usually best to rely on the chair to close the polls. When
everyone appears to have voted, the chair inquires, "Have all
voted who wish to do so?" If there is no response, he says, "If
no one else wishes to vote . . . [pause], the polls are closed,"
thus in effect declaring the polls closed by unanimous consent. Thereafter, if other members arrive who wish to vote, a
majority vote is required to reopen the polls (**30**). The tellers
proceed to count the ballots—in a secluded location or in another room if the meeting proceeds to other business during
the counting. Some small organizations have a custom that
ballots are counted in full presence of the meeting.

Recording the Votes. In recording the votes cast, the
tellers ignore blank ballots and do not credit illegal votes to
any candidate or choice. All blanks must be ignored as scrap
paper, since members who do not wish to vote may adopt
this method of concealing the fact. If in unfolding the ballots it is found that two or more filled-out ballots are folded
together, they are recorded as illegal votes—that is, each set
of ballots folded together is reported as one illegal vote on
each question, and is not credited. On the other hand, a
blank ballot folded in with one that is properly filled out is
ignored, but it does not cause the rejection of the ballot
with which it was folded.

1   Each segment of a ballot is treated as if it were a separate ballot, and the tellers must count the number of votes
cast for each office or issue. If a member leaves one or more
of the choices blank on a ballot containing several questions
5   or more than one office to be filled, the blank spaces in no
way affect the validity of the spaces he has filled, and for
each of these votes he should be given credit for one legal
vote. If he votes for too many candidates for a given office,
however, that particular section of the ballot is illegal, be-
10   cause it is not possible for the tellers to determine for whom
the member desired to vote.

Small technical errors, like the misspelling of a word or
name, do not make a vote illegal if the meaning of the ballot is clear. Unintelligible ballots or ballots cast for an
15   unidentifiable candidate or a fictional character are treated
as illegal votes. If the meaning of one or more ballots is
doubtful, they can be treated as illegal if it is impossible for
them to affect the result; but if they may affect the result,
the tellers should report them to the chair, who will imme-
20   diately submit to the assembly the question of how these
ballots should be recorded.

All illegal votes of the type described in the preceding
paragraph—that is, illegal votes cast by legal voters—are
taken into account in determining the number of votes cast
25   for purposes of computing the majority. On the other hand,
if one or more ballots are identifiable as cast by persons not
entitled to vote, and it can be established that there are no
other such ballots, these ballots are excluded in determining the number of votes cast for purposes of computing the
30   majority. If there is evidence that any unidentifiable ballots
were cast by persons not entitled to vote, and if there is any
possibility that such ballots might affect the result, the entire ballot vote is null and void and a new ballot vote must
be taken. The principle is that a choice has no mandate
35   from the voting body unless approval is expressed by more

than half of those entitled to vote and registering any evidence of having some opinion.

Tellers' Report and the Chair's Declaration of the Result. The chairman of tellers, standing, addresses the chair, reads the tellers' report, and hands it to the chair without declaring the result. In the case of an election, the report should follow this form:

TELLERS' REPORT

Number of votes cast	97
Necessary for election	49
Mr. Miller received	51
Mr. Wilson received	24
Mr. Strong received	14
Illegal Votes	
Mr. Friend (ineligible)	7
One ballot containing two for	
Mr. Wilson folded together, rejected	1

In the case of balloting on a motion, the tellers' report is as follows:

TELLERS' REPORT

Number of votes cast	102
Necessary for adoption (majority)	52
Votes for motion	69
Votes against	32
Illegal votes	
One ballot containing two	
no votes, rejected	1

The tellers' report should not include the number of members eligible to vote. In a local society or other body in which membership continues on a long-term basis, only the officer responsible for maintaining the membership roll, and in a convention only an immediate updated report of the credentials committee, can validly determine this figure if it becomes needed. The reporting teller never declares the result of a ballot vote. The result is always declared by the chair, who also reads the tellers' report before he does so. In an election, the chair separately declares the election of each officer (see also **46**). In balloting on a motion, the chair announces the result.

The tellers' report is entered in full in the minutes, becoming a part of the official records of the organization. Under no circumstances should this be omitted in an election or in a vote on a critical motion out of a mistaken deference to the feelings of unsuccessful candidates or members of the losing side.

After completion of an election or balloting on a motion, if there is no possibility that the assembly may order a recount (which requires a majority vote unless a special rule permits a lesser number to do so), the ballots can be ordered to be destroyed or to be filed for a certain length of time with the secretary (such as one month) before being destroyed.

MACHINE OR ELECTRONIC VOTING.   The voting process has been considerably changed in many organizations—especially in those comprising hundreds of voters—by the use, instead of paper ballots, of voting machines such as those used in political elections, or electronic devices similar to those used in the House of Representatives and many other legislative bodies but set up to provide for secrecy of the vote and the identity of the voters. It is important that the electronic device provided be programmed to comply with the rule stated on page 402 that each segment of a ballot be treated as if it were a separate ballot and that the votes cast for each office or issue be ascertained. Where such devices are to be used, the following considerations are important.

- Preparations for the election should be made in consultation with the person in charge of installing the devices, so that all adjustments required by the particular conditions of the election can be provided for.
- Persons who are to tend the devices during voting must be carefully instructed in their duties, and must be able to explain the use of the devices to voters.
- If there are likely to be many voters who have never used the devices, it may be advisable to have a device available for the voters' inspection on a day previous to the election.

ROLL-CALL VOTE.   Taking a vote by *roll call* (or by *yeas and nays,* as it is also called) has the effect of placing on the record how each member or, sometimes each delegation, votes; therefore, it has exactly the opposite effect of a ballot vote. It is usually confined to representative bodies, where the proceedings are published, since it enables constituents to know how their representatives voted on certain measures. It should not be used in a mass meeting or in any assembly whose members are not responsible to a constituency.

Ordering a Roll-Call Vote.   In a representative body, if there is no legal or constitutional provision specifying the size of the minority that can order a roll-call vote, the body should adopt a rule fixing the size of such a minority—for example, *one fifth of those present,* as in Congress, or some other portion of those present that is less than a majority. In the absence of such a special rule, a majority vote is required to order the taking of a vote by roll call—in which case a motion to do so is likely to be useless, since its purpose is to force the majority to go on record. In local societies having a large membership but relatively small attendance at meetings, a motion to take a vote by roll call is generally dilatory. It is in order, as one of the *Motions Relating to*

1   *Methods of Voting,* however, to move "that a signed ballot be taken by tellers;" and if such a vote is ordered, the voter writes "yes" or "no" on the ballot and signs it. The votes can be recorded in the minutes just as a roll call would be,
5 but the names of all members need not be called. A roll-call vote cannot be ordered in committee of the whole.

  Procedure for Roll-Call Vote. When a vote is to be taken by roll call (see **30** for the motion), the chair puts the question in a form like the following:

10

    CHAIR: As many as are in favor of the adoption of the resolution will, as their names are called, answer *aye* [or *"yes,"* or *"yea"*]; those opposed will answer *no* [or *"nay"*]. The secretary [or "the Clerk"] will call the roll.

15

    The roll is called in alphabetical order except that the presiding officer's name is called last, and only when his vote will affect the result. It is too late, after one person has answered to the roll call, to renew the debate. Each mem-
20 ber, as his name is called, responds in the affirmative or negative as shown above. If he does not wish to vote, he answers *present* (or *abstain*). If he is not ready to vote, but wishes to be called on again after the roll has been completely called, he answers *pass.*
25   The secretary repeats each member's name and answer aloud as it is given and notes the answers to the roll call in separate columns. A convenient method of noting the answers is to write the number *1* to the left of the name of the first member answering in the affirmative,the number *2* to
30 the left of the second name in the affirmative, and so on. The negative answers are treated similarly in a column to the right of the names; and those answering *present* are tallied in a third column, to the far right or left. In this way, the last number in each column shows how the vote stands
35 at any given point in the list.

At the conclusion of the roll call, the names of those *1* who failed to answer can be called again, or the chair can ask if anyone entered the room after his or her name was called. Each of these members who then responds can be assigned the final number for his or her vote or abstention *5* in the proper column, continuing from the last number previously in the column, although the member's number will appear in a position out of sequence. Changes of vote are also permitted at this time, before the result is announced. When this happens, the number beside the member's name *10* is struck through, the total for that column is adjusted accordingly, and the next, final number in the proper column is entered. Changes of vote may be limited when some electronic equipment is used.

The secretary gives the final number of those voting on *15* each side, and the number answering *present*, to the chair, who announces these figures and declares the result.

In roll-call voting, a record of how each member voted, as well as the result of the vote, should be entered in full in the journal or minutes. If those responding to the roll call *20* do not total a sufficient number to constitute a quorum, the chair must direct the secretary to enter the names of enough members who are present but not voting to reflect the attendance of a quorum during the vote.

In large conventions, the roll is sometimes called of en- *25* tire delegations rather than of the individual members. The secretary, in calling for the votes of a delegation, should state the vote entitlement, as: "Local No. 145: 8 votes." In such cases, the chairman or spokesman of each delegation, as it is called in alphabetical or numerical order, responds by giving *30* its vote, as: "Local No. 145 votes 5 'for' and 3 'against.'" The secretary repeats this for confirmation and calls the next delegation. If any member of the assembly doubts the chairman's announcement of the delegation's vote, he may demand a poll of the delegation, in which case each delegate's *35*

1 name is called by the secretary, and the delegation votes individually. When all delegates have voted, the secretary announces the totals for the delegation, which are recorded.

Electronic Roll-Call Vote Installation.   Various forms of
5 electronic devices have become available to take the place of
a roll-call vote. Any deliberative body can use such a system
with appropriate adjustments to conform as closely as possible with the rules given above for roll-call voting procedure.
When used, there is usually a presumption of technical, me-
10 chanical accuracy of the electronic system if properly used by
the members. Changes of votes after the result has been announced by the chair on the allegation of machine error are
not entertained. On the same grounds, a recapitulation (the
secretary reading the names of those voting "aye" or "no")
15 is not permitted. Where electronic voting is used, it should
be noted that, if it is impossible to erect a display board in the
hall, members of the same delegation will not be able to as-
certain how other members of the delegation vote. Also,
steps must be taken to prevent members from being able to
20 vote more than once by using a neighbor's keypad, or a
member lending his keypad to a friend so that the friend can
vote for him in his absence by "proxy."

INTERRUPTION OF VOTES.   Interruptions dur-
25 ing the taking of a vote are permitted only before any member has actually voted, unless, as sometimes occurs in ballot
voting, other business is being transacted during voting or
tabulating. For points of order regarding the conduct of a
vote, see pp. 243–44.
30

ABSENTEE VOTING.   It is a fundamental principle of
parliamentary law that the right to vote is limited to the
members of an organization who are actually present at the
time the vote is taken in a legal meeting, although it should
35 be noted that a member need not be present when the ques-

tion is put. Exceptions to this rule must be expressly stated in the bylaws. Such possible exceptions include: (a) voting by postal or electronic mail, or facsimile transmission (fax), and (b) proxy voting. An organization should never adopt a bylaw permitting a question to be decided by a voting procedure in which the votes of persons who attend a meeting are counted together with ballots mailed in by absentees. The votes of those present could be affected by debate, by amendments, and perhaps by the need for repeated balloting, while those absent would be unable to adjust their votes to reflect these factors. Consequently, the absentee ballots would in most cases be on a somewhat different question than that on which those present were voting, leading to confusion, unfairness, and inaccuracy in determining the result. If there is a possibility of any uncertainty about who will be entitled to vote, this should be spelled out unambiguously and strictly enforced to avoid unfairness in close votes.

A VOTE BY MAIL. A vote by mail, when authorized in the bylaws, is generally reserved for important issues, such as an amendment to the bylaws or an election of officers—on which a full vote of the membership is desirable even though only a small fraction of the members normally attend meetings. Situations of this kind frequently occur in scientific societies or in alumni associations whose members may be in many countries.

For a vote by mail—so that there may be no question of the result in the event that the vote is close—it is important that the mailing list used should exactly correspond to the current official roll of voting members. For this purpose, the secretary should furnish to the chairman of tellers or other official in charge of issuing the ballots a list of the names and mailing addresses of record of all persons legally entitled to vote, which the secretary should certify as corrected to the date as of which the ballots are issued.

If the vote is not to be secret, the following items should be sent to each qualified voter: (1) a printed ballot containing a space for the voter's signature, to ensure against votes being cast by other than legal voters, together with full instructions for marking and returning by the required date; and (2) a specially recognizable, self-addressed return envelope with the name and address of the secretary, the chairman of tellers, or other person designated to receive the marked ballot. If qualifications of the nominees may not be widely known to the membership, it is permissible to allow each nominee to furnish for enclosure a brief factual statement of his service and qualifications, provided that all nominees are accorded equal opportunity and space. Electronic mail and other means of electronic communication can be tailored to comply with these requirements (see footnote, p. 2).

If the vote is to be secret, an inner return envelope—with a space for the voter's signature placed on its face instead of on the ballot—should be sent to the voter with the ballot, in addition to the self-addressed outer return envelope described above. The ballot sent to the voter should be prefolded a sufficient number of times so that—when returned marked and refolded in the same manner and sealed in the inner envelope—there will be no chance of accidental observance of the member's vote by the teller who removes the ballot from the inner envelope. The person designated as addressee for the returned ballots should hold them in the outer envelopes for delivery, unopened, at the meeting of the tellers where the votes are to be counted. At that meeting all inner envelopes are first removed from the outer envelopes. In the procedure by which the tellers remove the ballots from the inner envelopes, each envelope and ballot is handled in the following manner: (1) the signature on the envelope is checked against the list of qualified voters; (2) the voter is checked off on the list as having voted; and

(3) the envelope is opened and the ballot is removed and placed, still folded, into a receptacle. When all inner envelopes have thus been processed, the ballots are taken from the receptacle and the votes are counted. In order to ensure the accuracy and the secrecy of such a vote by mail, special care should be taken in all phases of handling the ballots. The chairman of tellers or other person responsible must be able to certify the results from both of these standpoints. Should the recipient of the ballots receive two evidently sent in by the same voter, the above procedure permits the voter to be contacted for a determination of which is the voter's true vote and, if both are, which (the most recent) is to be counted. As with respect to nonsecret ballots, electronic mail and other means of electronic communication may be able to be tailored to comply with the above requirements for secret mail balloting.

Preferential Voting. The term *preferential voting* refers to any of a number of voting methods by which, on a single ballot when there are more than two possible choices, the second or less-preferred choices of voters can be taken into account if no candidate or proposition attains a majority. While it is more complicated than other methods of voting in common use and is not a substitute for the normal procedure of repeated balloting until a majority is obtained, preferential voting is especially useful and fair in an election by mail if it is impractical to take more than one ballot. In such cases it makes possible a more representative result than under a rule that a plurality shall elect. It can be used only if expressly authorized in the bylaws.

Preferential voting has many variations. One method is described here by way of illustration. On the preferential ballot—for each office to be filled or multiple-choice question to be decided—the voter is asked to indicate the order in which he prefers all the candidates or propositions, placing the numeral *1* beside his first preference, the numeral *2*

1 beside his second preference, and so on for every possible
   choice. In counting the votes for a given office or question,
   the ballots are arranged in piles according to the indicated
   first preferences—one pile for each candidate or proposi-
5 tion. The number of ballots in each pile is then recorded for
   the tellers' report. These piles remain identified with the
   names of the same candidates or propositions throughout
   the counting procedure until all but one are eliminated as
   described below. If more than half of the ballots show one
10 candidate or proposition indicated as first choice, that
   choice has a majority in the ordinary sense and the candidate is elected or the proposition is decided upon. But if
   there is no such majority, candidates or propositions are
   eliminated one by one, beginning with the least popular,
15 until one prevails, as follows: The ballots in the thinnest
   pile—that is, those containing the name designated as first
   choice by the fewest number of voters—are redistributed
   into the other piles according to the names marked as second choice on these ballots. The number of ballots in each
20 remaining pile after this distribution is again recorded. If
   more than half of the ballots are now in one pile, that candidate or proposition is elected or decided upon. If not, the
   next least popular candidate or proposition is similarly eliminated, by taking the thinnest remaining pile and redistrib-
25 uting its ballots according to their second choices into the
   other piles, except that, if the name eliminated in the last
   distribution is indicated as second choice on a ballot, that
   ballot is placed according to its third choice. Again the
   number of ballots in each existing pile is recorded, and, if
30 necessary, the process is repeated—by redistributing each
   time the ballots in the thinnest remaining pile, according to
   the marked second choice or most-preferred choice among
   those not yet eliminated—until one pile contains more than
   half of the ballots, the result being thereby determined. The
35 tellers' report consists of a table listing all candidates or

propositions, with the number of ballots that were in each pile after each successive distribution.

If a ballot having one or more names not marked with any numeral comes up for placement at any stage of the counting and all of its marked names have been eliminated, it should not be placed in any pile, but should be set aside. If at any point two or more candidates or propositions are tied for the least popular position, the ballots in their piles are redistributed in a single step, all of the tied names being treated as eliminated. In the event of a tie in the winning position—which would imply that the elimination process is continued until the ballots are reduced to two or more equal piles—the election should be resolved in favor of the candidate or proposition that was strongest in terms of first choices (by referring to the record of the first distribution).

If more than one person is to be elected to the same type of office—for example, if three members of a board are to be chosen—the voters can indicate their order of preference among the names in a single list of candidates, just as if only one was to be elected. The counting procedure is the same as described above, except that it is continued until all but the necessary number of candidates have been eliminated (that is, in the example, all but three).

When this or any other system of preferential voting is to be used, the voting and counting procedure must be precisely established in advance and should be prescribed in detail in the bylaws of the organization. The members must be thoroughly instructed as to how to mark the ballot, and should have sufficient understanding of the counting process to enable them to have confidence in the method. Sometimes, for instance, voters decline to indicate a second or other choice, mistakenly believing that such a course increases the chances of their first choice. In fact, it may prevent any candidate from receiving a majority and require

1 the voting to be repeated. The persons selected as tellers must perform their work with particular care.

The system of preferential voting just described should not be used in cases where it is possible to follow the nor-
5 mal procedure of repeated balloting until one candidate or proposition attains a majority. Although this type of preferential ballot is preferable to an election by plurality, it affords less freedom of choice than repeated balloting, because it denies voters the opportunity of basing their sec-
10 ond or lesser choices on the results of earlier ballots, and because the candidate or proposition in last place is automatically eliminated and may thus be prevented from becoming a compromise choice.

15   PROXY VOTING.   A *proxy* is a power of attorney given by one person to another to vote in his stead; the term also designates the person who holds the power of attorney. Proxy voting is not permitted in ordinary deliberative assemblies unless the laws of the state in which the society is incor-
20 porated require it, or the charter or bylaws of the organization provide for it. Ordinarily it should neither be allowed nor required, because proxy voting is incompatible with the essential characteristics of a deliberative assembly in which membership is individual, personal, and nontransfer-
25 able. In a stock corporation, on the other hand, where the ownership is transferable, the voice and vote of the member also is transferable, by use of a proxy. But in a nonstock corporation, where membership is usually on the same basis as in an unincorporated, voluntary association, voting by proxy
30 should not be permitted unless the state's corporation law— as applying to nonstock corporations—absolutely requires it.

If the law under which an organization is incorporated allows proxy voting to be prohibited by a provision of the bylaws, the adoption of this book as parliamentary authority by prescription in the bylaws should be treated as sufficient provision to accomplish that result (cf. footnote, p. 562). *1*

STRAW POLLS NOT IN ORDER.   A motion to take an informal straw poll to "test the water" is not in order because it neither adopts nor rejects a measure and hence is *5* meaningless and dilatory. If the assembly wishes to discuss and take a vote on a matter without the vote constituting final action by the assembly, it may instead vote to go into a committee of the whole or a quasi committee of the *10* whole (**52**). Under these procedures, the assembly considers the matter as would a committee, and its vote while in committee of the whole (or quasi committee of the whole) serves only as a recommendation to the assembly, which the assembly is free to reject just as would be the case with re- *15* gard to the report of any ordinary committee.

NOMINATIONS AND ELECTIONS

§46. NOMINATIONS AND ELECTIONS

Nominations

A nomination is, in effect, a proposal to fill the blank in an assumed motion "that _____ be elected" to the specified position. In choosing someone to fill an office or other elective position in a society or assembly, a more effective freedom of choice is maintained through the practice of nominating persons for the office, rather than moving that a given person be elected as in the older British procedure. Hence, a form of ballot on which provision is made for voting "for" or "against" a candidate or candidates, as distinguished from a motion, is not proper. Since such a ballot is improper, in order to defeat a candidate for an office it is necessary to vote for an opposing candidate, thus avoiding the anomaly of an assembly refusing to elect anyone to an office.

Strictly speaking, nominations are not necessary when an election is by ballot or roll call, since each member is free to vote for any eligible person, whether he has been nominated or not. In most societies, however, it is impractical to proceed to an election without first making nominations. Unless the members' choice is confined to a small number of persons, voting may have to be repeated many times before a candidate achieves the required majority.

Methods of nomination are: (a) by the chair; (b) from the floor (sometimes called "open nominations"); (c) by a committee; (d) by ballot; (e) by mail; and (f) by petition. If no method of nominating has been specified in the bylaws and if the assembly has adopted no rule on the subject, any member can make a motion prescribing the method (**31**).

As the following descriptions of the six methods of nomination indicate, not all of them are appropriate or desirable in average societies. The order in which they are listed corresponds to that in which they would be voted on if all six were proposed in motions prescribing the method of nomination.

NOMINATIONS BY THE CHAIR.   At a mass meeting it is a common practice to have the chairman nominated by the person who was designated to call the meeting to order, but an organized society should adopt other methods of nominating for office. The chair, however, can make nominations for committee membership and similar positions (an exception being made in the case of the nominating committee), as may be provided in the bylaws or by the adoption of a motion.

NOMINATIONS FROM THE FLOOR.   Under the procedure of nominations from the floor, the chair calls for nominations at the time established by rule or custom of the organization or assembly—which may be while the election is pending or earlier, but in any case is subsequent to the report of the nominating committee if there is such a committee. A member need not be recognized by the chair

1 to make a nomination. In a large meeting or convention a member should rise when making a nomination from the floor, but in small assemblies nominations frequently are made by members from their seats. No second is required, 5 but sometimes one or more members will second a nomination to indicate endorsement. Where more than one person is to be elected to an office or position, such as to a board of directors or trustees, or to a committee, no one may nominate more than one person for the office, if an ob- 10 jection is made, until every member wishing to nominate has had an opportunity to do so. In no event may a member nominate more persons than there are places to fill.

    The same person can be nominated for more than one office, even if voting for all offices is to take place at the same 15 time on a single ballot. If one person is elected to more than one office under these conditions, the case is resolved as described on page 425, line 30 to page 426, line 6.

    If there is no nominating committee and nominations are to be from the floor, the chair calls for them by saying, for ex- 20 ample, "Nominations are now in order for the office of President." If there is a nominating committee, the chair calls for nominations as shown on pages 421–22. When the presiding officer has called for nominations from the floor, a member rises and makes a nomination as follows:

25

    MEMBER: I nominate Mr. A. [Or, in a large assembly, "Mr. President, I nominate Mr. A."]

    CHAIR: Mr. A is nominated. Are there any further nominations [or "any further nominations for the office of President"]?

30

    The chair repeats each nomination in this way until all nominations for the office have been made. (For the procedure for closing nominations, see p. 422.) Nominations for the different offices are thus called for in the order in which 35 the offices are listed in the bylaws.

NOMINATIONS BY A COMMITTEE. In the election of officers of an ordinary society, nominations often are made by a nominating committee. Usually in such cases a nominating committee is chosen in advance to submit nominations for the various offices for which elections are to be held at the annual meeting.

Designation of the Nominating Committee. The nominating committee should be elected by the organization wherever possible, or else by its executive board. Although in organizing a new society it may be feasible for the chair to appoint the nominating committee, in an organized society the president should not appoint this committee or be a member of it—ex officio or otherwise. The bylaws may provide that "the President shall appoint all committees except the Nominating Committee" and that "the President shall be ex officio a member of all committees except the Nominating Committee"; the exception should not be omitted in either case.

Nominees. Although it is not common for the nominating committee to nominate more than one candidate for any office, the committee can do so unless the bylaws prohibit it. It is usually not sound to *require* the committee to nominate more than one candidate for each office, since the committee can easily circumvent such a provision by nominating only one person who has any chance of being elected (see also p. 431).

Members of the nominating committee are not barred from becoming nominees for office themselves. To make such a requirement would mean, first, that service on the nominating committee carried a penalty by depriving its members of one of their privileges; and second, that appointment or election to the nominating committee could be used to prevent a member from becoming a nominee.

It is desirable policy for the nominating committee, before making its report, to contact each person whom it wishes to

1 nominate, in order to obtain his acceptance of nomination—
that is, his assurance that he will serve in the specified office if
elected. The bylaws can make such a practice mandatory.

    Report of the Nominating Committee.   The time at
5 which the nominating committee's report is made is a matter
to be determined by rule or established custom of the particular organization—depending on its own conditions. In
some societies this report is not formally presented to the
voting body until the election is pending; but in any organi-
10 zation where advance interest in the election may develop,
the nominations submitted by the committee should be
made known to the membership earlier. These nominations
can be mailed to all members, for example, several days before the regular meeting—usually the election meeting it-
15 self—at which the chair calls for additional nominations from
the floor (see below). The report should always be formally
presented at a regular meeting, even if the names of the committee's nominees have been transmitted to the members of
the society beforehand. Sometimes—in societies that hold
20 frequent regular meetings—the nominating committee's report is presented at the regular meeting preceding the annual
meeting (**9**) at which the election is to take place.

    When the nominating committee is called upon for its
report at a meeting, its chairman rises and presents the re-
25 port as follows:

    NOMINATING COMMITTEE CHAIRMAN: Mr. President, the Nominat-
ing Committee submits the following nominations: For President, Mr.
A [or "John A"]; for Vice President, Mr. B; for Secretary, Mr. C; . . .
30 [and so on for each office to be filled, naming the nominees in the
order in which the offices are listed in the bylaws].

    A minority within a nominating committee, as a group,
may propose other nominees for some or all of the offices
35 in any case where nominations from the floor are permitted.

A nominating committee is automatically discharged when its report is formally presented to the assembly, although if one of the nominees withdraws before the election, the committee is revived and should meet immediately to agree upon another nomination if there is time.

Call by the Chair for Further Nominations from the Floor. After the nominating committee has presented its report and before voting for the different offices takes place, the chair must call for further nominations from the floor. This is another stage of nomination and election procedure for which a number of details should be established by rule or custom of the particular organization. In many organizations, nominations from the floor are called for immediately after the presentation of the nominating committee's report—while the election is pending or earlier. When the calling for nominations from the floor is about to begin, if some time has elapsed since the presentation of the nominating committee's report, the complete list of the committee's nominations should be read again before further nominations are called for.

In some organizations all nominations from the floor are completed and nominations are closed for each office before voting for any office takes place. In other organizations, when nominations for one office have been completed, votes are cast for that office and the result is announced before the chair calls for nominations for the next office (see also pp. 424ff.). A custom of the organization based on its own conditions should determine which of the two procedures is used. In either case, the different offices are taken in the order in which they are listed in the bylaws. The chair, as he calls for nominations, first repeats the name that was submitted by the nominating committee, thus:

CHAIR: For President, Mr. A is nominated by the Nominating Committee. Are there any further nominations for President? [If a

1   member nominates another person, the chair repeats the name of that
     nominee.] Mr. N. is nominated. Are there any further nominations?

     When it appears that no one else wishes to make a nom-
5   ination, the chair should again ask if there are any further
     nominations; and if there is no response, he normally de-
     clares that nominations (for that office) are closed, without
     waiting for a motion to that effect, as follows:

10   CHAIR: Are there any further nominations for President? . . .
     [Pause.] If not . . . [pause], nominations are closed. [Or, "Without
     objection, . . . nominations are closed."]

     (For use of the motion to close nominations, which re-
15   quires a two-thirds vote, see **31**.) After nominations have
     been closed, a majority vote is required to reopen them.
     After nominations have been closed, voting for that of-
     fice takes place, or nominations for the next office are called
     for by the chair, depending on the procedure being fol-
20   lowed by the particular organization.

     NOMINATIONS BY BALLOT.   The object of a
     nominating ballot is to provide the members with an indi-
     cation of the sentiments of the voting body, which they may
25   take into account in voting in the election. The value of the
     nominating ballot is that it shows the preferences without
     electing anyone. The nominating ballot is conducted in the
     same way as an ordinary electing ballot except that every-
     one receiving a vote is nominated; the tellers' report, there-
30   fore, does not state the number of votes necessary for
     nomination. Since each member has the opportunity to
     nominate on his ballot a candidate for every office, he does
     not have the right then to make nominations from the
     floor, unless the assembly by a majority vote authorizes such
35   nominations.

Impropriety of Making the Nominating Ballot the Elect- **1**
ing Ballot. Sometimes a motion is made to declare the
nominating ballot the electing ballot. Such action negates all
the advantages of a nominating ballot and is, in effect, the
same as having an electing ballot without any nominations. **5**
If there is to be only one ballot, it should be the electing ballot, with nominations from the floor, or by a nominating
committee and from the floor. A nominating ballot cannot
take the place of an electing ballot in an organization whose
bylaws require elections to be held by ballot. **10**

Impropriety of Limiting Voting in the Election to the Two
Leading Candidates. In some organizations using the
nominating ballot, an attempt is made to limit the voting
on the electing ballot to the two nominees for each office
receiving the highest number of votes on the nominating **15**
ballot. This—or any attempt to limit the number of candidates for an office to two, by whatever method they are
nominated—is an unfortunate practice and should be dis-
couraged. Often the two leading candidates for a position
will represent two different factions, and division within the **20**
organization may be deepened by limiting the election to
them. On the other hand, it may be possible to unite the
members if the assembly has the choice of a compromise
candidate.

25

NOMINATIONS BY MAIL. In organizations whose
membership is widely scattered, the method of nominating
by mail is often adopted. In such a case a nominating ballot
can be prepared, deposited, and counted in the same way as
an electing ballot—with the secretary of the organization **30**
mailing to every legal member a nominating ballot, plus instructions for completing and returning it as described on
page 410. Or, in some organizations, a blank on which each
member can submit the names of desired nominees, in a
signed ballot, is used instead of a secret nominating ballot. **35**

NOMINATIONS BY PETITION.   The bylaws may provide that a member shall be a nominee upon the petition of a specified number of members. Sometimes, a nominating petition blank is mailed to the members with a copy of the list of nominees submitted by a nominating committee. In large state or national societies composed of local units, the blanks are sometimes mailed to these units with instructions for their distribution or processing.

Elections

In an assembly or organization that does not have a rule or established custom prescribing the method of voting in elections, the voting can be by any of the accepted methods. While some form of election by ballot is generally appropriate in organized societies, each assembly should adopt—and each society should prescribe in its bylaws—the procedure best suited to its purposes and needs. Where there is no determining rule, a motion to fix the method of voting (or any other detail of nomination or election procedure) is an incidental main motion if made before the election is pending, or an incidental motion if made while the election is pending (**30, 31**). Such a motion can be offered containing a blank so that different methods are voted on in succession; or the chair can take votes on the methods in this way, assuming the motion, if no member objects. In the absence of a rule establishing the method of voting, the rule that is established by custom, if any, should be followed, unless the assembly, by adoption of an incidental motion or incidental main motion, agrees to do otherwise.

BALLOT ELECTION.   Two alternative procedures for the sequence of nominating and voting in elections by ballot can be prescribed or adopted, as mentioned above. The first method requires the least time, while the second affords greater flexibility in choosing officers. These proce- dures are as follows:

1) All nominations can be completed before any balloting takes place—in which case voting for all offices is com- monly done by a single ballot. This method is suitable for use in conventions where voting takes place at a "polling place" apart from the convention meetings. It may also be a preferred method in any large meeting where the time required for balloting is an important consideration. The elections should take place early in such a meeting, to allow time for any necessary addi- tional balloting for any office for which no candidate re- ceives a vote sufficient for election. Votes can be cast for any person who is eligible for election, even if he has not been nominated. The procedure followed in balloting, in counting the votes, and in reporting the results is de- scribed on pages 398–404. The tellers prepare a tellers' report for each office involved, in the form shown on page 403. When these reports are completed for all of- fices, the chairman of tellers, after reading them to the as- sembly, submits them to the chair, who, as he reads each one of them again, declares the result for that office. In each case where a candidate has a majority, the chair de- clares that candidate elected. For offices for which no candidate has a majority, the chair announces, "no elec- tion." When the tellers' reports for all offices have thus been read, the chair directs that new ballots be distrib- uted for those offices for which no candidate attained a majority (see also below). In balloting by this method, if a person has been nominated for a number of offices, it may happen that the same person is elected to more than one office. Although, strictly speaking, there is no prohi- bition against a person's holding more than one office, it is understood in most societies that a member can serve

1   in only one such capacity at a time, and sometimes the bylaws so provide. In such a case, if the person elected to two or more offices is present, he can choose which of the offices he will accept. If he is absent, the assembly should

5   decide by vote the office to be assigned to him, and then should elect person(s) to fill the other office(s).

   2) Under the usual form of the second election procedure, balloting for each office immediately follows nominations from the floor for that office. The ballots are

10   counted for one office and the result of that election is announced—after repeated balloting, if necessary—before the next office to be voted on is opened to nominations from the floor. The members are thus able to take into account the results for the offices voted on

15   first, in deciding upon both nominations and votes for the later offices. Under this method the ballots normally consist of small slips of blank paper handed out by the tellers as each ballot is taken—on which voters write the name of the candidate of their choice (who need not

20   have been nominated). This method is generally practical only in assemblies small enough that the votes from each balloting can be counted while the meeting briefly pauses—usually without recessing or proceeding to other business, although it can do either of these things

25   if it wishes.

   Whichever one of the preceding methods of election is used, if any office remains unfilled after the first ballot, as may happen if there are more than two nominees, the bal-

30   loting should be repeated for that office as many times as necessary to obtain a majority vote for a single candidate. The same is true where two candidates tie for a majority vote for an office. When repeated balloting for an office is necessary, the names of all nominees are kept on the ballot.

35   The nominee receiving the lowest number of votes is never

removed from the next ballot unless the bylaws so require, or unless he withdraws—which, in the absence of such a bylaw, he is not obligated to do. The nominee in lowest place may turn out to be a "dark horse" on whom all factions may prefer to agree.

In an election of members of a board or committee in which votes are cast in one segment of the ballot for multiple positions on the board or committee, every ballot with a vote for one or more candidates is counted as one vote cast, and a candidate must receive a majority of the total of such votes to be elected. In such a case, if more than the prescribed number receive a majority vote, the places are filled by the proper number receiving the largest number of votes. If less than the proper number receive a majority vote, those who do have a majority are elected, and all other candidates remain on the ballot for the necessary repeated balloting. Similarly, if some candidates receive a majority but are tied for the lowest position that would elect, all of those candidates also remain on the next ballot.

If the bylaws require the election of officers to be by ballot and there is only one nominee for an office, the ballot must nevertheless be taken for that office unless the bylaws provide for an exception in such a case. In the absence of the latter provision, members still have the right, on the ballot, to cast "write-in votes" for other eligible persons.

An election by ballot can be conducted by mail if the bylaws so provide, as explained on pages 408–14. For such an election, however—unless repeated balloting by mail is feasible in cases where no candidate attains a majority—the bylaws should authorize the use of some form of preferential voting or should provide that a plurality shall elect.

VIVA-VOCE ELECTION.   The viva-voce method of election finds application principally in mass meetings—or in cases where a candidate is unopposed or the election is

1 not strongly contested, and the bylaws do not require election by ballot.

When there is more than one nominee for a given office in a viva-voce election—or in an election by rising vote or 5 by show of hands—the candidates are voted on in the order in which they were nominated. When the nominations have ended, the chair repeats the nominations and continues:

CHAIR: As many as are in favor of Mr. A for President say *aye*. 10 . . . Those opposed say *no*. . . . The ayes have it and Mr. A is elected President.

If the noes are in the majority the wording is:

15   CHAIR: The noes have it and Mr. A is not elected. Those in favor of Mr. B [the next nominee] say *aye*. . . . Those opposed say *no*. . . .

As soon as one of the nominees receives a majority vote, the chair declares him elected and no votes are taken on the 20 remaining nominees for that office. The other officers are elected in the same way. When a number of members are to be elected to identical offices in the nature of a single office held by more than one person—as, for example, in electing four directors—the same procedure is followed; when four 25 have received a majority, the voting ceases.

It will be seen that, under the procedure just described, it is necessary for members wishing to vote for a later nominee to vote against an earlier one. This fact gives an undue advantage to earlier nominees and, accordingly, a voice vote 30 is not a generally suitable method for electing the officers of organized societies.

When only one nominee is put up and the bylaws do not require a ballot, the chair can take a voice vote, or can declare that the nominee is elected, thus effecting the elec- 35 tion by unanimous consent or "acclamation." The motion

to close nominations should not be used as a means of mov-   *1*
ing the election of the candidate in such a case.

The assembly cannot make valid a viva-voce election if
the bylaws require the election to be by ballot.

5

ROLL-CALL ELECTION.   Although unusual, an
election can be held by roll call. Either the first or second
procedure described on pages 425–26 for election by ballot
can be generally followed, and the member (or the chairman of a delegation, as the case may be), when called upon,   *10*
declares his vote or the votes of the members of his delegation for each office to be filled. The secretary should record
the vote(s) and then repeat them to be sure of their accurate recordation.

15

CUMULATIVE VOTING.   For ballot or roll-call elections of boards, committees, delegates, or other positions
held by more than one individual, the bylaws may provide for
cumulative voting. In this form of voting, each member is entitled to cast one vote for each position, so that, if, for exam-   *20*
ple, three directors are to be elected, each member may cast
three votes. These votes may all be cast for one, two, or three
candidates, as the voter chooses. A minority group, by coordinating its effort in voting for only one candidate who is a
member of the group, may be able to secure the election of   *25*
that candidate as a minority member of the board. However,
this method of voting, which permits a member to transfer
votes, must be viewed with reservation since it violates a fundamental principle of parliamentary law.

30

PROVIDING FOR COMPLETION OF AN ELEC-
TION.   If an assembly wishes to adjourn when an election
is incomplete, an adjourned meeting (**9**) should be provided for. If such an adjourned meeting is impossible or impractical and the organization will hold another regular   *35*

1 business session before a quarterly time interval has elapsed
(see p. 88), the election is completed at the next regular
meeting.

5   TIME AT WHICH AN ELECTION TAKES EFFECT.
An election to an office becomes final immediately if the
candidate is present and does not decline, or if he is absent
but has consented to his candidacy. If he is absent and has
not consented to his candidacy, the election becomes final
10 when he is notified of his election, provided that he does
not immediately decline. If he does decline, the election is
incomplete, and another vote can be taken immediately or
at the next meeting without further notice. After an election has become final as stated in this paragraph, it is too
15 late to reconsider (**37**) the vote on the election.

    An officer-elect takes possession of his office immedi-
ately upon his election's becoming final, unless the bylaws
or other rules specify a later time. If a formal installation
ceremony is prescribed, failure to hold it does not affect the
20 time at which the new officers assume office.

OFFICERS; MINUTES
AND OFFICERS' REPORTS

§47. OFFICERS

As stated on page 21, the minimum essential officers for
the conduct of business in any deliberative assembly are a
presiding officer and a secretary or clerk. The usual duties
of these and other officers generally required in an organized society are summarized and discussed in this section.
Every society should specify in its bylaws what officers it requires, how they shall be elected or appointed, their term of
office, and any qualifications for holding office or any duties different from or in addition to those stated in the parliamentary authority.

Principles Applying to Holding of Office

In most societies it is usual to elect the officers from
among the members; but in all except secret societies, unless the bylaws or an established practice provide otherwise,
it is possible for an organization to choose its officers from
outside its membership. In many legislative bodies the presiding officer is not a member of the body. In certain in-

1 stances in an ordinary society—for example, if an adjourned
meeting or a special meeting (**9**) must deal with a problem
that has intensely divided the organization—it may be that
such a meeting can accomplish more under the chairman-
5 ship of an invited nonmember who is skilled in presiding;
and such an arrangement can be made with the approval of
the assembly if the president and the vice-president(s) concur. A large society with complex financial affairs may wish
to employ a professional as treasurer.

10   An office carries with it only the rights necessary for ex-
ecuting the duties of the office, and it does not deprive a
member of the society of his rights as a member. If a person
holds an office in a society of which he is not a member and
the bylaws make that officer an ex-officio member of the
15 board, the nonmember is thereby a full-fledged board
member with all the accompanying rights; but this does not
make him a member of the society.

       The bylaws may contain a provision that "No person
shall be eligible to serve more than _____ consecutive
20 terms in the same office." In filling vacancies for unexpired
terms, an officer who has served more than half a term in
an office is considered to have served a full term. As stated
on page 430, the term of office begins as soon as the officer is elected, unless the bylaws establish a different time.

25

Elected Officers

       CHAIRMAN OR PRESIDENT.   The presiding offi-
cer of an assembly ordinarily is called the *chairman***** when
30 no special title has been assigned, or in a body not permanently organized, such as a mass meeting (**53**). In organized societies the presiding officer's title is usually

---

*See page 22 regarding variations of this term which have come into
use.

prescribed by the bylaws, that of *president* being most com- 1
mon. The term *the chair* refers to the person in a meeting
who is actually presiding at the time, whether that person is
the regular presiding officer or not. The same term also applies to the presiding officer's station in the hall from which 5
he or she presides, which should not be permitted to be
used by other members as a place from which to make reports or speak in debate during a meeting (see also p.
437). In assemblies where committee chairmen or others
will require a lectern for their papers, another lectern on the 10
side of the platform or on the floor at the front should be
provided so that the chair can maintain his presiding location. For the manner in which the chair should be addressed in a meeting, see pages 22–23.

The presiding officer of an assembly—especially of a 15
large one—should be chosen principally for the ability to
preside. This person should be well versed in parliamentary
law and should be thoroughly familiar with the bylaws and
other rules of the organization—even if he or she is to have
the assistance of a parliamentarian. At the same time, any 20
presiding officer will do well to bear in mind that no rules
can take the place of tact and common sense on the part of
the chairman.

Duties of the Presiding Officer of an Assembly. The
principal duties of the presiding officer of an assembly 25
under parliamentary law are listed below—with references,
where appropriate, to fuller descriptions elsewhere in this
book. Additional information relating to the duties of the
chair in particular cases will be found in the treatment of
the subjects involved. It is the duty of the presiding officer 30
of an assembly:

1) To open the meeting at the appointed time by taking the
   chair and calling the meeting to order (p. 24), having ascertained that a quorum is present (pp. 20–21; **40**). 35

2) To announce in proper sequence the business that comes before the assembly or becomes in order in accordance with the prescribed order of business, agenda, or program, and with existing orders of the day (**41**).

3) To recognize members who are entitled to the floor (pp. 28–30; **42**).

4) To state and to put to vote all questions that legitimately come before the assembly as motions or that otherwise arise in the course of proceedings (except questions that relate to the presiding officer himself in the manner noted below), and to announce the result of each vote (**4**); or, if a motion that is not in order is made, to rule it out of order. (For a discussion of the circumstances under which the chair votes, see pp. 392–93. See also the discussion of unanimous consent, pp. 51–53.)

5) To protect the assembly from obviously frivolous or dilatory motions by refusing to recognize them (**39**).

6) To enforce the rules relating to debate and those relating to order and decorum within the assembly (pp. 21–24, 41–42; **43**).

7) To expedite business in every way compatible with the rights of members.

8) To decide all questions of order (**23**), subject to appeal (**24**)—unless, when in doubt, the presiding officer prefers initially to submit such a question to the assembly for decision.

9) To respond to inquiries of members relating to parliamentary procedure (*Parliamentary Inquiry*, pp. 281–82) or factual information (*Point of Information*, pp. 282–83) bearing on the business of the assembly.

10) To authenticate by his or her signature, when necessary, all acts, orders, and proceedings of the assembly.

11) To declare the meeting adjourned when the assembly so votes or—where applicable—at the time prescribed in the program, or at any time in the event of a sud-

den emergency affecting the safety of those present (**8, 21**).

At each meeting, in addition to the necessary papers proper to that meeting's business, the presiding officer should have at hand:

- a copy of the bylaws and other rules of the organization;
- a copy of its parliamentary authority (that is, this book, if it is prescribed in the bylaws);
- a list of all standing and special committees and their members; and
- a memorandum of the complete order of business listing all known matters that are to come up, shown in proper sequence under the correct headings—or with their scheduled times—as applicable.

Except in a small board or a committee, the presiding officer should stand while calling a meeting to order or declaring it adjourned, and while putting a question to vote. He should also stand—without leaving the chair—while explaining his reasons for a ruling on a point of order (if the explanation entails more than a few words) or when speaking during debate on an appeal or a point of order that he has submitted to the judgment of the assembly (**23, 24**). When speaking for the first time during debate in either of the latter two cases, he can do so in preference to other members (see p. 246 and Standard Characteristic 5, pp. 242, 249–50). While a member is speaking in debate on any question, the presiding officer should remain seated—unless the view between him and the members would be obstructed, in which case he should step back slightly during the member's speech. At times other than those just mentioned, the presiding officer can stand or sit as he finds convenient for commanding the assembly's attention, preserving order, etc.—provided that his station is arranged so that even when seated he can see the entire hall and all present can see him (see also pp. 21, 433).

Whenever a motion is made that refers only to the presiding officer in a capacity not shared in common with other members, or that commends or censures him with others, he should turn the chair over to the vice-president or appropriate temporary occupant (see below) during the assembly's consideration of that motion, just as he would in a case where he wishes to take part in debate (see also pp. 382–83). The chair, however, should not hesitate to put the question on a motion to elect officers or appoint delegates or a committee even if he is included.

Temporary Occupants of the Chair.   If it is necessary for the president to vacate the chair during a meeting, or if the president is absent, the chair is occupied temporarily by another—who also must not be precluded from presiding by any of the impediments mentioned in the preceding paragraph—as follows:

1) *A vice-president.* If the president for any reason vacates the chair or is absent, the vice-president or first vice-president normally should take the chair unless he also, because of involvement in the debate or for any other reason, should disqualify himself from presiding in the particular case; and if the first vice-president is absent or must disqualify himself, the duty of presiding devolves on the other vice-presidents in order. For this reason, the bylaws should number the vice-presidencies if there are more than one, and persons should be elected to specific positions. It should be noted, however, that if the bylaws provide for a president-elect, they usually provide also that the president-elect shall precede the first vice-president in the right to preside.

2) *An appointed chairman pro tem.* If the president vacates   1
   the chair during a meeting and no vice-president is available, he can, subject to the approval of the assembly, as
   explained on pp. 382–83, appoint a temporary chairman
   who is called the *chairman pro tempore,* or *chairman pro*   5
   tem. The return of the president, the arrival of a vice-
   president, or the first adjournment puts an end to this
   appointment, and the assembly can terminate it even
   earlier by electing another chairman (see also p. 642).
   The regular presiding officer, knowing that he will be   10
   absent from a future meeting, cannot in advance authorize another member to preside in his place.

3) *An elected chairman pro tem.* If neither the president nor
   any vice-president is present, the secretary—or in the secretary's absence some other member—should call the   15
   meeting to order, and the assembly should immediately
   elect a chairman pro tem to preside during that session.
   Such office is terminated by the entrance of the president
   or a vice-president, or by the election of another chairman pro tem. If the assembly is to elect a chairman pro   20
   tem to hold office beyond the current session (in the
   event that the president and the vice-presidents are unable to perform their duties for that length of time), notice must be given at the preceding meeting or in the call
   of the meeting at which such election is held.   25

    The practice in some organizations of permitting the
chairman of a committee to preside over the assembly or
put questions to vote during the presentation and consideration of the committee's report violates numerous princi-   30
ples of parliamentary law relating to the chair's appearance
of impartiality and the inappropriateness of his entering
into debate, not to speak of the regular presiding officer's
duty to preside (see pp. 432–36).

1   *Suggestions for Inexperienced Presiding Officers.*   The
larger the assembly, the more readily it will detect the
slightest weakness in a presiding officer. Efforts to capital-
ize on any such failing may follow with sometimes disas-
5   trous results. It is often said that knowledge is strength, and
certainly that is true in this case. The presiding officer
should be thoroughly familiar with the "Duties of the presiding officer of an assembly," as stated on pages
433–36, and should have with him the documents listed
10 on page 435. There is no acceptable alternative to parliamentary procedure for the conduct of business in a deliberative assembly; yet many presiding officers try to get
along with a minimum of knowledge. This approach in-
evitably results in signs of unsureness. A presiding officer
15 should make every effort to know more parliamentary procedure than other members, and should at least become familiar with 1 through 9 of this book and memorize the list
of ordinary motions in their order of precedence, on tinted
page 4. The chair should be able to refer to the table of
20 rules relating to motions on tinted pages 6–29 quickly
enough that there will be no delay in deciding all points
contained there. These steps are simple and will enable a
president to master parliamentary procedure more quickly.
As more difficult points arise, a careful reading of the de-
25 tailed treatment of such points in the body of this book will
make them readily understood and mastered.

The presiding officer must not permit members to press
on so rapidly that the parliamentary steps are abridged or
go unobserved. When a motion is made, he should not rec-
30 ognize any member or allow anyone to speak until the motion is seconded (where that is required) and he has stated
the question.

The chair should take special care to make sure that the
members always understand what is the immediately pending
35 business—the *exact* question to be voted on the next time a
vote is taken. Failure of presiding officers to do so is one of

the greatest causes of confusion in meetings. The chair should carefully follow the directions for stating a question on a motion or resolution given on pages 36-37. Particularly in stating the question on an unwritten motion, the chair should always say, "It is moved and seconded that" and then give the precise words of the motion fully, no matter how clearly the motion may have been framed when moved by its maker. The chair should never try to avoid this critically important duty by saying, "You have heard the motion" or by saying, "The motion is moved and seconded" without repeating its words. The chair must be careful to be exact in stating any proposed amendment so as to make clear the effect its adoption would have on the motion to be amended. After the vote on an amendment, he should fully restate that motion as it stands as a result of the amendment's adoption or failure (see pp. 136–37). Above all, just before the vote, the chair must make clear the precise question the assembly is to decide. It is far better to risk taxing the patience of an assembly by repeating the wording of a motion on which all may be clear, than to risk taking a vote whose effect may be unclear to even a few members.

When a vote is taken, the result should be announced and also what question, if any, is then pending, before any member who addresses the chair is recognized. In a large assembly where a microphone is required, the chair should insist that a member go to it and identify himself. This brief delay is often very salutary in quieting heated feelings. Efforts to abbreviate the requirements of parliamentary procedure often signal an effort to substitute the member's will for the parliamentary leadership of the presiding officer. A not uncommon instance of this kind is described on page 368, lines 31–36, where a member attempts quickly to obtain the floor to offer a motion in competition with one arranged by the officers to be offered by another member. Firmness and, at the same time, calm insistence on the regular order is a technique essential to the development of a skilled presiding officer.

1   While a commanding presence and knowledge are essential in procedural matters, the president of an ordinary deliberative assembly, especially a large one, should, of all the members, have the least to say upon the substance of pending questions. While providing strong leadership, he should be fair. He should never get excited; he should never be unjust to even the most troublesome member, or take advantage of such member's lack of knowledge of parliamentary law, even though a temporary good might be accomplished thereby. The president should never be technical or more strict than is necessary for the good of the meeting. Good judgment is essential; the assembly may be of such a nature, through its unfamiliarity with parliamentary usage and its peaceable disposition, that strict enforcement of the rules, instead of assisting, would greatly hinder business. But in large assemblies where there is much work to be done, and especially where there is likelihood of trouble, the only safe course is to require a strict observance of the rules.

Administrative Duties of the President of a Society.   All of the duties of the presiding officer described above relate to the function of presiding over the assembly at its meetings. In addition, in many organized societies, the president has duties as an administrative or executive officer; but these are outside the scope of parliamentary law, and the president has such authority only insofar as the bylaws provide it. In some organizations the president is responsible for appointing, and is ex officio a member of, all committees (except the nominating committee, which should be expressly excluded from such a provision); but only when he is so authorized by the bylaws—or, in individual cases, by vote of the assembly—does he have this authority and status. As an ex-officio member of a committee, the president has the same rights as the other committee members, but is not obligated to attend meetings of the committee and is not counted in determining the number required for a quorum or whether a quorum is present.

PRESIDENT-ELECT. Some organizations desire to elect their president one entire term in advance, and in such cases, during the term following the election, the person chosen is called the *president-elect*. This office exists only if expressly provided for in the bylaws, in which case the members never vote on any candidate for the office of president, but elect a president-elect and the other officers of the organization. Accordingly, when a member has served his full term as president-elect, he automatically becomes president for a full term. Once a person has been elected president-elect, the assembly cannot alter its decision regarding the succession of that person to the presidency, unless he vacates office during his term as president-elect or unless ground arises for deposing him from that office (see pp. 642–43).

When the bylaws of an organization provide for a president-elect, it is usual to provide also that if the president should be absent, or if the office of the president should become vacant between elections, the president-elect shall preside, if present, or shall fill the vacancy. Unless such provision is made, the first vice-president would preside or complete the president's term. It is also customary to provide in the bylaws for some method to fill a vacancy in the office of president-elect, should one occur between elections. It is important to consider these provisions with great care. The bylaws can assign the president-elect specific responsibilities.

VICE-PRESIDENT. In the absence of the president, the vice-president serves in his stead; thus, it is important to elect a vice-president who is competent to perform the duties of president. When a vice-president is presiding, he or she should be addressed as "Mr. or Madam President" (unless confusion might result—for example, when the president is also on the platform—in which case the form "Mr. or Madam Vice-President" should be used).

1   Some societies elect several vice-presidents in an order of precedence: first, second, third, and so on. In case of the resignation or death of the president, the vice-president (if there is only one) or the first vice-president (if there are
5 more than one) automatically becomes president for the unexpired term, unless the bylaws *expressly* provide otherwise for filling a vacancy *in the office of president*. The second vice-president, if there is one, then becomes first vice-president, and so on, with the vacancy to be filled oc-
10 curring in the lowest-ranking vice-presidency. Sometimes the bylaws provide that the different vice-presidents shall have administrative charge of different departments.

    Although in many instances the vice-president will be the logical nominee for president, the society should have
15 the freedom to make its own choice and to elect the most promising candidate at that particular time.

    SECRETARY.   The secretary is the recording officer of the assembly and the custodian of its records, except those
20 specifically assigned to others, such as the treasurer's books. The recording officer is sometimes called the *clerk,* the *recording secretary* (when there is also, for example, a corresponding secretary or financial secretary), the *recorder,* or the *scribe.*

    Duties of the Secretary.   The duties of the secretary are:
25

1) To keep a record of all the proceedings of the organization—usually called the *minutes.*
2) To keep on file all committee reports.
3) To keep the organization's official membership roll (un-
30   less another officer or staff member has this duty); and to call the roll where it is required.
4) To make the minutes and records available to members upon request (see below).
5) To notify officers, committee members, and delegates
35   of their election or appointment, to furnish committees

with whatever documents are required for the perform- *1*
ance of their duties, and to have on hand at each meeting a list of all existing committees and their members.

6) To furnish delegates with credentials.

7) To sign all certified copies of acts of the society, unless *5*
otherwise specified in the bylaws.

8) To maintain record book(s) in which the bylaws, special
rules of order, standing rules, and minutes are entered,
with any amendments to these documents properly
recorded, and to have the current record book(s) on *10*
hand at every meeting.

9) To send out to the membership a notice of each meeting, known as the *call* of the meeting, and to conduct
the general correspondence of the organization—that
is, correspondence that is not a function proper to other *15*
offices or to committees (see also *Corresponding Secretary* and *Executive Secretary,* below).

10) To prepare, prior to each meeting, an order of business
(**41**) for the use of the presiding officer, showing in
their exact order, under the correct headings, all matters *20*
known in advance that are due to come up and—if applicable—the times for which they are set.

11) In the absence of the president and vice-president, to
call the meeting to order and preside until the immediate election of a chairman pro tem. *25*

In the absence of the secretary, a secretary pro tem
should be elected; the corresponding, financial, or executive secretary in organizations having such officers is not an
automatic replacement. If, under "Reports of Officers" in *30*
the order of business, correspondence of an official character is to be read, it is normally read by the recording secretary and not by the corresponding secretary.

Records of the Secretary. When reports are received
from committees, the secretary should record on them the *35*

1 date they were received and what further action was taken
   on them, and preserve them among his records. It is not
   necessary for an assembly to vote that a committee report
   be "placed on file," as that should be done without a vote.

5   The use by the secretary of a tape recorder can be of
   great benefit in preparing the minutes, but a transcription
   of it should never be used as the minutes themselves.

   Any member has a right to examine the minutes of the
   society at a reasonable time and place, but this privilege
10 must not be abused to the annoyance of the secretary. The
   same principle applies to the minutes of boards and committees, their records being accessible to members of the
   boards or committees but to no others. When a committee
   requires certain records for the proper performance of its
15 duties, the secretary should turn them over to the committee chairman—after consulting with the president in any
   cases where he or she is in doubt. The corporation law of
   each state frequently provides for the availability of records
   of any group incorporated in that state.
20

   CORRESPONDING SECRETARY.   In larger societies, the duties of issuing notices of meetings and conducting the general correspondence of the organization as
   described under item (9) on page 443 are frequently as-
25 signed to a separate elected officer, usually called the *corresponding secretary*. When there is a corresponding secretary,
   the unqualified word *secretary* used alone refers to the
   recording officer.

30   TREASURER, AND FINANCIAL SECRETARY.
   The treasurer of an organization is the officer entrusted
   with the custody of its funds. The treasurer, and any other
   officers who handle funds of the society, should be bonded
   for a sum sufficient to protect the society from loss. The
35 specific duties of the treasurer will vary depending on the

size and complexity of the society; but this officer cannot disburse funds except by authority of the society or as the bylaws prescribe. The treasurer is required to make a full financial report annually or as the bylaws may prescribe, and to make such interim reports as the assembly or the executive board may direct. (For the suggested form of this annual report in simple cases, see pp. 460–61.)

In ordinary societies, tasks incident to the collection of dues from members are a part of the treasurer's duties unless the bylaws provide otherwise. Much clerical work may be attached to this function, however, in large organizations, in societies where dues are payable in frequent installments, or in societies that suspend the voting-membership rights of members who fall in arrears in dues payments (see pp. 393–94). In such cases some organizations have, in addition to the treasurer, a *financial secretary*—an officer whose usual duties are to bill members for their dues and to receive payment of them, to maintain a ledger of each member's account, and to turn over to the treasurer and obtain his receipt for moneys received.

OTHER OFFICERS. In addition to the officers described above, an organization can provide in its bylaws for any other officers it may wish—including assistant officers. Officers sometimes included, and their usual duties, are:

- *Directors* (or *trustees,* or *managers*), who sit as members of the executive board (**49**)—usually in addition to the other officers—and perform such duties as the bylaws may require. In some organizations the term *trustees* refers to officers who perform the duties of elected auditors (see p. 462).
- A *historian,* who prepares a narrative account of the society's activities during his or her term of office, which,

1   when approved by the assembly, will become a permanent part of the society's official history.

- A *librarian,* who, if the society possesses a collection of books or other written or printed matter, has custody of these items, and—subject to the society's direction—control over members' access to them.

- A *curator,* who serves as custodian of any objects of value that may belong to the society (other than library holdings).

- A *chaplain,* who recites or leads invocations and benedictions where such prayers are offered at the opening and closing of meetings or other events, and who—if a clergyman—serves the organization in that capacity in such manner as it may require.

- A *sergeant-at-arms* (or *warden,* or *warrant officer,* as sometimes called), who, on the floor of the meeting hall, assists in preserving order as the chair may direct. In a convention or large meeting this officer may have charge of the ushers. He may handle certain physical arrangements in the hall as well, such as being responsible in some cases for seeing that the furnishings are in proper order for each meeting. In a legislative or public body that has the power to penalize or compel the attendance of its members, the sergeant-at-arms may have the duty of serving warrants or notices of fines, or of arresting absent members in the event of a *Call of the House* (pp. 339–40).

- A *doorkeeper* or *guard,* who, in meetings where only members or some other limited category of persons are permitted to enter, checks the credentials or eligibility of those arriving, and denies entrance to unauthorized persons.

Directors should always be elected. The other officers mentioned above are usually elected also, but the bylaws can provide for their appointment.

HONORARY OFFICERS (AND MEMBERS). An honorary office is in fact not an office but—like honorary membership—a complimentary title that may be bestowed on members or nonmembers. When it is desired to honor a nonmember, it is more usual to elect such a person to honorary membership. An honorary officer—for example, an honorary president or an honorary treasurer—is often elected at the time of retirement from the corresponding actual office, particularly when the person has filled it creditably for a long time. If there are to be honorary officers or honorary members, they must be authorized by the bylaws. Like an honorary degree conferred by a college or university, an honorary office or membership is perpetual—unless rescinded or unless its duration is limited by the bylaws. Rights carried with the honor include the right to attend meetings and to speak, but not to make motions or vote unless the person is also a regular member, or unless the bylaws provide full membership rights.* Honorary presidents and vice-presidents should sit on the platform, but they do not preside. An honorary office entails no duties and in no way conflicts with a member's holding a regular office or being assigned any duty whatever. It is not improper to include in the published list of honorary officers the names of those who are deceased, if that fact is clearly indicated.

Appointed Officers or Consultants

EXECUTIVE SECRETARY.   The term *executive secretary,* or *executive director,* is usually applied to a salaried

---

*Some societies provide in the bylaws for electing to "honorary life membership"—or even its automatic conferment upon—a person who has been an active member for a specified long period of years, sometimes with the added requirement that he shall have attained a certain age. The bylaws may prescribe that such an honorary member shall pay no dues but shall retain full voting privileges.

1 officer who devotes full time to the position of administrative officer and general manager of an organization, especially at the national, regional, or state level; and unless otherwise indicated the term is used in that sense in this
5 book. In most organizations, the executive secretary is employed by the board of directors under contract, but in some this officer is elected by the convention.

Duties of the Executive Secretary.   The executive secretary is in charge of the central office of the society and acts
10 under the immediate direction of the board and the executive committee, if there is one (see p. 468). He is sometimes ex officio the secretary of the executive committee (and sometimes of the board) and is responsible for seeing that the committee's instructions are carried out. He is expected
15 to recommend plans of work and to conduct the day-to-day business of the organization. He is often responsible for the work that would otherwise be carried out by an elected corresponding secretary. He usually hires, fires, and determines the salaries of other staff members with the approval of the
20 board or executive committee, which may regulate this function by adopting personnel policies. The bylaws should specify the duties of the executive secretary and should describe the manner in which he is to be selected, and for how long a term.

25 *Relationship to the President.*   The relationship between the office of executive secretary and that of president depends on the duties and authority of these officers as defined in the bylaws. In some organizations, the executive and managerial function that would otherwise be exercised
30 by the president is entirely split off and vested in the executive secretary. This arrangement leaves the president his duties as presiding officer and spokesman for the organization. In any case, the president should not attempt to give orders to the executive secretary independently unless the
35 bylaws so authorize; in the absence of such a provision, the

executive secretary receives his direction from the board or
executive committee.

PARLIAMENTARIAN. The parliamentarian is a consultant, commonly a professional, who advises the president
and other officers, committees, and members on matters of
parliamentary procedure. The parliamentarian's role during
a meeting is purely an advisory and consultative one—since
parliamentary law gives to the chair alone the power to rule
on questions of order or to answer parliamentary inquiries.

A small local organization should rarely require the
services of a parliamentarian, unless it undertakes a general
revision of its bylaws; but for large assemblies and conventions or organizations where the transaction of business is
apt to be complex, it is advisable to engage one. Some state
or national organizations find it advisable to employ a parliamentarian throughout the year to assist with any questions that may arise in interpreting bylaws and rules, or in
connection with the work of the board and of officers or
committees. In such a case, the parliamentarian's duties extend beyond giving opinions to the presiding officer during
meetings, and may include assisting in the planning and
steering of business to be introduced.

Appointment of the Parliamentarian. If a parliamentarian is needed by an organization, the president should be
free to appoint one in whom he has confidence. The board
or society must approve any fee that will be required, however. If needed for only one meeting, a parliamentarian
should be appointed as far as possible in advance of the
meeting at which he is to serve, since his main work should
be done outside the meeting.

Duties of the Parliamentarian. The president, knowing in advance the business to come before the assembly,
should confer with the parliamentarian before the meetings
open, and during recesses, in order to anticipate any prob-

1 lems that may arise and to avoid, as much as possible, frequent consultation during the meetings. There is no set
   rule for the number of additional functions a parliamentarian may be asked to perform as a permanent appointee,
5 such as teaching classes, holding office hours during conventions, and the like.

   During a meeting the work of the parliamentarian
   should be limited to giving advice to the chair and, when
   requested, to any other member. It is also the duty of the
10 parliamentarian—as inconspicuously as possible—to call the
   attention of the chair to any error in the proceedings that
   may affect the substantive rights of any member or may
   otherwise do harm. There should be an understanding between the parliamentarian and the presiding officer that
15 there will probably be occasions when it may be essential
   for the chair to listen to suggestions being made by the parliamentarian, even if it means momentarily not giving full
   attention to others or asking the assembly to *stand at ease*
   during the consultation (see p. 243). This practice will en-
20 able the chair to be in a position to act promptly at the correct time and be fully informed. In advising the chair, the
   parliamentarian should not wait until asked for advice—that
   may be too late. An experienced parliamentarian will often
   see a problem developing and be able to head it off with a
25 few words to the chair. Only on the most involved matters
   should the parliamentarian actually be called upon to speak
   to the assembly; and the practice should be avoided if at all
   possible. The parliamentarian should be assigned a seat next
   to the chair, so as to be convenient for consultation in a low
30 voice, but the chair should try to avoid checking with the
   parliamentarian too frequently or too obviously. After the
   parliamentarian has expressed an opinion on a point, the
   chair has the duty to make the final ruling and, in doing so,
   has the right to follow the advice of the parliamentarian or
35 to disregard it. But if the parliamentarian's advice on im-

portant procedural issues is habitually disregarded, he may find it necessary, at the end of the present engagement or session, to resign.

A member of an assembly who acts as its parliamentarian has the same duty as the presiding officer to maintain a position of impartiality, and therefore does not make motions, participate in debate, or vote on any question except in the case of a ballot vote. He does not cast a deciding vote, even if his vote would affect the result, since that would interfere with the chair's prerogative of doing so. If a member feels that he cannot properly forego these rights in order to serve as parliamentarian, he should not accept that position. Unlike the presiding officer, the parliamentarian cannot temporarily relinquish his position in order to exercise such rights on a particular motion.

Regarding the duties of the parliamentarian in connection with a convention, see also pages 589–90.

§48. MINUTES AND REPORTS OF OFFICERS

Minutes

The record of the proceedings of a deliberative assembly is usually called the *minutes,* or sometimes—particularly in legislative bodies—the *journal.* In an ordinary society, unless the minutes are to be published, they should contain mainly a record of what was *done* at the meeting, not what was *said* by the members. The minutes should never reflect the secretary's opinion, favorable or otherwise, on anything said or done. The minutes should be kept in a substantial book or binder.

CONTENT OF THE MINUTES. The *first paragraph* of the minutes should contain the following information (which need not, however, be divided into numbered or separated items directly corresponding to those below):

1 1) the kind of meeting: regular, special, adjourned regular, or adjourned special;

2) the name of the society or assembly;

3) the date and time of the meeting, and the place, if it is
5   not always the same;

4) the fact that the regular chairman and secretary were present or, in their absence, the names of the persons who substituted for them; and

5) whether the minutes of the previous meeting were read
10   and approved—as read, or as corrected—and the date of that meeting if it was other than a regular business meeting. Any correction is made in the text of the minutes being approved; the minutes of the meeting making the correction merely state that the minutes were
15   approved "as corrected" (see form, p. 454, l. 34–35).

The body of the minutes should contain a *separate paragraph for each subject matter,* giving, in the case of all important motions, the name of the mover, and should show:

20

6) all main motions (**10**) or motions to bring a main question again before the assembly (pp. 72–76; **34–37**)—except, normally, any that were withdrawn*—stating:

a) the wording in which each motion was adopted or
25   otherwise disposed of (with the facts as to whether the motion may have been debated or amended be-

---

*There may be certain instances in which a main motion is withdrawn under circumstances that require some mention in the minutes. In such a case, only as much information should be included in the minutes as is needed to reflect the necessary details clearly. For example, if, at one meeting, a main motion was made *the* special order for the next meeting (pp. 359–60), or a main motion was postponed after lengthy consideration to a meeting at which it was withdrawn by consent, action at the first meeting should always be recorded, and the withdrawal at the second meeting should be stated for completeness of the minutes.

fore disposition being mentioned only parentheti-
cally); and

b) the disposition of the motion, including—if it was
temporarily disposed of (pp. 88, 329–30)—any
primary and secondary amendments and all adhering
secondary motions that were then pending;

7) secondary motions that were not lost or withdrawn, in
cases where it is necessary to record them for completeness or clarity—for example, motions to *Recess* or to *Fix
the Time to Which to Adjourn* (among the privileged
motions), or motions to *Suspend the Rules* or grant a
Request to Be Excused from a Duty (among the incidental motions), generally only alluding to the adoption of
such motions, however, as ". . . the matter having been
advanced in the agenda on motion of . . ." or ". . . a
ballot vote having been ordered, the tellers . . . ";

8) all notices of motions (pp. 116–18); and

9) all points of order and appeals, whether sustained or
lost, together with the reasons given by the chair for his
or her ruling.

The *last paragraph* should state:

10) the hour of adjournment.

Additional rules and practices relating to the content of
the minutes are the following:

- The name of the seconder of a motion should not be
  entered in the minutes unless ordered by the assembly.
- When a count has been ordered or the vote is by ballot,
  the number of votes on each side should be entered;
  and when the voting is by roll call, the names of those
  voting on each side and those answering "Present"
  should be entered. If members fail to respond on a roll-

1 call vote, enough of their names should be recorded as
present to reflect that a quorum was present at the time
of the vote. If the chair voted, no special mention of this
fact is made in the minutes.

5 • The proceedings of a committee of the whole, or a
quasi committee of the whole, should not be entered in
the minutes, but the fact that the assembly went into
committee of the whole (or into quasi committee) and
the committee report should be recorded (see **52**).

10 • When a question is considered informally, the same information should be recorded as under the regular
rules, since the only informality in the proceedings is in
the debate.

• When a committee report is of great importance or
15 should be recorded to show the legislative history of a
measure, the assembly can order it "to be entered in the
minutes," in which case the secretary copies it in full in
the minutes.

• The name and subject of a guest speaker can be given,
20 but no effort should be made to summarize his remarks.

THE SIGNATURE.   Minutes should be signed by the
secretary and can also be signed, if the assembly wishes, by
the president. The words *Respectfully submitted*—although
25 occasionally used—represent an older practice that is not
essential in signing the minutes.

FORM OF THE MINUTES.   The principles stated
above are illustrated in the following model form for minutes:

30

The regular monthly meeting of the L.M. Society
was held on Thursday, January 4, 20__, at 8:30 P.M.,
at the Society's building, the President being in the
chair and the Secretary being present. The minutes of
35 the last meeting were read and approved as corrected.

The Treasurer reported the receipt of a bill from the Downs Construction Company in the amount of $5,000 for the improvements recently made in the Society's building. The question put by the chair "that the bill be paid" was adopted. 5

Mr. Johnson, reporting on behalf of the Membership Committee, moved "that John R. Brown be admitted to membership in the Society." The motion was adopted after debate.

The report of the Program Committee was received and placed on file. 10

The special committee that was appointed to investigate and report on suitable parking facilities near the Society's building reported, through its chairman, Mrs. Smith, a resolution, which, after debate and amendment, was adopted as follows: "*Resolved,* That . . . [its exact words immediately before being acted upon, incorporating all amendments]." 15

The resolution relating to the use of the Society's library by nonmembers, which was postponed from the last meeting, was then taken up. This motion and a pending amendment were laid on the table after the chair announced that the guest speaker had received a phone message which would require his early departure. 20

The President introduced the guest speaker, Mr. James F. Mitchell, whose subject was _____. 25

At the conclusion of Mr. Mitchell's talk, the resolution relating to the use of the Society's library by nonmembers was taken from the table. After amendment and further debate, the resolution was adopted as follows: "*Resolved,* That . . . [its exact wording immediately before being finally voted on]." 30

Mr. Gordon moved "that the Society undertake the establishment of a summer camp for boys on its lakefront property." Mrs. Thomas moved to amend 35 this motion by inserting the word "underprivileged" before "boys." On motion of Mr. Dorsey, the motion to establish the camp, with the pending amendment, was referred to a committee of three to be appointed by the chair with instructions to report at the next meeting. The chair appointed Messrs. Flynn, Dorsey, and Fine to the committee.

The meeting adjourned at 10:05 P.M.

Margaret Duffy, Secretary

READING AND APPROVAL OF THE MINUTES. *When the next regular business session will be held within a quarterly time interval* (see p. 88), *when the session does not last longer than one day, and when there will be no change or replacement of a portion of the membership before the next session,* procedures relative to the reading and approval of minutes are as follows:

- The minutes of the meeting are normally read and approved at the beginning of the next regular meeting, immediately after the call to order and any opening ceremonies. An adjourned meeting of an ordinary society approves the minutes of the meeting that established the adjourned meeting; its own minutes are approved at the next adjourned or regular meeting, whichever occurs first. A special meeting does not approve minutes; its minutes should be approved at the next regular meeting.

- Corrections, if any, and approval of the minutes are normally done by unanimous consent. The chair calls for the reading of the minutes, asks for any corrections, then declares the minutes approved, as shown on pages 343–44.

- By a majority vote without debate, the reading of the minutes can be "dispensed with"—that is, *not carried out at the regular time.* If the reading of the minutes is

dispensed with, it can be ordered (by majority vote 1
without debate) at any later time during the meeting
while no business is pending; and if it is not thus taken
up before adjournment, these minutes must be read at
the following meeting before the reading of the later 5
minutes. If it is desired to approve the minutes without
having them read, it is necessary to suspend the rules for
this purpose.

- A draft of the minutes of the preceding meeting can be
  sent to all members in advance, usually with the notice. 10
  In such a case, it is presumed that the members have
  used this opportunity to review them, and they are not
  read unless this is requested. Correction of them and
  approval, however, is handled in the usual way. It must
  be understood in such a case that the formal copy 15
  placed in the minute book contains all corrections that
  were made and that none of the many copies circulated
  to members and marked by them is authoritative (see
  also p. 344).

20

*When the next regular business session will not be held
within a quarterly time interval* (see p. 88), *and the session
does not last longer than one day, or in an organization in
which there will be a change or replacement of a portion of the
membership,* the executive board or a committee appointed 25
for the purpose should be authorized to approve the minutes. The fact that the minutes are not then read for approval at the next meeting does not prevent a member from
having a relevant excerpt read for information; nor does it
prevent the assembly in such a case from making additional 30
corrections, treating the minutes as having been previously
approved (see third paragraph below).

In sessions lasting longer than one day, such as conventions, the minutes of meetings held the preceding day are
read and are approved by the convention at the beginning 35

1

of each day's business after the first (and minutes that have not been approved previously should be read before the final adjournment)—except as the convention may author-
5 ize the executive board or a committee to approve the minutes at a later time.

When the minutes are approved, the word *Approved,* with the secretary's initials and the date, should be written below them.

10   If the existence of an error or material omission in the minutes becomes reasonably established after their approval—even many years later—the minutes can then be corrected by means of the motion to *Amend Something Previously Adopted* (**35**), which requires a two-thirds vote,
15 or a majority vote with notice, or the vote of a majority of the entire membership, or unanimous consent.

MINUTES TO BE PUBLISHED. When minutes are to be published, they should contain, in addition to the
20 information described above, a list of the speakers on each side of every question, with an abstract or the text of each address, in which case they may be called "proceedings," "transactions," or the like. In such cases the secretary should have an assistant. When it is desired, as in some
25 conventions, to publish the proceedings in full, the secretary's assistant should be a stenographic reporter or recording technician. The presiding officer should then take particular care that everyone to whom he assigns the floor is fully identified. Under these conditions it is usually
30 necessary to require members to use a public address system. Reports of committees should be printed exactly as submitted, the minutes showing what action was taken by the assembly in regard to them; or they can be printed with all additions in italics and parts struck out enclosed in
35 brackets, in which case a note to that effect should precede the report or resolution.

Reports of Officers

In principle, all reports of officers in a society are incident to administrative duties that these officers have by virtue of provisions in the bylaws or other rules. Strictly speaking, in a purely deliberative assembly, the officers make no reports.

In an organized society, the bylaws may require each of the principal officers to make a report of the year's work at the annual meeting (**9**). At any meeting at which officers' reports are made, they immediately follow the reading and approval of the minutes.

REPORTS OF EXECUTIVE OFFICERS.   In addition to their annual reports, the president and vice-president from time to time may wish or need to report on their activities in connection with administrative duties. Such reports are usually for purposes of information only, but may sometimes contain recommendations calling for action by the assembly. In either case, the reports should generally conform to the rules as to form, substance, and disposition that govern committee reports (**51**). Motions to adopt or implement any recommendations should be made from the floor by a member *other than the reporting officer.*

REPORTS BY THE TREASURER.   At each meeting of a society, the chair may ask for a "Treasurer's report," which may consist simply of a verbal statement of the cash balance on hand—or of this balance less outstanding obligations. Such a report requires no action by the assembly.

In addition, the treasurer is required to make a full financial report annually, and in some societies more often. Such an annual report should always be audited. It is compiled and dated as of the last day of the fiscal year, if there is one, or December 31 if no different financial year is stated in the bylaws.

Form and Content of the Financial Report. The best form for the financial report depends on particular conditions, such as the kind and size of the society, the nature of its activities, the frequency of reporting, and so on. The form used should be patterned after reports in similar organizations. In any case, since the financial report is made for the information of the members, it should not contain details of dates and separate payments, which are a hindrance to the report's being understood. The following brief model report is in a form suitable for most small societies whose financial affairs are simple and primarily involve cash.

REPORT OF THE TREASURER

OF THE L.M. SOCIETY FOR THE YEAR

ENDING DECEMBER 31, 20__

Balance on hand January 1, 20__		$1,253.25
Receipts		
Members' Dues	$630.00	
Proceeds from Spring Barbecue	296.75	
Fines	12.00	
Total Receipts		938.75
Total		$2,192.00
Disbursements		
Rent of Hall	$500.00	
Custodial Service Fees	175.00	
Stationery and Printing	122.40	
Postage	84.00	
Total Disbursements		$881.40
Balance on hand December 31, 20__		1,310.60
Total		$2,192.00

Richard Larson, *Treasurer*   *1*

Audited and found correct.
  Colleen Burke
  Randolph Schuler   *5*
    Auditing Committee

In organizations whose finances are more involved, a double-entry set of books may be advisable or required. *10* Such a system should be set up with the assistance of an accountant, and the report would normally consist of a balance sheet showing the society's assets, liabilities, and fund balance (or members' equity) as well as an income statement similar to the above report form without the opening *15* and closing cash balances. Other statements may be included as needed, such as a statement of changes in members' equity, a statement of sources and application of funds, and a cash forecast. This system may be on a cash or an accrual basis and will usually require review or audit by *20* an accountant.

Action on the Financial Report.   No action of acceptance by the assembly is required—or proper—on a financial report of the treasurer unless it is of sufficient importance, as an annual report, to be referred to auditors. *25* In the latter case it is the auditors' report which the assembly accepts. The treasurer's financial report should therefore be prepared long enough in advance for the audit to be completed before the report is made at a meeting of the society. *30*

When the amounts involved are very large and the reports complicated, or the organization's contributors or others require it, it is desirable to have the audits made by independent certified accountants. But in ordinary societies and those in which the expense of a professional cannot be *35*

1　justified, it is practical to have the financial reports audited by
an auditing committee of two or more members of the society—appointed in advance if there is not a standing auditing
committee. In some organizations the financial reports are
5　audited by elected officers known as "trustees." Where professional examination is desired but the organization does
not require a full audit, a "review" (as distinct from a mere
"compilation") by an accountant may supply sufficient test-
ing and verification to satisfy the organization. If the audi-
10　tors' report consists only of an endorsement on the financial
report—to the effect that it has been found correct, as
shown in the model above—the treasurer can simply read
out this certification as he concludes the presentation of his
own report. After the treasurer has made his report to the
15　assembly (and after any detailed report presented by the
chairman of the auditing committee, if it is needed), the
chair states the question on adopting the *auditors'* report.
The adoption of the auditors' report has the effect of relieving the treasurer of responsibility for the period covered
20　by his report, except in case of fraud.

　　If the treasurer presents an unaudited annual report or
other financial report that the bylaws require to be audited,
and if there is a standing auditing committee or if auditors
have already been chosen in some other manner, the chair,
25　without waiting for a motion when the treasurer has finished reading his report, immediately says, "The report is
referred to the Auditing Committee [or "to the auditors,"
or "to the Trustees for audit"]." If no auditors have been
chosen, the proper procedure is to adopt a motion to refer
30　the report to an auditing committee to be appointed by one
of the methods described in **50.**

　　REPORTS OF OTHER OFFICERS.　Other officers
as may be prescribed in the bylaws, such as a historian or a
35　librarian, may also have occasion to report to the assembly.

These reports are usually made annually and, like those of   *1*
the executive officers, are generally for purposes of information only. They can, however, contain recommendations
upon which it is hoped the assembly will act. If the report
is to become a permanent official document of the organi-   *5*
zation, it should be formally adopted by the assembly.
Thus, for example, historical accounts prepared by the historian do not become part of the official history of the society until the assembly formally adopts them, with any
desired changes, after their presentation by the historian.   *10*

CHAPTER

XVI

BOARDS AND COMMITTEES

§49. BOARDS

The essential characteristics of a *board* are stated on pages 8–9. All of the material under the heading "Types of Deliberative Assembly" on pages 5–9 should be read in connection with this section.

The authority by which a board is constituted commonly prescribes the times at which it shall hold regular meetings, and the procedure by which special meetings of the board can be called; or the board can establish such provisions to the extent that it has the authority to adopt its own rules (see p. 469).

The Executive Board of an Organized Society

Except in the simplest and smallest local societies, or those holding very frequent regular meetings, it is generally found advisable to provide in the bylaws for a board to be empowered to act for the society when necessary between its regular meetings, and in some cases to have complete control over certain phases of the society's business. Such a board is usually known as the *executive board,* or—in organizations where there is an executive committee within and subordinate to the board as described below—the *board of directors, board of managers,* or *board of trustees.* Any such body is referred to in this book as an executive board, however—regardless of whether there is an executive committee—in cases where the distinction is immaterial.

If a society is to have an executive board, the bylaws should specify the number of board members and how they are to be determined, should define the board's duties and powers, and should make provision for meetings of the board as stated above. An executive board commonly consists of the society's officers (**47**) who also have duties apart from the board, together with a number of directors, managers, or trustees who may or may not have other duties such as the chairmanship of important standing committees (**50**), but who usually should be classed as officers of the society, and who are elected in the same way and at the same time as its other officers. (See sample bylaws, Art. IV, Sec. 1, and Art. VI, Sec. 1, pp. 566–68.) Frequently it is provided that a specified percentage of the directors shall be chosen periodically in such a way that their terms of office overlap those of the others—as when, for example, there are six directors and it is provided that two shall be elected at each annual meeting for three-year terms.

A society has no executive board, nor can its officers act as a board, except as the bylaws may provide; and when so established, the board has only such power as is delegated to it by the bylaws or by vote of the society's assembly referring individual matters to it. The amount of regular power delegated to an executive board under the bylaws varies considerably from one organization to another. If the society as a whole meets less often than within quarterly time intervals (p. 88), or if its main purpose is other than to transact business, the entire administrative authority of the society is

1   best left to the board between the society's meetings. Usu-
    ally in organizations meeting monthly or oftener, and some-
    times in those meeting quarterly, the board is not given so
    much power, since the society can attend to much of its
5   business at its regular meetings. (For appropriate wordings
    for the governing provision in the bylaws in each of these
    two cases, see pp. 560, 568.) In any event, no action of the
    board can conflict with any action taken by the assembly of
    the society; and except in matters placed by the bylaws ex-
10 clusively under the control of the board, the society's as-
    sembly can give the board instructions which it must carry
    out, and can countermand any action of the board if it is not
    too late (as it would be, for example, when a contract has al-
    ready been made). It should be noted, however, that exactly
15 the opposite condition prevails in connection with boards of
    business corporations, in which the board has exclusive
    power and authority to operate the business.

Ex-Officio Board Members

20   Frequently boards include ex-officio members—that is,
    persons who are members of the board by virtue of an office
    or committee chairmanship held in the society, or in the par-
    ent state or national society or federation or some allied
25 group; or—sometimes in boards outside of organized soci-
    eties—by virtue of a public office. In the executive board of
    a society, if the ex-officio member of the board is under the
    authority of the society (that is, if he is a member, officer, or
    employee of the society), there is no distinction between
30 him and the other board members. If the ex-officio member
    is not under the authority of the society, he has all the priv-
    ileges of board membership, including the right to make
    motions and to vote, but none of the obligations—just as in
    a case, for example, where the governor of a state is ex offi-
35 cio a trustee of a private academy. The latter class of ex-offi-

cio board member, who has no obligation to participate, should not be counted in determining the number required for a quorum or whether a quorum is present at a meeting. Whenever an ex-officio board member is also ex officio an officer of the board, he of course has the obligation to serve as a regular working member.

When an ex-officio member of a board ceases to hold the office that entitles him to such membership, his membership on the board terminates automatically.

Concerning ex-officio members of committees, including the president, see page 480.

Officers of Boards

A board that is not an instrumentality of a parent assembly or membership body is organized as any deliberative assembly, with a chairman* or president, a secretary, and other officers as may be needed. In general, such a board elects its own officers if the authority under which the board is constituted makes no other provision as to how the officers are to be determined. A board that is to elect its officers should meet for this purpose as soon as possible after the selection of its members (see also p. 471). In most ordinary societies having executive boards, on the other hand, it is customary for the president and the secretary of the society to serve in the same capacity within the board even if the bylaws are silent on the subject. If any other arrangement is desired, it should be specified in the bylaws.

Bodies Subordinate to a Board

As a general principle, a board cannot delegate its authority—that is, it cannot empower a subordinate group to

---

*See page 22 regarding variations of this term that have come into use.

1 act independently in its name—except as may be authorized
by the bylaws (of the *society*) or other instrument under
which the board is constituted; but any board can appoint
committees to work under its supervision or according to
5 its specific instructions. Such committees *of the board* always
report *to the board*.

EXECUTIVE COMMITTEE.   In a society where the
board is large or its members must travel from a distance to
10 meet, it is usual for the bylaws to establish an *executive committee* composed of a specified number of board members,
which shall have all or much of the power of the board between meetings (just as the board has all the power of the
society between the society's meetings), but which cannot
15 modify any action taken by the board (just as the board cannot modify any action taken by the society). The executive
committee is thus in reality a "board within a board." Usually the membership of the executive committee is specified
in the bylaws, rather than being left to the choice of the full
20 board. The executive committee should be small and its
members should, if possible, live near enough to each other
to be able to hold frequent regular meetings, and emergency meetings when necessary. The executive secretary, if
there is one, should work closely with the executive com-
25 mittee, but should be appointed by the parent body or at
least by the board. A board cannot appoint an executive
committee unless the bylaws so authorize.

COMMITTEES OF A BOARD.   Where an organiza-
30 tion is local—for example, a society for sustaining a foster
home for children—the executive board usually divides itself into committees having charge of different branches of
the work during the interval between the monthly or quarterly meetings of the board. At the board meetings these
35 committees report on the fulfillment of their assigned re-

sponsibilities. In such cases the committees are genuinely
subordinate to the board and must ordinarily report back to
it for authority to act (in contrast to an executive committee, which usually has power to act as the board, and in contrast to standing committees of the *society,* which are not
subordinate to the board unless made so by a provision in
the bylaws). Any board can appoint committees of the kind
just described without authorization in the bylaws.

Conduct of Business in Boards

GENERAL PROCEDURE.   In an organized society
the board operates under the bylaws, the parliamentary authority, and any applicable special rules of order or standing
rules of the society, except as the bylaws may authorize the
board to adopt its own rules (see **2, 56**). A board that is not
a part of a society can adopt its own rules, provided that
they do not conflict with anything in the legal instrument
under which the board is constituted.

Under the general parliamentary law, business is transacted in large boards according to the same rules of procedure as in other deliberative assemblies. In smaller boards,
these rules apply as far as practicable, with the exceptions
noted below. In any case, a board can transact business only
in a regular or properly called meeting or at an adjournment
thereof (**9**), of which every board member has been notified and at which a quorum (a majority of the total membership unless otherwise specified in the bylaws or
established by the constituting power) is present. The personal approval of a proposed action obtained separately by
telephone or individual interview, even from every member
of a board, is not the approval of the board, since the members were not present in one room where they could mutu-
ally debate the matter. If action on such a basis is necessary
in an emergency, it must be ratified (pp. 118–20) at the next

regular board meeting in order to become an official act of the board.

A record of the board's proceedings should be kept by the secretary, just as in any other assembly; these minutes are accessible only to the members of the board unless the board grants permission to a member of the society to inspect them, or unless the society by a two-thirds vote (or the vote of a majority of the total membership, or a majority vote if previous notice is given) orders the board's minutes to be produced and read to the society's assembly.

At regular board meetings the executive committee, if there is one, should be required to make a report of its activities since the last board meeting. No action need be taken on this report, which is generally intended as information only.

PROCEDURE IN SMALL BOARDS. In a board meeting where there are not more than about a dozen members present, some of the formality that is necessary in a large assembly would hinder business. The rules governing such meetings are different from the rules that hold in other assemblies, in the following respects:

- Members are not required to obtain the floor before making motions or speaking, which they can do while seated.
- Motions need not be seconded.
- There is no limit to the number of times a member can speak to a question, and motions to close or limit debate (**15, 16**) generally should not be entertained.
- Informal discussion of a subject is permitted while no motion is pending.
- Sometimes, when a proposal is perfectly clear to all present, a vote can be taken without a motion's having been introduced. Unless agreed to by unanimous consent,

however, all proposed actions of a board must be approved by vote under the same rules as in other assemblies, except that a vote can be taken initially by a show of hands, which is often a better method in such meetings.

- The chairman need not rise while putting questions to vote.

- The chairman can speak in discussion without rising or leaving the chair; and, subject to rule or custom within the particular board (which should be uniformly followed regardless of how many members are present), he usually can make motions and usually votes on all questions.

EFFECT OF PERIODIC PARTIAL CHANGE IN BOARD MEMBERSHIP.   In cases where a board is constituted so that a specified portion of its membership is chosen periodically (as, for example, where one third of the board is elected annually for three-year terms), it becomes, in effect, a new board each time such a group assumes board membership. Consequently, all unfinished business existing when the outgoing portion of the board vacates membership falls to the ground under provision (c) on page 229; and if the board is one that elects its own officers or appoints standing committees, it chooses new officers and committees as soon as the new board members have taken up their duties, just as if the entire board membership had changed. The individual replacement of persons who may occasionally vacate board membership at other times, however, does not have these effects.

§50. COMMITTEES

A committee, as understood in parliamentary law, is a body of one or more persons, elected or appointed by (or by direction of) an assembly or society, to consider, investigate, or take action on certain matters or subjects, or to do

1   all of these things. Unlike a board, a committee is not itself
considered to be a form of assembly.

Although the term *committee* commonly implies a relatively small number of persons appointed to give a task more
5   detailed attention than is possible in a body the size of the assembly, this characteristic more accurately describes what are
known as *ordinary committees.* An assembly can also designate all of its members present to act as a committee, which
is called a *committee of the whole* and is distinguished from an
10   ordinary committee. In large assemblies, the use of a committee of the whole is a convenient method of considering a
question when it is desired to allow each member to speak an
unlimited number of times in debate. Committees of the
whole are treated separately in **52.** The statements in this sec-
15   tion apply principally to ordinary committees.

Ordinary committees are of two types—*standing committees* (which have a continuing existence) and *special committees* (which go out of existence as soon as they have
completed a specified task).*

20   Generally the term *committee* implies that, within the
area of its assigned responsibilities, the committee has less
authority to act independently for the society (or other constituting power) than a board is usually understood to have.
Thus, if the committee is to do more than report its find-
25   ings or recommendations to the assembly, it may be empowered to act for the society only on specific instructions;
or, if it is given standing powers, its actions may be more

---

*Under the general parliamentary law, a committee of the whole is in
the nature of a special committee, since each committee of the whole is regarded as going out of existence when it has completed its consideration of
the subject for which it was established. In the U.S. House of Representatives, however, this is not the case, and there are two standing committees
of the whole—the Committee of the Whole House, and the Committee of
the Whole House on the State of the Union.

closely subject to review than a board's, or it may be required to report more fully. Also, unlike most boards, a committee in general does not have regular meeting times established by rule; but meetings of the committee are called as stated on page 482. Some standing committees, however—particularly in large state or national organizations—function virtually in the manner of boards, although not designated as such.

When a committee is appointed "with power," this means with power to take all the steps necessary to carry out its instructions.

In large assemblies or those doing a great volume of business, much of the preliminary work in the preparation of subjects for consideration is usually done by committees. In many such bodies, in fact, it is advisable to have every main question go to a committee before final action on it is taken by the assembly.

Standing committees are constituted to perform a continuing function, and remain in existence permanently or for the life of the assembly that establishes them. In an ordinary society, the members of such a committee serve for a term corresponding to that of the officers, or until their successors have been chosen, unless the bylaws or other rules otherwise expressly provide. Thus, a new body of committee members is normally appointed at the beginning of each administration.

A standing committee must be constituted by name (a) by a specific provision of the bylaws or (b) by a resolution which is in effect a special rule of order and therefore requires notice and a two-thirds vote for adoption, if any of the following conditions are to apply:

- if the committee is to have standing authority to act for the society on matters of a certain class without specific instructions from the assembly;

- if all business of a certain class is to be automatically referred to the committee; or
- if some other rule of parliamentary procedure is affected by the committee's assigned function.

If a standing committee's assigned function does not affect a rule of parliamentary procedure in any of these three ways, it can be established by a standing rule adopted by a majority vote without notice, although, even in such a case, the committee is frequently constituted by name in the bylaws as indicated above. If certain standing committees are enumerated in the bylaws, an inference arises that there shall be no others unless the bylaws also include a provision authorizing their appointment; and without such a provision, no standing committee aside from those enumerated can be established unless the bylaws are amended to include it (see also pp. 560–61). A standing committee of a society reports to the assembly of the society, and not to the executive board or board of directors, unless the bylaws provide otherwise. In some societies, standing committees in effect have charge of certain branches of the organization's work, in which case these committees are really in the nature of boards.

A *special* (*select,* or *ad hoc*) *committee* is a committee appointed, as the need arises, to carry out a specified task, at the completion of which—that is, on presentation of its final report to the assembly—it automatically ceases to exist. A special committee may not be appointed to perform a task that falls within the assigned function of an existing standing committee.

Appointment of Committees

METHODS OF APPOINTMENT.   In an assembly or organization that has not prescribed in its bylaws or rules how the members of its committees shall be selected, the method can be decided by unanimous consent or by majority vote at the time the committee is appointed, as described on page 166; or (in the case of a special committee) the method can be specified in the motion to establish the committee. The power to appoint a committee carries with it the power to appoint the chairman and to fill any vacancy that may arise in the committee. The two paragraphs headed *Designating the Committee Chairman* on page 168 should be read in connection with the five methods of appointing a committee described below.

It is possible for persons who are not members of the assembly or the society to be appointed to committees—even to the position of committee chairman—but control over all such appointments is reserved to the assembly in the individual case, unless the bylaws provide otherwise. From this principle, it follows that, referring to these five methods of appointment, non–assembly members may be appointed to committees by methods (a), (b), (c), and (e), as listed below. When method (d) is used and the chair appoints either a standing or a special committee, however, the governing rule regarding the appointment of non–assembly members is as stated under "NAMING MEMBERS TO A SPECIAL COMMITTEE," on page 167.

Methods by which committees can be appointed are as follows:

a) *Election by ballot.* This method is principally applicable to important standing committees having extensive powers. Under this procedure, nominations for committee membership can be made by any of the methods described in **46;** then the nominees are voted on by ballot just as in an election of officers or a board, a majority vote being necessary to elect. In the event that more, or less, than the required number receive a majority, places on the committee are filled as explained on page 427, lines 6–19. If it is the assembly's practice—or its wish in the particular case—to select the committee chairman (rather than leave it to the committee to do so as explained on p. 168), the chairmanship can be treated as a separate position to be voted for on the same ballot with the other committee members; or, in a smaller assembly, if preferred, the chairman can be elected from among the committee's members on a second ballot, after their names have been announced.

b) *Nominations from the floor (open nominations) with viva-voce election* (usually called simply "nominations from the floor"). This is a common method of appointing members to a committee when the assembly wishes to reserve the selection to itself without requiring secrecy in the voting. When this method has been decided upon, the chair says, "Members will please nominate," or, "Nominations for the committee are now in order." The chair announces each nomination as he hears it, as shown on page 418. No one has a right to nominate more than one person to membership on the committee until every other member has had an opportunity to nominate a candidate; and thus the nomination of more than one person at a time by a single member can be entertained only by unanimous consent. If no more than the prescribed number of committee members are nominated, even after the chair calls for further nominations, the chair can put the question on the members named constituting the committee. A vote in such a case is unnecessary, however, since the fact that no more than the required number are nominated shows that there is unanimous consent that the committee should consist of these persons, which the chair declares as follows: "Messrs. A, B, and C, Mrs. D, and Mrs. E are nominated. Are there any further nominations? . . . Since there are none, the committee is composed of the persons just named [or he repeats the names if he feels it advisable]." If there are more nominees than the required number of committee members, then, when there are no further nominations, the chair repeats all of the names in the order in which they were nominated, and in the same order puts the question on the election of each nominee—one at a time until the proper number have been elected—as described for viva-voce elections (**46**). For reasons explained on pages 427–29, those nominated last in such a case have less chance of being elected. After the selection of committee members has been completed, the assembly can elect a committee chairman from among them, if desired; or a chairman can be elected separately, first.

c) *Nominations by the chair* (with confirmation by voice vote). This method is used when the assembly wishes to take advantage of the chair's knowledge and judgment as to suitable appointees, yet wishes to have veto power. In this case, the chair names the same number of persons as there are to be members of the committee, always naming his choice of committee chairman first, thus: "The chair nominates Mr. X as chairman, Mrs. Y, and Mr. Z.* The question is: Shall these persons constitute the committee?" Any member can then move to strike out one or more names—but not to insert new ones, which the chair must do if such a motion to strike out is adopted. After any changes in the original names have thus been made, the chair repeats the proposed

---

*The first person that the chair names is automatically chairman of the committee unless the assembly rejects that person as a committee member or unless he or she declines the chairmanship; but it is good practice for the chair to mention him or her as chairman (see p. 168).

1   names as they stand and puts the question on the entire
     list: "Mr. X, Mrs. Y, and Mr. W are nominated. As many
     as are in favor of these persons constituting the com-
     mittee, say *aye*. . . . Those opposed, say *no* . . . , etc."

5   d) *Appointment by the chair.* In the absence of special con-
     ditions, appointment of committees by the chair, or by
     the regular presiding officer, is usually the best method
     in large assemblies, and it is the ordinary procedure in
     many smaller societies as well. The president cannot as-
10   sume such power, however, unless it is given to him by
     the bylaws or by action of the assembly in the individ-
     ual case (pp. 164, 166, 561). When the bylaws provide
     that the *president* shall appoint all committees, this
     power does not transfer to the *chair* if someone else
15   presides. A clause in the bylaws assigning to the presi-
     dent the duty of appointing all committees should
     therefore contain appropriate provision for its own sus-
     pension if necessary (for example, if there is occasion to
     appoint a special committee during a meeting from
20   which the president is absent). In addition, a clause con-
     ferring on the president such power of appointment
     should exclude the nominating committee (see pp.
     567, 569). Whenever it is stated in the bylaws (with
     or without the proper exceptions just noted) that the
25   president "shall appoint all committees," this means
     that the president shall select the persons to serve on
     such committees as the bylaws prescribe to be estab-
     lished or the assembly may direct to be appointed; it
     does not mean that the president can himself decide to
30   appoint and assign a task to a group and thereby give it
     the status of a committee of the society. When the chair
     appoints a committee, no vote is taken on the ap-
     pointees, except any who are not members of the as-
     sembly in cases where there is no prior authorization for
35   the chair to appoint non–assembly members to the

committee—either in the bylaws or in a motion direct- *1*
ing the appointment of the particular committee (see
also p. 167). But the chair must announce the names of
the committee members to the assembly, naming the
chairman of the committee first, as in (c) above; and *5*
until such announcement is made the committee cannot act. If the assembly orders the appointment of a
special committee and it is desired to let the chair select
the committee members after adjournment, this delay
must be authorized by the assembly; the names of the *10*
committee members must then be announced at the
next meeting and recorded in the minutes.

e) *Appointment by adoption of a motion naming members of
a committee.* This method finds use in the case of special committees when the rules or particular conditions *15*
do not dictate the use of another procedure. The names
of the proposed committee members can be included in
the motion proposing to appoint the committee, either
as it is originally offered or by way of an amendment.
Or, if the motion to appoint the committee is adopted *20*
without prescribing the manner of appointment, a second motion can be made "That the committee be composed of Mr. X, Mr. Y, . . . " In either case, the motion
naming the committee members can specify the committee chairman or not as the assembly wishes. If other *25*
names (intended to replace one or more of those in the
motion) are proposed while the motion is pending, all
such names and those in the motion should be treated
as nominations and should be voted on as in the case of
an election (see also pp. 163ff.). *30*

Unless the bylaws or other governing rules expressly
provide that committee members shall serve ". . . *and* until
their successors are chosen" or for a fixed period, as ". . . for
a term of two years" (in which case the procedure for their *35*

1 removal or replacement is the same as that for officers described on p. 643, l. 6–14), committee members (including
the chairman) may be removed or replaced as follows: If appointment was as provided in paragraphs (a), (b), (c), or (e)
5 above, the removal or replacement of a committee member
requires the same vote as for any other motion to *Rescind* or
Amend Something Previously Adopted. If appointment was
by the president acting alone under paragraph (d), he may
remove or replace committee members by his own act (see
10 pp. 169–70).

A committee (except a committee of the whole, **52**) can
appoint subcommittees, which are responsible to and report to the committee and not to the assembly. Subcommittees must consist of members of the committee, except
15 when otherwise authorized by the society in cases where
the committee is appointed to take action that requires the
assistance of others.

The rules affecting ex-officio members of committees
are the same as those applying to ex-officio members of
20 boards (pp. 466–67). When the bylaws provide that the
president shall be ex officio a member of all committees
(except the nominating committee, as such a provision
should state), the president is an ex-officio member who
has the right, but not the obligation, to participate in the
25 proceedings of the committees, and he is not counted in
determining the number required for a quorum or whether
a quorum is present at a meeting.

The resignation of a member of a committee should be
addressed to the appointing power, and it is the responsi-
30 bility of that power to fill the resulting vacancy.

PROPER COMPOSITION OF COMMITTEES.
The members of a standing committee should be chosen so
as to provide the strongest possible group for the handling
35 of any task that may arise within the province of the com-

mittee. In the case of a special committee, the purpose for which it is appointed affects the desirable size and composition, as follows:

- When a special committee is appointed to implement an order of the assembly, it should be small and should consist only of those in favor of the action to be carried out. If anyone not in sympathy with the action is appointed, he should ask to be excused.
- When a special committee is appointed for deliberation or investigation, however, it should often be larger, and it should represent, as far as possible, all points of view in the organization, so that its opinion will carry maximum weight. When such a committee is properly selected, its recommendations will most often reflect the will of the assembly. By care in selecting committees, debates on delicate and troublesome questions in ordinary societies can be mostly confined to the committees. The usefulness of the committee will be greatly impaired, on the other hand, if any important faction of the assembly is not represented.

INFORMATION, INSTRUCTIONS, AND REFERRED PAPERS. Upon the appointment of a committee, the secretary of the society should see that all persons appointed are notified, and should furnish a list of the members of the committee to its chairman or, in the chairman's absence, to some other authorized committee member. When a subject or item of business is referred to the committee (normally at the time of its appointment if it is a special committee, or at any time if it is a standing committee), the secretary should provide the committee chairman or his representative with copies of the papers, motion, or other matter formally referred to it, and whatever instructions the assembly has given. Upon the committee's re-

1 quest, any other papers or books necessary for the proper performance of its duties should be made available to it by the appropriate officers of the society, who can first consult with the president if in doubt.

5 A committee should take care to preserve the papers referred to it from the society, since, after its assignment is completed, they must be returned in the same condition as when received. If the committee wishes to write on copies of the documents, therefore, it must obtain its own photocopies, 10 unless it has been provided with extra copies specified in its instructions as for that purpose. In any case, amendments prepared for recommendation to the assembly when the committee reports should be drawn up on a separate sheet.

15 **Conduct of Business in Committees**

COMMITTEE PROCEDURE.   When a committee has been appointed, its chairman (or first-named member temporarily acting—see p. 168) should call it together. If its 20 chairman fails to call a meeting, the committee must meet on the call of any two of its members, unless (for very large committees) the assembly's rules prescribe, or empower the assembly or the committee to require, a larger number. The quorum in a committee is a majority of its membership un- 25 less the assembly has prescribed a different quorum (**40**). All of the meetings of a special committee constitute one session (**8**).

The bylaws may authorize a board or committee (or even a relatively small assembly) to meet by videoconference or 30 teleconference. If they do, then such a meeting must be conducted by a technology that allows all persons participating to hear each other at the same time (and, if a videoconference, to see each other as well). The opportunity for simultaneous communication is central to the deliberative 35 character of the meeting, and is what distinguishes it from at-

tempts to do business by postal or electronic mail or by fax
(see p. 2). It is advisable to adopt special rules of order and
standing rules, as appropriate, to specify precisely how recognition is to be sought and the floor obtained during video-
conferences and teleconferences.

In small committees the chairman usually acts as secretary, but in large ones and many standing committees, a
secretary may be chosen to keep a brief memorandum in
the nature of minutes for the use of the committee.

In a standing or special committee—unless it is so large
that it can function best in the manner of a full-scale assembly—the same informalities and modifications of the
regular rules of parliamentary procedure generally prevail as
are listed for small boards on pages 470–71; also, the rules
governing the motion to *Reconsider* are modified as stated
on pages 318–19. In committees, the chairman not only
has the right to make and debate motions, but he is usually
the most active participant in the discussions and work of
the committee. In order that there may be no interference
with the assembly's having the benefit of the committee's
matured judgment, motions to close or limit debate (**15,
16**) are not allowed in committees.

Committees of organized societies operate under any
applicable rules stated in the bylaws, the special rules of
order, the parliamentary authority, and standing rules
adopted by the society. Committees may not adopt their
own rules except as authorized in the bylaws or in instructions given to the committee by the society (see p. 469
for the same rule as applicable to boards).

When a committee is to make substantive recommendations or decisions on an important matter, it should give
members of the society an opportunity to appear before it
and present their views on the subject at a time scheduled
by the committee. Such a meeting is usually called a *hearing*. During actual deliberations of the committee, only
committee members have the right to be present.

1   A committee has no power to punish its members for disorder or other improper conduct related to its proceedings, but should report the facts to the assembly.

5   ADJOURNMENT: MANNER AND EFFECT.   When a committee intends to reconvene, it can simply adjourn, or adjourn to meet at a later time. In the first case—when it adjourns without appointing a time for another meeting—it is considered as having adjourned to meet at the call of the
10   chair. In the second case—when it sets an adjourned meeting—it is advisable, though not obligatory, to notify absent members of the adjourned meeting.

When a special committee has finished with the business assigned to it, a motion is made for the committee to
15   "rise"—which is equivalent to the motion to adjourn sine die (or without day)—and for the chairman or some other member to make its report to the assembly. The motion to rise is never used in standing committees, or in special committees until they are ready to go out of existence.
20

CONTINUITY AND CONCLUSION OF COMMITTEE ASSIGNMENT.   Since members of standing committees in ordinary societies are appointed for a term corresponding to that of the officers, such a committee is
25   generally required to report at least once a year, usually at the annual meeting, on its activities and everything referred to it during the year. When a standing committee submits such a report at the conclusion of its members' term, the *committee* is not discharged from further consideration of referred mat-
30   ters on which it reports partially at that time, unless the assembly so votes (**36**); thus such matters normally go over to the new committee. The members of the old committee continue their duties until their successors are chosen.

A special committee—since it is appointed for a specific
35   purpose—continues to exist until the duty assigned to it is accomplished, unless discharged sooner (see **36**); and it

ceases to exist as soon as the assembly receives its final report. The fact that an annual meeting intervenes does not
discharge a special committee, but in an elected or appointed body, as a convention, special committees that have
not reported cease to exist when the new officers assume
their duties at the next annual meeting.

§51. REPORTS OF BOARDS AND COMMITTEES

A report of a subordinate board or a committee is an official statement formally adopted by, and submitted in the
name of, the reporting body, informing the parent assembly of action taken or recommended, or information obtained.

General Considerations Affecting Board and Committee Reports

LIMITATION OF REPORT CONTENT TO WHAT
HAS BEEN LEGALLY AGREED TO.   Except as noted
in this paragraph, a report of a board or committee can contain only what has been agreed to by a majority vote at a
regular or properly called meeting of the board or at a
meeting of the committee (or at an adjournment of one of
these meetings, pp. 90–91)—where every board or committee member was notified of the meeting and where a
quorum of the board or committee was present. An emergency presentation of facts or recommendations made
merely upon separate consultation with every member of a
board must be described thus to the parent assembly, and
not as an official report of the board (see also pp. 469–70).
In the case of a committee, however, if it is impractical to
bring its members together for a meeting, the report of the
committee can contain what has been agreed to by every
one of its members. If a committee is appointed from dif-

1 ferent sections of the country with the expectation that its
work will be done by correspondence, its report can contain
only what is agreed to by a majority of its members.

5   TYPES OF REPORTS.   For convenience in the discussions in this section, reports may be divided into two
general categories as follows:

a) *Annual or periodic reports of boards or standing commit-*
10   *tees* are usually submitted in accordance with requirements in the bylaws, are primarily for information, and
should summarize important work done by the board
or committee during the year or other period covered
by the report. They may also contain recommenda-
15   tions—which may relate to general policy to be followed by the organization, or may propose specific
action by its assembly (see next paragraph).
b) *Reports relating to single items of business arising during*
the year fall into a number of particular forms—which
20   are described for the case of committees beginning on
page 496. As will be seen from examples in the text on
those pages, these reports can often be quite brief unless special circumstances or instructions to the reporting body call for a detailed presentation of facts.

25

RECOMMENDATIONS IN A REPORT.   In any re-
port of a subordinate board or a committee (of type [a] or
[b] above), specific recommendations for immediate action
by the parent assembly should be grouped at the end—re-
30 peating them if they have already been noted at separate
places in the report—and should generally be cast in the
form of one or more proposed resolutions. Although it is
possible for a report, in the circumstances just described, to
present recommendations which are not in the form of res-
35 olutions or motions, the "adoption" of such recommenda-

tions by the parent assembly may, depending on their word- *1*
ing or that of the motion to adopt, lead to confusion as to
whether their adoption *authorizes action,* or only has the
force of a declaration of intent (requiring the adoption of
subsequent resolutions for implementation). A board or *5*
committee is usually best fitted to prepare resolutions to
carry out its recommendations, and it should never leave
this responsibility to others.

When a report is made for the purpose of presenting
recommendations on a single subject—especially if it is the *10*
report of a committee to which the subject was referred—
it is often best for the formal report to be confined as much
as possible to the recommendations, whether they are in the
form of resolutions or otherwise (see examples, pp.
497ff.). If this approach is followed and it is desired to *15*
bring supporting reasons to the attention of the assembly,
the reporting member (that is, the person who presents the
report) can include brief oral explanations with his presentation. Or, supporting reasons can be explained at greater
length during debate on the report—by the reporting *20*
member, who has the right to the floor first in debate, and
also by other members of the board or committee, if appropriate, as the debate progresses.

In the foregoing connection, it should be noted that
under parliamentary conditions the inclusion of supporting *25*
facts or reasoning in a report proposing certain action may
tend to work against the taking of that action, since some
members who might otherwise have been willing to accept
the proposals may be led to vote against them if they disagree with the factual background as reported or the rea- *30*
soning of the reporting body.

FORM OF DETAILED REPORT.   If special condi-
tions dictate that a report devoted to a single subject and presenting recommendations should include a full account of *35*

the details involved in the case, the body of the report is best organized according to the following topics, as applicable:

1) a description of the way in which the reporting body (usually a committee in such cases) undertook its charge;
2) the facts uncovered or information obtained;
3) the findings or conclusions derived from the facts or information; and
4) resolutions or recommendations.

If for any reason one or more resolutions or recommendations are placed within this type of detailed report before its conclusion, they should be repeated at the end, as stated above. In this way they can be more easily dealt with apart from any implied endorsement of reported facts and reasoning which some members may not accept.

PRESENTATION AND RECEPTION OF REPORTS.

A report of a board or committee to an assembly is presented at the proper time by a "reporting member" of the board or committee. For the report of a board whose chairman is also the presiding officer of the assembly, the secretary or another one of its members acts as reporting member. In the case of a committee, the committee chairman is the reporting member unless—because he does not agree with the report or for any other reason—he does not wish to give it, in which event the committee chooses another one of its members.

A reporting member *makes* or *presents* a report on behalf of a board or a committee when, having been assigned the floor for such a purpose in a meeting, he does one of the following things (depending on the nature of the report and other conditions): (a) renders the report orally, if it is not in writing; (b) reads the report to the assembly and passes it to the chair or the secretary; or (c) announces that

he is submitting it and passes it to one of these officers to
be read by a reading clerk. When the assembly hears the report thus read or orally rendered, it *receives* the report. The
terms *presentation* and *reception* accordingly describe one
and the same event from the respective viewpoints of the reporting member and the assembly.

MOTIONS FOR ACTION ON REPORTS.
Immediately after receiving a board's or a committee's report—unless it is a report containing only information on
which no action is taken (p. 507)—an assembly normally
considers whatever action may be recommended in or arise
out of the report. In the remaining pages of this section, it is
explained how such action under various conditions may involve the introduction of motions—to implement recommendations or, occasionally, to adopt the entire report.

Motions to Implement Recommendations.   When a report contains recommendations—except in cases where the
recommendations relate only to the adoption or rejection
of question(s) that were referred while pending (**13**) and
consequently become pending again automatically when reported (p. 499–507)—the reporting board or committee
member usually makes the necessary motion to implement
the recommendations at the conclusion of his presentation,
provided he is a member of the assembly (see examples, pp.
497–99 and 502ff., in which it is generally assumed that
the "reporting member" is a member of the assembly). If
the report is read by the secretary or a reading clerk in such
a case, the reporting member resumes the floor for the
purpose of making the motion immediately after the reading is completed. No second is required in these cases,
since the motion is made on behalf of the board or committee (see p. 35).

If the person presenting the report is not a member of
the assembly or for any other reason does not make the re-

1 quired motion to implement the recommendations as just
described, any member of the assembly can do so; but the
motion should then be seconded. Or, when the proper
motion is a matter of clear-cut procedure and must neces-
5 sarily be introduced to resolve the case, the chair may
sometimes expedite matters by *assuming* the motion—that
is, stating the question on it without waiting for it to be
made—*provided that the assembly is accustomed to this
method.**

10 *Motion to Adopt an Entire Report.*   In rare instances
after an assembly has received a report, it may have occasion
to adopt the (entire) report; an affirmative vote on such a
motion has the effect of the assembly's endorsing every
word of the report—including the indicated facts and the
15 reasoning—as its own statement (see also pp. 118–19). Unlike motions to take the action recommended in a report as
described above, a motion "to adopt the report" should be
made by someone other than the reporting member and requires a second. Adoption of an entire report is seldom wise
20 except when it is to be issued or published in the name of
the whole organization.

EQUIVALENCE OF TERMS; INCORRECT MO-
TIONS.   As applied to an assembly's action with respect to
25 board or committee reports or any of their contents, the expressions *adopt, accept,* and *agree to* are all equivalent—that
is, the text adopted becomes in effect the act or statement of
the assembly. It is usually best to use the word *adopt,* however, since it is the least likely to be misunderstood.

30 A common error is to move that a report "be received"
after it has been read—apparently on the supposition that

---

*Such a practice is justified by the fact that more than one person must
have voted for the recommendation within the board or committee and
must therefore wish it to come before the assembly.

such a motion is necessary in order for the report to be taken under consideration or to be recorded as having been made. In fact, this motion is meaningless, since the report has already been received. Even before a report has been read, a motion to receive it is unnecessary if the time for its reception is established by the order of business, or if no member objects (see also below).

Another error—less common, but dangerous—is to move, after the report has been read (or even before the reading), that it "be accepted," when the actual intent is that of the mistaken motion to receive, as just explained, or of a legitimate motion to receive made "before" the report is read. If a motion "to accept" made under any of these circumstances is adopted and is given its proper interpretation, it implies that the assembly has endorsed the complete report.

APPLICABILITY OF REGULAR RULES TO QUESTIONS ARISING OUT OF REPORTS. When a board or committee report has been received and the chair has stated the question on the adoption of the motion, resolution(s), recommendation(s), or report—whether the question became pending automatically, or the proper motion was made or was assumed by the chair as explained above— the matter is treated as any other main question, is open to debate and amendment, and can have any of the subsidiary motions applied to it. Similarly, if a committee to which the main question was referred has recommended that it be amended or definitely or indefinitely postponed, the motion to take such action is debatable and (for primary amendment or definite postponement) amendable, under the regular rules for these motions.

In the foregoing connection it should be noted that the consideration of a matter *that was referred* to a board or committee cannot be objected to (**26**) when it is reported on—regardless of whether the matter was referred as a pending question (**13**) or as a subject on which no question was pending. The reason is that an *Objection to the Consideration of a Question* can be raised only against an original main motion at the time of its introduction; and the reported matter in no case has this status since (a) if it was referred as a pending question, it was introduced at an earlier time, or (b) if it was referred as a subject on which no question was pending, the main question introduced following the report is an incidental main motion (see pp. 96ff.).

CONDITIONS FOR AMENDMENT OF A REPORT BY THE ASSEMBLY BEFORE ITS ADOPTION.   An assembly that is to adopt an entire report which it has received can amend the report, but the text as published or recorded must not make the reporting board or committee appear to say anything different from the wording that was actually reported. For this reason, the published or recorded text should show clearly the reported version and the changes that the assembly has made—for example, by enclosing in brackets all that was struck out and underlining or putting in italics all that was inserted, and including a note explaining this notation at the beginning of the report (see also pp. 490, 493).

Board Reports

OCCASION AND MANNER OF PREPARATION. The executive board (or board of directors) of a society reports to the assembly annually on the work done during the year, and at such other times and upon such subjects as the bylaws may prescribe or the society's business may require.

A board report is usually drafted by the president or secretary, and this draft often passes through the executive committee first, if there is one, before it comes up for consideration and adoption by the board at one of its meetings (see also pp. 485–86). A board report should be signed by the president or chairman of the board and its secretary only.

RECEPTION AND DISPOSITION OF BOARD RE-PORTS. In meetings at which the executive board is to make a report, the chair calls for it at the time provided in the order of business, or, if there is no such provision, before committee reports are received or unfinished business is taken up. After the reading of the report, the reporting member moves the adoption of any resolutions included in it, which, as indicated above, should be grouped or repeated at the end. If the annual report of the board is to be formally adopted by the society before being published, an appropriate wording for the minutes in such a case is the following: "The Executive Board [or "Board of Directors," etc.] submitted its report, which, after debate and amendment [if any], was adopted as follows, the words in brackets having been struck out and those underlined [or, "in italics"] having been inserted before the report was adopted." A society need not endorse the report of its board, and can even decline to allow the report to be printed, or it can adopt only a part; but whatever it prints or records from the report must show any changes clearly marked.

Committee Reports

GENERAL FORM OF COMMITTEE REPORTS. All committee reports should in general be submitted in writing, except as noted (for particular types of brief reports in a small assembly) on pages 508–10. In the case of such exceptions, a report can be given orally only if it is brief enough that the secretary can record its complete substance in the minutes on hearing it given—which he must do if no written copy is submitted for file.

1 Usually a written committee report is not addressed or dated. It is understood to be addressed to the assembly, and its date is that on which it is presented in a meeting of the assembly as recorded in the minutes.

5 A committee report should always be worded in the third person—that is, as shown in the next paragraph (not "I report . . ." or "We recommend . . . "). Similarly, in an assembly a committee report is always spoken of by the chair and others as, for example, "the report of the Finance Commit-

10 tee" or "the report of the committee to which was referred . . . [stating the subject]." It should never be spoken of as "the report of the chairman of the Finance Committee" and never as "Mr. Smith's report," even though it is usually presented by the committee chairman and even if he may have

15 personally drafted it or done most of the work reported.

A committee report should begin with an identification of the committee submitting it—the name of the committee in the case of a standing committee, or the subject that was referred in the case of a special committee; thus:

20

> [*For a standing committee:*] The Committee on . . . wishes to report [or, "reports"] that . . . [or, "submits the following report: . . . "].

25 Or:

> Report of the Committee on . . . :
> [*For a special committee:*] The committee to which was referred [stating the subject] reports [or "recom-
30 mends"] that . . .

Or:

> The committee appointed to [stating the purpose] re-
35 ports that . . . [or, "submits the following report: . . . "].

If a written committee report is of considerable importance, it should be signed by all the members concurring.* Otherwise, the committee can authorize its chairman to sign the report alone, in which case he adds the word *Chairman* after his signature. By so signing, the committee chairman certifies that the report has been adopted by the committee as explained on pages 485–86. When all concurring members sign the report, it is customary for the chairman to sign first, but this is not obligatory. In any case, he should not place the word *Chairman* after his name except when he signs alone on behalf of the entire committee. The use of the words *Respectfully submitted* preceding the signature(s) on a committee report is unnecessary and no longer customary.

RECEPTION OF COMMITTEE REPORTS. Reports of committees are called for or can be presented in a meeting as follows:

- If, as is usually the case, a place has been provided in the order of business for the reports of committees, the chair calls for the reports of standing committees first, in the order in which they are listed in the bylaws or other rules; after that he calls for the reports of the special committees, in the order of their appointment. (The chair omits calling for the report of any committee that he knows has no report to make; see also pp. 344–45.) As each report is called for, the committee chairman or other reporting member rises, addresses the chair, and presents the report.
- Or, if the order of business makes no provision for committee reports, the committee chairman or other re-

---

*Regarding signature with an expression of disagreement in a certain particular, see page 512.

porting member should obtain the floor when no business is pending and, addressing the chair, inform the assembly that the committee has agreed upon a report which he is prepared to submit. If the chair thinks that the assembly wishes to hear the report, the chair directs the member to proceed. If anyone objects to the report's reception or if the chair is in doubt as to whether the report should be received at that time, he puts the question to the assembly:

> CHAIR: The question is, "Shall the report be received now?" As many as are in favor of receiving the report now, say *aye*. . . . Those opposed say *no*. . . ., etc.

This question requires a majority vote. If the vote is in the negative, a later time for the reception of the report should be set, either by a vote or by unanimous consent. The manner of presenting the report is the same as described above.

(For the reception of "minority reports," see pp. 511–12.)

MANNER OF PRESENTATION AND DISPOSITION OF COMMITTEE REPORTS IN PARTICULAR CASES.   The proper method of presenting and disposing of different types of committee reports is explained below, with sample reports being given in certain cases. Whenever a motion by the reporting member is a normal part of the procedure in the examples, it is assumed that this member actually makes the motion rather than leaving it to the chair to state the question without a formal motion (see pp. 489–90).

A Report at the Initiative of a Standing Committee Recommending Action.   If a standing committee wishes on its own initiative to recommend action by the assembly on a matter within the committee's concern, it is generally desir-

able, as stated above, for the report to consist of or con-   1
clude with one or more proposed resolutions embodying
the committee's recommendations. Such resolutions
should always be in writing. Although the reporting member in a small assembly may sometimes give accompanying   5
explanations orally, it is usually better to submit a formal
written report if it is to contain anything other than the resolutions themselves. In any event, after giving or reading
the report, the reporting member moves the adoption of
the resolution(s). He may make such a presentation, for ex-   10
ample, as follows:

REPORTING MEMBER (reading written report):

The Buildings and Grounds Committee wishes to report that the club-   15
house roof was extensively damaged by the hurricane last week. The
committee therefore recommends the adoption of the following resolution: "*Resolved,* That the Buildings and Grounds Committee be authorized to request bids for repair of the clubhouse roof and to award
a contract for the same, provided that, without further authorization,   20
the cost shall not exceed $5,000."

George Wilson, Chairman
Mr. President, by direction of [or "on behalf of"] the committee, I
move the adoption of the resolution just read.

                                                          25

The chair then states the question on the resolution,
and it is considered just as any other main motion. If the report contains more than one resolution, the reporting
member makes a single motion for the adoption of them
all, and the rules given on pages 105–106 apply.   30
Although it is not generally the best procedure, a report
may sometimes contain recommendations not in the form
of motions or resolutions. In any case, as stated above, the
recommendations should be placed at the end of the report
even if they have been given separately before. Sometimes   35

1   also, in this connection, it is moved "to adopt the commit-
     tee's recommendation(s)," although, as noted on pages
     486–87, this can lead to confusion as to the precise effect
     of the motion. A better method of treating a committee
5   recommendation that is not in the form of a resolution—in
     a case, for example, where the recommendation is to au-
     thorize a $2,000 expenditure for a personnel consultant's
     fee—is to offer a motion like this: "In accordance with the
     recommendation in the committee's report, I move that
10   the expenditure of $2,000 for a personnel consultant's fee
     be authorized." The reporting member can make such a
     motion after reading the report, or another member can
     obtain the floor to do so. In cases where the committee has
     offered no resolutions embodying its recommendations and
15   the drafting of satisfactory resolution(s) covering them is
     likely to require the further attention of a committee, an-
     other member can move to refer the matter to the same or
     another committee for this purpose.*

         A Report on a Referred Subject on Which No Resolution
20   *or Motion Was Pending.*   If a subject on which no resolu-
     tion or motion was pending has been referred to a com-
     mittee for recommendations, the report usually should
     conclude with one or more resolutions, unless the commit-
     tee recommends that no action be taken. The committee's
25   report on the subject referred to it may be presented, for
     example, thus:

     REPORTING MEMBER (reading written report):

30   The committee that was appointed to recommend a suitable recre-
     ational facility for the Club to donate to the new Runnymede Park
     project finds that no provision has been made for tennis courts. The
     committee therefore recommends the adoption of the following reso-

     ---

     *The motion to refer in such a case is a main motion, since the matter
     being referred is not a pending question (see p. 161).

lution: "*Resolved,* That the Club underwrite the cost of two tennis   *1*
courts to be constructed in Runnymede Park."

Howard Ford, Chairman
Mr. President, on behalf of the committee, I move the adoption of the
resolution just read.   *5*

The resolution is treated as any other main question,
just as in the preceding case dealing with the recommendation of a standing committee. Recommendations not in the
form of resolutions are also handled as described in the pre-   *10*
ceding case.

*A Report on a Resolution Previously Referred to a Com-
mittee.*   When a committee reports on a resolution or
other main question which was referred to it (**13**) or which
the rules require to be considered by it before coming be-   *15*
fore the assembly with the committee's recommendation,
the form of the report and the type of action depends on
the nature of the case, as follows:

• *Recommending adoption, or rejection, or (when a major-*   *20*
  ity of the committee fail to agree) making no recommen-
  dation. Such a report in a small assembly can be given
  orally (provided that the secretary records it in the minutes); for example, thus:

25

REPORTING MEMBER: The committee to which was referred
the resolution, "*Resolved,* That the Federation endorse the so-
called Farnsworth Plan for financing the proposed new school
construction program," recommends that the resolution be
adopted [or "not be adopted"].   *30*

Or:

The committee to which was referred . . . has been unable to
arrive at a recommendation.   *35*

If the resolution is too long to fit into the form given above, a form such as the following may be used:

REPORTING MEMBER: The committee to which was referred the resolution relating to governmental reorganization reports it with the recommendation that it be adopted as referred.

The reporting member should then hand to the chair or the secretary the copy of the resolution that was turned over to the committee.

When the presentation of the report is concluded in each of the above cases, the resolution or main question becomes pending automatically and the chair states the question accordingly, no motion being necessary. If the committee recommends adoption or makes no recommendation, the chair, as soon as the reporting member has resumed his seat, proceeds:

CHAIR: The committee to which was referred the resolution on . . . recommends its adoption [or, "is unable to arrive at a recommendation"]. The resolution is . . . [reading it]. The question is on the adoption of the resolution.

The question is always stated and put on the *adoption* of the resolution (that is, so that a vote of *aye* is a vote in favor of it). Thus, when the committee's recommendation is in the negative, the chair states the question as follows:

CHAIR: The committee to which was referred . . . recommends that it not be adopted. The resolution is . . . [reading it]. The question is on the adoption of the resolution, the recommendation of the committee to the contrary notwithstanding. [Or, simply, "The question is on the adoption of the resolution," in which case the chair may add, "The committee recommends that the resolution be rejected."]

- *Recommending action on a resolution and an amend-* 1
  ment that were pending when referred. If an amendment
  was pending when the resolution was referred, the report can be given orally in a small assembly provided
  that it is recorded in the minutes; and it should first 5
  state the committee's recommendation as to the disposition of the amendment, then as to the disposition of
  the resolution. For example:

> REPORTING MEMBER: The committee to which was referred 10
> the resolution, "*Resolved,* That the proposed expansion of the
> yacht basin be authorized," together with the pending amend-
> ment, "to add the words, 'at a cost not to exceed $150,000,'" rec-
> ommends that the amendment be adopted and that the resolution
> as thus amended be adopted. 15

As in the preceding case, no motions are necessary,
and the chair states the question first on the amendment, and after it is voted on, then on the resolution.
The same principles apply if a primary amendment and 20
a secondary amendment were pending when the resolution was referred. The report should state the committee's recommendations first on the secondary
amendment, then on the primary amendment, and finally on the resolution; and the chair states the ques- 25
tions in that order.

- *Recommending definite or indefinite postponement.* If a
  resolution or other main question is referred to a committee while a motion to postpone it indefinitely is 30
  pending, that motion to *Postpone Indefinitely* (**11**) is ignored by the committee and by the assembly when the
  committee reports. But whether or not such a motion
  was pending at the time of referral, the committee can
  report the main question with a recommendation that it 35

be postponed indefinitely or that it be postponed to a certain time (**14**). Thus, if (a) no amendment was pending at the time of referral, or if (b) an amendment was pending and the committee recommends postponement to a certain time, the reporting member makes a motion for the postponement at the conclusion of his presentation. But if (c) an amendment was pending and the recommendation is for indefinite postponement, the motion to *Postpone Indefinitely* cannot be made until after the amendment has been voted on (see *Order of Precedence of Motions,* **5**). In each of the three cases, the report can be given orally in a small assembly, provided that it is recorded in the minutes, as follows:

a) If no amendment was pending at the time of referral:

> REPORTING MEMBER: The committee to which was referred the resolution, "*Resolved,* That . . . ," recommends, and on behalf of [or "by direction of"] the committee I move, that the resolution be postponed until . . . [or "be postponed indefinitely."].

> The chair then states the question first on the postponement, and if that is voted down, next on the resolution.

b) If an amendment was pending and the recommendation is for postponement to a certain time:

> REPORTING MEMBER: The committee to which was referred the resolution, "*Resolved,* That . . . ," together with the pending amendment [stating the amendment], recommends, and by direction of the committee I move, that the resolution be postponed until . . .

> The chair states the question first on the postponement as in (a); but if that is voted down, the question in this case is next on the amendment, and then on the resolution.

c) If an amendment was pending and the recommen- *1*
dation is for indefinite postponement (in which case
the motion to *Postpone Indefinitely* is not in order
when the report is made):

REPORTING MEMBER: The committee to which was re- *5*
ferred the resolution, "*Resolved,* That . . . ," together with
the pending amendment, [stating the amendment], recommends that the resolution be postponed indefinitely.

The reporting member resumes his seat without *10*
making a motion, and the chair immediately states
the question on the amendment. After it has been
voted on, he can state the question on the indefinite
postponement (thus assuming this motion), or he
can recognize the reporting member to move it by *15*
direction of the committee, and the procedure is
then as in (a) above.

• *Recommending amendments.* When a committee reports back a resolution or paper with amendments that *20*
it proposes, the amendments, at least, should be in writing unless they are very simple. In a small assembly, depending on the complexity of the case, the amendments
can be written out on a separate sheet that is handed to
the chair or the secretary at the conclusion of an oral *25*
presentation, or a more formal written report can be
submitted; the latter procedure should be followed in a
large body. In the report, the resolution can be included
in full and be followed by a statement of the proposed
amendments as in the example below; or, if the resolu- *30*
tion or document is long and copies are available to the
members, the report can contain only the amendments
with enough of the context of the resolution to make
them understood. If no amendment was pending at the
time of referral, the reporting member at the conclusion *35*

of his presentation moves the adoption of the amendments proposed by the committee, making a single motion covering them all. But if an amendment was
pending at the time of referral, the chair (unless the
committee recommends a secondary amendment,
whose adoption the reporting member would first
move) states the question on the referred amendment
first—the reporting member making no motion until
after that amendment has been voted on. The following
example (although equally suitable for treatment by the
method of reporting a substitute as on pp. 506–507) illustrates the presentation of a written report proposing
amendments to a resolution short enough to be read in
full, in a case where no amendment was pending at the
time of referral.

REPORTING MEMBER (reading written report):

The committee to which was referred the resolution relating
to a proposed scholarship in journalism hereby submits its report. The resolution is the following: "*Resolved,* That the Guild
establish a four-year scholarship in journalism at the State University, to be open to sons and daughters of Guild members, the
recipient to be chosen annually by the Board of Directors of the
Guild."

The committee recommends that the resolution be amended
as follows:

1) by striking out the words "four-year scholarship" and
   inserting the words "scholarship covering the last three
   undergraduate years";

2) by striking out the words "to be open to sons and daughters of Guild members"; and

3) by adding the words "upon the recommendation of the
   Dean of the School of Journalism";

and the committee further recommends that, as thus
amended, the resolution be adopted.

Milton Roth, Chairman *1*
[Or (see p. 495):]
Milton Roth
John Harley
Elizabeth Norton *5*
Elwood Quinn

Mr. President, by direction of the committee, I move the adoption of the amendments contained in the report.

After the chair states the question on the adoption *10* of the amendments proposed by the committee, the procedure is by one of the following methods:

a) Normally the chair immediately rereads or calls for a rereading of the first of these amendments, after which it is open to debate and secondary amend- *15* ment. A vote is then taken on the adoption of the first committee amendment, after which the next one is read, and so on. Until all of the committee's amendments have been voted on, no other primary amendments are in order, but only secondary *20* amendments as each committee amendment comes up. After all of the committee's amendments have been acted upon, other amendments which are not precluded by action taken on the committee amendments can be proposed from the floor. *25* When these have been voted on, the chair puts the question on adopting the resolution or paper as amended.*

b) If the amendments may be expected not to occasion debate or secondary amendment—for example, if *30*

---

*The step of taking a vote on the adoption of the entire paper applies only to cases where that paper is *pending*. This step does not apply in the case of a report on a series of amendments to something previously adopted (**35**), such as bylaws that are in effect (see also **57**).

they are reported from a committee of the whole (**52**) where they have already been open to debate and amendment—the chair puts a single question on all of the committee's amendments together, except those for which a member asks for a separate vote, thus: "As many as are in favor of adopting the amendments recommended by the committee, except those for which a separate vote has been asked, say *aye*. ... Those opposed, say *no*. ... " This is called putting the question on the amendments *in gross*. He then takes up the remaining amendments separately in their order.

c) By suspending the rules (**25**) or by unanimous consent (pp. 51–53), the assembly can allow the introduction of a motion to adopt all recommendations in the report, without considering the amendments separately.

• *Recommending a substitute.* If a committee reports back a resolution with a substitute that it recommends for adoption, at least the substitute should be in writing, just as in the case of any other report proposing amendments. If no amendment was pending when the resolution was referred, the reporting member concludes his presentation by making the motion to substitute; for example, thus:

REPORTING MEMBER: The committee to which was referred the resolution, "*Resolved,* That the proceeds from the recent bequest to the Association from the Asquith estate be invested in stock of the Consolidated Development Corporation," recommends that, for the resolution, the following substitute be adopted: "*Resolved,* That the Executive Board be authorized to retain reputable investment counsel with a view to determining appropriate investment of the proceeds from the Asquith bequest."

On behalf of the committee I move that the resolution last read be substituted for the referred resolution.   *1*

The chair then states the question on the motion to substitute. But if amendment(s) were pending when the   *5* resolution was referred, then, before the motion to substitute can be made, the question is first on the secondary amendment if one was pending, then on the primary amendment that was pending. When these amendments have been voted on, the reporting mem-   *10* ber makes the motion to substitute and the chair states the question on it (or the chair can state the question assuming the motion). In any event, the substitute proposed by the committee is treated as in the case of any other motion to substitute (see pp. 146ff.). If the mo-   *15* tion to substitute is lost, the "original" resolution is open to further amendment; but if the motion to substitute is adopted, the resolution thus substituted can be amended only by *adding*. (Regarding substitutes proposed by committees, see also p. 149.)   *20*

In regard to referred questions reported back, see also *Resolutions Committee*, pages 614–15, 619–21.

A Report Containing Only Information.   If the report contains only an account of work done or a statement of   *25* fact or opinion for the assembly's information, it should generally be in writing, and always so if there is any possibility of its adoption by the assembly. Apart from filing such a report, however, no action on it is necessary and usually none should be taken. (See also *Motion to Adopt an Entire*   *30* *Report*, p. 490, and *Conditions for Amendment of a Report by the Assembly Before Its Adoption*, p. 492.)

Membership and Nominating Committee Reports; Reports of Other Kinds of Committees.   When a membership committee reports on names of persons referred to the   *35*

1   committee as applicants for society membership, the report
    can be rendered orally, but a list of the names of the persons
    recommended for membership should be submitted in
    writing. When such a report is made, the chair at once
5   states the question on the admission to membership of the
    candidates recommended by the committee.

    The report of the nominating committee consists of a
    written list of candidates for office, just as in the case of the
    membership committee's report. No vote on the nominat-
10 ing committee's report should be taken, however; the pro-
    cedure is as described in **46**.

    For the handling of the report of an auditing commit-
    tee, see pages 461–62.

    For the report of a committee on bylaws, see **54** and **56**.

15 For the reports of the three principal committees that
    perform parliamentary functions in the organization of a
    convention– the Credentials Committee, the Committee
    on Standing Rules, and the Program Committee—see **59**.

    For the report of an investigating committee appointed
20 under disciplinary procedures, see **61**.

SUMMARY OF TYPES OF REPORTS THAT CAN BE RENDERED ORALLY IN A SMALL ASSEMBLY.

25 As stated on page 493, committee reports should be sub-
    mitted in writing, with the following permissible exceptions
    that apply to very brief reports in a small assembly, provided
    that the secretary records the complete substance of the re-
    port in the minutes as it is given orally:

30
    • With respect to a resolution or main question that was
      referred while pending:

    1) If the committee report consists only of a recom-
35   mendation as to the disposition of the referred res-

olution or motion, the report can be given orally if
implementation of the recommendation involves:

   a) no further motion, as when the committee rec
      ommends that the referred resolution or motion
      be adopted, or rejected; or

   b) the introduction of a subsidiary motion that can
      be made orally, as when the committee recom
      mends that the referred resolution be postponed
      definitely or indefinitely, or be amended by the
      change of only a few words.

2) If an amendment or a primary and a secondary
amendment were pending with a resolution or main
question that was referred and the committee has
no new amendments to propose, the report can also
usually be oral, in which case the reporting member
simply states the committee's recommendation as to
the adoption or rejection, first, of the secondary
amendment, and then of the primary amendment,
and finally its recommendation as to the disposition
of the resolution or main motion—all before any of
the referred questions are voted on.

3) When the committee wishes to propose amendments, the amendments themselves should always
be in writing if they involve more than a few words;
but the complete report—that is, the declaration on
behalf of the committee that it recommends the
amendments—can be oral or written depending on
the complexity of statement required by the resulting parliamentary situation.

• If a subject that was not in the form of a pending resolution or motion was referred to a committee for recommendations, and if the committee in its report
presents the recommendations in one or more resolutions offered with no comment, only the resolutions

1 need be in writing and the statement that the committee recommends their adoption can be given orally.

ACTION REQUIRED BY A PARTIAL REPORT.   A
5 partial report of a committee is handled in the same way as the final report. If it is a progress report only, with no recommendations or conclusions, it is treated as any other report for information only, and no action need be taken. But if the partial report recommends action, the question is put
10 on adopting its proposed resolutions, or its recommendations, or the report itself, just as if it were the final report. A committee can be discharged (**36**) by a majority vote at the time at which it makes a partial report.

15 FORMAL EXPRESSION OF MINORITY VIEW ("MINORITY REPORT").   The formal presentation of a so-called "minority report"—that is, the presentation of an expression of views in the name of a group of committee members not concurring with the committee report—is
20 usually allowed by the assembly when such permission is requested, as explained below. Regardless of whether a minority report is submitted, however, the report adopted by vote of a majority in the committee should always be referred to as "the committee report," never "the majority
25 report."

Nature of Committee Minority's Rights with Respect to Reports.   As indicated above, the formal presentation of a "minority report" is a privilege that the assembly may accord, not a matter of right—since the appointment of the
30 committee implies that the assembly is primarily interested in the findings of the majority of the committee's members. But in debate on any written or oral report in the assembly, any member of the reporting committee who does not concur has the same right as any other member of the assembly
35 to speak individually in opposition. No one can make allu-

sion in the assembly to what has occurred during the delib- 1
erations of the committee, however, unless it is by report of
the committee or by unanimous consent.

Form of Minority Report; Minority Recommendations.
A "minority report" in writing may begin: 5

> The undersigned, a minority of the committee ap-
> pointed to . . . , not agreeing with the majority, desire
> to express their views in the case. . . .

If the committee report concludes with a proposed res- 10
olution, the minority can (a) recommend rejection of the
resolution; (b) recommend amendment of it; or (c) recommend adoption of some other suitable motion designed to
dispose of the resolution appropriately.

If the committee report is for information only, the 15
views of the minority may be similarly constructed or may
conclude with a motion.

Reception of Minority Report. When the minority of a
committee wishes to make a formal presentation of its
views, it is customary, unless the assembly refuses permis- 20
sion, to receive its report immediately after the report of the
committee. In such a case, the member presenting the committee report can properly notify the assembly that the minority wishes to submit its views in a separate report. As
soon as the chair has stated the appropriate question on the 25
committee report, he should call for the minority presentation unless someone objects, in which case he should put
the question on the report's being received. A majority vote
is required to receive a minority report; the question is undebatable. 30

When the minority report is presented, it is for information, and it cannot be acted upon except by a motion to
substitute it for the report of the committee. Whether
the views of the minority are formally presented or not,
however, any member can move that resolutions proposed 35

1 by the committee be amended, or that they be postponed indefinitely, or that some other appropriate action be taken.

5 INDICATING AGREEMENT WITH A REPORT EXCEPT IN A SPECIFIED PARTICULAR.   If a written report of a committee is signed by all who concur and a committee member is in agreement with the report except in one particular, he can, after all who agree to the report *10* have signed, add a statement that he concurs with the report except the part that he specifies, and then sign the statement—regardless of whether a minority report is to be submitted. Similarly, a committee member who agrees with most of a minority report can sign it with an added note in-*15* dicating what he does not agree with, just as in the case of a committee report. If the committee members in the minority do not agree, the assembly can allow more than one minority report to be submitted.

20 ## §52. COMMITTEE OF THE WHOLE AND ITS ALTERNATE FORMS

The *committee of the whole* and its two alternate forms, the *quasi committee of the whole* (or *consideration as if in* *25* *committee of the whole*) and *informal consideration,* are devices that enable the full assembly to give detailed consideration to a matter under conditions of freedom approximating those of a committee. Under each of these three procedures, any member can speak in debate on the *30* main question or any amendment—for the same length of time as allowed by the assembly's rules—as often as he is able to get the floor. As under the regular rules of debate, however, he cannot speak another time on the same question so long as a member who has not spoken on it is seek-*35* ing the floor.

Each of these three devices is best suited to assemblies *1*
of a particular range in size and provides a different degree
of protection against disorderliness and its possible consequences—which are risked when each member is allowed
to speak an unlimited number of times in debate, such risk *5*
increasing in proportion to the size of the assembly.
With respect to this type of protection, the essential distinctions between the three procedures may be summarized as follows:

10

- In a *committee of the whole,* which is suited to *large assemblies,* the results of votes taken are not final decisions of the assembly, but have the status of
recommendations which the assembly is given the opportunity to consider further and which it votes on *15*
finally under its regular rules. Also, a chairman of
the committee of the whole is appointed and the
regular presiding officer leaves the chair, so that, by
being disengaged from any difficulties that may arise in
the committee, he may be in a better position to pre- *20*
side effectively during the final consideration by the
assembly.
- In the *quasi committee of the whole,* which is convenient
in *meetings of medium size* (about 50 to 100 members),
the results of votes taken are reported to the assembly *25*
for final consideration under the regular rules, just as
with a committee of the whole. But in this case the presiding officer of the assembly remains in the chair and
presides.
- *Informal consideration,* which is suited to *small meet- *30*
ings of ordinary societies,* simply removes the normal
limitations on the number of times members can speak
in debate, as stated in the first paragraph of this section.
The regular presiding officer remains in the chair; and
the results of votes taken during informal consideration *35*

1   are decisions of the assembly, which are not voted on
     again.

     The complete rules governing committees of the whole,
5   proceedings in quasi committee of the whole, and informal
     consideration are given below.

Committee of the Whole

10   Although the committee of the whole is not used ex-
     tensively except in legislative bodies, it is the oldest of the
     three devices described above and is the prototype from
     which the other two are derived. Unlike the processes of
     quasi committee of the whole and informal consideration, a
15   committee of the whole is a real committee in the parlia-
     mentary sense. Therefore, during the time that a meeting is
     "in committee of the whole," even though the committee
     consists of the entire body of members in attendance at the
     assembly's meeting, it is technically not "the assembly."
20   The parliamentary steps in making use of a committee
     of the whole are essentially the same as those involved in re-
     ferring a subject to an ordinary committee. The assembly
     votes to go into a committee of the whole (which is equiv-
     alent to voting to refer the matter to the committee), and a
25   chairman of the committee is appointed. The committee
     considers the referred matter, adopts a report to be made to
     the assembly, then votes to "rise and report." Finally, the
     committee chairman presents the report and the assembly
     considers the committee's recommendations—all as in the
30   case of an ordinary committee.

     GOING INTO COMMITTEE OF THE WHOLE.
     As implied above, the motion to go into a committee of the
     whole is a form of the motion to commit (**13**). When it is
35   moved as a subsidiary motion—that is, when it is applied to

a pending question—it takes precedence over all other forms of the subsidiary motion to *Commit*. The motion is made as follows:

MEMBER (obtaining the floor): I move to go into a committee of the whole [or, "I move that the assembly now resolve itself into a committee of the whole"] to consider the pending question [or "to take under consideration . . . (stating the subject)"]. (Second.)

Instructions to the committee of the whole can be included in this motion of referral.

If the motion of referral to the committee of the whole is adopted, the presiding officer immediately calls another member to the chair—frequently, but not necessarily, the vice-president—and takes his place as **a** member of the committee. In large assemblies, the secretary may also leave his seat, the committee chairman may preside from that position, and an assistant secretary may act as secretary of the committee. For the committee's use until it reports, its secretary should keep a temporary memorandum of the business it transacts, but the committee's proceedings are not entered in the minutes of the assembly. Those minutes should carry only the same kind of record of the referral to a committee of the whole, the committee's report, and the assembly's action on the report, as if the committee had been an ordinary one.

CONDUCT OF BUSINESS.   Like ordinary committees, a committee of the whole cannot alter the text of any resolution referred to it; but it can propose amendments, which it must report in the form of recommendations to the assembly. Amendments to a resolution *originating in the committee* are in order, however; and if such amendments are adopted within the committee, they are incorporated in the resolution before it is reported to the assembly for action.

1   A committee of the whole is under the rules of the assembly, except as follows:

1) The only motions that are in order in a committee of
5   the whole are to adopt (within the committee, for inclusion in its report), to amend (what it is proposed to report), and to "rise" or "rise and report"*—except that, among the incidental motions, a point of order (**23**) can be raised, an appeal from the decision of the
10   chair (**24**) can be made, a division of the assembly (**29**) can be called for, and applicable requests and inquiries (**32, 33**) can be made.
2) In debate on motions to adopt or amend, unless a limit is prescribed by the assembly before it goes into com-
15   mittee of the whole as explained below, each member can speak an unlimited number of times under the rules given in the first paragraph of this section.**

If the committee of the whole wishes action to be taken
20 which requires the adoption of any motion other than those that are in order in the committee as listed in (1) above, it must vote to rise and report a recommendation that the assembly take the desired action (see below). The motion to

---

*As applied to committees in general, the word *rise* simply describes the parliamentary step of ceasing to function as a committee, preparatory to making a report. As stated on page 484, the motion to rise is not used in ordinary standing committees, and in ordinary special committees it is used only when the committee is ready to make its final report and go out of existence. In a committee of the whole, on the other hand, the word *rise* applies to any case of the committee's returning to the status of the assembly—whether it is expected to be temporarily or permanently.

**Appeals in committee of the whole are debatable under the same rules as in the assembly—that is, each member (except the chair) can speak only once in debate on them.

rise is undebatable and cannot be amended, and it is always
in order in committee of the whole, except during voting or
verifying a vote and when another member has the floor.

Among the consequences of the rules stated in the preceding paragraph are the following:

- A committee of the whole cannot appoint subcommittees or refer a matter to another (ordinary) committee.
- An appeal from the decision of the chair must be voted
  on directly, since it cannot be postponed or laid on the
  table in the committee.
- The only way for debate to be closed or limited in the
  committee is for the assembly to specify such conditions
  before going into committee of the whole. If the committee develops a desire to have debate limited, it can
  only do so by rising and requesting the assembly to impose the desired limits, as explained below. If debate has
  been closed at a particular time by order of the assembly, the committee does not have the power, even by
  unanimous consent, to extend the time.
- A roll-call vote or a vote by ballot cannot be ordered in
  a committee of the whole, nor can a counted rising vote
  be ordered except by the chair.
- A committee of the whole has no power to impose disciplinary measures (**61**) on its members, but can only
  report the facts to the assembly. If the committee becomes disorderly and its chairman loses control of it,
  the presiding officer of the assembly should take the
  chair and declare the committee dissolved.
- A committee of the whole cannot adjourn or recess, but
  must rise in order that the assembly may do so.

RISING AND REPORTING.   When a committee of
the whole has completed its consideration of the matter referred to it, or when it wishes to bring the meeting to an

1 end, or wishes the assembly to take any other action requiring the adoption of a motion which is not in order in the committee, the committee rises and reports.

If the committee originates a resolution, it concludes by
5 voting to report the resolution, as perfected. If a resolution was referred to the committee, however, it votes only on any amendments that it will recommend, not on the resolution, which it reports back to the assembly with the recommended amendments. On a motion, or by unanimous
10 consent, the committee rises and the presiding officer of the assembly resumes the chair. The committee chairman returns to a place in the assembly in front of the presiding officer, at which, standing, he addresses the chair:

15   COMMITTEE CHAIRMAN: Mr. President, the committee of the whole has had under consideration . . . [describing the resolution or other matter] and has directed me to report the same as follows: . . .

The sample reports in the subsection *Manner of Presen-*
20 *tation and Disposition of Committee Reports in Particular Cases* (pp. 496ff.) may be used as guides for reporting similar cases from a committee of the whole, and the procedures for disposing of such reports as described in the same pages are likewise applicable. If no amendments are re-
25 ported, the chair states the question on the resolution that was referred to the committee or that it recommends for adoption; and this question is then open to debate and amendment in the assembly. If amendments proposed by the committee are reported, the committee chairman reads
30 them and hands the paper to the chair, who reads them again or has the secretary do so. The chair then states and puts the question on all of the committee's amendments in gross (that is, taken together), unless a member asks for a separate vote on one or more of them. If so, a single vote is
35 taken on all of the other amendments, and then the ques-

tion is stated separately on each of the amendments for
which a separate vote was asked. These amendments can be
further debated and amended in the assembly, as can the
main question after action on all the committee's amendments—under the same rules as when any other committee
reports.

If the committee, to facilitate completion of its work,
wishes the assembly to take an action outside the committee's powers that requires the adoption of an undebatable
motion—for example, to limit debate in the committee—a
motion to rise should be made in a form like the following:

MEMBER (obtaining the floor): I move that the committee rise and
request that debate be limited . . . [specifying the desired limitation].
(Second.)

If this motion is adopted, the committee chairman reports to the assembly as follows:

COMMITTEE CHAIRMAN: Mr. President, the committee of the whole
has had under consideration . . . [describing the referred matter] and
has come to no conclusion thereon, but asks permission [or "leave"]
to continue sitting with debate limited . . . [specifying the limitation].

The presiding officer then puts the question on granting the request, and if the result is affirmative, the committee chairman resumes the chair.

A committee of the whole can also rise, before completing its work, to request instructions, in which case the
nature or wording of the request should be agreed to before the motion to rise is made.

If the committee wishes to bring its proceedings to an
end because it believes the matter can be better handled
under the assembly's rules, or because it wishes the meeting
to be adjourned, the motion to rise can be made in this form:

1   MEMBER (obtaining the floor): I move that the committee rise.
(Second.)

The committee chairman then reports:

5

COMMITTEE CHAIRMAN: The committee of the whole has had
under consideration . . . [describing the matter] and has come to no
conclusion thereon.

10   With such a report, the committee passes out of existence unless the assembly directs it to sit again. In this connection, however, the committee in reporting can "ask
permission to sit again," with or without specifying a time;
and in granting such a request, the assembly can make the
15   sitting a general order or a special order (**41**) for a particular time. If the assembly grants the committee permission to
sit again without specifying a time, the sitting is unfinished
business. A committee of the whole cannot itself arrange a
future meeting.

20   If an hour for adjournment has been preset in the assembly and it arrives while the meeting is in committee of
the whole, the committee chairman announces, "The hour
for adjournment of the assembly has arrived and the committee will rise." The committee chairman then reports that
25   the committee has come to no conclusion on the referred
matter, as described in the preceding paragraph.

QUORUM IN COMMITTEE OF THE WHOLE.
The quorum of a committee of the whole is the same as
30   that of the assembly unless the bylaws provide, or the assembly establishes, a different quorum for the committee.
If the bylaws do not provide a different quorum for the
committee, the assembly can establish one in the particular
case before going into committee of the whole, regardless
35   of the quorum that the bylaws require for the assembly. If

at any time the committee finds itself without a quorum, it
must rise and report the fact to the assembly. If the assembly itself is thereupon without a quorum, it must then adjourn or take one of the other courses that are open in the
absence of a quorum (pp. 336–37).

Quasi Committee of the Whole
(Consideration As If in Committee of the Whole)

A somewhat simpler version of the committee of the
whole, in effect, is the procedure of consideration in quasi
committee of the whole (or consideration as if in committee of the whole), which is convenient in assemblies of
medium size. In contrast to a committee of the whole, the
quasi committee of the whole is not a real committee, but
is "the assembly acting as if in committee of the whole."

GOING INTO QUASI COMMITTEE OF THE
WHOLE.   The motion to consider in quasi committee of
the whole takes precedence over all other forms of the motion to *Commit* (**13**) except the motion to go into a (real)
committee of the whole, to which it yields. The motion for
consideration in quasi committee is made in a form like this:

MEMBER (obtaining the floor): I move that the resolution be considered in quasi committee of the whole [or "be considered as if in
committee of the whole"]. (Second.)

This motion is debatable as to the desirability of going
into quasi committee, just as any other motion to *Commit*.
If it is adopted, the chair concludes his announcement of
the result of the vote as follows:

CHAIR (after declaring the voting result): The resolution is before
the assembly as if in committee of the whole.

1   The presiding officer of the assembly does not appoint
a chairman of the quasi committee, but remains in the chair
himself throughout its proceedings. The assembly's secretary should keep a temporary memorandum of the business
5   transacted in quasi committee; but, just as in the case of a
real committee of the whole, the minutes of the assembly
should carry only a record of the report from quasi committee and the action thereon, as shown below.

10   CONDUCT OF BUSINESS.   In the quasi committee
of the whole, the main question and any amendments that
may be proposed are open to debate under the same rules
as in a real committee of the whole—each member being allowed to speak an unlimited number of times as explained
15   on page 512. In contrast to the case of a real committee of
the whole, however, any motion that would be in order in
the assembly is also in order in the quasi committee, where
it is debatable only to the extent permitted under the assembly's rules. But if any motion except an amendment is
20   adopted, it automatically puts an end to the proceedings in
quasi committee. Thus, for example, if a motion to refer the
main question to an ordinary committee is made in quasi
committee of the whole, such a motion to *Commit* would
be equivalent to the following series of motions if the mat-
25   ter were being considered in a real committee of the whole:
(1) that the committee of the whole rise; (2) that the committee of the whole be discharged from further consideration of the subject; and (3) that the question be referred to
an ordinary committee.
30

REPORTING.   The motion to rise is not used in
quasi committee of the whole. If the quasi committee is not
brought to an end as described in the preceding paragraph,
then, when no further amendments are offered in response
35   to the chair's call for them, the presiding officer immedi-

ately proceeds to report to the assembly and to state the
question on the amendments as follows:

> CHAIR: The assembly, acting as if in committee of the whole, has
> had under consideration . . . [describing the resolution] and has made
> the following amendments . . . [reading them]. The question is on the
> adoption of the amendments.

The proceedings in a quasi committee of the whole are
thus concluded, and from this point the procedure is the
same as in disposing of the report of a real committee of the
whole (pp. 518–20)—the chair putting the question on the
reported amendments in gross, except those for which a
separate vote may be asked, and so on.

Informal Consideration

As explained above, if a question is considered in either
a real committee of the whole or in quasi committee of the
whole, the recommendations of the committee or quasi
committee must be reported to the assembly and then the
assembly must take action on these recommendations. In
ordinary societies whose meetings are not large, a much
simpler method is to consider the question informally,
which in effect only suspends the rule limiting the number
of times a member can speak in debate on the main question and any amendments to it.

When it is desired to consider a question informally, a
member makes the motion that this be done:

> MEMBER (obtaining the floor): I move that the question be con-
> sidered informally. (Second.)

This motion ranks just below the motion "to consider
as if in committee of the whole," which in turn ranks just

1 below the motion "to go into committee of the whole," as
stated above. This is a variation of the motion to *Commit,*
and can be debated only as to the desirability of considering the question informally. If the motion is adopted, the
5 chair announces the result thus:

> CHAIR (after declaring the voting result): The question is now
> open to informal consideration. There is no limit to the number of
> times a member can speak on the question or any amendment.

10

The "informal" aspect of the consideration applies only
to the number of speeches allowed in debate on the main
question and its amendments; all votes are formal, and any
other motion that is made is under the regular rules of de-
15 bate. In contrast to the case of a committee of the whole or
quasi committee of the whole, the proceedings under informal consideration are recorded in the assembly's minutes, just as they would be if the consideration were formal.
While considering a question informally the assembly can,
20 by a two-thirds vote, limit the number or length of
speeches, or in any other way limit or close debate. As soon
as the main question is disposed of, temporarily or permanently, the informal consideration automatically ceases
without any motion or vote.
25 Before the main question is disposed of, the informal
consideration can be brought to an end, if desired, by
adopting by majority vote a motion "that the regular rules
of debate be in force," or "that the question be considered
formally."

30

Aids to the Crystallization of Opinion

The more traditional aids to the crystallization of opinion in societies have been, simply, to take a *Recess* or to refer
35 the matter to a committee—often a large committee com-

posed of members representing differing views in the society, such as a committee of the whole or one of its alternate forms. In more recent years, a practice has developed of establishing breakout groups with every member in attendance being urged to participate in a group. Each breakout group, of which there may be many, is usually kept small—frequently ten or twelve persons—and a moderator is appointed for each group. Often, the groups meet during a recess or adjournment of the assembly. Sometimes, the conclusions reached by the various breakout groups are conveyed to a committee that assembles them and attempts to report a consolidated response to the assembly. At other times, the breakout groups report through their moderators directly to the assembly after it has been reconvened and the matter under consideration is again pending. These reports are in the nature of debate. Whatever method is used, in the end, the pending measure must be returned to the full assembly for final consideration under normal parliamentary procedure—just as in the case of a referred question reported back by a committee—and the assembly must make the final decision, if whatever is to purport to be a product of the assembly is to be valid as the assembly's act.

MASS MEETINGS; ORGANIZATION OF A PERMANENT SOCIETY

§53. MASS MEETINGS

Distinguishing Characteristics of a Mass Meeting

A *mass meeting,* as understood in parliamentary law, is a meeting of an unorganized group, which in a publicized or selectively distributed notice known as the *call* of the meeting—has been announced:

- as called to take appropriate action on a particular problem or toward a particular purpose stated by the meeting's sponsors, and
- as open to everyone interested in the stated problem or purpose (or to everyone within a specified sector of the population thus interested).

To the extent that persons in the invited category are clearly identifiable—as, for example, registered voters of a particular political party, or residents of a certain area—only such persons have the right to make motions, to speak, and

to vote at the meeting, and none others need be admitted 1
if the sponsors so choose. In any event, a mass meeting is
convened—and those who attend are admitted—upon the
implied understanding that the sponsors (who have engaged the hall and assumed the expenses of promoting the 5
meeting) have the right to have the proceedings confined
to the overall object they have announced; but that the entire assembly (which is made up of persons whose help the
sponsors are seeking) has the right to determine the action
to be taken in pursuit of the stated object. With respect to 10
this limitation of the right of attendance—or, at least, of
participation—to persons in general sympathy with the announced object of the meeting, a mass meeting differs from
a "town meeting," a public forum, a "lecture-and-
discussion-period" type of meeting, or an open hearing 15
held by an instrumentality of government.

Organization of a Mass Meeting

CALL OF THE MEETING.   The call or announce- 20
ment of a mass meeting should specify the date, hour, and
place of the meeting, its purpose, and—where applicable—
who is invited to attend. It may also carry an identification
of the sponsorship. Depending on the funds available and
the people to be reached, the call can be given the desired 25
publicity or distribution by whatever means are expected to
be most effective—announcements in the newspapers or by
radio or television, a web site, mailings, posters, handbills or
flyers, or the like.

30

PREPARATION.   While a mass meeting should be
conducted so as to accord the assembly its proper role in
determining the outcome as described above, at the same
time, a certain amount of planning by the sponsors is advisable to avoid the risk of the meeting's foundering. 35

1   Before the meeting, the sponsors should agree on the
following:

- whom they prefer for its chairman;
5 - who shall call the meeting to order and nominate their
  choice of chairman;
- who shall be nominated for secretary and by whom;
- what rules—if any—shall be proposed for adoption; and
- who shall make the initial talk explaining the purpose of
10   the meeting.

(See also the detailed discussion of these steps below.)

   The person chosen as chairman should be competent as
15 a presiding officer and in sympathy with the object of the
meeting, and it is an advantage if he personally knows many
of the people who may attend. Depending on conditions, it
is sometimes good policy to have a set of resolutions drafted
in advance to submit to the meeting. Provision should also
20 be made for occupying the time of the gathering in the
event that resolutions are referred to a committee—or a
committee is assigned to draft them (see below).

25   THE "MEMBERSHIP" OF A MASS MEETING.   At
a mass meeting, the "membership" consists of all persons in
the invited category who attend. If no qualification was
placed in the call, anyone who attends is regarded as a
member and has the same rights as members in other as-
30 semblies—to make motions, to speak in debate, and to
vote. If the call specified only a particular category of persons as invited and if no attempt is made to screen the attendance at the door, anyone attending is presumed to be
entitled to participate as a member, subject only to his sub-
35 sequent identification to the contrary. If only those invited

are admitted, anyone legitimately admitted has the rights of *1*
a member, and a person who is discovered to have entered
fraudulently can be asked to leave.

RULES IN A MASS MEETING. Mass meetings *5*
frequently operate with no formally adopted rules, upon
the assumption that the meeting will proceed according
to the common parliamentary law—or that any differences of opinion on procedural questions can be resolved
by citing a recognized parliamentary manual as persuasive *10*
(see pp. 3, 16). Depending on the probable character of
the assembly, however, it may be wise to adopt a standard
parliamentary authority, which can be done by a majority
vote on the motion of a member—made, as prearranged
by the sponsors, immediately after the election of the sec- *15*
retary (see below). Other rules are seldom necessary at a
mass meeting unless it is desired to modify the general
rules (pp. 375–77) as to the allowable length and number
of speeches. If such a modification is desired, the assembly can adopt a standing rule covering the desired provi- *20*
sions at the same time as it adopts the parliamentary
authority, or at a later time. In regard to the vote required
for their adoption, or suspension, standing rules of a mass
meeting (or a series of mass meetings) are similar to
standing rules of a convention as described on pages *25*
600–602.

In any event, without adoption at a mass meeting and regardless of what rules the meeting may adopt, the provisions
of the call, specifying the meeting's purpose and those invited
to attend it, have a force equivalent to bylaws of an organized *30*
society; that is, they define the subject matter within which
motions or resolutions are in order, and determine who have
the right to participate as members (see also pp. 531–32).
This effect is a consequence of the sponsors' rights as explained in the first paragraph of this section. *35*

1   Any person at a mass meeting who, after being advised, persists in an obvious attempt to divert the meeting to a different purpose from that for which it was called, or who otherwise tries to disrupt the proceedings, becomes subject
5   to the disciplinary procedures described in **61.**

OPENING OF THE MEETING; ELECTION OF OFFICERS.   A chairman and a secretary are in general the only officers required by a mass meeting. Their election
10   takes place immediately after the meeting is called to order, a convenient method of electing them being by voice vote. As explained in **46,** the first person nominated is voted on first under this method. In the interest of electing competent persons, it is therefore advisable that a name chosen by
15   the sponsors be placed in nomination first for each office. Additional nominations can be made from the floor and the assembly can elect anyone it wishes, but except under unusual circumstances it is likely to elect the apparent choices of the sponsors.

20   Although the person who calls the meeting to order can call for nominations for chairman, and another can nominate the sponsors' choice, it is proper—and simpler—for one person to perform both functions (see *Nominations by the Chair,* p. 417). In the latter case, at the scheduled hour
25   or shortly thereafter, this person steps to the chair and, after waiting or signaling for quiet, says, "The meeting will come to order. I nominate Mr. A for chairman of this meeting." After any additional nominations from the floor, the chair puts the question on each name in succession, beginning
30   with the one he placed in nomination himself, as described under *Viva-Voce Election,* pages 427–29.

When the chairman of the meeting has been elected, he takes the chair and may say a few words of acknowledgment if he wishes, after which he says, "Nominations are now in
35   order for secretary of this meeting." The person agreed

upon to nominate the sponsors' choice for secretary should
promptly place that name in nomination; members can also
make additional nominations. The secretary is elected viva
voce in the same manner as the chairman. When the secretary has been elected, he should take his seat near the chairman and keep a record of the proceedings. If additional
officers are desired, they can be elected in the same way.

Transaction of Business Specified in the Call

EXPLANATION OF THE MEETING'S PURPOSE.
When the elections are completed, the chair says, "The Secretary will now read the call of this meeting." This reading
of the call should include the names of the sponsors. The
chair then recognizes the person who is to explain the purpose of the meeting more fully, or the chairman gives this
presentation himself if he has been selected to do so.

RESOLUTIONS TO ACCOMPLISH THE PUR-
POSE.   After the purpose of the meeting has been explained, it is in order for a member to offer a resolution, or
a series of resolutions, to accomplish this purpose; or, if believed more suitable to the conditions, it can be moved that
a committee be appointed to draft such resolution(s).

If the plan is for the resolution(s) to be offered immediately after the initial explanation, they can have been prepared
in advance—with double-spaced reproduced copies for distribution to those in attendance—and a preselected member can
now move their adoption. (For considerations to be observed
in the drafting of resolutions, see *The Framing of Main Motions,* pp. 99–106.) After another member has seconded the
resolution(s), the chair states the question on them, they are
open to debate and amendment, and the assembly proceeds
to consider them, the entire procedure being as described in
4 and (for a series of resolutions) on pages 105–106.

In stating the question, the chair should make sure that those present understand the means by which the assembly can modify the proposals contained in the resolutions, and should provide such explanations as he believes necessary (see pp. 108–11). With reference to the proposal of substitutes or other amendments—or alternative resolutions if those first introduced are rejected—any motion within the scope of the meeting's purpose as announced in the call is in order; but any motion outside of or contrary to that purpose is out of order. For example, if the announced purpose of a mass meeting is to oppose the construction of a proposed airport in a particular location, any motion or resolution directed toward preventing the airport's construction can be brought up at the meeting; but a motion whose effect would be to endorse the airport construction project is out of order.

The rules governing the assignment of the floor and debate, as given in **42** and **43**, are generally applicable. In a mass meeting, however, there is no appeal from the chair's decision in assigning the floor. The rule requiring the assembly's permission to speak for longer than ten minutes at a time in debate on pending questions applies if the meeting has adopted no other rule.

RESOLUTIONS DRAFTED BY A COMMITTEE APPOINTED AT THE MEETING.

If resolutions have not been prepared in advance, a committee should be appointed at the meeting to draft them. Such a procedure is appropriate when it is believed advisable to obtain expressions of opinion from persons who attend the meeting, before attempting to frame resolutions. In a small mass meeting, the chair at his discretion can permit those present to make brief statements of this nature after the initial explanation of the meeting's purpose and before the motion to appoint the committee is made. In that case, the chair should specify the time to be allowed each member—which is a matter entirely under the chair's control unless the meeting has adopted a special rule, since the procedure is in effect a relaxation of the general parliamentary rule prohibiting speeches when no question is pending (see pp. 32–33). In any event, the same kind of discussion can also take place in regular debate on the motion to appoint the committee, since it is relevant to the committee's instructions to draft resolution(s) "expressing the sense of the meeting" on the specified subject, as explained below.

The person who is to make the motion to appoint the committee should be agreed upon by the sponsors in advance, as well as the matter of whether preliminary discussion is to be permitted before the motion is made. The motion may be made in a form such as the following:

MEMBER (obtaining the floor): I move that a committee of five be appointed by the chair to draft resolutions expressing the sense of this meeting on ... [the subject for which the meeting was called]. (Second.)

This is a main motion, since it is made when no question is pending. It is debatable and amendable and can have any subsidiary motion applied to it.

In a mass meeting it is usually advisable to have all committees appointed by the chair—assuming that the chairman has been well chosen. If the assembly prefers a different method of appointment, however, the procedures that can be followed are as described in **50.** When the committee has been appointed, it should immediately retire and prepare the resolution(s).

During the committee's absence from the hall, the assembly can attend to any other business related to the object of the meeting; or it can occupy the time in listening to talks, in engaging in forums or seminar-type discussions, or in watching a relevant film; or it can recess (**20**).

If the assembly does not recess and the chair sees the committee return to the room, he should ask, as soon as the

1   pending business is disposed of (or as soon as the person giving a talk closes, etc.), "Is the committee that was appointed to draft resolutions prepared to report?"

When the committee chairman has answered affirma-
5   tively, the chair says, "If there is no objection, the meeting will now hear the committee's report. [Pause.] The chair recognizes the chairman of the committee appointed to draft resolutions." (See treatment of *unanimous consent,* pp. 51–53.)

10 If the chair does not notice the committee's return, the committee chairman, at the first opportunity, obtains the floor and says, "The committee appointed to draft resolutions is prepared to report." Unless objection is then made, the chair directs the committee chairman to proceed. If
15 anyone objects, the chair puts the question on the report's being received (see pp. 495–96).

The committee chairman, addressing the presiding officer of the assembly, presents the report as follows:

20 COMMITTEE CHAIRMAN: Madam President, the committee appointed to draft resolutions recommends, and on behalf of the committee I move, the adoption of the following resolution(s) . . . [reading them].

On the presentation of this report, the committee is dis-
25 charged automatically. The chair then states the question on the resolutions, and they are considered in the same way as summarized above for the case in which resolutions are offered by a member from the floor (see also **51**).

30 ## Adjournment

In a mass meeting, unless a time for another meeting has already been set (by adopting a motion to *Fix the Time to Which to Adjourn,* **22,** or by adopting temporary rules as
35 described below), a motion to adjourn is not in order while business is pending (see pp. 225–27).

When the business for which the mass meeting was
called has apparently been completed and no question is
pending, someone should move "to adjourn," or the chair
can call for such a motion. Unless a time has been set for another meeting, the adoption of this motion dissolves the assembly—so that, as explained in **21**, it is a main motion and
can be debated and amended just as any other main motion.
An example of an amendment to a main motion "to adjourn" might be "to add the words 'until eight o'clock
Wednesday evening,'" which would thereby include in the
motion a provision to set a time for another meeting.

In cases where it is desired to close the meeting before
its business has been completed, the rules are as follows:

a) If the time for another meeting has already been set, the
motion to adjourn is privileged, just as in a meeting of
an ordinary permanent society, and is subject to the
rules given in **21.**

b) If no time has been set for another meeting and a question is pending, a motion to *Fix the Time to Which to
Adjourn* (**22**) should first be moved and adopted, after
which the privileged motion to *Adjourn* (**21**) is in
order; the procedure is as shown on page 238, line 15
to page 239, line 6.

c) If no time has been set for another meeting and no
question is pending, any member can move, for example, "to adjourn until eight o'clock Wednesday
evening," which is a main motion.

When a motion to adjourn a mass meeting has been
adopted and no time is set for another meeting, the chair
should say, "The ayes have it and the meeting is adjourned." This announcement in effect declares the assembly dissolved. If a time for an adjourned meeting has been
set, on the other hand—either previously or by means of a
provision included in the motion to adjourn—the chair an-

nounces the result by saying, "The ayes have it and this
meeting is [or "stands"] adjourned until eight o'clock
Wednesday evening." Before declaring the adjournment,
or even taking a vote on adjourning, the chair should
make sure that all necessary announcements have been
made.

Series of Mass Meetings; Temporary Society

If more than one mass meeting is necessary to achieve a
certain objective, or if the group is working toward the formation of an organized society, a temporary organization to
continue beyond a single mass meeting may become necessary. If so, the officers elected at the first meeting are designated *chairman pro tem* and *secretary pro tem*—although the
words *pro tem* are not used in addressing these officers. If a
permanent society is the aim of the group, the temporary officers serve until the election of permanent officers. If special
rules were not adopted at the first meeting, a committee on
rules can be appointed to recommend a few rules, providing
for the hour and place for holding the meetings, the number
and length of speeches allowed (if the general rules given on
pp. 375–77 are not satisfactory), and a work on parliamentary law to be used as parliamentary authority. If such rules
specify periodic dates on which meetings are to be held, each
meeting is a separate session (**8**) as in an ordinary society; but
if the time of each succeeding meeting is set at the previous
meeting or is "at the call of the chair," the entire series of
meetings constitutes a single session.

§54. ORGANIZATION OF A
PERMANENT SOCIETY

When it is desired to form a permanent society, the or-
ganizers proceed in much the same way as for a mass meeting, except that the meetings while the organization is

being formed should usually be carefully limited to persons
whose interest in the project is known. For this reason, it
may be desirable to solicit attendance for these meetings by
personal contact or by letter, rather than by public announcement.

First Organizational Meeting

The first meeting, at which the business portion should
be kept brief, sometimes follows a luncheon or dinner. At
these meetings for purposes of organization, the call to
order can be delayed a few minutes beyond the scheduled
time, if desired.

ELECTION OF TEMPORARY OFFICERS, AND
INTRODUCTORY TALKS.   When the person designated for the purpose has called the meeting to order, he
announces, "the first business is the election of a chairman." As in a mass meeting, the one who calls the meeting
to order can either nominate a chairman pro tem or immediately call for nominations from the floor, and the nominees are voted on by voice. After the chairman pro tem has
taken the chair, a secretary is elected, also as in the case of
a mass meeting (see pp. 530–31).

The chair then calls on the member most interested in the
formation of the society to provide background information,
or he himself can make the talk. Others can also be asked to
give their opinions on the subject, but the chair should not
permit any one person to monopolize the meeting.

ADOPTION OF A RESOLUTION TO FORM A SO-
CIETY.   After a reasonable time for such informal discussion, someone should offer a resolution proposing definite
action. Those who planned the meeting should have prepared in advance a suitable resolution, which may be in a
form essentially as follows:

1 *Resolved*, That it is the sense of this meeting that a society for . . . [the object of the proposed society] now
be formed [or "shall now be formed"].

5   This resolution, when seconded, is stated by the chair,
and is then open to debate and amendment. Such a resolution, it should be noted, is only a declaration of intention;
its adoption does not bring the organization into being,
which is accomplished by the adoption of bylaws and the
10 signing of the membership roll by those who initially join
the society, as described below. If the meeting is a large one,
it is usually better that, except for a brief statement of purpose, the resolution be offered before the introductory
talks mentioned above.
15

FURTHER BUSINESS RELATING TO ORGANI-
ZATION. After the resolution to organize the society is
adopted, the succeeding steps generally are:

20 1) Introduction and adoption of a motion that a committee
of a specified number be appointed by the chair to draft
bylaws* for the society—and, where incorporation may
be necessary, to consult an attorney as described below.

2) Introduction and adoption of a motion to fix the date,
25   hour, and place of the next meeting (**22**), at which the
report of the bylaws committee will be presented. If it
is impractical to set a time and place for the next meeting, the motion can be that "when the meeting adjourns, it adjourn to meet at the call of the chair."

30 3) Introduction and adoption of a motion authorizing
the committee on bylaws to provide reproduced

---

*Called the *constitution* or *constitution and bylaws* in some organizations (see pp. 12–14). For factors affecting the appropriate size of this committee, see pages 549–50.

copies of the completed draft for distribution to all
who attend the next meeting. In this connection, persons seeking to form a society should take into account the fact that expenses may be involved, whether
or not an organization materializes. Initiation fees or
dues cannot be collected or received in the name of
the society until its organization, as described in this
section, is completed. Expenses advanced can be reim-
bursed.

Other business before adjournment may include informal discussion of aims and structure of the proposed society—which may serve to guide the bylaws committee (see
also below).

When the business of the first meeting is concluded and
a motion to adjourn is adopted (see pp. 534–36), the chair
says either: (1) "The meeting stands [or "is"] adjourned to
meet again at . . . [the date, hour, and place of next meet-
ing]"; or (2) "The meeting is adjourned to meet again at
the call of the chair."

Work of the Bylaws Committee

General principles for guidance in the drafting of bylaws
are given in **56**. The drafting committee may find it helpful
to procure and study copies of the bylaws of other organizations similar to the one being formed, although the possible applicability of their provisions must be carefully
evaluated in the light of expected conditions within the new
society. The committee may also find it advisable to consult
a professional parliamentarian.

If it is expected that the society will own real estate, become a beneficiary under wills, engage employees, or the
like, it may need to be incorporated according to the laws
of the state in which it is situated (see pp. 10–11). In

1 such a case, the bylaws committee should be authorized to
have one or more of its members consult an attorney to secure information and advice regarding the legal requirements that must be taken into account in drawing up the
5 society's bylaws. If the society is to be incorporated, the
same attorney should draft the charter or other instrument
of incorporation, which the committee submits for approval
at the second organizational meeting, before the bylaws are
considered, unless there is some reason for delay (see
10 below).

As indicated above, it is advisable to prepare double-
spaced reproduced copies of the proposed bylaws—as
drawn up by the committee—for distribution to each person entering the hall for the second organizational meeting.
15 If desired, such copies can be mailed in advance to everyone who attended the first meeting.

Second Organizational Meeting

20 READING AND APPROVAL OF THE MINUTES.
With the temporary officers elected at the first organizational meeting serving until the regular officers are elected,
the first item of business at the second meeting is the reading and approval of the minutes of the first meeting, with
25 corrections if necessary.

CONSIDERATION AND ADOPTION OF PRO-
POSED BYLAWS.   After the minutes are approved, the
report of the bylaws committee normally is received. If
30 there is a proposed corporate charter, that document is presented first. The assembly can amend the draft of the charter, but any resulting modification should be checked by
the attorney, to whom the charter is returned after its adoption, for processing under the legal procedure for incorpo-
35 ration in the particular state.

If there is no proposed corporate charter, the bylaws committee chairman, when recognized for the purpose of presenting the report, begins somewhat as follows:

COMMITTEE CHAIRMAN: Mr. Chairman, the committee appointed to draw up proposed bylaws has agreed upon the following draft and has directed me to move its adoption. [Reads proposals in full—members following on their own copies—unless the first reading is dispensed with; then moves the adoption of the document, as follows:] Mr. Chairman, by direction of the committee, I move the adoption of the bylaws.

No second is necessary, since the motion is offered by a committee of more than one person. Since a complete set of bylaws is commonly considered *by article or section* (see **28**), the chair states the question as follows:

CHAIR: The question is on the adoption of the bylaws as proposed by the committee. The committee chairman [or "the Secretary"] will now read the proposed bylaws, one article or section at a time. After each article or section is read, it will be open to debate and amendment. When amendment of one article or section is completed, the next one will be read and considered. No section or article will be adopted until all have been opened to amendment.

Each article or section is read separately, each provision being carefully explained by the chairman of the bylaws committee, as described above; and after the last one has been completed, the chair gives opportunity to insert additional paragraphs or sections and to correct any inconsistency or oversight that may have arisen during the process of amendment, as follows:

CHAIR: The entire set of bylaws is now open to amendment. Are there any further amendments?

1   If, at any point during the consideration of the bylaws,
it develops that important additions or amendments are desirable but will require time or investigation to prepare, it is
in order to move to recommit (**13**) the proposed bylaws,
5   with instructions that the committee report at another
meeting for which the time can be fixed. Or, further consideration of the bylaws can simply be postponed (**14**) to
such a meeting. This third meeting in forming an organization, although in many cases unnecessary, in others often
10   pays dividends in increased understanding and a larger
membership. In any event, at the second or third meeting,
when there are no further amendments, the question is put
on adopting the bylaws:

15   CHAIR: The question is on the adoption of the bylaws as amended.
As many as are in favor of adopting the bylaws, say *aye*. . . . Those opposed, say *no*. . . [and so on, taking a voice vote in the regular man-
ner].

20   In case of doubt, the chair should call for a rising vote
and, if necessary, direct that a count be made; or a member
can call for a division (**29**), and can move that the vote be
counted, as described on pages 48–50. Unlike the case of
amending or revising the bylaws of an organization already
25   established (**57**), the adoption of the bylaws through which
a society is brought into being requires only a majority
vote. The bylaws take effect immediately upon their adoption. A negative vote on their adoption can be reconsidered, but not an affirmative one.
30

RECESS TO ENROLL MEMBERS.   After the adop-
tion of the bylaws, only those who join the society are entitled to vote in further proceedings. At this point, therefore,
the meeting recesses to enroll initial members. Immediate
35   admission to membership is contingent upon signing a per-

manent record sheet provided in advance by the secretary *1*
pro tem—to be filed with the original papers of the organization. This signature constitutes agreement to abide by
the bylaws, and is a commitment to prompt payment of the
initiation fee (if there is one) and dues for the first year or *5*
other period prescribed by the bylaws. Persons thus signing
become "charter members."* The secretary pro tem should
record and give receipt for payments received from members until the treasurer is elected and takes office.

10

READING OF THE ROLL AND ELECTION OF
PERMANENT OFFICERS.   After the recess the chairman pro tem calls for the reading of the roll of members,
and the secretary pro tem does so. The chair then says,
"The next business in order is the nomination and election *15*
of the permanent officers as prescribed in the bylaws."

The nomination and election processes are as described
in **46,** the election being by ballot if the bylaws so prescribe,
which they usually should. The members for whom one can
vote are not limited to nominees, since each member is free *20*
to vote for any member who is not made ineligible by the
bylaws. After the election is completed, the chair declares
the results. Unless a proviso attached to the bylaws (pp.
578–79) prescribes otherwise, the newly elected officers
immediately replace the temporary ones. *25*

ANY OTHER ESSENTIAL BUSINESS.   When the
offices have been filled and the new president has taken the
chair, he should call for any business requiring immediate
attention. In a new society it is generally important that the *30*
president have time to give careful thought to committee

---

*Sometimes, in forming a society, all who join before a specified date
after the actual establishment of the organization are included in the roll of
charter members.

appointments after examining the list of members. It is therefore often advisable to provide for an adjourned meeting to complete the organization before the first regular meeting. The president may find it essential, however, to name the chairmen of certain committees, such as the membership or program committees, immediately.

When the business of the meeting has been completed, or when an adjourned meeting has been provided for, a motion to adjourn is in order. If it is adopted, the chair announces the result and declares the meeting adjourned.

Subsequent meetings of the society are conducted as described in **3** and **4**. For additional information regarding the organization of a federation by a convention of delegates from prospective member societies, see **60**.

§55. MERGER, CONSOLIDATION, AND DISSOLUTION OF SOCIETIES

Combining of Societies

DISTINCTION BETWEEN MERGER AND CONSOLIDATION. In cases where two existing societies wish to combine, there are two possible procedures, which are legally distinct:

- In the case of a *merger,* one of the two organizations continues, while the other loses its independent identity and ceases to exist, since it is merged—that is, absorbed—into the former.
- In the case of a *consolidation,* two or more organizations each discontinue their independent existence, and a new entity is formed that includes the memberships of the consolidating organizations, continues their work, and assumes their assets and liabilities.

In either a merger or a consolidation, the resulting organization may be given a new name, which may include, for example, elements of the names of each of the combining organizations.

CASES INVOLVING INCORPORATED SOCIETIES.   If one or more of the organizations involved in a merger or a consolidation are incorporated, an attorney should be consulted to draw up the proper papers and advise as to all steps necessary to fulfill the legal requirements.

CASES INVOLVING UNINCORPORATED SOCIETIES.   If none of the organizations involved in a merger or a consolidation is incorporated, the respective procedures are as follows:

- In the case of a merger, the organization that is giving up its independent identity should adopt a resolution substantially as follows: "*Resolved,* That the A Society be, and hereby is, merged into the B Society as of [date] or when such merger shall be accepted by the B Society." For its adoption, such a resolution requires the same notice and vote as for amending the bylaws (see pp. 562–63). This resolution should be joined with, or its adoption should be followed by the adoption of, resolutions transferring all of the assets and liabilities to the organization into which it is merging, and providing for whatever other administrative details will be required in the mechanics of transition. The society into which the first organization is being merged should adopt a resolution accepting the merger, and this motion similarly requires the same notice and vote as to amend the accepting organization's bylaws, because it so greatly alters the per-capita interest of each member.

1   Often, resolutions authorizing and approving mergers
      contain stipulations and qualifications, sometimes even
      to the extent of naming the officers who will serve dur-
      ing the first year after the merger. Usually these resolu-
5   tions are the work of a joint committee of the two
      organizations and form a part of its recommendations.

   • In the case of a consolidation, the two or more consoli-
     dating organizations adopt resolutions authorizing the
     consolidation, similar to the resolutions described in the
10   preceding item relating to merger. Often—but not neces-
     sarily—these meetings are held simultaneously in the
     same building. As in the case of a merger, the resolutions
     containing details relating to the mechanics of transition
     are usually drafted by a joint committee. After the con-
15   solidating organizations have each adopted resolutions
     which are substantially identical and which provide for
     consolidation as of a stated date, a joint meeting of the
     members of the consolidating groups is held for the pur-
     pose of organizing the new society that is to emerge. In
20   contrast to the case of a merger, a new set of bylaws must
     be drawn up and adopted. The procedure is similar to
     that for the original establishment of a society as described
     in **54,** except that the necessary resolutions and motions
     normally are worded so that the date on which the new
25   organization is established, its bylaws take effect, and its
     officers assume office coincides with the date on which
     the consolidating groups discontinue separate existence.

Dissolution of a Society

30   It may sometimes happen over a period of time that the
      needs which led to the formation of a society have largely
      disappeared, and the organization may wish formally to dis-
      band or dissolve.

DISSOLUTION OF AN INCORPORATED SOCI-
ETY.   If a society is incorporated, the laws of the state in
which it is incorporated provide in some detail the legal requirements for the dissolution of the corporation. An attorney should be consulted to draw up the necessary papers
and advise the society as to the procedure to be followed.

DISSOLUTION OF AN UNINCORPORATED SO-
CIETY.   In the case of an unincorporated society, a resolution should be prepared, such as: "*Resolved*, That the X
Society be dissolved as of March 31, 20__." This resolution
may be preceded by a preamble setting forth the reasons for
the dissolution. It is in effect a motion to rescind the bylaws,
and therefore requires for its adoption the same notice and
vote as to amend them (see pp. 562–63). The required notice should be sent by mail to all members of record.

Such a resolution can be coupled with other resolutions
stating the manner in which the society's assets shall be disposed of and attending to other administrative details—or
these can be adopted separately. In certain tax-exempt organizations of a charitable or educational character, federal
and state tax laws must be adhered to in the disposal of the
organization's assets. Often such assets are distributed to
societies with similar objectives, or to a superior body.

BYLAWS

§56. CONTENT AND COMPOSITION OF BYLAWS

Nature and Importance of Bylaws

The constitution and/or bylaws of a society, as explained in **2**, contains its own basic rules that relate to itself as an organization, except for what must be included in the corporate charter of an incorporated society. Under the preferred practice for ordinary societies today, the constitution and the bylaws—once usually separate—are now combined in a single instrument, referred to in this book as the *bylaws* (although in some organizations called the *constitution*, or—even though only one document—the *constitution and bylaws*). A precise statement of the essential characteristics of bylaws, in the sense of the combination-type instrument, and their relation to the other kinds of rules that an organization may have is given in **2**, which should be read in connection with this chapter. Because bylaws in this sense are the most important rules which an organization must compose for itself, and because certain considerations must be taken into account that affect their construction as a unified document rather than a series of separate rules, bylaws are given more detailed treatment below.

The content of a society's bylaws has important bearing on the rights and duties of members within the organization—whether present or absent from the assembly—and on the degree to which the general membership is to retain control of, or be relieved of detailed concern with, the society's business. Except as the rules of a society may provide otherwise, its assembly (that is, the members attending one of its regular or properly called meetings) has full and sole power to act for the entire organization, and does so by majority vote. Any limitation or standing delegation of the assembly's power with respect to the society as a whole can only be by provision in the bylaws—or in the corporate charter or separate constitution, if either of these exists.

Committee to Draw Up Bylaws

APPOINTMENT OF COMMITTEE.   A committee to draw up proposed bylaws is usually appointed at the first organizational meeting when a new society is being formed, as described in **54;** or, if an existing society wishes to undertake a general revision of its bylaws, a committee to draw up the proposed revision can be appointed at any regular meeting, just as any other special committee.

A committee to draw up proposed bylaws should generally be large, and should include the most judicious persons available, those who have a special interest in the rules of the society, and those who would otherwise be likely to consume much time in discussing the bylaws when they come before the assembly for adoption. Persons having writing ability of the kind required should also be included, unless a professional parliamentarian is to do the actual drafting of the bylaws. Even if the drafting is to be done by members of the committee, a parliamentarian can often be of great assistance as a consultant.

1   The committee should consult an attorney with reference to the considerations indicated on pages 539–40 if there is any possibility that the society should be incorporated. If it is to be incorporated, the committee works with the attorney
5 to provide him with the necessary information for drafting an appropriate corporate charter, to which the bylaws must conform. The committee should review the draft of the charter before submitting it to the assembly.

10   INITIAL DISCUSSIONS; FACTORS INFLUENCING CONTENT OF BYLAWS. The committee normally begins its work—with the entire committee present—in general discussion of the desired content of the bylaws. Besides reviewing the existing bylaws (in the
15 case of a revision), it is well for the committee to study the bylaws of a number of similar organizations, or—if applicable—of other subordinate units within the same state or national society. Before any provisions from other documents are used as a pattern, however, possible differences
20 between the conditions in the other organizations and the one for which the bylaws are being prepared should be carefully analyzed.
    If the unit for which the bylaws are to be drawn up is subject to a parent organization or superior body, such as a state
25 or a national society (or both), or a federation, the bylaws governing at these higher levels should be studied for provisions which are binding upon subordinate units in a way that must be taken into account. The bylaws of a subordinate unit need to conform to those of a superior body only on clearly
30 requisite points. For example, if the superior body limits the size of its subordinate units to 200 members, the bylaws should contain this limit or one that is lower. But the subordinate unit should not adopt provisions from the other document that have no local application, and the bylaws of the
35 superior body should not require it to do so.

In order to give the organization the greatest freedom to act within its object, bylaws should be made no more restrictive nor more detailed in specification than necessary.

The description of the basic bylaw articles beginning on page 553 provides a brief indication of the framework within which the particular needs of the society should be considered in determining the content of its bylaws. A sample set of bylaws of the type that might be adopted by a small and independent local society is shown beginning on page 565. Such a model can only illustrate how a typical document of this kind is put together, however; and the provisions must be varied, additional ones inserted, or inapplicable ones omitted, as appropriate to the individual organization.

DRAFTING OF BYLAWS; APPOINTMENT OF SUBCOMMITTEE(S). After conferences on the topics described above, the committee should appoint a drafting subcommittee, or several of them for various articles if the bylaws are expected to be long and complex. Another subcommittee may be needed in the latter case to eliminate inconsistencies, make the style uniform, and make sure that, as far as possible, everything relating to a single subject is placed in the same or adjacent articles.

The composition of bylaws is somewhat different from ordinary expository writing, in that it places greater demand on a "tight" clarity and precision in word choice, sentence structure, and punctuation. In bylaws, as in legal documents of any kind, every punctuation mark may have an important effect; and what is omitted may carry as much significance as what is included. Indisputability of meaning and application is a more important consideration than "readability," and the latter must be sacrificed when both cannot be achieved. Each sentence should be written so as to be impossible to quote out of context; that is, either its

1 complete meaning should be clear without reference to sentences preceding or following, or it should be worded so as
to compel the reader to refer to adjoining sentences—as by
beginning, "Any member so elected . . ." Exceptions or
5 qualifications to statements should be included, as far as
possible, within the sentence to which they apply—which
can often be accomplished by ending sentences with clauses
beginning "except that . . ." or "provided, however,
that . . ." Where such a technique is impractical, a sentence
10 should contain at least an allusion or reference to any exceptions to its own applicability—as in "Except as provided
in Article VI, Section 2 of these bylaws, officers shall . . . "

Provisions of a temporary nature or relating to the mechanics of transition from old to revised bylaws should not
15 be included within bylaws (see pp. 578–79).

Regarding the inclusion of provisions in the nature of
rules of order within bylaws, see pages 16–17.

CRITICAL REVIEW BY FULL COMMITTEE.
20 After the first draft of the bylaws has been completed, it
should be given thorough critical examination in discussions by the full committee. The probable long-range effect
of each provision should be weighed, and particular care
taken to detect and eliminate any remaining inconsistencies
25 or ambiguities. It is much better to take a good deal of time
in consideration of bylaws before their adoption than to
find an early need for extensive amendment.

PRESENTATION OF REPORT.   After the proposed
30 bylaws are approved by the committee, the report of the
committee is presented to the assembly and is considered
seriatim—article by article and, whenever an article consists
of more than one section, section by section. The procedure is as described on pages 540–42 and in 28—
35 except that:

a) especially in the case of a revision of bylaws, the motion
   to adopt them may include provisos relating to transition, as explained on pages 578–79; and

b) a revision of bylaws is adopted by the vote required to
   amend the existing ones (pp. 562-64), rather than by a
   majority vote as in the case of bylaws that bring a society into being.

In presenting the report of the bylaws committee to the
assembly, the committee chairman should explain each section and—in the case of a proposed revision of bylaws—
make clear what is new about each provision or how it
differs from the corresponding provision of the existing bylaws.

Content of Bylaw Articles

BASIC BYLAW ARTICLES.   While the number of
bylaw articles will be determined by the size and activities
of the organization adopting them, and more than those
listed below will be needed in some cases, the average society will find it sufficient to include articles on the following
numbered headings. The description of appropriate provisions in these articles, while in no sense exhaustive, should
prove of help in framing bylaws. Articles are commonly designated with Roman numerals, and sections with Arabic
numerals (see also sample bylaws beginning on p. 565).

Article I: Name.   In unincorporated societies, the full,
exact, and properly punctuated name of the society should
be given. In incorporated societies or those with separate
constitutions, however, the bylaws can omit this article,
since the official name of the organization is then stated in
the corporate charter or constitution. If the name is in both
locations, conflicts may creep in, and it is the name as stated
in the superior document that is official.

1 *Article II: Object.* In unincorporated societies, the object of the society should be concisely expressed in a single sentence, the various aspects or phases being written in sequence, set off by semicolons, or in lettered subparagraphs, 5 also set off by semicolons. The statement should be general in its application, since it sets boundaries within which business can be introduced at the society's meetings—a two-thirds vote being required to allow the introduction of a motion that falls outside the society's object. For the same 10 reason stated above in reference to the society's name, this article also can be omitted from the bylaws in incorporated societies or in those having a separate constitution. Some societies prefer to set forth the object in a preamble to the bylaws rather than in an article, in which case the preamble 15 precedes Article I, and the numbering of the remaining articles described below is modified as necessary. This device is especially useful in societies incorporated many years before, whose charter no longer states its object in modern terms or with the specificity now desired.

20 *Article III: Members.* Usually the article on members consists of several sections, covering, for example: (1) classes of members—as "active," "associate," and the like—with any distinctions between them being set forth, and, as applicable, the rights of each, and any limitation on their 25 number; and (2) qualifications or eligibility for membership, with application and acceptance procedures, including the method of reviewing and voting on applications. Unless the financial obligations of members are especially complicated, a section of this article should also state: (3) the required 30 fees and dues, the date(s) when payable (whether annually, semiannually, quarterly, etc.), the time and prescribed procedure for notifying members if they become delinquent in payment, and the date thereafter on which a member will be dropped for nonpayment of dues. Before a member in 35 arrears has been finally dropped under such a provision,

his voting rights cannot by suspended unless the bylaws so 1
provide. Members cannot be assessed any additional payment aside from their dues unless it is provided for in the
bylaws. If the necessary provisions relating to the financial
obligations of members to the society are too complex to be 5
included in this article, such provisions can be set out in a
separate article immediately following.

Some organizations require attendance at a certain proportion of the meetings or a specified minimum participation in the society's activities as a requirement for 10
continued membership; this also can be done only by provision in the bylaws.

Sometimes this article also contains provisions for: (4)
resignations; and (5) honorary members (see p. 447).

In a state or national body or a federation, local units or 15
constituent clubs, rather than individuals, may be the
"members" referred to in this article.

Article IV: Officers. As stated in **47,** every society
should specify in this article of its bylaws the officers it requires, including honorary ones, and how they shall be 20
elected or appointed. The officers rank in the order listed,
so that the president should be named first, the vice-president or first vice-president next (unless there is to be a president-elect; see p. 441), and so on. Directors should usually
be classed as officers. 25

Normally all that need be said about the duties of officers (apart from occasional references in other articles,
under the topics to which specific duties relate) can be included in the section designating the officers, to the effect
that "These officers shall perform the duties prescribed by 30
these bylaws and by the parliamentary authority adopted by
the Society." In cases where the extraordinary duties of officers are numerous, however, a separate article titled "Duties of Officers" may sometimes follow this article, and treat
the duties for each office in a separate section. Such a pro- 35

cedure is advantageous in collecting related information in one place, but it results in repetition and may occasion problems of interpretation. Great care must be taken in the writing of the article not to omit any duty, since an implication that the duty is not required could be read into the omission. For this reason, if such an article is to be included, it is well to conclude the section on each office with a clause such as ". . . and such other duties applicable to the office as prescribed by the parliamentary authority adopted by the Society."

A method of nominating officers (see **46**) may be prescribed in a section of this article; in the absence of such a provision or an established custom of the society, nominations are made from the floor or as otherwise directed by vote of the society at the time of each election (see also **31**). If the bylaws provide for a nominating committee and prescribe that the committee shall nominate "candidates for each office," the committee is not limited to one candidate for each office. If it is desired to impose such a limitation, the provision should state that the committee shall nominate "a candidate for each office."

Election by ballot should usually be prescribed in the section pertaining to elections and terms of office—often with additional details of election procedure as discussed in **46**. A provision can be included to dispense with the ballot when there is only one candidate for an office, although this deprives members of the privilege of voting for "write-in" candidates in such a case. If it is desired to elect by mail, by plurality vote, by preferential voting, or by cumulative voting, this must be expressly stated, and necessary details of the procedure should be prescribed (see **45**). The length of the terms of office should be prescribed; and unless the terms are to begin at the instant the chair declares each officer elected, the time when they are to begin must be specified. To ensure the continued services of officers in the event, for example, of public emergency or of difficulty in obtaining a nominee for an office, it is well to provide that officers "shall hold office for a term of . . . year(s) or [or "and"*] until their successors are elected." The unqualified wording "for a term of . . . year(s)" should be avoided, because at the end of that time there would be no officers if new ones had not been elected.

Since a reasonable rotation in office is desirable in almost all organizations, a section of this article may well provide that "No officer shall be eligible to serve for more than . . . consecutive terms [specifying the number] in the same office." For purposes of determining eligibility to continue in office under such a provision, an officer who has served more than half a term is considered to have served a full term in that office.

The method of filling vacancies may also be provided. Unless the bylaws clearly provide otherwise, notice of filling a vacancy must always be given to the members of the body that will elect the person to fill it. If the bylaws are silent as to the method of filling a vacancy in the specific case of the presidency, the vice-president or first vice-president automatically becomes president for the remainder of the term, and the vacancy arises in the vice-presidency or lowest-ranking vice-presidency; if another method of filling a vacancy in the presidency is desired, it must be prescribed and specified as applying to the office of president in particular.

Article V: Meetings. The first section of the article on meetings should fix the day on which regular meetings of the society are to be held—as by specifying, for example, "the first Friday of each month." If the words "unless otherwise ordered by the Society [or "Executive Board"]" are added, the date can be changed in an unusual circumstance,

---

*For the difference in effect between "or" and "and" when used here, see pages 642–43.

1 but only for that single meeting on that particular occasion,
and not for a period of time including several meetings. To
change the general rule fixing the time for meetings would
require amendment of the bylaws. The hour at which meet-
5 ings are to held should not be specified in the bylaws, but
should be established by a standing rule (**2**).

Some organizations prefer to schedule meetings by resolution. If so, the bylaws should provide for the number of
days' notice required before regular meetings, since under
10 such a practice members cannot determine the meeting
dates by consulting the bylaws.

In a separate section it should be provided that "The
regular meeting . . . [specifying which one, as "on the last
Tuesday in May"] shall be known as the annual meeting."
15 As explained in **9**, this meeting is conducted in the same
way as any regular meeting, except that officers are elected
and annual reports are received from officers and standing
committees.

A section authorizing the calling of special meetings
20 (without which they are not permitted; see pp. 89–90)
should state by whom such meetings can be called—such as
the president, the board, or a specified number of members
nearly equal to a quorum—and the number of days' notice
required. It may be well to provide that no business shall be
25 transacted except that mentioned in the call (that is, the notice) of the special meeting, although this rule would apply
even if not expressly stated.

The quorum for all meetings should be established in a
section of this article (see **40**).

30 In state or national bodies where one session—usually
called a *convention*—is held annually, biennially, or at less
frequent intervals—the article on meetings is titled "Conventions." While much that is stated above would be generally applicable to such an article, considerable adaptation
35 is needed, as described on pages 582–83.

Article VI: Executive Board (or Board of Directors).   As   1
explained on pages 464–66, all but the smallest societies
usually find it advisable to establish a board whose members
are the officers of the society, such a body being entrusted
with administrative authority and responsibility to a degree   5
that varies with the organization. If there is to be such a
board, sections of this article should:

- specify the board's composition;
- delineate the powers of the board; and   10
- set forth any special rules by which the board is to conduct its business, such as when and how often it is to
  meet, its quorum, and the like.

                                                                 15
In most societies this body is called the *Executive Board*
unless there is to be a smaller body within it to act for the
board between its meetings, in which case the full board is
usually designated the *Board of Directors* and the smaller
body is called the *Executive Committee* (see p. 468). The   20
Executive Committee is then established in a separate article following the one on the complete board, with similar provisions. Organizations may sometimes give varied
names to their full boards, such as *Board of Managers,
Board of Trustees, Board of Governors, Administrative*   25
Council, etc.. In such cases, the nature of the particular
body as one of the types described above can be determined from the bylaw article that establishes it.
     Article VI, Section 2 of the sample bylaws (p. 568)
shows an appropriate wording for defining the board's   30
powers so that the society's assembly will retain full control
but can leave to the board such details as it may wish. If the
organization desires to turn all of its business over to the
board—as may occur, for example, in some social clubs—
the same section should be reduced to: 35

1   The Executive Board [or "Board of Directors," etc.]
shall have full power and authority over the affairs of
the Society except . . . [specifying classes of business
the society may wish to reserve to its assembly].

5

    Article VII: Committees.   The article on committees
should provide for the establishment of each of the standing committees (**50**) that it is known will be required. A
separate section devoted to each of these committees
10 should give its name, composition, manner of selection,
and duties. If this article names certain standing committees, no other standing committees can be appointed without amending the bylaws, unless a provision is
included—usually in a separate section of the article as de-
15 scribed below—permitting the establishment of such other
standing committees as are deemed necessary to carry on
the work of the society. In any event, if a standing committee is to have standing authority to act for the society without specific instructions, if business of a certain class is to be
20 automatically referred to it, or if some other rule of parliamentary procedure is affected by the committee's assigned
function, such procedure must be prescribed in a provision
of the bylaws or in a special rule of order, establishing the
committee by name.
25   The number and nature of the standing committees
that may be named in individual sections of this article will
depend on the size and object of the organization. The
standing committees most frequently established by local
societies are few in number; they may include a committee
30 on membership, a program committee, and sometimes a finance committee. (A section relating to the nominating
committee, when included, is usually located not in this article but in the article on officers, where nomination and
election procedures are usually prescribed.) In national or
35 state bodies more committees may be needed, but local

units should not try to establish a committee to correspond to each one in the superior body, and the superior body generally should not require them to do so.

Appointment of special committees is usually provided for in a separate section that may also, as indicated above, provide for the appointment of additional standing committees. When this section empowers the president to appoint such special committees or additional standing committees as the society or the board shall direct, he is not thereby authorized to appoint other committees on his own initiative. If the president is to appoint committees and it is desired that he have standing authority to appoint non–assembly members to positions on the committees without submitting these persons' names to the assembly for approval, this section should contain a provision to that effect (see pp. 167, 475, 478–79). This section may also provide that certain officers—for example, the president—"shall be ex officio a member of all committees except the Nominating Committee." In that case, the president has the right, but not the duty, of participating in the work of the committees (see also pp. 466–67, 480). Without such a provision, he has no vote within the committees, nor can he attend their meetings except as invited by a particular committee. The nominating committee should always be expressly excluded in a provision making the president an ex-officio member of committees.

If no article on committees is included in the bylaws, standing and special committees are established as directed by the society (see **13, 50**).

Article VIII: Parliamentary Authority. The parliamentary authority—through the adoption of which a society establishes its rules of order—should be prescribed in a one-sentence article reading: "The rules contained in the current edition of . . . [specifying a standard manual of parliamentary practice, such as this book] shall govern the Society in all cases to which they are applicable and in which

they are not inconsistent with these bylaws and any special rules of order the Society may adopt."* Societies can adopt special rules of order as they are needed to supplement their parliamentary authority, as explained in **2.** When a particu-
5 lar work is adopted as the parliamentary authority, what any other book may say on any point is of no authority if in conflict with the adopted work. In other cases, it may be persuasive but is not binding upon the society.

Article IX: Amendment of Bylaws.   The bylaws should
10 always prescribe the procedure for their amendment, and such provision should always require at least that advance notice be given in a specified manner, and that the amendment be approved by a two-thirds vote. If the bylaws contain no provision for their amendment, they can be amended at any
15 business meeting by a two-thirds vote, provided that *previous notice* (in the sense defined on p. 116) has been given; or, without notice, they can be amended at any regular meeting by vote of a majority of the entire membership. In making a requirement that notice be given by submitting the amend-
20 ment at a meeting in advance of the one at which it is to be considered, the provision should always specify submission at "*the* previous meeting," and not "a" previous meeting, since the latter would permit indefinite delay and would defeat the object of giving notice—namely, to alert the members to the
25 proposed amendment so that all those interested can arrange to be present at its consideration. The requirement of notice

---

*Where a particular type of organization is subject to local, state, or national law containing provisions relating to its procedure—as for certain procedures in a labor organization, in condominium associations, or in an incorporated association—it may be desirable to add at this point a phrase such as, "and any statutes applicable to this organization that do not authorize the provisions of these bylaws to take precedence." However, such statutes (those that do *not* authorize bylaws to take precedence) supersede all rules of the organization which conflict with them, even if no mention is made of it in the bylaws.

restricts amendment of the proposed bylaw amendment to   *1*
changes within the scope of the notice, as explained on pages
576–77 (see also Standard Characteristic **6,** p. **295**).

The manner prescribed for giving notice should suit the
needs of the particular assembly. For some, oral notice is suf-   *5*
ficient; others may require written notice. Some may require
only a general statement of the purport of the amendment;
others may require that the exact wording of the amendment
be given. If the bylaws require only previous notice of an
amendment without limitation of the period within which it   *10*
must be acted upon, and a committee is appointed to revise
the bylaws and report at a specified meeting, the appointing
action is all the notice required, and the amendments can be
immediately acted upon at the time the committee reports.
But if it is required that the amendment itself, or "notice of   *15*
such amendment," be submitted at the previous regular
meeting, the revision cannot be taken up until the meeting
following the meeting at which the committee submitted its
report. In societies having very frequent regular meetings primarily for presentation of a program, and also monthly or   *20*
quarterly business meetings (p. 88), it is well to permit action
on amendments to the bylaws only at a quarterly or annual
meeting or their adjournments. Where assemblies meet regularly only once a year, instead of requiring amendments to
be submitted at the previous annual meeting, the bylaws   *25*
should provide for both notice and copies of the proposed
amendment to be sent by mail to the member delegates or
constituent societies.

If there is a constitution separate from the bylaws, the
requirement for amendment of the constitution should be   *30*
made more difficult than that for amendment of the bylaws;
otherwise there would be no purpose in having separate
documents. In either case, however, the necessary vote
should be at least two thirds.

In prescribing the vote necessary for the adoption of an   *35*
amendment, the expression "a vote of two thirds of the

members" should never be used in ordinary societies, especially in large organizations. In such societies two thirds of the entire membership would rarely, if ever, be present at a meeting. It is more reasonable to require "a two-thirds vote" (see p. 388–89).

The wording of this article should avoid redundant phraseology such as "amend, alter, add to, or repeal," or "alter or amend," or "amend or in any way change." The word *amend* covers any change, whether a word or a paragraph is to be added, struck out, or replaced, or whether a new set of articles is to be substituted for the old one. Efforts to define the meaning of such expressions as "two-thirds vote" should also be avoided in the wording of this article, since these definitions are found in the parliamentary authority.

ADDITIONAL BYLAW ARTICLES. Some societies may have cause to include additional bylaw articles, such as those mentioned above, bearing on the subjects of finance, duties of officers, and an executive committee of the board of directors. In a national organization, an article providing for constituent societies or units at regional, state, or local levels and establishing their relationships within the organizational structure may be required. In associations divided into departments, the article establishing them—titled "Departments"—follows the article establishing committees. In professional and some other societies there may be an article on disciplinary procedure; and such an article can be simple or very elaborate. Most such provisions, however, are generally unnecessary in ordinary societies, at least at the local level (see **61**).

Sample Bylaws

Regarding the applicability of the following model, see page 551, lines 4–14. Titles of sections are optional, but they may be felt to be desirable, particularly if the bylaws

become elaborate, as may be the case, for example, in a
complex national organization.

BYLAWS

OF THE _____ SOCIETY

OF _____

ARTICLE I

Name

The name of this Society shall be _____.

ARTICLE II

Object

The object of this Society shall be to _____;
to _____; and to _____.

ARTICLE III

Members

Section 1. Maximum Membership. The membership of this Society shall be limited to two hundred
members.

Section 2. Membership Eligibility and Admission
Procedure. Any adult resident of _____ shall be
eligible for membership, provided that such resident
shall be proposed by one member and seconded by another member of the Society. A proposal for membership, signed by the two endorsers, shall be sent to the
Recording Secretary, who shall report it, together with
the names of the sponsors, at the next regular meeting
of the Society. Voting upon the admission shall take
place at the next regular meeting thereafter. A two-

thirds vote shall elect to membership. A person so elected shall be declared a member of the Society upon payment of the initiation fee and the annual dues for the first year.

Section 3. Initiation Fee and Dues. The initiation fee shall be _____ dollars. The annual dues shall be _____ dollars, payable in advance on or before _____ of each year. The Treasurer shall notify members _____ months in arrears, and those whose dues are not paid within _____ thereafter shall be automatically dropped from membership in the Society.

Section 4. Resignation from Membership. Any member desiring to resign from the Society shall submit his resignation in writing to the Recording Secretary, who shall present it to the Executive Board for action. No member's resignation shall be accepted until his dues are paid.

Section 5. Honorary Life Membership. Upon the signed recommendation of one member, seconded by another member, and by a three-fourths vote by ballot at the annual meeting, honorary life membership may be conferred upon an adult resident of _____ who shall have rendered notable service to the Society. An honorary member shall have none of the obligations of membership in the Society, but shall be entitled to all of the privileges except those of making motions, of voting, and of holding office.

ARTICLE IV

Officers

Section 1. Officers and Duties. The officers of the Society shall be **a** President, a First Vice-President, a Second Vice-President, a Recording Secretary, a Corresponding Secretary, a Treasurer, and four Directors. These officers shall perform the duties prescribed by these bylaws and by the parliamentary authority adopted by the Society.

Section 2. Nomination Procedure, Time of Elections. At the regular meeting held on the second Tuesday in February, a Nominating Committee of five members shall be elected by the Society. It shall be the duty of this committee to nominate candidates for the offices to be filled at the annual meeting in April. The Nominating Committee shall report at the regular meeting in March. Before the election at the annual meeting in April, additional nominations from the floor shall be permitted.

Section 3. Ballot Election, Term of Office. The officers shall be elected by ballot to serve for one year or until their successors are elected, and their term of office shall begin at the close of the annual meeting at which they are elected.

Section 4. Office-Holding Limitations. No member shall hold more than one office at a time, and no member shall be eligible to serve more than two consecutive terms in the same office.

ARTICLE V

Meetings

Section 1. Regular Meetings. The regular meetings of the Society shall be held on the second Tuesday of each month from September to May inclusive unless otherwise ordered by the Society.

Section 2. Annual Meetings. The regular meeting on the second Tuesday in April shall be known as the annual meeting and shall be for the purpose of electing officers, receiving reports of officers and committees, and for any other business that may arise.

Section 3. Special Meetings. Special meetings may be called by the President or by the Executive Board and shall be called upon the written request of ten members of the Society. The purpose of the meeting shall be stated in the call. Except in cases of emergency, at least three days' notice shall be given.

Section 4. Quorum. Fifteen members of the Society shall constitute a quorum.

ARTICLE VI

The Executive Board

Section 1. Board Composition. The officers of the Society, including the Directors, shall constitute the Executive Board.

Section 2. Board's Duties and Powers. The Executive Board shall have general supervision of the affairs of the Society between its business meetings, fix the hour and place of meetings, make recommendations to the Society, and perform such other duties as are specified in these bylaws. The Board shall be subject to the orders of the Society, and none of its acts shall conflict with action taken by the Society.

Section 3. Board Meetings. Unless otherwise ordered by the Board, regular meetings of the Executive Board shall be held on the first Tuesday of each month from September to June, inclusive. Special meetings of the Board may be called by the President and shall be called upon the written request of three members of the Board.

ARTICLE VII

Committees

Section 1. Finance Committee. A Finance Committee composed of the Treasurer and four other members

shall be appointed by the President promptly after each
annual meeting. It shall be the duty of this committee
to prepare a budget for the fiscal year beginning the first
day of April, and to submit it to the Society at its regular meeting in March. The Finance Committee may
from time to time submit amendments to the budget
for the current fiscal year, which may be adopted by a
majority vote.

Section 2. Program Committee. A Program Committee of five members shall be appointed by the President promptly after the annual meeting, whose duty it
shall be to plan the annual program of the Society. This
committee's report shall be submitted to the Society for
its approval at its regular meeting in September.

Section 3. Auditing Committee. An Auditing Committee of three members shall be appointed by the President at the Society's March meeting, whose duty it
shall be to audit the Treasurer's accounts at the close of
the fiscal year and to report at the annual meeting.

Section 4. Other Committees; President's Ex-Officio
Committee Membership. Such other committees, standing or special, shall be appointed by the President as the
Society or the Executive Board shall from time to time
deem necessary to carry on the work of the Society. The
President shall be ex officio a member of all committees
except the Nominating Committee.

ARTICLE VIII

Parliamentary Authority

The rules contained in the current edition of
Robert's Rules of Order Newly Revised shall govern the
Society in all cases to which they are applicable and in
which they are not inconsistent with these bylaws and
any special rules of order the Society may adopt.

ARTICLE IX

Amendment of Bylaws

These bylaws may be amended at any regular meeting of the Society by a two-thirds vote, provided that the amendment has been submitted in writing at the previous regular meeting.

Some Principles of Interpretation

In preparing bylaws and interpreting them, the following principles of interpretation—which have equal application to other rules and documents adopted by an organization—may be of assistance.

1) *Each society decides for itself the meaning of its bylaws.* When the meaning is clear, however, the society, even by a unanimous vote, cannot change that meaning except by amending its bylaws. An ambiguity must exist before there is any occasion for interpretation. If a bylaw is ambiguous, it must be interpreted, if possible, in harmony with the other bylaws. The interpretation should be in accordance with the intention of the society at the time the bylaw was adopted, as far as this can be determined. Again, intent plays no role unless the meaning is unclear or uncertain, but where an ambiguity exists, a majority vote is all that is required to decide the question. The ambiguous or doubtful expression should be amended as soon as practicable.

2) *When a provision of the bylaws is susceptible to two meanings, one of which conflicts with or renders absurd another bylaw provision, and the other meaning does not, the latter must be taken as the true meaning.* For example, assume the bylaws define the officers as "a president, a vice-president, a secretary, a treasurer, and five other

members, all of whom shall serve as members of the
Board . . ." Assume also that elsewhere the bylaws speak
of "Directors" being board members. A suggestion that
the "Directors" are not officers and are additional
members of the board would create a conflict within the
bylaws and cannot be taken as the true meaning. The
"other members" are the same as the "Directors."

3) *A general statement or rule is always of less authority than
a specific statement or rule and yields to it.* It is not practical to state a rule in its full detail every time it is referred to. General statements of rules are seldom strictly
correct in every possible application. The specific statement of the rule that gives the details applying to the
particular case must always be examined. For instance: in
the Sample Bylaws, Article III, Section 2 (pp. 565-66),
it is provided that any "adult resident" shall, by a two-
thirds vote, be elected to membership. This is a general
statement which yields to the proviso stated in Section 1
of the same article that restricts membership to two
hundred. Thus, the Society is not empowered to elect a
two-hundred-and-first member by a two-thirds vote. No
one has a right to quote a general statement as of authority against a specific statement.

4) *If the bylaws authorize certain things specifically, other
things of the same class are thereby prohibited.* There is a
presumption that nothing has been placed in the bylaws without some reason for it. There can be no valid
reason for authorizing certain things to be done that
can clearly be done without the authorization of the
bylaws, unless the intent is to specify the things of the
same class that may be done, all others being prohibited. Thus, where Article IV, Section 1 of the Sample
Bylaws (pp. 566–67) lists certain officers, the election
of other officers not named, such as a sergeant-at-arms,
is prohibited.

1　5) *A provision granting certain privileges carries with it a right to a part of the privileges, but prohibits a greater privilege.* The Sample Bylaws, in Article VI, Section 2 (p. 568) provide that the executive board may "fix the

5　hour and place of meetings" of the society. The board may, therefore, change the time or the place, or both, of a society's meeting. But it may not change the day for which the meeting is scheduled.

　　6) *A prohibition or limitation prohibits everything greater*

10　*than what is prohibited, or that goes beyond the limitation; but it permits what is less than the limitation, and also permits things of the same class that are not mentioned in the prohibition or limitation and that are evidently not improper.* The Sample Bylaws, Article IV, Section 4 (p.

15　567) limits a member to holding one office at a time. This limitation carries with it, of course, the prohibition of holding more than two or three offices as well. The next clause in Article IV, Section 4 (p. 567) limits officers to two consecutive terms in the same office. Hence,

20　an officer cannot serve three or four consecutive terms, but may serve less than two such terms. Article IX of the Sample Bylaws (p. 570) limits amendments to the bylaws to those of which notice has been given and which are adopted by a two-thirds vote. Thus, the change of a

25　single word is prohibited unless these conditions are met, and a revision of the entire bylaws requires that the same steps be taken.

　　7) *The imposition of a definite penalty for a particular action prohibits the increase or diminution of the penalty.* If

30　the bylaws state that a member shall be dropped from membership on a board if he misses three consecutive regular meetings of the board, he cannot be retained by vote of the board, nor can more severe penalties be imposed, such as a fine in addition. If, for example, it is

35　desired to allow the board to diminish or waive the penalty, or increase it, the bylaw must not make it definite or must specifically provide for diminution, waiver, or enlargement.

8) *In cases where the bylaws use a general term and also two or more specific terms that are wholly included under the general one, a rule in which only the general term is used applies to all the specific terms.* Where the bylaws provide in the basic enumeration of the classes of membership that "members may be active, associate, or honorary," the general term "member" is used to apply to all three classes of members. But if, in the article on Members, it is stated that members may be either active or associate members, or if that article simply describes "members" without classification, as in the Sample Bylaws, Article III (pp. 565–66), the term "member" applies only to those classes or that class of members, even if honorary members are provided for elsewhere—in which case honorary membership is not real membership. Similarly, if the bylaws provide for "elected officers" and "appointed officers," the word "officers" or the expression "all officers," used elsewhere in establishing the term during which office shall be held, applies to both the elected and the appointed officers.

§57. AMENDMENT OF BYLAWS

A motion to amend the bylaws is a particular case of the motion to *Amend Something Previously Adopted* (**35**); it is therefore a main motion, and it is subject to the same rules as other main motions with the following exceptions:

1) Special requirements for this motion's adoption should be specific in the bylaws, and they should always include at least notice *and* a two-thirds vote, which (with a vote of a majority of the entire membership as an allowable alternative) are the requirements for its adoption if such specification in the bylaws is neglected (see p. 562).

2) Permissible primary and secondary amendment of the motion to amend the bylaws is usually limited by the extent of change for which notice was given, as explained below.

3) An affirmative vote on the motion to amend the bylaws cannot be reconsidered (**37**).

4) The rule that, when a main motion is adopted, no other conflicting main motion is thereafter in order is not applicable to the motion to amend the bylaws, since several notices of proposals representing different approaches to the same problem may have been given, and all such bylaw amendments are entitled to be considered (see pp. 575–76).

Method of Handling Bylaw Amendments

The extensiveness of amendments to the bylaws will determine the method of handling them, as follows:

ISOLATED CHANGES.   If only an isolated change is to be made in the bylaws, it can be treated as any motion to *Amend Something Previous Adopted* (**35**), subject to the particular rules indicated immediately above. Sometimes a more extensive change is proposed involving the substitution of an entire section, group of sections, or article. In such a case, often only a few separated passages are actually involved in the changes, and they are offered in the form of a single proposed substitute in order to avoid time-consuming separate action on each change. The text of the substitute should then be given with the notice of proposed amendment, or the notice should delineate each of the actual changes, and only changes within the scope of those contained in the substitute can be considered. Portions of the substitute which remain as in the existing version cannot be amended, since they involve areas for which no notice of proposed change was given.

GENERAL REVISIONS.   Changes of the bylaws that *1* are so extensive and general that they are scattered throughout the bylaws should be effected through the substitution of an entirely new set of bylaws, called a *revision*. Notice of such a revision is notice that a new document will *5* be submitted that will be open to amendment as fully as if the society were adopting bylaws for the first time. In other words, in the case of a revision, the assembly is not confined to consideration of only the points of change included in the proposed revision as submitted by the committee that *10* has drafted it. The revision can be perfected by first-degree and second-degree amendments, but as in the case of any other bylaw amendment, the old document is not pending; and therefore, while the revision can be rejected altogether, leaving the old bylaws intact, the old document cannot be *15* altered with a view to retaining it in a changed form.

PROCEDURE OF CONSIDERATION.   A revision of bylaws or a lengthy amendment involving more than one section should be considered seriatim as described in **28**. If *20* notice is given of several amendments which conflict so that all cannot be given effect, the chair should arrange them in a logical order, much as in the case of filling blanks (**12**), generally taking the least inclusive amendment first and the most inclusive last so that the last one adopted is given ef- *25* fect. Such arrangement of the amendments can be altered by the assembly by a majority vote without debate. Adoption of such an arrangement by unanimous consent or a formal vote is not subject to a motion to *Reconsider,* nor may a later, separate amendment be offered as a substitute for a pending *30* one. However, as already stated on page 574, all bylaw amendments of which notice was given should be considered, as a matter of the rights of their proposers, and a bylaw amendment is not dropped simply because it would conflict with one previously adopted. This procedure does not vio- *35* late the normal parliamentary rule as might appear, because

1　when any bylaw amendment is adopted, that amendment
becomes a part of the bylaws immediately; and it is the bylaw
language *as thus amended,* rather than the previous language, which any bylaw amendments subsequently consid-
5　ered would now propose to modify. If an amendment that
has not been considered no longer presents a rational proposition because it was applicable only to language which has
disappeared from the bylaws in this process, such a bylaw
amendment must, of course, be dropped; but this situation
10　should generally not arise if the amendments are taken up in
proper order as indicated above.

　　The final vote on a bylaw amendment should be counted
and recorded in the minutes unless it is nearly unanimous.

15　　## Amending a Proposed Amendment to the Bylaws

　　While amendments to a proposed bylaw amendment
can be made in both the first and the second degrees (as applicable) and can be adopted by a majority vote without no-
20　tice, they are subject to restrictions on the extent of the
changes they propose.

　　If the bylaws require previous notice for their amendment (as they should), or if they do not but notice *has* been
given and a majority of the entire membership is not pres-
25　ent, no amendment to a bylaw amendment is in order that
increases the modification of the article or provision to be
amended (see Standard Characteristic 6, p. 295). This re-
striction prevents members from proposing a slight change
and then taking advantage of absent members by moving a
30　greater one as an amendment to the amendment. Thus, if
the bylaws place the annual dues of members at $10 and an
amendment is pending to strike out 10 and insert 25, an
amendment to change the 25 to any number between 10
and 25 would be in order, but an amendment to change the
35　number to less than 10 or greater than 25 would be out of
order, even with unanimous consent. Had notice been given

that it was proposed to increase the dues to more than $25 or to reduce them below $10, members who opposed such a change might have attended the meeting to vote against the amendment. The same principle applies to an amendment in the nature of a substitute for sections or articles (short of a revision), as already indicated above; the proposed substitute is open to amendments that diminish the amount of change, but not to amendments that increase it or that introduce new changes. Thus, if an amendment is pending to substitute a new rule for one that prescribes the initiation fee and the annual dues, and the substitute proposes to alter the initiation fee but does not propose any change in the annual dues, then an amendment which recommends changing the annual dues would be out of order.

Amendments to strike out a sentence, paragraph, or section deserve special care. In such cases, the existing bylaw is not itself open to consideration, but only the amendment. If notice is given to strike out a provision of the bylaws and some members feel it should be retained with certain changes whose substance would be outside the scope of that notice, those members should immediately give notice of the amendments to the existing provisions which they think are advisable. Otherwise, friends of the existing provision will be cut off from opportunity to work out compromises for its partial retention by perfecting the existing language.

Giving Notice of Amendments

Notice of a bylaw amendment should be formally worded in a form such as "To amend Article IV, Section 2, by striking out 'March' and inserting 'April' after the words 'second Tuesday in.'" If required to be in writing, the notice should be signed by two members, who thus serve as mover and seconder. When the bylaws do not place a limitation on those who can give notice of a bylaw amendment, any member is entitled to do so. If notice is to be given at a meeting, this is

1 usually done under new business, although it can be done at
any time, even after it has been voted to adjourn if the chair
has not actually declared the meeting adjourned. A bylaws
committee can give notice in that part of the order of busi-
5 ness set aside for committee reports. If notice is to be given
by mail, the society is responsible for paying the cost of sending such notice, not the member proposing the amendment.
When notice has been given of a bylaw amendment, it becomes a general order for the meeting at which it is to be
10 considered. The notice should fairly inform the members of
the changes contemplated. Showing the existing bylaw and
the bylaw with the proposed changes in parallel columns is a
good device so long as the exact amendment, stated in a formal manner, is set out at the top across both columns. When
15 notice of a bylaw amendment is given in open meeting, it
cannot be considered at that time, except to be discussed informally and briefly at the discretion of the presiding officer
(see also pp. 383–84).

20 ## Time at Which a Bylaw Amendment
Takes Effect

An amendment to the bylaws goes into effect immediately upon its adoption unless the motion to adopt specifies
25 another time for its becoming effective, or the assembly has
set such a time by a previously adopted motion. While the
amendment is pending, a motion can be made to amend
the enacting words of the motion to amend by adding a
clause such as this: ". . . with the proviso that [or, ". . . pro-
30 vided, however, that"] this amendment shall not go into effect until after the close of this annual meeting." Or, while
the amendment is pending, an incidental motion can be
adopted that, in the event of the amendment's adoption, it
shall not take effect until a specified time. Either method re-
35 quires only a majority vote. It is a mistake to encumber the
bylaws themselves with provisions which have effect for

only a limited time. If the mechanics of transition to operation under a revised set of bylaws will be complicated in ways for which the act of adoption must provide temporarily, such provisions can be numbered and attached to the revision draft on a separate sheet headed "Provisos Relating to Transition." The motion to adopt the revision can then be made in this form: "I move the adoption of the revised bylaws with the provisos attached thereto."

Amendments to the article on officers may raise difficulties in relation to the time at which adopted changes take effect, unless special care is taken. A society can, for example, amend its bylaws so as to affect the emoluments and duties of the officers already elected, or even to abolish an office; and if it is desired that the amendment should not affect officers already elected, a motion so specifying should be adopted before voting on the amendment, or the motion to amend can have added to it the proviso that it shall not affect officers already elected. There is virtually a contract between a society and its officers, and while to some extent action can be taken by either party to modify or even terminate the contract, such action must be taken with reasonable consideration for the other party.

It is important to note that, although the time when a bylaw amendment *takes effect* can be delayed by the assembly, the amendment becomes part of the bylaws immediately upon adoption. If the amended bylaws are printed, a footnote or similar device should indicate that the amended language is not yet in effect and, if language was removed by the amendment, the text of that provision should be given if it is still applicable in the organization.

Captions, Headings, and Article and Section Numbers

It was formerly customary to permit the secretary to fill in captions, headings, and article, section, or paragraph

1   numbers or letters, and the like, after the assembly had
    adopted bylaws or other long documents. Such designa-
    tions were treated as mere marginal notations which could
    be clerically modified. It is now the usual practice to include
5   these subtitles or identifying numbers or letters as an inte-
    gral part of what is adopted by action of the assembly.

      In the process of amending previously adopted docu-
    ments of this kind, indisputably necessary changes in desig-
    nation by number or letter may be presumed to have been
10 included in the assembly's action even if they were not men-
    tioned. For example, if an assembly adopts a motion "to in-
    sert after Article III a new Article IV reading as follows: . . .
    ," the secretary or a committee should, of course, raise the
    numerical designation of each of the later articles by one,
15 even if the enacting motion made no reference to doing so.
    Only the assembly can amend captions or headings under the
    rules applicable to bylaws or other papers if such change
    could have any effect on meaning, and this authority may not
    be delegated. Corrections of article or section numbers or
20 cross-references that cannot result in a change of meaning
    can be delegated, however, to the secretary or, in more in-
    volved cases, to a committee. An assembly may delegate its
    authority in this connection in a particular case, by adopting,
    for example, a resolution such as the following:

25
      Resolved, That the secretary [or, "the . . . committee"]
      be authorized to correct article and section designa-
      tions, punctuation, and cross-references and to make
      such other technical and conforming changes as may
      be necessary to reflect the intent of the Society in con-
30   nection with . . .

CONVENTIONS

§58. CONVENTIONS OF DELEGATES

As commonly understood in parliamentary law and as used in this book, the word *convention* refers to an assembly of *delegates* (other than a permanently constituted public law-making body), who are usually chosen specially for each session as representatives of the constituent units or subdivisions within a larger group of people, to sit as a single deliberative body acting in the name of the entire group. The most common type of convention is that of an established state or national society—in which the delegates are selected by, and from among, the members of each local unit. Other terms by which such a convention may be described in some organizations include *congress, conference, convocation, general assembly, house of delegates,* and *house of representatives.*

The term *house of delegates,* or *house of representatives,* is often applied particularly in the case of learned or professional associations, to distinguish the voting body of delegates from large numbers of other members of the constituent units, who come to the convention to attend seminars, workshops, educational or social activities, or the like. In some societies, also, *house of delegates* or *house of representatives* may describe a body of delegates who, instead

1　of being elected only for a convention session, are elected for a fixed term during which they hold sessions from time to time as the bylaws may prescribe.

　　　Conventions vary in size, duration, and complexity of
5　operation. A relatively small state society may hold a one-day convention consisting of two or three meetings at which all delegates are present. A week's convention of a national scientific or educational association, on the other hand, may be divided into a number of specialized sections
10　meeting separately at the same time, with only a few meetings when the entire body of delegates gathers in one hall.

　　　In addition, a convention is sometimes called for the purpose of forming an association or federation; or (like a mass meeting, **53**) it may be convened to draw interested
15　parties or representatives of interested organizations together in acting upon a particular problem.

　　　This chapter is limited to the features common to most conventions and relates principally to the convention of an established society. (For variations of procedure applying to
20　other types of conventions, see **60**.)

Basic Provisions in Bylaws

　　　In the case of an established state, regional, or national
25　society composed of constituent units, the bylaws (see pp. 12–14, 558) or other governing instrument of the association or parent body should:

- authorize a periodic convention;
30　• define its powers and duties;
- fix its quorum;
- specify its voting members;
- prescribe the qualifications of its delegates and alternates, the basis of determining their number, and the
35　method of electing them; and

- make such provision as the particular convention may require for its organization and operation.

Basic provision for the voting body of members may be worded in the bylaws as appropriate to the particular organization—for example, as follows:

> The voting members of the State Convention shall be the state officers (including members of the Executive Board of the State Association), the president (or, in his absence, the vice president) of each club within the Association, and the elected delegates of each club.

In addition, the bylaws at the level on which the convention is held should prescribe: (1) the conditions for a constituent unit to be in good standing for purposes of the right to representation—commonly including a minimum membership requirement; and (2) the number of delegates to which a unit shall be entitled depending on its size—usually by specifying, for example, that each unit shall be represented by its president, plus one additional delegate if the unit has more than a certain number of members, or two additional delegates if the unit has more than twice that number of members, and so on.

The bylaws at the level at which the convention is held should also provide for the election of alternates as described on page 585.

To avoid a change of officers during the convention (see p. 556), the bylaws should provide that newly elected officers shall take up their duties at the close of the convention.

Convention Members and Alternates

WAYS IN WHICH VOTING MEMBERSHIP COMES ABOUT. Voting membership in a convention of an established society generally comes about in one of the following ways:

1) through being an accredited delegate elected by a constituent body especially to act as its authorized representative (or one of several representatives) in a particular convention;
2) through provision in the bylaws, as in many organizations, that the president or chief officer (or, in his absence, the vice-president) of each constituent local unit shall be the delegate or one of the delegates;
3) through being an incumbent elective officer of the organization on the level at which the convention is held—for example, an officer of a state society in a state convention, where the officers of the state society as listed in the bylaws are ex officio the officers of the convention as well as members of it, irrespective of the number of delegates that the local unit to which an officer belongs is entitled to elect; or
4) through being an accredited elected alternate and replacing, at the time of the convention, a delegate who is unable to attend or who withdraws from registered status.

FILLING OF VACANCIES ARISING IN A DELEGATION.   If the president of a constituent unit is unable to be present at the convention of an established society, his place there is taken by the vice-president (or by the second, third, or ranking available vice-president if necessary and if there are such officers), just as for any other duty in which the vice-president acts in the president's place. If the vice-president is himself an elected delegate but takes the president's place, the vice-president's original position as an elected delegate is filled by an elected alternate in the manner explained below—just as when any other elected delegate does not serve.

Provision for Alternates.   To ensure as complete representation at the convention as possible, the bylaws at the convention level should provide that each unit shall elect a certain number of alternates—frequently equal to the number of delegates. To maintain a uniform standard of representation, the qualifications for election as an alternate—which may include membership in good standing for a prescribed number of years—are made the same as for a delegate.

Alternates normally are elected with a designated order, in which they will be called to serve, if available, as vacancies arise in the delegation of their constituent unit. When a unit has more than one delegate, an elected alternate (other than the vice-president) is not associated with any particular delegate. The vacancy that occurs first in point of time (except one involving the president when the vice-president is able to serve in his stead) is filled by the first elected alternate or the ranking one available, and so on.

In cases where the individual delegates within a unit's delegation represent particular areas or groups, it may sometimes be desirable to make exception to the foregoing rule by providing, in the bylaws at the convention level, for the pairing of each alternate with a specific delegate. The disadvantage of such a system arises when both a particular delegate and his only alternate are unable to attend the convention—thus depriving a constituent unit of part of the representation to which it is entitled.

Status and Seating of Alternates; Replacement Procedure.   Alternates registered as such are usually provided with badges of a different color or shape from those of delegates and are seated in sections apart from them. (In large conventions, assigned seats in the assembly hall ordinarily can be guaranteed only to the voting body.) When an alternate is officially registered by the Credentials Committee (pp. 592ff.) as taking the place of an elected delegate, however, he is supplied with a delegate's badge and becomes a voting delegate with the same duties and privileges as if originally so elected.

If an alternate is to replace a delegate who has registered, proper evidence of that delegate's withdrawal from such status must be presented to the Credentials Committee, and the alternate must be reregistered as the new delegate before he can sit or vote as a member of the convention. It is the duty of any registered delegate who ends his presence at the convention to see that his departure is promptly reported to the Credentials Committee, and to whatever authority is concerned with locating the proper accredited alternate if one is available. Unless the rules of the body provide otherwise, no alternate or other person can "substitute" for a delegate who remains registered. In other words, a delegate's temporary absence from the convention hall does not entitle an alternate to make motions, speak in debate, or cast the delegate's vote—even with the delegate's authorization—unless a rule of the body permits this procedure.

DUTIES OF DELEGATES. When a member of a constituent unit has accepted election as a delegate, he has the obligation to attend the convention, with such expense allowance as the unit may provide; he should not leave it to an alternate to serve in his place except for serious reason. At the convention, the delegate has the duty to be present at the business meetings, and to be prepared on returning from the convention to present to his unit an information report of what transpired. A delegate is free to vote as he sees fit on questions at the convention, except as his constituent unit may have instructed him in regard to particular matters scheduled for consideration.

Caucuses

Prior to or during a convention, members of a delegation may need or wish to meet as a group to decide how they will act with reference to certain matters to come before the convention; a meeting of this kind is usually called a *caucus*. Unless such a caucus is so large that it must necessarily proceed in the manner of an assembly, it is governed by the rules of procedure applicable to committees (**50**), since the delegation is in effect a committee to represent and act at the convention for the constituent society or unit that chose it. If the president of a constituent society (or in his absence the vice-president) is automatically a delegate to a convention, he usually acts as chairman of his delegation; otherwise the delegation chairman is selected as outlined for the case of any other committee (p. 168).

Sometimes caucuses are held of different groupings of delegates, as, for example, all delegates from a certain district, territory, or other geographic area as defined by the organization; and they are similarly governed by the rules generally applicable to committees.

As in the case of any committee, in the absence of a superior rule to the contrary a constituent society or unit can instruct its delegation, although this is not always a good practice in ordinary societies. Such instructions are binding upon the delegation to the extent that the convention's presiding officer and other officials should enforce instructions of which they have been properly and officially notified. Such instructions, for example, frequently require a delegation to take a position for or against a measure expected to come before the convention, or to vote for certain candidates. As stated above, the delegates are free to vote as they see fit except where an instruction has been given; but a society can, by instructing its delegation, bind it to vote as a unit (that is, to cast all of its votes in accord with the decision of the majority of the delegation) on all issues, on a particular class of business, or on certain matters to be acted on by the convention.

1   The term *caucus* is also sometimes applied to a similar
    meeting of all the known or admitted partisans of a partic-
    ular position on an important issue—in a convention or any
    other deliberative assembly—who meet to plan strategy to-
5   ward a desired result within the assembly. Such a meeting
    may be held on the presumed informal understanding that
    those who attend will follow the decisions of the caucus.

§59. ORGANIZATION OF A CONVENTION
10 OF AN ESTABLISHED SOCIETY

    Most conventions must operate on a closely controlled
    schedule and transact a large amount of business quickly—
    often with rented facilities available only for a prearranged
15 length of time and with each added day of meetings entailing
    considerable expense both to the association and to the del-
    egates personally. Maximum effort toward a well-organized
    convention is therefore essential.

20 **Advance Preparation**

    The work of organizing and preparing for a convention
    normally begins weeks or months in advance and involves
    many committees, under the general direction of the offi-
25 cers and the board of the association.

    The principal parliamentary functions most directly
    connected with the formal organization of the convention
    itself are performed by three committees, each of which has
    been appointed by the president or the board as prescribed
30 in the bylaws. These three committees are: (1) the Creden-
    tials Committee, which prepares and certifies to the con-
    vention the list of officers, delegates, and alternates that it
    has registered after finding them entitled to accreditation;
    (2) the Committee on Standing Rules, which drafts rules of
35 operating procedure specially required for the particular

convention; and (3) the Program Committee, which works *1*
out a convention program combining a suitable *order of
business* (**41**) with special features designed to promote and
develop the association or society as a whole. Because the
duties of these committees are exacting, a member should *5*
never be appointed to one of them for any other reason
than his ability in the field involved.

In addition, depending on the size of the convention,
one or more committees concerned with the necessary physical arrangements, such as securing the hall, hotel accommo- *10*
dations, and related services, should be appointed. If a single
committee is responsible for all of these matters, it may be
known as the Convention Arrangements Committee.

Another important committee that usually works before
as well as during the convention is the Resolutions Com- *15*
mittee. This committee screens and recommends appropriate action on resolutions and original (as distinct from
incidental) main motions to come before the convention.

The duties of the convention committees are more fully
explained in the succeeding pages of this chapter. *20*

Each of the regular standing committees of the association—in consultation with the presiding officer, the executive
body or board, and the Program Committee—should also
carefully plan the presentation and management of the convention business that is the particular committee's concern. *25*

A preconvention meeting of the board of the association is often held in the convention city a day or more in
advance of the convention opening. A number of decisions
bearing on business to come before the convention may be
made at this meeting. *30*

Services of a Parliamentarian

A key consultant in the preparation for a convention
should be the parliamentarian, *who should be engaged well in* *35*

advance. It is desirable that this person be a professional— the more seasoned in actual operating experience within organizations, the better. Although he has the duty of giving parliamentary advice and opinions (see pp. 449–51) at convention meetings (where he should be seated next to the presiding officer), the parliamentarian's most important work may well be performed before the convention opens. During the period of preparation and while the convention is in progress, he should serve as the principal adviser to the president, the officers, and the committee chairmen regarding management of the convention as it relates to the actual transaction of business. The chairmen of the Credentials Committee, the Committee on Standing Rules, the Program Committee, the Resolutions Committee, the Elections Committee if there is one, and the standing committees who are to present business to the convention should all consult with the parliamentarian during this time; and it may be advisable that he should attend certain meetings of these committees. The parliamentarian should always be present at the preconvention board meetings mentioned above.

Formal Organization Procedure at the Convention

Before a convention can transact any other business, it must officially form itself into a single voting body—which is done at the first *business* meeting. Preliminary ceremonies—whether at the commencement of the convention or at the beginning of each day—are not regarded as business. A separate formal opening of inspirational nature can be held, if desired, before the convention is officially organized. When the assembly of delegates of an established society has been so organized in accordance with the bylaws or other governing rules as described below, it then acts as

and in the name of the whole society and may be referred *1*
to as "The Tenth Annual Convention of the National Society of _____" or, as common formerly, "The National Society of _____ in convention assembled."

The official organization of the convention is brought *5*
about by the separate consideration and adoption of the reports of three committees mentioned above—the Credentials Committee, the Committee on Standing Rules, and the Program Committee, in that order.

As each report comes up for consideration, it is pre- *10*
sented to the convention by a reporting member, normally the respective committee chairman. This person should conclude his report with a statement that "by direction of the committee" he moves its adoption—unless he is not a voting member of the convention, in which case anyone *15*
who is such a voting member can make this motion; a convenient practice is for the recording secretary of the convention or a qualified member of the committee to do so. No second is required if the motion is made by a member of the committee. If no one offers the motion promptly, the *20*
chair can call for it, or can assume it by stating, for example, "The question is on the adoption of the report of the Program Committee."

Each of these committee reports is debatable and amendable. In an ordinary convention of a society, how- *25*
ever, debate or proposals for amendment of any of them seldom occur, and the reports are likely to be adopted without dissenting vote—if the committees have done their work well. (The vote *required* for their adoption is a majority for the reports of the Credentials Committee and *30*
the Program Committee, and normally a two-thirds vote for that of the Committee on Standing Rules, as explained on pp. 600–601.) With the adoption of these three separate reports, the convention is officially organized for conducting business. *35*

Credentials Committee

RESPONSIBILITIES.   The specific duties of the Credentials Committee are listed below. Items (1) through (4) must of necessity be spread over a considerable period of time in advance of the convention. Items (5) and (6) must be performed at the convention location during the period leading up to the convention opening. Items (7) and (8) relate to the committee's duties during the convention.

1) Distribution well in advance, to each constituent body entitled to representation, of (a) information, in accordance with the bylaws, as to the authorized number of representatives and alternates, eligibility requirements, and the time and manner of their election;* and (b) credentials forms with instructions that they are to be returned by a specified date after having been filled in with the names of the representatives and alternates designated by the constituent unit, and having been signed by the unit's secretary and sometimes also by its president. A single form can be used for all representatives and alternates, or a separate form in the form of a card can be used for each delegate and each alternate, with different colors to distinguish delegates from alternates. If alternates are paired with specific delegates as described on page 585, double cards can be used.

2) a) Examination of all forms returned, to verify the eligibility of each member listed; and (b) notification to the proper constituent unit whenever an elected delegate or alternate is found ineligible (through nonpayment of dues, insufficient duration of membership, etc.), advising the unit of its right to designate one of the elected

---

*Some organizations include this information in a printed, general "Call to Convention."

alternates named on its credentials form to take the
place of any ineligible delegate (unless replacement is
automatic because of pairing of alternates with individual
delegates).

3) Compilation of the list of members entitled to register
and the basis of this right (officer who is a convention
member ex officio, unit president, elected delegate, alternate,
etc.) arranged for quick reference—as alphabetically
by districts, clubs, sections, or as may be suitable.

4) Arrangements for registration to take place at the convention—beginning
one or two days before the convention
opens (see p. 594).

5) Registration—which normally includes these steps:
   a) Submission, by the member intending to register, of
      evidence that he is entitled to do so;
   b) Verification by the committee, or a subcommittee of
      it, that the member's credentials are correct;
   c) Recording of the member as officially registered,
      upon his paying the registration fee (which is sometimes
      sent in in advance) and signing the list of registrations;
      and
   d) Issuing of the particular badge to which the member
      is entitled, the official program, and additional
      necessary information, such as time and place of individual
      section or committee meetings or workshops.

6) Preparation of the committee's first report to the convention,
which can include registrations only to such an
hour as will enable the chairman of the Credentials
Committee to present this initial report as the first item
of official business of the convention.

7) Continuation of the committee until the convention
ends—to record changes in the registration rolls occasioned
by: (a) additional registrations (which the bylaws
or the convention's standing rules [pp. 599ff.] may

1   require to be closed at a specified time slightly earlier than
the final adjournment); or (b) the departure of delegates
and the reregistration of alternates who replace them.

8) Submission of a supplementary credentials report—at
5   the beginning of the first business meeting each day and
at other times when required—as resulting from
changes in the registration rolls.

In societies that maintain a permanent administrative
10 headquarters, most of the clerical duties required of the
Credentials Committee in advance of the convention usually develop into a routine technique preserved from year to
year and performed largely by the regular paid staff; but the
authority and responsibility for general direction of this
15 work remain with the Credentials Committee.

TIMES AND PLACE OF REGISTRATION. The
times and the place of registration should be announced in
the printed convention program. In a convention of any size
20 lasting for a number of days, registration may begin one or
two days before the convention opens, and provision should
be made to handle a heavy volume of registrations during the
afternoon and evening before the opening business meeting,
as well as on the morning of that meeting. This registration
25 normally takes place in a separate room or hall whose size and
equipment depend on the probable total number of registrants. Throughout the convention, a registration desk of the
Credentials Committee in a convenient location should be
manned a reasonable time before each business meeting be-
30 gins, and should always remain open during meetings. Near
the end of the convention, usually only one or two committee members stay on duty.

METHOD OF REGISTRATION. The method used
35 by the Credentials Committee to register the delegates and

alternates will vary according to the size of the convention.   *1*
A procedure in common use is outlined as follows: The entire association holding the convention is divided into parts,
such as states, districts, or counties, and a separate section of
the register—often prepared in triplicate, as noted below—   *5*
is set up for each subdivision. Each section of the register
contains—arranged in an appropriate logical order—the
typed names of the constituent societies or units located
within the corresponding geographical area; and under each
unit's name are typed alphabetically the names of the dele-   *10*
gates and alternates that have been sent in on the unit's credentials blanks, provided that these persons have been found
eligible by the committee. During the initial period when
the bulk of registrations take place, usually two committee
members are assigned to a separate and conspicuously   *15*
marked table or station for each section of the register. In a
large convention, ushers may be helpful in guiding delegates
and alternates to the proper section, where they present
their credentials and sign the register to the right of their
typewritten names. At least one, and frequently two, dupli-   *20*
cate registers (or photo-copy-reproduced sets of the register
pages) are desirable in addition to the Credentials Committee's master copy—one duplicate list to be submitted as an
attachment to the committee's report, the other for later use
by election tellers in verifying the eligibility of voters. By use   *25*
of the latter copy, counting procedure in an election can be
expedited by dividing the tellers into subcommittee groups
for each section of the register, according to the same pattern as in the case of the Credentials Committee members
during registration. The delegates' badges can also be corre-   *30*
spondingly labeled or numbered to facilitate identification
with the correct section.

Cases of contested seats in a delegation will seldom arise
except in political conventions. In the rare event of a contest
between two delegates or groups of delegates and serious   *35*

1 doubt as to which is entitled to be seated, the committee
should omit both from the list and report the fact of the
contest to the convention as explained below. If, on the
other hand, after hearing the facts, the committee thinks the
5 contest is not justified, it should enter on the list only the
names of the delegates whose claim it finds to be legitimate.
The same rules apply to the more common case of delegates
chosen by a local unit that is not entitled to representation
or has chosen delegates in excess of its entitlement.
10

    ADOPTION OF REPORT.   Before the receipt of the
Credentials Committee report, since the membership has
not been established, no motion whatever is in order under
any pretext except those that are in order in the absence of
15 a quorum. (But see pp. 621–22 for necessary variations in
the case of conventions not of a permanent organization.)
Even, for example, a motion relating to the validity of the
holding of the convention is not in order. It is, therefore,
essential that the committee establish and hold itself to a
20 deadline for registrations to be included in its first report,
which will leave it time to prepare that report. The opening
ceremonies will afford some opportunity for this work, and,
while it is in process, delegates can continue to register—
but not to be included in the committee's initial report. If
25 the report is not ready in time, the convention may continue with other nonbusiness matters, such as speakers, or
may stand at ease or take a recess.
    The Credentials Committee report, which is read by the
committee's chairman, should state in substance that, "At-
30 tached is the list of the names of the voting members of the
convention and their alternates who have been registered
up until . . . [indicating the hour to which the list is cor-
rected]." This statement should be followed by whatever
statistical summary is customary in the particular organiza-
35 tion (frequently including a breakdown according to basis

of voting membership as indicated in item [3] on p. 593), and should always give the total number of convention members *entitled to vote* and the number of registered alternates. Normally the list of delegates and alternates is not read unless a portion of it is read upon request, for information. If there is an unresolved contest between delegates, the particulars should be stated, as well as the fact that the names of the contesting or contested delegates do not appear on the roll. The committee chairman concludes the report by saying, "On behalf of the committee, I move that the roll of delegates hereby submitted be the official roll of the voting members of the convention." The report with the attached list of names should then be handed to the chair or to the secretary.

Unless there is debate or proposed amendment, the chair, before taking the vote on the adoption of the report, asks, "Are there any questions on the report?" If seat(s) are contested, an amendment can be offered substantially in this form: "To amend by adding 'provided that the name of George J. Morse be added to the roll of delegates as submitted, as a delegate from the state of Missouri.'" The name of the rival delegate can then be offered in a secondary amendment, for example, "to strike out 'George J. Morse' and insert 'Frank Norton.'" Whether or not a contest is reported, it is in order to move such amendments or even to move to substitute an entirely different set of delegates for any delegation in the reported list, but no such amendment is permitted to include more names than those of a single challenged delegate or delegation all of whom are challenged on the same grounds, together with any claimants involved. On an amendment proposing changes in the list of delegates, none of the delegates involved in the case can vote. Those seated by the committee, though contested in a case not yet reached, can vote on all cases except their own. On the question of adopting the Credentials

1 Committee's report or on motions connected with its consideration, only those persons whose names are on the list
   of voting members reported by the committee (as this list
   stands after any amendment already approved by the con-
5 vention) are entitled to vote.

   ROLL OF VOTING MEMBERS; SUPPLEMENTARY
   REPORTS.   When the report of the Credentials Committee is adopted, it is thereby ratified as the official roll of vot-
10 ing members of the convention—subject to changes through
   later reports. A voting member who registers after the submission of the first report assumes his full status as soon as he
   has done so, if his status is not questioned; if it is, it must
   await a decision by the committee or the convention itself.
15 Although the Credentials Committee normally makes a supplementary report only at the beginning of each day, it may
   be called upon to do so at other times, such as immediately
   before an important vote. If there has been no change in the
   roll of registered delegates since the last report, no motion or
20 vote is required; but if there are changes, the committee
   chairman should conclude his report by saying, "On behalf
   of the committee, I move that the revised roll of delegates
   hereby submitted be the official roll of voting members of
   the convention." Although this motion might appear to be
25 one to amend something previously adopted (**35**), it requires
   only a majority vote for its adoption, since it is always understood that the roll will be added to and subtracted from as
   delegates arrive late or leave early, and alternates may thereby
   be shifted in status.

30   The Credentials Committee's master roll of currently
   registered voting members of the convention should be
   maintained at all times in such a way that their exact
   number can be promptly determined. Accuracy of the list
   of registrants is essential, since it may affect the outcome
35 of elections or closely contested issues. If the bylaws or

the convention's standing rules do not prescribe a quorum (**40**)—which they should do—the quorum is a majority of the number of voting members who have actually registered, irrespective of whether some may have departed.

Committee on Standing Rules

RESPONSIBILITIES.   The Committee on Standing Rules drafts and submits for consideration a group of rules known as "The Standing Rules of the Convention," which, as adopted, will apply to that one convention only. These rules must in no way conflict with the bylaws of the society, but (in contrast to ordinary standing rules in a local society) they can involve modifications of rules contained in the parliamentary authority prescribed by the bylaws. The standing rules of a convention usually contain both "parliamentary" rules relating to the conduct of business, and nonparliamentary rules, so that in some ways they resemble a combination of special rules of order and ordinary standing rules (**2**). Since their effect expires at the close of the session that adopts them, however, they differ from either of the latter types of rules in certain respects.

The standing rules of successive conventions held by a society often become developed to a point where little change in the rules adopted by the preceding convention is necessary. On the other hand, the work of this committee may sometimes require extensive research into past proceedings of the organization. In any case, the parliamentarian should always be consulted regarding the convention's standing rules, and he often prepares a first draft for submission to this committee.

A copy of the "Proposed Standing Rules of the Convention" that the committee is to recommend—usually

1 printed in the official program—should be handed to each
person when he registers.

PRESENTATION AND ADOPTION OF CONVENTION STANDING RULES.

5 The report of the
Committee on Standing Rules is presented to the convention immediately after the adoption of that of the
Credentials Committee by offering a motion in a form
similar to item 9, tinted page 31, and by reading the pro-
10 posed rules in their entirety—regardless of their previous
distribution—unless, in cases where every delegate has
been provided with a copy and the rules generally do not
change from year to year, a firmly established custom of
the organization permits this reading to be omitted. After
15 debate or amendment (if any), a single vote normally is
taken on the complete body of rules. It should be understood that seriatim consideration (**28**) is not applicable
because, although the rules may be organized to have the
appearance of being a single document, they are, in fact,
20 a group of separate main motions being offered by the
committee under one enacting motion. By the demand of
a voting member of the convention, a separate vote can
be required on any individual rule (see p. 265), although
such a demand is advisable only if a serious matter ap-
25 pears to be at stake. If such a demand is made, the remainder of the rules are acted on first, and then those
separated out are acted on individually. Under the usual
procedure of voting on the standing rules as a "package,"
a two-thirds vote is required for their adoption—because,
30 if they are to fill the needs of the convention, they nearly
always include provisions which can be imposed only by
a two-thirds vote. If a new rule is proposed, either during
the consideration of the committee's proposed rules or
later during the convention, it should be acted on sepa-
35 rately after the adoption of the committee's proposals as
discussed below.

VOTE REQUIRED FOR ADOPTION OF AN INDI-   1
VIDUAL RULE.   If a standing rule of a convention is
voted on individually, the vote necessary for its adoption is
in some cases two thirds and in others a majority, depending on the nature of the rule: 5

1) Convention standing rules requiring a two-thirds vote
   for adoption (even individually) are, in principle, distinguished by the same characteristics as provisions which,
   in an ordinary local society or assembly, would need a   10
   two-thirds vote to be placed in effect for the duration of
   a meeting or session, or would require adoption as a *special rule of order* to continue in force from session to
   session (see **2**). An example would be a rule limiting the
   time allowed for debate. Rules in this class are described   15
   by the term *parliamentary standing rules in a convention* as used in this book.
2) A standing rule is individually adoptable by a majority
   vote in a convention if it does not fall in class (1) above,
   and consequently could be adopted in a local assembly   20
   as an *ordinary standing rule* (see **2**). Examples of such
   convention rules would be those relating to the wearing
   of badges or to the format in which written reports or
   resolutions shall be submitted.

   25

VOTE REQUIRED TO AMEND OR RESCIND A
CONVENTION STANDING RULE.   To amend or re-
scind a standing rule of a convention requires a two-thirds
vote or the vote of a majority of all the delegates or other
"voting members" of the convention who have been regis-   30
tered, except that a rule individually adoptable by a majority vote can be amended or rescinded by a majority vote
after notice on at least the preceding day.

SUSPENSION OF A CONVENTION STANDING   35
RULE.   Any standing rule of a convention (except one

1 prescribing the parliamentary authority) can be suspended
for a particular specified purpose by a majority vote, even if
the rule required a two-thirds vote for its adoption. Under
such a suspension, however, the applicable rules in the par-
5 liamentary authority prescribed by the bylaws (or by a rule
of the convention) come into force—as if the standing rule
had not been adopted. To suspend a convention standing
rule and also the general parliamentary rule normally applying to the same situation requires a two-thirds vote, just
10 as to suspend the general rule when no standing rule is involved (**25**).* No standing rule of a convention can be suspended for the remainder of the session, and no standing
rule which has only a single application can be suspended,
since this would be equivalent to rescinding the rule, and
15 the case would have to be treated accordingly.

    SAMPLE SET OF CONVENTION STANDING
RULES.   The standing rules of a convention must vary
20 with its size, type, and responsibilities. While it is not possible to frame model rules which are universally applicable,
the following sample set illustrates the nature of the standing rules adopted by many conventions.

---

    *The reason why a parliamentary standing rule of a convention can be
suspended by a majority vote even though it requires a two-thirds vote for
its adoption is as follows: In a convention, parliamentary standing rules—
which are in the nature of suspensions of the regular rules of order for the
duration of the convention session—generally arise from a need to give the
majority more power to transact business with minimum delay, even when
the majority is not large enough to command a two-thirds vote. Since it is
thus likely to reduce the protection of a minority greater than one third, a
parliamentary standing rule of a convention requires a two-thirds vote for
its adoption; but since the same rule tends to protect a majority of less than
two thirds, such a majority should have the right to suspend the rules for a
particular purpose and allow the regular rules of order to come into force.

STANDING RULES OF THE _____ CONVENTION
                    OF _____

Rule 1. (a) The Credentials Committee, directly after the opening ceremonies of the first business meeting,* shall report the number of delegates and alternates registered as present with proper credentials, and shall make a supplementary report after the opening exercises at the beginning of each day that business continues.

(b) A member registered as an alternate may, upon proper clearance by the Credentials Committee, be transferred from alternate to delegate at any time during the continuance of business meetings.

Rule 2. For admission to the assembly hall, to facilitate identification and seating, members, alternates, and others shall be required to wear the badge issued by the Credentials Committee upon registration.

Rule 3. A resolution offered by an individual member shall be in writing, signed by the maker and the seconder—each of whom shall be a voting member of the convention—and shall be sent directly to the desk of the Recording Secretary.

Rule 4.** (a) All resolutions except those proposed by the Executive Board [or "Board of Directors," "Board of Managers," etc.] or by committees, and all recommendations made in reports of officers or committees of the convention that are not in the form of resolutions, shall be referred without debate to the Resolutions Committee; resolutions proposed by the

---

*See pages 590–91.

**Regarding variations in the rules and practices of societies relating to the handling of resolutions at a convention, see pages 614–17.

Executive Board or by committees shall be presented by the Board or proposing committee directly to the convention.

(b) Each member who offers a resolution shall be given an opportunity to explain it to the Resolutions Committee if he so requests.

(c) The Resolutions Committee shall prepare suitable resolutions to carry into effect recommendations referred to it, and shall submit to the convention, with the Committee's own recommendation as to appropriate action, these and all other resolutions referred to the Committee, except questions which the Committee by a vote of two thirds of its members may decide not to report.*

(d) The convention by a majority vote may suspend this Rule 4 and may immediately consider a question, or may order the Resolutions Committee to report a question at a certain time, even if the Committee has voted not to report it.

Rule 5. No member shall speak in debate more than once on the same question on the same day, or longer than two minutes, without permission of the convention granted by a two-thirds vote without debate.

Rule 6. All reports and other material for the permanent record or printed proceedings shall be in typing and, immediately on presentation, shall be sent to the Recording Secretary.

Rule 7. Nominations for each office to be filled by the convention shall be limited to one nominating speech of three minutes and one seconding speech of one minute for each nominee.

Rule 8. Notices for announcement to the convention shall be in writing, signed by the person (or a proper representative of the persons) under whose au-

*See pages 616–17.

thority the announcement is issued, and shall be sent to the desk of the Recording Secretary.

Rule 9.* The rules contained in the current edition of *Robert's Rules of Order Newly Revised* shall govern the convention in all cases to which they are applicable and in which they are not inconsistent with the bylaws of the Society [or "Federation," "Association," etc.] and these standing rules.

Program Committee

The Program Committee plans and submits the proposed schedule of meetings, proceedings, and special events of the convention. When the program is adopted by the voting body, with or without amendment, it becomes the *order of business* of the entire convention session (**41**). The program also commonly includes—interwoven throughout the convention timetable—a series of addresses, forums, workshops, exhibits, tours, and other activities designed for membership-training, motivational, or entertainment value.

RESPONSIBILITIES.   The nature of a convention Program Committee's responsibilities is considerably more complex than for a committee of the same name in a local society that includes a "program" as a part of each meeting. The overall program must cover all aspects of the society's work and commitments on the level at which the convention is held (district, state, national, etc.)—reviewing the period

---

*A rule on "Parliamentary Authority" is included in the standing rules of a convention only if the bylaws of the organization do not prescribe the authority. If this rule is included, it cannot be suspended as such, although a particular rule stated in the parliamentary authority can be suspended by a two-thirds vote.

since the preceding convention and anticipating the course of the society until the next convention. In addition to enabling the convention to handle all business that it should consider within the time available, the program should be of such nature as to stimulate each delegate to an evaluation of the society's policies, accomplishments, and opportunities, inasmuch as benefit from the convention to the general membership may depend largely on the impression that each local president or delegate transmits to the unit he represents.

The Program Committee usually begins work soon after the preceding convention closes, and its duties continue throughout the convention that it plans—so that it functions as virtually a standing committee of the organization. The Program Committee should work in close contact with the president and the parliamentarian.

PLANNING THE PROGRAM. Although the program must come before the convention for adoption and can be amended by it, many details must be decided far ahead. Prior to the convention, the Program Committee must have the authority (sometimes with designated members of the executive committee or board as advisers, and often acting in cooperation with a Convention Arrangements Committee) to engage outside speakers or entertainers, to work out an order of business allotting appropriate amounts of time to each subject, and to make all necessary advance arrangements.

Some societies mail a tentative skeleton program to the constituent units several weeks beforehand as part of a printed "Call to Convention." The complete program that the committee expects to recommend should be printed at the latest practical time for handing to each person as he registers at the convention.

The order of business for the complete series of a convention's business meetings normally includes, in expanded form, the elements of the one followed in ordinary meet-

ings of the society's constituent units (**41**). In the case of
the convention, however, greater detail and precision are
necessary for two principal reasons: (1) Adherence to a prearranged schedule is imperative if the convention is to complete its work—timing being an especially important factor
if there are to be features carried by radio and television at
particular hours, addresses by government officials, or ap-
pearances by professional artists. (2) Each member has the
right to know at which meeting and at what approximate
time a particular matter can be expected to come before the
convention, so that he may avoid absence from the hall during important debates or votes.

Some organizations divide the printed convention program into two parts, the first of which gives the times and
places of special events and—for each business meeting—only
the hours of the call to order, adjournment, and any scheduled recesses. The second part, listing the items or classes of
business set for each meeting, is then known as the *agenda*
(**41**). Use of this term does not alter the fact that the items
must be brought before the convention in the order named,
and not until the meeting or hour for which they are set.

While it is not possible to set out a model program that
would be suitable for all conventions, the following principles are commonly applicable:

- Notice of the times of registration should be given early
  general distribution by mail, and should also be printed
  in the convention program. Handing out—with the
  program—a schedule of preconvention meetings of the
  board and of committees is often advisable, although
  the persons directly concerned with these meetings may
  need to be separately informed at an earlier time.
- When the invocation is offered, the national anthem is
  played or sung, and the pledge of allegiance is recited in
  opening ceremonies, they should always be in that
  order—that is, the invocation first and the pledge last.

- If there is an address of welcome—often given by a local public official at the opening of the convention—it should, as a matter of courtesy, be followed by remarks of acknowledgment and appreciation by the presiding officer or his designee on behalf of the organization.

- For each meeting, the program should specify the hour of opening and closing, and the program or the agenda should specify the order in which the subjects or classes of subjects assigned to that meeting are to come up. The extent to which such classes are subdivided should be guided by the particular conditions and probable timing problems of the individual convention. Sufficient time should be allotted for thorough consideration of each important policy question that is expected to come before the convention. For such an item of business, it is frequently advisable to set a particular hour—which *automatically* makes the matter a *special order* unless otherwise specified (see p. 360). Listed subjects for which no hour is specified are general orders for the meeting to which they are assigned.

- Reports of officers are commonly presented in the order in which the officers are listed in the bylaws, the president reporting first, unless it is the desire or practice of the organization to vary from such an order. Action on the report of the auditors should immediately follow the treasurer's report. Often reports of officers that are for information only and do not require action by the convention are printed and distributed in advance. In such a case it may not be necessary to have the report read; the chair can simply pause for any questions by delegates to the reporting officer, and the reporting officer can make additional comments on his report at that time. The report of the board, if any, usually should follow the reports of officers.

- Reports of committees that are for information only and that do not require action by the convention should, as far as possible, be brought up in succession at the same point in the order of business. Time can frequently be saved by reproducing and distributing these reports in advance, in which case it may be unnecessary to read them aloud to the convention. The chair can then simply call the name of each committee in sequence, pausing for any questions. The chairman of any committee can be permitted to make additional comments upon his committee's report at that time.

- The report of a committee having a resolution or other motion to offer can be received at any appropriate time, but it should usually be before the report of the Resolutions Committee.

- A time for announcements should immediately precede the adjournment of each meeting of the convention.

- Beginning with the second day of the convention (unless a rule or resolution is adopted providing for the approval of the minutes of the entire convention by the board or a committee), the minutes of the preceding day's meetings should be read immediately after any opening ceremonies at the first meeting of each day. Authority to approve such minutes is then usually delegated to the board or to a special committee, by means of a standing rule of the convention or an adopted resolution introduced by the Resolutions Committee.

- Business unfinished at the end of a day normally is taken up after the reading of the minutes (or after the opening of the meeting, if the minutes are not read) at the resumption of business the next day—provided that the program makes no special provision for unfinished business on that day and there is no conflict with a special order. If unfinished business is not listed as such in the program each day, the planned timing should nevertheless allow for it; a listed heading of "Unfinished Busi-

1 ness" should then be provided near the end of the last business meeting, and at any point where it is advisable because special orders have been scheduled early in the day (see also **41**).

5 • Nominations and the election of officers should take place relatively early in the convention, if possible, so that there will be time to complete balloting if more than one ballot must be taken.

• If there is to be a formal installation of officers, this cer-
10 emony is often made a part of a closing banquet meeting, at which any presentations of gavels, pins, awards, or the like are also made.

It is often advisable to schedule a meeting of the exec-
15 utive body or board of the association a day after the close of the convention, asking the board members and other necessary personnel to remain in the convention city for this purpose. If such a meeting is to be held, its time and place may be announced in the printed convention
20 program.

ADOPTION OF THE CONVENTION PROGRAM. The program is the president's guide as to the order of business during the initial proceedings, even before it has
25 been formally adopted by the convention. Directly after the adoption of the standing rules, the report of the Program Committee is presented—normally by the committee chairman—somewhat as follows: "Mr. President, a printed copy of the program as proposed by the Program Committee is
30 in the hands of each registrant for the convention. By direction of the committee I move the adoption of the program as printed." (If the chairman or other person presenting the report is not a voting member of the convention, he omits the motion for adoption. For procedure
35 in such a case, see p. 591.)

If last-minute changes in the program have become necessary, the chairman can make his report by saying: "Mr. President, because of . . . [briefly indicating reasons], the Program Committee recommends the following modifications in its proposed program which has been printed and placed in the hands of each registrant for the convention: . . . [clearly stating each change, with reference to page and line in the printed program]. By direction of the Program Committee, I move that, with these changes, the printed program be adopted." This motion is debatable and amendable. A majority vote adopts the program—even if it contains special orders. While the making of a special order requires a two-thirds vote under ordinary circumstances, the situation is different in the case of a convention program, where the special order is part of a complete order of business being adopted for the current session.

To change the program after its adoption requires a two-thirds vote or the vote of a majority of all the delegates or other "voting members" of the convention who have been registered—or unanimous consent, which can usually be obtained with no difficulty in cases where a departure from the program is justified. Thus, an affirmative vote to adopt the program cannot be reconsidered. (See pp. 51–53; see also *Program* and *Taking Up Business Out of Its Proper Order,* pp. 351–53). Changing the program to add additional meetings within the same session requires such a vote except that during the last meeting scheduled by the program an additional meeting may be set by majority vote through the use of the motion to *Fix the Time to Which to Adjourn* (**22**). Any proposed changes except those to which there is obviously no reasonable alternative are best referred to the Program Committee. The committee can recommend changes if and when needed while the convention is in progress, but neither the presiding officer nor the Program Committee is free to alter the program as adopted—which only the convention can do.

1   (For parliamentary rules applying at the expiration of the time allotted to a subject, and procedure at scheduled times of adjournment, see pp. 215, 230–32, 359, 362.)

5   **Convention Arrangements Committee**

The complex arrangements necessary to a convention generally require the coordination of many additional details that are outside the province of any of the other committees mentioned in this chapter. In the simplest case a Convention Arrangements Committee is appointed—usually by the board at the convention level. Most often the committee's membership is largely made up of members of the constituent society or societies acting as convention hosts; it should, however, include persons who have had experience in similar work at prior conventions. In cases where there has been competition between cities for the convention site, it is often well to place on this committee local members who were instrumental in obtaining the selection of their city.

The Convention Arrangements Committee may be empowered to consult experts, who may include professional convention managers. Assistance frequently is obtainable also from staff members of hotels where conventions are held, and from convention bureaus in many cities.

Depending on the size and duration of the convention, duties ordinarily assigned to the Convention Arrangements Committee are sometimes delegated to subcommittees or even distributed among separate committees. At the outset, the convention headquarters must be selected and advance arrangements made concerning room accommodations in as many hotels or motor inns as may be necessary. The committee may work with the Credentials Committee in coordinating room reservations for delegates with their registration for the convention. While the Program Committee may arrange for all speakers and entertainment, details relating to the overnight and other accommodations for these guests are usually a responsibility of the Convention Arrangements Committee. Ensuring that dignitaries and honored guests are met at the airport or other point of arrival may also be one of the latter committee's functions.

Printed or reproduced material assembled in cooperation with the Program Committee for distribution to the delegates in advance of the convention should include directions for getting to the convention by the various means of transportation available, and information about the locality, points of interest, restaurants, entertainment, tours arranged by the Program Committee, and parking facilities for those driving to the convention.

Careful attention should be given to seating arrangements within the hall, voting members always being located in a separate section if other persons are assigned seating space on the convention floor. Pages, messengers, ushers, and doorkeepers—who are essential to the good order of all but the smallest conventions—should be trained to perform their duties in a calm and courteous manner. During the convention, liaison should be maintained with the Program Committee to ensure, for example, proper seating on the platform, as the needs may change from meeting to meeting.

The staffing of an information desk throughout the convention may lie within the province of the Convention Arrangements Committee, together with additional functions in the areas of communications and public relations. If the meetings are to be covered by the press, the representatives of the various media must be kept informed of developments and provided with an area on the floor near the platform, or in some other point of vantage in the hall. It is often helpful to have facilities for typing and copying close at hand, as well as for the distribution of literature. In very large conventions it is wise to investigate existing telephone and other communication facilities and to provide for their augmentation if necessary.

1 **Resolutions Committee**

The Resolutions Committee—also sometimes called the *Reference Committee* or, in certain cases described below, the
5 *Platform Committee*—has as its basic purpose the screening of all original main motions (**10**) that have not been screened by another committee and that come—or are to come—before the convention. It is usually not intended to require purely formal or incidental main motions to be submitted to the Res-
10 olutions Committee, or to refer to it resolutions reported to the convention by other committees (see also **51**).

VARIATIONS IN RULES RELATING TO THE RES-
OLUTIONS COMMITTEE.   The establishment of a Res-
15 olutions Committee in a convention represents a limitation on the ordinary right of members to propose any number of motions from the floor without notice—such limitation arising from the need for keeping within a schedule and disposing of a large amount of business within a short time. The
20 degree of limitation imposed and the manner in which the committee functions vary considerably, depending on the organization, in particulars such as the following:

Variations in the Time When a Resolution Can Be Introduced.   In the simplest situation a resolution is offered from
25 the floor of the convention in the way it would be in an ordinary meeting. Such an arrangement is outlined in Standing Rules 3 and 4(a) on pages 603–604. A place in the program or agenda should then be provided at each meeting, under a heading such as "New Business," for the introduction of res-
30 olutions. Under this system, the proposer of the resolution says, "Mr. President, I move the adoption of [or "I offer"] the resolution which I have sent to the Secretary's desk." The secretary reads the resolution, announcing the names of the mover and the seconder, and the chair says, "Under the rules
35 the resolution is referred to the Resolutions Committee."

To save even this time in a convention, an arrangement can be made whereby resolutions are submitted to the recording secretary without being formally moved and read in open meeting, and the secretary then must promptly deliver them to the chairman of the Resolutions Committee. The convention can suspend such a rule at any time, however—by a majority vote if it is a standing rule of the convention, or by a two-thirds vote if it is a higher-ranking rule (p. 17)—and can thus take up a resolution without sending it to the Resolutions Committee.

If many resolutions are customarily proposed by members, a permanent rule or provision in the bylaws can be adopted by the organization requiring all resolutions to be submitted to the committee, or to the executive secretary for delivery to the committee, a number of days, weeks, or even months in advance of the convention. This system can be arranged to allow time for sending copies of all resolutions considered by the Resolutions Committee to the constituent societies and their delegates in advance of the convention, thereby giving time for consultation and, possibly, instruction of delegates. In such cases it is advisable to provide that resolutions can also be introduced at the convention if permitted by a two-thirds vote in the individual case.

Variations in Permitted Origin of Resolutions.   In the ordinary case only the members of the convention—that is, the delegates—are allowed to introduce resolutions for consideration by the assembly, and other members of constituent societies (who are not convention members) are allowed to speak for the purpose of suggesting motions only with the consent of the convention. Such consent can be granted in an individual case, or a rule can be adopted specifying persons who, in addition to the delegates, can submit resolutions; the latter practice has particular value when resolutions are required to be submitted in advance of the convention meetings.

In some cases any member of a constituent society, whether he is a delegate or not, is permitted to offer a resolution. In other organizations a resolution is required to have the sponsorship of a constituent society itself. A number of organizations require even the resolutions offered by standing and special committees of the organization to be screened and reported by the Resolutions Committee. In some types of organizations the Resolutions Committee originates and drafts its own resolutions for submission to the assembly. In any society, when an officer or committee simply makes one or more recommendations, the Resolutions Committee is customarily assigned the task of putting the recommendation(s) in the form of resolution(s).

Variations in the Power of the Resolutions Committee. In the simplest arrangement, the Resolutions Committee has only the power to put resolutions in proper form, eliminate duplication where similar resolutions are offered, and ensure that all resolutions relating to a specific subject will be offered in a logical sequence. In other cases the committee is given the authority to make substantive alterations in a resolution, but only with the sponsor's consent; while in still others, by vote of the committee—sometimes a two-thirds vote—the substance of the resolution can be altered and the resolution can be reported to the assembly in the altered form as though the committee had originated it.

Except as the rules may provide otherwise, the Resolutions Committee is required to report all resolutions referred to it; but the committee can, if it wishes, report a resolution with "no recommendation." If the committee is given the power "not to report" a resolution—thus withholding it from consideration by the convention—a requirement of an unusually high vote within the committee (such as a three-fourths vote or a vote of two-thirds of the committee's members) should always be imposed; and the convention should always be given power to override such a decision of the Resolutions Committee and order the committee to report the resolution, by a majority vote (see Rule 4(d) in the sample standing rules of a convention, p. 604). In this connection, it should be noted that voting "not to report" a resolution, reporting it with "no recommendation," and reporting it with the recommendation that it be rejected by the convention are each quite different.

PLATFORMS OR POLICY STATEMENTS.   In political and certain other types of organizations, the Resolutions Committee is required to prepare and report a platform for adoption by the organization, setting forth its views, aims, and aspirations. Other associations occasionally require the committee to draft statements of policy or similar documents that take the form of a platform rather than of a resolution. In such a platform or statement, many of the principles applicable to drafting resolutions are followed.

If there is a preamble, instead of beginning each paragraph with the word "Whereas," a participle is used; thus, "Believing in the . . . , [etc.]." Each paragraph is terminated by a semicolon and, in the case of the next-to-the-last paragraph, the word "and." The last paragraph of the preamble may be followed by the word "therefore." Each new paragraph of the preamble begins with another participle. In the body of the paper, each paragraph, instead of opening with the enacting words "*Resolved,* That," begins with a verb denoting an attitude or position—for example, "Affirms . . . ," "Assures . . . ," "Condemns . . . ," "Calls upon . . . ," and the like. As in a resolution, no paragraph should contain a period within its structure. The paragraphs of the body of the document can be linked by a semicolon and the word "and," as in the preamble, or a semicolon only can be used. The first paragraph of the body of the statement is often somewhat general. The preamble and the body of the statement may be connected by words such as "Issues this statement of . . . ; and. . . ." The full name of the organization can precede these words, or it can be placed before the preamble; for example, thus:

> Believing . . . ;
> Recalling . . . ; and
> Noting . . . ;
> The Phoenix Improvement Association issues this
> statement of its basic governing principles; and
> Affirms . . . ;
> Assures . . . ; and
> Condemns . . .

Or:

> The Phoenix Improvement Association,
> Believing . . . ; and
> Holding . . . ; therefore
> Issues this statement of its basic governing princi-
> ples; and
> Affirms . . . ;
> Assures . . . ; [and so on].

COURTESY RESOLUTIONS.   In addition to its duties in regard to the resolutions which are referred to it and which usually relate to policy matters, the Resolutions Committee is often charged with the duty of drafting and presenting to the assembly any courtesy resolutions that may seem appropriate. Ordinarily, courtesy resolutions express the appreciation of the convention to those who arranged accommodations for its physical needs or rendered it service.

MEETINGS OF THE COMMITTEE.   Ordinarily the Resolutions Committee should make known, through

the program or announcements, the times and places it will
meet. It is best to allow any sponsor of a resolution to appear before the committee to explain it and answer any
questions about it; and interested delegates also may be allowed to attend and even participate in discussion. Many
times such free discussion reduces friction that may have
developed concerning a resolution, and the convention as a
result goes more smoothly. After any open "hearings"
of this type, the committee meets in executive session (**9**)
to review each resolution and prepare its report. The
parliamentarian may be asked to attend the committee's
meetings.

REPORT OF THE RESOLUTIONS COMMITTEE.

In reporting, the Resolutions Committee follows the procedure of any committee reporting back a resolution referred to it, as described in **51**. Even when resolutions are
submitted to the committee before the opening of the convention, the report on each resolution is treated as if it had
been moved and seconded in the assembly before being referred to the committee. It is never necessary for the Resolutions Committee chairman or reporting member to move
the adoption of a resolution being reported—unless the
committee itself originated it, as in the case of courtesy
resolutions.

When the committee recommends amendments to a
resolution, in cases where it is not empowered to incorpo-
rate them itself, its chairman reports as follows:

RESOLUTIONS COMMITTEE CHAIRMAN: Mr. President, the Resolutions Committee recommends that the resolution relating to . . . [or
"Resolution No. 6," etc.] be amended by striking out the words ". . . "
and inserting the words ". . . ," and that, as thus amended, the resolution be adopted. By direction of the Resolutions Committee, I move
the adoption of the recommended amendment.

1   If the convention members do not have reproduced copies of the resolution, the chair should read it before stating the question on the amendment. He then proceeds:

5   CHAIR: The Resolutions Committee recommends the adoption of the resolution with the following amendment ... [rereading the amendment]. The question is on the amendment.

     In instances where it is advisable for a resolution of
10 overriding importance to be considered as a special order rather than as a part of the main body of resolutions reported by the Resolutions Committee, this is arranged through liaison with the Program Committee. The chairman of the Resolutions Committee then reports the reso-
15 lution at the time prescribed for it in the agenda. If desired, the committee's report can include a preliminary motion establishing special rules for the consideration of the resolution, similar to the practice of the U.S. House of Representatives. The following is an example of such a rule:
20
     Resolved, That at the time prescribed in the agenda the resolution relating to _____ be considered as a special order, the general debate to be limited to two hours and equally divided between, and controlled by,
25   Mr. A, the leader for the affirmative, and Mr. B, the leader for the negative; that at the expiration of general debate the resolution shall be open to amendment, debate on said amendment(s) to be limited to two minutes for each member.
30
     Under such a rule, the leaders for the two sides are recognized alternately by the presiding officer and can speak themselves or yield the floor to other member(s) for a portion of the time at their disposal. The leaders are usually the
35 more ardent or persuasive advocates of the two positions,

and frequently they speak first and save themselves enough
time so that at the end they can close debate for their side.
An alternative procedure is to assign a longer period of debate to Mr. A and Mr. B, and require other members to adhere to a shorter limit. Often it is helpful to require general
debate to be conducted first before amendments are allowed, but this provision can be dispensed with.

§60. CONVENTIONS NOT OF
A PERMANENT SOCIETY

A convention called only for a specific purpose not involving a permanent organization, or one called to form a
state or a national society or a federation, is similar to a mass
meeting as described in **53** in that when called to order it
has no bylaws or officers. Because it has no bylaws, added
difficulty may be encountered in determining who are the
properly appointed delegates.

The group sponsoring the convention should appoint a
Convention Arrangements Committee, as described above,
to secure the hall and accommodations for the delegates,
make the preliminary arrangements for the convention, and
perform the other coordinating and arranging duties assigned to it. Someone designated by the sponsoring group—
sometimes the chairman of the Convention Arrangements
Committee—should call the meeting to order and preside
during any opening exercises and the election of a temporary
chairman. The sponsoring group's choice for temporary
chairman and the person who is to nominate him should be
agreed upon in advance. After the elected temporary chairman has taken the chair, a temporary secretary is elected.
Next should come the appointment of the Credentials,
Rules, and Program Committees, or the ratification of the
prior selection of these committees. In a convention of this
type, if these committees have not been appointed in ad-

1 vance, all committees should be appointed by the chair. Until
the report of the Credentials Committee is received, no business can be transacted except to authorize the presiding officer to appoint the above-mentioned committees, or to ratify
5 the previous appointment of them.

   If the Credentials Committee and other organizing
committees were not appointed in advance and are not,
therefore, ready to report, the time they need to prepare
their reports is usually spent in listening to talks, perhaps on
10 various phases of the convention's object. Otherwise the reports of the organizing committees are received in the same
manner as that described for organizing a convention of an
established association. If a permanent organization is not
contemplated, a permanent chairman and secretary can, but
15 need not, be elected at this time, after which the convention proceeds with the business for which it was called together. The principal purpose in electing a temporary
chairman first and a permanent chairman later in a convention of this kind is to enable the temporary chairman to pre-
20 side over the convention while it acts upon any matters
relating to contested seats (see pp. 595–98), so that the
permanent chairman can be elected by the delegates on the
permanent roll of the convention as it is finally determined
after all such contests have been resolved.

25   If the convention is called to form a permanent organization, permanent officers are not elected until later (after
the adoption of the bylaws), but a resolution should be
adopted at this point in the proceedings expressing an intention to form such a permanent association, as in the case
30 of forming a permanent local society (see **54**). A set of bylaws should have been carefully drawn up before the meeting of the convention, either by a Bylaws Committee
appointed by the organizing group, with the appointments
being ratified by the convention, or by members of the
35 sponsoring group who thereafter hand them to a Bylaws

Committee appointed at the convention. In the latter case   *1*
some of those who drafted the bylaws should be appointed
to the committee to avoid delay in reporting them.

After adoption of the bylaws, a Nominating Committee, selected in a manner as close as possible to that pre-   *5*
scribed in the bylaws, nominates candidates for office, and
those elected to these permanent offices take up their duties immediately, unless other provision is made.

DISCIPLINARY PROCEDURES

§61. DISCIPLINARY PROCEDURES

In most societies it is understood that members are required to be of honorable character and reputation, and certain types of associations may have particular codes of ethics to enforce. Although ordinary societies seldom have occasion to discipline members, an organization or assembly has the ultimate right to make and enforce its own rules, and to require that its members refrain from conduct injurious to the organization or its purposes. No one should be allowed to remain a member if his retention will do this kind of harm.

Formal disciplinary procedures should generally be regarded as a drastic step reserved for serious situations or those potentially so. When it appears that such measures may become necessary, proper and tactful handling of the case is of prime importance. It is usually in the best interests of the organization first to make every effort to obtain a satisfactory solution of the matter quietly and informally.

Punishments that a society can impose generally fall under the headings of reprimand, fine (if authorized in the bylaws), suspension, or expulsion. The extreme penalty that an organization or society can impose on a member is expulsion.

Cases of conduct subject to disciplinary action divide themselves into: offenses occurring in a meeting; and offenses by members outside a meeting.

Offenses Occurring in a Meeting

PRINCIPLES GOVERNING DISCIPLINE AT MEETINGS. A society has the right to determine who may be present at its meetings and to control its hall while meetings are in progress; but all members have the right to attend except in cases where the bylaws provide for the automatic suspension of members who fall in arrears in payment of their dues, or where the society has, by vote and as a penalty imposed for a specific offense, forbidden attendance.

Nonmembers, on the other hand—or a particular nonmember or group of nonmembers—can be excluded at any time from part or all of a meeting of a society, or from all of its meetings. Such exclusion can be effected by a ruling of the chair in cases of disorder, or by the adoption of a rule on the subject, or by an appropriate motion as the need arises—a motion of the latter nature being a question of privilege (**19**). A motion to exclude all nonmembers (except absolutely necessary staff, if any) is often referred to as a motion to "go into executive session" (see **9**).

All persons present at a meeting have an obligation to obey the legitimate orders of the presiding officer. Members, however, can appeal from the decision of the chair (**24**), move to suspend the rules (**25**), or move a reconsideration (**37**)—depending on the circumstances of the chair's ruling. A member can make such an appeal or motion whether the order involved applies to him or not.

In dealing with any case of disorder in a meeting, the presiding officer should always maintain a calm, deliberate tone—although he may become increasingly firm if a situation demands it. Under no circumstances should the chair attempt to drown out a disorderly member—either by his own voice or the gavel—or permit himself to be drawn into a verbal duel. If unavoidable, however, proper disciplinary proceedings to cope with immediate necessity can be conducted while a disorderly member continues to speak.

BREACHES OF ORDER BY MEMBERS IN A MEETING. If a member commits only a slight breach of order—such as addressing another member instead of the chair in debate, or, in a single instance, failing to confine his remarks to the merits of the pending question—the chair simply raps lightly, points out the fault, and advises the member to avoid it. The member can then continue speaking if he commits no further breaches. More formal procedures can be used in the case of serious offenses, as follows:

Calling a Member to Order. If the offense is more serious than in the case above—as when a member repeatedly questions the motives of other members whom he mentions by name, or persists in speaking on completely irrelevant matters in debate—the chair normally should first warn the member; but with or without such a warning, the chair or any other member can "call the member to order." If the chair does this, he says, "The member is out of order and will be seated." Another member making the call rises and, without waiting to be recognized, says, "Mr. President, I call the member to order," then resumes his seat. If the chair finds this point of order (**23**) well taken, he declares the offender out of order and directs him to be seated, just as above. If the offender had the floor, then (irrespective of who originated the proceeding) the chair should clearly state the breach involved and put the question to the assembly: "Shall the member be allowed to continue speaking?" This question is undebatable.

"Naming" an Offender.   In cases of obstinate or grave breach of order by a member, the chair can, after repeated warnings, "name" the offender, which amounts to preferring charges and should be resorted to only in extreme circumstances. Before taking such action, when it begins to appear that it may become necessary, the chair should direct the secretary to take down objectionable or disorderly words used by the member. Although the chair has no authority to impose a penalty or to order the offending member removed from the hall, the assembly has that power. It should be noted in this connection that in any case of an offense against the assembly occurring in a meeting, there is no need for a formal trial with witnesses, since the witnesses are all present and make up the body that is to determine the penalty.

The declaration made by the chair in naming a member is addressed to the offender by name and in the second person, and is entered in the minutes. An example of such a declaration is as follows:

CHAIR: Mr. J! The chair has repeatedly directed you to refrain from offensive personal references when speaking in this meeting. Three times the chair has ordered you to be seated, and you have nevertheless attempted to continue speaking.

If the member obeys at this point, the matter can be dropped or not, as the assembly chooses. The case may be sufficiently resolved by an apology or a withdrawal of objectionable statements or remarks by the offender; but if not, any member can move to order a penalty, or the chair can first ask, "What penalty shall be imposed on the member?" A motion offered in a case of this kind can propose that the offender be required to make an apology, that he

1 be censured, that he be required to leave the hall during the remainder of the meeting or until he is prepared to apologize, that his rights of membership be suspended for a time, or that he be expelled from the organization. The offend-
5 ing member can, by majority vote, be required to leave the hall during the consideration of his penalty, but he should be allowed to present his defense briefly first. If he denies having said anything improper, the words recorded by the secretary can be read to him and, if necessary, the assembly
10 can decide by vote whether he was heard to say them. A single member can require the vote on the imposition of a penalty to be taken by ballot. Expulsion from membership requires a two-thirds vote.

If the assembly orders an offending member to leave the
15 hall during a meeting as described above and he refuses to do so, the considerations stated below regarding the removal of offenders apply; but such a member exposes himself to the possibility of more severe disciplinary action by the society.
20

PROTECTION FROM ANNOYANCE BY NON-MEMBERS IN A MEETING; REMOVAL OF AN OFFENDER FROM THE HALL. Any nonmembers allowed in the hall during a meeting, as guests of the or-
25 ganization, have no rights with reference to the proceedings (p. 625). An assembly has the right to protect itself from annoyance by nonmembers, and its full authority in this regard—as distinguished from cases involving disorderly members—can be exercised by the chair acting alone. The
30 chair has the power to require nonmembers to leave the hall, or to order their removal, at any time during the meeting; and the nonmembers have no right of appeal from such an order of the presiding officer. However, such an order may be appealed by a member. That appeal is undebatable
35 (see Standard Descriptive Characteristic 5[a], p. 249). At a

mass meeting (**53**), any person who attempts to disrupt the proceedings in a manner obviously hostile to the announced purpose of the meeting can be treated as a nonmember under the provisions of this paragraph.

If a person—whether a member of the assembly or not—refuses to obey the order of proper authority to leave the hall during a meeting, the chair should take necessary measures to see that the order is enforced, but should be guided by a judicious appraisal of the situation. The chair can appoint a committee to escort the offender to the door, or the sergeant-at-arms—if there is one—can be asked to do this. If those who are assigned that task are unable to persuade the offender to leave, it is usually preferable that he be removed by police—who may, however, be reluctant to intervene unless representatives of the organization are prepared to press charges. The sergeant-at-arms or the members of the appointed committee themselves have the legal right to use such force as is necessary to remove the offender from the hall, *and no more.* But such a step should generally be taken only as a last resort, since, if the ejected party is maltreated, the person(s) who applied the excessive force, and not ordinarily the organization or the presiding officer, may be held liable for damages; and a person who would refuse to leave upon legitimate request may be the type most likely to bring suit, even if with little justification. In cases where possibly serious annoyance by hostile persons is anticipated—in some mass meetings, for example—it may be advisable to arrange in advance for the presence of police or guards from a security service agency.

Offenses Elsewhere Than in a Meeting; Trials

If there is an article on discipline in the bylaws (p. 564), it may specify a number of offenses outside meetings for which penalties listed on page 624, line 20 to page 625, line 3 can be imposed on a member of the organization. Frequently such an article provides for their imposition on any member found guilty of conduct described, for example, as "tending to injure the good name of the organization, disturb its well-being, or hamper it in its work." In any society, behavior of this nature is a serious offense properly subject to disciplinary action, whether the bylaws make mention of it or not.

If improper conduct by a member of a society occurs elsewhere than at a meeting, the members generally have no first-hand knowledge of the case. Therefore, if disciplinary action is to be taken, charges must be preferred and a formal trial held before the assembly of the society, or before a committee—standing or special—which should be required to report its findings and recommendations to the assembly for action.

RIGHTS OF THE SOCIETY AND THE ACCUSED. Since a society has the right to prescribe and enforce its standards for membership, it has the right to investigate the character of its members as may be necessary to this enforcement. But neither the society nor any member has the right to make public any information obtained through such investigation; if it becomes common knowledge within the society, it should not be revealed to any non-member. Consequently, a trial must always be held in executive session; and the introduction and consideration of all resolutions leading up to the trial also should take place when nonmembers are not present.

If (after trial) a member is expelled, the society has the right to disclose the fact that he is no longer a member—circulating it only to the extent required for the protection of the society or, possibly, of other organizations. Neither the society nor any of its members has the right to make pubic the charge of which an expelled member has been found guilty, or to reveal any other details connected with the case. To make any of the facts public may constitute libel. A trial by the society cannot legally establish the guilt of the accused, as understood in a court of law; it can only establish his guilt as affecting the society's judgment of his fitness for membership.

Ordinarily it is impossible for the society to obtain *legal* proof of facts in disciplinary cases. To get at the truth under the conditions of such a trial, hearsay evidence has to be admissible, and judgment as to the best interests of the society may have to be based on it. Witnesses are not sworn. The persons with first-hand knowledge may be nonmembers, who probably will decline to testify, and may be willing only to reveal the facts privately to a single member on condition that their names in no way be connected with the case. Even members may be reluctant to give formal testimony against the accused. A member can be required to testify at a trial on pain of expulsion, but it is very seldom advisable to force such an issue.

A member has the right that allegations against his good name shall not be made except by charges brought on reasonable ground. If a member is thus accused, he has the right to due process—that is, to be informed of the charge and given time to prepare his defense, to appear and defend himself, and to be fairly treated.

If a member is guilty of a serious offense and knows that other members are in possession of the facts, he may wish to submit his resignation from membership. When the good of the society appears to demand the separation of an offending member, it is usually best for all concerned to offer the member the opportunity to resign quietly before charges are preferred. The society has no obligation to suggest or accept such a resignation at any stage of the case, however, even if it is submitted on the offender's own initiative.

STEPS IN A FAIR DISCIPLINARY PROCESS.
Most ordinary societies should never have to hold a formal

1   trial, and their bylaws need not be encumbered with clauses
on discipline. For the protection of the society and members alike, however, the basic steps which, in any organization, make up the elements of fair disciplinary process
5   should be understood. Any special procedures established
should be built essentially around them, and the steps
should be followed in the absence of such provisions. As applying to offenses elsewhere than in a meeting, the important steps are as follows:

10   *Confidential Investigation by Committee.*   A committee whose members are selected for known integrity and
good judgment should conduct a confidential investigation
(usually including an interview with the accused) to determine whether further action, including the preferring of
15   charges if necessary, is warranted.

Accordingly, if the bylaws do not provide for the
method of charge and trial, a member should, at a time
when nonmembers are not present, offer a resolution to appoint an investigating committee. This resolution should be
20   in a form similar to the following:

> *Resolved,* That a committee of . . . [perhaps "five"]
> be appointed by the chair [or "be elected by ballot"]
> to investigate rumors affecting the character of our
25   > member, Mr. N, which, if true, render him unwor-
> thy of membership [or "cast doubt on his worthi-
> ness for membership"], and that the committee be
> instructed to report resolutions covering its recom-
> mendations.

30

For the protection of parties who may be innocent, the
first resolution should avoid details as much as possible. It
is best that an individual member not prefer charges, even
if he has proof of another's wrongdoing. If a member in-
35   troduces a resolution preferring charges unsupported by an

investigating committee's recommendation, another member should move to postpone this resolution indefinitely, saying that if the indefinite postponement is approved, he will move the appointment of such a committee (by a resolution, as in the example above). A resolution is improper if it implies the truth of specific rumors or contains insinuations unfavorable to a member, even if he is to be accused. It is out of order, for example, for a resolution to begin, "Whereas, It seems probable that members of the Finance Committee have engaged in graft, . . . " At the first mention of the word "graft" in such a case, the chair should instantly call to order the member attempting to move the resolution.

An investigating committee appointed as described above has no power to require the accused or any other member of the society to appear before it, but it should quietly conduct a complete investigation, making an effort to learn all relevant facts. Information obtained in strict confidence may help the committee to form an opinion, but it should not be reported to the society or used in a trial—except as may be possible without bringing out the confidential particulars. Before any action is taken, fairness generally demands that the committee or some of its members meet with the accused for frank discussion and to hear his side of the story. It may be possible at this stage to point out to the accused that if he does not rectify the situation or resign, he probably will be brought to trial.

Report of Resolutions Either Exonerating the Accused or Preferring Specific Charges. If after investigation the committee's opinion is favorable to the accused, it should prepare and report a resolution exonerating him. But if the committee from its investigations finds substance to the rumors and cannot resolve the matter satisfactorily in any other way, it should make a report in writing—which should be signed by every committee member who

1   agrees—outlining the course of its investigation and preferring charges. The preferral of charges is accomplished by
recommending in the report the adoption of resolutions, as
in the following example:

Resolved, That when this meeting adjourns, it adjourn to meet at 8 P.M. on Wednesday, November 15,
20__.
[For variations depending on conditions, see the
first paragraph following these resolutions, below.]
Resolved, That Mr. N be, and hereby is,* cited to
appear at said adjourned meeting for trial, to show
cause why he should not be expelled from the Society
on the following charge and specifications:
Charge. Conduct unworthy of a member of this
organization.
Specification 1. In this that Mr. N has so conducted himself as to establish among a number of his
acquaintances a reputation for willfully originating
false reports against innocent persons.
Specification 2. In this that on or about the
evening of August 12, 20__, in the Matterhorn
Restaurant, Mr. N was seen by patrons to be the apparent provoker of a needless and violent disturbance,
causing damage to the furnishings.
Resolved, That Messrs. S and T act as managers for
the Society at the trial. [See below.]

With reference to an appropriate date for which to set
the trial, thirty days is a reasonable time to allow the accused to prepare his defense. When a trial is to be before the
assembly of the society as in the example above, it is generally not good policy to hold it at a regular meeting. If there

---

*Regarding the effect of the words "and hereby is," see pages 636–37.

is to be another regular meeting between the date of adoption of these resolutions and the date desired for the trial, the first resolution should be to establish a special meeting instead of an adjourned meeting (see **9**). If believed advisable—and particularly when the trial is likely to be delicate, involve potential scandal, or be long and troublesome, or when the assembly of the organization is large—the resolutions reported by the investigating committee, instead of providing for trial before the entire assembly, can be worded so as to establish a committee to hear the trial and report its findings and recommendations to the assembly for action. In such a case, the first two of the resolutions above would be worded as follows:

> *Resolved,* That a trial committee consisting of Mr. H as chairman and Messrs. A, B, C, D, E, and F be appointed to try the case of Mr. N and report its findings and recommendations. [A special committee appointed to hear a trial should be composed of persons different from those on the preliminary investigating committee. This resolution can either be offered with the names of the members of the proposed trial committee specified as in the example, or it can contain a blank so as to leave the manner of their selection to the assembly.]
>
> *Resolved,* That Mr. N be, and hereby is, cited to appear before the said trial committee at the Society hall at 8 P.M. on Wednesday, November 15, 20__, to show cause why he should not be expelled from the Society on the following charge and specifications: . . . [setting them forth, as above.]

The third resolution would be the same whether the trial is to be before the assembly or before a special committee (see above).

1 A *charge* sets forth an *offense*—that is, a particular kind
of act or conduct that the governing rules define as entailing liability to prescribed penalties—of which the accused is
alleged to be guilty. A *specification* states *what the accused is*
5 *alleged to have done* which, if true, constitutes an instance of
the offense indicated in the charge. An accused must be
found guilty of a *charge* before a penalty can be imposed.
Ordinarily each separate charge contained in the resolutions
should be accompanied by at least one specification, unless
10 the investigating committee and the accused agree in preferring that this information not be disclosed outside the
trial. Each specification should be carefully worded so as to
make no broader allegation than is believed sufficient to establish the validity of the charge if the specification is found
15 to be true.

The "managers" at the trial—referred to in the third
resolution of the complete set shown above—have the task
of presenting the evidence against the accused, and must be
members of the society. Their duty, however, is not to act
20 as prosecutors—in the sense of making every effort to secure conviction—but rather to strive that the trial will get
at the truth and that, in the light of all facts brought out,
the outcome will be just.

Formal Notification of the Accused.   If the society
25 adopts resolutions ordering trial before the assembly or a
committee, the secretary should immediately send to the
accused by registered mail a letter notifying him of the
date, hour, and place of the trial, containing an exact copy
of the charge(s) and specifications with the date of their
30 adoption, and directing him to appear as cited—even if the
accused was present when the resolutions were adopted. If
the resolutions contain all the necessary information as illustrated on the two preceding pages, and if the second
resolution includes the words *and hereby is* before the word
35 *cited* (see first line), the secretary's letter of notification can

reproduce the resolutions in full and can be worded as
follows:

Dear Mr. N:
    Your attention is called to the fact that the . . . So-
ciety, at its meeting on October 14, 20__, adopted the
following resolutions:
    . . . [Text of resolutions].
    Kindly be present at the Society hall at the time in-
dicated above.
Sincerely
John Clark, Secretary

If, however, the words *and hereby is* were omitted from
the second resolution, the secretary's notice to the accused
should be worded as a formal citation, thus:

Dear Mr. N:
    You are hereby cited to appear for trial at the . . .
Society hall at 8 P.M. on Wednesday, November 15,
20__, to show cause why you should not be expelled
from the Society on the following charge and specifications: . . . [Text of charge and specifications].
    By order of the . . . Society, adopted at its meeting
on October 14, 20__.
John Clark, Secretary

Whichever form of letter is sent to the accused as described above, the secretary should have at hand at the trial
a photo-copy, printout, or other direct reproduction of it
with the return receipt attached, as proof that the accused
was informed of the charges against him. In any event, from
the time the accused has been thus notified, all of his rights
as a member of the society (except as relate to the trial) are
suspended pending disposition of the case.

1   *Trial Procedure.* The trial is a formal hearing on the validity of the charges, at which the evidence against the accused is presented by the managers for the society, at which the accused has the right to be represented by counsel and
5 to speak and produce witnesses in his own defense, and after which, if the charges are found to be true, a penalty is imposed or recommended, but if the charges are not substantiated, the accused is exonerated and his privileges of membership are automatically restored. The managers, as
10 previously stated, must be members of the society. Defense counsel can be attorney(s) or not, but must be member(s) of the society unless the trial body (that is, the assembly or the trial committee as the case may be) by vote agrees to permit attorney(s) who are not member(s) to act in this ca-
15 pacity. Nonmembers who consent to testify can be brought in as witnesses at the trial, but such a witness should be allowed in the room only while he is testifying.

    If the accused fails to appear for trial at the appointed time as directed, the trial proceeds without him.

20   At the trial, in calling the meeting to order, the chair should call attention to the fact that the meeting is in executive session (**9**), and to the attendant obligation of secrecy. Preliminary steps then include the secretary's reading from the minutes the resolutions adopted by the society relating to
25 the trial, the chair's verification—by inquiring of the secretary—that the accused was furnished with a copy of the charges, the chair's announcement of the names of the managers for the society, and the chair's inquiry of the accused as to whether he has counsel. The trial then proceeds as follows:
30

    a) The chair directs the secretary to read the charge and specifications.

    b) The chair asks the accused how he pleads—*guilty* or *not guilty*—first to each of the specifications in order, and
35   then to the charge.

c) If a plea of *guilty* is entered to the charge, there need be no trial, and the meeting can proceed directly to the determination of the penalty after hearing a brief statement of the facts.

d) If the plea to the charge is *not guilty,* the trial proceeds in the following order, the chair first explaining all the steps, then calling for each of them in sequence: (1) opening statements by both sides—the managers first; (2) testimony of witnesses produced by the managers for the society; (3) testimony of defense witnesses; (4) rebuttal witnesses on behalf of the society; and then on behalf of the defense, if any; and (5) closing arguments by both sides. Up until the completion of the closing arguments, no one is entitled to the floor except the managers and the defense; and they must address the chair except when questioning witnesses. Cross-examination, re-direct-examination, and re-cross-examination of witnesses is permitted, and witnesses can be recalled for further testimony as the occasion may dictate.

e) When the closing arguments have been completed, the accused must leave the room. If the trial is before the assembly rather than a trial committee, the managers, defense counsel (if members of the society), and member witnesses for both sides remain, take part in discussion, and vote as any other members. The chair then states the question on the finding as to the guilt of the accused, as follows: "The question before the assembly [or "the committee"] is: Is Mr. N guilty of the charge and specifications preferred against him?" Each of the specifications, and then the charge, is read, opened to debate, and voted on separately—although the several votes can be delayed to be taken on a single ballot. The specifications or the charge can be amended to conform to facts brought out in the trial—but not in such a way as to find the accused guilty of a charge not wholly in-

1   cluded within charge(s) for which he has been tried. If
    the accused is found guilty of one or more of the spec-
    ifications but not of the charge, a lesser charge should
    be moved and voted on. If the accused is found guilty,
5   the chair announces that the next item of business is the
    determination of the penalty. One of the managers for
    the society usually makes a motion for a penalty the
    managers feel appropriate (see pp. 624–25); this motion
    is debatable and amendable. As in the case of an offense
10 committed at a meeting, on the demand of a single
    member both the question of guilt and the question of
    the penalty must be voted on by ballot. For expulsion,
    a two-thirds vote is required.

    f) After voting is completed, the accused is called back
15 into the hall and advised of the result.

    In general, in any trial within a society, an accused
    should be found guilty of a charge only when his guilt, by
    its nature, has created a situation such that the best inter-
20 ests of the organization or the profession it represents re-
    quire a finding of guilty and the imposition of a penalty. A
    member who votes for a finding of guilty at a trial should
    be morally convinced of the existence of this kind of guilt
    on the part of the accused, on the basis of the evidence he
25 has heard.

    Assembly's Review of a Trial Committee's Findings.   If
    the trial has been held before a trial committee instead of the
    assembly of the society, this committee reports to the assem-
    bly in executive session (**9**) the results of its trial of the case,
30 with resolutions—in cases where its finding is one of *guilty*—
    covering the penalty it recommends that the society impose.
    The report should be prepared in writing and should include,
    to the extent possible without disclosing confidential infor-
    mation which should be kept within the committee, a sum-
35 mary of the basis for the committee's finding. Unless the

report exonerates the accused, he should then be permitted—himself, or through his counsel, or both, as he prefers—to make his statement of the case, after which the committee should be given the opportunity to present a statement in rebuttal. The accused—and his counsel if not member(s)—then leave the room, and the assembly acts upon the resolutions submitted by the committee. The members of the committee should remain and vote on the case the same as other members of the society. Under this procedure, the assembly can decline to impose any penalty, notwithstanding the trial committee's recommendation; or it can reduce the recommended penalty; but it cannot increase the penalty. The assembly cannot impose a penalty if the trial committee has found the accused not guilty.

COMMITTEE ON DISCIPLINE.   In some professional societies and other organizations where particular aspects of discipline are of special importance, the handling of such matters is simplified by providing in the bylaws for a standing Committee on Discipline (see **50, 56**). Its prescribed duties are normally to be alert to disciplinary problems, to investigate them, to introduce all necessary resolutions, and—in event of a trial—to manage the case for the society. This committee may also have the duty of hearing the actual trial, in which case it should be large enough that a subcommittee can perform the confidential investigation as described on pages 632–33. Under the latter practice, the full Committee on Discipline adopts the charge and specifications, and the chairman of the committee sends the citation to the accused and presides at the trial, which is conducted just as it would be if held before the assembly. It is generally best not to empower the committee to *impose* a penalty, however, but to require it to report its recommended disciplinary measures to the society for action, just as in the case of a special committee to hear a trial. In organizations where disciplinary matters may arise with some frequency, the system of having a Committee on Discipline has the advantages of not unduly inconveniencing the society, and of promoting the avoidance of scandal and the settlement of disciplinary problems without an actual trial.

Remedies Against Misconduct or Dereliction of Duty in Office

If the chair at a meeting ignores a motion apparently made and seconded in good faith, and neither states the question on the motion nor rules it out of order, the maker of the motion should raise a *Point of Order* (**23**) covering the case, and from the chair's decision he can *Appeal* (**24**). If the chair also ignores the point of order, the member can repeat the motion; and if it is seconded and the chair still ignores it, the maker of the motion can himself put it to a vote standing in his place. If the regular presiding officer of an organized society culpably fails to perform the duties of the chair properly in a meeting, a motion can also be made to censure him, which can be put to a vote by the maker of the motion as just explained, if necessary (see also p. 436). If the offending occupant of the chair is not the regular presiding officer of a society, a motion can be made to "declare the chair vacant and proceed to elect a new chairman." Such a motion is a question of privilege affecting the assembly (**19**).

Except as the bylaws may provide otherwise, any regularly elected officer of a permanent society can be deposed from office for cause—that is, misconduct or neglect of duty in office—as follows:

- If the bylaws provide that officers shall serve "for __ years *or* until their successors are elected," the election of the officer in question can be rescinded and a successor can thereafter be elected for the remainder of the term. The vote required for removing the offender from office in such a case is the same as for any other motion to *Rescind* (**35**).

- If, however, the bylaws provide that officers shall serve *only* a fixed term, such as "for two years" (which is not a recommended wording; see p. 557), or if they provide that officers shall serve "for __ years *and* until their successors are elected," an officer can be deposed from office only by following the procedures for dealing with offenses by members outside a meeting; that is, an investigating committee must be appointed, it must prefer charges, and a formal trial must be held.

CHARTS, TABLES
AND LISTS

I. CHART FOR DETERMINING WHEN EACH SUBSIDIARY OR PRIVILEGED MOTION IS IN ORDER

In the chart on the two following pages, the privileged, subsidiary, and main motions are listed in order of rank, the motion at the top taking precedence over all the others, and each of the remaining ones taking precedence over all those below it. A main motion is in order only when no other motion is pending.

When a given one of the motions listed is immediately pending, then: (a) any other motion appearing *above* it in the list is *in order*, unless a condition stated opposite the other motion causes that motion to be out of order; and (b) motions listed *below* the given motion which are not already pending are *out of order* (except for the application of *Amend* or the *Previous Question* to certain motions ranking above them as noted in the next paragraph; see also Standard Characteristic 2, pp. 126–27 and 190–91).

With respect to arrowed lines in the chart, (———) indicates applicability of all of the subsidiary motions to the main motion; (——), applicability of *Amend* to certain other motions in the order of precedence; (— — —), applicability of *Limit or Extend Limits of Debate* to debatable motions in the order of precedence; and (— — —), applicability of the *Previous Question* to the motions that are debatable or amendable.

I. CHART FOR DETERMINING WHEN EACH SUBSIDIARY OR PRIVILEGED MOTION IS IN ORDER (cont.)

Order Of Precedence of Motions

P
R
I
V
I
L
E
G
E
D

Fix the Time to Which to Adjourn (when privileged as explained on pp. 234–35)

Adjourn (when privileged as explained on pp. 225–27)

Recess (when moved while a question is pending)

Raise a Question of Privilege

Call for the Orders of the Day

U
N
D
E
B
A
T
A
B
L
E

S
U
B
S
I
D
I
A
R
Y

Lay on the Table

Previous Question (immediately to close debate and making of subsidiary motions except *Lay on the Table*)

Limit or Extend Limits of Debate

Postpone to a Certain Time (or **Postpone Definitely**)

Commit (or **Refer**)

Amend

Postpone Indefinitely

MAIN MOTION

D
E
B
A
T
A
B
L
E

Other Conditions Affecting Admissibility
MOTION DIRECTLY TO LEFT ON FACING PAGE IS OUT OF ORDER WHEN:

- a motion to *Suspend the Rules* relating to priority of business is pending

- a *Point of Order*, undebatable *Appeal*, or one of the five *Requests and Inquiries*—not adhering to main question—is pending

- a motion which cannot be debated or amended is immediately pending

- any undebatable question is immediately pending; also when motion(s) under an order for the *Previous Question* remain to be voted on

- any undebatable question except *Division of the Question* or *Consider by Paragraph or Seriatim* is immediately pending; also when motion(s) under an order for the *Previous Question* remain to be voted on

- a motion to *Reconsider* is pending, or any undebatable question except *Division of the Question* or *Consider by Paragraph or Seriatim* is immediately pending; also when motion(s) under an order for the *Previous Question* remain to be voted on

- the application would be to the main question, and any motion except *Postpone Indefinitely* is pending; also, in any application, when motion(s) under an order for the *Previous Question* remain to be voted on

- any motion except the main question is pending; also when the *Previous Question* has been ordered

- any motion is pending

II. TABLE OF RULES RELATING TO MOTIONS

MOTION	CLASS[1]	IN ORDER WHEN ANOTHER HAS THE FLOOR	MUST BE SECONDED[2]
1. Main motion or question (**10**)	M	No	Yes
2. Adjourn, ordinary case in societies (**21**)	P	No	Yes
3. Adjourn at or to a future time, or in advance of a time already set, or when the assembly will thereby be dissolved (**8, 10, 21**)	M	No	Yes
4. Adopt, accept, or agree to a report (**10, 51**)	M	No	Yes
5. Adopt bylaws or constitution, initially in forming a society (**10, 56, 56**)	M	No	Yes[3]
6. Adopt revised bylaws or constitution (**35, 56, 57**)	M/B	No	Yes[3]
7. Adopt special rules of order (**2, 10**)	M	No	Yes
8. Adopt ordinary standing rules (p. 18) (**2, 10**)	M	No	Yes

[1]Key to classification symbols: M—main motions; S—subsidiary motions; P—privileged motions; I—incidental motions; B—motions that bring a question again before the assembly; M/B—incidental main motions classed with motions that bring a question again before the assembly (see pp. 72ff.).

(For forms used in making motions, see Table III.)

DEBATABLE	AMENDABLE	VOTE REQUIRED FOR ADOPTION	CAN BE RECONSIDERED
Yes	Yes	Majority, except as explained on pages 98–99	Yes
No	No	Majority	No
Yes	Yes	Majority	No
Yes	Yes	Majority	Yes
Yes	Yes	Majority	Negative vote only
Yes	Yes	As provided in existing bylaws. (In absence of such provision, same as in next line)	Negative vote only
Yes	Yes	(a) Previous notice *and* two-thirds; or (b) majority of entire membership	Negative vote only
Yes	Yes	Majority	Yes

[2]Motions listed as requiring a second do not need to be seconded when made by direction of a board or committee.

[3]In practice, motion is usually made by the reporting member of a committee, in which case it does not require a second.

II. TABLE OF RULES RELATING TO MOTIONS (cont.)

MOTION	CLASS[1]	IN ORDER WHEN ANOTHER HAS THE FLOOR	MUST BE SECONDED[2]
9. Adopt parliamentary standing rules in a convention (**10, 59**)	M	No	Yes[3]
10. Adopt agenda or program (**10, 41, 59**)	M	No	Yes[3]
11. Amend a pending motion (**12**)	S	No	Yes
12. Amend an amendment of a pending motion (**12**)	S	No	Yes
13. Amend Something Previously Adopted, general case, including ordinary standing rules (**35**)	M/B	No	Yes
14. Amend parliamentary standing rules in a convention, when they are not pending (**35, 59**)	M/B	No	Yes
15. Amend adopted agenda or program with reference to items not yet reached (**35, 41, 59**)	M/B	No	Yes[3]

[1]Key to classification symbols: M—main motions; S—subsidiary motions; P—privileged motions; I—incidental motions; B—motions that bring a question again before the assembly; M/B—incidental main motions classed with motions that bring a question again before the assembly (see pp. 72ff.).

[2]Motions listed as requiring a second do not need to be seconded when made by direction of a board or committee.

(For forms used in making motions, see Table III.)

DEBATABLE	AMENDABLE	VOTE REQUIRED FOR ADOPTION	CAN BE RECONSIDERED
Yes	Yes	Two-thirds	Negative vote only
Yes	Yes	Majority	Negative vote only
If motion to be amended is debatable[4]	Yes	Majority	Yes
If motion to be amended is debatable[4]	No	Majority	Yes
Yes	Yes	(a) Majority with notice; or (b) two-thirds; or (c) majority of entire membership	Negative vote only
Yes	Yes	Two-thirds; or majority of all having convention voting rights who have been registered	Negative vote only
Yes	Yes	As immediately above, though often by unanimous consent after Program Committee's recommendation	Negative vote only

[3]In practice, motion is usually made by the reporting member of a committee, in which case it does not require a second.

[4]Debate on motion must be confined to *its* merits only, and cannot go into the main question except as necessary for debate of the immediately pending question.

II. TABLE OF RULES RELATING TO MOTIONS (cont.)

MOTION	CLASS[1]	IN ORDER WHEN ANOTHER HAS THE FLOOR	MUST BE SECONDED[2]
16. Amend bylaws or constitution, when not pending (**35, 57**)	M/B	No	Yes
17. Amend special rules of order, when not pending (**2, 35**)	M/B	No	Yes
18. Appeal, general case (**24**)	I	Yes, at time of appealed ruling	Yes
19. Appeal, relating to indecorum or transgression of rules of speaking, or to the priority of business, or if made while an undebatable question is pending (**24**)	I	Yes, at time of appealed ruling	Yes
20. Ballot, to order the vote on pending question to be taken by (**30, 45**)	I	No	Yes
21. Blank, to create by striking out (**12**)	I	No	Yes
22. Blanks, proposals for filling (**12**)	—	Can be called out when chair asks for them	No

[1]Key to classification symbols: M—main motions; S—subsidiary motions; P—privileged motions; I—incidental motions; B—motions that bring a question again before the assembly; M/B—incidental main motions classed with motions that bring a question again before the assembly (see pp. 72ff.).

(For forms used in making motions, see Table III.)

DEBATABLE	AMENDABLE	VOTE REQUIRED FOR ADOPTION	CAN BE RECONSIDERED
Yes	Yes	As provided in bylaws or constitution. (In absence of such provision, same as in No. 17, following)	Negative vote only
Yes	Yes	(a) Previous notice *and* two-thirds; or (b) majority of entire membership.	Negative vote only
Yes,[4] under rules stated on pages 249–50	No	Majority in negative required to reverse chair's decision	Yes
No	No	Majority in negative required to reverse chair's decision	Yes
No	Yes	Majority	Yes
No	No	Majority	No
Yes[4]	No	Majority	Yes

[2]Motions listed as requiring a second do not need to be seconded when made by direction of a board or committee.

[4]Debate on motion must be confined to its merits only, and cannot go into the main question except as necessary for debate of the immediately pending question.

II. TABLE OF RULES RELATING TO MOTIONS (cont.)

MOTION	CLASS[1]	IN ORDER WHEN ANOTHER HAS THE FLOOR	MUST BE SECONDED[2]
23. Change or depart from adopted convention agenda or program, immediately to take up a matter out of its proper order (**25, 35**)	I	No	Yes
24. Commit, Refer, or Recommit a pending question (**13**)	S	No	Yes
25. Committee, to refer a matter that is not pending to (**10, 13**)	M	No	Yes
26. Consider informally (**13,52**)	S	No	Yes
27. Consider by Paragraph or Seriatim (**28**)	I	No	Yes
28. Continue speaking after indecorum, to grant permission to (**23, 61**)	I	No	Yes, if in form of a motion
29. Debate and amendment, to obtain immediate closing of	(See *Previous Question*, No. 65)		
30. Debate, to Limit or Extend Limits of, on a pending question (**15**)	S	No	Yes

[1]Key to classification symbols: M—main motions; S—subsidiary motions; P—privileged motions; I—incidental motions; B—motions that bring a question again before the assembly; M/B—incidental main motions classed with motions that bring a question again before the assembly (see pp. 72ff.).

[2]Motions listed as requiring a second do not need to be seconded when made by direction of a board or committee.

(For forms used in making motions, see Table III.)

DEBATABLE	AMENDABLE	VOTE REQUIRED FOR ADOPTION	CAN BE RECONSIDERED
No	No	Two-thirds; or majority of all having convention voting rights who have been registered	No
Yes[4]	Yes	Majority	If committee has not begun consideration of the question[8]
Yes	Yes	Majority	If committee has not begun work on the matter
Yes[4]	No	Majority	Negative vote only
No	Yes	Majority	No
No	No	Majority	Yes
No	Yes	Two-thirds	Yes; but if vote was affirmative, only unexecuted part of order[8]

[4]Debate on motion must be confined to its merits only, and cannot go into the main question except as necessary for debate of the immediately pending question.

[8]A negative vote on this motion can be reconsidered only until such time as progress in business or debate has made it essentially a new question.

II. TABLE OF RULES RELATING TO MOTIONS (cont.)

MOTION	CLASS[1]	IN ORDER WHEN ANOTHER HAS THE FLOOR	MUST BE SECONDED[2]
31. Debate, to Limit or Extend Limits of, for the duration of a meeting (**10, 15**)	M	No	Yes
32. Discharge a Committee (**36**)	B or M/B[5]	No	Yes
33. Discharge a Committee, when it has failed to report at prescribed time, or while assembly is considering partial report of committee (**36**)	B or M/B[5]	No	Yes
34. Division of the Assembly (call for verification of a voting result by an uncounted rising vote) (**29**)	I	Yes	No
35. Count of vote on Division, to order, if chair does not do so (**4, 29, 30, 45**)	I	Yes	Yes
36. Division of a Question (**27**)	I	No	Yes

[1]Key to classification symbols: M—main motions; S—subsidiary motions; P—privileged motions; I—incidental motions; B—motions that bring a question again before the assembly; M/B—incidental main motions classed with motions that bring a question again before the assembly (see pp. 72ff.).

(For forms used in making motions, see Table III.)

DEBATABLE	AMENDABLE	VOTE REQUIRED FOR ADOPTION	CAN BE RECONSIDERED
Yes	Yes	Two-thirds	Yes
Yes; debate can go into question in hands of the committee	Yes	(a) Majority with notice; or (b) two-thirds; or (c) majority of entire membership	Negative vote only
Yes; debate can go into question in hands of the committee	Yes	Majority	Negative vote only
No	No	Demand of single member compels Division	No
No	Yes	Majority	No
No	Yes	Majority	No

[2]Motions listed as requiring a second do not need to be seconded when made by direction of a board or committee.

[5]B if committee is discharged from consideration of question that was pending at time of referral and was referred by subsidiary motion to *Commit;* M/B if subject was referred by a main motion (see pp. 302-303).

II. TABLE OF RULES RELATING TO MOTIONS (cont.)

MOTION	CLASS[1]	IN ORDER WHEN ANOTHER HAS THE FLOOR	MUST BE SECONDED[2]
37. Call for a separate vote on a resolution which is one of a series *on different subjects* offered by a single motion (pp. 106, 265) (**10, 27**)	I	Yes	No
38. Duty, to be excused from (**32**)	I	Yes	Yes, if motion is made by member to be excused, no, if made by another member
39. Effect, fix time for taking (**10, 12, 57**)	M,S or I[6]	No	Yes
40. Extend time for consideration of pending question, or time until scheduled adjournment or recess (**18**)	I	Yes; when orders of the day are announced or called for	Yes
41. Fix the Time to Which to Adjourn, if moved while a question is pending *and* no other meeting is scheduled for the same or the next day (**22**)	P	No	Yes
42. Fix the Time to Which to Adjourn, when another meeting is scheduled for the same or the next day, or if the motion is made while no question is pending (**10, 22**)	M	No	Yes

[1]Key to classification symbols: M—main motions; S—subsidiary motions; P—privileged motions; I—incidental motions; B—motions that bring a question again before the assembly; M/B—incidental main motions classed with motions that bring a question again before the assembly (see pp. 72 ff.).

(For forms used in making motions, see Table III.)

DEBATABLE	AMENDABLE	VOTE REQUIRED FOR ADOPTION	CAN BE RECONSIDERED
No	No	Demand of single member compels specified separate vote	No
Yes	Yes	Majority	Negative vote only
Yes	Yes	Majority	Yes[7]
No	No	Two-thirds	No
No	Yes	Majority	Yes
Yes	Yes	Majority	Yes

[2]Motions listed as requiring a second do not need to be seconded when made by direction of a board or committee.

[6]See pp. 578–79. This motion can be made as a main motion, as an amendment to enacting words, or as an incidental motion, and the same rules apply.

[7]See, however, Standard Characteristic 2, pp. 307–308 and pp. 317ff.

II. TABLE OF RULES RELATING TO MOTIONS (cont.)

MOTION	CLASS[1]	IN ORDER WHEN ANOTHER HAS THE FLOOR	MUST BE SECONDED[2]
43. Information, Point of (**33**)	I	Yes	No
44. Lay on the Table (**17**)	S	No	Yes
45. Minutes, to approve (when done by a motion) (**10, 48**)	M	No	Yes
46. Minutes, to correct before adoption (when done by a motion) (**12, 48**)	S	No	Yes
47. Minutes, to correct after approval	(See *Amend Something Previously Adopted*, No. 13.)		
48. Minutes, to dispense with reading of (**48**)	I	No	Yes
49. Nominations, to make (**46**)	—	No	No
50. Nominations, to close (**31**)	I	No	Yes
51. Nominations to reopen (**31**)	I	No	Yes
52. Nominations, motions relating to (except to close or reopen nominations) made while election is pending (**31**)	I	No	Yes

[1]Key to classification symbols: M—main motions; S—subsidiary motions; P—privileged motions; I—incidental motions; B—motions that bring a question again before the assembly; M/B—incidental main motions classed with motions that bring a question again before the assembly (see pp. 72 ff.).

[2]Motions listed as requiring a second do not need to be seconded when made by direction of a board or committee.

(For forms used in making motions, see Table III.)

DEBATABLE	AMENDABLE	VOTE REQUIRED FOR ADOPTION	CAN BE RECONSIDERED
No	No	Is not voted on	No
No	No	Majority	Negative vote only[9]
Yes	Yes	Majority	Yes
Yes	Yes	Majority	Yes
No	No	Majority	No
Yes	No	Majority for election unless bylaws provide otherwise.	Election cannot be reconsidered after person elected learns of it, and has not declined
No	Yes	Two-thirds	No
No	Yes	Majority	Negative vote only
No	Yes	Majority	Yes

[9]A negative vote on this motion can be reconsidered only until such time as either (a) progress in business or debate has made it essentially a new question, or (b) something urgent has arisen that was not known when the assembly rejected the motion.

II. TABLE OF RULES RELATING TO MOTIONS (cont.)

MOTION	CLASS[1]	IN ORDER WHEN ANOTHER HAS THE FLOOR	MUST BE SECONDED[2]
53. Nominations, motions relating to, made while election is not pending (**10, 46**)	M	No	Yes
54. Objection to Consideration of a Question (**26**)	I	When another *has been assigned* the floor, until debate has begun or a subsidiary motion has been stated by chair	No
55. Order, to make a special, when question is not pending (see No. 63) (**10, 41**)	M	No	Yes
56. Orders of the Day, to Call for (**18**)	P	Yes	No
57. Orders of the day, to proceed to (**18**)	—	Chair at his discretion puts this question when orders of the day are due to be taken up or are called for	—
58. Orders of the day, when pending (**10, 18, 41**)	M	—	—
59. Order, Point of, Question of, or Calling a Member to (**23**)	I	Yes	No
60. Parliamentary Inquiry (**33**)	I	Yes	No

[1]Key to classification symbols: M—main motions; S—subsidiary motions; P—privileged motions; I—incidental motions; B—motions that bring a question again before the assembly; M/B—incidental main motions classed with motions that bring a question again before the assembly (see pp. 72 ff.).

(For forms used in making motions, see Table III.)

DEBATABLE	AMENDABLE	VOTE REQUIRED FOR ADOPTION	CAN BE RECONSIDERED
Yes	Yes	Majority	Yes
No	No	Two-thirds against consideration sustains objection	Negative vote (sustaining objection) only
Yes[4]	Yes	Two-thirds	Yes
No	No	Must be enforced on demand of one member unless set aside by a two-thirds vote (see p. 215)	No
No	No	Two-thirds in negative required to refuse to proceed to orders of the day	No
Yes	Yes	Majority, except as explained on pages 98–99	Yes
No (but chair can permit full explanation and can submit question to assembly, in which case rule is as for *Appeal*; see No. 18)	No	Is ruled upon by chair (unless he submits question to judgment of majority in assembly)	No
No	No	Is not voted on, but is responded to by chair	—

[2]Motions listed as requiring a second do not need to be seconded when made by direction of a board or committee.

[4]Debate on motion must be confined to its merits only, and cannot go into the main question except as necessary for debate of the immediately pending question.

II. TABLE OF RULES RELATING TO MOTIONS (cont.)

MOTION	CLASS[1]	IN ORDER WHEN ANOTHER HAS THE FLOOR	MUST BE SECONDED[2]
61. Postpone Indefinitely (**11**)	S	No	Yes
62. Postpone to a Certain Time, or Definitely, applied to a pending question (**14**)	S	No	Yes
63. Postpone a pending question to a certain time and make it a special order (see No. 55) (**14**)	S	No	Yes
64. Postpone an event or action previously scheduled (**35**)	M/B	No	Yes
65. Previous Question (immediately to close debate and the making of subsidiary motions except the motion to Lay on the Table) (**16**)	S	No	Yes
66. Proviso (**10, 12, 57**)	M, S, or I[6]	No	Yes
67. Question of Privilege, to Raise while regular introduction as main motion is not in order (**19**)	P	Yes, but should not interrupt a person who has begun to speak, unless unavoidable	No; but if the question of privilege thereby raised is in the form of a motion, the motion must be seconded

[1]Key to classification symbols: M—main motions; S—subsidiary motions; P—privileged motions; I—incidental motions; B—motions that bring a question again before the assembly; M/B—incidental main motions classed with motions that bring a question again before the assembly (see pp. 72 ff.).

[2]Motions listed as requiring a second do not need to be seconded when made by direction of a board or committee.

(For forms used in making motions, see Table III.)

DEBATABLE	AMENDABLE	VOTE REQUIRED FOR ADOPTION	CAN BE RECONSIDERED
Yes; debate can go into main question	No	Majority	Affirmative vote only
Yes[4]	Yes	Majority, unless it makes question a special order	Yes[8]
Yes[4]	Yes	Two-thirds	Yes[8]
Yes	Yes	(a) Majority with notice; or (b) two-thirds; or (c) majority of entire membership	Negative vote only
No	No	Two-thirds	Yes; but if vote was affirmative, only before any vote has been taken under it[8]
Yes	Yes	Majority	Yes
No	No	Admissibility of question is ruled upon by chair	No

[4]Debate on motion must be confined to its merits only, and cannot go into the main question except as necessary for debate of the immediately pending question.

[6]See pp. 578–79. This motion can be made as a main motion, as an amendment to enacting words, or as an incidental motion, and the same rules apply.

[8]A negative vote on this motion can be reconsidered only until such time as progress in business or debate has made it essentially a new question.

II. TABLE OF RULES RELATING TO MOTIONS (cont.)

MOTION	CLASS[1]	IN ORDER WHEN ANOTHER HAS THE FLOOR	MUST BE SECONDED[2]
68. Question of privilege (a) when brought up while an ordinary main motion is in order; and (b) when pending (irrespective of how brought up) (**10, 19**)	M	Floor should be obtained in usual manner if question is brought up while main motion is in order	Yes
69. Ratify, or Confirm (**10**)	M	No	Yes
70. Read Papers, to grant permission to (**33**)	I	If not granted by unanimous consent, can be moved by person requesting permission or by another while the former has the floor	Yes, if motion is made by person requesting permission; no, if made by another member
71. Recess, to take a, if moved while business is pending (**20**)	P	No	Yes
72. Recess, to take a, if moved while no question is pending (**10, 20**)	M	No	Yes
73. Reconsider (**37**)	B	When another *has been assigned* the floor, but not after he has begun to speak	Yes

[1]Key to classification symbols: M—main motions; S—subsidiary motions; P—privileged motions; I—incidental motions; B—motions that bring a question again before the assembly; M/B—incidental main motions classed with motions that bring a question again before the assembly (see pp. 72 ff.).

(For forms used in making motions, see Table III.)

DEBATABLE	AMENDABLE	VOTE REQUIRED FOR ADOPTION	CAN BE RECONSIDERED
Yes	Yes	Majority	Yes
Yes	Yes	Majority, except as explained on pages 98–99	Yes
No	No	Majority	Yes
No	Yes	Majority	No
Yes	Yes	Majority	No
If motion to be reconsidered is debatable, in which case debate can go into that question	No	Majority	No

[2]Motions listed as requiring a second do not need to be seconded when made by direction of a board or committee.

II. TABLE OF RULES RELATING TO MOTIONS (cont.)

MOTION	CLASS[1]	IN ORDER WHEN ANOTHER HAS THE FLOOR	MUST BE SECONDED[2]
74. Reconsider, in a committee (**37**)	B	Cannot interrupt a person speaking	No
75. Reconsider, call up motion to (**37**)	—	No	No
76. Rescind and expunge from minutes (**35**)	M/B	No	Yes
77. Rescind, Repeal, or Annul (**35**)	M/B	No	Yes
78. Refer	(See *Commit, Committee*, Nos. 24 and 25.)		
79. Substitute	(See *Amend a pending motion*, No. 11.)		
80. Suspend the Rules (as applied to rules of order) (**25**)	I	No	Yes
81. Suspend ordinary standing rules, or standing rules in a convention (**25, 59**)	I	No	Yes
82. Take from the Table (**34**)	B	No	Yes
83. Take up a question out of its proper order	(See *Suspend the Rules [as applied to rules of order]*, No. 80; cf. also No. 23)		

[1]Key to classification symbols: M—main motions; S—subsidiary motions; P—privileged motions; I—incidental motions; B—motions that bring a question again before the assembly; M/B—incidental main motions classed with motions that bring a question again before the assembly (see pp. 72 ff.).

(For forms used in making motions, see Table III.)

DEBATABLE	AMENDABLE	VOTE REQUIRED FOR ADOPTION	CAN BE RECONSIDERED
As in No. 73, preceding	No	Two-thirds; but majority if every committee member who voted with prevailing side is present or was notified	No
—	—	—	—
Yes	Yes	Majority of entire membership	Negative vote only
Yes	Yes	(a) Majority with notice; or (b) two-thirds; or (c) majority of entire membership	Negative vote only
No	No	Two-thirds—except where rule protects a minority of less than one third (see p. 253)	No
No	No	Majority	No
No	No	Majority	No

[2]Motions listed as requiring a second do not need to be seconded when made by direction of a board or committee.

II. TABLE OF RULES RELATING TO MOTIONS (cont.)

MOTION	CLASS[1]	IN ORDER WHEN ANOTHER HAS THE FLOOR	MUST BE SECONDED[2]
84. Voting, motions relating to, if made while subject is pending (**30**)	I	No	Yes
85. Voting, motions relating to, if made while no question is pending (**10, 30, 45, 46**)	M	No	Yes
86. Withdraw or Modify a Motion, to grant maker permission to, after motion has been stated by the chair (**33**)	I	If not granted by unanimous consent, can be moved by person requesting permission, or by another while the former has the floor	Yes, if motion is made by person requesting permission; no, if made by another member

[1]Key to classification symbols: M—main motions; S—subsidiary motions; P—privileged motions; I—incidental motions; B—motions that bring a question again before the assembly; M/B—incidental main motions classed with motions that bring a question again before the assembly (see pp. 72 ff.).

(For forms used in making motions, see Table III.)

DEBATABLE	AMENDABLE	VOTE REQUIRED FOR ADOPTION	CAN BE RECONSIDERED
No	Yes	Majority, except two-thirds for motion to close polls	To close polls, no; to reopen polls, negative vote only; all others, yes
Yes	Yes	Majority	Yes
No	No	Majority	As to withdrawal, negative vote only; as to modification, yes

[2]Motions listed as requiring a second do not need to be seconded when made by direction of a board or committee.

III. SAMPLE FORMS USED IN MAKING MOTIONS

1. Main motion or question (original)

> [For forms see pp. 32; 99–103]

2. Adjourn, ordinary case in societies

> I move to adjourn.

3. Adjourn at or to a future time, or in advance of a time already set, or when the assembly will thereby be dissolved

> I move to adjourn at 4 P.M.
>
> I move that the meeting adjourn to meet at 8 P.M. Tuesday.
>
> I move to adjourn.
>
> I move to adjourn sine die.

4. Adopt, accept, or agree to a report

> I move that the report be adopted.

5. Adopt bylaws or constitution, initially in forming a society

> On behalf of the committee appointed to draw up bylaws, I move the adoption of the bylaws submitted by the committee.

6. Adopt revised bylaws or constitution

> On behalf of the committee on revision of the bylaws, I move that, as a substitute for the present bylaws, the bylaws submitted by the committee be adopted with the following provisos:...

7. Adopt special rules of order

> In accordance with notice given at the last meeting, I move that the following resolution be adopted as a special rule of order: *"Resolved,* That..."

8. Adopt ordinary standing rules (p. 18)

> I move that the following resolution be adopted as a standing rule: *"Resolved,* That..."

9. Adopt parliamentary standing rules in a convention

> By direction of the Committee on Standing Rules, I move the adoption of the Standing Rules of the Convention as just read.

10. Adopt convention agenda or program

> By direction of the Program Committee, I move the adoption of the Convention Program as printed.

11. Amend a pending motion

> I move to amend by adding...
>
> I move to amend by inserting the word...before the word...
>
> I move to amend by striking out the second paragraph.
>
> I move to amend by striking out "concrete" and inserting "blacktop."
>
> I move to substitute for the pending resolution the following resolution: *"Resolved,* That..."
>
> [For manner in which above forms are varied in the particular case, see subsections under *Rules for the different forms of amendment in* **12**.]

12. Amend an amendment of a pending motion

> I move to insert in the pending amendment the word...before the word...
>
> I move to amend the pending amendment by...[varying form to fit particular case, as under *Amend a pending motion,* No. 11].

III. SAMPLE FORMS USED IN MAKING MOTIONS (cont.)

13. Amend Something Previously Adopted, general case, including ordinary standing rules

> I move to amend the resolution relating to..., adopted at the September meeting, by...

14. Amend parliamentary standing rules in a convention, when they are not pending

> I move to amend Standing Rule No. 6 by...

15. Amend adopted convention agenda or program with reference to items not yet reached

> I move to amend the agenda [or "program"] by...

16. Amend bylaws or constitution, when not pending

> In accordance with notice given, I move the adoption of the following amendment to the bylaws...

17. Amend special rules of order, when not pending

> In accordance with notice given, I move to amend Special Rule of Order No. 3 by...

18. Appeal, general case

> I appeal from the decision of the chair.

19. Appeal, relating to indecorum or transgression of rules of speaking, or to the priority of business, or if made while an undebatable question is pending

> [Same form as No. 18]

20. Ballot, to order the vote on a pending question to be taken by

> I move that the vote on the pending question be taken by ballot.

21. Blank, to create by striking out

>I move to create a blank by striking out "$10,000."

22. Blanks, proposals for filling

>I suggest $20,000.

23. Change or depart from adopted convention agenda or program, immediately to take up a matter out of its proper order

>I move to suspend the rules and take up...

24. Commit, Refer, or Recommit a pending question

>I move to refer the motion to the Program Committee.

>I move that the motion be referred to a committee of three to be appointed by the chair.

>[For additional variations see p. 170]

25. Committee, to refer a matter that is not pending to

>I move that a committee [stating number and manner of selection] be appointed to conduct a survey relating to...

26. Consider informally

>I move that the question be considered informally.

27. Consider by Paragraph or Seriatim

>I move that the resolution be considered by paragraph.

28. Continue speaking after indecorum, to grant permission to

>[Chair usually puts question without a motion. When done by a motion:] I move that the member be permitted [or "allowed"] to continue speaking.

III. SAMPLE FORMS USED IN MAKING MOTIONS (cont.)

29. Debate and amendment, to obtain immediate closing of

[See *Previous Question*, No. 65]

30. Debate, to Limit or Extend Limits of, on a pending question

I move that debate be limited to one speech of three minutes for each member.

[For variations in particular cases see p. 188.]

31. Debate, to Limit or Extend Limits of, for the duration of a meeting

I move that during this meeting debate be limited to five minutes for each member.

32. Discharge a Committee

[For a standing committee:] I move that the Finance Committee be discharged from further consideration of the resolution relating to...

[For a special committee:] I move that the committee to which was referred...be discharged.

33. Discharge a Committee, when it has failed to report at prescribed time, or while assembly is considering partial report of committee

[Same forms as No. 32]

34. Division of the Assembly (call for verification of a voting result by an uncounted rising vote)

Division!

I call for a division.

35. Count of vote on Division, to order, if chair does not do so

    I move that the vote be counted.

    I move for [or "demand"] tellers.

    I move that the vote on this motion be by counted division.

36. Division of a Question

    I move to divide the resolution so as to consider separately...

37. Call for a separate vote on a resolution which is one of a series *on different subjects* offered by a single motion (pp. 106, 265)

    I call for a separate vote on the third resolution.

38. Duty, to be excused from

    I move [or "ask"] that I be excused from...

    I move that the resignation be accepted.

39. Effect, fix time for taking

    I move that the amendment to the...take effect as of...

40. Extend time for consideration of pending question, or time until scheduled adjournment or recess

    I move that the time for consideration of the pending resolution be extended for twenty minutes.

    I move to suspend the rules which interfere with continuing the consideration of the motion.

    I move that the time until the recess be extended ten minutes.

III. SAMPLE FORMS USED IN MAKING MOTIONS (cont.)

41. Fix the Time to Which to Adjourn, if moved while a question is pending *and* no other meeting is scheduled for the same or the next day

> I move that when this [or, "the"] meeting adjourns, it adjourn to meet next Tuesday at 8 P.M.

42. Fix the Time to Which to Adjourn, when another meeting is scheduled for the same or the next day, or if the motion is made while no question is pending

> [Same form as No. 41]

43. Information, Point of

> I rise to a point of information.
>
> Point of information!
>
> Will the member yield for a question?

44. Lay on the Table

> I move that the motion be laid on the table.

45. Minutes, to approve

> [Normally done by unanimous consent. When done by a motion:] I move that the minutes be approved as read [or "as corrected"].

46. Minutes, to correct before adoption

> [Usually suggested informally and done by unanimous consent except in cases of disagreement. When done by a motion:] I move to amend the minutes by...

47. Minutes, to correct after approval

> [See *Amend Something Previously Adopted*, No. 13.]

48. Minutes, to dispense with reading of

> I move that the reading of the minutes be dispensed with.

49. Nominations, to make

> I nominate George Beall.

50. Nominations, to close

> I move that nominations be closed.

51. Nominations, to reopen

> I move that nominations for...be reopened.

52. Nominations, motions, relating to (except to close or reopen nominations) made while election is pending

> I move that candidates for service on the committee be nominated from the floor.

53. Nominations, motions relating to, made while election is not pending

> [Same form as No. 52]

54. Objection to Consideration of a Question

> I object to the consideration of the question.

55. Order, to make a special, when question is not pending

> I move that the following resolution be made a special order for 3 P.M.: *"Resolved,* That..."

56. Orders of the Day, to Call for

> I call for the orders of the day.

III. SAMPLE FORMS USED IN MAKING MOTIONS (cont.)

57. Orders of the day, to proceed to

> [Chair at his discretion puts this question when orders of the day are due to be taken up or are called for.]

58. Order of the day, when pending

> [Will have been introduced earlier as a main motion.]

59. Order, Point of, Question of, or Calling a Member to

> Point of order!
>
> I rise to a point of order.
>
> I call the member to order. [Applying to indecorum]

60. Parliamentary Inquiry

> I rise to a parliamentary inquiry.
>
> Parliamentary inquiry, Mr. President!

61. Postpone Indefinitely

> I move that the resolution be postponed indefinitely.

62. Postpone to a Certain Time, or Definitely, applied to a pending question

> I move to postpone the question to the next meeting.

63. Postpone a pending question to a certain time and make it a special order

> I move that the resolution be postponed until 3 P.M. and made a special order.

64. Postpone an event or action previously scheduled

> I move that the dinner previously scheduled for September 15 be postponed until October 17.

65. Previous Question (immediately to close debate and the making of subsidiary motions except the motion to Lay on the Table)

> I move the previous question.
>
> I demand the previous question.
>
> I move the previous question on the motion to commit and the amendment.

66. Proviso

> I move to add the following to the motion: provided that this shall not take effect until....

67. Question of Privilege, to Raise while regular introduction as main motion is not in order.

> I rise to a question of privilege.

68. Question of Privilege (a) when brought up while an ordinary main motion is in order; or (b) when raised, immediately admitted, and offered as a motion under No. 67 above

> [Is moved as a main motion.]

69. Ratify, or Confirm

> I move that the action of the Executive Board on...be ratified.

70. Read Papers, to grant permission to

> [Usually done by unanimous consent. When done by a motion:] I move that the member [or "I"] be permitted [or "allowed"] to read...

III. SAMPLE FORMS USED IN MAKING MOTIONS (cont.)

71. Recess, to take a, if moved while business is pending

    I move to recess for five minutes.

72. Recess, to take a, if moved while no question is pending

    [Same form as No. 71]

73. Reconsider

    I move to reconsider the vote on the motion relating to...
    I move to reconsider the vote on the amendment striking
    out...and inserting...

74. Reconsider, in a committee

    [Form similar to No. 73]

75. Reconsider, call up motion to

    I call up the motion to reconsider the vote...

76. Rescind and expunge from the minutes (**35**)

    I move that the entry relating to ... be rescinded and ex-
    punged from the minutes.

77. Rescind, Repeal, or Annul

    I move that the resolution relating to...adopted on [date] be
    rescinded.

78. Refer

    [See *Commit, Committee*, Nos. 24 and 25.]

79. Substitute

    I move to substitute for the pending resolution the follow-
    ing resolution: "*Resolved,* That..."

80. Suspend the Rules (as applied to rules of order)

> I move to suspend the rules which interfere with...

81. Suspend ordinary standing rules, or standing rules in a convention

> [Form similar to No. 80]

82. Take from the Table

> I move to take from the table the motion relating to...

83. Take up a question out of its proper order

> I move to suspend the rules and take up...

84. Voting, motions relating to, if made while subject is pending

> I move that the vote on this question be taken by rising and be counted.

85. Voting, motions, relating to, if made while no question is pending

> [Form similar to No. 84]

86. Withdraw or Modify a Motion, to grant maker permission to, after motion has been stated by the chair

> [Usually done by unanimous consent. When done by a motion, for the case of withdrawal:] I move that the member [or "I"] be permitted [or "allowed"] to withdraw the motion. [For the case of modification by a motion, see *Amend a pending motion*, No. 11.]

IV. MOTIONS AND PARLIAMENTARY STEPS

- **Which Are in Order When Another Has the Floor and Do Not Require a Second**

Can interrupt a person speaking in debate if urgency requires it.	Calling a member to order (p. 626–27) Call for the Orders of the Day (**18**) Call for Division of the Assembly (**29**) Call for separate vote(s) on one or more of a series of unrelated resolutions that have been offered by a single motion (pp. 106, 265), or on one or more of a series of amendments on which the chair has stated the question in gross (pp. 505–506, 518–19, 523) Parliamentary Inquiry (pp. 281–82) Point of Information (pp. 282–83) Point of Order (**23**) Raise a Question of Privilege (**19**) Requests, or motions to grant the request of another member, as follows: For Permission to Withdraw or Modify a Motion (283–86) For Permission to Read Papers (pp. 286–87) For any Other Privilege (pp. 287–88) Request To Be Excused from a Duty (**32**)
In order when another has been assigned the floor but has not begun to speak. (See particular rules under references given.)	Notice of intent to introduce a motion requiring such notice (pp. 116–18) Objection to the Consideration of a Question (**26**)

- **Which Are in Order When Another Has the Floor But Must Be Seconded**

Can interrupt a person speaking in debate if urgency requires it.	Appeal (**24**) Formal motion to grant maker's own request, if it is not granted by unanimous consent (**32, 33**; pp. 277–78, 283–88)
In order when another has been assigned the floor but has not begun to speak. (See particular rules under references given.)	Reconsider (to *make* the motion, but not to have it considered at that time; **37**) Reconsider and Enter on the Minutes (to *make* the motion; pp. 321–24)

- **Which Are Out of Order When Another Has the Floor But Do Not Require a Second**

Call up a motion to Reconsider or a motion to Reconsider and Enter on the Minutes (**37**)

Nominations* (**46**)

Proposals for filling blanks* (pp. 155–60)

---

*When chair calls for them, can be offered without obtaining the floor.

V. MOTIONS AND PARLIAMENTARY STEPS

- **Which Are Not Debatable and Not Amendable**

  Adjourn (when privileged; **21**)

  Appeal, if it: (a) relates to indecorum or a transgression of the rules of speaking; (b) relates to the priority of business; or (c) is made while an undebatable question is pending (**24**)

  Amend an amendment to an undebatable motion (**12**)

  Calling a member to order (pp. 626–27)

  Call for the Orders of the Day (**18**)

  Call for Division of the Assembly (**29**)

  Call for separate vote(s) on one or more of a series of unrelated resolutions which have been offered by a single motion (pp. 106, 265), or on one or more of a series of amendments on which the chair has stated the question in gross (pp. 505–506, 518–19, and 523)

  Call up a motion to Reconsider, or a motion to Reconsider and Enter on the Minutes (**37**)

  Dispense with reading of the minutes (pp. 456–57)

  Grant permission to continue speaking after indecorum (pp. 626–27)

  Lay on the Table (**17**)

  Objection to the Consideration of a Question (**26**)

  Parliamentary Inquiry (pp. 281–82)

  Point of Information (pp. 282–83)

  Point of Order (except one referred to assembly by chair on which appeal would be debatable, or one where debate is permitted at chair's discretion by way of explanation; **23**)

  Previous Question (**16**)

  Raise a Question of Privilege (**19**)

  Reconsider an undebatable motion (**37**)

  Requests or motions to grant requests, in these cases:
    For Permission to Withdraw a Motion (pp. 283–86)
    For Permission to Read Papers (pp. 286–87)
    For Any Other Privilege (pp. 287–88)

  Request for Permissions to Modify a Motion (283–86)

  Suspend the Rules (**25**)

Take from the Table (**34**)
Take up a question out of its proper order (**25**; pp. 351–53)

- **Which Are Not Debatable But Are Amendable**
  Amend an undebatable motion (**12**)
  Consider by Paragraph or Seriatim (**28**)
  Division of a Question (**27**)
  Fix the Time to Which to Adjourn (when privileged; **22**)
  Limit or Extend Limits of Debate (**15**)
  Motions relating to methods of voting and the polls (**30**)
  Motions relating to nominations (**31**)
  Recess (when privileged; **20**)

- **Which Are Not Amendable But Are Debatable**
  Amend in amendment to a debatable motion (**12**)
  Appeal, in all cases except those listed at the top of the facing page,
    as undebatable (**24**)
  Blank, proposals for filing (pp. 155–60)
  Consider informally (**13, 52**)
  Nominations, to make (**46**)
  Postpone Indefinitely (**11**)
  Question of Order, when it has been referred to the assembly by
    the chair and an appeal on the same point would be debatable
    (see above, and **23**)
  Reconsider a debatable motion (**37**)

- **On Which Debate Can Go into Merits of the Main Question
  or the Question Which Is the Subject of the Proposed Action**
  Amend Something Previously Adopted (**35**)
  Discharge a Committee (**36**)
  Fix the time at which a motion shall take effect (**10, 12, 57**)
  Postpone Indefinitely (**11**)
  Ratify (pp. 119–20)
  Reconsider a debatable motion (**37**)
  Rescind (**35**)

VI. MOTIONS WHICH REQUIRE A TWO-THIRDS VOTE

Amend or Rescind constitution, bylaws, or rules of order, previous notice also being required (**2, 35, 57**)

Amend or Rescind Something Previously Adopted (other than constitution, bylaws, or rules of order), if notice has not been given (**35**)

Close nominations (**31**)

Close the polls (**30**)

Depose from office where trial is not required (see pp. 642–43), and notice has not been given

Discharge an order of the day before it is pending (**41**)

Discharge a Committee, if notice, or a partial report, has not been given (**36**)

Extend time for consideration of pending question (**18**), or time until scheduled adjournment or recess (**20, 21**)

Expel from membership, notice and a trial being also required unless the offense is committed in a meeting of the assembly (**61**)

Limit or Extend Limits of Debate (**15**)

Make a special order (**14, 41**)

Previous Question (**16**)

Reconsider in committee, when someone who voted with the prevailing side is absent and has not been notified that the reconsideration will be moved (pp. 318–19)

Refuse to proceed to the orders of the day (**18**)

Suspend the Rules (**25**)

Take up a question out of its proper order, or take up an order of the day before the time for which it has been set (**14, 25, 41**)

VII. MOTIONS WHOSE RECONSIDERATION IS PROHIBITED OR LIMITED

- **Cannot be reconsidered at all:**

    Adjourn (**21**)
    Close nominations (**31**)
    Close the polls (**30**)
    Consider by Paragraph or Seriatim (**28**)
    Create a blank (pp. 155–56)
    Dispense with the reading of the minutes (pp. 456–57)
    Division of the Assembly, or ordering a rising vote counted (**29**)
    Division of a Question (**27**)
    Extend time for consideration of pending question (**18**), or time until scheduled adjournment or recess (**20, 21**)
    Parliamentary Inquiry (pp. 281–82)
    Point of Information (pp. 282–83)
    Point of Order (**23**)
    Proceed to the orders of the day (**18**)
    Raise a Question of Privilege (**19**)
    Recess (**20**)
    Reconsider (**37**)
    Suspend the Rules (**25**)
    Take from the Table (**34**)
    Take up a question out of its proper order (**14, 25, 41**; pp. 351–53)

- **A negative vote cannot be reconsidered (although an affirmative vote can be):**

    Postpone Indefinitely (**11**)

(continued on next page)

VII. MOTIONS WHOSE RECONSIDERATION IS PROHIBITED OR LIMITED (cont.)

- **An affirmative vote cannot be reconsidered (although a negative vote can be):**

Accept resignation or grant Request to Be Excused from a Duty, if person was present or has been notified (**32**)

Adopt or amend agenda or program (**41, 59**)

Adopt or amend bylaws or constitution, rules of order, or any other rules that require previous notice for their amendment (**2, 54, 57, 59**)

Amend Something Previously Adopted (**35, 57**)

Commit, if committee has begun work on referred matter (**13**)

Consider informally (**13, 52**)

Discharge a Committee (**36**)

Election, if person elected was present and did not decline, or has been notified and has not declined (**46**)

Grant Permission to Withdraw or Modify a Motion (pp. 283–86)

Lay on the Table (**17**)

Objection to the Consideration of a Question (**26**)

Previous Question, after any vote has been taken under it (**16**)

Reopen nominations (**31**)

Reopen the polls (**30**)

Rescind (**35**)

INDEX

*Numbers following index entries refer to pages;
a letter* t *preceeding a number indicates reference to
the tinted section preceeding the index.*